Børge Schantz and Reinder Bruinsma
Editors

Exploring the Frontiers of Faith

Festschrift in Honour of Dr. Jan Paulsen

Congratulatory Edition

ADVENT-VERLAG

Editors: Børge Schantz and Reinder Bruinsma
Copy editor: Jonquil Hole
Cover design: Sislak Design, Bad Soden-Salmünster, Germany
Graphic design and layout: rimi-grafik, Celle, Germany
Printing: Thiele & Schwarz, Kassel, Germany
Photos: Archives General Conference of Seventh-day Adventists (cover)
         fotolia.com / Andrea Danti (background cover)
         Joel D. Springer/Adventist Review (facing page 16)

© 2009 Advent-Verlag, Pulverweg 6, 21337 Lueneburg, Germany
Website: www.advent-verlag.de, e-mail: info@advent-verlag.de

ISBN: 978-3-8150-0118-9

Table of Contents

PART IV: Education

PART V: Mission and Christian Witness

List of Contributors

Wim Altink
Niels-Erik Andreasen
Radiša Antić
Kai Arasola
Roberto Badenas
Bryan W. Ball
Bert B. Beach
Peter P. J. Beyerhaus
Reinder Bruinsma
John Graz
Stefan Höschele
Sakae Kubo
Michael M. Kulakov Jr.
Richard P. Lehmann
Richard Müller
Svein Myklebust
Anders Eyvind Nielsen
Bjørn Ottesen
Michael Pearson
Gunnar Pedersen
Paul Birch Petersen
Zdravko Zack Plantak
Rolf J. Pöhler
Børge Schantz
Steven Thompson
Sigve Tonstad
Laurence A. Turner
Bertil Wiklander

Biographical information about the authors is found at the end of their essay.

List of Abbreviations

AALE	American Academy for Liberal Education
AUSS	Andrews University Seminary Studies
AUSDD	Andrews University Seminary Doctoral Dissertation Series
AV	Authorised Version
BEN	Bibliana's Elektroniske Nyhedsbrev
BETL	Bibiotheca Ephemeridum Theologicarum Lovaniensium
DKNT	Dansk Kommentar til Det Nye Testamente
ESV	English Standard Version
GCA	General Conference Archives of Seventh-day Adventists
IDB	Interpreter's Dictionary of the Bible
JAE	Journal of Adventist Education
JATS	Journal of the Adventist Theological Society
JBTh	Journal of Biblical Theology
JSNTSup	Journal for the Study of the New Testament, Supplement Series
JSOT	Journal for the Study of the Old Testament
JTS	Journal of Theological Studies
KJV	King James Version
RSN	Religious Studies News
LXX	Septuagint
NASB	New American Standard Bible
NEB	New English Bible
NID	New International Dictionary
NIV	New International Version
NKJV	New King James Version
NovT	Novum Testamentum
NRSV	New Revised Standard Version
NT	New Testament
RSN	Religious Studies News
RSV	Revised Standard Version
SBL	Society of Biblical Literature
SBS	Stuttgarter Bibelstudien
SNTS	Society for New Testament Studies
TDNT	Theological Dictionary of the New Testament
OT	Old Testament
VT	Vetus Testamentum
WUNT	Wissenschaftliche Untersuchungen zum Neuen Testament

Abbreviations for Books of the Bible

Genesis	Gen	Matthew	Mat
Exodus	Ex	Mark	Mk
Leviticus	Lev	Luke	Lk
Numbers	Num	John	John
Deuteronomy	Deut	Acts	Acts
Joshua	Josh	Romans	Rom
Judges	Judg	1-2 Corinthians	1-2 Cor
Ruth	Ruth	Galatians	Gal
1-2 Samuel	1-2 Sam	Ephesians	Eph
1-2 Kings	1-2 Kgs	Philippians	Phil
1-2 Chronicles	1-2 Chr	Colossians	Col
Ezra	Ezra	1-2 Thessalonians	1-2 Thess
Nehemiah	Neh	1-2 Timothy	1-2 Tim
Esther	Esth	Titus	Titus
Job	Job	Philemon	Phlm
Psalms	Ps	Hebrews	Heb
Proverbs	Prov	James	Jas
Ecclesiastes	Eccl	1-2 Peter	1-2 Pet
Song of Solomon	Song	1-2-3 John	1-2-3 John
Isaiah	Isa	Jude	Jude
Jeremiah	Jer	Revelations	Rev
Lamentations	Lam		
Ezekiel	Ezek		
Daniel	Dan		
Hosea	Hos		
Joel	Joel		
Amos	Amos		
Obadiah	Obad		
Jonah	Jonah		
Micah	Mic		
Nahum	Nah		
Habakkuk	Hab		
Zephaniah	Zeph		
Haggai	Hag		
Zecharaiah	Zech		
Malachi	Mal		

Copyright Information for the Bible Versions Used

The most frequently used Bible version in this *Festschrift* is the NIV. In addition, the authors of the essays in this book have used the KJV and several other Bible versions:

ESV   *The Holy Bible, English Standard Version,* © 2001 by Crossway Bibles, a division of Good News Publishers.

NASB   *New American Standard Bible,* © 1960, 1971, 1995 by The Lockman Foundation, La Habra, California.

NEB   *The New English Bible,* © 1961, 1970 by The Delegates of the Oxford University Press and the Syndicates of the Cambridge University Press.

NIV   *Holy Bible, New International Version®,* © 1973, 1978, 1984 by the International Bible Society.

NRS   *New American Standard,* © 1960, 1971, 1995 by The Lockman Foundation.

NRSV   *New Revised Standard Version Bible,* © 1989 by the Division of Christian Education of the National Council of the Churches of Christ in the United States of America.

RSV   *Revised Standard Version of the Bible,* © 1952, 1971 by the Division of Christian Education of the National Council of the Churches of Christ in the United States of America.

Preface

It has been both a privilege and an honour to be so heavily involved with the preparation of this *Festschrift* for Dr. Jan Paulsen, long time church leader in the Seventh-day Adventist Church and since March 1999 its nineteenth world president. This collection of essays is a fitting tribute to Dr. Paulsen at a significant moment in his life.

We (Børge Schantz, Denmark, and Reinder Bruinsma, The Netherlands) have known Jan Paulsen for many years as a personal friend, esteemed colleague and our 'boss'. We have appreciated him in those roles, while we ourselves were still in active church service, and we have also enjoyed his collegiality and friendship—and still do. In many ways we have looked up to him, and continue to do so, as an inspiring role model.

Børge Schantz came up with the idea of honouring Jan Paulsen with a *Festschrift* on the occasion of his 75th birthday in January 2010. This moment was a fitting opportunity to express appreciation for his 54 years of committed service to the world church. He approached Reinder Bruinsma with the request to serve as his co-editor—a request that was gladly accepted. For some fifteen months we have invested a significant amount of our time in this special project. The fact that we have both retired from 'regular' church service enabled us to do so. It has been a deeply satisfying experience.

When we approached leaders and academics (in many cases these qualities being united in the same person) to contribute a chapter to this extraordinary publication, we received many enthusiastic responses. The result, which you now hold in your hands, is a rich collection of essays on a wide variety of topics. All twenty-eight authors have a strong European connection. They either live or lived in Europe, work or have worked on the same continent where Jan Paulsen also lived and worked for most of his distinguished career. All are either active or retired Seventh-day Adventist workers, except two contributors who are Lutherans. But everyone of them has had personal associations with Paulsen, either as his professor, student, colleague or co-worker, or as part of a team with him as leader.

We are, in particular, delighted with the positive response from Prof. Dr. Peter P. J. Beyerhaus, who was Paulsen's *Doktorvater* when he received his doctoral degree from the University of Tübingen. Professor Beyerhaus' contribution is a special tribute to one of his most prominent students. For this reason, and because of its very personal content, it fittingly opens the collection of essays.

The authors of this book, who combine thirteen different nationalities and currently live in ten different countries, are, of course, not truly representative of all the leaders and academics who serve or have served the Adventist Church worldwide. (As far as this lack of representativeness is concerned: we are acutely aware that there is, in spite of our efforts to avoid this, a lamentable disparity in the gender balance!) Yet, in a very real way the contributors are representative of the quality of leadership and intellectual strength that is so abundantly present in the Adventist Church, and of which Jan Paulsen himself is such a prominent example.

All contributors to this *Festschrift* have chosen a topic within the area of their particular expertise. Each essay, in its own way, fits well within the Adventist Christian tradition and, we believe, also to a large extent coincides with the interests of Dr. Paulsen. As the editors, however, we want to underline the fact that not all opinions expressed by the authors necessarily concur in every detail with our own. Nor do we assume that the opinions that are expressed and the conclusions that are reached represent in all cases the thinking of Dr. Paulsen. From our association with him we are, however, quite sure that he does not expect everyone to think in all matters, theological and otherwise, as he does.

The essays have been organized into four sections: (1) biblical and theological studies; (2) church administration; (3) education; and (4) mission and Christian witness. We realize that in a few cases a particular essay could fit in more than one category. The wide diversity of topics defies easy categorization.

A very special feature in the book is the Congratulatory List (*tabula gratulatoria*) with about one thousand names of colleagues and friends from around the world who have expressed their desire to also send their best wishes to the person to whom this *Festschrift* is dedicated. Those who are listed, and many others, cherish the direction and inspiration Paulsen has provided in the various phases of his ministry.

Before we come to the final paragraphs of this preface it should be pointed out that, since this project has been initiated on European soil, we have chosen to employ British spelling throughout.

A few words of appreciation are in order. First of all, we thank the authors for their willingness to invest so much time and energy in the essays they have produced, and also for reacting so positively to our reminders regarding deadlines and to our editorial decisions regarding details of style and formatting. We know from experience that it is quite challenging to achieve full consistency and correctness in any major publication.[1]

---

[1] There are, admittedly, some inconsistencies in the editorial format of the book. We have accepted some variations in the way Greek words have been transcribed by the different authors. We have also accepted some variations in the footnote format with regard to the way authors refer to a source they previously quoted. The sources that are referred to or quoted are from publishers located in a wide range of countries. As a rule the country is indicated with the place name where the publisher is (or was) located. Since the majority of the publications that are referred to or quoted are, however, from American publishers, as the rule only the place name, with the abbreviation of the state are mentioned, without the addition of 'USA'.

If we approach the ideal of consistency to some extent, it is due to the sharp eye and the English language skills of Mrs. Jonquil Hole (who taught in the School of English at Newbold College, when Paulsen was the school's principal). We greatly value her assistance. Likewise we are indebted to Bettina Krause and Lynda and John Baildam for preparing the bibliography of the publications of Dr. Paulsen.

Preparing a *Festschrift* is a complex enterprise. In addition to intense communication with authors, there are other important aspects concerning biography, bibliography, finance, time and place for the presentation of the book, and so on. The organization of the extensive Congratulatory List required a great deal of time and care. Many people have given us a helping hand in these matters. Special mention deserve Weslynne Sahley, Tor Tjeransen, Øivind Gjertsen, Randi and Svein Myklebust, Steven Thompson and Esti Pujic.

In addition, we like to thank the management of the Advent Verlag in Lueneburg, Germany, for their willingness to publish this volume as a non-commercial venture. We have benefited greatly from their technical advice and practical support.

Producing a substantial *Festschrift* demands an outlay of funding that will not be fully met by income from sales. Our thanks go to the church entities and a few private donors who have helped to provide the support that we needed. Among these generous church entities are a number of world divisions of the Adventist Church (the Trans-European, North American, South Pacific and Euro-Africa divisions) and church organizations in Britain, Finland, Norway, Iceland, Denmark and the Netherlands as well as some private contributors. These donations have also made it possible to send out more than five hundred free copies to theological libraries operated by Adventist and other Christian traditions. Copies of the *Festschrift* have also been made available worldwide to public affairs agencies in the Adventist Church for use in their contacts with other churches. In addition, some free copies have been reserved for special friends of the church around the world.

Together with about one thousand men and women whose names are listed on pages 437-464, and with the authors of the essays in this book, we congratulate Jan Paulsen on his 75th birthday. May the Lord, whom he has served so well for so many years, continue to give him, with his wife Kari, good health and sustained energy for many happy years to come.

Reinder Bruinsma

Jan Paulsen: Select Bibliography

Monographs

When the Spirit Descends
(Hagerstown, MD: Review & Herald, 2001).

Let Your Life So Shine: The Uncommon Rewards of Living Like Jesus
(Boise, ID: Pacific Press, 2003).

The following list comprises a chronological selection of articles, news reports, editorials, (condensed) sermons, devotional messages, comments, interviews and conversations by and with Jan Paulsen, published in the English language in the following Seventh-day Adventist periodicals:

AR	*Adventist Review* (until 1971 *Review and Herald*)
AW	*Adventist World*
DE	*Dialogue*
GR	*Gleaner*
IT	*Insight*
JAE	*Journal of Adventist Education*
LT	*Northern Light/Light*
LUH	*Lake Union Herald*
LY	*Liberty*
MN	*Mission*
MR	*British Advent Messenger/Messenger*
MY	*Ministry*
NV	*News and Views*
OK	*Outlook*
RD	*Record*
SAT	*(New) Southern Asia Tidings*
SM	*Spectrum*
SSL	*Sabbath School Leadership*
SWUR	*Southwestern Union Record*
VR	*Visitor*
YMA	*Youth Ministry Accent*

'A Church Building Project at Bekwai, Ghana', MR, 69.5 (28 February 1964), 3-4.

'Adventist College of West Africa Conducts Field Schools', AR, 143.56 (15 December 1966), 24.

'West African College Conducts Branch Sabbath Schools, Wins 20', AR, 144.24 (15 June 1967), 25.

'Will Adventists Speak in Unknown Tongues?' LT, 23.5 (May 1973), 6.

'Other Voices of Objection', LT, 24.9 (September 1974), 6.

'Youth Searching for Right Answers', LT, 24.1 (January 1974), 4-5.

'Submission or Freedom? A Matter of Authority', LT, 25.6 (June 1975), 4-5.

'Feeder Schools', LT, 26.5 (May 1976), 4.

'Newbold's New Staff', MR, 81.20 (1 October 1976), 2.

'In the Interest of Unity', LT , 27.12 (December 1977), 1, 7.

'Ointment, So That You May See', AR, 157.20 (GC Bulletin 5, 23 April 1980), 2-4.

'Report of Church Activities in Poland', AR, 159.13 (1 April 1982), 1, 14-15.

'A Meditation on "Newness" ', LT, 34.1 (January 1984), 2.

'The Reaping Principle', LT, 34.6 (June 1984), 2.

'The Beauty of Preaching', LT, 34.10 (October 1984), 2.

'The Gift of Openness', LT, 35.1 (January 1985), 2.

'Manhood—Womanhood—Priesthood', LT, 35.4 (April 1985), 2.

'Partners in Service', AR, 162.28 (1 July 1985), 8-10.

'Northern European Division', JAE, 47.5 (Summer 1985), 36-37.

'Post-Winter Meetings: Reflections', LT, 36.1 (January 1986), 2.

'1986—Year of Peace?', LT , 36.4 (April 1986), 2.

'Adventists for Prevention', LT, 36.11 (November 1986), 3-4.

'Everyone for Prevention', LT, 36.11 (November 1986), 4-5.

'Trans-Europe—A Variety of Challenges', MN, 75.4 (Winter 1986), 5-6.

'What the Lord's Supper Means to Me', AR, 163.51 (18 December 1986), 11-13.

'Mission Institutes in Pakistan Mark a First for SDAs', AR, 164.31
(30 July 1987), 29.

'Paulsen Shares Plans for Trans-European Division', AR, 164.38
(17 September 1987), 19-20.

'On Being Wiser', LT, 37.12 (December 1987), 2.

'Pakistan Union Gets New President', LT, 38.5 (May 1988), 4.

'The Church is Growing Rapidly', LT, 38.11 (November 1988), 3-5.

'Give the People Life', MY, 61.7 (July 1988), 6-7.

'Witness or Renewal: A Choice?' LT, 38.7 (July - August 1988), 2.

'On "Trying Again" ', LT, 39.1 (January 1989), 2.

'Believing and Trusting', AR, 166.6 (9 February 1989), 8-10.

'Acquitted: The Glorious Commencement of our Walk with God', AR, 166.7
(16 February 1989), 10-11.

'Growing in Christ: The Intimate Connection between Justification and
Sanctification', AR, 166.8 (23 February 1989), 8-9.

'Reflections on a Visit', LT, 39.3 (March 1989), 3.

'Healing in Hungary', SM, 20.2 (December 1989), 18-20.

'Trans-European Challenge', MN, 78.2 (Summer 1989), 5-6.

'Comments on Ecumenical Relationships', LT, 39.6 (June 1989), 4.

'Is Social Service our Mission?' AR, 166.35 (31 August 1989), 16-20.

'Divided Church in Hungary Sets Date for Unity', AR, 166.40 (5 October 1989), 6.

'1990! So What's New?', LT, 40.1 (January 1990), 2.

'Something Special for Christ in 1990', LT, 40.1 (January 1990), 5.

'Opening Doors', AR, 167.27 (GC Bulletin 3, 9 July 1990), 18-20.

'Revitalized Church Life', LT, 40.11 (November 1990), 4.

'ADRA Registered', LT , 40.11 (7 November 1990), 7.

'Should We Slow Down?' LT, 41.1 (January 1991), 4-5.

'We are Bonded to One Another', LT, Jun. - Jul. 1991, 3-4.

'To the Readers of Light Magazine', LT, 41.11 (November – December 1991), 4.

'Church in South Africa Votes to Unite', SAT, 87.2 (February 1992), 10.

'Who Owns the Church?' MR, 99.2 (21 January 1994), 1, 8.

'God Will Do It!' MN, 83.2 (Summer 1994), 4-5.

'The Community of the Spirit' (Silver Spring, MD: Ellen G. White Estate), 1995.

'Refugee or Pilgrim?' AR, 172.10 (9 March 1995), 8-10.

'The Flame Still Burns', AR, July 2, 1995, 18-20.

'Open Borders, Open Minds', AR, 172.50 (9 November 1995), 8-10.

'Beyond the Platitudes', AR, 174.49 (4 December 1997), 13-15.

'"An Open Person" - Pastor Jan Paulsen', AR, 176.10 (11 March 1999), 10-13.

'Acceptance Speech Excerpts', GR, 94.4 (19 March 1999), 26.

'New GC President: "An Open Person" ', RD, 104.10 (27 March 1999), 10-11.

'World Leader Echoes His Concerns', SAT, 94.4 (April 1999), 4-6.

'The Urgency of the Gospel', AR, 176.14 (8 April 1999), 14-17.

'The Dynamics of "Present Truth" ' AR, 176.30 (29 July 1999), 18-19.

'Reaching for a Better Humanity', AR, 176.35 (2 September 1999), 20-22.

'Reflections on a Personal Journey', AR, 176.35 (2 September 1999), 46.

'Openness of Identity', AR, 176.38 (23 September 1999), 5.

'Experiencing the Bonding of God's Family', AR, 176.39 (30 September 1999), 36-38.

'Glorious Days Ahead for the Family of God', AR, 176.39 (30 September 1999), 48.

'Openness of Identity', MY, 72.10 (October 1999), 4.

'An Agenda for the New Millennium', AR, 176.48 (2 December 1999), 35-39.

'The Tapestry of Humanity', AR, 176.52 (30 December 1999), 36-38.

'Three Laws of Spirituality', DE, 12.2 (January 2000), 24-25.

'Welcome/Bienvenue', AR, 177.26 (GC Bulletin 1, 30 June 2000), 2.

'Until the Day Dawns', AR, 177.26 (30 June 2000), 18-23.

'Extreme Answers', IT, 31.25 (1 July 2000), 5-6.

'A Conversation with Jan Paulsen', AR, 177.27 (GC Bulletin 2, 2 July 2000), 4-5.

'Steady as You Go', AR, 177.34 (13 July 2000), 5-8.

'The Certainty of His Coming', RD, 105.34 (2 September 2000), 18-21.

'Time for a New Commitment', RD, 105.34 (2 September 2000), 32.

'Ten Years of Harvest', AR, 177.42 (14 September 2000), 10.

'Idols and Realities', AR, 177.45 (5 October 2000), 17-21.

'The Certainty of His Coming', AR, 177.53 (30 November 2000), 26-29.

'Time for a New Commitment', AR, 177.53 (30 November 2000), 40.

'This Strange Journey', AR, 178.8 (22 February 2001), 22-23.

'Message for Pilgrims', MR, 106.18 (17 August 2001), 20.

'Growing Together', AR, 178.36 (6 September 2001), 16-20.

'The Word Unites Us in Mission', AR, 178.39 (27 September 2001), 11-13.

'Coming Together around the World', AR, 178.39 (27 September 2001), 40.

'The Only Secure Future', AR, 178.40 (4 October 2001), 7.

'Leading an Exploding Church', AR, 178.40 (4 October 2001), 21-24.

'At Such a Time as This', RD, 106.39 (6 October 2001), 8.

'Swept Up in Christ', AR, 178.48 (29 November 2001), 4-12.

'Mission in a Troubled World', AR, 178.50 (13 December 2001), 8-11.

'In Times Like These: A Conversation with the President … After September 11', AR, 179.1 (3 January 2002), 24.

'In Times Like These: A Conversation with the President … On Africa', AR, 179.7 (14 February 2002), 17.

'In Times Like These: A Conversation with the President … On Go One Million', AR, 179.12 (21 March 2002), 13.

'In Times Like These: A Conversation with the President … ' [No further title], AR, 179.18 (2 May 2002), 12-13.

'The Theological Landscape', AR, 179.24 (13 June 2002, Supplement), 1-8.

'Mission and Vision', VR, 107 (15 June 2002), 4.

'In Times Like These: A Conversation with the President … ' [No further title], AR, 179.28 (11 July 2002), 17.

'Whom Do We Worship?' AR, 179.39 (26 September 2002), 11-13.

'For Times Like These', AR, 179.39 (26 September 2002), 40.

'Living It. That's What It's All About!', MY, 74.10 (October 2002), 5-7.

'In Times Like These: A Conversation with the President … On Mission', AR, 179.50 (12 December 2002), 16.

'In Times Like These: A Conversation with the President … ' [No further title], AR, 180.2 (9 January 2003), 22.

'Let's Talk', YMA (January - March 2003), 3-7, 8-19.

'Religion, 'Pure and Faultless'', AR, 180.10 (6 March 2003), 36-40.

'In Times Like These: A Conversation with the President … On Remuneration', AR, 180.11 (13 March 2003), 22.

'In Times Like These: A Conversation with the President … Re-Imagining the Pastor', AR, 180.14 (n.d. April 2003), 32-33.

'Committed to Liberty & Mission', LY, 98.3 (May - June 2003), 16-19.

'Meaningful Grace: Why We Need It So Desperately', RD, 108.35 (6 September 2003), 3-5.

'Grace for Troubled Times', AR, 180.39 (25 September 2003), 32.

'In Times Like These: A Conversation with the President … A View from Abroad', AR, 180.41 (9 October 2003), 22-23.

'Evangelism? Yes! But Also Mission', AR, 181.11 (11 March 2004), 8-13.

'Giving Our Youth a "Voice" ', AR, 181.36 (2 September 2004), 40-43.

'United in the Fellowship of Christ', AR, 181.40 (30 September 2004), 3-5.

'In the Warmth of Fellowship', AR, 181.40 (30 September 2004), 32.

'The General Conference President Says', MR, 110.2 (28 January 2005), 3.

'GC President Responds to Tsunami Disaster', AR, 182.5 (3 February 2005), 42.

'To Delegates and Attendees at the 2005 General Conference Session', SWUR, 104.6 (June 2005), 27.

'I-Chat with the President', IT, 36.25 (2 July 2005), 8-10.

'Welcome to Delegates', AR, 182.27 (GC Bulletin 1, July 2005, 2.

'Compelled by Mission', AR, 182.27 (GC Bulletin 1, July 2005), 16-19.

'Mission is Our Objective', AR, 182.28 (GC Bulletin 2, 3 July 2005), 3.

'If My People', AR, 182.34 (GC Bulletin 8, 14 July 2005), 18-20.

'Seventh-day Adventist World President Invites Delegates to the 2005 World Session', OK, 91.3 (July - September 2005), 4.

'The Church of the Open Door', AW, 1.1 (September 2005), 8-9.

'United in Witness of Truth', AR, 182.40 (15 September 2005), 3-5.

'Unity and Mission', RD, 109.38 (1 October 2005), 8-9.

'A Tapestry of Adventism', AW, 1.2 (October 2005), 8-10.

'One in Christ', AW, 1.3 (November 2005), 8-9.

'A Vital Role', SAT, 4.6 (November-December 2005), 4.

'Our Youth: A Still Vastly Untapped Resource for God', AW, 1.4 (December 2005), 8-9.

'Embracing the Unique', AW, 2.1 (January 2006), 8-9.

'Focused on the Kingdom, Bonded by the Spirit', MY, 79 [sic] = 78.1 (January 2006), 14-17.

'The Aroma of Christ', AW, 2.2 (February 2006), 8-9.

'The Pilgrim's Journey', AR, 183.5 (16 February 2006), 8-11.

'Teaching Religion for the Church: An Interview with Jan Paulsen', JAE, 68.3 (February - March 2006), 4-9.

'Let's Talk', AR, 183.7 (9 March 2006), 8-13.

'Holy Spirit: Personable Power. The Old Testament Presence', SSL, 10.4 (April 2006), 10.

'Holy Spirit: Personable Power. The Enabler', SSL, 10.4 (April 2006), 11.

'Let's Talk', AW, 2.5 (May 2006), 8.

'A World-Embracing Vision', AW, 2.6 (June 2006), 8-10.

'Freedom and Deference: A Testing Bond', AW, 2.7 (July 2006), 8-10.

'No Time to be Spectators', AW, 2.8 (August 2006), 8.

'Eve: Hope Ignited', AR, 183.27 (28 September 2006).

'The Openness that Lies before Us', AW, 2.10 (October 2006), 8-10.

'Seeing through God's Eyes', AW, 2.11 (November 2006), 8-9.

'Images of Africa', AW, 2.12 (December 2006), 8-9.

'Service: An Attitude', AW, 3.1 (January 2007), 8-10.

'Crossroads in My Life', AW, 3.2 (February 2007), 8-9.

'A Church Rejoicing', AW, 3.3 (March 2007), 8-9.

'Leadership: True Christian Leadership', SSL, 11.3 (March 2007), 12.

'Leadership: Advice from a President', SSL, 11.3 (March 2007), 13.

'Women and Ministry: A Good Combination', AW, 3.4 (April 2007), 8-10.

'Serving our World, Serving our Lord', AW, 3.5 (May 2007), 8-10.

'Telling the World Who We Are', AW, 3.6 (June 2007), 8-9.

'When Words Are Not Enough', AW, 3.7 (July 2007), 8-9.

'A Healthy Church: Part 1', AW, 3.8 (August 2007), 12-13.

'A Healthy Church: Part 2', AW, 3.9 (September 2007), 8-9.

'A Word from President Jan Paulsen', AR, 184.27 (27 September 2007), 32.

'Do Not Let your Hearts be Troubled', AR, 184.27 (27 September 2007), 3-5.

'A Healthy Church: Part 3', AW, 3.10 (October 2007), 8-9.

'Beyond Stereotypes', AW, 3.11 (November 2007), 8.

'In Conversation with Pastors', AW, 3.12 (December 2007), 8-9.

'Shared Responsibility, Shared Trust', AW, 4.1 (January 2008), 8-10.

'Working Together, Seeking Consensus', AW, 4.2 (February 2008), 8-10.

'Clear Thinking about Military Service', AW, 4.3 (March 2008), 8-10.

'Reflections on Grace', LUH, 100.3 (March 2008), 30-31.

'Five Things the World Needs to Know about Us', AW, 4.5 (May 2008), 8-9.

'Freedom to Care', AW, 4.7 (July 2008), 8-10.

'Help Along the Way', AW, 4.8 (August 2008), 8-10.

'Going Forward Thoughtfully', AW, 4.9 (September 2008), 8-10.

'The Adventist Church and the Signs of the Times', AR, 185.27
    (25 September 2008), 3-5.

'Signs of Hope', AR, 185.27 (25 September 2008), 2.

'Looking Back at Let's Talk', AW, 4.10 (October 2008), 8-10.

'Is the General Conference Necessary?' AW, 4.11 (November 2008), 8-10.

'A New Humanity', AW, 4.12 (December 2008), 16-20.

'A Dynamic Church for Difficult Times', AW, 5.1 (January 2009), 8-10.

'Follow the Bible: A Journey to Spiritual Renewal', MY, 81.1 (January 2009), 5-8.

'5 Reasons I Rest Well at Night', AW, 5.2 (February 2009), 8-9.

'A Climate for Growth', AW, 5.4 (April 2009), 8-9.

'5 Things I Have Learned', AW, 5.5 (May 2009), 8-10.

'Look after Your Own Spiritual Growth', NV (May - June 2009), 16-17.

'Integrity = Openness + Trust', AW, 5.6 (June 2009), 8-10.

'Paulsen Speaks on Issues of Origins', AR, 186.19 (9 July 2009), 8-9.

'Finding Faith in China', AW, 5.8 (August 2009), 16-19.

'Christ's Healing in a Changing World', AW, 5.9 (September 2009), 8-10.

Unpublished Academic Papers and PhD Thesis

'The Coming of Methodism to West Nigeria with Particular Attention to its Growth among the Ijebu People' (unpublished PhD thesis, Eberhard-Karls-Universität zu Tuebingen, 1972).

'The Charismatic Movement: A Report of the Special Committee Meeting in Camp Cumby-Gay, Georgia', General Conference of Seventh-day Adventists, January 1973.

'The Holy Spirit and the Church [Prepared for the European Bible Conferences]', General Conference of Seventh-day Adventists, 1977.

'The Sanctuary/Judgment in the Book of Revelation' (General Conference of Seventh-day Adventists Daniel and Revelation Committee), 198- [n.d.].

Video Media

Let's Talk Series (Silver Spring, MD: General Conference of Seventh-day Adventists; People of Hope Production):

'Let's Talk', 2003.

'Let's Talk—Andrews University', 2004.

'Let's Talk—Avondale College', 2005

'Let's Talk—Cameroon', 2005.

'Let's Talk—Europe', 2005.

'Let's Talk—South Pacific', 2005.

'Let's Talk—World Session', 2005.

'Let's Talk—Oakwood College', 2006.

'Let's Talk—South Africa', 2006.

'Let's Talk—Uganda', 2006.

'Let's Talk—Brazil', 2007.

'Let's Talk—Caribbean', 2007.

'Let's Talk—New York City', 2007.

'Let's Talk New York City—Behind the Scenes', 2007.

'Let's Talk—Pacific Union College', 2007.

'Let's Talk—South America', 2007.

'Let's Talk—Hong Kong', 2008.

'Let's Talk—Manila', 2008.

'Let's Talk—Romania', 2008.

'Let's Talk—India', 2009.

'Let's Talk—Northern Asia-Pacific', 2009.

'Let's Talk—Ukraine', 2009.

'Let's Talk—Washington, DC', 2009.

Pastors: In Conversation Series (Silver Spring, MD: General Conference of Seventh-day Adventists; People of Hope Production):

'Pastors: In Conversation—North America', 2007.

'Pastors: In Conversation—Africa', 2008.

'Pastors: In Conversation—Europe', 2008.

'Pastors: In Conversation—South America', 2008.

'Pastors: In Conversation—Inter-America', 2009.

'Pastors: In Conversation—Northern Asia-Pacific', 2009.

Sundry

'Social Service/Social Action – Is that also God's Mission?', in *Adventist Missions Facing the 21st Century: A Reader*, ed. by Hugh I. Dunton, Baldur Ed. Pfeiffer and Borge Schantz, Archives of International Adventist History, 3 (Frankfurt am Main: Peter Lang, 1990), pp. 139-148.

Foreword for 'A Path Straight to the Hedges,' by Borge Schantz (Silver Spring, MD: Ministerial Association, 2000), pp 9-12.

'Compelled to Mission: Report to General Conference Session' (Silver Spring, MD: General Conference of Seventh-day Adventists), 2005.

'Bridge to the Future' (Silver Spring, MD: General Conference of Seventh-day Adventists), 2006.

'Time to Talk: Conversation with Women' (Silver Spring, MD: General Conference of Seventh-day Adventists, People of Hope Production), 2006.

'Almost Home—Completing the Journey' (Silver Spring, MD: Adventist Communication Network), 2008.

'Five Things I Want the World To Know' (Silver Spring, MD: General Conference of Seventh-day Adventists, People of Hope Production), 2008.

'Night Talk with Mike Schneider: Interview with Jan Paulsen' [webcast], Bloomberg Television, New York, NY, http://adventplanet.com/page/page.php?id=67 (February 11, 2008).

Book Reviews

Gottfried Oosterwal, Mission: *Possible. The Challenge of Mission Today* (Nashville, TN: Southern Publishing Association), 1972, in *Spectrum* 5.2 (February 1973), 63-66.

_____, *Modern Messianic Movements as a Theological and Missionary Challenge* (Elkhart, IN: Institute of Mennonite Studies), 1973, in *Andrews University Seminary Studies*, January 1976, 317-318.

Jan Paulsen—a Visionary Viking at the Helm

Børge Schantz

There are days in the land of the midnight sun when, in the winter, the sun does not rise above the horizon. It was into this dark world that Jan Paulsen was born on January 5, 1935, and during the first two weeks of his life the sun did not have a chance to shine on the newborn baby. However, five months later there was no sunset for fifty days.

Narvik, Norway, some 140 miles beyond the Arctic Circle, is one of the most northerly 'midnight sun' towns in the world. This means that Jan with his family—father Reidar Paulsen, a shoemaker; dedicated mother Alfhild, caretaker of the local Adventist church; and three brothers and one sister—lived the first fifteen years of his eventful life in an area where winter was like one long dark night and summer a time without sunset.

Early in his childhood Jan had his first cross-cultural experiences. The Laplanders (the Sámi people) with their Finno-Ugric language are known as nomadic reindeer keepers and sheep herders. Here the young boy had his first 'pastoral' experience as a shepherd for a Lapland neighbour.

Life in the thriving, isolated town followed a quiet, predictable and steady rhythm. Narvik, having very few roads, depended on its rail connection to Sweden. Connections to others towns in Norway were by ship. Port activities were one of the main sources of income in the town, because of its extensive transit facilities for the precious iron-ore from Sweden, destined for ports in Germany and England.

This rhythm was brutally disrupted by the outbreak of the Second World War. Both the Germans and the British wanted to secure Swedish iron ore for their war industries. On April 9, 1940, Narvik became a theatre of war. Armies and navies— with the Germans on one side, facing Norwegian, British, French and Polish soldiers on the other—were soon engaged in serious combat. For a short time the Norwegian general Fleischer had the upper hand and forced the Germans to retreat. However, German attacks continued, resulting in five years of German occupation of the town and of Norway. Repeated British air attacks made it necessary for the civilian population, including the Paulsen family, to be evacuated to safer places. These tragic events of war, experienced by Jan in his formative childhood years, no doubt made a deep impression on his thinking.

Jan Paulsen has his roots in the lands of the Vikings. Their voyages, a thousand years ago (800-1100 AD), reached countries which today stretch from Newfoundland to Iran, and from Norway to Algeria. The romanticized picture of Vikings as raiders is only one side of their history. With few men, simple organization and primitive means they colonized, ruled, bartered and settled in distant lands. But, more importantly, they also opened trade routes. They met Orthodox and Catholic Christians, and even Muslims on their far-ranging expeditions. Christianity put a stop to their exploits. Norsemen were probably the first Europeans to discover America. Interestingly, a descendant of these adventurous people, a millennium later, was elected leader of a missionary movement with the main goal of reaching into the far corners of the world.

Church membership and continued education
At age fourteen Jan decided to be baptized and to join the Adventist church in Narvik. The officiating pastor, Paul Frivold, who passed away just a few months ago, was also the pastor who encouraged Jan to study for the ministry and later, as conference president, called him to join the ministerial work.

Jan studied in local schools up to university entrance level. But from that point onwards he wanted to continue his education at an Adventist institution. At that time the West-Nordic Union was still in the process of building the Norwegian Junior College, Tyrifjord. So, in 1952, Jan had to travel 2,000 kilometers (1,200 miles) south to Vejlefjord, Denmark, for the first phase of his ministerial training. Danes and Norwegians studied together. The language posed no problem and the teachers were both Norwegians and Danes. The Bible teacher was Viggo Norskov Olsen, later president of Loma Linda University. At Vejlefjord Jan met another student from Norway: Kari Trykkerud. These two Norwegians, far away from home, soon developed an interest in each other. They married three years later and have now been happily together for fifty-five years.

The next eight years were spent in a ministerial internship in Stavanger, and studies at Andrews University in Michigan, USA (then Emmanuel Missionary College), which resulted in a Bachelors degree in 1957, and a Master of Arts degree in 1958. Then, after serving as pastor/evangelist in Haugesund (1958-1960), the young family returned to the United States—this time to the Theological Seminary in Washington, DC, where Jan obtained a Master of Divinity degree (MDiv) in 1962. It became clear that Jan's interests in Adventist ministry were, in particular, along educational and administrative lines. Interestingly, during this period of study Jan made his living as a night watchman at the old General Conference headquarters in Takoma Park, Washington.

Africa and Europe
In 1962 the Paulsen family, with their daughter Laila (born in 1961), accepted a call to serve as Bible teacher and chaplain at the Bekwai Seventh-day Adventist Secondary School and Teachers Training College in Ghana. Here Jan Paulsen served

with fellow Norwegian principal Øivind Gjertsen. Among the students was a young Ghanaian, Mathew A. Bediako, the current general secretary of the General Conference.

In 1963 Jan was ordained. In the same year Jan-Rune, their second child, was born. A year later the West African Union transferred the family to Nigeria to serve at the newly established Adventist College of West-Africa. Here Jan was to lead out in setting up one of the first ministerial training programmes in sub-Sahara Africa. Later he became the president of that institution — now Babcock University. At just 34 years of age, Jan Paulsen was probably the youngest principal of an Adventist seminary.

The family returned to Europe in 1968, when Jan Paulsen accepted a call from Newbold College. Here they would stay for twelve years. Jan served as the head of the theology department, and then, in 1976, became the principal — a position he held until 1980. During that period he obtained a study leave, which he spent in Tübingen, Germany. The university conferred the degree of Dr. theol. on him in 1972. Jan's doctoral dissertation, *The Coming of Methodism to West Nigeria, With Particular Attention to its Growth Among the Ijebu People*, was, according to his *Doktorvater* Peter Beyerhaus, an excellent evaluation of the Wesleyan mission to Nigeria.

The emphasis in his studies and in the dissertation was on mission theology. Jan's interests also included biblical and systematic theology. At Tübingen University he had the opportunity to attend lectures from outstanding Lutheran theologians such as Jürgen Moltmann.

The eighteen years of direct involvement with Adventist higher education ended in 1980. During these years Jan had proven himself not only a good teacher but also a solid administrator. Church administration was to be his main focus in the following three decades.

At the Dallas (Texas) General Conference session in 1980 Dr. Jan Paulsen was elected general secretary of the Trans-European (then Northern-European) Division. In 1983 he became the president of the same division, an appointment confirmed by the world church in session at the New Orleans (Louisiana) General Conference session in 1985. The Trans-European Division consists of thirty-seven countries on three continents, stretching across five times zones, from Pakistan to Iceland and extending North-South from Norway to Sudan. Inside the division borders are the world's greatest concentrations of Lutherans, Anglicans, Greek Orthodox, Jews and Muslims. The nations represent republics, kingdoms, Muslim governments (some with Shari'ah law) and new governments established in former Communist Eastern Europe. In truth, it is a division that demands diplomacy, cultural adaptations and religious adjustments. Jan Paulsen stayed in this position until 1995.

At the front line

I met Jan and Kari for the first time fifty-seven years ago. They were students at Vejlefjord, while I was conscripted into national service. Nine years later we met again in West Africa. Although we worked in different countries and positions, we met regularly at union committee meetings and other occasions. Subsequently we were together in England for thirteen years—he in division administration and I at Newbold College and the Islamic Study Centre. When Jan and Kari moved to Washington we kept in contact with each other. We have common field experiences, we share acquaintances and friends, and use a similar language. Over the years we have been in touch, socially and professionally. We have worked together, socialized together and dialogued on issues. We have agreed as well as disagreed.

Jan was prepared to dialogue with students in the classroom and lecture halls. Even the most vexing questions on doctrine, biblical themes and church issues were not dismissed but accepted for debate. However, the lecturer always made clear where he stood and always presented the church's position. His students appreciated this.

I have watched Jan preach in shirt sleeves in the open air to small groups in African villages, but also as the main speaker at annual sessions, held in elegant halls in Europe, with large audiences. We have worked together under primitive conditions, teaching Bible, pastoral care and evangelism for ministers with limited formal education. But we also shared an experience where Jan was in dialogue about a biblical theme with experienced theologians. I have watched Jan in a confidential situation, as he tried to persuade a fellow-worker to remain loyal to church principles; in a committee room as he led out in a tense discussion on financial matters, and in a cordial meeting with the world leader of another Christian tradition. We have been together in a tent in a desert area, under primitive conditions, where in an act of exorcism he laid his hands on a demon-possessed woman. For budgetary reason we once had to live in a two-star hotel (the bed being too short for the more than six-feet-tall Jan). It was during an evangelistic campaign in a Muslim country. It was worth all the hardships when, with the other pastors, often two or three in the same pool, we baptised about 400 people as the result of different campaigns.

The entire world

At the General Conference Session in the Netherlands in 1995 Dr. Jan Paulsen was elected as one of the vice-presidents of the world church, and thus moved to the General Conference headquarters near Washington, DC. He remained in that position until 1999, when, in special circumstances, the Executive Committee of the world church elected him, between sessions, as the nineteenth world president. This election was confirmed at the Toronto, Canada, General Conference Session in 2000. Jan was re-elected in 2005 at the Saint Louis, Missouri, session.

Briefly stated, this means that Dr. Jan Paulsen is the administrative leader of the world-wide Seventh-day Adventist Church with about 16 million members. The movement has more than 200,000 employees, which means that one in every 80 members works for the church. There are currently 7,500 Adventist educational and health institutions. The number of students from the primary to the doctoral level exceeds 1.4 million. The world 'field' is divided into 13 divisions, 103 unions, 571 conferences and missions, with a total of about 65,000 churches. The president chairs dozens of committees and is an *ex officio* member of all councils and committees of the world church. The consolidated annual budget of the church is more than US$ 2.6 billion. All these activities take place in 201 of the world's 230 countries. Jan Paulsen's official trips—travelling on a Norwegian passport—have taken him to all continents, across the 24 time zones. In his fifteen years on the presidential floor in the General Conference building he has, so far, visited 84 of the nations of the world. In addition to all the demanding tasks that have to do with the church, the president of the world church also represents the denomination to the secular as well as to the religious world. It is part of his assignment to meet heads of state, international political leaders, church leaders and representatives from world religions.

The pilgrimage of the boy who fled from fighting armies in Norway, via Denmark, Ghana, Nigeria and England to the United States, where, as a mature man, he ended up occupying the top position at the General Conference, has been a remarkable journey. As in the case of Abraham of old, it could be argued that important developments in Jan's career took place in each new geographical stage of his journey. There have been Shechems, Bethels, Hebrons and even Mt. Moriahs in Jan's life. His acceptance of various 'calls' provided him and his family with international experiences and challenges. Each station granted useful opportunities for further development. As the years passed, Jan acquired cross-cultural flexibility, learned new languages, experienced increased educational opportunities, and sharpened his executive skills. To travel is to learn. In order to learn one needs an open mind. Life experience is transformed into useful leadership skills, when it is based on healthy ambitions. Personal aspirations are not only useful professionally, for the church and its progress in all aspects. They are also incentives for performance that lead to personal acceptance and a good reputation. They have to be combined with sincere humility. A good leader of an international church—with a membership three times the population of his home country, Norway—demands, in addition to these qualities, the sense of a spiritual need for dependence on, and acceptance of, divine guidance.

A Scandinavian Lutheran church leader described the solution to his theological/administrative tensions in this way: 'I sought counsel from the Word and he told me to go to Experience. I went to Experience and she referred me back to the Word. And I became a happy messenger between the two of them.' This may well at times also have been Jan Paulsen's administrative experience, when decisions on practical matters seemed to conflict with theological/doctrinal creeds.

The results of Jan Paulsen's pilgrimages were residence on three continents, the ability to preach in three languages (Norwegian, English and German) and obtaining various academic degrees culminating in a Dr. theol. degree from a renowned German university. He acquired executive experience in an educational as well as a general church setting. Jan Paulsen is a leader. There is something about him and his imposing stature that, when he enters the room, leaves no doubts in anyone's mind that he is the chief.

Jan Paulsen responsibilities, his work, assignments, travels, comments, expressions and appointments, are well known to Adventists in general. He is the Adventist world leader who has the most comprehensive coverage on television, the internet, and in the Adventist magazines and church papers. It stands to reason that many of these activities, even awards and honorary degrees, are almost automatically bestowed on a General Conference president. However, Jan Paulsen's style of administration and leadership has made him highly respected and esteemed beyond what generally goes with the office.

Unity in diversity

At the turn of the century Jan was elected to guide the church from its twentieth century 'modernist' style into the twenty-first century with its 'post-modernist' tendencies. Highly significant, often revolutionary, factors emerge, which, on occasion, challenge the more traditional emphasis on spiritual values and the 'remnant' concepts of Adventism. It would be difficult to point to what could be termed a common denominator for Jan Paulsen's administration of more than a decade. But perhaps it is best encapsulated by the slogan I have chosen as the title for this paragraph: *unity in diversity*. In all Jan Paulsen's administrative activities and spiritual instructions—theologically and organizationally—with regard to all kinds of topics, the underlying premise was to stay united. For him unity is not necessarily to be interpreted as *uniformity*. He has always called for an acceptable balance between the beliefs and practices of Adventism. Because of his balanced theological views and doctrinal interpretations, the majority of both conservative and liberal church members share a confidence in his leadership.

Pursuing the goal of unity in the Seventh-day Adventist Church is next to an impossible task. The 16 million believers live in over 200 nations. They represent more than 1500 ethnic groups and cultural subdivisions, and speak 700 languages. Among them are rich and poor, educated and illiterate, young and old, liberal and conservative, and now also 'modern' and 'postmodern' people. At his level, Jan's contribution is to keep unity and balance in the diversity of the many components of spiritual, ethnical, cultural, linguistic and administrative categories in the world church. It is obvious that to achieve a unity in world-wide observances, even in the interpretation of fundamental beliefs as well as of church policies, is an extremely difficult, perhaps even impossible, task. The more so, since fundamental beliefs, church ordinances and policies are generally expressed in terms and concepts that have been influenced by western styles and cultures. They must to a greater or lesser extent not only be translated but also be adapted to the various geographical areas where the church has a presence.

Jan Paulsen, in addition to his desire to keep the church united, often stresses that Adventist Christians should be positively involved in the life of the local community. The church must not only preach the everlasting gospel to the world, but also has a responsibility to promote human rights and social justice by community involvement. God's call to reconciliation is also a call to a Christian involvement in society. Seventh-day Adventists should be part of the community in which they live and use their opportunities to take part in activities in the domains of welfare and development. A specific emphasis is to be seen in areas of public health, as in the fight against HIV/AIDS and against drugs. Adventists who live in geographical areas where civil strife and ethnic cleansing are current, or have taken place in the recent past, have been admonished by Paulsen to be loyal citizens and to work for peace and understanding.

Leaders of world religions and international Christian denominations will unavoidably on their trips to various countries be met by reporters who are keen on getting brief statements on controversial questions that are important, but often touchy, in their religious/political environments and special situations. This, of course, also regularly happens to the head of the Seventh-day Adventist church with members in countries with all kinds of political governments and religious belief systems. Even local Adventist reporters are often keen to get the president's assessment of a critical issue. His comments may be widely published and used in the general press and in church periodicals.

It is next to impossible for an international world leader in his itineraries to be aware of all pitfalls of a political or religious character hidden in questions. Ready and unprepared answers, reactions and opinions will always run the risk that they are generally not enlightened by a thorough knowledge of the facts. 'Politically correct' statements are convenient but, as it happens, often not trustworthy. Every statement will, however, be open to criticisms, gainsays and interpretations in such a way that they will on occasion not express the true position of the church or help the local community. It has, however, been observed that Jan Paulsen generally has been careful in that respect.

A genuine understanding and concern for the future of the movement is revealed in Jan Paulsen's televised encounters with Adventist youth on all six continents. In a relaxed way he answered questions of a theological or organizational nature, and dealt with some of the positive and negative aspects of postmodernism.

Middle-of-the-road approach

I happen to belong to Jan's contemporaries in both age and employment. Together with friends and colleagues in various countries and in different lines of responsibility, I have had the opportunity, during more than a half century, of following Jan in his service to the church. Many of us, as his contemporaries, have worked with him, supported him through the years and even voted for him in elections that brought him to ever higher responsibilities.

At the time when Jan became the helmsman, the Adventist world was in need of stability. He has rightly been praised for contributing to this stability and for his attempts in all situations to maintain unity in diversity. We have, naturally, observed and dialogued with him as a friend about the way in which he has dealt with certain issues. His consistent efforts to keep the balance, in order to maintain unity, lead us to describe him as a middle-of-the-road driver—always aiming for a centre line on the road of church administration.

With Jan in the driver's seat and taking the lead, other drivers in the 'entourage' of the church have tended to follow the same course. A steady middle-of-the-road journey has the advantage that the vehicle will stay safely away from alluring but often dangerous ditches, both to the right and to the left. However, some may feel that safe driving in the middle of the road on occasion did not provide sufficient opportunities to develop and try new plans and strategies that may be found along some of the by-ways.

When it became known in 1999 that the new president was Jan Paulsen, many heads of institutions and departments expressed their approval and indicated they were pleased with the choice. Various reasons could be listed for this welcome for the new president. Educators felt that they now had a president who could understand their situation, as his initial experience on two continents had been in the field of education. Bible teachers were pleased that a theologian was now in charge, for they faced severe issues and tensions that needed attention. Those involved with foreign missions appreciated having a missiologist at the helm. All the various church departments, no doubt, felt they could draw on a president with international experience as educator, theologian and missiologist. Some might even have entertained the idea that Paulsen's election could be to their advantage, as they possibly assumed that, because of his previous experience, he might have a special interest in precisely their field of work. As an administrator with practical and international experience Jan Paulsen had, no doubt, valuable contributions to make to various departments. But he was determined to serve the entire church and to foster unity in the multitude of departments and activities. Many assignments are normally delegated to fellow-leaders who have the president's backing. Only reluctantly is Jan Paulsen prepared to reconsider decisions and actions by appointed committees and their chairpersons. Jan has shown himself to be a president and an administrator with a clear responsibility for all branches and activities.

In his writing and sermons strong biblical, theological and spiritual concerns and insights are apparent. They are safe and sound in their promotion of Adventist biblical theology, a Christian life-style, a personal relationship with the Saviour, Jesus Christ, and a call to the readers and listeners to contribute to the society around them. They provide solid, well-thought-out biblical principles that are presented in a dignified manner. A genuine pastoral care has always been the core of his messages. Careful listeners and readers will get sound spiritual food. However, they have to be alert. Innovations, such as overhead projectors and power-point presentations, are rarely, if ever, used. Personal experiences and suitable incidents from the Adventist world field are seldom used to illustrate a point. Pure biblical principles are set forth.

Leadership style

Jan is a hardworking president. He wastes no time and is well-organized in his activities. The Skype section on my laptop reveals that sometimes as early as 5:00 am Jan deals with some of his email correspondence. The president of the General Conference has fast and direct communication with all fields and institutions. It is, however, a two-way stream. A continuous flow of reports and suggestions, praise and even disapproval and criticism comes his way. He has a staff in his office that will take care of many matters and will deal with insincere and unwanted messages. Various responsibilities are delegated to fellow-leaders and associates.

I see Jan Paulsen as a balanced leader in his work, influence and achievements. Given the size of the Adventist movement in the early twenty-first century, there will unavoidably be reactions and disagreements to any administrative and leadership style, whether of a theological, organizational, missiological or personal character. It is unavoidable that at times mistakes are made and wrong decisions are arrived at, by the leader as well as the team members. Jan is known for fairness in accepting blame, even for actions and decision made by fellow-workers to whom certain assignments have been delegated.

A Scandinavian

Jan's leadership is undoubtedly influenced by his Norwegian culture and up-bringing. Typical Scandinavian characteristics are—perhaps a little negatively—expressed in the *Jante Law* which is based on the book *A Refugee Crosses his Tracks*, written in 1933 by the Norwegian/Danish author Aksel Sandemose. The plot is set in an imaginary small town called Jante and is about the Scandinavian mentality as expressed in unspoken rules in communities. The *Jante Law* in essence says: Who do you think you are? Don't think you are better than us! Don't think that you are special!

In its more comprehensive form the *Jante Law* can be positively interpreted to mean,
- that there is a borderline between the private sphere and work;
- that rational reasons have a strong precedence over emotional reasons (emotions are regarded as a signal for unhappiness with life or fate);
- that quietness is the commonly accepted norm (noisy people are strongly disapproved of. Vociferous stubbornness is deemed very ill-mannered);
- that you think twice before you speak (only utter your most firmly held beliefs when there is a considered intention);
- that to be kind and good-natured is important. (One prefers to be quiet or agreeable, instead of uttering an opposing opinion, unless one really aims at hurting others);
- that you try not to lose your temper even when severely provoked.

Parts of the *Jante Law* could spiritually have been based on the words of the apostle Paul in Romans 12:3. 'For I say, through the grace given to me, to everyone who is among you, not to think of himself more highly than he ought to think, but to think soberly, as God has dealt to each one a measure of faith.'

Applying these Scandinavian norms to the Norwegian Jan Paulsen, one finds that he is not inclined to promote himself by talking about his own actions, deeds and achievements. In his reports he does not make a habit of dropping names, although he has met more heads of state and religious world leaders and other celebrities than any other General Conference president. He is not given to flattery. He is really rather sparing in his compliments to fellow workers for their achievements. When dealing with people and issues, even with difficult personalities and in knotty situations, he is known to be calm, not easily losing his temper. However, his stand on issues will be revealed in a quiet way, by carefully chosen words or body language. Jan stands no nonsense. He has a direct, sometimes frank—nonetheless diplomatic—way of letting others understand when he feels that one has gone too far.

Jan has many friends, but probably very few close friends. The contemporary fashion for many executives to consult so-called 'spin-doctors,' who are expected to know what is going on and help devise shrewd strategies, is not part of Jan's administrative style. But although having few close friends and no spin-doctors could be a strength—possibly even a necessity— it can also at times make senior leadership a very lonesome experience. 'It can be very cold at the top,' another Norwegian leader told me years ago.

The president in private

Jan is a husband, father, father-in-law and grandfather, and until recently also a son. Kari, his wife for more than fifty-five years, has been an intelligent partner. Kari has served as a good and balanced counsellor to her husband. Not only in family and household affairs, but also in church matters. As a student at Vejlefjord, when Viggo Norskov Olsen was their main instructor, Kari received the commendation that she was an extremely capable student with insights into theological and biblical themes that surpassed most other students, and even equalled Jan's. Kari has been a hostess for the many social gatherings that also are part of the president's public function. She has been a representative first lady on the public platform, both when meeting with church officials and in government settings.

Kari is not robust by nature. For years she has suffered from various serious ailments that would have caused many other people to give up or, at least, demand a life that is less taxing than the role of a first lady. Her state of health has required constant supervision by various medical specialists. During the years in the tropical climate in the part of Africa where they were missionaries, Kari, however, never asked for 'permanent return.' But after six years it became necessary to return to Europe.

Jan could probably not have accepted the subsequent demanding assignments without Kari's approval and support. Their marriage gave them three children. The oldest, their daughter Laila, lives in England with her husband Vladimir. Laila has an advanced degree in nursing and is an instructor in that field in the school of nursing connected with a British university. Jan-Rune, born 1963, decided that his field was to be more practical, and he travelled as a technician. It was on of these assignments in Kiel, Germany, in 2000, that he tragically fell ten meters (thirty feet) and landed on a concrete slab. He is still undergoing rehabilitation. The youngest son, Rein Andre, born in 1970, has a leading position in a prestigious relief and welfare organisation. He is married to Aimée, who came from Congo. They have provided the Paulsens with two grandsons, Jan Reidar and Hans Olav. They currently live and work in Switzerland.

One of the issues in missiology is to understand what it means to be a MK (a missionary kid). Missionary families are called to serve in other countries. They are enriched by multicultural encounters. However, the children—the MKs—may pay a high price for the advantages of cross-cultural understanding and mastering a foreign language. They can suffer from the loss of steady friends, and may even feel somewhat rootless in their home countries. One of the consequences of the 'one hundred percent Norwegian Paulsen family's international experience' is that they now live in four different countries.

Jan Paulsen's mother died in 2006. She was in her nineties when she passed away. Jan was close to his mother and counted her as the person who has had the greatest influence on his life and Christian experience. The loss of a mother, although she passed away well beyond the Psalmist's norm of seventy or even eighty years, is always hard. It is a final *good bye*.

A short time after her departure from this life (but not as a result of it), the Adventist church in Narvik was dissolved and the church building sold. The church in the town where Jan was born and was baptized thus ceased to exist. This must no doubt have been a tragic reminder to Jan that, although the growth of the Advent movement has gone from 11 million in 2000 until it now has passed the 16 million mark, the remarkable increase in membership is generally in areas south of the Tropic of Cancer. In the traditional Christian nations, stagnation, or even a membership decline, is a sad part of the reports.

Appreciation expressed

Authors of various chapters of the *Festschrift* and many whose names are on the Congratulatory List wanted to express their personal appreciation for Dr. Paulsen's leadership, as well as for his personal interest in them. As the editors of this book, we feel that the chapters in themselves and the many names on the Congratulatory List are tributes to Jan as a leader. The hours of research and work put into them are, no doubt, a heart-felt thank-you to Jan for his leadership and friendship. A few specially chosen greetings which cover the general spirit of admiration and personal thankfulness from various contributors have, however, been chosen.

A former student of Jan Paulsen summarizes the result of Jan's teaching by stating that for him the Bible was never the same again, as Paulsen presented a new way of engaging with Scripture. 'Our horizons were expanded and stimulated in exegetical creativity.'

A fellow leader remarked that Jan should be recognized for his many important contributions, such as his *outstanding Christian leadership*, but also for his *ethical integrity*. This was confirmed by a lecturer who emphasized Jan Paulsen's 'remarkable outstanding ability to sustain tensions of various kinds.' The positive evaluation of Dr. Paulsen continues: 'He managed to speak to the liberal and conservative wings of the church and to all those in between, in such a way as to avoid any major ruptures in the body of the church. He shows himself capable of deep theological reflection. You might even call him mystical at times. And yet he has responded to the demands of the modern world of television interviews and podcasts, having always believed that the young people of the church may be entrusted with responsibility at an age earlier than thought wise by some of his peers.'

Another author states that it is a refreshing pleasure to write a chapter in the *Festschrift* as 'we are honouring a church leader and not just a scholar. In other words, we are honouring a church leader with scholarly leanings, rather than a church scholar with leadership leanings.'

The rule we (the editors) established, that the names of persons who made these comments of praise should not be mentioned, will in one case be ignored. The exception is Dr. Peter Beyerhaus, former professor and director of the Institute of Missiology and Ecumenical Theology at Tübingen University, Germany. Dr. Beyerhaus is a renowned Lutheran missiologist, and in his younger years served as a missionary to Southern Africa. During Jan's studies, which in 1972 allowed him to add the letters Dr. theol. to his name, Peter Beyerhaus was not only his *Doktorvater*. He became a special friend, as strong bonds developed between the Beyerhaus and Paulsen families. Mrs. Beyerhaus is originally from Sweden.

Dr. Peter Beyerhaus introduced his special chapter of the *Festschrift* with these words:

> That Dr. Paulsen's career 27 years later would end up at the top of the world-wide Seventh-day Adventist Church we could never have imagined. Now his high position and, moreover, the fact that consequently Tübingen University lists President Paulsen amongst the Notable Laureates in Theology—together with Pope Benedict XVI, Dietrich Bonhoeffer and Hans Küng—fills us with pardonable pride!

Autobiography

It is a common trend that, following their retirement, leaders write their memoirs. There are many interesting and enlightening autobiographies by statesmen and -women, politicians, business people, religious leaders and many others. They show how people in retirement may feel inclined not only to emphasize the highlights of their careers, but also to acknowledge wrong decisions, negligence in some areas, or even mistakes they may have made during their administration. When a person is no longer in charge, no longer carries heavy responsibilities, and, as a result, is less exposed to criticism and opposition, it may be easier to speak of things that have not gone so well. Such memoirs may help to explain past history and may contain lessons for future leaders.

It would be interesting if one day, after Jan Paulsen retires, we will be able to benefit from his life story and memoirs in an autobiography. Perhaps in those memoirs we will find interesting paragraphs on his personal views on such issues as the theology of ordination (including the ordination of women), a re-organization of the church to achieve greater efficiency, the question as to how much the Advent message can be contextualized, and the unavoidable challenges and tensions that may exist between theological propositions and administrative resolutions, and a few other interesting issues.

Final words

Wikipedia states that 'a *Festschrift* is typically published on the occasion of the honoree's retirement, sixtieth or sixty-fifth birthday, or other notable career anniversary.' The 'excuse' for this *Festschrift* is a seventy-fifth birthday. As editors we find ourselves in the interesting situation that the person we want to honour and appreciate is still in a demanding and active global leadership role, while we ourselves, and half of the contributors, are contemporaries of Jan, but have already entered the 'sustentation' phase of our lives. We decided therefore, that if we as seniors are going to initiate a *Festschrift*, we have to use the seventy-fifth birthday as the excuse. We realize, however, that Moses was eighty years old when he was called by God for the most demanding and important task in not only his life but also in the history of God's people. Jan, with his good health and clear mind, could possibly follow the example of the patriarch. With this *Festschrift*, however, we confine ourselves to wishing Jan a happy seventy-fifth birthday, and express our appreciation for his first seventy-five years, and sincerely hope that he will yet have many more anniversaries to celebrate.

May the good Lord of Mission bless the Paulsen family and the world-wide church he so ably is serving.

The Backbone of Spiritual Leadership: Battling in Prayer

Peter P. J. Beyerhaus

The aim of this presentation is to point out that prayer involves spiritual struggle, especially in connection with mission and evangelism, and that such wrestling prayer is an indispensable prerequisite for spiritual leadership.

I Theological Foundation

The place of intercession in the divine drama of salvation

Prayer and battle—can these two go together? Do they not exclude each other, since prayer sets our mind at rest, whilst battling inflames? 'Sweet hours of prayer' runs the opening line of a well known hymn, and I hope that many readers can confirm this from their own experience. Yes, such an experience is a reality, a precious gift of the Holy Spirit to God's children—at least for certain times—which we can never value highly enough.

But we would be fatefully wrong, if we thought that this is the whole truth about prayer. For there is also another side to it, no less important. We learn from the Bible that many a time the believer's spiritual life is not a mystical enjoyment, but rather a serious task, and at times even a fierce battle. And so prayer, too, can assume the form of a hot struggle. Think of such well known examples as *Jacob*, who in the valley of the Jabbok river fell on his knees to pray, and all of a sudden found himself wrestling desperately with a stranger, a battle that lasted that entire night and brought him to complete exhaustion (Gen 32:23-33)! Think of *Moses* who had to pray with his arms lifted up all through the battle with the Amalekites (Ex 17:8-13). Have you ever tried to keep up your arms in that position for more than five minutes? Or think of *Jesus* himself, who in his prayer in the garden of Gethsemane was overwhelmed by such agony that he shed drops of sweat, mingled with tears and blood! (Lk 22:44; Heb 5:7).

The whole history of the world, from its creation to its final consummation, can be described as a cosmic drama. Adventists will be eager to agree with this. The drama has its catastrophic beginning with the fall of Adam; it has its decisive turning point in the middle—when God sent his Son to our rescue. And it will end with a great triumph, when God will send him for the second time to set up his messianic kingdom in power and glory. Evangelism is the way in which believers become involved in this drama. For world-evangelization is the most important task of the church in the time between the two comings of Christ. To evangelize means to proclaim the dual victory of our Lord: The victory which he has already won over Satan, sin and death at his cross and in his resurrection; and the future victory which we are expecting at his Second Coming.

In the meantime, however, we are engaged in an on-going warfare with Satan. Although he has already been decisively defeated, even during his retreat he renders a furious resistance to the redemptive work of God amongst men. Jesus himself called him the *prince of this world* (John 12:31; 14:30; 16:11)—even at this present stage! Satan knows that his days are numbered. He also knows he cannot oppose Christ directly any more. Therefore he tries to attack him indirectly through his believers by frustrating their spiritual life and work. In this struggle the church has a twofold task: She has to defend the position which she holds as the body of Christ; and she is to go out in mission to claim for Christ's saving rule such new territories as are still occupied by the kingdom of darkness. In view of this dual assignment the church in her present state on earth is called the 'church militant'; once the battle is over she will be called the 'church triumphant.'

That future is already enjoyed by the martyrs, for they live in the presence of Christ whom they confessed until death. In its triumphant state the whole church will be rewarded for her faithful struggle by receiving a share in Christ's own eternal bliss. It was to the members of the struggling church at Thyatira that the heavenly Lord sent the message: 'He who conquers and who keeps my words until the end, I will give him power over the nations ... even as I myself have received power from my Father, and I will give him the morning star' (Rev 2:26-27).

But even now God has not left his church to herself in her struggle. He has given to her some most effective tools: He has endowed her and he is constantly ready to endow her anew with his Holy Spirit and his divine Word—mighty weapons indeed. And Paul has shown in Ephesians 6:10-19 how these weapons are attained and reinforced in us, i.e. by prayer. It is by prayer that we plead with God for the equipment we need in the battle, particularly that of evangelism and world mission, and, generally, in guarding the church against the attacks of the gates of hell (Mat 16:20). One of the final acts of Jesus Christ, the head of the church, before he went to the cross was to commend his disciples to the protection of his Father in heaven. Thereby he set an example for every future leader in the church.

Without prayer we remain unarmed, and without arms we cannot win. On the contrary: We will lose any spiritual battle, both on the individual level in personal evangelism and on the corporate level when trying to win a new people for Christ. So the fulfilment of God's eternal plan of salvation, which is carried out in evangelizing every nation on earth before the kingdom of God can come in power, depends on our faithfulness in becoming armed by praying, and involving ourselves in this spiritual warfare by witnessing to the gospel in the power of the Holy Spirit, which we receive in answer to such prayer.

The three opponents in our spiritual warfare

If our Christian life is marked by a continuous warfare, we need to know who actually are our opponents in the battle. Basically, they are three in number, but they are very unlike each other.

a. The devil

We have already pointed at Satan as the basic enemy of Christ and his church. He does not fight alone but commands a whole host of demonic forces. Through the messianic work of Jesus, God's Son, Satan has already received his decisive blow. Once an archangel in a very exalted position in the angelic hierarchy, he rebelled against God and caused disruption, confusion and disintegration in the entire visible and invisible world. But by the redemptive work of Christ he lost his original position. Jesus himself saw him falling down like lightning from heaven (Lk 10:18). He reacts to his defeat furiously, trying to sweep along with him as many souls as possible to make them share his eternal damnation. Yet his power is restrained by Christ. Those who cling faithfully to him cannot be overcome by the devil, because Jesus protects them (1 John 4-5, 18). Satan, however, tries hard to cut our spiritual connection with our Lord by infusing his own spirit into our hearts. He has many different approaches to attack us: he tempts us individually, and he uses the fascination of foreign religions and modern ideologies to make us think, feel and act contrary to the Spirit of God and his way of salvation. In our times he even enters into the churches themselves by substituting an ideologically infected pseudo-gospel for their biblical preaching. This is a special challenge to all church leaders, as Paul shows in his 'pastoral letters' to Timothy and Titus (1 Tim 6:3-5; 2 Tim 3:1-5; Titus 1:10-16).

Today we are also experiencing an incredible emergence of occultism: astrology, divination, magic practices, eastern mysticism. Even open Satanism has intruded into our formerly Christian countries, using many means, including certain types of pop music. Christians are not always sensitive to these dangers and therefore they are spiritually weakened without recognizing the cause. They ought to be on their guard, making use of Bible study and prayer. Satan knows this is their best weapon to counteract his temptations. Therefore he tries his utmost to dissuade Christians from praying, telling them that they have so many other important duties to do right now, or that at this late hour of the day they are too tired. I can imagine that the president of a world-wide church with more than 16 million members in more than 200 countries may be especially tempted by such a thought time and again, but I trust that my dear disciple and friend will not give in to such insinuations. Indeed, really great people in church history, who were in extraordinary measure used by the Lord to achieve great things, in the midst of hard work still took enough time for prayer. Martin Luther once told his friends that he usually prayed two hours every morning, except on those days when he had to cope with an especially hard task. 'Then,' he said, 'I take four hours.'

Another demonic way to impress Christians is to let them fall into sin, causing a guilty conscience in them, so that they do not dare to approach God's throne of mercy. Or, in extraordinary cases, Satan might venture an open attack on the Christian, giving him a vision of his ghastly power and scaring him to despair. Especially in pagan countries, where magic and spiritism still have their stronghold, this can be experienced both by national converts and by foreign missionaries. It is, therefore, important for them to learn how they can defend themselves, even in a demonized situation.

I once visited a German lady missionary in Tokyo, who told me how she had gone through such an experience. She had been invited by a Shinto priest to give English lessons to his daughter. He himself was of course in daily contact with the ancestral and national spirits through invocations, divination and sacrifices. When he discovered that his girl was not only gaining secular knowledge but had started to read the Bible and to believe in Jesus, he began to hate the missionary. One night Miss Müller was suddenly awakened by a dreadful vision. She saw the appearance of the Shinto priest slowly approaching her bed and throwing a net around her. She was quite unable to make the slightest movement, and when she even felt fingers clutching around her throat to choke her, she feared that this was the end of her life. But in this moment she remembered a short prayer that her grandmother had taught her when she still was a child: 'Jesus, cover me with your blood!' She exclaimed these words; at first silently in her mind and then out loud, and this instantaneously changed her situation: The appearance of the priest slowly retreated and dissolved; she could breathe and felt quite free again and could also move her limbs normally.

Satan is still very forceful, that is true. But his force ends where the realm of Jesus breaks into his dark dominion. And this is the case wherever the victory of Christ is invoked, which was won once and for all when he shed his blood at the cross. His blood atoned for our sins and opened free access for all those who accept his offer in repentance and faith (1 John 1:9).

b. Our carnal nature as opposed to God

The second opponent in our spiritual warfare is not an outward enemy, but we find him in ourselves: It is *our old sinful nature* that tenaciously tries to draw us away from God. In principle, Christians in their regeneration have done away with that old nature. They have given their sinful self into death, they have crucified themselves with Christ and risen with him to a new life in the Holy Spirit. But as long as we still live in our body, the flesh—as the New Testament calls this old nature—with its sinful desires, is still around us. It tries to counteract every good resolution of our new, inner man. This is an experience which we have almost as often as we want to be with the Lord in prayer and by listening to his holy word. It is this inner cleavage in us, to which Jesus alerted his three intimate disciples Peter, John and James in the garden of Gethsemane, on the night of his betrayal, with the warning: 'Watch and pray, that you may not fall into temptation; the spirit indeed is willing, but the flesh is weak' (Mat 26:41).

Our old nature is Satan's most convenient ally: In most cases he need not even approach us himself, because our old self is already busy doing its job: It makes us lazy in our spiritual life; it distrusts the promises given in answer to faithful prayer; it tempts us with sensual pleasures and an inner-worldly self-fulfilment which appear far more attractive than a life as followers of Jesus. We have to be aware of this inner situation. We must learn that a healthy spiritual life cannot be built on just spontaneously following our own unstable religious desires. God calls us to an unconditional dedication to his call; and often this implies fighting sacrificially against a violent or tough inner resistance from our own old self. Paul exhorts us to renew our decision daily to opt for life in the Spirit rather than life according to the flesh: 'If you live according to the flesh, you will die; but if by the Spirit you put to death the deeds of the body you will live. For all who are led by the Spirit of God are sons of God' (Rom 8:13).

c. God himself as our opponent!

Truly, God has destined us to be his own dear sons and daughters and to live with him in a most intimate fellowship of mutual love. Having been re-assured of this marvellous privilege, it may sound absolutely incredible to us that we might encounter a third and even more terrifying opponent in our prayer struggle: It is no one less than *God himself* ! Yes, that sounds most paradoxical and difficult to accept, since it seems to contradict our entire Christian concept of God as a God of love. How can he meet a human being in opposition, at the very moment when he or she tries to seek his presence and help in prayer?

There is a story in the Old Testament, which we have already referred to, that tells us about precisely such an incident. Who was the stranger who attacked Jacob, just when he had started to pray, and who wrestled with him the entire night? At first Jacob did not know who it was, but rather believed him to be a mortal enemy. But he was able to identify him when the battle was over, and his superhuman opponent had departed: *'Jacob called the name of the place Peniel, saying: "I have seen God face to face, and yet my life is preserved"'* (Gen 32:31).

Why had God decided not to give a quick and positive hearing to the prayer of Jacob that evening? The answer lies in Jacob's previous life and in the plan that God had made for his future. Jacob had been elected by God to be the bearer of his blessing and to be the mediator of these blessings to his own children and through them—as the elected people of Israel—to all the nations on earth. But Jacob had proved to be unworthy of this high calling. He had behaved as a deceiver and as a ruthless egoist. He had cheated his twin brother Esau (Gen 25:29-34), and his dying father Isaac (Gen 27), as well as his father-in-law Laban: (Gen 30:25-43). God would not use a deceiver and a brutal egoist as an instrument in his plan of salvation. He first had to change his character by bringing him to a realization of his true wicked nature, and to bring him to repentance and to a total surrender to him. And God accomplished this goal by encountering Jacob that night, not as a merciful God, but—to start with—as the terrifying God of justice and holiness, whom to meet face-to-face is fatal to sinful man. Even Isaiah, when he had his awe-inspiring heavenly vision in the temple, exclaimed fearfully, 'Woe to me! For I am lost; for I am a man of unclean lips ... for my eyes have seen the King, the Lord of hosts' (Isa 6:5)!

Prayer, according to a classical definition, is lifting up our soul to God. When we pray, we must be mindful of our real relationship to him. God is holy and immensely exalted; we are poor creatures, and on account of our sinful nature separated from him by an unbridgeable gap.

It was only God himself who through the cross of Jesus Christ could close that gap and restore our broken relationship with himself. The struggle of prayer, therefore, is ultimately the struggle with God himself. In this struggle God reminds us of our utter unworthiness to approach his majestic throne. And he reminds us that it is only on account of his infinite mercy, which he extended to us by giving his only begotten Son as an atoning sacrifice, that we could become acceptable to him again—acceptable even as his beloved children. On our side, this means that we have to come to repentance and to a grateful faith in Christ, before a vital contact by prayer can be established with God.

In this sense, struggling with God in prayer means fleeing from the God of holiness, who appears as our greatest adversary, to the God of mercy, who is our Saviour. If we do not realize this tension, our petitions remain just empty words and have no power to ascend to heaven. Worse than that: Our petitions might even sound like abominations in the ears of God, in cases when they are evidently in contrast to the real condition of our hearts and lives (cf. Isa 1:15: 'When you spread forth your hands, I will hide my eyes from you; even though you make many prayers, I will not listen; your hands are full of blood.') Then God may intervene in such a shocking way as he did in the case of Jacob, when Jacob tried to appease God in a self-deceiving assurance in the valley of Jabbok. God had to bring him to his senses; he had to purify him by an agony of spiritual trial; he had to change his character by giving him a new name that indicated his new relationship to him: *Israel*, meaning: the one who fought with God, and also: the one who in his fight trusts in the God who will fight for him.

We are wrong if we believe that the purpose of prayer is to change the heart of *God*. No, in prayer *we* ourselves are to be changed first, so that the obstacles in our own character and life are removed—the obstacles that we have put on the road by which God wants to come into our hearts and fill us with his divine grace and strength. Such a cleansing prayer is a hard struggle. It might cost us an entire night's watch or even longer. Our battle with God is won when our mind has come into full harmony with God's mind, and when we can confidently pray, 'O Lord, let your will be done, come and make me a suitable instrument to execute your will; come and bless me again, dear Lord!'

II Pastoral Application

Ten rules for fighting the spiritual battle

Having accepted that prayer is a part of our threefold battle with Satan, with our old nature and with God himself, we must also become aware of the rules for fighting a good fight in prayer. Just as there are rules of engagement for soldiers at war, and also rules in sports, there are certain rules for our fight in prayer, which we must know and observe if we want to win.

When we kneel or sit down to pray, we are engaging ourselves in a very important task. We are not just performing a pious exercise; we want to achieve an important purpose. Some people regard prayer simply as a kind of ceremony that is prescribed for believers. They perform it half-heartedly, without expecting much as its outcome. There is indeed a vast difference between just *praying* and *praying effectively*. There are people who never experience an answer to their prayers, although they pray daily; but there are other Christians who can fill complete diaries with recorded answers to their prayers. How can we explain the difference?

The difference is that the second category of praying Christians faithfully observes Gods rules for praying to him in a way that is pleasing to him, whilst the first group ignores those rules.

What then are the rules for an effective and victorious life of prayer? The answer could be given in one single word: We have to pray in *faith*. For Jesus himself said: 'If you have *faith* as a grain of mustard seed, you will say to this mountain, "Move away to another place," and it will move; and nothing will be impossible to you' (Mat 17:20, 21).

But then again we are left with the question: What does it mean to 'pray in faith'? A Christian who prays in faith is a person whose heart is totally united with the heart of God, who does not allow anything to come between God and himself. But this is the definition of a perfect saint, and no genuine Christian would boast that he has already become such a saint while he is still here on earth. It is a state which we can only strive to reach step by step as obedient followers of Christ. And, therefore, it is good to have certain rules for effective prayer, for praying in faith, rules which we can extract from the Bible. As I have pondered over this subject, I found, by study and through personal experience, that the following ten rules apply and prove helpful in our endeavor to become warriors of prayer:

1. In opening our prayer we surrender ourselves to God in humility.

Like Isaiah in the temple (Isa 6:5) we have to realize the awful majesty of God in contrast to our own sinfulness and utter unworthiness to approach him. Therefore, we must begin our prayer by a dual movement of giving glory to God and confessing our sin.

2. We can approach God only through the one way God has opened to us: Jesus Christ.

Christ is the one way that leads to the throne of grace. Jesus himself has clearly pointed out this way to us: He advised us to pray in his name (John 14:13f). Jesus is God's beloved Son, he is the one man who on account of his perfect obedience is wholly acceptable to God. By his self-sacrifice he has bridged the abyss between God and fallen mankind. Our prayer will be acceptable if we are united to Christ in his intercessory ministry as our High Priest, and if we are filled with his Holy Spirit.

3. Our prayer must fit into God's master plan for salvation.

God's great objective is to save lost mankind through the redemptive work of Jesus Christ. Every prayer must fit into this great design. We must be neither selfish nor foolish in our prayer.

4. A highly acceptable prayer is the one in which we are united with fellow Christians.

Such prayer is endorsed by an explicit promise of Jesus himself: 'If two or three of you agree on earth about anything they ask, it will be done for them by my Father in heaven' (Mat 18:19). Jesus says this in connection with his prescriptions for a future church order. It shows that church leaders have a particular responsibility to stimulate an orderly and enduring prayer life in their flock (1Tim 2:1-3; cf. 1 Thes 5:17). How much time do we spend with our friends in such meaningful action? I had a Korean girl student—a convert from Buddhism—who fought her way through great material and spiritual obstacles right along to the doctorate and finally to a professorship in Seoul by constant prayer fellowship with her girl friend. On the day of her promotion another friend of hers gave a moving account of this story.

5. Our prayer will be victorious, if we put on the whole armour of God.

It can be very helpful to ponder the specific meaning of each of the weapons that belong to this armour (Eph 6:10-18). A friend of mine always recites this passage in his morning prayer and very consciously puts on these weapons one by one, to arm himself for the struggle that awaits him. I have experienced myself in my missionary ministry in Africa how indispensable and how powerful these weapons are, when you encounter the invisible forces of pagan witchcraft and spiritism.

6. Plead the promises of God!

In our struggle with God in prayer we can overcome his pedagogical resistance to us, if we boldly invoke the biblical promises that he gave us. How was Jacob able not only to endure God's wrestling with him, but even to overcome him? He cried, 'I will not let you go unless you bless me!' (Gen 32:26). What an insolent approach to God, it seems! Yes, it would be insolent if thereby we were presumptuously attempting to force our selfish will upon the sovereign will of God, as the magicians try. We are not presumptuous, however, but act in obedience, if we remind God of previous promises which he himself has given us. That he had done, indeed, to Jacob at Bethel, when he saw the heavenly ladder, and the angels of God ascending and descending on it. 'I am the Lord,' he heard him saying, 'of Abraham your father and Isaac, ... and by you and your descendants shall all the nations on earth bless each other' (Gen 28:1-15).

A young Christian worker was astonished by the contrast between the feebleness of his own prayer life and the bold and effective prayer of his elderly pastor. His prayers seemed to shoot to heaven like a rocket. Asking the pastor to explain this secret to him, he received the reply, 'Young man, plead the promises of God!' God cannot act against his own promises, if we trust in them and in full assurance remind God of them at the critical moment, pleading with him like this: O God, you have said to your people, and you have said it to me as well: *"Fear not, for I have redeemed you; I have called you by your name, you are mine."* Now, O Lord, the moment has come when I need your help, come to my redemption again!' Surely, such a plea will not remain unanswered!

7. Meet Satan's attacks by proclaiming to him Christ's victory at the cross.

We cannot counteract Satan in our own strength; because his power is superhuman. But he has been overcome already by Someone stronger than he, and those who belong to him as members of his body share in his victory. Satan knows this, and he shudders each time he is reminded of this. Just think of the experience of that lady missionary with the Shinto priest. Martin Luther in his famous hymn 'A mighty fortress is our God' triumphantly sings: 'The prince of darkness grim, we tremble not for him; his rage we can endure, for lo! his doom is sure; one little word shall fell him.'

8. Follow a definite strategy of prayer!

Prayer is neither a retreat into mystical tranquillity, nor is it is a pouring out of spontaneous religious thoughts. Prayer is a very serious task with very definite objectives. Therefore, we should structure it properly. This includes developing a real strategy of prayer. It is advisable to draw up a schedule for thanksgiving and petition, in which we include all the objectives the Lord has laid as prayer items upon our heart. Such a schedule will conveniently cover the seven days of the week, so that each prayer object will receives the attention it is due.

9. Pray perseveringly like Jacob, Elijah and Jesus!

The battle of prayer is a very tough one and often time-consuming. Rome was not built in one day, and Christ's total destruction of Satan's bulwarks will take the entire course of salvation history, not ending before his Second Coming. God can, and sometimes does, fulfil our petitions instantaneously; but this is not the rule. He might even deliberately delay his answer in order to test the seriousness of our dedication and our trust in him (Jas 5:16-18). Therefore, never give up praying before you have the inner assurance that God has heard your prayer, and that he will attend to it at that time which he finds appropriate, right now, tomorrow or in some years' time.

10. Pray sacrificially and as a priest!

One of the most cherished biblical persuasions of evangelicals is that every Christian shares in the priesthood of all believers. But what does the Bible mean by this promise and calling which God gave both to the ancient people of God, Israel (Ex. 19:5), and to the New Testament people, the church (1 Pet 2:5)? It means that God has called us to a ministry of priestly mediation between our fellow men and him. By this I do not invalidate the sole mediatorial role of Jesus Christ, who sacrificed himself once and for all at the cross for our atonement with God. But Christ himself, our High Priest, has made all members of his body of fellow priests with him: he entrusted us with the task of being ambassadors of his reconciliation to the world; and he wants us like priests to plead in our intercession for those who are perishing because they do not know or have not accepted God's offer of reconciliation. Such intercession in virtue of Christ's atoning self-sacrifice is a priestly function. It means that we deeply empathize with the sufferings and weaknesses of our fellow men, knowing that we are sinners ourselves who live only by the mercy of God. And it also means that we pray sacrificially for them, supporting our supplications by fasting and watching, just as Jesus himself spent whole nights on mountains or in desert places in supplication for his disciples and for the whole world.

The reward for fighting the battle

It may appear that I have given a rather austere description of the spiritual battle in prayer to which we are called. To some it might even seem to be a great exaggeration and unnecessary complication. But do we know of any high goal in life that we can attain in an easy-going way? Just think of the tough self-discipline that sportsmen take upon themselves as they run in competition! Or think of all endurance and sacrifices it costs to study for an academic degree! Our spiritual battle has a reward of a much higher and a longer lasting value than anything people fight for in secular enterprises.

Conclusion

All real victories in the advancement of God's kingdom are won in prayer in the heart of God before the results appear before the eyes of man. The reward of prayer is found on many different levels, personal and corporate. Individual Christians become more mature and sanctified, capable of being instruments in the hands of God. The church of Christ is built up by growing in depth and in width. Spiritual captives are liberated from their satanic bonds and won for Jesus Christ. Demons are expelled and forced to retreat.

I read of a congress of parapsychologists in Bogotá who tried to experiment with spiritistic forces. It failed completely. Why? Some concerned Christians in that city were meeting at the same time and implored God's Holy Spirit to bring to naught the efforts of those parapsychologists and thus to prevent their city from being flooded by a wave of occultism. I myself had a similar experience at the time of the world-wide students' neo-Marxist unrest in 1970. I had to address an evangelistic rally in Berlin which a group of hostile students tried to disturb and disrupt. But just with a few words, taken from the Bible, I was able to silence them, and then the whole meeting proceeded in a blessed atmosphere. Neither the conveners nor I myself had any idea how this change had come about. I learned the explanation only when I had arrived home in Tübingen. On my desk I found a postcard written by an elderly 'sister,' who worked for an evangelical mission society. She informed me that she planned to convene a prayer group just at the hour when our meeting in Berlin was to take place, in order to give us spiritual support!

The entire way of the gospel through the world is prepared and secured by fervent prayer. How could the Korean church grow by leaps and bounds, so that Korea by now has become the country from which the largest number of missionaries is sent for service in about 170 countries all over the world? Korean Christians have one primary answer to this question: The reason is that the Korean church spends much time and energy in private and corporate prayer—possibly more than any other church in the world.

Even secular events are influenced by the unobtrusive power of prayer: What was the decisive reason why Hitler, after having crushed France in just a few weeks, could not invade and conquer England? It might very well be, as British Christians claim, that their island was fortified by a wall of intercession. Likewise Catholic Christians in Austria believe that their country got rid of the Soviet occupation in 1946 because they had started a crusade of prayer to that effect.

I do not suggest that by prayer all the political problems of mankind may be resolved within the history of this fallen world. But certainly by being prayer warriors we do participate in the ultimate defeat of Satan at the end of history, when Christ will come again to remove him from his usurped position as the prince of this world. Then his messianic kingdom in glory can be established—that universal state of peace, justice and perfect happiness which people in vain try to set up themselves by following their own ideologies.

The greatest objective, however, of our Christian prayer struggle is not the fulfilment of all the desires that men have for themselves, whether physical or spiritual. The highest goal, to which all other goals are subordinate in importance, is the honour of God himself. When God hears our prayer and when he honours his own promises on which our prayer is based, he proves before the entire world that he is both faithful and omnipotent, and that in spite of all hindrances and opposition he is able and determined to accomplish his eternal plan of salvation. Then, in the end, our present prayer of supplication will give way to one great prayer of praise and thanksgiving in the radiant city of God which has come down to earth (Rev 21:2).

But even now, in the midst of all turmoil and anxiety, the 'militant' church in her worship confidently anticipates this final triumph by joining in the chorus of the heavenly company of angels and perfected saints (Heb 12:22-23), that is assembled around the throne of God, in a jubilant prayer of adoration (Rev 7: 9-12).

Peter P. J. Beyerhaus. Born in Germany. Retired in 1997. Since 1965 professor and director of the Institute of Missiology and Ecumenical Theology, Tübingen University, Germany. Education and administrative experience in South Africa and Germany. Author of books and articles. Member of numerous missiological societies and requested world-wide as guest-lecturer. Th.D. from Uppsala University (1956).

Exploring the Frontiers of Faith

PART I
Adventist Studies

Towards an Authentic Adventist Identity

Bryan W. Ball

In 1988 the South Pacific Division of the Seventh-day Adventist Church sponsored a commemorative 'Righteousness by Faith'-conference, co-ordinated by the late Dr. Arthur Ferch. In the book that emerged after that 1988 event Ferch wrote of the 1888 Minneapolis General Conference and the Ministerial Institute that preceded it, 'The proceedings at Minneapolis, both during the institute and the session, highlighted that Christ and his righteousness are and must remain central to the Seventh-day Adventist message and mission.'[1] We do not know precisely what Dr. Ferch had in mind when he chose the title for that book, but perhaps we can detect in it a certain wistful longing for something not yet fully realised: *Towards Righteousness by Faith: 1888 in Retrospect.* If that is true, as well it may be, it underlines the continuing need for a thoroughly Christian Adventism or, perhaps it could be said, an Adventist identity rooted and grounded in the essentials of the basic Christian gospel, with a corresponding emphasis on the person and work of Christ.

The first paper at the 1988 Conference, and subsequently the first chapter of the book, was delivered by Dr. Arthur Patrick. In discussing the need at the time for the church to move beyond what he termed its 'seemingly immoveable posture,' represented by Uriah Smith and George Butler with regard to basic Christian doctrine and the distinctive doctrines of the nascent Advent movement, Dr. Patrick observed, 'The internationalisation of Adventism intensified its need to be seen, unmistakably, as a Christian movement.'[2] With thanks to Dr. Patrick for that important emphasis and with apologies to him for a rather liberal paraphrase, it might be said with equal aptness today, 'The secularisation of Adventism (we refer here chiefly to the church in the Western world) intensifies its need to be and to be seen fundamentally as a thoroughly Christian movement.' The continuing challenge for the church, now with even greater internationalisation and increasing secularisation, is to *be* a thoroughly Christian movement both in doctrine and lifestyle. It is even less acceptable today than it was in 1888 to preach and live merely within the prescriptive guidelines of our name. Seventh-day Sabbath keeping and insistent proclamation of the approaching Second Advent, if indeed these two features may still be claimed as definitive of our church in the Western world, are not enough.

---

[1]   A. J. Ferch, ed., *Towards Righteousness by Faith: 1888 in Retrospect* (Wahroonga, Australia: South Pacific Division of Seventh-day Adventists, 1989), 1.

[2]   A. N. Patrick, 'Smith, Butler and Minneapolis: The Problems and the Promise of Historical Enquiry,' in: Ferch, ed., *Righteousness by Faith,* 17.

Our task,[3] then, is to go beyond and behind Righteousness by Faith as a mere theological declaration to the substance of what have traditionally been known in Christian theology as christology and soteriology. They are defined in one respected source respectively as, 'The study of the Person of Christ, and in particular of the union in him of the divine and human natures, and of His significance for the Christian faith,' and 'the section of Christian theology which treats of the saving work of Christ for the world.'[4] Our task also is to take these crucial theological categories from the shelf of formal academic consideration and place them once more at the heart of contemporary Adventist Christianity or, if we prefer our own terminology, at the heart of our message and mission.

Before we attempt that, a word or two about the title of this chapter. The word 'authentic' is, I believe, important. It can and should be applied to both Adventism and to the wider Christian faith. There are, it is said, at least twenty-seven different interpretations of Jesus available today and probably as many different versions of Christianity itself. Clearly, not all can be regarded as expressions of authentic Christian faith. Somewhere, at some point, the authentic shades into the spurious and Christianity shades into pseudo-Christianity. There can only be an authentic Adventism if there is an authentic Christianity and if Adventism itself is grounded in that authentic Christianity. Authenticity may prove to be the church's greatest need in the face of the encroaching pressures of secularism, materialism and nominalism which undeniably dog our heels as we continue our journey to the kingdom in a new century few, if any, of our forefathers expected.

We may take our lead from one of evangelical Christianity's most influential and articulate twentieth-century spokesmen. In *Christian Basics* John Stott begins by defining what Christianity is *not*. It is not, he says, primarily a creed, nor a code of conduct, nor a cult, in the sense of cultus, a system of worship. If the essence of Christianity is neither creed, code of conduct, nor cult, then, he asks, What is it? Stott's answer is simple, 'It is Christ.'[5] That may, indeed, sound trite and superficial. It is, however, the truth. 'Christianity without Christ is a frame without a picture, a casket without a jewel, a body without breath,'[6] he says. Obvious as this may seem and regardless of how many times it has been said, it must be re-stated and re-affirmed in any meaningful discussion of Adventist identity. Within the constraints of space and time, we will attempt to extend this simple but essential definition in five directions, each of which we suggest will help to identify authenticity in both historic Christianity and in contemporary Adventism.

---

[3]   Most of the material in this essay was presented at a Bible conference in Australia in 2006.

[4]   F. L. Cross and E. A. Livingstone, eds., *The Oxford Dictionary of the Christian Church* (London, UK: Oxford University Press, 3rd ed. 1997), 336, 1520.

[5]   J. R. W. Stott, *Christian Basics: A Handbook of Beginnings, Beliefs and Behaviour* (Grand Rapids, MI: Baker Book House, 1991), 14-16.

[6]   Ibid., 18.

The person of Christ

The person of Jesus, who he was and who he remains today, is the foundation of all else that can be said about him. Everything that Jesus himself said and did, including his death and resurrection, are only meaningful in the light of who he was. So who was he?

It took the Christian church four centuries or more to work out the answer to this question—not because it was doubted, or because the New Testament or the early documents were unclear, but to defend orthodoxy against unorthodoxy and heterodoxy. The formulations of Nicaea and Chalcedon concerning the person of Christ have been re-affirmed in one way or another in statements of faith produced by mainstream Christianity ever since. The Thirty-Nine Articles of the Anglican Church and the Presbyterian Westminster Confession of Faith, to mention only two, assert the divine-human nature of the Son in the context of a trinitarian theology. A. H. Strong began his persuasive discussion of Christ by considering his 'deity and humanity indissolubly united,' and by arguing 'no mere human genius, much less the genius of Jewish fishermen, could have originated this conception.'[7] The incarnation, in which God became man while retaining divinity, is the irreplaceable cornerstone of all Christian doctrine and practice.

In his classic work on the incarnation, *God Was in Christ,* D. M. Baillie defends the traditional understanding of that event against twentieth-century attempts to revive various christological heresies of the early church period. He speaks of 'the coming into history of the eternally pre-existent Son of God,' and says, 'We confess that while the life lived by Jesus was wholly human, that which was incarnate in Him was of the essence of God, the very Son of the Father, very God of very God.'[8] It was not coincidental that the first section proper of *Seventh-day Adventists Answer Questions on Doctrine,* published in 1957 in response to problems perceived by leading evangelical Christians in Adventist theology, was entitled, 'Questions about Christ,' or that it dealt with the incarnation, the deity of Christ and his eternal pre-existence.[9] It is illuminating, to say the least, that after more than a century of vigorous preaching and publishing, much of it substantially theological, Adventism in the mid-twentieth century had to re-affirm its commitment to the very foundations of Christian orthodoxy. The publication of *Questions on Doctrine* was, after 1888, a defining moment in Adventist history and the pursuit of authenticity.

---

[7]   A. H. Strong, *Systematic Theology* (London, UK: Pickering and Inglis, 29th Printing, 1981), 186f.

[8]   D. M. Baillie, *God Was in Christ* (London, UK: Faber and Faber, 1949), 150f.

[9]   *Seventh-day Adventists Answer Questions on Doctrine* (Washington, DC: Review and Herald Publishing Association, 1957), 35-86. Section I dealt with 'Preliminary Questions,' including doctrines shared with other Christians, in which it was noted that 'practically all Seventh-day Adventist beliefs are held by one or more Christian groups,' 21.

Few have expressed the beauty and the mystery of the divine-human union better than did Ellen G. White in the aftermath of 1888. Whatever else may be said about Ellen White's writings, they articulated for the church the essential truths of the incarnation and the nature of Christ at a crucial point in our history. *Ministry* magazine did the church a great service in publishing the pamphlet *Christ's Nature During the Incarnation* in 1956, bringing together a comprehensive collection of these Ellen White statements. It is still difficult to find a clearer or more balanced expression of these most basic of Christian truths. Under the sub-headings, 'The Mystery of the Incarnation' and 'Miraculous Union of Human and Divine' we find, amongst much else in this pamphlet, the following:

> Christ was a real man; He gave proof of His humility in becoming a man. Yet He was God in the flesh.[10]

> Divinity and humanity were mysteriously combined, and man and God became one.[11]

> Was the human nature of the Son of Mary changed into the divine nature of the Son of God? No; the two natures were mysteriously blended in one person—the man Christ Jesus. In Him dwelt all the fullness of the Godhead bodily.[12]

> He was God while upon earth, but He divested Himself of the form of God and in its stead took the form and fashion of a man.[13]

> He veiled his divinity with the garb of humanity but He did not part with His divinity.[14]

In his fine book, *The Man Who is God*, Dr. Edward Heppenstall noted the importance of these truths for the church at large, for the Adventist community in particular, and for lost humanity as a whole, in saying,

---

[10] E. G. White, *The Youth's Instructor,* October 13, 1898.
[11] E. G. White, *The Signs of the Times,* July 30, 1896.
[12] E. G. White, *Seventh-day Adventist Bible Commentary* (Washington, DC: Review and Herald Publishing Association, vol. 5, 1956), 1113.
[13] E. G. White, *The Review and Herald,* July 5, 1887.
[14] E. G. White, *The Review and Herald,* June 15, 1905. All the preceding Ellen White quotations, together with many others dealing with various aspects of the nature of Christ, were published in *Ministry* magazine in September, 1956, and were reprinted and widely circulated in pamphlet form under the title *Christ's Nature During the Incarnation.*

That God the Creator should Himself condescend to become a creature and imprison Himself within matter He created is an event that defeats logical analysis and rational explanation. But God in Jesus did become flesh, a complete human being. This is the greatest miracle of all time and eternity. It cannot be fully comprehended. It can only be received in grateful adoration.[15]

Heppenstall concludes, 'There is no way to get rid of the incarnation without getting rid of Christianity.'[16] Authentic Adventism stands firmly with historic Christendom in this foundational truth, and is defined by the person of Jesus, God incarnate, the One in whom humanity and divinity were mysteriously and forever conjoined.

The life and death of Christ
There is no possibility of doubt about the death of Jesus as a defining characteristic of true Christianity. For centuries the cross has been the central symbol of the Christian faith. From the very beginning, Jesus' death on Calvary has been crucial to the true faith and to all genuine interpretation of the biblical revelation concerning God's redemptive activity for lost humanity. We shall return to it from an Adventist perspective shortly. But here we emphasise the life, as well as the death, of Jesus to bring a biblical balance to the Catholic and more extreme evangelical emphases on the cross and the sufferings of Christ as the sole expression of God's redeeming activity. Jesus was born, not only to die, but also to live, for lost humanity. God was in Christ, reconciling the world to himself, from the moment the incarnation took place. One reputable source equates atonement with reconciliation and says, 'It means the work of Christ, culminating at Calvary.'[17] The Christ-event as a whole brings reconciliation, and the Christ-event is God's intervention in human history through the Son, beginning with the incarnation and ending with Christ's return to complete what he initiated during his earthly life. John Macquarrie puts it even more clearly in his *Principles of Christian Theology*:

Just as we cannot separate the two doctrines of the person and the work, so, when we turn to the doctrine of Christ's work, we may not separate His life and His death ... The cross does, of course, occupy the central place in the doctrine of the atonement, but the cross cannot be understood apart from

---

[15] E. Heppenstall, *The Man Who is God* (Washington, DC: Review and Herald Publishing Association, 1977), 20. Heppenstall is still regarded by many as one of the most influential Adventist theologians of the later twentieth century.

[16] Ibid., 21.

[17] A. Richardson, ed., *A Dictionary of Christian Theology* (London, UK: SCM Press Ltd., 1969), 18.

the life which it ended ... We must try to avoid any separation of the life and death. Our attention will indeed be focussed on the death of the cross, but only because this is the finish and culmination of Christ's work. It has its significance only in the context of Christ's life as its climax and summation.[18]

We de-emphasise the life of Christ as part of God's reconciling activity at the serious risk of misunderstanding, even minimising, his great work of expiation and reconciliation. Constrained by space, we will note just three aspects of Christ's work in human flesh that are definitive for both basic Christianity and authentic Adventism.

His sinless life. The classic definition of Chalcedon regarding the sinlessness of Christ has come ringing down through the ages: 'Like us in all things except sin.'[19] This is, of course, but a re-statement of the Pauline assertion in 2 Corinthians 5:21, 'God made him who had no sin to be sin for us.'[20] There are again many statements from the pen of Ellen White which affirm the sinlessness of Jesus in words it is impossible to misunderstand. One must suffice. She wrote of Christ taking human nature:

> Christ did not in the least participate in its sin ... He was touched with the feeling of our infirmities, and was in all points tempted like as we are. And yet He 'knew no sin.' He was the Lamb 'without blemish and without spot ...' We should have no misgivings in regard to the perfect sinlessness of the human nature of Christ.[21]

This sinlessness is not something that can be discarded as peripheral. It is the crucial foundation of that righteousness which Jesus provided by living above sin in the flesh as a son of Adam, and which is, in this end-time, Adventism's special contribution to the understanding of God's plan of salvation. Again, in explaining Christ's role in reconciliation and atonement, historic Christianity declares:

> Only the Son of God made flesh could qualify in his righteousness, sinlessness and obedience. Christ is the new Adam of a renewed race which, sin-

---

[18] J. Macquarrie, *Principles of Christian Theology* (London, UK: SCM Press, Ltd., 1966), 280f.

[19] Richardson, ed., *op. cit.*, 57. See also H. Bettenson, ed., *Documents of the Christian Church* (Oxford University Press, 2nd ed., 1963), 51. On the Council of Chalcedon, see, for example, the *Dictionary of Christian Theology*, 57f and *The Oxford Dictionary of the Christian Church*, 315.

[20] Biblical references cited in this chapter are taken from the New International Version, unless otherwise stated. The NIV translation of this verse, as is that of the NKJV, is obviously preferable to the AV rendering.

[21] E. G. White, *Signs of the Times*, June 9, 1898; cited in:, *Seventh-day Adventist Bible Commentary*, vol. 5, 1131.

ners though they are, have been begotten of Christ into a new people, acceptable in a righteousness which is Christ's and which he imparts.[22]

His death at Calvary. Of the many things that could be said and re-affirmed of the death of Jesus, we will mention only one. The ninth of the Adventist Fundamentals categorically states, among other things, 'The death of Christ is substitutionary and expiatory ...'[23] This accurately reflects the historic Christian interpretation and is in harmony with Paul's declaration in Romans 5:8, 'While we were still sinners, Christ died for us.' On the cross, Christ took our place. His death was substitutionary, and in being substitutionary it was redemptive. There has been little doubt about that in Adventist theology, although one recent comment is worth noting. Dr. Raoul Dederen speaks of the substitutionary act of Christ that is central to the New Testament specifically in contradistinction to the exemplarist and moral influence interpretations that have found favour with some twentieth-century theologians, including even a few within Adventist ranks. Commenting on the Greek word *antilutron* (literally translated 'ransom-in-lieu-of') he states,

> the force of this combined word ... attests that in Jesus' crucifixion the apostles saw a death endured by one both on behalf of and instead of others, so that in his death Christ took our place, and we no longer need to die eternally if we accept Him as our substitute ... It is on the ground of such biblical statements that a penal substitutionary understanding of the atonement is justified, even enjoined.[24]

When explaining the death of Jesus, John Stott similarly affirms, 'He bore in our place the penalty which our sins had deserved.'[25] Christian literature and Christian hymns repeatedly affirm the substitutionary nature of Jesus' death on the cross as, of course, does Scripture.

His resurrection. The third defining aspect of Christ's earthly life and ministry is his resurrection. It is impossible to over-estimate the significance of the resurrection of Jesus as a defining feature of true Christianity—perhaps *the* defining feature. It was the central theme of the early Christian proclamation, repeatedly emphasised

---

[22] Richardson, ed., *op. cit.*, 19.

[23] See, for example, *Seventh-day Adventists Believe ... A Biblical Exposition of Fundamental Doctrines* (Silver Spring, MD: Ministerial Association, General Conference of Seventh-day Adventists, 1986), 106.

[24] R. Dederen, 'The Death of Jesus,' in: Bryan W. Ball and William G. Johnsson, eds., *The Essential Jesus* (Boise, ID: Pacific Press Publishing Association, 2002), 160. See also R. Dederen, 'Atoning Aspects in Christ's Death' in: A. V. Wallenkampf and W. R. Lesher, eds., *The Sanctuary and the Atonement: Biblical, Historical, and Theological Studies* (Hagerstown, MD: Review and Herald Publishing Association, 1981), 292-325.

[25] Stott, *Christian Basics*, 69.

and explained in the preaching of the apostles in the book of Acts. Without it the cross would have been an empty victory. As Michael Green so aptly says, 'The cross and the resurrection of Jesus belong together ... It is not the cross which saves. It is Jesus crucified and risen.'[26] Green defends the resurrection persuasively and at length in his book *The Empty Cross of Jesus*, reminding us that its 'implications are immense.'[27]

Let us be in no doubt here. It is the resurrection which is the real sticking point between belief and unbelief. Modern man can believe easily enough in a dead Jesus, particularly if he was only a wandering Jewish rabbi or a social revolutionary bent on disturbing the present order. But contemporary man finds it difficult, impossible, to believe in a risen, living Jesus. If Adventists are to be authentically Christian, they must defend and proclaim the resurrection of Christ with as much conviction and authority as they proclaim Daniel 2, the Sabbath, the sanctuary, or any other aspect of truth which they regard as important for our age to hear. The sinless life and substitutionary death of Jesus, culminating in his bodily resurrection, are definitive of the original first-century faith and of authentic twenty-first-century Adventism.

The words of Christ
It is not what others say about Jesus, but what he himself says that is ultimately decisive in terms of Christian authenticity. We recall the unsolicited testimony of two disciples on the road to Emmaus as they shared their personal knowledge of him with an unrecognised stranger, 'He was a prophet, powerful in word and deed before God and all the people' (Lk 24:19). Likewise, the objective testimony of the temple guards who had heard Jesus themselves, 'No-one ever spoke the way this man does,' they said (John 8:46). We only have to look at a red-letter edition of the New Testament to know how much of the gospel records are given over to the words of Jesus. These words, even if debatable in the minds of some scholar or another, clearly set forth the beliefs and teachings of Jesus himself, and are therefore fundamental to any interpretation of Christian faith, original or for our time. Again, we attempt the impossible in trying to distill the words of Jesus into two or three paragraphs, but suggest, however, that they fall into at least two crucial categories, which we will propose as definitive — his claims and his teachings.

Firstly, the claims of Jesus. They are truly breath-taking, considered either individually or collectively. The 'I am' claims alone set Jesus apart from any other teacher or religious leader in the history of the human race: '*I am* the light of the world'; '*I am* the bread of life'; '*I am* the good shepherd'; '*I am* the vine'; '*I am* from above'; '*I am* the resurrection and the life'; and of course, '*I am* the way, the truth,

---

[26] M. Green, *The Empty Cross of Jesus* (London, UK: Hodder and Stoughton, 1984), 3.
[27] Ibid., 124.

and the life.' Then there are all the other claims, equally astounding: 'I and my Father are one'; 'Anyone who has seen Me has seen the Father'; 'No one comes to the Father, except through Me'; 'He who comes to Me will never hunger, never thirst'; 'Come unto Me ... and I will give you rest'; 'He who hears my word and believes ... has everlasting life.' C. S. Lewis so rightly said in defending the biblical Jesus against the claim that he was no more that a great moral teacher, 'A man who was merely a man and said the things Jesus said would not be a great moral teacher ... ' Either this man was, and is, the Son of God, or else a madman.'[28] We may quite legitimately preach, teach, and publish about prophecy, Daniel and Revelation, archaeology, the sanctuary, conditional immortality, the spirit of prophecy, or indeed any one of the '28 fundamentals,' but we must never forget that authentic Christianity presses upon people the claims of Jesus.

Then there are his teachings. Where do we start? Again, that which distinguishes Christ and Christianity from all other teachers and world religions is the grandeur, the loftiness, the depth, the universal and eternal relevance of his moral and ethical teachings. We may take the Sermon on the Mount, once described as the 'Magna Carta of the Kingdom,' as representative. Lenski says, 'It presents the entire life in the kingdom, from the first entrance into the kingdom here on earth, to the final consummation of the kingdom in the last judgment.'[29] Consider its teachings again: 'Love your enemies'; 'Do good to those who hate you'; 'Judge not, that you be not judged'; 'Do not lay up for yourselves treasures on earth'; 'Whoever slaps you on your right cheek, turn the other to him also'; 'Whatever you want men to do to you, do also to them.'

Then there are all the kingdom teachings of Jesus, the parables of the kingdom pre-eminent amongst the rest. John Bright introduced his seminal study of the kingdom in the teachings of Jesus with this observation, 'The concept of the kingdom of God involves, in a real way, the total message of the Bible.'[30] We who continually remind people that the preaching of the gospel in all the world is the final sign of the end-time, should remember that the gospel to be preached as a witness to all nations is the gospel of the kingdom, and that the kingdom involved is the kingdom which Jesus inaugurated at the beginning of his ministry and which he said was within those who were true believers. These, together with all the other words Jesus spoke, are truly definitive of authentic Christianity, as they must also be of authentic Adventism. In a sermon preached in an Oxford college

---

[28] C. S. Lewis, *Mere Christianity* (London, UK: Fontana, 1958), 52. The argument has been borrowed and repeated frequently in the last half century. It is irrefutable.

[29] R. C. H. Lenski, *The Interpretation of St. Matthew's Gospel* (Minneapolis, MN: Augsburg Publishing House, 1964), 179.

[30] J. Bright, *The Kingdom of God: The Biblical Concept and its Meaning for the Church* (Nashville, TN: Abingdon Press, 1984), 7.

in 1968, shortly after his re-conversion to the Christian faith, Malcolm Muggeridge spoke specifically of the words of Jesus, 'I have conscientiously looked far and wide, inside and outside my own head and heart, and I have found nothing other than this man and his words which offers any answer to the dilemmas of this tragic, troubled time.'[31]

The compassion of Christ

Our considerations to this point have focused on theological truths and conceptual expressions of what constitutes the true Christian faith. For centuries confessions of faith, however limited, have helped both believers and those on the outside to understand just what it is that Christians believe. The written and the spoken word have been highly effective in defending and communicating that faith. Only in relatively recent times, as existentialism has gained ground, have some Christians placed more emphasis on feeling than on understanding. E. L. Mascall's ever-timely plea for the recovery of 'a clear and coherent understanding of the Christian doctrines about God, Christ, man, and redemption'[32] is perhaps even more appropriate today than it was nearly thirty years ago. He gave his book a title in the form of a question, *Whatever Happened to the Human Mind?* We lose the significance of that question in relation to authentic faith at great loss. True Christianity *does* take root in the mind, in the understanding, even though we often talk about Christian experience. 'What *think* ye of Christ?' is perhaps still the most fundamental question of all.[33] But there is another dimension, which we also neglect at great loss.

From the very beginning, Christianity has been marked by compassion and concern for others. Good works *are* the evidence of true faith and we should not allow fear of legalism or the charge of legalism to hide this truth or to prevent us from putting it into practice. Deeds of mercy and the tangible expression of compassion begin with the One of whom it is recorded, 'When he saw the multitudes, he was moved with compassion.' That is what true Christian compassion always does. It moves people to action. Jesus was moved by compassion throughout his ministry. The first miracle recorded as having been performed by the early disciples after Pentecost centred on a disabled cripple. Christian literature is full of stories of those who have been moved to action in disinterested service for the poor, the needy and the disinherited. The Florence Nightingales and the Mother Teresas

---

[31]   M. Muggeridge, 'Unto Caesar,' a sermon delivered in the chapel of Hertford College, Oxford, UK, November 3, 1968, in *Jesus Rediscovered* (Collins, 1982), 110.

[32]   E. L. Mascall, *Whatever Happened to the Human Mind?* (London, UK: SPCK, 1980), ix.

[33]   In *The Christian Mind* (1963), Harry Blamires lamented the decline in Christian intellectuals in the latter half of the twentieth century, noting 'the loneliness of the thinking Christian,' 21. It was a valid comment on the growing tendency of the times to emphasize feeling and experience above reason. That trend has not declined.

of this world are of equal value in demonstrating what true Christianity is and explaining it to an unbelieving world as are the Billy Grahams and the George Vandemans.

Francis Schaeffer spoke of the need to practise truth as well as to proclaim it. In an age and in a culture which question the possibility of truth in any absolute sense, and which frequently equate religious truth with psychological truth, Schaeffer argued that if Christians only preach and proclaim what they believe they have thereby undermined their credibility. He points out that the watching world has a right to judge whether Christians are authentic 'on the basis of observable love.'[34] In terms of communicating truth to a sceptical culture Schaeffer states:

> If you think that those who have rejected the plastic culture and are sick of hypocrisy are going to be impressed when you talk about truth and at the same time practice untruth, you are wrong. They will never listen. You have cut the ground from under yourself. We live in a generation that does not believe that such a thing as truth is possible, and if you practice untruth while talking about truth, the real thinkers will just say, 'Garbage!'[35]

Strong words, indeed. In commenting on the Lausanne Covenant for world evangelisation, a document that still shapes the thinking of many evangelicals, and which proposed both preaching and social involvement as necessary to reach the unsaved, John Stott similarly argues that the true gospel of Christ is always defined by 'simple, uncomplicated compassion.'[36]

There is a message here of fundamental importance for people with a long heritage of words, theological arguments and a list of 'fundamentals' which continues to grow.[37] A religion which majors only in words, written or spoken, to the exclusion of actual involvement in meeting the needs of the disadvantaged is never authentic Christianity, regardless of however articulate its advocates may be. Ellen White used the phrase, 'the unwearied servant of man's necessity' in describing the incarnate Christ and stated that the work of his disciples now, as

---

[34] F. A. Shaeffer, 'The Church at the End of the Twentieth Century' in *The Complete Works of Francis A. Shaeffer* (Wheaton, IL: Crossway Books, 1982), vol. 4, 'A Christian View of the Church,' 33.

[35] Ibid.

[36] John Stott, *Christian Mission in the Modern World* (London, UK: Falcon Books, 1975), 29, 30.

[37] In 1956, when *Questions on Doctrine* was published, Adventists held 22 Fundamental Beliefs. This represented a considerable increase from earlier years. In 1988, when *Seventh-day Adventists Believe ...* appeared, there were 27. In 2005 a further 'fundamental' was added, bringing the total to 28. Given the length of most of these official statements of belief, one wonders just how much is actually 'fundamental,' or whether they could be expressed more succinctly.

always, is 'to feed the hungry, clothe the naked, and comfort the suffering and the afflicted.'[38] Howard Snyder even calls for a radical lifestyle that is intentionally counter-cultural and opposed to the contemporary, materialistic lifestyle which insidiously invades the lifestyle of the church. Arguing that affluent Christians are a contradiction in terms and 'out of sequence' with the times, Snyder claims, 'We have forgotten, or rejected, the values of simplicity, plainness and frugality held by our forefathers and most of the world's peoples.'[39] While speaking from within the world's most affluent society, Snyder's comments seem to have something to say to the church in the rest of the Western world, particularly to a church that is concerned with authenticity. If Christians, Adventists included, do not spread the gospel by involvement with the people they are trying to reach, how else can they be the salt of the earth? The question refuses to go away.

The presence of Christ

We have now touched on a number of issues that have traditionally been regarded as crucial to the definition of authentic Christianity.[40] There is one more that demands consideration, for without it Christianity can never be complete or authentic. From the outset it has claimed the attention of Christian writers, mystics and missionaries, saints and sinners, rich and poor, beginning with the writers of the New Testament itself. It concerns two dimensions of the Christian journey, one personal, one corporate, one at either end of the spectrum of Christian life and purpose. At one end is the inner life of the believer, the struggle with temptation and sin and the quest for personal authenticity in an alien world—in Adventist terminology the 'Great Controversy,' in all its facets and as it is played out daily on the battleground of each heart and life. And at the other end, the final accomplishment of the church's mission, a seemingly huge and increasingly impossible task

Throughout the Christian centuries untold millions of believers struggling with the world, the flesh and the devil, have found comfort and strength in the promise of Jesus, 'I am with you always.' One of the most challenging tasks for Christian leaders and those called to explain the word of God to the people has been to make this promise real and to keep it before the church. Paul speaks of 'Christ in you, the hope of glory.' But how can Jesus be with us, when the Bible says that after the resurrection he returned to heaven? And for Adventists, how can he be in us, when we know that he is seated at the right hand of God? Of course, we know the

---

[38] E. G. White, *The Ministry of Healing* (Mountain View, CA: Pacific Press Publishing Association, 1942), 17, 106.

[39] H. Snyder, *Liberating the Church* (Downers Grove, IL: InterVarsity Press, 1983), 206, 194.

[40] Many of the aspects of christology and soteriology briefly examined in this chapter are dealt with more extensively in Ball and Johnsson, eds., *The Essential Jesus*, published by Pacific Press in 2002, and written by twelve highly-qualified and respected Adventist scholars.

answer, theoretically at least, to this seeming paradox, as Christians through the centuries have known it. They have defined it in terms of a trinitarian theology which recognises the Holy Spirit as the third person of the Godhead, and the One who makes the presence of Jesus a reality.

It is not necessary to recount again the biblical basis of this trinitarian theology, or even the overwhelming evidence of the New Testament for the reality of the Holy Spirit or his indispensable work in the plan of salvation. Let us merely be reminded again that he has been a vital player in the outworking of Christian history at both the personal and the corporate levels from the very earliest days. It is impossible to speak of true Christianity without giving him a prominent place. The so-called Athanasian Creed clearly spelled it out centuries ago: 'The Godhead of the Father, and of the Son, and of the Holy Spirit, is all one ... So the Father is God, the Son is God, and the Holy Spirit is God. And yet they are not three Gods, but one God.'[41] Adventists believe that too, or at least, most of them do, thankfully. But here again comes the tension between belief and practice, between words and reality, between experience and nominalism, between the normal and the ideal. We cite John Stott once more. After all, we are re-affirming basic Christianity and defining Adventism in terms of that Christianity, and few have expounded basic Christianity in our time better than he has. In *Christian Basics* Stott explains the role of the Spirit in terms which Adventists, especially Adventist leaders, ought readily to understand:

> The Holy Spirit has sometimes been called the 'executive' of the Godhead, meaning that what the Father and the Son desire to do in the world and in the church today, they execute through the Holy Spirit.[42]

He then goes on to explain seven areas in which the Holy Spirit plays a crucial role in the corporate life of the church and in the life of the individual believer, qualifying each of them as specifically Christian: Christian conversion, Christian assurance, Christian holiness, Christian understanding, Christian fellowship, Christian service and Christian mission. At least four of these categories relate to the personal life of the believer, the challenge of *being* a Christian, of *being* an Adventist, in the midst of a very non-Christian culture and surrounded continually by sights and sounds that are definitely non-Christian, if not completely pagan. It is precisely the same kind of culture that surrounded the first Christians, fortified by the promise of Jesus to be with them as they set out to conquer a pagan world. The other three categories relate to the life and witness of the Christian community,

---

[41]   Cited in Stott, *Christian Basics*, 77. On the Athanasian Creed, see for example *The Oxford Dictionary of the Christian Church* (3rd ed.), 119.

[42]   Stott, *Christian Basics*, 78.

all to be influenced, if not dominated, by the presence of Jesus through the activity of the Spirit. We might summarise all this in two words, substance and purpose, content and task, or perhaps, message and mission.

'Message and Mission' is a phrase that has become very familiar to Adventists in the past decade or so. Indeed, it might not be too much to say that for many it has become the catch-phrase which encapsulates our identity. It is a good phrase. It puts succinctly, and in relation to each other, the two essential aspects of our existence and our task as a people. We *do* have a message, and it *is* to be shared. We do have a mission, and it drives us, quite literally, from dawn to dusk, at least at the administrative and pastoral levels, as indeed it should. The message is the content of what we believe, and the mission is the task of sharing it with the unbelieving world—no easy task, as we are constantly reminded. But the message is to be the *whole* Christian message, not just Adventism's prophetic or distinctive features. And the mission is to share *that* message. How can it be accomplished? Only by the presence of Jesus himself, as he promised, specifically with regard to witness, through the presence of the Spirit at every level of activity in the church, not least at the individual and local church levels, where the battle is fought with increasing intensity every day and where Christianity and Adventism are first seen and encountered by the unreached and by them judged as authentic or not.

In our quest for authenticity the presence of Jesus, realised and realisable through the Spirit, is as indispensable as are all other characteristics which distinguish the genuine from the spurious. So, one final quotation:

> There is perhaps no greater need in the contemporary church than that we should be filled with the Holy Spirit (Eph 5:18). We need Him not only to bring us conversion and assurance, not only to sanctify, enlighten, unite and equip us, but also to reach out through us in blessing to an alienated world like rivers of living water which irrigate the desert.[43]

That could easily be a quotation from any one of a dozen of more Adventist authors. It is, in fact, the statement of an evangelical Anglican and it reminds us in conclusion of the basic affinity, as well as the same fundamental needs, that we share with many of our brothers and sisters in the wider Christian community. Many Adventist writers and preachers have said essentially the same thing many times over. The presence of Jesus, through the agency of the Holy Spirit, is the greatest and most urgent need of the church today, as it has ever been, at every level, to make her message and her daily life before the watching world authentic and her mission a dynamic success. That divine and enabling presence, as indeed

---

[43] Ibid.

every other feature of the historic faith we have considered in these few pages, is still a defining characteristic of authentic Christianity and of authentic Adventism.

Concluding considerations

Our quest in the foregoing pages has been to identify authentic twenty-first century Adventist Christians. From that perspective it might be said that the substance of what has been written above is more theoretical than experiential, cerebral rather than existential. That could be equally true of those sections of this chapter that deal with the church's mission and the role of the Holy Spirit as it is of those which concern the more obviously theological concepts of christology and soteriology. Indeed, missiology and pneumatology are both recognised categories of academic enquiry and reflection, indexed in many systematic theologies together with christology, soteriology, protology, eschatology, and all other branches of theology as traditionally understood. Moreover, it must be said again that understanding is always prerequisite to action, even in the life of faith and witness. Paul's assertions that he serves God with his mind (Rom 7:25), and that believers are to be transformed by the renewal of their minds (Rom 12: 2), continually call for thoughtful consideration.

Any such criticism would, however, reflect a legitimate concern. Understanding must be translated into experience, both in the life of the individual believer and in the corporate life of the believing community. Authenticity, the central theme of these reflections, must prevail at both levels, the intellectual and the experiential, and in both the personal and corporate life of the church and its members. The stifling, stultifying, stagnating effects of nominalism, secularism and materialism, to say nothing of superficial, uninformed 'belief' which frequently passes for authentic Christianity, must be recognised, understood and rejected.

There is, then, one final consideration. It flows from one word and the concept inherent in that word. The word encapsulates all that we have attempted to articulate with reference to Christian authenticity, in whatever context it may be pursued. This word is used repeatedly throughout the four gospels and the book of Acts. It is one of the best-known words in the Christian vocabulary. It takes us back to Christian origins and to Jesus himself. It has been resurrected in recent years as a vibrant expression of Christian life and responsibility.[44] It is the word 'disciple.' The two-fold meaning of this word, as commonly understood and its actual inherent meaning, together point us clearly in the direction of true Christian

---

[44] E.g. in the works Donald McGavran, one of the pioneer exponents of Church Growth in the 1970s: *Understanding Church Growth* (Grand Rapids, MI: William B. Eerdmans Publishing Company, 1970), ch. 15, 'Discipling Urban Communities,' where discipling clearly means bringing people to believe in Christ and commit their lives to him. Many have since adopted McGavran's terminology.

authenticity. Jesus called men and women, young people and even children, to be disciples. That was his primary concern, the focus of much of his preaching and teaching. If there were but one defining feature of his entire ministry, it would be this. To be an authentic believer in Jesus' day was to be a disciple. It has been so throughout the Christian era.

So, in conclusion we emphasise again the two meanings of this defining and evocative word. For centuries it has been understood that a disciple is primarily a follower of Christ. True disciples are not merely believers, or sympathisers, or those who understand, but those who actually follow. Their initial interest or sympathy or comprehension results in action. 'Come, follow me,' Jesus said to Peter and Andrew, and 'at once they left their nets and followed Him' (Mk 1:17, 18). Kittel states that throughout the New Testament the word almost invariably denotes those 'who have attached themselves to Jesus as their Master,' and that it 'always implies the existence of a personal attachment which shapes the whole life' of the one so described.[45] A disciple is a person who has heard the call of Jesus and who has freely decided to follow him as Lord and Master. Kittel, again, speaks of 'the personal allegiance of the disciples to Jesus' and points out that Christ's call to discipleship results in 'acceptance into personal fellowship.'[46] A disciple is a follower in fellowship with Christ himself.

But there is another, inherent, meaning to the word 'disciple.' There is only one word in the original Greek that is translated 'disciple' in all the more than 250 times that the word appears in the New Testament. It is the Greek word *mathētēs*, and it literally means 'one who is taught,' a 'trained one.' It carries the ideas of 'learner' and 'pupil,' and explains why on occasion the apparent lack of understanding on the part of the disciples was 'a severe burden to Jesus.'[47] An authentic disciple is a follower of Jesus who has been taught. Disciples have been instructed and informed; they have heard, understood and accepted Jesus and all he stands for. And, moreover, they have willingly assented to identify with him and his mission. The call to discipleship is also 'a call to work with Jesus.'[48] It is the outcome of instruction and understanding, no matter what the pedagogical methods may have been or how long the learning process has taken. They *know* that they are disciples, and they know *why*. Authentic discipleship can never be divorced from understanding.

Authentic disciples, then, today as in the first century AD when Christian discipleship first became a reality, understand who Jesus was, and who he now is.

---

[45] G. Kittel, *Theological Dictionary of the New Testament* (transl. G. W. Bromiley, Grand Rapids, MI: William B. Eerdmans Publishing Company, 1981), vol. IV, 441.
[46] Ibid., 446.
[47] Ibid., 451.
[48] Ibid., 452.

They accept the New Testament record of his life, death and resurrection as fact and the significance of those facts as reflected in the historic Christian declaration. They have heard the words of Jesus, his claims and his teachings, and have accepted them without condition or reservation. Like Jesus, they see the unheeding, shepherdless multitudes plunging inexorably to oblivion like the Gadarene swine, and they are moved to compassion. They feel drawn to Jesus as did the first disciples, comfortable yet challenged in his presence, continually called by the Spirit to higher ground and to share what they themselves have learned and experienced. Yes, discipleship accurately defines authentic Christians, as it does authentic Adventists, living as they claim to believe they do, in the last age. It always has done, and it always will.

Bryan William Ball. Born in Great Britain. Retired in 1996. Pastoral, educational and administrative positions, including presidency for North England Conference, principal Avondale College, and president South Pacific Division 1990-97. Author of book and articles. Recipient of Australian Government Centenary Medal. PhD, University of London (1971).

Is the Postmodern Adventist a Threat to the Unity of his Church?

Reinder Bruinsma

The unity of the church has consistently been an important theme in Adventist history and thought. In recent times church leaders as well as members in the pew have frequently expressed their fear that today this unity is not as secure as it once was. This concern is certainly justified, for the Adventist denomination is not immune to the dangers of being torn into various modalities, or of spending a major portion of its energy in internal struggles between competing or opposing theological camps.

A reality check reveals, in fact, that Adventism worldwide manifests a significant degree of diversity in thought and praxis. It has been argued that there are at least four distinct streams in Adventism: Mainstream Adventism, Evangelical Adventism, Progressive Adventism and Historic Adventism.[1] Former *Adventist Review* editor William G. Johnsson refers to the 'many different voices and gurus' in contemporary Adventism, who all place their own emphases and often differ significantly in the way they interpret Scripture.[2] Another author refers to 'five different Adventist gospels.'[3]

Until quite recently I firmly believed that the divide between liberal and conservative Adventists presents the greatest threat to the church's unity. Of course, I have long realized that labels such as 'conservative' and 'liberal' are only of relative value. An Adventist who considers himself quite liberal may still look hopelessly conservative to a 'progressive' person in one of the historic Protestant churches. Yet there is no doubt that there are major differences in the way Adventists relate to doctrinal and practical issues. Lately I have, however, concluded that Adventism is not just confronted with a gap between varying degrees of liberalism on the one hand and a range of conservative positions on the other, but that it increasingly faces a much more fundamental split, namely between *modern* Adventists and *postmodern* Adventists.[4] In the following pages I will attempt to give a fair and accurate description of the 'postmodern adventist.' I believe this description should lead us to conclude that, although some of the ideas of the *postmodern* Adventist

---

[1] David J. Newman, 'How much diversity can we stand?' *Ministry* (April 1994), 5, 27.

[2] The *Fragmenting of Adventism* (Boise, ID: Pacific Press Publishing Association, 1995), 91-95.

[3] Martin Weber, *Who's Got the Truth? Making Sense out of Five Different Adventist Gospels* (Silver Spring, MD; Home Study Institute Press, 1994).

[4] I have argued this in a recent article in *Ministry*: 'Modern versus Postmodern Adventism: the Ultimate Divide?' (June 2005), 16, 17, 19-21.

may be challenging to the church's unity, he poses no greater threat to it than the *modern* Adventist.[5]

Is the suggestion about the enormous gap between modern and postmodern Adventism merely a hunch or do I have a reasonably solid basis for such an assessment? It seems to me that, once you have intensely studied the phenomenon of postmodernity, you cannot help but recognize it when it confronts you. When interacting with many of the church members in Europe and other regions in the Western world, it stares me in the face, time and again. I cannot but conclude: There is a significant percentage of church members—young and not so young—who think and act in a postmodern way. And there is a far greater group of those who manifest some definite postmodern trends, even though they are still quite 'modern' in many other respects.

Many church members are still solidly modern. But postmodern Adventists are certainly not rare exceptions—and their number and influence are growing, not just in many countries in Europe but also elsewhere in the world. Seventh-day Adventists live in a world which is in transition: from modernity to postmodernity. And, unavoidably, many of them change as the world they inhabit is changing.

Disinterested in doctrinal fine print

One of the foremost characteristics of the postmodern Adventist is his attitude to 'truth' and doctrine. Postmodern Christians, in general, still believe, in varying degrees, in the basic Christian doctrines. But they pick and choose as they compose their own collection of truths, and they feel they ought to be allowed to do so without being criticized or condemned. If they still hold that there is 'absolute' truth, they will attach that label to far fewer propositions than earlier generations of Christians were inclined to do. They look at the past and see how minute variants in doctrinal convictions have led to bitter conflict and, often, to more heat than light. They have noticed how doctrinal positions have shifted, even among those who once believed they were one hundred percent correct and possessed the unchangeable truth. This de-emphasis on doctrine is seen by many as a manifestation of superficiality, worldliness, or liberalism. But although there may be similarities with liberalism, there is more to it. It is not primarily a matter of theology, but of world-view and mindset.[6]

---

[5]   The term 'modern' is used in this essay in the meaning of pertaining to the historical period following the Middle Ages, with a strong emphasis on the rationalistic approach that resulted from the Enlightenment world-view. 'Postmodern' refers to the recent reaction to this mode of thinking.

[6]   Numerous studies have been written about the issue of Truth in postmodernity. Among the many books that have appeared in the evangelical world about this topic and provide a lucid survey of the matter, see Gene Edward Veith, *Postmodern Times: A Christian Guide to Contemporary Thought and Culture* (Wheaton, IL: Crossway Books, 1994) and Douglas Groothuis: *Truth Decay* (Downer's Grove, IL: InterVarsity Press, 2000).

The postmodern Adventist may at first sight be taken for a liberal—someone whose theology deviates from main-line Adventism. And, true enough, some of his viewpoints may be considered 'liberal,' but the issue goes far beyond the divide between conservative and liberal Adventism. Postmodernity does indeed have its impact on one's theological views, but this is just one aspect. It colours the entire way of life, one's attitude to everything and everybody. A postmodern Adventist not only *believes different things*, he also *believes in a different way* and lives his life in a different manner.

Reason versus experience

For the traditional (modern) Adventist, faith is predominantly rational. It is a set of propositions. What he believes can be formulated in a set a fundamental beliefs. In this, Adventists have tended to be quite similar to other Christians. Just like most other Christian denominations, Adventists have formulated creedal statements. Even though they have long maintained that their doctrinal statements are not to be compared with the creeds of other churches, these do in fact function as such. They are not just (and, in any case, no longer) a tentative, informal summary of what most Adventist agree to be the essential tenets of their faith, but have developed into a very detailed formal document, in which every word, period and comma counts. The cumbersome process involved in adding a non-controversial paragraph (in 2005) to the *Statement of Fundamental Beliefs* (which was first adopted as recently in 1980)[7] clearly shows the extent to which this statement has become, in the mind of many, an almost verbally inspired document to which nothing should be added and, even more decidedly, from which nothing should ever be subtracted!

But there is a growing number of Adventist believers who view this state of affairs with substantial misgivings. They wonder whether they need such an extensive statement of what 'we' believe. And they ask themselves (and others) whether it is really necessary to believe in *all* 28 fundamental beliefs to qualify as an Adventist in good standing. Moreover, they are not so sure that all doctrines have been put in their most logical sequence, and that all have equal weight. Are some issues not far more vital than others? The church does not make it unequivocally clear *how many* of these doctrinal truths one must accept before one can be baptised and join the church.

---

[7] For the full text, see the *Seventh-day Adventist Church Manual* (Silver Spring, MD: Secretariat of the General Conference of Seventh-day Adventists, 2005 ed.), 9-19. Commentaries on this document which carry considerable authority are: *Seventh-day Adventists Believe: An Exposition of the Fundamental Beliefs of the Seventh-day Adventist Church* (Silver Spring, MD: Ministerial Association of the Seventh-day Adventist Church, 2005 ed.) and Raoul Dederen, ed., *Handbook of Seventh-day Adventist Theology* (Hagerstown, MD: Review and Herald Publishing Association, 2000).

Some would say it is vital that all the doctrines which are listed in 'the 28' must be taught and understood before a person can be baptised. Others would insist that this is not enough and point to a range of other convictions which must first be communicated and accepted, in particular those related to the Adventist prophetic scenario. Yet, somewhat inconsistently, the 'baptismal questions' are more limited in scope than the list of fundamental beliefs. And one cannot but get the impression that many of those who are baptised, in particular in developing countries after a short evangelistic campaign, are admitted—with the full approval of church leadership—into membership with only a limited understanding of Adventist doctrine.

But the doctrinal concerns (or the lack thereof) of the postmodern Adventist are largely of another nature. He[8] has a different attitude to doctrine. He will agree that members of a faith community must have certain basic theological understandings in common. But when it comes to doctrinal issues his first question is not: *Is it true?* Is this what the Bible says? Is this what the Adventist pioneers discovered or confirmed as biblical truth, and is this what the church officially teaches? No, the most vital question is rather: *What does it do for me* if I believe these things? How does this affect my life and make me a better and happier person?[9] A growing number of church members have come to the conclusion that doctrines must not only be true, but that they *must make a practical difference*. They must do something for you! If not, why bother?

Until just a few decades ago, people who became interested in the Seventh-day Adventist message would receive a series of Bible studies, either in their home, or in a Bible seminar or a Bible study group in the church, in which all the important Adventist viewpoints would be reviewed in some depth. The person who 'taught' the prospective member (who 'gave the Bible studies'), usually followed a predetermined outline, carefully leading the interested person to a number of spaced-out decisions, before he would be challenged to make the ultimate decision to be baptised. In 'western' Adventism this is no longer the rule, but rather the exception. The person who is willing or even eager to discuss his faith with us, usually to a large extent sets the agenda for the interaction. He decides on the questions he wants to ask, and determines the order in which the topics come to the table. But, more importantly, he will be selective in what he chooses to accept and what he sees as relevant for him. He is like a shopper who goes through the aisles of the su-

---

[8]   I am using here, and in the rest of this chapter, the masculine pronoun, rather than the more accurate designation 'he or she.'

[9]   My conviction that this observation is correct was considerably strengthened by the many reactions I received from readers of my book: *It's Time To Stop Rehearsing What We Believe and Start Looking at What Difference It Makes* (Nampa, ID: Pacific Press Publishing Association, 1998). In this little book I looked at each of the fundamental Adventist doctrines and discussed their practical relevancy.

permarket and picks what he likes and ignores what does not take his fancy. While in the past, after a period of building trust, an interested person would be inclined to accept the entire doctrinal package, even if there might still be some lingering doubts about some aspects of some doctrines, the postmodern 'seeker' is different. He accepts what appeals to him, and that is it. And he refuses to be pressured into affirming beliefs of which he is not totally convinced or considers as immaterial.

This, of course, makes the issue as to how many of the church's doctrines a prospective Adventist must accept before he can be baptised, even more pressing. All agree that the baptismal candidate must have faith in God and in Jesus. And that he must affirm his belief in the return of Jesus, in the Seventh-day Sabbath and a few other key doctrines. But what happens if he is not (yet) convinced that tithing is a biblical concept, and simply cannot see that it would be wrong to have a glass of wine at dinner time? What, if he is not convinced of the traditional Adventist understanding of the millennium, and is not impressed by 'little horn' and 'mark of the beast' language? Can such a person be baptised? The postmodern person will see this as a false dilemma. What counts is not his understanding of doctrinal minutiae but his budding relationship with his Lord. His baptism is a seal and a public acknowledgement of that *relationship* rather than an acknowledgement that he *understands* and accepts as valid a list of doctrinal *propositions*. To belong to a group of people with similar ideas and ideals is important, but that faith community is not so much thought of in terms of a national or global organization which has inflexible rules of admittance, but rather as a *local* group of like-minded individuals.

Thus it happens more and more often that people ask for baptism without the corollary of church membership. They may plan to attend church, but do not want to become church members at this point in time. Of course, from a church political point of view, it is vital that baptism and church membership are kept together.[10] But is it also a theological necessity?[11] Whatever pastors and other church officials may think, the postmodern people in their congregation, in particular the newcomers, will simply follow their own inner conviction or postpone their final choice.

The quest for experience

Most Adventists will agree that feeling and emotion are aspects of their religion that cannot be ignored. But, at the same time, they also tend to be wary of too much emotion. Their religion is a *rational* religion. Adventists do not simply *read*

---

[10] See *Seventh-day Adventist Church Manual* (Silver Spring, MD: Secretariat of the General Conference of Seventh-day Adventists, 2005 ed.), 30.

[11] Herbert Kiesler, 'The Ordinances: Baptism, Foot Washing, and the Lord's Supper,' in: Raoul Dederen, ed: *Handbook of Seventh-day Adventist Theology* (Hagerstown, MD: Review and Herald Publishing Association, 2000), 586.

the Bible, they *study* the Bible. Truth is propositional truth, and faith therefore has strong rational overtones. This is hardly surprising. The Adventist 'pioneers' had to define and defend their beliefs in an environment in which their teachings were under constant attack as unbiblical and sectarian. They were also regularly faced with outbursts of charismatic phenomena which threatened to destroy the unity and cohesiveness of the tiny movement they were trying to build.

But let us not forget that the Adventist pioneers lived in a country and at a time when every believer was a potential theologian. Nathan O. Hatch, a well-known expert in the area of American religious history, wrote about this in his fascinating book on *The Democratization of American Christianity*.[12] In describing the mid-nineteenth century religious scene in the United States, he paints a world in which everyone who owned a Bible and a concordance and had access to a few library books, and then sat down to put his views in writing, could expect a hearing. An enormous array of books, journals, pamphlets found their way to a public that was eager to compare and judge, and valued the products of these amateur theologians as much as, or at times even more, than the learned tomes of the professionals. William Miller and, a little later, Adventist pioneers Joseph Bates, James White, Uriah Smith, and John N. Andrews set the standard for the kind of carefully constructed argumentation that underpinned the 'present truth.' They selected Bible texts that would give logical support to their theses, and they read widely and explored historical facts which would give further credence to their prophetic interpretations. They wanted to find convincing proof for their ideas, and were eager to instruct and to persuade.

Modern Adventism still very much operates this way. It is not hard to find examples of this in a wide range of 'independent ministries.' However, much of what is published by the regular denominational publishing houses and is promoted by the departments at the various levels of the church also reflects this traditional emphasis on logical argument and on propositional truth that is well argued and is aimed at convincing the seeker for truth.

Adventism is not unique in this respect. A large section of nineteenth and even twentieth century Protestant Christianity in the United States, as well as in Europe and Australia, was very similar. Adventists argued among themselves about points of biblical exegesis, and Adventists debated with other Christians about a range of doctrines. Many of these other Christians were just as eager to argue among themselves and with Adventists! But things have changed. And not just because very few people nowadays know enough about the Bible to engage in serious debate about points of doctrine. There is a more fundamental issue at stake. Most Christian no longer have their heart in doctrinal disputes.

---

[12] New Haven/London, UK: Yale University Press, 1989.

There has been a major paradigm shift among Christians in the Western world. The postmodern Christian wants first and foremost to *experience* his religion in ways that are *culturally relevant* to him. This is also true for major segments of the Adventist Church and it has a major impact on the way many Adventists like to worship and 'do' church, as well as on their private devotional life and the way they approach religious and ethical issues. Personally, I am still struggling with some recent trends in Christian, including Adventist, worship. There is a 'still small voice' in me that says that a church organ is more suitable for praising God than a guitar or a set of percussion instruments. I continue to regard a good sermon as the most central element of the Sabbath morning service. And I am happy when the worship leader has had the good taste to choose a few traditional hymns from the Adventist Hymnal, that have some literary merit, rather than the simplistic 'praise songs' with a few simple lines which must be repeated, it seems, *ad infinitum.*

I realize that this part of me is hopelessly modern! Postmodern Adventists, like their brothers and sisters in other denominations, have a different concept altogether about meaningful worship. They tend to prefer a lively service, with contemporary Christian music and drama. They want to look at the screen where the beamer projects the inevitable praise songs. Here and there participants are beginning to overcome the Adventist inhibition against raising their hands while singing and praying.

Postmodern Adventists do not necessarily attend the church that is closest to where they live, but they often shop around until they find the congregation that suits them best. Surely, the question whether they are likely to hear a good sermon remains a factor that influences their choice, but it is just one among many criteria a 'good' church must possess. Atmosphere, music, drama, social events, children's programmes, and even parking space, are at least as important.

A previous generation of Adventist believers would attend church, often regardless of whether or not they actually enjoyed the type of worship and the social interaction they were going to experience. They went to their Adventist church, because that is where they found the Truth—and that is what counted above everything else. The postmodern Adventist is still very much aware of the 'Adventist connection,' but he will far more likely stop attending church if the service does not 'do' anything for him. Or, he may even decide to attend another evangelical church where he 'feels' more at home and finds the kind of worship that satisfies his spiritual longings, even if there may be some doctrinal points he does not subscribe to.

There are a number of interrelated aspects. In many parts of the Western world, the 'planting' of new churches for the unchurched has become part of the Adventist strategy. Traditional methods fail to reach the secular audience and traditional congregations do not easily attract the nominal Christian who is biblically illiterate. The 'church plants' which try to reach secular people tend to de-emphasize doctrine. 'Friendship evangelism' that stretches over a long period, even years, has replaced the short, crusade-type evangelism which deals fairly quickly with key Adventist doctrines. The approach of the 'church plants' is *relational* rather than doctrinal. Their ultimate aim is that people will accept Jesus Christ as their Saviour, and experience salvation, rather than to lead them to assent to a series of propositional truths. People who eventually enter the church via this route will have become used to a type of worship which is a far cry from the traditional Adventist worship service and cannot be expected ever to 'do' church in the traditional way.

Those who are active in this church planting movement (and it is indeed becoming a *movement*) do so because they felt an urgent call to witness to their Lord. They have not been chosen by a nominating committee during the annual or biannual ecclesial process as outlined in the *Church Manual*. Often, it is not clear at all who has decided which people will form the church planting team. It begins with someone who has a vision, with people talking, dreaming and brainstorming. When duties are distributed among team members, a 'spiritual gifts inventory' may provide the basis for the allocation of various responsibilities. This approach is also beginning to find its way into the 'regular' organizational process of the local Adventist congregation. The idea is that assigning church offices and administrative tasks should not happen on a merely pragmatic basis: who is willing, often after some pressure, to do what? The spiritual gift-oriented approach starts from a different premise: You do not begin by listing the jobs to be done, but you start with finding out how the Spirit has distributed his gifts among the members, and then you challenge the people to use their specific gifts of ministry in their church. This approach fits well with the postmodern person, who is highly suspicious of bureaucratic ecclesiastical rules and inflexible church manuals and the like. But it requires little imagination to see that those who opt for the postmodern gift-oriented approach to the internal organisation of the church can easily clash with the traditionalists with their modern allegiance to ecclesial law and order!

The gap between modern and postmodern Adventism is also very apparent in the approach to church discipline. It becomes a very pressing issue in congregations which consist of a mix of modern and of postmodern Adventists. The modern Adventist will insist that members who commit substantial mistakes ought to be disciplined. That is what the *Church Manual* prescribes and it is a prerequisite for maintaining order. But to the postmodern Adventist church discipline is largely a relic of the past. The postmodern Adventist will hardly pay attention to what others, even his fellow-believers in his local church, feel and say about his doctrinal aberrations or about his non-conformist behaviour. In that situation the main function of discipline—to bring people back to the 'straight and narrow' path—has been lost.

The end of the meta-narrative of Adventism?

The prophets of postmodernity have stressed the end of the 'meta-narrative' as one of its key concepts.[13] They have declared that the *grand narratives* of the past, which proclaim an all-embracing meaning to life, and provide a cohesive world-view, have been replaced by a much more fragmented view of life.[14]

It is not difficult to see the impact of this way of thinking on the postmodern Adventist. A very significant paradigm shift is taking place in the Adventist church in the Western world in this regard. The modern Adventist proudly views Advent-ism as a *grand* story, as a *meta-narrative* that goes far beyond the local congregation or the conference or union. He believes Adventism plays a key role in the final phase of the *Great Controversy*. His church is a divinely-ordained movement with a worldwide mission, which from a very modest beginning in the eastern part of the United States grew into a world church with millions of members, with a pres-ence in every corner of the world, and which will continue to grow and eventually gather all God's faithful into a 'remnant' that will be saved when Christ returns.

The modern Adventist believes in a worldwide movement, which may have some local variations in forms of worship and in the ways in which people ex-press themselves, but is firmly united in doctrine, in organisation and policy. He cannot imagine there could be any other church structure than that of General Conference, divisions, unions, conferences and local churches, and fully expects that the higher units will provide a constant stream of initiatives, programmes and resources to the lower echelons. He is quite happy to see a substantial amount of financial support channelled from the local base to the 'higher' organisational levels, which he regards as more than a merely pragmatic structure that can and should be adapted to ever-changing needs.

For postmodern Adventists all of this is a totally different story. They may think globally in quite a number of respects, but they tend to act locally. Although they take pride in the fact that they can find Adventist churches all over the world, and appreciate that the church is more than just a local faith community, they are much more sceptical about the organizational aspects of global Adventism. And they are far more likely to focus on the differences within worldwide Adventism

---

[13] For a concise discussion of this aspect of postmodernism, see Stanley J. Grenz, *A Primer on Postmodernism*, (Grand Rapids, MI: William B. Eerdmans Publishing Company, 1996), 39-56.

[14] See the section 'Worldview and Postmodernity,' in: David K. Naugle, *Worldview: The History of a Concept* (Grand Rapids, MI: William B. Eerdmans Publishing Company), 173-184.

than on its unity and uniformity. They do not really care whether the church uses the same Bible lessons all over the world, or whether it has well developed unified church policies. In fact, they tend to think that it might be better to intentionally choose different routes where cultures and historical, educational, economic and geographical contexts differ. They have very little interest in the church's hierarchical system and wonder whether all these levels of church administration are still needed. They wonder how all this expensive bureaucratic infrastructure helps the *local* church to do better in responding to the needs they are facing in their own congregation and their local community.

Postmodern Adventists have ceased to buy in to slogans and programmes that are pushed 'from the top down.' Sure, they are looking for resources, but these do not necessarily have to come from denominational offices. Seldom will they implement an existing programme in every detail, but they will pick and choose, and, as postmodernists do, collate the components they have assembled from a wide array of sources into something they feel suits their particular local needs.

Postmodern Adventists will almost invariably manifest a substantial degree of suspicion regarding the institutional church and its hierarchy. They have little regard for leaders simply because they happen to have been elected to a particular post at some administrative meeting. They are much more interested in natural leaders who have proven that they have something relevant to say, and who demonstrate, in how they speak and write, that they are at the right wave-length.

This suspicion towards the institutional church has far-reaching financial consequences. Many postmodern Adventists have a hard time to be convinced that the only 'store house' into which their tithes must be brought (Mal 3:6) is the conference bank account. Collecting tithes in this way has been a practical arrangement which may have served the church well in the past. But what theological backing, they say, is there for this practice? Why can the tithe, or at least a major portion of it, not stay at the local level? The postmodern Adventist does not believe in a complicated multi-layered system over which he has little or no influence, but would like to send his money directly to the place where he wants it to be used. And, as soon as he feels uncertain about the way the money is actually spent, he tends to reconsider his giving pattern.

But the grand story of Adventism has evaporated in an even more fundamental respect. The modern Adventist derives his entire identity, or at least the core of his identity, from his membership in the Adventist Church. His own story, to a large extent, is a chapter or a paragraph, or at the very least a footnote in the grand story of Adventism. His social networks coincide to a large extent with the congregation to which he belongs. He is an Adventist first, and only then, at some distance, also a citizen of a country or town, a doctor or a bookkeeper, a soccer enthusiast or a tennis fan.

The postmodern Adventist has a multiple identity, or, to put it even more succinctly, a fragmented identity. Being an Adventist Christian is an important part
of his life. But there are other sectors of life which hardly intersect with his religious identity. His professional life and his social life may be worlds apart from
each other and from his religious life. His professional network will be at least as
important to him as his church network, and his social network may only very
partially coincide with his church network and only to a very limited extent with
his professional network. The postmodern Adventist is an Adventist, but at the
same time he is just as much a professional who wants to succeed in his career,
an enthusiastic volunteer for Green Peace or for the local Amnesty chapter, and a
person who enjoys country living or zealously collects Civil War memorabilia. He
will keep these various compartments of his life far more separate than his modern
brother or sister does.

Are the walls coming down?
Until relatively recently it was often quite tough to become or remain a Seventh-
day Adventist. Many regarded the Adventist Church as a sect at the fringe of Christianity, and people were warned against allowing themselves to be brainwashed
by these strange, Sabbath keeping, prophecy-enthused, people. Adventists were
usually forced onto the defensive, as they were fighting ignorance and misconcep-
tions about their church, and saw their beliefs constantly challenged. There has,
however, been a gradual but very real change, and today Adventism is regarded
by many other Christians, who know anything about it, as a legitimate part of the
evangelical stream of Christianity.

This process has caused considerable internal confusion. On the one hand, it
feels good to be recognized as true Christians and to discover that the sectarian label has almost disappeared. But, on the other hand, many Adventists still operate
with an eschatology which positions them as a vulnerable minority—the faithful
'remnant'—over and against a majority of other Christian believers who belong to
the spiritual axis of evil, called Babylon. For modern Adventists this is still very
much the end-time scenario they keep in the back of their minds, in spite of the
considerable tension it creates. For, while they enjoy the PR of good relationships
with other Christians in the present, they know they must remain vigilant, for
sooner rather than later the battle lines will be drawn in the final confrontation
between those who are Christ's and those who are not.

The postmodern Adventist is much less sure about how things are going to
play out in the final phase before Christ's second coming. The prophecies of Daniel and Revelation no longer provide him with a precise timetable of future events.
After all, his postmodern reading of the Bible has made him aware of, and comfortable with, constant shifts in the interpretation of the Bible—and most definitely

of the prophetic portions of Scripture. His attitude is characterized by a 'wait and see' approach rather than by a firm conviction about the chronological order of future events and the identity of the key-players therein. He is less inclined than his modern fellow-believer to see clear and absolute lines of demarcation between Adventists and other Christians. Adventism has a role and brings an extra dimension to his Christian faith, but the postmodern Adventist hesitates to affirm that he has the absolute truth and that all others are totally wrong. In any case, when he looks at others and at religious and social developments, he is more concerned about common issues of justice and morality than doctrinal differences. It follows that the postmodern Adventist is more open to ecumenical dialogue and cooperation than traditional Adventism has been and is.

Finally, one other important characteristic of the postmodern Adventist must be highlighted. Postmodern people, including those in the Adventist Church, detest hypocrisy. They have no time for people who live a lie, who say one thing and then turn around and do something else. If you want to talk religion to a postmodern person, you have to be authentic. Nothing turns the postmodern (and even more so the *young* postmodern) person away from the church and from 'churchy' people as hypocrisy. The postmodern Adventist will accept a lot of things. But a lack of integrity is not one of them!

Is postmodernity all bad?

The description of the postmodern Adventist given above is certainly not exhaustive. But enough has been said to show why several of the ideas and attitudes of the postmodern Adventist cause a lot of concern to many of his fellow-believers. With this in mind we return to the question posed in the opening paragraphs of this essay. Is the postmodern trend, which is gaining influence, a threat to the unity of the church? Many modern Adventists would argue that it is. However, it could be maintained that the modern Adventist is, in fact, a greater threat to the unity of his church. The modern Adventist defends 'the truth' and usually does not want to provide much space for the postmodern believer. In his view the postmodern Adventist no longer represents 'true' Adventism, but, at best, a watered-down version of it. He believes it is important to counteract his influence as much as possible. The postmodern Adventist does not 'fight' for his view point. He accepts that there are differences of opinion and approach. He simply asks for tolerance and space.

It would be too simplistic, however, to argue that postmodern Adventism does not pose major challenges to the unity of the church. How can people who have firm convictions about the Truth and who sense a calling to defend a series of doctrinal 'truths,' peacefully cohabit in one faith community with others who regard truth and ethical standards as far more relative? It may well be that there are fewer 'truths' than traditional Adventism has defended. And it should be conceded (I believe) that Adventism has often manifested a lack of balance between the rational and the experiential. But the *language* of faith must have a propositional *grammar*: faith must be about something that goes beyond feeling, something that is real, or rather about Someone who is more than a product of our own imagination. If not, what common platform is there?

It may well be that Adventism must try harder in formulating a response to the philosophies that undergird postmodernity. Fortunately there are Christian theologians and philosophers who have accepted this challenge and it is worth listening to what they have to say.[15] It is good to see Adventist efforts to build on this and to develop resources that will help in the dialogue with postmoderns.[16] I have also tried to make a contribution in this respect.[17]

The philosophical and theological challenges are significant. And, for people who still think largely 'modern,' to have meaningful dialogue with people who have imbibed postmodernity with their entire being, is tremendously difficult. Yet, at the same time, it would be wrong to declare postmodernity nothing but a threat to the church and its unity. Postmodernity has positive aspects. It emphasises the value of spirituality. It corrects a one-sided obsession with doctrinal purity at the expense of religious experience. It is suspicious of the uncontested reign of science. It recognizes the fragility of our world and the finiteness of its resources and demands responsible stewardship and justice. It emphasizes personal integrity and the relational aspect of religion. It demands pluriformity, space for individual opinion, and tolerance.

The major philosophical and theological premises of postmodernity must be taken seriously. They are often challenging but they are not unanswerable. Moreover, many aspects of postmodernity are, in fact, akin to important facets of Adventist Christianity and have the potential to enrich rather than destroy the unity of the church. They provide important stepping stones to reach postmodern secular people around us with 'present truth.' The postmodern Adventist will indeed present a threat to the unity of his church, if no meaningful dialogue between *moderns* and *postmoderns* in the church can take place. Views from both camps can,

---

[15] I have benefited greatly from such books as: Nancey Murphy, *Beyond Liberalism and Fundamentalism. How Modern and Postmodern Philosophy Set the Theological Agenda* (Harrisburg, PA: Trinity Press International, 1996), and, in particular, Alvin Plantinga, *Warranted Christian Belief* (New York: Oxford University Press, 2000).

[16] These include the resources that are provided by the *Centre for Secular and Postmodern Studies* that has been established by the world church of Seventh-day Adventists (www. reframe.info). Jon Paulien, theology professor at Loma Linda University, recently wrote a stimulating book that deals with the approach to the postmodern public: *Everlasting Gospel in an Ever-changing World* (Nampa, ID: Pacific Press Publishing Association, 2008).

[17] Reinder Bruinsma, *Faith, Step by Step: Finding God and Yourself* (Grantham, UK: The Stanborough Press, Ltd, 2006).

I believe, be woven into a promising and inspiring synthesis that is faithful to the Scriptures and to the basics of Adventist tradition. Hopefully, some of the most creative Adventist thinkers will see it as their God-given calling to dedicate their talents to that important task.

Reinder Bruinsma. Born in the Netherland. Retired 2007. Pastoral, editorial, educational, lecturing and administrative experience in the Netherlands, the Cameroons, Ivory Coast, United States and Great Britain. Executive secretary of the Trans-European Division, 1995-2001. President Dutch Adventist Church, 2002-2007. Author of books and articles. PhD, University of London (1994).

Why Adventists Defend Religious Freedom:
The Biblical Roots

John Graz

'Why has the Seventh-day Adventist Church been so involved in religious free-dom since its beginning?' We hear this question regularly when people learn of our activities and our history in support of religious freedom.[1] We cannot pretend that religious freedom is the number one activity of the Adventist Church; but you will never hear a church leader stating publicly, 'We do not need to defend reli-gious freedom.' Why is this so? Religious freedom is deeply rooted in the church's history. From the beginning of their movement, Adventists have tended to see themselves as champions of religious freedom. They believe they have been called to 'lift up the banner of the truth and religious liberty.' Religious liberty is part of the church's mission, and it has a significant place in its vision of the end time.[2]

There are a number of reasons why Adventists defend religious freedom in the twenty-first century. I will mention just six: 1. Religious freedom is a fundamental right; 2. Religious freedom is threatened around the world; 3. Religious freedom is a gift from God, the Creator and Saviour; 4. Religious freedom is part of the prophetic message of the church; 5. Religious freedom makes the preaching of the gospel possible; and 6. Religious freedom is the sign of the kingdom of God and of his church. All of these points could be extensively developed, but in this study I will underline primarily the biblical roots of religious freedom. We promote and defend religious freedom for all people everywhere because, first of all, religious freedom is, according to the Bible, a gift from God.

Freedom of choice at creation
The founders of the Seventh-day Adventist Church followed the principle of *Sola Scriptura*. They saw religious freedom as a biblical principle.[3] We can sum up their thoughts in a few sentences. Religious freedom is the natural result of God's love.

---

[1] We use the term 'religious freedom' and keep 'religious liberty' for the official title of organizations and for quotations.

[2] In 1889 Adventists chartered the National Religious Liberty Association, and in 1893 the International Religious Liberty Association (IRLA). In 1901 they organized the Department of Religious Freedom as part of the General Conference. In 2007 they celebrated the 100th Anniversary of their magazine, *Liberty*, which is printed every two months with a circulation of 200,000. Every year the IRLA organizes international congresses, symposia, meetings of experts, and mass celebrations called Festivals of Religious Liberty. Every five years they hold a World Congress which has become one of the largest meetings for religious freedom activists and religious and political leaders.

[3] 'Religious Liberty,' *SDA Encyclopedia* (1976), vol. 10, 1197-1199.

The kingdom of God is built on love. Creation is the outworking of that love. But there is no love without freedom and no freedom without freedom to choose.

In 1907, W. A. Gosmer wrote: 'As in heaven there was the liberty born only of love, as a consequence, He who came as heaven's representative would bring only the principles of love and liberty which were found in heaven.'[4]

1. God's love is creation's essential principle

The story of the creation of human beings, according to Genesis 1 and 2, is embedded in God's love for his creatures. 'Then God said, "Let us make man in our image, according to our likeness ..."' There is a clear distinction between the creation of people and the creation of light, animals, and water. We are told: 'Then God said: "Let there be light."' The same expression is used for 'the waters' and for 'the firmament.' When it comes to man, it is written, 'Let *us* make man.' God is totally involved in human creation.

The word 'image' is repeated three times in Genesis. Gen 1:27 says, 'In the image of God he created him.' And for those who may think that God created only 'him,' it is written: 'male and female he created them.'[5] Then he blessed them and gave them a mission and the power to accomplish it. In each act of the creation of humans we can see God's love in action. The best definition of God comes from the apostle John: 'God is love' (1 John 4:8). 'He who does not love does not know God.' God's love is at the very beginning of mankind's history. God's love is the foundation of human dignity.

We as human beings have been created by love in the image of God, and there is no love—real, absolute love—without the freedom to love. For Augustine, using the classification provided by Aristotle, man was created in the image of God who is free, and he was given free memory, mind, and will.[6]

2. Freedom to choose implies access to information

Love cannot be dissociated from the freedom to love. God did not force his creatures to love him. He did not force them to obey him. In Genesis 2, God describes organizing the best environment for his creatures. A beautiful garden was 'planted eastward in Eden.' Then God 'took the man and put him in the Garden of Eden,' with the mission 'to take care of it' (vs 15).

Everything is perfect, but everything has to be tested. Then God the Creator 'commanded the man, "You are free to eat from any tree in the garden; but you

---

[4]   W. A. Gosmer, 'Religious Liberty,' *Liberty*, 2:4, (1907), 31.
[5]   Augustine believed man received a soul with a free will. I do not agree with him when it comes to his theology of the soul. All Church Fathers believed that Adam and Eve were created with the freedom to choose. Luther thought it could be dangerous to give the impression that we have a free will. See Luther's work, *Lectures on Genesis,* vol. 1, chapters 1-5, 50, 60, 84-85, edited by Jaroslav Pelikan (St Louis, MS: Concordia Publishing House, 1958). Luther quoted Augustine, 'On the Trinity,' X, chapters 11-12.
[6]   See Augustine, 'On the Trinity,' X, chapters 11-12, quoted by Martin Luther in *Lectures on Genesis.*

must not eat from the tree of the knowledge of good and evil'"' (vs 16-17). In the perfect environment which had just been created for humankind, there was a choice.

God created Adam and Eve innocent and as candidates for perfection—perfection defined not as a state of being, but as the result of a process consisting of a succession of free choices.[7] Perfection could not be achieved without the exercise of the will to gain the necessary knowledge to make a decision. There is no perfection without freedom of choice and without obedience to God's will.

Freedom to choose is a gift from our Creator. It is an inherent part of our human dignity. We need reason and God's guidance to make the right choice. Every tendency to disguise or to destroy this God-given freedom is an attack against God's purpose for humankind, a negation of God's love, and an annihilation of our human dignity.

Frank B. Holbrook writes: 'Like the angels, Adam and Eve were created free moral agents. The prohibition against eating the fruit from the tree of the knowledge of good and evil placed a simple test before them, providing an option to obey God because they loved him, or to disobey him by asserting their own wills in opposition to his.'[8] Today freedom is often described as: 'Do what you wish, whatever you want.'

According to the Bible, our first parents were created with the freedom to choose and they had to exercise it, to make a choice. God gave them the most important information they needed—the consequence of their choice: 'For in the day that you eat thereof you shall surely die.'

Freedom of choice includes the freedom to gather all the information needed. Reason will help us to make our decision. But reason is fed by knowledge. When the choice has been made, the consequences will follow. In theological terms, this means the judgement. Where there is freedom, there is access to knowledge, responsibility, choice, and judgement.

3. Consequences of the wrong choice.

'God made Adam after his own character, pure and upright. There were no corrupt principles in the first Adam, no corrupt propensities or tendencies to evil. Adam was faultless as the angels before God's throne.'[9]

In Genesis 3 a new actor challenges God's information. He was 'more subtle than any' beast of the field which the Lord God had made' (vs 1, KJV). He did not

---

[7]   I will use 'freedom of choice' or 'free choice'or 'freedom to choose' instead of 'free will' which is far more complex in its philosophical approach. 'Freedom to choose' makes an easier relation with religious freedom than 'free will.' 'Free choice' is also used by Church Fathers, including Augustine.

[8]   'The Great Controversy,' *Handbook of Seventh-day Adventist Theology* (Hagerstown, MD: Review and Herald Publishing Association, 2000), 979.

[9]   Ellen G White, letter 191, 1889.

directly oppose God's words, but interpreted them and distorted their meaning. Verse 4 says, 'You will not surely die.' Verse 5 continues, 'You shall be as gods, knowing good and evil.' Having this information, Adam and Eve used their reason to compare the information they received. They then made their choice, using their will, to eat the fruit.

William Barclay wrote, 'Before man, there stands an open choice; and it has to be so. A coerced goodness is not real goodness; and a coerced love is not love at all. If men deliberately choose to turn their backs on God after he has sent his Son Jesus Christ into the world, not even he can do anything about it.'[10]

In his book, *Liberty, Rethinking an Imperiled Ideal*, Glenn Tinder writes: 'Evil can be due only to human beings. This is not, of course, because God created them evil. It is because he created them free. He gave them the power of choosing evil and thereby mutilating their created nature.'[11]

Reason only was not enough to ensure the right choice. A good use of reason would have been to believe the Creator, God, rather than the creature, the serpent. But when it comes to making a choice, other factors intervene such as covetousness, selfishness, and pride. The devil cannot win on the ground of reason alone. He seduces us, and seduction is his most effective weapon.

4. Freedom of choice in an unfavourable environment.

Freedom to choose existed in heaven before the fall of the angels,[12] and it was in Eden before the fall of Adam and Eve. In Eden, it was not an 'absolute' freedom because of the presence of the devil who was acting as an external call to disobedience. Absolute freedom will be a reality in the Kingdom of God. Luther wrote, 'But when it is finished in the Kingdom of the Father, then the will will be truly free and good, the mind truly enlightened, and the memory persistent.'[13] The external call to rebellion will no longer exist.

After being expelled from the Garden of Eden, Adam and Eve were no longer in a favourable environment. Temptations became part of their life. The fall weakened their humanity, and disobedience to God's word became natural. Ellen G. White wrote: 'The fall of our first parents broke the golden chain of implicit obedience of the human will to the divine.'[14] Their reason had been affected. Their per-

---

[10] William Barclay, *The Letter to the Romans*, rev. ed. (Philadelphia, PA: The Westminster Press, 1975), 29.

[11] Glenn Tinder, *Liberty, Rethinking an Imperiled Ideal* (Grand Rapids, MI: Wm. B. Eerdmans Publishing Company, 2007), 31.

[12] See Isaiah 14:12-16.

[13] Luther's *Works*, Vol. 1, 'Lectures on Genesis,' chapters 1-5, edited by Jaroslav Pelikan, (St Louis, MS: Concordia Publishing House, 1958), 65.

[14] 'He [Satan] tempts them to it [sin], and makes sin look enticing and pleasant, but he has to leave it to their own wills whether they will do it or not. He does not force men to become intoxicated ... but he presents temptations in a manner to allure to evil, and man is a free moral agent to accept or refuse' (*Testimonies*, vol. 2, 294).

ception of the truth was no longer as clear as it had been. They now had 'corrupt propensities or tendencies to evil.'[15] But they still had the power to exercise their freedom to choose.

It is interesting to notice that, according to the Latin and Greek Church Fathers who lived prior to Augustine, the human will is fully free and able to resist sin's seduction. They considered human freedom as the essential condition of morality. Augustine agreed for a while as he dealt with the Manicheans: 'The free will, naturally assigned by the Creator to our rational soul, is such an essential power ... he [man] received naturally when he was created.'[16] But in his answer to Pelagius he gave exclusive choice to God. 'God has chosen us to become saints. After the fall God ... does not deprive the wicked of the free will. But this will, which is free in evil things is not free in good things, for the reason that it has not been made free.'[17] Augustine had a great influence on Martin Luther and John Calvin who both denied 'free will.' They felt a free will would restrict God's sovereignty and his absolute grace.

On the same issue, Luther wrote, 'In a certain way, we indeed have a free will in those things that are beneath us ... But in those matters that pertain to God and are above us, no human being has a free will ... For those we don't choose, we do not do anything; but we are chosen, we are equipped, we are born again, we accept as Isaiah says, "You are the Potter; we, your clay" (Isa 64:8).'[18]

The Bible contains so many texts in favour of free choice that it is difficult to follow Augustine, Luther and Calvin on this issue.[19] Deuteronomy 30:20 reads: 'See, I have set before you today life and good, death and evil, in that I command you today to love the Lord your God, to walk in his ways and to keep his commandments.'

In every human being there is still this print of God's love which is the freedom to choose. Sin made human salvation impossible without Jesus' sacrifice, but God, through Christ, did not allow the fall to eliminate the freedom to choose. Christ, by his death and resurrection, provided salvation for all humanity.[20] We are not in any way saved by our own power, but as human beings and God's creatures we are free to accept or refuse God's grace.

---

[15] Ellen G White, MS I, 1892.

[16] St. Augustine, *Acts or Disputation Against Fortunas, A Selected Library of the Nicene and Post – Nicene Fathers of the Christian Church,* edited by Philipp Schaff (Grand Rapids, MI: Wm. B. Eerdmans Publishing Company, May 1983), vol. IV, 121.

[17] A *Treatise Against Two Letters of the Pelagians,* op cit., vol. 1, ch. 7, 379.

[18] Luther's *Works,* Vol. 1, 'Lectures on Genesis,' chapters 1-5, edited by Jaroslav Pelikan (St Louis, MS: Concordia Publishing House, 1958,) vol. 7, ch. 2, 84.

[19] Deut 30:15-16; John 14:15; John 15:7; Rom 2:10; 1 Cor 9:24.

[20] The seed of the woman 'shall bruise your head, and you shall bruise his heel' (Gen 3:15).

Nobody can be saved against his free choice. It is interesting to note this comment of Ellen G. White: 'It is not the plan of God to compel men to yield their wicked unbelief. Before them are light and darkness, truth and error. It is for them to decide which to accept. The human mind is endowed with power to discriminate between right and wrong. God designs that men shall not decide from impulse, but from weight of evidence, carefully comparing scripture with scripture.'[21]

Adam and Eve had the freedom to choose. When they disobeyed God, they died. Jesus came, and by his blood he gave to everyone a new freedom. The story of creation forms the basis of our understanding of free choice as a gift of God. Does Jesus' life and teaching confirm it?

Jesus honoured freedom of choice

For Jesus religion is a matter of conviction and choice. Nobody is spared from making a choice. As the Son of God, he had to choose. At the beginning of his ministry, Satan suggested to him that he could avoid the cross and still have the whole world (Mat 4:1-10). Resisting temptation was a choice. Contrary to Adam, he chose to obey God, and he responded to Satan, 'It is also written ...' (vs 7). A few hours before he was crucified, he was again tempted to save his life and avoid torture and the cross. It was a very painful choice, but he made it. He chose to be obedient until the end: 'Yet not what I will, but what you will' (Mk 14: 32-41). The Son of God himself was free to follow or not follow his Father. As in Eden, obedience was the test of faithfulness. 'If you love me, keep my commandments' (John 14:15). If God did not force his Son to obey him, would he force his human creatures to follow him? No! Because God loves his creatures and there is no love without freedom to choose.

1. The disciples were free to choose.

After the temptations in the wilderness, Jesus confirmed his choice and he called his disciples (Lk 8:18-22). All the disciples had good reasons to say No! Later on, Jesus had to face a major crisis with his disciples when he saw them leaving him one after another. It could have been the end of his team, the end of the dream. Opportunists would have manipulated the small group of the faithful. Jesus could have performed miracles to impress or terrorize those who were hesitating. But instead, he simply asked the twelve: 'Do you want to go away?' (John 6:67). This means that even those who are baptised, even those who made a commitment to follow him—they are still free to choose, free to stay, free to leave. Their choice should be respected.[22]

---

[21] The *Study Bible* (Harrah, OK: Academy Enterprises Inc, 1993), 243. See Joshua 24:15.

[22] About eleven countries have the death penalty for those who convert from Islam to another religion. See Tad Stahnke and Robert C. Blitt, *The Religion-State Relationship and the Right to Freedom of Religion or Belief: A Comparative Textual Analysis of the Constitutions of Predominantly Muslim Countries*, USCIRF, research@uscirf.gov, March 2005.

The freedom to choose is also given to the members of the church. The church is the assembly of those who believe and who obey God. The risen Christ says to his church through the message to Laodicea, 'Listen! I am standing at the door knocking; if you hear my voice and open the door; I will come in to you and eat with you' (Rev 3:20). The One who received the kingdom, the power, and the glory does not force the church to invite him into her life.

Jesus confirms the entire Bible when he makes it crystal clear what are the consequences of our choices. For Jesus, just as for Moses and Joshua, the choice is between life and death. Those who choose to obey God will be saved (Deut 30:19). We are free to choose, but our choice has consequences: 'Whoever believes and is baptised will be saved, but whoever does not believe will be condemned' (Mk 16:16).[23]

2. Jesus did not force people to choose him.

Jesus met people of other faiths. He shared the good news but never forced anyone to change. He did not preach with the sword in one hand and a cross in the other. He did not order his disciples to destroy pagan temples. When a Roman centurion asked him to heal his servant, he answered his prayer without any condition (Mat 8:5-8). In the area of Tyre, when a Greek woman asked him to heal her little daughter, Jesus did not heal her daughter on condition of her becoming his follower. Look at the way he talked with the Samaritan woman. He could have argued with her about who has the right religion. She opened the discussion with a challenge to him. But he just brought her the good news without coercion or harassment.

A few days before his arrest in Jerusalem, Jesus decided to go through the territory of the Samaritans. He sent his disciples to the village to find a place to stay for the night. The Samaritans refused to give him hospitality. It is an interesting episode because two of his disciples, John and James, were so furious that they wanted to pray God to destroy the village. That is exactly what religious fanaticism has done for centuries and is still doing today: Destroy those who are different and refuse to welcome them! Jesus rebuked his disciples and said: 'Ye know not what manner of spirit ye are of ' (Lk 9:55-56, KJV). Religious intolerance and religious violence are not part of Jesus' teaching.

I love the way Luke concluded his story: 'They went to another village.' That is all. No need to curse them or threaten them. They made their choice and Jesus respected it. They went to another village where people would be happy to welcome them.[24] That should have been a clear enough example for all Christians that

---

[23] See the parable of the Last Judgement in Matthew 25.
[24] The story of the ten lepers is a good example. Jesus healed all ten but only one came back and glorified God. Jesus did not use his healing to force them to follow him (Lk 17:12).

they should reject the use of force and violence in their mission. Unfortunately it was not.

Augustine tried to justify religious coercion by using Jesus' words: 'Compel them to come in.' Facing the heresy of Donatism, Augustine made an unfortunate interpretation of Jesus' parable of the great banquet (Lk 14:16-24).[25] A master organized a great supper and invited his friends. They declined the invitation. This was very humiliating for the master. The dinner was ready and nobody came. The man decided to send his servants out to bring back everyone they could find. His order is in verse 23: 'Compel them to come in.' The Greek verb *anagkazo*, can be translate as 'to constrain' or 'to compel'—whether by force or by persuasion.[26] As Augustine saw it, the Donatists did not want to accept the truth. What should the church authorities do? To use civil law to force them to accept the truth (orthodoxy) was acceptable. Their will, according to the great theologian, was in a state of ignorance and trouble. Like their habits it needed to be broken.[27] Augustine interpreted the words: 'Compel them to come in' in terms of: 'Use compulsion outside, so freedom can arise once they are inside (par. 112.8).' It is interesting that, when Donatists were persecuted, Augustine tried to make bridges: 'We love you, please accept the truth. We love you, but we want to correct you.'[28] He believed correction in this world would save heretics from eternal punishment in the next.

Augustine's view formed the basis of the doctrine and the practice of the Middle Ages. It opened the way for the Inquisition and justified the use of violence against Anabaptists by the Reformers.[29] No Christian theologian now supports this interpretation of Jesus' words. However, the example of Augustine shows how fragile we are when what we consider to be the truth is directly or indirectly challenged.

3. Jesus respected people's choices.

Jesus respected people's decisions and he stated that beautiful and universal principle: 'Therefore, whatever you want men to do to you, do also to them for this is the Law and the Prophets' (Mat 5:12).

I want to be free to choose my religion and I have to respect that freedom for others. I want to teach my religion to my children and share my religion with others. The golden rule is the basic principle of human rights and religious free-

---

[25] According to James Carroll, it was the late Augustine who, no longer depending on the force of reason, justified the use of coercion in defending, and spreading, the orthodox faith, 'in being first compelled by fear or pain, so that they might afterwards be influenced by teaching.' James Carroll, *Constantine's Sword, The Church and the Jews* (Boston, New York: Houghton Mifflin Company, 2001), 211.

[26] See *The Expositor's Bible Commentary*, Frank E Gaebelein, gen. ed. (Grand Rapids, MI: Zondervan Publishing House, revised 1984), vol. 8, 978.

[27] In Lib. arb. 3. 18; 51-52.

[28] Garry Wills, *Saint Augustine*, (New York: Viking Press, 1999), 109.

[29] In: *De Civitate Dei*, XXIII, 51.

dom. When a teacher asked Jesus about the greatest commandment, his answer was: 'Love the Lord your God with all your heart and with all your soul and with your entire mind and your strength.' And he added, 'The second is this: "Love your neighbour as yourself." There is no commandment greater than these' (Mk 12: 31-31). Jesus made clear that the neighbour is any human being. The story of the Good Samaritan illustrated his teaching (Lk 10:29-37). When someone is suffering or is a victim of injustice, there is a human and a Christian obligation to help. Religion is not a criterion when it comes to helping people. Everyone is a child of God and should have his or her freedom of religion protected.

4. Persecuted when exercising freedom of choice.

Persecution is the most brutal negation of the freedom of choice. In the gospels, persecution is omnipresent. It appeared from the beginning with the slaughter of the first born sons in Bethlehem. It continues with the beheading of John the Baptist and the crucifixion of Jesus and the persecution of the apostles. Jesus saw persecution as inevitable and he wanted to prepare his disciples to face it. The world is under the control of the 'Prince of this world.' It will not accept the disciples, just as it did not accept the prophets or Christ, the Son of God. When they decided to follow Jesus, the disciples became candidates for persecution. The possibility of persecution confronts every Christian. Jesus has never hidden that cruel reality: 'Then you will be persecuted and put to death, you will be hated by all nations because of me!' (Mat 24:9). That has happened for centuries, and it will happen again in the last days.

5. The Christian's response to persecution.

Instead of invoking the self-defence principle, Jesus said, 'Blessed are those who are persecuted because of righteousness, for theirs is the kingdom of heaven. Blessed are you when people insult you and falsely say all kinds of evil against you because of me. Rejoice and be glad, because great is your reward in heaven, for in the same way they persecuted the prophets who were before you' (Mat 5:10-11). How do we react? With love!

'But I tell you: Love your enemies and pray for those who persecute you, that you may be sons of your Father in heaven' (vs 44). If Jesus did not recommend that his disciples use violence when they were persecuted, how would he have justified violence to persecute those who do not want to follow his teachings?[30] Inspired by this teaching and by the example of his Master, the apostle Paul wrote: 'Beloved, do not avenge yourselves.' And quoting Scripture, he added, 'overcome evil with good' (Rom 12:19-21).

---

[30] See Roland Minnerath, 'Tertullien précurseur du droit a la liberté de religion,' Méditerranées, Moyen Age chrétien et Antiquité, L'Harmattan (no 18-19, 1999), 42.

Freedom of choice and eschatology
1. The 'Great Controversy'.

Adventists did not, of course, invent eschatology, but inherited the message of the New Testament and of Christians through the ages. Most of the Protestant reformers and independents gave importance to eschatology. According to LeRoy E. Froom, 'It was prophecy that formed the basis of his [Rogers Williams'] immortal appeal for full religious liberty.'[31] Adventists see the issues of religious freedom in the context of eschatology.

In 1888 the book *The Great Controversy between God and Satan* was published, and it was later re-edited several times.[32] The author, Ellen G. White, wrote it during the Sunday law agitation and the strong religious movement to make America a 'Christian nation.' Her vision of history has deeply influenced the Seventh-day Adventist mindset.

This book presents the cosmic battle between God and Satan which began when Lucifer challenged the law of God and denied his infinite love, justice and authority (1 John 3:4; 4:8). Frank B. Holbrook wrote: 'Every intelligent being in God's created universe is subject to authority. Absolute freedom does not exist in the natural order or in human society. The question is not how to escape authority, but rather under what authority will life be made the most meaningful, now and eternally.'[33]

When seduction does not work, coercion and persecution are the methods the devil uses. He forces those who accept God's authority and obey his commandments to change their allegiance. According to Revelation 12:17, faith in Jesus and obedience to his commandments are the test of belonging to God's people. Obedience is the test in the last days at it was in the Garden of Eden, and in 'the great controversy,' religious freedom is the test *par excellence* which draws the line between good and evil. It is a gift from God and a principle of his kingdom. In persecuting and oppressing God's people, Satan and his disciples follow a path in direct opposition to God's ways.

The statement *Seventh-day Adventists and the Ecumenical Movement* contains the following remark about final events: 'In fact, the eschatological picture of the final events is a dramatic tableau of religious persecution, as the massive forces of apocalyptic Babylon try to squeeze the church of the remnant into the mold of united apostasy.'[34]

---

[31] LeRoy Edwin Froom, *The Prophetic Faith of our Fathers* (Hagerstown, MD: Review and Herald Publishing Association, 1954), vol. III, 49. Williams had studied history in the light of prophecy.

[32] Mountain View, CA: Pacific Press Publishing Association, 1888, 1907, 1911.

[33] Frank B. Holbrook, *The Great Controversy*, 976.

[34] Statements, *Guidelines & Other Documents, General Conference, Seventh-day Adventist Church*, 2000, 127.

Adventists recognize that Vatican II, and later Pope John-Paul II, and Benedict XVI, claimed religious freedom as a Christian principle. Adventists believe, however, that this relatively recent adoption of religious freedom will not survive the eschatological testing during the final turmoil prior to the Second Advent. This view was reaffirmed in the statement: *How Seventh-day Adventists View Roman Catholicism.*[35]

2. Truth and freedom.

The end-time scenario does not limit Adventists to a passive strategy. They see themselves in the role of defending religious freedom against intolerance, injustice and oppression: 'The banner of the truth and religious liberty held aloft by the founders of the gospel church and by God's witnesses during the centuries that have passed since then, has, in this last conflict, been committed to our hands.'[36]

Truth and liberty are interrelated. The truth is important, but many of its advocates have been oppressed. Truth and freedom have to go together. Preaching the truth also means promoting, protecting, and defending the right to accept or to refuse it. In the last days those who will fight the truth will also fight the freedom to accept it. With such a stress on freedom, Adventist eschatology keeps alive the focus on human rights. Eschatology is not an escape from the responsibility in society and in the world, but it is a stimulation for more justice and less discrimination.

In Revelation 13, the apostle John described the vision he had about the persecution of Jesus' disciples in the last days. They will be persecuted by a power called the 'beast coming up out of the earth' (vs 11). What are the characteristics of that evil beast? We read that it causes 'as many as would not worship the image of the beast, to be killed' (vs 15). It will be a systematic persecution: 'He causes all, both small and great, rich and poor, free and slave, to receive a mark on their right hand or on their foreheads, and that no one may buy or sell except one who has the mark or the name of the beast, or the number of his name' (vs 16-17). In that eschatological vision of history, the anti-Christ coalition uses force to impose its worship. That illustrates the fundamental difference between the kingdom of God and the kingdom of Satan.[37]

Persecution is a denial of human dignity. It is the product of intolerance, which is the product of many sins. Persecution is the opposite of Christ's message which respects freedom of choice. Disciples of Jesus will not force people to give up or to keep a religion against their will. They will not discriminate against people based on their religion or beliefs. They will not permit an organization or a government

---

[35] Ibid, 57.
[36] Ellen G White, *The Acts of the Apostles,* (Mountain View, CA: Pacific Press Publishing Association, 1921), 68-69.
[37] See the retribution of the persecutors in Revelation 12:20.

to take the role of God or violate conscience. They will not permit violence against innocent people, including innocent believers. Individuals will do their best to listen to and to help the voiceless, homeless, persecuted and poor.

Anything which threatens free choice does not come from God. No one, either church or government, has the right to force someone to adopt, to change, to stay in the same religion, or to have no religion. In order to protect free choice, church and state are best kept separate. One deals with spiritual issues, the other with society. Jesus said: 'My kingdom is not of this world: if my kingdom were of this world, then would my servants fight' (John 18:36).

Why should we, as Christians, defend religious freedom for all people everywhere, knowing that persecution will happen anyway?[38] I am tempted to respond with another question: Why do we build hospitals when we know that people will finally die? Why do we help the poor when Jesus said: 'You will always have the poor with you'? Why do we defend religious freedom when we know that persecution will arise again? Why? Persecution bears the signature of the devil.[39] Free choice is a gift from God and religious freedom bears his signature!

From freedom of choice to religious freedom

Believing in freedom of choice leads naturally to the defence of religious freedom. Believing in free choice and its consequences for eternity leads Adventists to the defence of religious freedom. Believing in Jesus' mission to preach the good news to all nations leads Christians to protect religious freedom. Every aspect which could favour and make choice possible has to be protected. Freedom of expression, freedom of association, and global human rights[40] are positive conditions for using the freedom of choice we received from the Creator. Of course, religious freedom may also be protected by people who do not believe in free choice. We recognize that those who believe in double predestination may see religious freedom as one of the fruits of their election. It may be protected by non-believers. We should, of course recognize the extremely important influence of the philosophers of the Enlightenment in implementing religious freedom in the laws of many

---

[38] For Baptists or Adventists, it is a little easier than for some other Christians, because in both communions there has been a strong tradition in favour of religious freedom. Adventists believe they have a prophetic mission to defend and promote religious freedom for all. Ellen G. White stated: 'The banner of the truth and religious liberty held aloft by the founders of the gospel church and by God's witnesses during the centuries that have passed since then has in this last conflict been committed to our hands.' *The Acts of the Apostles*, 68-69.

[39] 'Any use of force or persecution in matters of religion is a policy inspired by the devil not by Christ.' *The Seventh-day Adventist Bible Commentary* (Hagerstown, MD: Review and Herald Publishing Association, revised 1980), vol. 5, 810.

[40] The *Universal Declaration of Human Rights*, Article 18, and several fundamental documents of the United Nations protect religious freedom as a fundamental right.

countries.[41] They underlined the rights of individuals. Catholics may insist on the freedom to choose as an instrument given by God to find the truth. For Adventists, who have followed the Mennonite and Wesleyan tradition, religious freedom is the consequence of the freedom of choice given by God as an expression of his love and character.

Freedom of choice is not just an instrument to reach the truth. It is an aspect of human dignity, given by the Creator and regenerated by the Saviour. Everyone should have the freedom to choose his or her religion and everyone has the right not to choose any. For both believers and non-believers, it is essential that they obtain the information they need and know the result of their choice, so they can take responsibility. Nobody can be saved against his or her will. This is religious freedom!

John Graz. Born in France. Since 1995 director of the Department of Public Affairs and Religious Liberty at the General Conference of Seventh-day Adventists. Pastoral, youth leadership and communication experience in France, Switzerland and USA. Memberships in societies and committees that deal with religious liberty and interchurch relationships. Author of books and articles. Doctorate, Sorbonne University, Paris (1986).

---

[41] Garry Wills, *Head and Heart, American Christianities* (New York: The Penguin Press, 2007), 1.

A critique of an appraisal:
Seeking a Sanctuary Revisited

Sakae Kubo

Malcolm Bull and Keith Lockhart were both students at Newbold College (UK) when I was Principal there. But they have both gone beyond Newbold and have done exceedingly well. Their book is a testament of their skills as researchers, scholars, and writers.[1] They show evidence that they have scoured every aspect of Adventism and have put together a solid piece of scholarly work, and not least of their accomplishment is that it is written in a most interesting fashion. Most impressive is how they are able within an overarching thesis to make every piece fit in apparently just as multitudinous, seemingly incongruous, pieces of a puzzle, which eventually come together perfectly to make a realistic picture. Although there are statistics and dates and people, they write so interestingly, it is difficult to stop reading. My critique does not in any way lessen my admiration for their work but does raise some questions concerning some of their overarching theses and analyses. The book has received rave reviews by every reviewer even when they offer criticism.[2] The first edition of the book was published in 1989. When referring to their work or the authors, I will, henceforth, use the initials BL.

---

[1] Malcolm Bull and Keith Lockhart, *Seeking a Sanctuary: Seventh-day Adventism and the American Dream*, 2d ed. (Bloomington, IN and Indianapolis, IN: Indiana University Press, 2007). The first edition was published in 1989. All references will be from the second edition.

[2] The second edition updated maps, graphs, and tables, reworked several chapters, and added the chapter on schisms. **First edition**: Eileen Barker, *Sociological Analysis* 52 (1991): 416-17; Jonathan Butler, *Spectrum* 21 (December 1990): 44-45; Stephen Hunt, *Journal of Religious History* 32 (2008): 123-24; Bill J. Leonard, *Review and Expositor* 99 (1991): 277; Richard C. Osborn, *Journal of Adventist Education* 53 (Summer 1991): 44-45; R. Laurence Moore, *Spectrum* 21 (December 1990): 46-47; Gary M. Ross, *College and University Dialogue* 2:2 (1990): 26-27; Gregory Schneider, *Church History* 60 (1991): 579-80; Richard W. Schwarz, *Andrews University Focus* (Fall 1990), 15, 25; Brian Eugene Strayer, *Andrews University Seminary Studies* 28 (Autumn 1990): 255-56. **Second edition**: Michael Campbell, *Ministry* 81 (Feb 2009): 27; Lisa Clark Diller, *Adventist Today* (Jan-Feb 2008): 9; Fabrice Desplan, *Archives de Sciences Sociales des Religions* 140 (2007): passim; Herbert Douglass 'From American Export to Global Product,' *Spectrum* 35 (Spring 2007): 56-60; Roger Dudley, *Andrews University Seminary Studies* 46 (Spring 2008): 125-28; Gary Land, *Spectrum* 35 (Fall 2007): 12-13; Douglas Morgan, 'Golden Age Distortions,' *Spectrum* 35 (Fall 2007): 14-18; Julius Nam, 'Thoughts on the Future of Adventism: A Response to Malcolm Bull and Keith Lockhart,' *Spectrum* 35 (Fall 2007): 18-20. Besides these we have one-line blurbs on the back of the first edition by Martin Marty, 'We do not often pause to point to a denominational history, but when one this good comes along, we pause'; Harold Bloom, 'The most informed study of Adventism,' and Ronald Numbers, 'A masterpiece. It is by far the best book on Adventism that has ever appeared.'

One has to keep in mind that a book review is quite limited in space, an average of a little over one page, so we cannot expect lengthy and substantial critiques. However, some have done well within these limits, not only surveying the contents of the book but offering some criticism. BL's work is comprehensive, covering numerous topics—history, theology, education, sociology, culture, the arts, philosophy, etc., of Adventism, so it is difficult to deal in detail with the scope of material presented, to say nothing about the expertise one would have to have to do so. My critique of BL, therefore, will be focused on a few selected key chapters with which I am in fundamental disagreement. The reviews referred to above can provide general evaluation and some more comprehensive coverage of the contents.

The book has an Introduction—Public Images, then Part 1 on Theology, Part 2 on the Adventist Experience and the American Dream, and Part 3 on Adventist Subculture and Conclusion. My treatment deals with Chapter 13: Adventism and America (Part 2), Chapter 14: Gender, Chapter 17: Medicine (Part 3), and Conclusion.

Part 2: Chapter 13 Adventism and America

BL place a lot of emphasis on their thesis that because of Adventism's interpretation of the beast which 'had two horns like a lamb' and 'spoke like a dragon' (Rev 13:11) as the United States, it turned away from the American Dream to set up its own alternative dream. They support their thesis on several fronts.

1. Since Miller proclaimed a cataclysmic end to the world over against the common view that the earth was getting better and better and moving to an earthly millennium, and Adventists are his descendants, Adventists became opposed to an American dream.[3]

2. With the disappointment, Adventists 'sought their sanctuary in heaven.'[4]

3. Their interpretation of Rev. 13 led them more pronouncedly to turn away from America as the land of their dreams.

4. Their adoption of the Seventh-day Sabbath and their interpretation of Rev 13 with the USA as a 'diabolical monster bent on the destruction of the saints'[5] led to a complete alienation with the American dream.

They develop further their thesis that the Adventist movement works within the sheep's clothing of the American dream. Until America is toppled, they are willing to appear to integrate superficially with American society. 'Deviance is both disguised and reinforced by a willingness to clothe Adventist practices in American dress.'[6] They say that 'the Sabbath is the key to understanding the

---

[3] *Seeking a Sanctuary* (2007), 244.
[4] Ibid., 246.
[5] Ibid., 246.
[6] Ibid., 248.

Adventist relationship with America.' The American people thought that Sunday sacredness would bring about the perfection of American society but Adventists, rejecting the American dream, chose the alternative route by using another sacred day, the Seventh-day Sabbath, as a means to achieve their dream. It is a stretch for BL to claim so much for the aims of Sunday observance for America and even of Sabbath observance for Adventists.[7]

I must admit that their sociological analysis of the relationship of Seventh-day Adventists to the United States is ingenious and makes for very interesting reading. It is amazing how they are able to fit everything into this pattern. However, I find some troubling aspects of this.

1. Adventists adopted the Seventh-day Sabbath (1847) before they interpreted the lamblike beast in Rev 13 as referring to the United States (1851).

2. The adoption of the Seventh-day Sabbath has to do with the church's desire to follow the Bible and the practices of the early church rather than any antipathy to the United States.

3. I do not sense any intended antipathy in Adventism to the American way of life as such but a more general antipathy to a worldly lifestyle. While the Seventh-day Sabbath is a significant difference, the antipathy to the worldly lifestyle is much more comprehensive. This is more so as the church has gone beyond the American boundary to the whole world. The difference over the day of worship has no specifically anti-American overtones among Adventists throughout the world. It is not an opposition to America with its emphasis on Sunday keeping but rather a rejection of Sunday keeping anywhere.

4. I do not see that Adventists uniquely created an alternative form of civil religion any more than other conservative churches such as the Nazarenes.

5. This interpretation is faulty because it is too much occupied with the relationship of Adventism to the United States rather than to the world.

According to Jonathan Butler, the Millerites had an apolitical orientation, obviously and necessarily because of their very imminent expectation of the end. Where they had previously been connected to temperance and anti-slavery organizations, they dropped these to concentrate on preaching the imminent return of Christ.[8] 'The sense of apocalyptic time left derelict any long-range earthly concerns.' He describes this as 'apolitical apocalyptic.'[9]

While BL see a turning away from the American dream to a new sanctuary, i.e., the alternative society of their own, Butler sees the Adventists, after understanding the USA as the lamblike beast of Rev 13, become more involved in the affairs of state. He describes this period as 'political prophetic.' James White, owner of

---

[7]   Ibid., 246-247.
[8]   Jonathan Butler, 'Adventism and the American Experience' in: Edwin S. Gaustad, ed., *The Rise of Adventism* (New York: Harper & Row Publishers, 1974), 176.
[9]   Ibid., 177.

the Review and Herald Publishing House, suggested that this be transferred to corporate ownership, as well as the numerous church buildings throughout the Adventist community. Since incorporation was obtained through the state and only after the formal organization of a denomination, many Adventists believed such a move would return them to Babylon, for they would become just another church in union with the state. Here White identified such an utter apolitical viewpoint as part of the Millerite mentality and sought to dissociate Sabbath keeping Adventists from it.[10]

Their view of the lamblike beast was not all negative. Rev 13:11 describes the beast as 'coming up,' and this was interpreted as 'a figure of American progress' — 'railroads, steam engines, postal service, population and territorial expansion were the great wonders of verse 13.'[11] But there was a negative side, and for Adventists this was the attempt at Sunday legislation and secondly, the millions of slaves held in bondage. Surprisingly, this latter issue occupied a major portion of their attention during this period. Instead of withdrawing into their own sanctuary and alternative world, they engaged the country by their writings and their acts, even by being involved in underground railroads. 'The Seventh-day Adventists, unlike the Millerites, drew upon political rhetoric to describe the national decline and therefore may be termed *political apocalyptics*.'[12]

From the mid-70s on, after the Civil War and the abolition of slavery, the beast of Revelation had been domesticated.

> They permitted the contours of the beast to soften in the third phase of Adventist development. Pictorial illustrations in Adventist journals and books denote the iconographic metamorphosis. In the 1850s the beast gradually lost teeth, pictorially, until by 1905 it had become an affable American buffalo. Within another generation, the onetime harsh woodcut gargoyle had mollified into the gambolling little lamb of 1940's Adventist evangelistic charts.[13]

Adventism became a 'between the times eschatology.'[14] Adventists became involved politically but only where their own particular interests were involved, especially in the areas of temperance, religious liberty, and Sunday legislation. Their involvement in religious liberty issues is described fittingly by Butler. 'They wished to delay the end in order to preach that the end was soon.'[15] He describes

---

[10] Ibid., 179.
[11] Ibid., 181.
[12] Ibid., 185.
[13] Ibid., 191.
[14] Ibid., 194.
[15] Ibid.

this period as *political prophetic*. This portrayal by Butler does not conform to that of BL who picture Adventists, because of their interpretation of Revelation 13, as obsessed with the Sabbath as opposed to Sunday and interested in establishing and withdrawing into an alternative society to fulfil their version of the American dream. Morgan[16] and Ross also oppose BL here.[17]

Part 3: Chapter 14 Gender

To understand this chapter it is necessary first to look at the thesis which underlies BL's conclusions. Since Adventism was founded by a woman, and because of its high preponderance of women members, it presents a feminine response to the conditions it faces (American society), i.e., the church responds in a feminine way to the 'norms of western culture.'[18] This response is characterized by quietness and malleability, 'avoidance of explicit sexuality and violence, and seeks to disarm its opponent through promoting temperance, health reform, and self-control.'[19] 'Like women, Adventists have tended to play caring, healing, and nurturing roles. And also like women, they have not claimed the right to their own space but have defined themselves through time—not by the monthly cycle of menstruation, but through the weekly observance of the Sabbath.'[20] Their feminine role 'helps to explain the church's stance toward organizations situated at the opposite end of the gender spectrum, such as secret societies and trade unions.'[21]

They go on to state that, in its history, the church first emphasized the equality of men and women but by 1900 the church sought to differentiate the roles of women and men for the first time. This resulted in women losing their positions in the church hierarchy. But in the second half of the twentieth century, the feminist movement arose, calling for equality of women in all areas of life and this affected the church. BL say that, 'the feminine movement produced two major results: equal pay for women, and the belated reincorporation of women into the church hierarchy.'[22] Regarding these they refer to the Merikay Silver case and point to women being hired as ministers and the controversy over their ordination. In their conclusion they write,

> Resistance to the women's movement within Adventism may thus derive, not just from the feeling that women should not usurp male roles, but also from the belief that male roles are, in themselves, less than desirable. The

---

[16] Morgan, ibid., 14-15.
[17] Ibid.
[18] *Seeking a Sanctuary* (2007), 259.
[19] Ibid.
[20] Ibid., 260.
[21] Ibid.
[22] Ibid., 268.

male dominated hierarchy of the church was, after all, originally permitted only as a necessary evil. Adventism itself is a women's movement, for
it takes its inspiration from a woman, is composed chiefly of women, and
espouses 'feminine' values. But though this may appeal to Adventist men
on a certain level, it does make it more difficult for them to find a role in the
denomination. Eschewing traditional forms of male expression such as self-
assertion, violence, intemperance, competitive sports, and sexual license,
Adventist men have therefore concentrated their energies on the few chan-
nels open to them—notably the creation and perpetuation of bureaucratic
and institutional structures. If women were permitted to participate fully
in these areas, men might find there was almost no scope for them to play
stereotypically masculine roles within the Adventist context.[23]

Presumably, BL are dealing with the church from the very beginning. My question
is whether the statistics they give are valid for the early period, i.e., particularly for
the mid-nineteenth century. Where are the statistics for this? Are the statistics they
give for the present or the average for the whole period? This question is important because they base their whole chapter on those statistics.

I challenge also the statement that the church was founded by a woman. What
constitutes 'founding'? There is no question that Ellen White had played an important part in the founding of the church but her husband, James, probably played a
more prominent role though others were involved as well.

Another question in regards to BL's analysis is their description of feminine
qualities and masculine qualities. They place in the former category, quietness,
malleability, temperance, health reform, self-control, caring, healing, and nurturing and in the latter self-assertion, violence, intemperance, competitive sports, and
sexual license. When I look at these descriptions, they fit better the categories of
Christian and non-Christian rather than feminine and masculine qualities.

BL make a weird and inscrutable statement that Adventists like women have
not 'claimed their own space but have defined themselves through time—not
by the monthly cycle of menstruation, but through the weekly observance of the
Sabbath.'[24] What are we to make of this statement?[25] They mean that since Adventists are acting like women they must have a menstrual cycle—only theirs is a
weekly one. It may sound reasonable to some but it just sounds ridiculous to me.
The whole analogy appears to be artificial and manufactured. Is the reason for the
menstrual cycle the same as the weekly one? Why the necessity to find an analogy
here?

---

[23] Ibid., 271.
[24] Ibid., 260.
[25] Butler regarded BL's explanation of Adventists relations to visual arts as 'fanciful.' This
explanation also seems to fit that description.

In regards to the equality of men and women in the church in the nineteenth century, the evidence presented is not sufficient to prove their point. It is true that the role of a prophet was not limited to men but was in fact recognized in a woman: Ellen White. But this did not mean that the role of women changed as they themselves indicate.[26] If BL's thesis is true it should have led to a higher role for women in the church but it did not. The fact that a church 'founded by a woman and a woman as prophet should treat women by not paying them equally and ordaining them openly' is a puzzle. If BL's thesis is true that Adventists favoured the feminine, then these things should not have happened. In other words, Adventists were not acting the feminine role. Otherwise, why did not the church eagerly accept women's ordination? It seems to me that regarding the role of women in the church, the controlling factor was the role of women in society in general. Adventists simply conformed to its culture on this point. This was true with almost all conservative churches regardless of the sexuality of their membership.

The next sentence raises a lot of questions. Why is it wrong for Adventist men to eschew 'traditional forms of male expression such as self-assertion, violence, intemperance, competitive sports, and sexual license'? It seems to me that all Christians, including men in 'masculine' churches, would want to eschew these things as well. And it seems somewhat simplistic to state that 'the creation and perpetuation of bureaucratic and institutional structures' was basically the only option left for men to express their maleness. They go on to state that if women were permitted to participate in these bureaucratic and institutional structures, there would be virtually nothing left for men to do within the church that was masculine. Because of this, they insinuate that Adventist men, as long as they are part of the church, will never allow women within the hierarchy.

BL state that Adventists respond like women in a patriarchal society who are marginalized and powerless. 'What is particularly interesting about Adventism is that it represents a feminine response to these conditions. At no stage have they attempted to confront the state.'[27] Butler, Ross, and Morgan contradict this depiction as we have indicated earlier.[28] In the following paragraphs, BL give examples of masculine responses such as Snook and Brinkerhoff who left the church because of a female prophet, Koresh, and the Mormons.

Koresh's masculine response was to bring in guns and claim 'first rights to the center's women.' The Mormons also reacted in a 'masculine' way which was 'loud, often violent, and controversially polygamous.'[29] If what BL state is true, that the

---

[26] Ibid., 261.
[27] Ibid., 259.
[28] Butler, 178-201, Morgan, 16-17.
[29] *Seeking a Sanctuary* (2007), 260.

Mormon type behaviour they described and Koresh's behaviour are vintage masculine responses, then Adventists can be justly proud to have behaved the way
they did. BL call it a 'feminine' reaction. I would call it a Christian reaction. To act
in the 'masculine' way as Koresh did and the Mormons as described by them is no
virtue, however one describes it.

Part 3: Chapter 17 Medicine
My view of Seventh-day Adventism is one of a dynamic organism, not a static
group like the Amish. This has been the history of the church from the very beginning from their Millerite connection until the present. They have evolved from
the date-setting of Millerism to not-date-setting, from the 'shut door' to the 'open
door,' from a Sunday keeping to a Sabbath keeping church, from a 6 to 6 to a sunset to sunset Sabbath keeping, from a concept of 'general benevolence' to a tithe-
paying group, from Arian to trinitarian, from legalistic to the salvation by faith
emphasis (1888), etc. Ellen White has also developed with time.[30]

BL have seen this development as well, as indicated in their book. They point
out the changes that took place in the church's educational and medical work.
Adventists do change when the circumstances change. But in certain analyses they
still seem to assume that Adventists should be static. They seem to waver in their
view regarding the church as static and dynamic. This is true of their view on the
development of the medical and educational work in the Adventist Church.

I take issue, therefore, with their analysis of the medicalization of the Adventist
Church. They refer first to Kellogg's influence on the medical work. BL speak of
Kellogg 'redefining the nature of Adventism' and challenging 'the way Adventism related to American society' and that he presented a 'form of Adventism that
threatened to upset the balance of the church's relationship with the republic.'[31]

When we look at how Kellogg viewed health according to BL, it does not appear at all that Kellogg's major stamp remains today. His obsession regarding the
importance of health above everything else has not been inherited by Adventist
doctors today. Schwarz states, 'Adventist history is replete with individuals who
fasten onto a particular aspect of doctrine and seek to make all else subservient to
it. Ellen White found it frequently necessary to warn Kellogg against thinking that
the health teachings and medical work were all-important and censoring those
who did not agree with him.' He illustrates this by a letter Kellogg wrote to her
stating that it seemed ...

... very clear that those who meet the Lord when he comes will be above the

---

[30] See Alden Thompson, 'Ellen White's Pilgrimage to Golgotha,' *Adventist Review* (December
24, 1981), 7-9 and 'The Theology of Ellen White: The Great Controversy Story,' *Adventist
Review* (December 31, 1981), 12-13.
[31] *Seeking a Sanctuary* (2007), 302.

power of disease as well as above the power of sin and that they will reach this condition by obedience to the truth [health reform] ... It seems to me very clear ... that the sealing of God is a physical and moral change which takes place in the man as the result of truth and which shows in his very countenance that it is the seal of God, and that the mark of the beast is the mark of the work of the beast in the heart and it changes the body as well as the character and also shows in the countenance. It seems to me our people have been wrong in regarding Sunday observance as the sole mark of the beast. The mark of the beast is simply the change of character and body which comes from the surrender of the will to Satan.[32]

BL's paraphrase of the above Kellogg statement shows how they fully understand its meaning and implications. They state that the seal of God and the mark of the beast 'had less to do with adherence to different days of the week than with obedience to the law of life.'[33]

Kellogg's letter above is crucial in understanding him and how for him everything revolved around the ultra-importance of health. He made it the sun around which the rest of the planets revolved and not just an important planet revolving around the sun. It shows also why there was conflict with Ellen White and the church authorities. It was not the medical work as such but Kellogg's view of the medical work. It was this extreme, lopsided medical centric view that caused the conflicts.

BL concur with this assessment. According to BL, 'Kellogg's Adventism revolved around an almost fanatical devotion to health reform.' He promoted '"biologic living"—a system of human perfection that could be reached through obedience to natural law and the strict control of diet.'[34] They claim that Kellogg was one of a few Adventists who took White's view on health seriously. But, in actual fact, he distorted it by subordinating everything else to it. He did not fully grasp the holistic view of the importance of the whole person, the spiritual, mental, and physical aspect of human beings. This view of Kellogg is crucial to his handling of the medical work and how he ran it.

Surely Kellogg is not representative of Adventist doctors today. Kellogg's extreme fanatical view of the importance of health is not Adventist. Adventists have always had a somewhat unique holistic view, maintaining the importance of the spirit, the mind, and the body. Obviously the body is important, but so is the spirit and the mind. This understanding comes from Ellen White who views redemption as including the whole person as sin affected the whole person. She states,

---

[32] Richard Schwarz, 'The Kellogg Schism: the Hidden Issues,' *Spectrum* (Autumn 1972), 24.
[33] *Seeking a Sanctuary* (2007), 303.
[34] Ibid., 302.

Through sin the divine likeness was marred, and well-nigh obliterated. Man's physical powers were weakened, his mental capacity was lessened, his spiritual vision dimmed. To restore in man the image of his Maker, to bring him back to the perfection in which he was created, to promote the development of body, mind, and soul, that the divine purpose in his creation might be realized—this was to be the work of redemption. This is the object of education, the great object of life.[35]

Since the mind and the soul find expression through the body, both mental and spiritual vigor are in great degree dependent upon physical strength and activity; whatever promotes physical health, promotes the development of a strong mind and a well-balanced character. [36]

This holistic view has been one of the great benefits of being an Adventist.[37] It has been for me personally. It is because of the educational emphasis of Adventism that I went on to college, the only one in a family of nine children. My wife is the only one that completed college in her family of ten. It is also because of its emphasis on healthful living that I have lived a healthy life. The benefits of an Adventist health style have been well documented by Gary Fraser and others. Of course, the primacy of a relationship with God puts all life in proper perspective. Very few if any other church has this kind of complete holistic emphasis. Everyone is familiar with the Adventist emphasis on health which BL have written much about. The educational emphasis is also unusual. BL say that 'in 1926, Adventist colleges were producing more than twice the number of college graduates that might be expected for a group of its size.'[38]

Instead of having this holistic view, Kellogg went to a one-sided, lopsided and radically extreme view in giving the body priority over the spirit. This kind of emphasis surely is completely different from Adventism's and its doctors' balanced holistic view of life today.

BL state that after Kellogg's expulsion, 'the clerical leadership did maintain control of the church, but it was unable to eradicate the form of Adventism Kellogg advocated. Adventist doctors continued to enjoy a special status within the

---

[35] Ellen G. White, *Education* (Mountain View, CA: Pacific Press Publishing Association, 1903), 15-16.

[36] Ibid., 195.

[37] See *Spirituality, Health, and Wholeness*, eds. Siroj Sorajjakool and Henry H. Lamberton (New York, London, UK, Oxford, UK: Haworth Press, 2004), where this concept is applied to health care and, especially, Richard Rice's chapter, 'Toward a Theology of Wholeness: A Tentative Model of Whole Person Care,' which introduces the book.

[38] *Seeking a Sanctuary* (2007), 353.

church, continued to practice an "undenominational" Adventism, and maintained the tradition of medical innovation.'[39]

Kellogg obviously did not leave his mark in making the medical work not only the right arm but the whole body, but BL see his heritage in the three things they mention above. The special status that doctors have today is regarding difference in pay. Obviously we know they have a different pay scale but that is true also for administrators who are working with the medical work regardless of whether they are doctors.

BL claim, to visit Adventist hospitals today is to see an Adventism that is 'of an undenominational, unsectarian, humanitarian and philanthropic nature.' Chief executives emphasize that they seek to preserve a 'Christian' rather than a specifically 'Adventist' atmosphere.[40] The quoted phrase comes from the new charter's declaration of principles included when the original charter of the sanitarium expired in 1897. Over the objections of some church leaders to this phrase,

> Kellogg assured them that this wording was necessary in order for the sanitarium to 'have the advantages of the statutes of the State; as a hospital, it must be carried on as an undenominational institution. It cannot give benefits to a certain class, but must be for the benefit of any who are sick. The institution may support any work it chooses with the earnings of the Association, but cannot discriminate against any one because of his beliefs.'[41]

Whether this was true or only a subterfuge is difficult to ascertain, although understanding Kellogg's inclination, it probably was the latter. Whatever the situation at Kellogg's time, we know that today we clearly describe our institutions as Seventh-day Adventist, that is, our hospitals are not 'undenominational.' This has never been a problem. It is always clearly indicated as such. If 'unsectarian' is a synonym for 'undenominational,' then what we have said above holds true here.

BL state regarding our hospitals that 'looser attitudes toward the Sabbath generally prevail. Employees are also paid at vastly higher rates than other church workers.'[42] Regarding the latter statement, Wayne Judd, Assistant Vice-President for Mission and Strategic Planning, Adventist Health, states that this is not correct. 'Executives are paid significantly higher rates; employees in general are not.'[43] In regards to the first statement Judd vociferously disagrees and he points to the Naples Statement and Guidelines where this document mentions that the Sabbath is one of the distinguishing marks of Adventism, but so is its understanding

---

[39] *Seeking a Sanctuary* (2007), 306.
[40] Ibid., 309.
[41] R. W. Schwarz, 'The Kellogg Schism: the Hidden Issues,' *Spectrum* (Autumn 1972), 27-28.
[42] Ibid.
[43] Wayne Judd, email letter to the author, March 3, 2009.

of caring for the sick. In the Guidelines the first point is that whatever is best for the patient must be done on the Sabbath. They go on to establishing transitions for the beginning and end of the Sabbath, deferral of any medical work that can reasonably be deferred including surgery, the need for professionals to rest, and encouraging Adventist employees to take their fair share of Sabbath shifts.[44]

It is interesting in this regard to give Alonzo Baker's side of the Kellogg story. He said he 'was closely associated with John Harvey Kellogg from September 1939 to June 1942, serving in the dual capacity of field secretary for his eugenics and genetics organization, the Race Betterment Foundation, and associate editor of his monthly journal, *Good Health*.'[45] He maintains that Kellogg kept the Sabbath right up to the last Sabbath of his life [Kellogg died December 14, 1943] and that his two institutions, one in Michigan and one in Florida, always observed the Seventh-day Sabbath.[46]

BL give an additional reason to show that Adventist hospitals are 'unsectarian,' i.e. 'by the fact that at least two-thirds of the medical and nursing staff are usually non-Adventist.'[47] Perhaps it would be better to have a higher percentage of Adventist employees. Judd says in regard to non-Adventist employees, 'I doubt that any of our SDA administrators and caregivers, including my corporate colleagues, would want to work with all Adventists. As the ecumenical spirit that gave birth to Adventism in the Millerite years, so today the fact that our employees so closely resemble the communities out of which they come, is a positive component in our culture.'[48] Obviously, it would be better to have a majority of Adventist doctors, nurses, and workers but the real question is whether it would be better to have an Adventist-oriented and directed hospital even if its employees are not all Adventists or none at all.

Besides Kellogg's one-sided view of the health work, his arrogance and intransigence were also significant factors in the problems between Kellogg and the church. A picture of the character of Kellogg painted by Schwarz shows us how we should evaluate what he espoused and what the Adventist medical work is about today. It is true that Kellogg was not as concerned about 'promulgating the perpetuity of the moral law or even the imminence of the second advent.'[49] As a person he was stubborn and domineering, jealous of potential rivals, and wanted

[44] 'The Mission of Adventist Healthcare: Defining and Fulfilling the Mission of Seventh-day Adventist Healthcare Institutions in North America in the Twenty-First Century,' Naples [FL] Healthcare Conference, 1991-1996, Ron M. Wisbey, Chairman; Lincoln, NE, AdventSource..
[45] Alonzo L. Baker, 'My Years with John Harvey Kellogg,' *Spectrum* (Autumn 1972), 40.
[46] Ibid., 44.
[47] *Seeking a Sanctuary* (2007), 310.
[48] Judd, email letter to the author, March 3, 2009
[49] R. W. Schwarz, *Light Bearers to the Remnant* (Boise, ID: Pacific Press Publishing Association, 1981), 282.

to be a 'one man show.' Although publicly Kellogg stated that he had no intent to make the Sanitarium independent of the church, privately he did plan to make it independent of the denomination. He personally drew up the sanitarium association's charter so that he would not be at the mercy of the General Conference, 'but would be able to stand alone if I should have to.'[50] Later his promoting of pantheistic ideas, constant financial squabbles, his determined desire for personal control and dominance of the medical work, and his intransigent attitude led to a final and unfortunate break with the dropping of his membership.

Kellogg's anti-denominationalism, non-sectarian spirit, toning down and deliberate neglect of the moral law or the second coming are not found today. The desire to be completely free of denominational oversight is not found. Kellogg's pantheism is not found. We do not find Kellogg's oversized ego that wanted total control of everything or obsession with complete independence from church control. The kind of ongoing deeply entrenched opposition between the medical personnel and the church depicted by BL goes far beyond reality. In fact just about the time Kellogg was disfellowshipped, what is now Loma Linda Medical School was founded. And soon after under Percy Magan's leadership it became accredited. BL look negatively at accreditation from the Adventist viewpoint and it is true that there are some Adventists who would look at it this way but not the majority. The same is true with our colleges and university accreditation. Here again Adventism is a dynamic, not a calcified, organization. Just because it viewed something negatively in the past does not mean it will do so forever. What it does now has to be determined on the basis of the present situation. Times change, situations change, and so we must change.

Of course, there may be some medical personnel who fit the description given by BL but I daresay that the majority do not. The religion professors at Loma Linda University I am sure do not feel opposition from the medical faculty and staff. In fact, I sense that they feel highly respected. Graham Maxwell and Jack Provonsha were highly respected. Although the latter was a physician, it was his theological contribution that was highly appreciated. The graduates of the medical school that we have had in the church at Chico generally have been faithful and strong supporters of the church. My son is a physician in Bakersfield and he has been very active in the church there, presently serving as an elder and Sabbath School teacher. I do not sense any anticlerical or antichurch attitude in him.

Of course, at times concern has been expressed concerning the medical work, but I sense at present that there is a rather amicable relationship existing between the church and its medical institutions. Church leaders continue to chair the medical boards of these various medical institutions.

---

[50] Ibid., 285.

Conclusion: The revolving door

In their conclusion, BL deal with the question of whether Adventists are moving toward a denomination or a sect. I would assume from their Prologue[51] that this book is focused not on Seventh-day Adventists as a world-wide organization but on Seventh-day Adventists in America. However, it seems to me that they do not always direct their comments to Seventh-day Adventists in America. For example, their chapter 'Conclusion,' deals on point 4 with global Adventism.[52]

After listing the six points that Niebuhr/Bainbridge (positive and negative) list as factors in determining whether a sect is moving toward a denomination, BL conclude that Bainbridge's tension-maintaining factors 'are always either stronger than, or a counterbalance to, the first'[53] regarding Adventists. The first two points in the Niebuhr/Bainbridge list are:

1. Arrival of a second generation versus continuing preponderance of converts.

2. Upward socioeconomic mobility versus failure to achieve upward mobility.

BL favour the second parts of the tension, i.e., 'continuing preponderance of converts' and 'failure to achieve upward mobility' as better fitting the Adventist experience and thus conclude that Adventists are not moving from sect to denomination. They state:

1. After more than 150 years, Adventism is still predominantly a religion of converts, thanks both to the church's continued success in attracting new recruits and to its rather low birth-rate and its inability to retain more than about 60 percent of those born into the church.

2. Although many individual Adventists do achieve impressive levels of socio-economic advancement, it does not have impact on the membership as a whole because new poor converts are constantly entering the church and wealthier life-long members are leaving.[54]

Statement one sounds too good to be true. Assuming that the remarks are directed toward the North American Division, Adventist administrators would consider it glad tidings were it true that the church is having continuing success 'in attracting new recruits.' Instead one hears only about the sad state of affairs in the North American Division when it comes to evangelism. There are also several questions one has to raise here. What are the implications of the statement that 'Adventism is still predominantly a religion of converts'? It is assumed that an established convert is no different from a new convert when it comes to upward socio-economic movement. A convert may have been a member for 67 years as I

---

[51] *Seeking a Sanctuary* (2007), xiv.
[52] Ibid., 361.
[53] Ibid., 360.
[54] Ibid.

have been. Does that not affect the conclusion? They give the figure of percentage of the membership from a non-Adventist background. However, how many of these are long-time members of the church? And how does that fact affect socio-economic development?

In the year 2007, in the North American Division, there were 37,359 additions to the church or a little over 3 ½ percent. We don't know how many of these were rebaptisms, professions of faith, and from Adventist families. Suppose we say one third of the total is included in this group. That means that a little over two percent would be converts from a non-Adventist background. The Pennsylvania study cited (which is too limited a sample) indicates that 78 percent of converts remain in the church after two years but only about half with normal attendance at this point. What would be the retention after five years? The fifty percent with normal attendance at this point would indicate that perhaps only fifty percent would remain after five years. In a church of one hundred, if two converts from a non-Adventist background are added a year and if they all remain faithful for five years, they would be ten percent of the congregation in five years. If half of them leave, then only five percent would remain or five. Those who remain after five years should no longer be considered 'new' converts since they are probably already beginning their socio-economic development. While hard statistics are rather limited, it seems that the statement 'Adventism is still predominantly a religion of converts' has to be qualified and if that is the case both of their conclusions have to be modified.

Moore in his review stated: 'The model, offered by Bull and Lockhart, suggesting the inevitability of lost membership, is a long way from proved. The "revolving door" thesis is argued more as a matter of inference from questionable survey material than as a matter of solid evidence.'[55] Dudley questions BL's statement that a sect moving toward a denomination no longer attracts members from lower social orders, pointing to the Baptists and Pentecostals as denominations that continue to do so. He thinks also that no evidence is produced by BL to show that as Adventists become more prosperous, they tend to leave the church and states that he has not seen statistics that indicate this.[56]

The other four points in the Niebuhr/Bainbridge list are:
    3. Assimilation of ethnic group versus non-assimilation.
    4. Membership growth versus failure to grow.
    5. Bureaucratization and institutionalization versus revivalism.
    6. Regression to the mean versus anchoring traditions.[57]

---

[55] Moore, 47.
[56] Dudley, 127.
[57] *Seeking a Sanctuary* (2007), 360.

They obviously choose the second half of the equation for Adventists to show that they are not moving to a denominational situation. But in regard to point 3 they have no solid evidence but simply an assertion that non-assimilation is happening in ethnic churches. On point 4 surprisingly they select the second half 'failure to grow,' when earlier they indicated that Adventism is 'predominantly a religion of converts,' because of the 'church's continued success in attracting new recruits.' Here they needlessly refer to the global growth of Adventism but discount it as 'extensive rather than intensive so it continues to remain a tiny minority in most places in the world, including the United States.' On point 5 they admit that bureaucratization and institutionalism have been notable features of Adventism but this has not led to lower tension with the outside world but to 'internalize upward social mobility and create low-tension ghettoes.' To the church as a whole, 'the Adventist leadership addresses repeated calls for revival and evangelism.' Whether this meets the criterion of revivalism versus bureaucratization and institutionalization is questionable at the least. On point 6 they point to Ellen White whose teaching anchors the church to high-tension positions.[58] Yet throughout the book BL have argued consistently that in their view the church has moved away from her positions regarding the medical and educational work and how the self-supporting institutions have been anchored to her teachings.

Their conclusion: 'Taking all these things together, there is thus little evidence to suggest that Adventism is reducing rather than maintaining tension with its environment and thus no basis for assuming that it is a sect in the course of transformation into a denomination.'[59] The evidence and support for this conclusion is wanting. BL by this statement assert that once a sect has become a denomination, tension with its environment disappears. Every viable Christian church ought to have some significant tension points with worldly society. If it means the removal of all of these to be what we want to be, we are in deep trouble. The early Christian Church was not a Seventh-day Adventist Church, yet it had 'significant tension points with worldly society.' It seems to me that the principles and teachings of Christ are so different from worldly society that if it does not have 'significant tension points' it would not really be a Christian Church, not to mention an Adventist Church. It is a bit simplistic to define a sect or a denomination simply with this yardstick. If this is the yardstick Adventists should not be concerned about this problem. Rather it should concern itself with whether it is remaining true to its mission to fulfil Christ's mission of extending his kingdom with its teachings and principles until his second advent. I am not contending that the church is moving from sect to denomination. What I am contending is that BL have not proved by their case that the church is not moving toward a denomination.

---

[58] Ibid., 361.
[59] Ibid.

The above critique, while limited to a few chapters, indicates some of the weaknesses of the broad generalizations that are made and some of the theses on which BL's arguments and conclusions are built. My original draft included a critique of the Introduction and Chapter 1 on Authority, but I excised them because of lack of space. It is hoped that others will deal with the remaining chapters of the book, either sustaining their positions or modifying them.

Sakae Kubo. Born in USA. Retired 1989. Last position: President of Academic Affairs and Dean of Atlantic Union College. Pastoral, teaching and administrative experiences. Taught at Andrews University (1955-1960), Theological Seminary (1960-1978). Dean Walla Walla College (1978-1980), principal Newbold College, (1980-1984). Author of books and articles. PhD, University of Chicago (1966).

The Waldensian Heritage: *Lux Lucet in Tenebris*

Richard W. Müller

Introduction

My first fascination with the Waldenses started in my teenage years when I read *The Great Controversy* by Ellen G. White for the first time. Many years later, when lecturing at Newbold College, this fascination increased during a summer pilgrimage with my family to the Alpine valleys of the Waldenses. The immediate impulse for choosing this topic comes from reading what I believe is the most comprehensive history ever written about the Waldenses by a Waldensian himself. A few years ago I inherited this volume from Thomas Christensen, in his younger years a pastor of the Adventist Church in Denmark. The author is Jean Léger (1615 – c.1670), pastor and moderator (superintendent) of the Waldensian Church. The book is entitled: *A Common History of the Waldenses or of the Evangelical Churches in the Valleys of Piemont*.[1]

Léger tells us how he collected and secured a number of original sources of the Waldenses and official documents relating to their history.[2] Through his foresight these precious sources escaped the flames of the Inquisition of the Roman Church and the destruction of the pillaging soldiers who stood at her service.[3] Most of these documents were personally handed over by Léger to Samuel Morland, an ambassador under Oliver Cromwell, the Lord-Protector of England, in order to be preserved at the Cambridge University Library. Other sources have been brought to the Library of Geneva for safe keeping.[4]

In this chapter we will present Léger's view of the Waldenses. This differs greatly from modern presentations of the Waldenses,[5] even those written by Waldenses themselves of more recent date.[6] The heritage of the Waldenses has to be preserved, in particular their great concern for: (a) the apostolic faith (unaltered doctrines); (b) the freedom to believe according to one's conscience (religious lib-

---

[1] First published in French: Jean Léger, *Histoire Generale des Eglises Evangeliques des Vallées de Piemont ...*, Leiden 1669. For this chapter the German translation was used: Johan Léger, *Algemeine Geschichte der Waldenser oder der evangelischen Kirchen in den Thälern von Piemont*. Translated from French by Hans Friedrich Freyherr von Schweinitz (Breslau, Johann Jacob Korn, 1750).

[2] Special thanks to Knud Larsen Capion, lecturer at the Danish Junior College (Vejlefjordskolen), for helping with the translation of some ancient texts and the analysis of some key words.

[3] See list of Waldensian manuscripts at the Cambridge University Library, Léger, 54-59.

[4] Léger, 60.

[5] See various modern works on church history.

[6] See e.g. Giorgio Tourn, *The Waldenses – The first 800 Years, 1174-1974* (Turin, Italy: Claudiana, 1980); *Prescot Stephens, The Waldensian Story* (Lewes, UK: The Book Guild Ltd, 1998).

erty); (c) the moral living of Christ's followers (the Ten Commandments); (d) the simple lifestyle of the believers; and (e) the willingness to die for one's faith.

On the basis, primarily, of Léger's extensive *History of the Waldenses,* we will concentrate in this chapter on some of these issues. What have Adventists, standing squarely on Protestant ground, done with this heritage? With the help of one of the prominent writers in the early history of the Seventh-day Adventist Church, Ellen G. White, we will illustrate how part of this heritage is treasured by the Adventist Church. This chapter will conclude by looking at one specific aspect: the Waldenses, like the Seventh-day Adventists, honoured the Ten Commandments to the extent that some also celebrated the Sabbath.

I Léger's portrait of the Waldenses

Their origin

Léger begins his history of the Waldenses by describing very briefly the person of Petrus Waldus (c. 1140-c. 1218; his name is also found in a variety of other spellings), who is regarded by many historians as the founder of the Waldensian Church. This section concludes with Waldus and the Poor Men of Lyon's travels to Picardy, the Netherlands, Germany, England, Poland, Moravia and Bohemia, where Waldus is said to have died. [7]

Over twenty pages are devoted to supporting Léger's conviction that there were Waldenses, even by that name, long before the second half of the twelfth century, the time of Petrus Waldus.[8] Many church historians and other witnesses are quoted to prove his case. It was not possible for me, within the confines of this chapter, to check Léger's sources. Some sources push the Waldenses back to the ninth and eighth centuries. One source even states that there was an early Waldo, who may have given his name to the movement.[9] Others go back even further, to the time of Pope Sylvester (314-335), as the time of their origin. They point to the time of Constantine the Great (306-337), the time of compromise when the alleged corruption of the church started.[10] Theodore Beza (1519-1605), the successor of John Calvin, is referred to as saying that the Waldenses, especially those who lived in the valleys of the Alps, 'are the true remnant of the first and true Christians ...'[11] Beza suggests that the name 'Waldenses' simply comes from 'des Vallées,' the valleys from where most of these believers came.[12]

---

[7] Léger, 26-31. 48.
[8] Léger, 32-53,
[9] Léger, 32-37.
[10] Léger, 34.
[11] Léger, 37.
[12] Léger, 41.

Léger also tries to prove that the Waldenses existed before Petrus Waldus by pointing to the writings they used. The most precious piece of literature, besides the Bible, *Lá Noble Leçon* (The Noble Lesson), comes from the year 1100. One copy of this important work is in Cambridge University Library, the other in Geneva.[13] Other publications are presented in Léger's work, sometimes both in the original language and with translation, and at other times only in translation, which Léger dates quite early.[14]

Léger turns also to the adversaries of the Waldenses and uses the statements of Catholic scholars and church authorities to demonstrate the age of the Waldenses.[15] We find expressions such as 'from antiquity,' or 'from ancient times,' or 'many centuries ago,' or 'from time immemorial.'[16] Léger further emphasizes the apostolic origin of the teachings of the Waldenses. They are, he maintains, the true followers of the apostles, while the Church of Rome fell from the truth.[17] Léger turns also to his friends, i.e. other Protestants, who are of the opinion that the Waldenses are not of recent date but reach far back in time. As reference he especially uses Olivetan (c. 1506-1538), best known for his translation of the *Olivetan Bible* into French, but also Beza (1519-1605), Calvin's successor, and Comenius (1592-1670), educator and bishop of the Moravian Brethren.[18]

Their doctrine

It is difficult to summarise the teachings of the Waldenses in this short chapter. It is even more difficult to show in detail where they differed from the Church of Rome. I will concentrate on those teachings which they denied and which put them under the ban of the dominant church and were the reasons for their severe persecution.

But first we want to introduce this section by pointing to Léger's work to see how he wants to provide evidence for the 'orthodoxy' of their faith. Many have accused the Waldenses and other dissenting groups of being Arians, Manichaeans or Cathari. This is strongly denied by Léger. He points out that the Waldenses stand on genuine apostolic ground, as expressed in the first four ecumenical councils.[19] From their many confessions of faith, including the Apostolic Confession,[20] and

---

[13] Léger, 66. According to Stephens this is a summary of Waldensian beliefs in the fourteenth/fifteenth century.
[14] Léger, 178, 212, 223, 146.
[15] See e.g. the entire chapter 26 of book I, 428-441.
[16] See chapter 18 of book I, 301-325.
[17] See chapter 20 of book I, 340-357: Proof concerning the apostolic succession and kinship.
[18] See chapter 20 of book I, 442-444): Concerning the age of the Waldenses from companions of faith.
[19] Léger, 326 ff.
[20] Léger, 125 ff; 234 ff.

in their Catechisms[21] Léger wants to show that they are in agreement with the reformed theology of the reformers of the sixteenth century.[22]

When one of the fierce opponents of the Waldenses, Claudius Seissel, the archbishop of Turin (around 1200), described the doctrinal convictions of the Waldenses, he gave a detailed list of many Catholic teachings which the Waldenses vehemently rejected. He stated: 'They say, that the Roman Popes and other teachers have falsified the sacred Scripture through their explanations and additions,' while they themselves claim 'to be alone the true evangelical and apostolic church, which holds the truth in purity.'[23]

The main charges which the medieval church raised against the Waldenses and which give us an insight in their beliefs, may be listed as follows:

- They rejected all churchly powers.
- They claimed that the Roman Church is the true 'Babylonian Harlot.'
- The miracles of the Roman Church are not true miracles.
- They rejected the feast days.
- They did not keep the fast days and the vigils.
- They rejected the sacrament of confirmation.
- They rejected transubstantiation.
- They did not pray for the dead or bring offerings for the dead.
- The saints do not hear our prayers and they do not intercede for us.
- They proclaim the word of God in the vernacular.
- It is enough to confess your sins before God. You do not need to confess them before the priest.
- The work of Christ is enough for your salvation. You do not need to plague yourself with your own works.
- One should not make any vows.
- No man should forbid the state of marriage.
- Pictures should be rejected. The devotion with which one honours 'holy' pictures is adultery.
- The Pope of Rome is nothing more than another bishop.
- The orders of monks and nuns are from the devil.
- Everyone should be allowed to preach.
- One should baptise in ordinary water.
- Work is allowed on all days, except Sundays. Therefore one does not need to keep special days for saints.
- The marriage of priests is not only allowed, but necessary.[24]

---

[21] Léger, 146 ff.
[22] Léger, 36 et al.
[23] Léger, 309-311.
[24] Léger, 312-320.

On the basis of these differences in doctrine, which the Roman Church acknowledged existed between their church and the Waldenses, the Waldenses came to the conclusion that the Roman Church is Antichrist. The Waldensian view of Antichrist, as Léger presented it, is not that of a single person. It is a religious institution, which developed through the centuries, especially from the time of Constantine the Great and the Roman bishop (pope) Sylvester.[25]

Their daily life
The lifestyle of the Waldenses can only be described in a general way, since we have adopted Léger's view of the 'Waldenses' in this chapter. Thus, we are not talking about one little homogeneous church group living in the western valleys of the Italian Alps with Torre Pelice as its modern centre. We are talking about a reformation movement which consisted of individual believers, and small groups of believers, spread throughout the Alpine valleys, southern France, Spain, Picardy, the Netherlands, Germany, Switzerland, Bohemia, Moravia, Austria, yes, even as far northeast as Poland. There was no hierarchical structure which held these followers of Christ together. What held them together was their God-given conviction to 'fight' for the truth, whatever the cost—even if it meant death.

When Léger describes the life of the Waldenses, he focuses on the valleys of the Alps, which he knew best and from where we have most written information.[26] For the true follower of Christ, there must be harmony between what one teaches and how one lives. James' letter, as a favoured book, is quoted: 'Faith without works is dead.'[27] In spite of this genuine understanding of the moral life of the follower of Christ, the Waldenses were often described by leaders of the Roman Church as 'monsters' and a 'pest' for society and the church.[28] The most disgusting vices were attributed to them, especially in connection with their clandestine meetings.[29] Fortunately, there also were honest witnesses among those who did not belong to the Waldenses, who gave a positive report about the moral life of these people. Léger quotes from some other sources that were directed against the Waldensian teaching, but had to acknowledge: 'In their conduct they are decent and modest. In their clothing pride is not seen.'[30]

---

[25] See chapter 23, book I, 380-393: Concerning the revelation of Anti-Christ in the eleventh century. Chapter 24, book I, 393-415: The state of the church during the time of the eleventh century, when Anti-Christ revealed himself. See also chapter 14 of book I, 178-211, where Léger quotes from a Waldensian source, both in the vernacular tongue of the Waldenses and in translation, their understanding of Anti-Christ and the reason why they had to leave the Roman Church. This writing is dated by Léger around 1120.

[26] Chapter 30 of book I, 492-520: About the lifestyle and customs of the Waldenses. Chap. 31 of book I, 521-543: About church discipline and church order.

[27] Léger, 493.

[28] Léger, 494.

[29] Léger, 496.

[30] Léger, 500.

Léger speaks of his people as a hard working, diligent group. Since the farms were too small to survive on, the husbands often tried to find work in other regions. The women would take care of the household and the small farms.[31] Their hard labour could easily be demonstrated by pointing to the terraces carved out of the mountains, with small patches of fertile soil. They lived primarily on grains and fruits, grapes and chestnuts and their limited livestock.[32]

Very early we read of the Waldenses' interest in educating their children. During the long winter months they taught their children in the basic subjects. Bible reading in their local tongue was mandatory, according to their famous early writing 'The Noble Lesson.'[33]

When the Roman Church accused the Waldenses of amoral behaviour, these were lies from an evil tongue. Their 'Book on Church Discipline and Order' gives ample proof that the pastors and local elders watched over their flock. They encouraged the people not to worship images, but to carry the image of God in their hearts and to follow Christ's example.[34] They did not allow any mixed marriages between Waldenses and people from the Roman Church or other religions.[35] Marriage was understood as a lifelong covenant which cannot be dissolved except by death.[36] The Holy Scripture were understood to include moral teaching.[37] Numerous places could be cited from the chapter on discipline, but also from the rest of Léger's book, to show how the Waldenses emphasized the importance of the Ten Commandments.[38]

Their persecution

The entire book II of Léger's Waldensian history is devoted to the horrors of religious persecution, which they encountered from fellow Christians who claimed to be the true church with roots going back to the apostle Peter.[39] The copperplate engravings that are included in Léger's work, which depict actual scenes of torture and massacre, imprint on our brains an indelible memory of the sufferings of people who simply wanted to follow God's revelation engraved in Holy Writ.

The records of a very early church council in northern Italy, the Council of Verona (1184), mention the Poor of Lyon, the city of Petrus Waldus' birth. Accord-

---

[31] Léger, 422f.
[32] Léger, 424f.
[33] Léger, 175, 431.
[34] Léger, 134f.
[35] Léger, 505.
[36] Léger, 511.
[37] Léger, 521.
[38] For a few examples, see Léger 70, 74f., 90, 128ff, 149, 151, 158, 200, 202, 369.
[39] In the German edition of 1750 both books are combined in one cover. Here we refer to pages 585-1577. The entire volume concludes with a chapter on the 'Wrath of God over the enemies and persecutors of the Evangelical-Waldensian Churches (1577-1634),' an autobiographical appendix, (1635-1720) and an index.

ing to Prescot Stephens this is the first official church document that refers to the Waldenses in connection with other so-called heretics: 'We therefore decree that the Cathars and Patarines, and those who call themselves by the false names of the Humble or the Poor of Lyons, the Passagians, the Josephini and the Aranaldists, should be struck with a perpetual anathema.'[40]

Landon, in his introduction to the Council of Verona, makes the following observations with regard to the beginnings of the Inquisition: 'In this council, we perceive the commencement of the system of Inquisition, since the bishops are ordered, by means of commissaries, to inform themselves of persons suspected of heresy, whether by common report or private information ... After all the spiritual penalties of the Church have been employed in vain, it is ordered that the offenders be given up to the secular arm, in order that temporal punishments may be inflicted.'[41]

The readers should not be left in any doubt as to who is punishing whom. The civil authorities carried out the physical punishment, but under pressure from the church. Actually, the civil authorities did not have much choice, for they were threatened with excommunication or, what was worse, with the interdict that put a whole village, town or city under the papal ban. This meant that no ecclesiastical services would be available. No sacraments would be offered, no burials in holy ground, nor baptisms. If people died in the state of excommunication, or while under the interdict, this meant eternal suffering in hell. In this state of fear the civil leaders felt they could do little other but comply with the wishes of church authorities.

Pope Innocent III (1198-1216), a few years later, was also confronted with various groups, including the Waldenses, who stood in opposition to the papal church. These groups were, in particular, strongly represented in south-western France, (i.e. Languedoc, Provence, Dauphiny). After some complaints from the bishop of Metz about Waldensian preaching on the basis of a vernacular translation of the Scriptures, Innocent sent Cistercian monks to correct this bad praxis. They did a thorough job. All vernacular copies of the Bible, and any other spiritual books they could lay their hands on, were burned.[42] Innocent III also ordered that a crusade be held, in order to stamp out what were regarded as heretical groups.[43] In the middle of this religious war, Innocent III called together the Fourth Lateran Council

---

[40] Here quoted from Stephens, 21.

[41] Edward E. Landon, A *Manual of Councils of the Holy Catholic Church* (Edinburgh, UK: John Grant, 1900), Vol. II, 166.

[42] Stephens, 25. On the burning of Waldensian books, see also Léger, 65. The systematic destruction of the sources is the reason for the dearth of information concerning the Waldenses and other groups within this reform movement.

[43] Stephens, 36. See also Karl Heussi, *Compendium der Kirchengeschichte*, 11th rev. ed. (Berlin, Germany: Evangelische Verlagsanstalt, 1958), 224.

(1215). Over 400 bishops and 800 priors and abbots from all parts of Western Europe gathered in Rome.[44] The primary purpose of the council was to deal with the threat of 'heresies.' Large-scale persecutions resulted in the period that followed. Any suspected person was brought before the inquisitional tribunals. If people did not recant and repent of their 'errors,' they would be handed over to the civil authorities who would punish them for heresy. This could include confiscation of property, banishment, or branding. In later years long periods of imprisonment, burning at the stake, drowning, etc. were added.[45]

Things get worse as we move into the late Middle Ages, and even into the time of the Reformation. In 1487, Pope Innocent VIII (1484-1492) issued a 'Bull against the Waldenses.' This bull pleads for the total eradication of the Waldenses.[46] They are described as a 'highly harmful' and 'abominable' sect of 'evil people.'[47] In this bull the pope calls upon the King of France and the Duke of Savoy to organise a crusade against the heretics in order 'to crush them like venomous asps.'[48]

The worst was yet to come: in the year 1655 an attempt was made to annihilate the Waldenses totally from their valleys. Léger himself was an eyewitness of the many massacres that happened during this time. His people were slaughtered in their houses and valleys like pigs in the slaughterhouse. Contemporary sources clearly illustrate the brutality of these efforts to get rid of all Waldenses once and for all.

II Ellen G. White's interest in the Waldenses

The Great Controversy

Against this background we can appreciate what E. G. White wrote about the Waldenses, and why she showed a special interest in them. The main source for this section is *The Great Controversy*, a book written by Ellen White in 1888. Other information comes from her three visits to the Waldensian valleys during the years she was in Europe, i.e. August 1885 to August 1887.

We will begin this section with some general statements concerning the Waldenses in order to show the similarity between Ellen White's description of these people of the Alps and what we find in Léger's extensive work. In comparison to other movements in church history, Ellen White devotes a relatively large number of pages to the Waldenses. While common college textbooks on church history

---

[44] Stephens, 36.

[45] Stephens, 44.

[46] For the entire text, see Léger, 619-649. A copy of this bull was originally part of the MS collection brought to the University Library in Cambridge for safe keeping. Unfortunately this author discovered that this manuscript is missing.

[47] Léger, 622.

[48] Stephens, 105.

deal with the Waldenses in one or two pages,[49] and the more popular versions may have a few more pages,[50] Ellen White devotes sixteen pages to the Waldenses in *The Great Controversy*. Although this book was published after she had visited the Waldensian valleys, she wrote as much, or even a little more, about the Waldenses in *The Spirit of Prophecy*, vol. IV, the forerunner of *The Great Controversy*.[51] This volume was published two years before she visited the valleys in northern Italy. Some sections are left out in the new edition of *The Great Controversy*, others are rewritten and enlarged, but the basic understanding of the Waldenses and the basic description of the people are the same, including the reference that some Waldenses kept the Sabbath. Even though she visited the Waldensian valleys three times, and saw with her own eyes that the Waldenses of her time were celebrating Sunday, she did not change this portion of the text when she wrote about the Waldenses four years later, i.e. in 1888. I emphasize this because it has been claimed that she made an inaccurate statement, when she stated that some Waldenses were Sabbath keepers.

Let us, however, before returning to this matter, look at some descriptions of the Waldenses in *The Great Controversy*. I have chosen a few quotations which match some of the issues discussed above, when we looked at Léger's work. Ellen White's description of the Waldenses is introduced by a general statement that during the long period of church history 'there were witnesses for God—men who cherished faith in Christ as the only mediator between God and man, who held the Bible as the only rule of faith, and who hallowed the true Sabbath.'[52] She is aware of the fact that there are only few traces of those people who deviated from the Roman Church. Where possible, both persons and writings were destroyed. The little information we have comes from their opponents, and often in a falsified way. After this general introduction, she speaks about the spread of Christianity that was accomplished independently of Rome. Here she focuses especially on the British Isles, where we have clear evidence for Sabbath keeping among the early Celts.[53] This was also true for other places which were outside the jurisdiction of the Roman pontiff, as we will see in the next section. But even where Rome was strong, there was opposition. Of 'those who resisted the encroachments of the papal power, the Waldenses stood foremost.' With this statement White introduces

---

[49] As e.g. Williston Walker et al., *A History of the Christian Church*, 4th ed. (New York: Scribner, 1965), 305f.

[50] Tim Dowley, ed., *The History of Christianity—A Lion Handbook* (Berkhamstead, UK: Lion Publishing, 1977), 315-318.

[51] Ellen G. White, *The Spirit of Prophecy*, (Oakland, CA: Pacific Press Publishing Association, 1884), vol. IV.

[52] Ellen G. White, *The Great Controversy* (Mountain View, CA: Pacific Press Publishing Association, n.d.), 61.

[53] White, 62. See also Leslie Hardinge, *Beliefs and Practices among the Celtic Church in Britain* (Unpublished PhD dissertation, University of London, 1963).

the Waldenses.[54] Then the focus shifts to the differences in doctrine that caused the Waldenses to leave the Roman Church and to call this institution the 'Antichrist.'

'The faith which for centuries was held and taught by the Waldensian Christians was in marked contrast to the false doctrines put forth from Rome. Their religious belief was founded upon the written word of God, the true system of Christianity.'[55] Like Léger, Ellen White was of the conviction that the Waldenses were not of a recent date. 'Theirs was not a faith newly received. Their religious belief was their inheritance from their fathers. They contended for the faith of the apostolic church.'[56] Therefore, she can utter the next statement, which has been challenged by some, not least by some Waldenses:[57] 'Through ages of darkness and apostasy there were Waldenses who denied the supremacy of Rome, who rejected image worship as idolatry, and who kept the true Sabbath. Under the fiercest tempests of opposition they maintained their faith.'[58]

This statement must be seen within its context. She does not mean that all Waldenses kept the Sabbath. Again in a later statement from the same book, she makes it very clear that we are only talking of *some* Waldenses who celebrated the Sabbath. 'A striking illustration of Rome's policy toward those who disagree with her was given in the long and bloody persecution of the Waldenses, some of whom were observers of the Sabbath.'[59]

Space does not allow us to present more quotations from this chapter. There are some significant statements about the importance of having the Bible in the vernacular—of reading the Bible and teaching it to our children; of the assurance of salvation; of Christ being the only mediator and helper; of the simple lifestyle; of the hope in the soon coming of Christ; of the missionary spirit, and of the severe persecutions. The chapter concludes with the thought that the Waldenses scattered the truth of the gospel to many countries in Europe, long before the birth of Luther, and that the truth from the Word of God must be proclaimed to the end of time.[60]

---

[54] White, 64.
[55] Ibid.
[56] Ibid.
[57] See: http://lifeassuranceministries.org/studies/waldenses.html. Here you find an e-mail from pastor Thomas Soggin of the Waldensian Church in Bergamo to Andras Szalai, director of Apologia Research Centre, Hungary, June 21, 2006, which maintains that the Waldenses never kept the Sabbath. Some Adventists have also challenged this statement. See e.g.. Bacchiocchi's *Endtime Issue* no. 87. Bacchiocchi not only questions White's reference concerning the Sabbath, but also her understanding, which is also part of Léger's understanding, that the roots of the Waldenses go further back in time than the times of Petrus Waldus.
[58] White, 65.
[59] White, 577.
[60] White, 61-78.

Ellen White's visits to the Waldensian valleys

Three times during her stay in Europe, Ellen White took the opportunity to cross the Alps and visit the places of her spiritual forefathers.

First visit: Nov. 27–Dec. 13, 1885. Ellen White and some others left Basel and went over the St. Gotthard pass to Turin, and then to Torre Pelice. She describes the beautiful scenery, which fascinated her. They arrived at Pastor A. C. Bourdeau's home on a Friday. Next Sabbath she was preaching in a hired hall to a small group of believers. In her sermon she explained why Adventists are separated from other churches: 'The question may arise in some minds why we as a people are separated from the world into little companies. We answer, it is not because we choose to differ from those around us, but because we see the necessity of obeying all the requirements of God.'[61] A little later she continues her sermon with these words: 'We want the truth, the whole truth as it is in Jesus. We cannot afford to cherish error on any point.' She encourages the small company of believers not to get discouraged. Then follows an interesting statement: '... if I lived in this place, I would mark the spot where so many suffered in ages past for the truth, and taking courage from them, would lift up the cross and obey the truth at any cost.'[62]

Second visit: April 16–c. May 1, 1886. This time her son W. C. White and his wife accompanied Ellen White. On this occasion she not only spoke on Sabbath to a little flock of brothers and sisters, but went to Villar Pellice on a Sunday and spoke to over 400 people in a rented hall. She also had other public speaking appointments during this visit.[63]

Third visit: Nov. 4–8, 1886. Little is recorded of this visit.

Did the Waldenses keep the Sabbath?

In order to answer this question, we have to look at the question of Sabbath versus Sunday in a wider context. Quite a number of academic studies have been undertaken to trace the change from Sabbath to Sunday in the early church.[64] But very little has been done to write a comprehensive history of the Sabbath-Sunday question during the Middle Ages.[65] Various forces in the early church period led to the abandonment of the *Sabbath as a day of rest* and the acceptance of *Sunday as a day of worship*, such as: (a) the allegorical method of interpreting the Old Testament; (b) anti-Judaism; (c) sun worship; (d) the Quartodeciman Controversy, about the

---

[61] Further information concerning the first visit is found in: *Historical Sketches of the Foreign Missions of the Seventh-day Adventists. Notes on Travel* (Basel: Imprimerie Polyglotte, 1886), 226-249.

[62] White, *Historical Sketches*, 232f.

[63] *Advent Review and Sabbath Herald*, January 1, 1886 and June 29, 1886.

[64] See my doctoral dissertation: Richard Müller, *Adventisten-Sabbat-Reformation* (Lund, Sweden: C.W.K. Gleerup, 1979), 3f.

[65] Müller, 13.

change of Easter from a date in the year (14 Nisan) to a day in the week, the Sunday; (e) Constantine's Sunday laws; (f) the fact that Christ rose on the first day of the week.

But how did our spiritual forefathers convert Sunday from *a time for worship* into *a day of rest,* and use the Sabbath commandment of the Decalogue for this purpose? It was a slow process which took centuries. An important stage was reached with Thomas Aquinas (1225-1274) and his 'semi-sabbatarian compromise.'[66] Aquinas divided the Sabbath commandment into a ceremonial part—the seventh day Sabbath—and a moral part—to have time to worship God, which cannot be disturbed by servile work. The ceremonial part is abrogated with the coming of Christ; the moral part is still binding and is applied to the Sunday.[67] This does not mean that the Roman Church did not try to enforce Sunday keeping before Aquinas' time. Indeed it did, as we will see, but Thomas provided a theological argument for doing so.

To this should be added the development in the regions where, initially, Rome did not have any influence. There many Christians indeed continued to rest on God's Sabbath as commanded in the Ten Commandments. Here we may point to the British Isles, before they came under Roman jurisdiction, beginning with Augustine of Canterbury (early sixth century-604).[68] We could also mention some of the Eastern Churches, and especially Christians in Ethiopia, who honoured the day of the resurrection, Sunday, but rested on Sabbath—until the sixteenth century, when Rome sent missionaries to that part of the world, who forbade Sabbath rest.[69] Of great interest is the development in the Eastern Churches, where the Sabbath as memorial of the creation and the Sunday, as the Lord's Day, i.e. the memorial of Christ's resurrection, were celebrated. This was done nearly everywhere, with the exception of Alexandria and Rome. As witness we can refer to the Apostolic Constitutions (fourth century), which even speaks of a five-day week for slaves.[70] Also the two church historians, Socrates of Constantinople (c. 380-?) and Sozomen (c. 400-c. 450) clearly speak of celebrating the Eucharist both on Sabbath and on Sunday.[71] To this could be added the conflict concerning Sabbath fasting which developed between the Eastern Churches and Rome. While Rome introduced the Sabbath fast, to make it a day of gloom, and thereby further increased the divide between Sabbath and Sunday, fasting on Sabbath was never allowed in

---

[66] Ibid.
[67] Müller, 17 – 20.
[68] See note 53.
[69] Ernst Hammerschmidt, *Stellung und Bedeutung des Sabbats in Äthiopien* (Stuttgart, Germany: W. Kohlhammer,1963).
[70] See the source collection of W. Rordorf, *Sabbat und Sonntag in der Alten Kirche* (Zürich, Switzerland: Theologischer Verlag, 1962), 101.
[71] Rordorf, 123. See also Heussi, 113.

the East, nor kneeling in church on Sabbath, to emphasize the festive character of the Sabbath in memory of God's creation. This is clear from the Council of Constantinople (691), which forbade fasting on the Sabbath.[72]

The question of the Sabbath fast was also one of the dividing issues at the time of the Great Schism between East and West in 1054.[73] After this final break, the patriarch of Constantinople, Michael Cerularius, wrote to the patriarch of Antioch to explain what had happened, giving the reasons for not submitting to Rome. On the question of Sabbath observance he said: 'For we are commanded also to honour the Sabbath equally with the (Sunday) Lord's (day), and to keep (it) and not to work on it.'[74] After the breakdown Cardinal Humbert, who led the Roman side in the discussions with Cerularius, wrote a treatise with the title: *Adversus Calumnias Graecorum* (Against the Calumnities of the Greeks), in which, among many other issues, he also refers to the question of Sabbath observance.[75] Even as late as the Council of Constantinople (1450), where all four patriarchs of the East were present, the old issues of the Sabbath fast and of kneeling in church both on Saturdays and Sundays, were on the agenda.[76]

The origin of and reason for the Sabbath fast are uncertain. All indications point to Rome as its origin. Together with anti-Jewish tendencies, the obligatory Sabbath fast tended to make the Sabbath a negative experience, a day of gloom, so that people would truly appreciate the Sunday, the day of the resurrection, on which they could enjoy eating meat. It is important to note that the Sabbath fast, at least at the end of the early church period, was not accepted in all places under Roman jurisdiction, as for instance in northern Italy, Milan, and certain cities in North Africa.[77]

Enforcement of Sunday keeping

The first traces of Sunday *as a day of worship* can already be found from around the middle of the second century. Even before Constantine the Great issued his civil Sunday laws, we already find the Council of Elvira (300 or a little later) threatening with the excommunication of those who do not regularly attend church on Sundays.[78] While Augustine of Hippo[79] and others spiritualized the fourth com-

---

[72] Landon, I, 210.
[73] R. L. Odom, 'The Sabbath in the Great Schism of A.D. 1054,' *AUSS*, I (1963), 74-80.
[74] Cerularius, Letter 1 to the Patriarch of Antioch, chapter 24, in Migne's *Patrilogia Graeca*, Vol. CXX, cols. 777, 778. Quoted from Odom, 79.
[75] Humber, 'Adversus Calumnias Graecorum,' chapter 6, in Migne's *Patriologica Latina*, Vol. CXI, III, cols. 936, 937. Quoted from Odom, 77-79.
[76] Landon, I, 225.
[77] See original sources in an article by Kenneth Strand, 'Sabbath Fast in Early Christianity,' *AUSS*, III (1965), 167-174.
[78] Rordorf, 177.
[79] Rordorf, 204-206.

mandment for the Christians, namely that the abstention of servile work means the abstention from sin and works of evil, at the beginning of the Middle Ages we find a shift in emphasis: one also should abstain from physical labour on Sunday. In the time up to Charlemagne (768-814), we find the legendary 'Letters from Heaven' which equate Sabbath with Sunday. At about the same time we find several books on penance, which contain detailed regulations concerning Sunday observance. Many church councils, some more important than others, enforce Sunday observance, in varying degrees. For the period of the Middle Ages, that is from about 600 until 1500, I have counted some thirty church councils that had the strict observance of Sunday on their agenda.[80] Apparently, the medieval church was facing major challenges in ensuring that people kept the Sunday sacred.

Sunday markets must have been especially difficult for the church to regulate.[81] In order not to encroach on Sunday holiness and to be rightly prepared for Sunday worship, many church councils demanded that one should start Sunday keeping at vespers on Saturday in the late afternoon/early evening. A few church councils went as far as demanding that Sunday keeping should begin at Saturday noon.[82]

Evidence of Sabbath keeping among the Waldenses

Space does not allow us to provide more general background from the complex times of the Middle Ages. Anti-Judaism, for example, was one of the main contributing factors in the early church in pushing the Sabbath aside and adopting Sunday. Several church councils had the Jews on the agenda. We find regulations from forbidding fellowship with Jews from Holy Thursday to Easter, or paying tithe, to the more extreme regulations of singling out the Jews by requiring marks of distinction on their clothes.[83] Since the Sabbath was one of the distinguishing marks of the Jews, not many Christians wanted to be identified with them by keeping the same day of rest, especially during the times of the crusades or the Inquisition. But in spite of this, we find evidence that some Waldenses kept the Sabbath, even though most written sources were burned or otherwise destroyed by the dominant church.

Writers who want to show that Waldenses kept the Sabbath, often start with

---

[80] See Landon, vol. I and II.

[81] Council of Gratlea (925), Landon, I, 294; Council of Anse (990), Landon I, 27f; Council of Cognac (1238), Landon I, 163f; Council of Apt (1365), Landon, I, 38f; Council of Westminster (1534), Landon, II, 313; Council of Cologne (1536), Landon II, 168, 170.

[82] Council of Anse (990), canon 7: 'Forbids all work on the evening of the Sabbath, after the hour of noon, and permits no buying and selling on Sundays.' Landon, I, 28. Council of Perth (1202), canon 2: 'That every Saturday from twelve o'clock be kept as a day of rest, by abstaining from work; the holy day to continue till Monday morning.' Landon, II, 37.

[83] See e.g. the Council of Ravenna (1311), requiring them to wear a distinguishing badge, Landon, II, 66; Council of Cologne (1452), requiring all clothing both of males and females to be marked by a circle in order to distinguish them, Landon, I, 167.

some words which resemble the word 'Sabbath' and which were used when referring to the Waldenses. These words are 'Insabbati,' 'Insabbatati,' 'Sabbatati,' 'Xabatati,' and 'Ençabots.' The Waldenses, however, never referred to themselves by these terms. Only their opponents used them. Did they want to indicate that the Waldenses kept the Sabbath? This has been denied by a number of scholars, including some Adventist researchers, like Earle Hilgert[84] and Daniel Augsburger.[85] Bacchiocchi agrees with Augsburger's interpretations of these words.[86] The main argument is that the above mentioned words do not refer to the Sabbath but to sandals or some kind of open shoes, as is clear from Latin and French dictionaries.

There is, however, one word that is not identified correctly. Both Hilgert and Augsburger claim that the Latin word for 'sandal' is 'sabbatum.' But according to a standard etymological dictionary, 'sandal' comes from the Latin 'sandalium,' which again comes from the Greek 'sandalon.'[87] 'Sabbatum,' according to Lewis and Short, does not have the meaning of footwear in classical Latin.[88] According to Bloch and Wartburg we do indeed find a connection between 'sabot' and footwear. The word appears for the first time in a twelfth-century document, but spelled as 'çabot,' with the meaning 'peg-top.' The word 'sabot' is first used in the fifteenth century and is found in some texts from northern France. This word is a combination of 'savate' and 'bot(te).' The word 'savate' is found, according to Bloch and Wartburg, for the first time in the twelfth century in French. It exists also in medieval Provençal ('sabata'; Italian: 'ciabatta'; Spanish: 'zapato'), and refers to some kind of footwear. The origin of the word is uncertain. This may support the theory that it comes from the Arabic 'sabbât.'[89] According to another etymological dictionary, a similar word existed in some other languages, which could point to a near-oriental origin. But this may just be accidental and may rather be a case of sound-imitation, a so-called 'onomatopoietikon.'[90]

This interpretation that 'insabbatati' and 'sabbatati' has a relationship to footwear has recently been challenged in a paper by P. Gerhard Damsteegt.[91] He focuses especially on the word 'insabbatati' and feels that it remains meaningless if

---

[84] W. E. Hilgert, *Religious Practices of the Waldenses and their Doctrinal Implications to A.D. 1530*, (Unpublished MA Thesis, 1946), 50-59. [Hilgert was an Adventist when he wrote this thesis.]

[85] Daniel Augsburger, 'The Sabbath and the Lord's Day during the Middle Ages,' in: Kenneth Strand, ed., *The Sabbath in Scripture and History* (Washington, DC: Review and Herald Publishing Association, 1982), 190–214.

[86] See his *Endtime Issues*, No 87

[87] O. Bloch and W. von Wartburg, *Dictionnaire Étymologique De La Langue Française* (Paris, France: Les Presses Universitaires de France, 1932).

[88] C. T. Lewis and C. Short, *A Latin Dictionary* (Oxford, UK: The Clarendon Press, 1975).

[89] Bloch and Wartburg, *op.cit.*

[90] Joan Cormonias, *Breve Diccionario Etimológico De La Lengua Castellana* (Madrid, Spain: Gredos, 1994).

[91] P. G. Damsteegt: 'An Analysis of Insabbatati and Sabbatati in Medieval and Reformation Sources.' Presented at the Evangelical Theological Society, Nov. 17, 2005.

it is made to refer to footwear. Damsteegt, however, appears to make the unfortunate mistake of focusing exclusively on the Latin prefix 'in-' (like the English prefix 'un-'), 'with the meaning of negation, i.e. in this context, meaning the opposite, namely wearing no shoes.' However, in Latin the prefix 'in-' also has the meaning of the English 'in,' in the sense of 'into.' Damsteegt concludes that 'insabbatati' refers to the fact that the Waldenses did not accept any of the feasts and holy days in honour of the saints and Mary, which the Catholic Church required its members to keep.[92]

According to the present writer, it is very difficult to be too dogmatic on this issue since we do not have enough information on how these words were originally used. But all this does not mean that there is no evidence that some Waldenses did not rest on the Sabbath. In fact, Damsteegt has brought to light some good examples that they indeed did. Let us briefly look at some of the evidence.

Farmers in northern Italy kept the Sabbath. Canon 13, issued by the Council of Friuli (791), discusses the greater blessedness of Sunday, as the Lord's Day, over Sabbath and comes with this interesting remark, that the Jews are celebrating the Sabbath, the last day of the week 'which also our farmers are celebrating.'[93] For our present purpose this is only of interest, if we accept the wider definition of 'Waldenses,' as given by Léger.

Passagini in northern Italy kept the Sabbath. In the region where the Waldenses preached in the twelfth and thirteenth century we find a group called Passagini, who according to their opponents kept the Sabbath.[94]

The testimony of the Roman Catholic priest Moneta of Cremona (northern Italy) from 1244. This priest accuses the Cathari and Waldenses of Sabbath keeping, while trying to defend the Catholics who do not transgress the Sabbath commandment by celebrating the Lord's Day as an ordinance of the church.[95]

A group of Sabbath keepers before the tribunal of the Inquisition in 1420. Several charges were brought against a group of 16 or 18 persons from Douai, as they were brought before the tribunal of the Inquisition. One of the charges was that they kept Sabbath on Saturdays. The preacher of the group, Bertoul Thurin, was executed 'for keeping Saturdays as his Sabbath.'[96]

Some Picards of Bohemia kept the Sabbath. Léger and others believe that the Picards of the late medieval time were Waldenses. The Waldenses, as has been shown above, were active in Picardy and many other places. In Bohemia they were

---

[92] Damsteegt, 12.
[93] Mansi XIII, 851. Quoted from: L. R. Conradi, *Geschichte des Sabbats und des ersten Wochentages* (Hamburg, Germany: Internationale Traktatgesellschaft, 1912), 474f.
[94] See Daniel Augsburger, 208f for the original sources.
[95] See Damsteegt, 10 for the original sources.
[96] See Daniel Augsberger, 209, for the original sources.

often referred to under the name of Picards. In a significant document[97] various teachings and doctrines of the Picards are mentioned. At times they are referred to as Picards in Bohemia, at other times as Picards in Moravia, at other times again as Waldensians or Picards, and again as Moravian Waldenses. It is very clear from this document that there was a close link between the presence of Waldenses/Picards in Bohemia and in Moravia. After a discussion of various doctrinal items we find a section on 'Matrimony,' where the following statement is made: 'There are few hindrances in regard to marriage; without any declaration they are united and they never contract a (marriage) with the understanding of the church. They do not take part in the Christian mass, they have no respect for sacraments, they avoid pictures of the Crucified as if it was the devil, they do not celebrate the holy virgin Maria's and the Apostles' holy days, some only the Lord's day. Some celebrate the Sabbath with the Jews, they do not accept the holy virgin's, the angels' and the saints' mediation.'[98] Here we have a very clear statement about a Waldensian/Picardian celebration of the Sabbath. Somewhat later follows other interesting information, namely that these people were, at the same time, Anabaptists. Twice in this document the relationship to the Anabaptists in Bohemia and Moravia is established. It is known that some Anabaptists in Bohemia and Moravia, with Nickolsburg as one of their centres, kept the Sabbath during the time of the Reformation. The spiritual impulse for this seems to have come from the Waldenses.[99]

Desiderius Erasmus refers to Sabbath keepers in Bohemia. Erasmus (1466/69–1536), the famous humanist at the time of the Reformation, speaks about people in Bohemia who keep the Sabbath like the Jews.[100]

There should not be any doubt in people's minds that the majority of Waldenses kept Sunday as the Lord's Day. This is clearly shown in several places and is found in a document referred to in Léger's work: *An Explanation of the Ten Commandments*.[101] It is of interest that here the Sabbath commandment is called the fourth commandment, in agreement with the Eastern Churches and the Reformed Churches, and in contrast with the Catholic and later Lutheran method of counting the Ten Commandments, which lists it as the third commandment. But this interpretation of the commandment leaves no doubt that the Sabbath means the Lord's Day, i.e. Sunday. The spiritual explanation of the fourth commandment

---

[97] Summa Picardicarum rerum tum in Bohemia tum in Moravia (Cod. Viennens. Lat. 967 a. Denis 1, 3258), Publishing by J. Døllinger, *Beiträge zur Sektengeschichte des Mittelalters*, Vol. 2: *Dokumente vornehmlich zur Geschichte der Valdesier und Katharer* (München, Germany: Beck, 1890), 632–662 et al.

[98] Döllinger, 662.

[99] See my dissertation, Part I, chapter 5: 'The understanding of the Sabbath amongst the sabbatarian Anabaptists,' 110–130.

[100] See Daniel Augsberger, 209 for the original sources.

[101] Léger, Book I, 128 ff.

sounds quite Augustinian. This, of course, did not prevent some Waldenses from resting on the Sabbath of the Bible. This might be expected, especially when we remember that they strongly emphasized the importance of the Ten Commandments, and that they refused to fast on Saturdays—possibly out of respect for the day of creation, as was done in the Eastern Church.

Conclusion

Lux lucet in tenebris—The light shines in the darkness. This is an allusion to John 1:5, where the text continues: 'and the darkness has not understood it.' This truth applies in a special way to the Middle Ages, when our spiritual forefathers had to undergo so much suffering. But the heritage of the Waldenses, especially the emphasis on the proclamation of the Word of God in the local tongue, has been handed down from generation to generation. We have the written Word and with the written Word, we have also the Living Word, Jesus Christ, amongst us. We often have not treasured this precious diamond as we should—the treasure for which our forefathers so often had to give their lives.

There is still much to learn and to treasure from our spiritual forefathers, not least concerning more evidence for their Sabbath keeping. More research, especially in the many protocols of the Inquisition which may have survived, is needed. There is also need for a new edition in a modern language of all the documents related to the Waldenses which are preserved in Cambridge and Geneva. Some of the documents would have to be dated anew, if at all possible, to see if there has been a development from the 'older' Waldenses, which Léger often refers to, to the Waldenses at the time of the Reformation.

It is, in particular, important that these valiant martyrs are not forgotten. Let me be so bold as to make a suggestion: Could not the leaders of the Adventist Church establish contact with the modern Waldensian Church and explore the possibility of erecting a simple memorial somewhere in the Waldensian valleys? In addition to serving as a fitting tribute to the Waldenses of old, it would also serve as a powerful reminder of the need to guard against all religious intolerance— present and future!

Richard Müller. Born in Germany. Pastoral, preceptorial, youth ministry and teaching experience in Germany, Denmark, England and Lebanon. Lecturer Newbold College 1977-81 and head of theology Middle East University 1992-95. Secretary Danish Union 1995-98. Director, Danish Correspondence School 1998-2004. Retired 2009. Dr. theol., University of Lund, Sweden, 1979.

A Prophetic Community Today:
Imaginative Visionaries and Social Activists for the Third Millennium

Zdravko Zack Plantak

A crisis comes when people least expect it. This was such a moment. The people of Israel were getting into a serious crisis. It was the time of weeping and anger, of 'hunger' and overindulgence, or, as one commentator put it, 'a tangled tale of manna and quails, greed and prophecy.'[1] Here, at what was later to be known as Kibroth-hattaavah, or the Graves of Craving, the Israelites wept and complained that the bread of angels was just too plain for them and that they were craving the Egyptian cuisine. The rabble or riffraff of their community had a strong craving for Egyptian fish, and the juicy cucumbers and melons, the leeks, the onions and the garlic. They complained because the sufficiency of God's provisions was just too bland and 'nothing at all but this manna to look at' (Num 11:6).[2] This was crisis time for Moses, who 'heard the people weeping throughout their clans, everyone at the door of his tent' (vs 10). Crisis time for the people of Israel who wanted to go back into slavery and the bondage of hard labour in Egypt, in order to indulge in leeks and garlic. Crisis time even for God, as his anger was 'kindled against the people' and 'blazed hotly' (vs 33, 10.) Moses is actually so upset that he asks God to kill him on the spot (vs 15).

The key to this story of crisis is the double answer that God provides to their craving. First there is the angry answer which can be paraphrased as, 'You want meat. I will give you meat until it comes out of your nostrils and makes you sick' (vs 20). However, God's second answer is even more puzzling and extravagant—and almost bizarre—nevertheless more kindly. God poured out prophecy: a spirit of prophecy so abundant and unexpected that clergy and laity alike started speaking the word of the Lord. The flood of prophecy in different areas of the camp made Joshua uncomfortable and insecure, as he felt that God's pouring out of the Spirit of prophecy had to be 'administratively controlled.' And he cries to Moses, 'My Lord, Moses, *stop them!*'

But the first *nabhi*—the role model for all other prophets—responds, 'Are you jealous for my sake? Would that all the Lord's people were prophets, that the Lord would put his Spirit on them!' (vs 29).

---

[1] Ellen Davis, *Getting Involved with God: Rediscovering the Old Testament* (Cambridge, UK: Boston, MA: Cowley Publications, 2001), 202.

[2] The translation used in this chapter, unless otherwise noted, is the English Standard Version (ESV).

So, what is the connection between what happened and this outburst of prophecy? The basic function of these prophets, I imagine, is to give God's perspective on the situation. So here, at the Graves of Craving, prophets were trying to reroute the people from craving for meat to gratitude for manna.

But what does this have to do with us? At times we have had a few lonely prophetic voices in the Adventist community, calling us to have a more generous and giving spirit, to a greater awareness and concern for the poor and disadvantaged, for those 'have-nots' of society that we so easily forget in our craving and greed. And, at times, I hear the rest of the church and maybe some Joshuas among us come and say in a loud voice: 'Moses, my Lord, stop them!' (Num 11:28). But the right response must be the reply of Moses: 'I wish that *all* God's people were prophets.' We, Adventist believers, must call for a clearer prophetic attitude and prophetic vision and imagination than ever before, to accomplish our prophetic ministry and fulfil all the necessary prophetic tasks before God establishes a new heaven and a new earth.

Jan Paulsen called for such prophetic vision in 1988 when I first heard him address the crucial issue of social and prophetic involvement in the world. He has repeated this in different forms and in different forums throughout his career:

> There are certain vestiges of injustice, inequality, and deprivation in the world, expressions of the devil's work, which the church as community must expose and take part in discrediting. The evil which is alien to God's kingdom is under God's judgment ... God must be able to express himself through the church. Concerns which are God's must by definition be the church's.[3]

Miguel de Cervantes' Don Quixote said to his friend: 'There are only two families in the whole world, my old grandmother used to say, the "haves" and the "have-nots."'[4] In addition to this timeless truth which, almost 400 years later, we must still seriously contemplate, I shall suggest that there are also only two ways to respond to this premise and that 'the greatest prophet of all time' addressed this most eloquently in his famous prophetic speech. But we shall not come to this 'prophet' until the end of this essay. Let's start from the beginning of what we

---

[3]   Jan Paulsen, 'Social Service/Social Action: Is That Also God's Mission?' (Presentation on Symposium of Seventh-day-Adventist Missiologists, Newbold College, Bracknell, Summer 1988), 4-5. Also quoted in Zdravko Plantak, *The Silent Church: Human Rights and Adventist Social Ethics* (Basingstoke and New York: Macmillan Press and St Martin's Press [now Palgrave], 1998), 56. Later this presentation was published with the same title in *Adventist Mission Facing the 21st Century: A Reader*, edited by Hugh I. Dunton, et al. (Frankfurt am Main, Germany: Peter Lang, 1990), 142-3.

[4]   Miguel de Cervantes, *Don Quixote*, II, xx, (1615).

know about prophets and about the prophetic role to which we are called at the end time.

It goes almost without saying that the Adventist understanding of the role of prophets and prophecies is primarily of a futuristic and apocalyptic nature. However, predicting the future through an eschatological emphasis was only a secondary role of the prophets of ancient Judaism. Their primary prophetic role was socio-ethical, as they were visionaries of what can be and should be. Since Adventists claim to constitute the prophetic minority at the end of the world's history,[5] we may learn from the prophets in Jewish society, whose role, in the view of the biblical evidence, was primarily that of social reformers and prophetic visionaries.

The Hebrew term *nabhi* comes from the root Akkadian form *nabu*, which means 'to call,' 'to announce.' The passive form of the noun *nabhi* and the verb *nabu* appears in Hammurabi's code, where *nabi* means 'called' —describing a person who received a divine call without any hereditary rights. In that very sense the Adventist movement and its pioneers were convinced that they had received the prophetic calling to be a peculiar people: God's true kingdom in the last days of earth's history.

Nabhi is first used in connection with Abraham (Gen 20:7). However it becomes a popular term with Moses (Deut 34:10). Moses, as the provider of the moral law, becomes a standard of comparison for all other prophets (Deut 18:15ff). As Joseph Blenkinsopp in his remarkable study suggested, 'prophets continue the role and activity of Moses the proto-prophet.'[6]

Enid Mellor rightly suggested that 'the biblical prophets wrote about the times in which they lived, and that prediction was less important than warning and exhortations. They believed themselves to be commissioned and inspired by Yahweh, to speak his word to their contemporaries—to point them away from their foolish ways and to show them true religion and morality.'[7] Mellor, like many modern students of prophetic literature, realizes that prophets had several roles. They were (1) social, political and religious leaders who proclaimed the law; (2) they guarded the spiritual life of the nation by being visionaries. They dared to imagine how life was supposed to be lived, with, as the title of Walter Brueggeman's famous book suggests: *Prophetic Imagination*;[8] (3) the prophets mediated be-

---

5   On Seventh-day Adventism's self-understanding as a 'Prophetic Minority' see: Charles Teel, 'Withdrawing Sect, Accommodating Church, Prophesying Remnant: Dilemmas in the Institutionalization of Adventism' (unpublished manuscript of his presentation at the 1980 Theological Consultation for Seventh-day Adventist Administrators and Religion Scholars, Loma Linda University, 1980).

6   Joseph Blenkinsopp, *Sage, Priest, Prophet: Religious and Intellectual Leadership in Ancient Israel* (Louisville, KY: Westminster John Knox, 1995), 120.

7   Enid Mellor, 'Reading the Prophets Today,' in: *Prophets and Poets* (Nashville, TN: Abingdon Press, 1997).

8   Walter Brueggeman, *Prophetic Imagination* (Minneapolis, MN: Augsburg Fortress, 1978).

tween the people and their God; and (4) they predicted future judgment, but also hope, that God would remember the most disenfranchised members of society. They were interested in international affairs and the future, as they counseled and influenced the social structures of their own generation in their own locality. They may, therefore, be described as theological and social reformers and visionaries.

Elements of prophetic teaching

Four essential elements[9] emerge from prophetic teachings. First, the warnings which prophets bring are always a *matter of life and death.* We see, for example, in Isaiah 40-55 the serious consequences that awaited Israel: captivity and exile. The prophets called Israel to reject evil and death, and choose God, moral behaviour and, consequently, life.[10] Deuteronomy 30:15-20 provides a clear example of this.

The second element in prophetic teaching deals with *God's care for those who are without proper protection within the existing social structures (i.e. slaves, widows, orphans, debtors, the homeless, strangers, etc).* Theologian and philosopher Cornel West suggested that a rich life is fundamentally a life of serving others, trying to leave the world a little better than you found it. This echoes the words of Rabbi Hillel 2000 years ago: 'If I am not for myself, who will be for me? And if I am only for myself, what am I?'[11]

The biblical law (Ex 23:3; Deut 16:19-20) requires that there should be no unjust differences between people. But in real life the economics of equality are exchanged for the economics of affluence. The prophetic alternative must mean what Brueggeman calls, 'the primary prophetic agenda,' which is the 'possibility of passion; ... passion as the capacity and readiness to care, to suffer, to die, and to feel' for other people. Ultimately, God 'is one whose person is presented as passion and pathos, the power to care, the capacity to weep, the energy to grieve and to rejoice.' And prophets must think like God, 'not whether it is realistic or practical or viable but whether it is imaginable.'[12]

Furthermore, God promises to be a support and help to those who do not have anybody: he hears their cries, sees their suffering, and brings help when his human agents fail to do so. The prophets talk about the alienation of those who grab land and 'add house to house and join field to field' until they become alone in the land (see Isa 5:8). This process of materialism, mirrored in our own time and expressed in the accumulation of material goods beyond the point of realistic needs,

---

[9] For this division into four elements of prophetic ethics, I am indebted to Walter Harrelson. See his 'Prophetic Ethics,' in *A New Dictionary of Christian Ethics* (1986), 508-512.

[10] As quoted in Paul Rogat Loeb, *Soul of a Citizen: Living with Convictions in a Cynical Time* (New York: St. Martins' Griffins, 1998), 14.

[11] Ibid., 13.

[12] Ibid., 41, 42, 44.

ends in isolation and existential alienation and in the loss of any meaningful human existence and relationship among people.

Thirdly, *God seeks obedience and justice rather than formal worship or sacrifice.* The sacrificial system and religious festivals (including the observance of Sabbath) were important; but ethical behaviour springing from right motives was even more important ('doing the truth' instead of only 'having the truth'). The basic motive was love which responds to God's love, God's choice and God's calling (Deut 7:6-11). Therefore, the motive for ethical behaviour and social action is an answer to God's love, which he expressed in covenants with human beings (1 John 4:9, 10). Philosopher Seneca's words echo this truth when he said, 'The real compensation of a right action is inherent in having performed it.' The question that must be deeply relevant and ingrained in our Sabbath-keeping consciousness is: How can we truly serve the Lord on the Sabbath in our worship and not be rejected as were those legalistic Sabbath keepers described in Amos 5:21-24:

> I hate, I despise your feasts, and I take no delight in your solemn assemblies.
> Even though you offer me your burnt offerings and grain offerings,
> I will not accept them;
> > and the peace offerings of your fattened animals,
> I will not look upon them.
> Take away from me the noise of your songs;
> > to the melody of your harps I will not listen.
> But let justice roll down like waters,
> > and righteousness like an ever-flowing stream.

Lest we be unsure whether this is about true prophetically imagined Sabbath keeping, Amos continues in the same breath, 'Hear this, you who trample on the needy and bring the poor of the land to an end, saying, "When will the new moon be over, that we may sell grain? And the Sabbath, that we may offer wheat for sale, that we may make the ephah small and the shekel great and deal deceitfully with false balances, that we may buy the poor for silver and the needy for a pair of sandals and sell the chaff of the wheat?"' (Amos 8:4-6). Reading these and many similar passages in the prophetic rage against injustice should make us spend less time arguing what kind of music we should utilize in our worships on Sabbath morning, what instruments are acceptable or should be banned, and more on what kind of people we are and how we pursue a just and compassionate living among ourselves and whether we fight for such values as are close to God's heart.

David Noel Freedman observed that 'the characteristic way of a prophet in Israel is that of poetry and lyric. The prophet engages in future fantasy. The prophet does not ask if the vision can be implemented, for questions of implementation are of no consequence until the vision can be imagined. The imagination must come before the implementation.'[13]

The fourth element of the prophetic role is *eschatological-apocalyptic*. In this element of prophetic teaching, the prophet goes outside his immediate domain and speaks about the global picture of human history. And, ultimately, the prophet speaks about *hope* that is so often non-existent among people who live their lives in a hopeless day-to-day survival mode. At its centre, prophetic eschatology is an affirmation that God *will* succeed in his desire for his creation, that he will win the battle between good and evil and inevitably bring salvation to his people both in a spiritual sense and also in the physical liberation from the bondage of hopelessness, poverty and this earth's disadvantage and groaning.

'It is the vocation of the prophet to keep alive the ministry of imagination, to keep on conjuring and proposing alternative futures to the single one that the establishment of the day wants to urge as the only thinkable one.'[14] The prophets are ultimately the seers and visionaries.[15]

Seventh-day Adventists have usually emphasized the fourth aspect of the prophetic role, especially in its evangelistic and theological sense. However, rather than portraying the theology of hope in the manner of Moltmann,[16] we have made doom and gloom out of these eschatological prophetic deliberations, which are more concerned with frightening people than with the hope and encouragement that God is in control and will finally conquer evil and establish the good rule of his heavenly government. In its self-understanding as a 'prophetic movement,' Adventism has usually been regarded as 'a movement preoccupied with making predictions' as well as 'a movement with a special interest in studying and interpreting predictive prophecy.'[17] But, as Jack Provonsha pointed out, Adventism as a prophetic movement should be defined more in terms of function and role; in other words, we should think of ourselves as a people with a mission to the world.[18] Therefore, we should also consider other aspects of prophetic ministry, if we desire to be faithful to our prophetic calling. One of these aspects, and perhaps the first one we should be more sensitive to, is the primary or socio-ethical role of prophets.

---

[13] Brueggemann, 44.
[14] Ibid., 45.
[15] Cf. Blenkinsopp, op. cit, 125.
[16] Jurgen Moltmann, *Theology of Hope: On the Ground and the Implications of a Christian Eschatology* (London, UK: SCM Press and New York: Harper and Row, 1967); N. T. Wright, *Surprised by Hope: Rethinking Heaven, the Resurrection, and the Mission of the Church* (New York, NY: HarperOne, Harper Collins Publishers, 2008).
[17] Jack Provonsha, *A Remnant in Crisis* (Hagerstown, MD: Review and Herald Publishing Association, 1993), 50.
[18] Ibid., 50-51.

When we begin the prophetic task of criticizing the present world order or the way injustice is committed through economic globalization, criticism will certainly come. But in spite of this, we must refocus on the biblical and theological underpinnings and foundations.

Examples of the primary prophetic role

The prophets of the Old Testament did not invent new social, economic or moral responsibilities. They believed and affirmed that the ideal for Jewish society as a whole, and its people as individuals, was set in the legislation of *the covenant* between God and Israel. Justice, as a basis of the law and the pillar of society, was regarded by the prophets as binding for all ages. The guidance the prophets gave to Israel regarding social, ethical and economic relationships was clearly based on the Mosaic Law as expressed in the Ten Commandments.

The moral law, as an expression of the character of God and as God's desire for human fulfilment, was always high on the agenda of Adventist theology. For us the Decalogue is still the great moral guideline binding upon all people in every age who desire to live in harmony with God and with other human beings. It is not, and has never been, the means of salvation (Rom 4:1-3; Heb 11). However, the fruitage of salvation is obedience to these precepts that God himself gave to humanity (Ex 31:18).

For a full understanding of what God means by his moral law, a Christian must turn to the God Incarnate. Jesus, in his most remarkable sermon about the law,[19] claimed that he did not come to abolish the law but to fulfil it (Mat 5:17). He stated: 'Anyone who breaks one of the least of these commandments and teaches others to do the same will be called least in the kingdom of heaven, but whoever practices and teaches these commands will be called great in the kingdom of heaven' (Mat 5:19).

When challenged to give an account of what he thought was the most important commandment, Jesus did not allow himself to be drawn into making the mistake of selecting one and overemphasizing it. Rather, he summed up the law and the prophets into a remarkably concise but powerful phrase borrowed from Deuteronomy 6: 'Love the Lord your God with all your heart and with all your soul and with all your mind. This is the first and the greatest commandment. And the second is like it: Love your neighbour as yourself' (Mat 22:37-39; cf. Deut 6:4-5). Asked on another occasion the question 'Who is my neighbour?' Jesus answered eloquently in a parable that our neighbour is everyone who is in need, regardless of race, nationality or caste (Lk 10:29-37).

---

[19] See, for example, C. H. Dodd, *Gospel and Law: Bampton Lectures in America* (Cambridge, UK: Cambridge University Press, 1951), 62-63.

The universality of the Old Testament account of the moral law (Ex 20:1-17 and Deut 5:1-22) and Jesus' elaboration of it (Mat 5-7) require respect for and guarding of human rights. Considering that God is interested in relationships between human beings, and that he demonstrated the desire to regulate these relationships with the last six commandments of the Decalogue and with the numerous sayings of Jesus, the body of Christ today (i.e. his embodied community) should uplift these regulations and apply them to every situation in life.

Thus Seventh-day Adventists, who desire to keep the commandments, should be the first to foster good relations with their neighbours. Whenever there is a violation of the love-principle in the world, they ought to be among the first to condemn it and to seek ways to eliminate injustice, inequality, bad relationships, and violation of human rights in general, in order to be true to their calling of the people of the law. However, at times we have made these wonderful divine instructions into limitations and burdens that have oppressed rather than liberated people.

Though the theme of social concern is reflected throughout all the prophets, three 'major' prophets (Isaiah, Jeremiah and Ezekiel) and seven 'minor' prophets (Hosea, Amos, Micah, Habakkuk, Zephaniah, Zechariah and Malachi) illustrate this most emphatically. Of all these prophets dealing with social justice, Isaiah is a foremost example. It is essential to understand the primary social role of the prophets in order to become a twenty-first century prophetic voice and a true prophetic community. Therefore, let us briefly consider Isaiah's concerns and his invitation.

Isaiah marked the sins of God's people of his time as idolatry (2:8), injustice (5:7; 59:8), bloodshed (59:7), rebellion (1:5; 57:4), neglect of widows (1:23; 10:2), heavy drinking (5:11; 28:1-7) and oppression of the poor (3:14-15; 10:2). Again, like other prophets, Isaiah saw the solution either in repentance and God's forgiveness, or in facing judgment, punishment and destruction. Inevitably, Isaiah emphasized that the Messiah will come and establish social justice in his millennial kingdom.

Isaiah was a citizen of the vibrant city—Jerusalem. He lived in the eighth century BC. He did not shy away from political involvement, or from getting involved with issues of justice and the socio-economic evils of his day. He was probably an aristocrat, and issues of state and national security greatly concerned him. He was active, charismatic and passionate. In Joseph Robinson's words, 'For [Isaiah] the integrity, more, the very existence of his faith, was dependent upon the decisions taken on political issues.'[20]

The message tells of God's punishment of Israel, in particular the kingdom of Judah and of punishment of the nations for their idolatry and injustice; and of

---

[20] In *Prophets & Poets* (Abingdon, 1997), 32.

God's subsequent redemption of the people of Israel. Both the punishment and redemption begin in Jerusalem/Zion, reaching from there to encompass the nations of the world. Although the message is universal in scope, it is never separated from its historic centre—the people of Israel. James Ward in his book *Thus Says the Lord* emphasizes how the message of punishment and redemption is 'summarized in the first chapter, which thus serves as an introduction. The theme of Zion's eventual redemption, stated briefly in 1:26-27, is developed in 2:2-5; 4:2-6.'[21] It is not until chapter 6 that the prophet gets his call and says, 'Send me!' Therefore, the first five chapters serve as a preliminary introduction. In particular, chapters 1 and 2 appear to be a resumé of the collected oracles of the eighth century prophet, explaining why his call was needed and why he accepted that prophetic calling with the words: 'Here am I. Send me!' (Isa 6:6).

Isaiah's dramatic expression is full of expressive colours and shades, many levels and layers of meaning. For example, there are distinctions between the people of God, the remnant, the servants of the Lord. And yet these distinctions between the nations and other groups within Israel are not hard and fast. The divisions and distinctions are a major part of Isaiah's concern. And yet, as Peter Miscall put it, 'we cannot resolve Isaiah into a simple narrative, nor can we resolve it into a morality tale of good versus evil, with Israel good and the nations evil. The story of sin, judgment (2:9-22) and restoration applies to all (2:2-4).'[22]

The richness is in the dramatic speeches in which the characters are not presented as distinct and historic individuals; they are constructs in the poetic form of Isaiah.[23] For example, Israel is masculine singular in 1:4, masculine plural in 1:5-7 and feminine singular in 1:21-26. Jerusalem is a woman, and the capital city a metonym for Israel. 'Israel is judged and condemned, desolate and devastated, and comforted and redeemed ... Generally male, God at times is female, whether as a woman and mother (42:14; 45:10; 66:9-13) or as mother nature (35:1-7; 41:18-19). God is powerful, judging and even savage; chapters 34 and 63:1-6 contain some of the most unattractive descriptions of God in the Bible. He is also mild, forgiving and comforting. God is described in human, animate and even inanimate terms. He is a bull (1:24), a lion and birds (31:4-5), a gem (28:5), light and fire (10:17) and sun and the moon (60:19-20).'[24]

As we turn to the first chapter, prophetic and pastoral concerns permeate this text. This passionate reflection breathes moral clear-sightedness and courage under the threat of disaster. Walter Brueggemann, in his commentary on Isaiah, calls Isaiah's canonical method of treatment an 'open-ended' theological interpretation.

---

[21] James Ward, *Thus Says the Lord* (Nashville, TN: Abingdon, 1991), 40.
[22] Peter Miscall, *Isaiah* (JSOT Press, 1993; Sheffield Academic Press), 15.
[23] I owe this section to Miscall.
[24] Ibid., 15

Each subsection begins with a helpful geopolitical, historical, and theological summary, followed by a running commentary structured according to his outline. He generally assumes that historical contexts and theological meaning of the texts are often only loosely linked, due to the perceived, rigorous 'reshaping' of the historical material.[25]

Stephen T. Hague stresses that the theological concerns of Isaiah take precedence over geopolitical concerns, the most important of which is the theme of judgment and the hope that that judgment brings. It is also suggested that for us moderns, as in Isaiah's day, evils gone unnoticed may lead to 'a supernatural swoop of nullification directly from heaven.'[26] Brueggemann rightly points out how Isaiah includes contemporary themes, such as consumerism, the 'wanton exhibitionism of the wealthy,' 'shameless luxury,' exploitation of the vulnerable, the greed of 'avaricious landowners,' self indulgence, injustice, urban decline, hypocrisy, militarism, social exploitation, and the geopolitics of superpowers. He uses modern language well to describe biblical realities: 'terrible againstness' for God's judgment, 'commodity fetishism' for the spiritual force of silver and gold that illustrates the self-deception that things can secure. In light of these themes, Brueggemann often writes as a preacher or prophet himself. So, for example, concerning the judgment announced in Isaiah 8, he says, 'We ourselves are now members of churches so secularized that Isaiah's rhetoric sounds obscurantist, if we hear it at all.'

Just scanning through selected verses of Isaiah 1 to 3, you will notice the strength of prophetic conviction. Isaiah is not timid; he speaks with full prophetic conviction and imagination when he declares,[27] 'Seek justice, correct oppression; bring justice to the fatherless, plead the widow's cause ... The Lord will enter into judgment with the elders and princes of his people: It is you who have devoured the vineyard, the spoil of the poor is in your houses. What do you mean by crushing my people, by grinding the face of the poor? declares the Lord God of hosts' (Isa 1:17 and 3:14-15).

As Michael Ignatieff in his highly acclaimed book *The Needs of Strangers*, points out in commenting on Shakespeare's King Lear, 'the test of human respect is in life's hardest cases: not in one's neighbor, friend or relation, but the babbling stranger, the foul and inconsistent inhabitant of the back wards of the state hospitals, the Mongol child [the insane, the retarded, the deaf and dumb, the crippled and deranged].'[28] And the prophetic role calls us to see these, to get dirty in the

---

[25] Walter Brueggemann, *Isaiah 1-39*, Westminster Bible Companion 1 (Louisville, KY: Westminster John Knox, 1998).

[26] Stephen T. Hague, Review of Walter Brueggemann's *Isaiah 1-39*, Westminster Bible Companion 1 (Louisville, KY: Westminster John Knox, 1998).

[27] Cf. Isa 1:11, 13-17, 21, 23; 2:3, 4, 7, 10, 19, and 3:14, 15.

[28] Michael Ignatieff, *The Needs of Strangers* (New York: Picador USA, 2001), 44.

trenches of human hubris, to imagine different options and to 'speak up for those who cannot speak for themselves' (Prov 31:6), and nurture the hopes of prophetic renewal.[29]

The role of the New Testaments prophets

The role of the prophets in the New Testament was not very different from that in the Old Testament. John the Baptist, whom Jesus called the greatest prophet of all times (Mat 11:9-11), invited the people of Israel to repent and to produce good fruit (Mat 3:2-10). After querying whether Jesus was the Messiah, he received a message from Jesus which he could understand, appreciate, and identify with. Jesus said: 'Go back and report to John what you hear and see: The blind receive sight, the lame walk, those who have leprosy are cured, the deaf hear, the dead are raised, and the good news is preached to the poor' (Lk 7:22b). No doubt only a true prophet would recognize the Messiah in such a description. That is why Jesus used this approach in explaining his mission to the imprisoned prophet. Just imagine if people around us came and asked, 'Are Seventh-day Adventists true representatives of Christ?' 'Are they true prophets?' Would they be able to describe our mission in similar terms to those Jesus used when describing his work?

John the Revelator was concerned about social as well as eschatological matters. Writing both about and to the Christian minority in a society that did not favour them a great deal, the writer of the book of Revelation was concerned for their safety, their well-being and their rights, which were being violated through persecution[30] (Rev 2:2, 9-10, 13, 21-22; 12:1-7; and 13:4, 15-16). He wrote about the new Jerusalem, which will serve prophetically for the healing of the nations in the new and just earth that God will establish on our planet as originally intended.

Jesus of Nazareth was greatly concerned with the social and economic justice of his time. In his inaugural speech he said that he had come to proclaim freedom to the captives, to release the oppressed and to proclaim the acceptable year of the Lord.[31] However, Jesus not only preached about issues of social concern, he also practiced his social beliefs. St. Augustine's famous quote came from the observation of Jesus: 'Fill yourselves first and then only will you be able to give to others.' (Read Matthew 4:23 and 15:30.) To use words of Meredith Gould from her book *Deliberate Acts of Kindness*: 'Compassion, [which is] the awareness of another suffering, [was] a quality-of-[his]-being.'[32] He proved through his ministry that

---

[29] See such significant occasions through the same passages, for example, in Isaiah 1: 18-19; 2:4.

[30] Cf. Rev 2:2, 9-10, 13, 21-22; 12:1-7; and 13:4, 15-16.

[31] Luke 4:18-21. Cf. Karl Barth, *Deliverance to the Captives*, translated by Marguerite Wieser with Preface by John Marsh (London, UK: SCM Press, 1961).

[32] Meredith Gould, *Deliberate Acts of Kindness: Service as a Spiritual Practice* (New York: Image Books/Doubleday, 2002), 13.

virtually nobody was outside of his interest. And he demanded nothing less from his followers. Even in the most famous of his eschatological discourses, when his closest followers asked him when his *parousia* would take place, Jesus not only answered in terms of external events, but also in terms of what his followers must do as they 'occupy until he comes again' (Mat 24:1-25:46).

It is essential for us, who have always called upon Matthew 24 and its signs of the times, to connect Jesus' sermon with his appeal to his disciples and followers to feed the hungry and to give drink to the thirsty, to welcome a foreigner and to clothe those who have no means as if they were doing it directly to Jesus himself. Mother Teresa expressed this powerfully when she said, 'Whoever the poorest of the poor are, they are Christ for us—Christ under the guise of human suffering.'[33] Again, Jan Paulsen calls for the same kind of lifestyle in a recent article on the meaning of the soon coming of the Lord: 'I wait [for the second coming] with the conviction that how I live today matters, that, although I yearn for the moment of ultimate healing, God is calling me today to be a healer, an agent of transformation and renewal in society.'[34]

Dietrich Bonhoeffer asked half a century ago a question that remains as urgent today as when it was first raised: 'Who is Jesus Christ for us today?' 'The hungry need bread,' he wrote in his book *Ethics* while he was in a Nazi camp awaiting execution, 'and the homeless need a roof; the oppressed need justice and the lonely need fellowship; the undisciplined need order and the slave needs freedom ... Because Jesus had entered into our world of sorrows, and because he had taken up the cause of those in need, making their cause to be his own, to allow the hungry to remain hungry would be blasphemy against God and one's neighbor, for what is nearest to God is precisely the need of one's neighbor.'[35]

This is not that dissimilar to what one of our founders wrote: 'Christ's chief work was in ministering to the poor, the needy, and the ignorant ... Christ's life is an example to all His followers.'[36] Paulsen, on another recent occasion, spoke about the well documented 'passion of early Adventist pioneers for causes such as the abolition of slavery, temperance, and religious liberty ... They, too, struggled to know how they should relate to the civil realm. But, with the guidance of Ellen White and other church leaders, concluded that inaction was not an option.'[37] Then Paulsen quotes Ellen White from a 1914 *Review and Herald* article: 'Many deplore the wrongs which they know exist, but consider themselves free from all

---

[33] Mother Teresa, *Mother Teresa: Her Essential Wisdom*, ed. Carol Kelly Gangi (New York: Fall River Press, 2006), 28.
[34] Jan Paulsen, 'When Words are Not Enough,' *Adventist World* (July 2007), 9.
[35] Dietrich Bonhoeffer, *Ethics*, 137.
[36] Ellen G. White, *Welfare Ministry*, 59
[37] Jan Paulsen, 'Serving Our World, Serving Our Lord,' *Adventist World*, NAD Edition (2007, v. 3, May 2007), 10.

responsibilities in the matter. This cannot be. Every individual exerts an influence in society.'[38]

Parallel to proclaiming the gospel, the task of the church is to feed the hungry, give drink to the thirsty, be hospitable to the stranger, clothe the poor, visit the prisoner, and look after the sick. The social concern thus expressed is to be one of the primary tasks of the prophetic community awaiting the final realization of the kingdom of Jesus. It is living in two kingdoms, here and now and not yet, but nevertheless very soon.

In the middle of the nineteenth century most Christian scholars perceived the kingdom of God as the present kingdom that Christians should work towards and establish on earth. By contrast, the early Seventh-day Adventists initially interpreted the kingdom of God as the eschatological-apocalyptic kingdom established by God at the end of the millennium.[39] Because of Ellen White, this emphasis within Adventism shifted. Ellen White proposed the concepts of the 'kingdom of grace' and the 'kingdom of glory,' and on this basis other Adventist thinkers further developed the idea. Initially in the 1950s, with the appearance of *Questions on Doctrines*, and especially in the last three decades, with a new generation of Adventist theologians and ethicists, Seventh-day Adventists placed a new emphasis on a number of issues and doctrines, including that of the kingdom of God. This time, the dual nature of the kingdom expressed as the two phases or stages not only affected the theological discussion of the timing of the kingdom, but also opened up a discussion about the moral and ethical effects of the kingdom of God. For the first time the doctrine of the kingdom of God resulted in considerations of a socio-ethical nature. And the conclusion was that 'eschatology and ethics must go hand in hand.'[40]

The ethical reasoning that springs from the concept of the kingdom of God must be taken very seriously. There is no doubt that Jesus, both in the Synoptic gospels and in the Gospel of John, reiterated the dual concept of the kingdom.[41] While Jesus proclaimed that his kingdom would come with power and glory after he had gone to the Father, and while he taught the disciples to pray for this future kingdom and instructed them to wait for him, Jesus also encouraged them to proclaim that this same kingdom was within them, and that they needed to make a personal commitment in order to enter it.[42] Jesus' proclamation of the kingdom

---

[38]   Ellen G. White, *Review and Herald* (Oct 15, 1914).

[39]   See for a more extensive discussion about the Kingdom of God concept and the Adventist contribution to this significant theological idea, Zdravko Plantak, *The Silent Church*.

[40]   John Brunt, 'Going About Our Daily Business,' in: *Pilgrimage of Hope*, edited by Roy Branson (Association of Adventist Forums, 1986), 28.

[41]   Although written at different times and from very different standpoints, the Synoptics and John give us the *ipsissima vox* of Jesus' sayings on the Kingdom of God.

[42]   Cf. Mk 14:23; Mat 24:30-31; Mat 10:7; Lk 10:9; Mat 25:3, 46; Lk 11:2; Lk 17:21; John 3:3-5; John 14:1-3.

included serious ethical implications: Preaching the good news to the poor, proclaiming freedom for the prisoners, healing the sick, releasing the oppressed and proclaiming God's favour and the Jubilee year (Lk 4:18-19).

Jesus' ethical implications of the kingdom are expressed in the most explicit way in the Sermon on the Mount. There, the inhabitants of the kingdom are the poor, those who mourn, the meek, the hungry and those who thirst for righteousness, the merciful, the pure in heart, the persecuted and the peacemakers. These are the true salt and light of the world (Mat 5:1-16). In order to enter the kingdom, Christians cannot just talk—they must do 'the will of my Father who is in heaven' (Mat 7:21). In such a way God's will was fully manifested in Jesus' life: the unselfish life for others in every moment of his earthly existence as he 'made himself nothing, taking the very nature of a servant' (Phil 2:7). Employing this kind of humility of Jesus, looking after the 'least of these brothers of mine,' is the true Christian response to the message of the kingdom. For, as Brunt pointed out, 'how can we possibly be committed to the principles of God's kingdom without showing now that we accept and live by them?'[43]

However, commitment to the principles of God's kingdom here and now does not take away from the anticipation of the final fulfilment of the promises of the second phase of the same kingdom when Jesus comes. The 'kingdom of glory' is a biblical concept of the eschatological kingdom to be established by God in his own time. Jesus' command, 'Occupy till I come' has ethical implications for human rights in the world we live in. For the contemporary Christian the 'eschatological vision of our future hope actually contributes to the content or shape of our daily lives. It helps us see how we should live responsibly here and now.'[44] How we treat others in this world will not bring about the kingdom of God, but it should prove that this kingdom is in our hearts, that we are the new creatures who have entered the sphere of the kingdom of grace, and that we anticipate the fulfilment of promises of the kingdom of glory in the near future.

Applications to a modern prophetic community
Throughout our history we have concentrated on the prophets' eschatological role. However, in reality, this part of prophetic ministry is secondary to the prophets' role of calling the people back to the God-given socio-economic and ethical principles enshrined in the Ten Commandments and Jesus' elaboration in Matthew 5:17-48, and summarized in Luke 10:27. As a 'prophetic movement,' we should balance the proclamation about future events and eschatological prediction with calling people back to God-given principles of socio-economic justice, Christian ethics

---

[43] John Brunt, *Now and Not Yet* (Washington, DC: Review and Herald Publishing Association, 1987), 73. See N. T. Wright, *Surprised by Hope*.
[44] Ibid, 16.

and human rights, based on the moral law of the Old Testament and the explanation of it by the greatest of all Jewish prophets, and the founder of the Christian church—Jesus Christ. Not only should we proclaim these principles, we should also embody them in our existence. And that is where imaginary visionaries and social actionaries of the contemporary prophetic community should find their proper and needed place. As O'Mahony rightly observed: 'In biblical times justice needed a prophet. Today, as ever, prophets are needed. From its very beginnings, the Christian community had a prophetic role.'[45] We, as Seventh-day Adventist Christians, are called to fulfil this role in the contemporary world. Paulsen in his recent article 'Serving Our World, Serving Our Lord' in *Adventist World* rightly concluded:

> There is a vast difference between seeking a voice in the public discourse, and seeking to wield political power. As a church—and individuals—we have not only the right but the obligation, to be a moral voice in society; to speak clearly and eloquently on that which touches our core values. Human rights, religious freedom, public health, poverty, and injustice—these are some of the areas in which we have a God-given responsibility to advocate for those who cannot speak for themselves ...
> Through His words and actions, Christ continually reached out His hand to improve the quality of life—both spiritually and physically—of the people around Him ... In serving our neighbors with love and integrity, we also serve our Lord.[46]

This finally brings us back to our initial story in Numbers 11, the story of the unbridled greed and free-flowing prophecy. The central message of the story lies in the connection between the apparent incompatibilities. This story is particularly pertinent to us living in the twenty-first century and, I suppose, especially to those who are on the cutting edge of dealing with poverty and human injustice. Greed is the governing attitude of our world. 'Our craving for *more than enough* is the deadly sin that is already wrecking havoc on a global scale.'[47] Globalization of the world has meant that the greedy have more while there are many that have no other option but to die or fight back with undignified means. Taking Scripture seriously will enable us to see how our greed, like Israel's, may result in devastating consequences. For that we just need to glance at verses 33 and 34.

---

[45] O'Mahony, *The Fantasy of Human Rights* (1978), 139.
[46] Jan Paulsen, 'Serving Our World, Serving Our Lord,' *Adventist World*, NAD Edition, vol. 3 (May 2007), 9-10.
[47] Davis, (2001), 203.

That some of us have much more than we need is indisputable. At no time in the history of the world have people lived so much beyond the level of subsistence as we do today, and 'there is no doubt that the earth cannot indefinitely sustain the burden that our accustomed lifestyle imposes on us.'[48] The Psalmist describes their problem in a poem (Ps 78:22-25):

> ... because they had no faith in God,
> and did not trust his saving power
> [though] he had opened the doors of heaven.
> He had rained upon them manna to eat;
> The grain of heaven he had given them.
> Mortals ate bread of angels,
> He sent food *enough*.

There was enough and the Psalmist is explaining that there should have been no craving for more, as there was sufficient provision from the hand of God as, with the daily dew, he sent them manna from heaven. But we often perceive emptiness where there is sufficient provision from the hand of God. Greed, however, is simple but deadly: it kills by a kind of spiritual malnutrition. The psalmists, those brilliant spiritual diagnosticians, call it 'leanness in the soul' (Ps 106:15). 'Sufficiency is one of the chief arts of spiritual life, so that we come to see the beauty of "enough" and actually prize it over "too much."'[49]

In Numbers 11, the greed of the Israelites quite literally killed them. When the meat they had craved 'was still between their teeth, not yet chewed, they died and the place was called Graves of Craving' (vs 33.) We have to learn this lesson, bearing in mind the needs of those who will come after us in this world and those who live in other parts and are already 'have-nots.' 'We make room for them by leaving the air and water as clean as we found them, by not taking more than our share of resources that can be depleted in a few generations but take geological ages to rebuild—like oil, coal, mineral deposits, or fertile soil. The motivation for voluntary simplicity is, of course, a hunger for justice: when a few have far too much, many have too little.'[50]

This biblical story is quite disturbing, but it also contains an element of hope. One may ask how this is connected with the issue at hand—the prophetic role and what we could learn as a prophetic movement. In Numbers 11 the hope here lies in God's second extravagant answer to Israel's greed: a spirit of prophecy that

---

[48] Ibid.
[49] Ibid., 204.
[50] Ibid., 205.

fills the seventy officially appointed elders. And, subsequently, the overflow of prophetic activity runs out into the camp of ordinary Israelites, so that Eldad and Medad start speaking God's truth. And when Joshua complains that things are getting out of hand, Moses replies in verse 29: 'Would that all the Lord's people were prophets!' As Ellen David put it in the conclusion to her commentary on this passage:

> Another [important] function of the biblical prophets is to speak on behalf of the poor: those people, generally invisible to us, who suffer because of our selfishness. If we read the daily news in the light of their prophecy, we will recognize with increasing clarity that our lifestyle extracts a price from people most of us will never see in person, at least this side of the Resurrection. Third World countries have little to sell on the global market but the bones of their land—its minerals and forests—and the cheap labor of their people. They are exchanging short-term gain for ever-deepening long-term poverty as their land is stripped and their water and air are polluted, in no small part by First World industries.[51]

And Joshuas, even contemporary Christian Joshuas, dare, in their ignorance, to come and complain 'Stop them, make them shut up and quit prophesying! We should not be involved in such a prophetic task. The Lord will come and take care of this problem. Stop them!' But the proto-*nabhi* responds, 'What, are you jealous for me?' Do you think that there is no space for me, and for Eldad and Medad? 'If only all God's people were prophets!'

May God give us more Adventist prophets, with more moral prophetic imagination and more stamina for prophetic living and acting, daring to speak out for the poor, daring to challenge the powers of imperial selfishness and of globalized greed in this third millennium.

Zdravko Zack Plantak. Born in Croatia. Since 1999 chair and professor for the Religion Department, Columbia Union College, Washington, DC, USA. Pastoral experience in Great Britain, 1988-98. His book: 'Silent Church: Human Rights and Adventist Social Ethics' deals with the relationship of Seventh-day Adventism and social justice issues. PhD, University of London (1995).

---

[51] Ibid., 202.

Keepers of the Flame or Preservers of the Ashes?
To Be Faithful to the Past Means to Move Forward in the Spirit of Our Predecessors

Rolf J. Pöhler

Seventh-day Adventists like to see themselves as heirs of the Protestant Reformation. What does it mean to walk in the footsteps of the Reformers? Will the spiritual and doctrinal renewal of the church ever be completed? What implications does the *ecclesia semper reformanda* have for us today?[1]

Introduction

Five hundred years ago, on the 18th of October in the year 1502, the University of Wittenberg was founded by Frederick III, called the Wise, elector of Saxony. He named it 'Leucorea,' which means 'White Mountain.' It was here that fifteen years later a young university professor by the name of Martin Luther started a public debate on some controversial religious issues, which threw the small town of Wittenberg into the spotlight of world history. There is hardly an event that has shaped the history of Europe to a larger extent than the Protestant Reformation of the 16th century. Within a century the 'Alma Mater Vitebergensis' became the largest university in Germany, a champion of modernity known under the names of 'Humanism' and 'Renaissance,' and the intellectual and spiritual centre of European Protestantism. With fewer than 5,000 citizens, the 2,000-3,000 students who came to Wittenberg each year made up a third of the population—an unprecedented ratio.

What was it that made Wittenberg such an attractive place? What were the ideas that inspired so many German youth to choose this place as their academic home and future *alma mater*? What is the genius of Protestantism that inspires us even today to study the Reformation and its impact on the contemporary church? What makes the short (5 ft. 4 in. or 162 cm) and depressed monk-turned-rebel so fascinating? What does he have to tell us today?

The question to be asked is this: Can Seventh-day Adventist Christians, particularly young believers, walk in the footsteps of the Reformers? What does the 16th-century Reformation mean to us today? Can, should, or must we share their beliefs, imitate their behaviour, copy their attitudes? The question I am raising in this essay is even somewhat more narrowly focused: Are we as Seventh-day Ad-

---

[1] This essay was originally presented at the Second European Congress of the Students' Association of the Euro-Africa Division of Seventh-day Adventists, held in Eisenberg, Germany, November 1-3, 2002.

ventists true heirs of the Reformers or are we simply paying lip service to them? Do we merely claim their name or are we, indeed, moved by their spirit? In other words: *Are we keepers of the flame or preservers of the ashes?*

The Adventist claim revisited

Seventh-day Adventists see themselves as heirs of the Reformers, continuing and completing what they had begun. There is hardly an evangelistic series during which it is not intimated that Adventists are rightly wearing the cloak of the Reformers. The story usually goes like this: All Protestant churches began as genuine reformation movements. However, in the course of time, they became satisfied with their beliefs, stopped advancing in understanding, codified their doctrines, and ceased to grow in faith. When new, genuine reformation movements arose, they resisted and opposed them. In this way, they became traditionalists and lost their high claim to be genuine reformers. They declined spiritually as well as morally and became part of apocalyptic Babylon.

Then the Seventh-day Adventists came onto the scene. They too started as a small but genuine renewal movement. They preached the neglected Advent message, restored the biblical Sabbath, discovered the true sanctuary in heaven, and founded the remnant church having the spirit of prophecy in their midst. At this point the story usually ends. The lecture is finished, the altar call is given: Come and join the Adventists, the true reformation movement of today!

But there are some questions that need to be addressed: What has happened to Seventh-day Adventists since the time of the birth of their movement? How is our record as a reformation movement? Are we still on track, do we continue the Reformation with vigour and zeal? Or have we perhaps already completed it, having reached the culmination point after which there is no more truth to be discovered, no more doctrine to be reformed, no more behaviour to be changed? Or—allow me to ask this somewhat disturbing question—do we follow in the footsteps of our predecessors by resting on our laurels, satisfied with what we have achieved, stifling further growth, resisting the advance of truth, becoming dull traditionalists ourselves? Are we perhaps promising more than we can actually deliver? *Are we keepers of the flame or just preservers of the ashes?*

The paradox of reformation movements

There seems to be a certain paradox involved in the history of all reformation movements. Usually they begin with the firm determination to return to the Scriptures and to be faithful to all of its teachings. This sound and admirable attitude allows them to discover biblical truths that had been neglected or forgotten. Their new exegetical and doctrinal insights are then passed on to the following generations, sooner or later in some codified form (in creeds or statements of faith). Valuable as they are, these truths are highly prized and carefully protected. Any deviation from them is regarded as a denial of biblical truth and branded as error or heresy. New insights are shunned, doctrinal change is regarded as a betrayal of truth, and those claiming to have new insights are treated as heretics. Strange as it may seem, it is exactly by trying to preserve their valuable tradition that the would-be reformers of ecclesiastical traditions have become stiff traditionalists themselves.

Are Adventists an exception to this? Or are there indications that this paradoxical turn of events applies even to us? Imagine for a moment that we as Adventists had not yet discovered the biblical truth about the Sabbath, or had not yet resumed the practice of footwashing at the communion service. Suppose your pastor were to preach a sermon on Isaiah 58:12, claiming that Adventists are called to be the 'repairers of the breach.' He would then argue from Scripture that Saturday, not Sunday, is the seventh day of the week to be kept holy as a day of rest, and that we should also practice footwashing before celebrating communion.

How would we react to this? Would we be ready to accept these biblical teachings and reform our practices? Would we perhaps start a Bible study group in order to find out whether the pastor is right or not? Would we refer this issue to the General Conference for further study and decision? Or would we tell him: 'Come on, pastor, who do you think you are? There is nothing in our doctrinal tradition to support your views. If God wanted the church to accept these ideas, he would have given these insights to our pioneers long ago. Do you really think that God wants the remnant church to change its beliefs and practices at this late hour of earth's history? And, by the way, nowhere in the writings of Ellen White do we find support for your strange views. They are not found in our fundamental beliefs. Besides, it is unrealistic to expect our church members to jeopardize their jobs in order to keep the Sabbath. Neither do we see light in washing one another's feet; we serve each other in love and humility—isn't this the true meaning of footwashing, after all? No, brother, forget it. We have never done this, and we are not ready to do so now. This is no time to change our beliefs and practices; rather we should preach the truths we have and call people out of the Babel of false teachings to the true remnant church proclaiming the last message for this world.'

Honestly, I suspect that my church—and I myself—would rather search for arguments to oppose such challenging ideas than welcome and accept these insights. True, there is in our own tradition the strong impulse to accept truth whatever it may cost and wherever it may lead. For example, in 1849 John Nevins Andrews, who later became the first missionary sent by the Seventh-day Adventist church to Europe, exclaimed: 'I would exchange a thousand errors for one truth.'[2] I wonder, would we be willing today to change ten errors for one truth, or perhaps five, or

---

[2] Life *Sketches of Ellen G. White* (Mountain View, CA: Pacific Press Publishing Association, 1915), 127.

even a single one? Is the radical and idealistic attitude of young John (he was only 20 years of age at the time) still representative of us Adventists? Do we still share the *naïveté* and optimism of our pioneers? Or have we become realists shunning such high-flying dreams? Have we matured, have we come of age, or have we just become traditionalists ourselves? *Are we still keepers of the flame or preservers of the ashes?*

The true spirit of the Reformers

What, then, is the true spirit of the Reformers that should inspire us today, challenge our thinking and guide our actions? Let me give you two examples of what I think represents the true spirit of the Reformation—and of the Adventist spirit as well.

a. The early reformer Jan Hus (c. 1372-1415) wrote late in his life, 'From the beginning of my studies I have made it a rule that whenever I come to know a sounder opinion on an issue, I will gladly and humbly give up the first opinion knowing that what we know is very little in comparison to what we do not know.'[3] This attitude had made him a worthy chancellor of the University of Prague. It was the same attitude, however, that would cost him his life when he refused to deny his biblical convictions at the Diet of Constance in 1414.

For many years I have quoted this statement to my theology students at Friedensau Adventist University; was I right in doing so? I have also repeatedly asked Adventist congregations whether they thought it proper for me to challenge my students in this way. Invariably they have agreed that this attitude represents Adventism at its best! Former General Conference President Neal C. Wilson once wrote, 'No serious student of Adventist history can study our past without noting that one constant factor in Adventism has been its willingness to change.'[4]

b. When in 1521 Martin Luther was challenged at the Diet of Worms in no uncertain terms to renounce his views or face excommunication and possibly even death, he was fearful to take a clear stand and asked for some time to reconsider his views before giving a final answer. After a night of intense inner struggle, he faced the assembled authorities of state and church, courageously giving what was unquestionably his most famous testimony. After pointing out that even church councils can err and have, in fact, erred in the past—a truth which his opponents did not want to hear but could not deny—he added, 'My conscience is bound in the Word of God; therefore, I cannot and will not retract, as it is neither safe nor upright to act against one's conscience.'[5] The criterion used by Luther in evaluat-

---

[3] John Hus, 'Defensio liberi De Trinitate Magistri Joannis Wiclif,' presented in Prague on 27 July, 1410.

[4] Quoted in the *Adventist Review*, 9 July 1981.

[5] 'Mein Gewissen ist gefangen in Gottes Wort; daher kann und will ich nichts widerrufen,

ing claims of religious truth was his conscience, bound by the Scriptures and enlightened by human reason *(ratione evidente)*. As a contemporary and representative of the spirit of Humanism, he regarded reason and conscience, shaped by faith in God's Word, as proper judge of church teachings.

Centuries later Ellen G. White, the most important of the early Adventist reformer-pioneers, reflected this view when she wrote, 'In matters of conscience the soul must be left untrammeled. No one is to control another's mind, to judge for another, or to prescribe his duty. God gives to every soul freedom to think, and to follow his own convictions.'[6]

W. C. White, Ellen White's son and companion during her later years, once wrote, 'Seventh-day Adventists claim to be different from all other denominations in this: That they are willing to receive new light.' Then he hesitated and added, 'Is this so?'[7] Today, we still have reason to ask ourselves: *Are we still keepers of the flame or merely preservers of the ashes?*

The human limitations of the Reformers

The Reformers were humans, not superhuman saints. They shared in the finiteness of all humanity. They were neither inerrant in their views nor infallible in their behaviour. We should not claim more for them, nor for any other messenger or prophet sent by God to guide his church through perilous times. To turn these saintly men and women into superhuman heroes, to ignore their intellectual, moral and spiritual limitations, to treat them as the final authority on each and every issue faced by the church today, is to misuse what God has given to them and to us.

To illustrate this, let me give a few examples from the lives and times of the 16th-century Reformers.

a. There is, for example, Luther's well-known attitude towards the peasants who were yearning, not only for spiritual freedom, but also for liberation from earthly oppression, hoping for social justice. When he realized that the cause of the Reformation was seriously threatened by the peasants' uprising, Luther turned strongly against them and advised the political authorities in no uncertain terms to use all available means to stop it. Kill them! was his clear-cut advice. When the East German socialist regime in the 1980s tried to use the popular sympathies for the Reformer for their own political ends, they clearly overstated their case. Luther was no social reformer, no champion of human rights, and no pre-democratic freedom fighter.

---

da es weder sicher noch recht ist, gegen das Gewissen zu handeln.' (WA 7, 838, 4-8)
[6] Ellen G. White, *The Desire of Ages* (Mountain View, CA: Pacific Press Publishing Association, 1940), 550.
[7] W. C. White to F. E. Belden, 9 February 1888.

b. Then there is Luther's anti-Semitic language and thinking, which was in harmony with the spirit of the time. If you visit the town of Wittenberg and take a tour of the city, you will be shown at the outside wall of the city church the so-called Jewish pig ('Judensau'), a sculpture mocking Jewish religious scruples and dietary restrictions. It was already there in Luther's time, and apparently no one thought of removing it because of its slanderous nature. After all, even the great Reformer obviously didn't mind.

c. You may also have heard of Luther's strong language used in dealing with some of his opponents. These were at times true invectives ('Schimpfkanonaden'). We would hardly consider it acceptable for a sincere Christian today to use such insulting language.

d. In addition, Luther was not exactly a model representative of Christian, let alone Adventist, temperance and health reform. For example, he liked to drink beer and even had a brewery in his own house.

e. Last but not least, there is the shocking intolerance of John Calvin, the Reformer at Geneva, who even had one fellow Protestant preacher burned at the stake because he rejected infant baptism and questioned the doctrine of the Trinity. (I suspect we would have to burn quite a few church members if we followed his example today.)

Would we today be justified in holding similar views or in behaving in like manner? Can we turn our backs on the burning social issues of our societies, claiming to be in harmony with Luther himself? Is there any justification in harbouring anti-Semitic ideas or using anti-Semitic language, even in seemingly harmless jokes, by pointing to the Reformers' example? Is it morally *kosher* to denounce one's opponents—be they Roman Catholics or confessing Adventists—in abusive language by referring to the professor from Wittenberg? Should we abandon the concept of health reform because the Reformers were oblivious to it? And is it acceptable to treat those within the church who hold differing views on some doctrinal points as hopeless heretics? In other words: *Are we keepers of the flame or preservers of the ashes?*

Ecclesia semper reformanda

One of the famous Latin phrases characterizing the Protestant Reformation was the slogan *ecclesia semper reformanda*, meaning that the church of Christ is constantly and permanently in need of change and reform. Spiritual renewal, liturgical adjustment, organizational restructuring, and doctrinal change are never just a thing of the past or of the future, but also of the present. There is always a need for *aggiornamento*, the improvement of the church, the upgrading of its heritage, the reformulation of its belief, and the deepening of its faith. This is one of the most basic and important insights of the Reformers.

The 95 theses that Martin Luther posted on the door of the palace church at Wittenberg on October 31, 1517 were an attempt by a young university professor to get a scholarly debate going on the letters of indulgences *(Ablasshandel)* that enraged the conscience of Luther who was about to discover the biblical gospel of grace. In the first of his theses, the author expressed a biblical truth that is so important that it became foundational to the Protestant Reformation as a whole—and to any true reformation at that. I believe it should guide all of our thinking even today. It reads: 'As our Lord and Master Jesus Christ says, "Repent" etc. (Mat 4:17), he wanted the whole life of the believers to be repentance.'

Applying this basic insight to the church as a whole, the Reformers were fully convinced that the Christian church is in constant need of reformation: *ecclesia semper reformanda.* Do we still believe this? Does our Adventist view of the church as God's last-day remnant leave enough room for true repentance, confession of denominational sins, and the genuine desire to change for the better? Or have we become so self-assured that we no longer feel the need to change our thinking, to review our teachings critically, and to revise our actions? In other words: *Are we keepers of the flame or preservers of the ashes?*

What about our Protestant heritage?

The lasting influence of the 16th-century Reformers, particularly of Martin Luther, can be felt even today—and rightly so. As the towering figure of the Reformation, he remains important to us as exegete and theologian, Bible translator and hymn writer, university professor and confessing Christian. His deep insight into the radical nature of human failure and sin, his liberating discovery of the divine way—and the assurance—of salvation, his high regard for the Scriptures as the authoritative Word of God, his courage in the face of stiff opposition, his firm eschatological hope—all this and more can and should inspire us to become better Christians, to grow into a better church, and to build a better society.

At the same time, we should not try merely to copy the Reformers' views, to imitate their behaviour, or to duplicate their words and deeds. Not everything they believed and did is exemplary, or even normative, for us living today. We need to make sound and informed judgements with regard to the lasting aspects of our Protestant heritage, proving everything, holding fast to what is good, while discarding that which belongs on the rubbish heap of history (1 Thess 5:19-22). This task requires spiritual discernment, intellectual rigour and moral strength. In the face of this challenging and risky task of distinguishing the outstanding from the outworn, differentiating the time-proven from the time-conditioned, and selecting the valuables from the basket of tradition, I suggest that we should apply the following guiding principles.

Firstly, we should strive to emulate the *spirit (Gesinnung)* of the Reformers. Their undivided heart wholly given to God, their determination to follow the Word and will of God, their loyalty to his church on earth, their zeal and dedication—these are truly admirable and inspiring. We have every reason to follow them in this respect, to develop the same attitudes in our own lives.

Secondly, we should uphold the basic *principles (Grundsätze)* which guided the Reformers in their times. The fourfold *sola* of Reformation theology *(sola scriptura, sola gratia, sola fide, solus Christus)* is a lasting contribution to the church of all ages. It has also become foundational to Adventist thinking and we should take pains that it will remain so in the future.

Thirdly, we should learn from the *experience (Erfahrungen)* of the Reformers, applying their insights to our own times and cultural contexts. Just as following Jesus does not require us to wear sandals or beards, so following in the steps of the Reformers does not imply that we think and act exactly as they did.

In short, we should always bear the question in mind: *Are we keepers of the flame or preservers of the ashes?*

What about our own Adventist tradition?

In the context of the intense debate preceding and following the General Conference of 1888, Ellen G. White made a number of highly significant statements that have not lost their urgency and appeal a century and more later. Here are some:

> The truth is an advancing truth, and we must walk in the increasing light ... No true doctrine will lose anything by close investigation ... This light [of present truth] should lead us to a diligent study of the Scriptures, and a most critical examination of the positions which we hold. God would have all the bearings and positions of truth thoroughly and perseveringly searched, with prayer and fasting. Believers are not to rest in suppositions and ill-defined ideas of what constitutes truth ... It is important that in defending the doctrines which we consider fundamental articles of faith, we should never allow ourselves to employ arguments that are not wholly sound ... We should present sound arguments, that will ... bear the closest and most searching scrutiny.[8]

Here the prophet of the Seventh-day Adventist Church is challenging her fellow believers to study their doctrinal and other ecclesiastical traditions, to review their adequacy, to grow in their theological understanding, and even to revise their teachings, if necessary. The Preamble of the 28 Fundamental Beliefs of Seventh-

---

[8] Ellen G. White, 'Attitude to New Light,' in: *Counsels to Writers and Editors* (Nashville, TN: Southern Publishing Association, 1946), 33-42.

day Adventists, voted at the General Conference Session in 1980 and enlarged in 2005, is an impressive contemporary reflection on these inspired quotations. Recent studies in Adventist theological history, undertaken by authors like George Knight[9] and myself[10], have demonstrated that Adventists have improved and adjusted their theology repeatedly in the course of time. It can be expected that we will also do so in the future—unless we stop growing in faith and refuse to advance in our beliefs. In this case we would become traditionalists, just like others about whom we have spoken critically.

There is, then, a crucial difference between esteeming one's own tradition, on the one hand, and revering it in an almost idolatrous manner to the detriment of the church and its advancement, on the other. Containing the richness of the experiences and insights of our spiritual predecessors (warps and woofs included), tradition is an invaluable source of information, inspiration and motivation. However, it should never be used to prevent deeper studies into the truth, to stifle the intellectual progress of believers, or to hamper the doctrinal growth of the church. Tradition is like the crash barriers on an *Autobahn*, allowing cars of all shapes and sizes to travel safely at an appropriate speed. Or, to use a nautical term, tradition is like an anchor used by sailors to move a vessel stuck in a sandbar into deeper waters. This process of using an anchor to move a ship ahead, not to tie it in place, is called kedging. In this sense we should use our tradition as a kedge, i.e., as a proper means to move forward, not to stay put or even move backward. As Richard O. Stenbakken wrote: 'We can use the past to assist our progress into the future. Anchors can help us live *from* the past rather than *in* the past. Kedging keeps us sailing ahead, keeps us salient, current, and futuristic. Without values and virtues we are, literally, dangerously adrift.'[11]

Thus, while we should respect and revere our tradition, we should beware of traditionalism. One cannot be a Christian without having a high regard for the past. After all, Scripture is an ancient book, and our salvation was accomplished by Christ many centuries ago. In fact, to believe in Christ means accepting the testimony of others who lived long before us. However, in order to have a living faith, it is mandatory for us personally and individually to share the faith that is alive in the church of Christ. In the words of church historian Jaroslav Pelikan: 'Tradition is the living faith of the dead; traditionalism is the dead faith of the living.'[12]

---

[9] George R. Knight, *A Search for Identity: The Development of Seventh-day Adventist Beliefs* (Hagerstown, MD: Review and Herald Publishing Association, 2000).

[10] Rolf J. Poehler, *Continuity and Change in Adventist Teaching: A Case Study in Doctrinal Development*, Friedensauer Schriftenreihe, Series A: Theologie, vol. 3 (Frankfurt, Germany, New York, Oxford, UK, etc.: Lang, 2000).

[11] Richard O. Stenbakken, 'Kedging the Future,' *College and University Dialogue*, 14:1 (2002), 3.

[12] Jaroslav Pelikan, *The Christian Tradition: A History of the Development of Doctrine*, 5 vols. (Chicago and London, UK: University of Chicago Press, 1971-1989), 1:9.

This also holds true for Seventh-day Adventism. One can hardly be an informed Adventist without realizing how much good has come to us from our denominational past. At the same time, one cannot help but realize that Adventist church history also saw its share of errant doctrinal views and outworn practices. Some in the church attempt to restore the past, trying to lead us back to an earlier level of theological understanding. Claiming to be 'historic Adventists,' they have become champions of a fossilized faith, wooing our children and youth with their siren songs. Do we really want to follow them? *Are we keepers of the flame or preservers of the ashes?*

So what about us today?

Samuele Bacchiocchi, the widely-read Adventist author and lecturer who was known for his conservative views on issues of ethics and lifestyle, once wrote in an e-mail message, 'We need to be open minded and be willing to re-examine our beliefs. I have changed my thinking on numerous issues, as my books show. One day I may write a book on my theological development. The issue is not age but the capacity to think critically and to have the courage to change our thinking, when confronted with compelling facts.'[13] Is this view typical of Seventh-day Adventists? Or does it rather sound as if it's coming from the schismatic or heretical fringes of Adventism?

Ellen White once wrote this challenging statement: 'Ignorance does not increase the humility or spirituality of any professed follower of Christ. The truths of the divine word can be best appreciated by an intellectual Christian. Christ can be best glorified by those who serve him intelligently.'[14] Do we believe this? Are we indeed striving to be intellectual Christians, capable of giving a logical and convincing exposition of our faith? Is it our personal priority to serve God intelligently, to truly understand the Scriptures, to discover its deeper meaning which requires much time and effort? Or are we satisfied by a mediocre theological understanding? *Are we still keepers of the flame or merely preservers of the ashes?*

Summary and conclusion

Seventh-day Adventists like to see themselves as true heirs of the Protestant Reformation. In this essay, we have repeatedly asked ourselves the intriguing question: What does it mean to walk in the footsteps of the Reformers? Do we actually honour, or rather betray, their cause by codifying their religious and theological insights? What implications does the *ecclesia semper reformanda* have for us today? How can we honour our Protestant (and Adventist) tradition without becoming

---

[13]   Samuele Bacchiocchi, Email to <sdanet.org> 20 April 2000.
[14]   Ellen G. White, *Counsels to Parents, Teachers, and Students Regarding Christian Education* (Mountain View, CA: Pacific Press Publishing Association), 361.

traditionalists? The answer I have suggested can be summarized like this: To be faithful to the past means to move forward in the spirit of our predecessors. This is to say that we should emulate their attitude, uphold their principles, and learn from their experiences while, at the same time, constantly advancing in the understanding and appreciation of revealed truth. Or, in the words of Jean Juares: *'Take from the altar of the past the fire, not the ashes!'*

Rolf J. Pöhler. Born in Germany. Since 2007 lecturer at Friedensau Adventist University, Germany. Pastoral, teaching and administrative experience. President of the North German Union Conference 2002-2004. Theological Advisor to the North German Union Conference. Author of books and articles. ThD, Andrews University (1995).

Exploring the Frontiers of Faith

PART II
Biblical and Theological Studies

1 Chronicles 16:8-36 as Literary Source and Theological Frame of Reference for Revelation 14:6-7

Wim Altink

That the book of Revelation is replete with Old Testament allusions is generally recognized by New Testament scholarship. The purpose of this chapter is to probe the Old Testament literary background to one such passage in the Apocalypse, Rev 14:6-7.[1]

Introductory observations

It will be noted that in Rev 14:7 the proclamation of the first angel (in the series of three messages from vs 6 to vs 11) contains four key words or expressions: 'fear' (phobeō), 'glory' (doxa), 'judgement' (krisis), and 'worship' (proskuneō).[2] These four words can be traced back to 1 Chr 16:8-36, David's psalm of thanksgiving at the return of the ark of the covenant and its reinstatement into the tent of worship in Jerusalem (cf. vs 1-7).

This psalm has parallels in three other psalms of the Psalter, which either have drawn upon it or provide the source from which it is constituted: Ps 96 (1 Chr 16:23-33); 105:1-15 (1 Chr 16:8-22); and 106:1, 47-48 (1 Chr 16:34-36). In addition, Ps 29 has a partial parallel with 1 Chr 16:23-33.[3] Among these various sections in the Psalter, only Ps 96 contains the four key expressions of Rev 14:7. However, in one case a different Greek word is used in Ps 96 (LXX, Ps 95); and the broader contextual parallels between 1 Chr 16 and Rev 14 are also lacking in Ps 96. For these reasons, 1 Chr 16:8-36 gives the best evidence for being the basic biblical literary background for Rev 14:6-7.[4]

---

[1] This chapter is an adaptation of two articles that I wrote for *Andrews University Seminary Studies*: '1 Chronicles 16:8-36 as Literary Source for Revelation 14:6-7.' *AUSS* 22 (1984), 187-196 and 'Theological Motives for the Use of 1 Chronicles 16:8-36 as Background for Revelation 14:6-7.' *AUSS* 24 (1986), 211-221.

[2] The combination of these four key words can also be found in Rev 11:13-19 and 19:1-10, the only other New Testament passages where all four do occur in combination.

[3] It is not of significance for our study whether the three sections in the Psalter provided the sources for 1 Chr 16:8-36, or whether 1 Chr 16:8-36 was the original piece from which materials were taken and placed into separate Psalms. For a discussion of the issues, see, e.g., E. L. Curtis and A. A. Madsen, *A Critical and Exegetical Commentary on the Books of Chronicles*, ICC (Edinburgh, UK: Charles Scribner's Sons, 1965), 221-224; H. Gese, 'Die Entstehung der Büchereinteilung des Psalters,' in Josef Schreiner, ed., *Wort, Lied, und Gottesspruch: Beiträge zu Psalmen und Propheten. Festschrift für Joseph Ziegler* (Würzburg, 1972), 2:61-62; T. C. Butler, 'A Forgotten Passage from a Forgotten Era (1 Chr. XVI 8-36),' *VT* 28 (1978), 142-150; and A. E. Hill, 'Patchwork Poetry or Reasoned Verse? Connective Structure in I Chronicles 16,' *VT* 33 (1983), 97-101.

[4] It must be recognized, of course, that the book of Revelation often has multiple literary sources for a given passage or even a given symbol.

With regard to extra-biblical sources, there are two passages in the Qumran 'War Scroll' (1QM) that have some parallels with Rev 14:6-7, primarily with respect to the occurrence of the four key words or expressions that have been mentioned above. These passages are 1QM 12:6-17 and 19:1-8, with the latter being basically a repetition of the former (with some minor changes). Both of these 1QM passages are so contextually different from 1 Chr 16 and Rev 14:6-7 that they can categorically be dismissed as furnishing the basic literary background for the wording of the latter text.

The four key words
phobeō, 'fear' — In 1 Chr 16:8-36 and Rev 14:6-7, there is a call to 'fear God.' The first angel in Rev 14:7 begins his message thus—phobēthēte ton theon. In 1 Chr 16:8-36, LXX, two forms of phobeō occur: phoberos in vs 25, within the statement, 'Great is the Lord and most worthy of praise; he is to be feared' (megas kurios ... phoberos ...); and phobethetō in vs 30, in the command, 'Fear before his presence, all the earth' (phobēthētō apo prosōpou autou pasa ē gē).

doxa, 'glory' –As with phobeō, doxa is linked with God in the two passages under consideration. The second clause in the angel's proclamation in Rev 14:7 is a command to 'give him [God] glory' (dote autoi doxan). In 1 Chr 16:8-36, the word doxa occurs four times: 'Declare his glory [doxan] among the nations' (vs 24); 'glory [doxa] and majesty are before him' (vs 27); 'ascribe to the Lord the glory [doxan] and strength' (vs 28); and 'ascribe to the Lord the glory [doxan] due to his name' (vs 29).

krisis/krinō, 'judgement'/'judge' —The third clause in the angel's message in Rev 14:7 refers to judgement: 'for the hour of his [God's] judgement has come' (oti ēlthen hē ōra tēs kriseōs). This statement is remarkably close to a statement in 1 Chr 16:33 – 'for he [God] is come to judge the earth' (oti ēlthe krinai tēn gēn).

Moreover, the term 'judgements' occurs in 1 Chr 16:12, 14—in the expressions, 'Remember his [the Lord's] marvellous works that he has done, his wonders, and the judgements [krimata] of his mouth'; and 'he is the Lord our God; his judgements [krimata] are in all the earth.' It is noteworthy that in each instance 'judgement' or 'judgements' are ascribed to God.

It is of interest to notice, too, that in David's psalm of thanksgiving, several aspects of judgement are in view—the historical and local, on the one hand, and the eschatological and universal, on the other. By way of contrast, only the universal dimension is depicted in Rev 14:7. Here all nations, peoples, etc., are envisaged in this apocalyptic picture.

proskuneō, 'worship'—The last of the four key words in Rev 14:7 is 'worship': 'Worship [proskunēsate] him who made the heavens ...' The same verb is found in 1 Chr 16:29, LXX: 'Worship [proskynēsate] the Lord.'

The foregoing survey concerning the four key words or expressions in Rev 14:7—*phobeō, doxa, krisis, and proskuneō* – shows that the Apocalypse uses a combination of words (and the related themes) appearing in 1 Chr 16:8-36. This survey is a first, and important, step in the line of evidence that reveals David's psalm of thanksgiving to be a basic literary source for the language of Rev 14:6-7. To some further evidences in support of this conclusion we now turn.

Other similarities in language and conceptualization between 1 Chr 16:8-36 and Rev 14:6-7
Besides the four words discussed above, there is another remarkable similarity in expression between 1 Chr 16:8-36 and Rev 14:7, and we find additional similarities that may be noted when comparing the preceding verse in Rev 14 (vs 6) with the passage in 1 Chronicles.

ouranos kai gē ... ('heaven and earth ...'). The concluding command of the first angel's proclamation in Rev 14:7 is to worship 'him who made the heaven and the earth and the sea and springs of water' (*toi poiēsanti ton ouranon kai tēn gēn kai tēn thalassan kai pēgas udatōn*). The words *toi poiēsanti ton ouranon* are very close to some phraseology in 1 Chr 16:26: 'o theos ēmōn ouranon epoiēsen', 'our God made the heavens.'

It should also be noted that in 1 Chr 16:31-32 the triad of 'heaven,' 'earth,' and 'sea' is mentioned, as in Rev 14:7, though in a somewhat different setting: 'Let the heaven [o ouranos] be glad, and let the earth [hē gē] rejoice ... Let the sea [hē thalassa] roar, with all that fills it.' (Nevertheless, this statement, though not explicitly referring to creation, is within the general context of the praise of God in vs 26 because 'the Lord made the heavens.') The one phrase in Rev 14:7 without parallel in 1 Chr 16:8-36 is *pēgas udatōn*, 'springs of water.'

On the other hand, 1 Chr 16:32b-33 adds further expressions too: 'Let the fields rejoice, and all that is in them; then shall the trees of the forest sing at the presence of the Lord, because he comes to judge the world.' The import of the last clause should not be overlooked when drawing parallels with Rev 14:6-7; for the reference to heaven, earth, sea, etc., in David's psalm, vs 26-33, is related to the reference to God's coming in judgement—just as in the Apocalypse the reference to heaven, earth, sea, and springs of water is also connected with the mention of the coming of God's judgement.

Expressions in Revelation 14:6
Several expressions in Rev 14:6 deserve notice here because of their use also in 1 Chr 16:8-36, LXX, though in somewhat different ways or contexts. The most striking of these pertains to the proclamation of the gospel to every 'nation [*ethnos*], kindred, tongue, and people [*laon*]' (Rev 14:6), as compared with the phraseology about the wilderness wanderings of ancient Israel (1 Chr 16:20)—'They went from

nation to nation [apo ethnous eis ethnos], and from one kingdom to another people [laon heteron].' The terms *ethnos*, 'nation,' and *laos*, 'people,' are obviously key
ones here. And it should also be noted that the same is true in 1 Chr 16:24, which
furnishes another close parallel to the wording in Rev 14:6. The text in 1 Chr 16:24
reads, 'Declare among the nations [exēgeisthe en tois ethnesi] his [God's] glory,
among all the peoples [pasi tois laois] his marvellous deeds.'

A further commonality in expression involves the phrase 'eternal gospel' in
Rev 14:6 [*euaggelion eiōnion*]. 1 Chr 16:36 proclaims a beatitude to the Lord 'from
everlasting to everlasting' [apo tou aiōnos kai eōs tou aiōnos]. And although the
term euaggelion, 'gospel,' in Rev 14:6 does not occur in 1 Chr 16:8-36, a statement
in vs 23 does provide an interesting point of comparison in thought: 'Proclaim
his [God's] salvation from day to day' [anaggeilate ex ēmeras eis ēmeran sōtērion
autou].

Synopsis of 1 Chronicles 16:23-26 and Revelation 14:6-7

The closest parallels structurally between David's psalm of thanksgiving and Rev
14:6-7 may be limited to the section of 1 Chr 16: 23-26. The parallels here are sufficiently close that a synopsis may be outlined as follows:

1 Chronicles 16		*Revelation 14*	
vs 23:	Sing [asate] to the Lord, all the earth [pasa hē gē];	vs 3:	And they sing [adousin]...
vs 23: (cont.)	proclaim ... his salvation [anaggeilate ... sotērion autou].	vs 6:	Then I saw another angel flying in the midst of heaven, having the eternal gospel to proclaim [euaggelisai euaggelion aiōnion]
vs 24:	Declare ... his glory [exēgeisthe ... tēn doxan autou]*		
vs 24: (cont., with some repetition)	... among the nations [en tois ethnesi] ...* among all the peoples [en pasi tois laois] his marvellous deeds.	vs 6: (cont.)	,to those who dwell on the earth [tous kathēmenous epi tēs gēs], to every nation [pan ethnos] and tribe and language and people [laon], saying in a loud voice:
vs 25:	... He [God] is to be feared [phoberos estin] ...	vs 7:	'Fear God [phobēthēte ton theon]: worship him
vs 26:	... our God made the heavens [ho theos ēmôn ouranous epoiēse].		who made the heavens [tō poiēsanti ton ouranon] ...

(* In vs 24, the expression 'among the nations' belongs in the ellipsis within the first excerpt, and 'declare' and 'his glory' belong within the two ellipses of the second excerpt. Thus, the literal rendering is as follows: 'Declare among the nations his glory, among all the peoples his marvellous deeds.')

A theological frame of reference

A point of particular interest theologically is the direct relationship of the ark of the covenant not only to David's psalm of thanksgiving, mentioned earlier (cf. 1 Chr 16:1), but also to the scene in Rev 14:6-7. It has been shown that in the structure of the book of Revelation, the vision of the ark of the covenant seen in heaven (11:19) is a prelude or 'victorious vision' for the entire section of Revelation from 12:1 to 14:20.[5] Thus, there is a striking parallel between the settings or occasions for the similar language used in 1 Chr 16:8-36 and Rev 14:6-7. Both passages are placed within the setting of some sort of manifestation of God's ark of the covenant, with its double feature of containment of God's Ten-Commandment law and the presence of the mercy seat. That the Apocalypse thus draws attention to the ark of the covenant by employing vocabulary of 1 Chr 16:8-36 finds further illumination in Rev 14:12, where 'the commandments of God' and 'the faith of Jesus' are mentioned. This indicates that the three angels' messages stress both the 'everlasting gospel' (cf. Rev 14:6) and the 'commandments of God' (note the implications in all three messages in vs 6-11).

The central theological concern in both instances embraces the covenant, as represented by the ark of the covenant. David's Psalm is prepared for, and sung in, the setting of the bringing of the ark of the covenant into Jerusalem after its having remained twenty years in Kirjath-jearim subsequent to its recapture from the Philistines. The section of the book of Revelation in which the proclamation of the first angel occurs is similarly introduced by a reference to 'the ark of testimony'—on this occasion, in the 'temple in heaven' (11:19).[6] In the two passages themselves—1 Chr 16:8-36 and Rev 14:6-7—as well as in their broader contexts, there are evidences of this underlying theological motif and of other, related, theological affinities between these passages.

The ark of covenant in the context of David's psalm of thanksgiving

As already noted above, the occasion for David's psalm of thanksgiving in 1 Chr 16:8-36 was the bringing of the ark of the covenant into Jerusalem, 'David's own city.' Indeed, the psalm of thanksgiving is introduced as follows: 'That day David

---

[5] Cf. K. A. Strand, *Interpreting the Book of Revelation*, 2nd ed. (Naples, FL: Ann Arbor Publishers, 1979), 48. Cf. also the outline on 51 and the diagram on 52.

[6] It seems clear that Rev 11:19 furnishes the introductory heavenly vision for the major section in Revelation that concludes with 14:20. See K. A. Strand, *Interpreting the Book of Revelation*, 2nd ed. (Naples, FL: Ann Arbor Publishers, 1979), 48.

first committed to Asaph and his associates this psalm of thanks to the Lord.' Thus, 1 Chr 16:8-36 was written with a special focus on the ark—a fact that is further substantiated by statements in 16:37 and 17:1, after the conclusion of the psalm itself.

As we look at the broader context for David's psalm of thanks, it is interesting to note that there is a remarkably high frequency of the terms 'ark of the covenant' and 'ark' (in reference to the ark of the covenant) in chapters 13-17, second only to the frequency of these terms in the book of Joshua. In these chapters of 1 Chronicles in the LXX the terms kibōtos tēs diathēkēs ('ark of the covenant') and kibōtos ('ark') occur, in fact, no fewer than thirty-one times.[7] Thus, in comparison with the whole of the Old Testament, the emphasis on the ark of the covenant in these chapters is by no means insignificant and is surely more than incidental.

Other key terms in the psalm of thanksgiving referring to the ark of the covenant
Apart from the terms 'ark of God,' 'ark of the Lord,' and 'ark of the covenant' that occur in 1 Chr 16 (see vs 1, 4, 6, 37), there are other words and expressions in the psalm of thanksgiving itself that appear to stand as synonyms for this ark. G. Henton Davies has pointed out, for example, that in the Psalter such terms as 'might,' 'before Yahweh,' and 'glory, beauty, honour' are at times used in this way.[8] Although his argument relates to certain psalms in the Psalter, it seems pertinent also for David's psalm of thanksgiving in 1 Chr 16.

Redemption and law
The basic double feature of the ark of the covenant is its containment of the Decalogue and the presence of the mercy seat. Thus, law and redemption are two major aspects that stand out clearly in the very existence and function of the ark.

Redemption—Taking a closer look at 1 Chr 16:8-36 and Rev 14:6-7, we find a parallel between the two in the motif of mercy and redemption. In the psalm of thanksgiving there are statements such as these, for example: 'He [Yahweh] remembers his covenant for ever; ... to you will I [Yahweh] give the land of Canaan as the portion you will inherit. When they [Israel] were but few in number, few indeed and strangers in it, they wandered from nation to nation ... He allowed no man to oppress them; for their sake he rebuked kings: do not touch my anointed ones; do my prophets no harm' (1 Chr 16:15, 18-22). The same motif is underscored by the call to 'remember the wonders he [Yahweh] has done' (vs 12).

The connection with the covenant (and the ark of the covenant) must not be overlooked here. Also, it is important to note that the LXX term for the ark's cover, 'mercy seat' (ilastē rion) is the very same word used in the New Testament with

---

[7] See Edwin Hatch and Henry A. Redpath, *A Concordance to the Septuagint*, vol. 2 (Grand Rapids, MI: Baker Academic, 1954), 763-764.

[8] G. Henton Davies, 'Ark of the Covenant,' *IDB*, 1:222-226.

respect to Christ's redemptive sacrifice: 'For all have sinned and fall short of the glory of God and are justified freely by his grace and redemption that came by Christ Jesus. God presented him as a sacrifice of atonement [ilastērion] through faith in his blood' (Rom 3:23-25; cf. also Heb 9:5).[9] Thus, the mercy-seat in the Israelite tabernacle became a type of the redemptive mission of Jesus—which is the heart of the 'everlasting gospel' (in addition to Rom 3 and other references in the Pauline epistles, cf. Lk 2:10-11, 30-32, 39; 4:18-19; John 3:14-18; Rev 1:5-6; 5:6-10; et al.).

Another theme which points to the redemptive motif represented by the ark of the covenant is that of divine judgement. In both Rev 14:6-7 and 1 Chr 16:8-36 the joy of gospel ('good news') is connected with judgement: the proclamation of the 'eternal gospel' by the first angel includes the statement that 'the hour of his [God's] judgement has come' (Rev 14:7), while in the psalm of thanksgiving there is reference to 'singing for joy before the Lord, for he comes to judge the earth' (1 Chr 16:33). Judgement for the believer is basically good news, inasmuch as it assures deliverance. As stated by W. Schneider, 'He who judges brings salvation, peace and deliverance, especially to the persecuted and oppressed (cf. Deut 10:18).'[10]

The law—Aside from the 'mercy-seat' cover on the ark of the covenant, the other main feature of the ark to which we have referred is the Ten-Commandment law of God that was placed inside it. In this connection, the four key words of Rev 14:6-7 treated in the first part of this chapter— 'glory,' 'fear,' 'judgement,' and 'worship'—have a correlating significance, to which we may give brief attention here.

'Glory' –In the Old Testament the term 'glory' (kabod) is used for the revelation of God himself. As stated by S. Aalen, it 'expresses itself above all in salvation history, i.e. in God's great acts (Ex 14:17f; Ps 96:3), and especially in God's presence in the sanctuary (Ex 40:34f; 1 Kgs 8:10f; Ps 26:8).'[11] And W. Dyrness has pointed out that 'it [glory] rested in particular where God was to be worshipped, in the temple.'[12] In 1 Sam 4:21, the loss of the ark of God to the Philistines meant that 'the glory was departed from Israel' (vs 21). The event was reflected in the name Ichabod ('Where is glory?'). Dyrness also points out that in biblical use, the term 'glory' has a double meaning: 'The idea of glory is used in the double sense of showing respect (or glorifying) and of that which inspires such respect.'[13] This double meaning of glory (glory from God, and glory to God) fits well with the

---

[9] In the LXX, all the occurrences of ilastērion refer to the mercy-seat. See Ex 25:17, 18, 19, 20, 21, 22; 31:7; 35:11; 37:6, 7, 8, 9; Lev 16:2, 13, 14, 15; Num 7:89; Ezek 43:14, 17, 20; Amos 9:1.

[10] W. Schneider, 'κρίμα,' *New International Dictionary of New Testament Theology* (hereinafter *NID New Testament*), ed. Colin Brown (Grand Rapids, MI: Zondervan, 1975), 2:363.

[11] S. Aalen, 'δόχα,' *NID New Testament*, 2:45.

[12] W. Dyrness, *Themes in Old Testament Theology* (Downers Grove, IL: InterVarsity Press, 1979), 43.

[13] Ibid., 42.

overall concept regarding the ark of the covenant, where the love from God (his presence) meets man's love to God (in keeping his commandments).

'*Fear*'–In referring to the biblical term 'fear,' W. Mundle states: 'God's grace and favour do not abolish the solemnity of the address [to fear]. It demands man's total obedience.'[14] Fearing God is not merely a feeling or a certain state of the mind, but is expressed in one's action. The fear of God and the commandments are linked together. As Mundle further states, 'The fear of God is the first essential motive in the laws of the Pentateuch (Lev 19:14, 32; Deut 13:11; 17:13 etc.).'[15]

'*Judgement*'— We have noted in the previous section of this article the relation of the judgement theme to that of redemption. It is important at this juncture to note, as well, its connection to the concept of law. In both 1 Chr 16:8-36 and Rev 14:6-7 there is an obvious link between judgement and God's commandments. For instance, 1 Chr 16:33 states: 'They will sing for joy before the Lord, for he comes to judge the earth.' This is a reference in which, as we have already noticed, judgement is correlated with the ark of the covenant. In Rev 14:6-7, the call is sent forth to 'fear God ... because the hour of his judgement has come.' In the same general context, we find an explicit reference to God's commandments: 'This calls for patient endurance on the part of the saints, who keep God's commandments and have the faith of Jesus' (vs 12).[16]

'*Worship*' –The original meaning of 'worship' (proskuneō) is 'to kiss.' In the ancient Greek world, one prostrated oneself on the ground in order to worship a deity. This heathen worship was connected with images; but 'the God of Israel is worshipped without images and therefore is not within the grasp of the worshipper. Proskuneō retains its physical sense of bending, however, except that this is understood as bowing to the will of the exalted One (cf. Ex 12:17f).' [17] Moreover, the root concept of proskuneō as 'kissing [the soil]' (or in the biblical context, 'bending [to the will of God]') indicates a connection between worship and God's commandments, in that a person's attitude in worship expresses itself foremost in willingness to do the will of God (i.e. to keep his commandments). H. Schönweiss and C. Brown have put it nicely, in stating that 'man's relation to God is expressed principally in worship, and above all in prayer. The call to conversion can therefore be put in the form: "Worship God!" i.e. recognize him in all his power and glory as creator and judge, acknowledge his exclusive sovereign rights and claim upon you (Rev. 14:7).'[18]

---

[14] Mundle, 'φόβος,' *NID New Testament*, 1: 622.

[15] Ibid.

[16] Another link between judgement and the commandments is the fact that divine judgement proceeds from the sanctuary, where the commandments were; cf. 1 Kgs 22:19; Ps 9:4, 7, 8, ll; 76:8, 9; 102:19, 20; Mic 1:3-5; Ezek 1:8-10; Mal 3:1-5; Isa 18:4; Amos 1:2; Rev 7:15; 11:19; 14:15, 17; 15:5, 6, 8; 16:1, 17.

[17] H. Schönweiss and C. Brown, 'προσκυνέω,' *NID New Testament*, 2: 876.

[18] Ibid., 2:877.

In the book of Revelation proskuneō has a high frequency of occurrence: 24 times of the New Testament total of 59! Those who 'remain faithful to Jesus' (Rev 14:12) are those who worship Jesus in spirit and truth (cf. John 4:22-24), who are not deceived or intimidated by the dragon of Rev 12 and the two beasts of Rev 13. It is not accidental that the main section of the book of Revelation in which the message of 14:6-7 occurs is introduced by a vision of the 'ark of the testimony' in 'the temple in heaven' (11:19). Nor is it coincidental that the 'commandments of God'are specifically mentioned in conjunction with the 'testimony of Jesus' in identifying God's loyal 'remnant'—those against whom the dragon manifests special wrath (12:17).

The creation motif and the law of God

In addition to the occurrence of the four key-words, 'glory,' 'fear,' 'judgement,' and 'worship,' a further connecting link between the Decalogue and the message of Rev 14:6-7 is the mention of God as Creator: 'Worship him, who made the heavens, the earth, the sea and the springs of water' (Rev 14:7). A marginal note to Rev 14:7 in Nestle-Aland's Greek edition of the New Testament refers to Ex 20:11 ('the Lord made the heavens and the earth, the sea ...'), a part of the Sabbath commandment in the Decalogue.[19]

Paralleling aspects of the covenantal form in 1 Chronicles 16 and Revelation 14

W. H. Shea and K. A. Strand have drawn attention to the occurrence of a covenantal form, similar to that of the ancient Hittite suzerainty treaties, in the seven letters to the seven churches in Revelation[20] and in the entire book of Revelation.[21] The two authors refer to the work of George Mendenhall, who pioneered the study of the Hittite suzerainty-treaty formulary as it was reflected in ancient Israel.[22] Five of the most basic elements in that particular formulary are the following:[23] (1) preamble, in which the king as author of the covenant mentioned his name, titles, attributes, etc.; (2) historical prologue, which looked back upon the earlier relationship between the two parties of the covenant; (3) the stipulations, mentioning the obligations of the vassal; (4) the witnesses, which were the gods of the two parties in the extra-biblical treaties, but were other elements in monotheistic

[19] Nestle-Aland, *Novum Testamentum Graece* (Stuttgart, Germany: Deutsche Bibelgesellschaft, 1927).

[20] W. H. Shea, 'The Covenantal Form of the Letters to the Seven Churches,' *AUSS* 21(1983), 71-84.

[21] K. A. Strand, 'A Further Note on the Covenantal Form in the Book of Revelation,' *AUSS* 21(1983), 251-264.

[22] G. E. Mendenhall, *Law and Covenant in Israel and the Ancient Near East* (Pittsburgh, PA: Biblical Colloquium, 1955).

[23] The summary is from Shea, 72.

Yahwism; and (5) the blessings and curses, pertaining to the matter of the vassal's future obedience or disobedience to the covenant.

Interestingly, elements of these five basic aspects of the formulary can also be found in both 1 Chr 16:8-36 and Rev 14:6-7—albeit, not in a clear-cut sequence (which was not necessarily even the case with regard to the Hittite examples themselves). The occurrence of this kind of covenantal language in both of these passages is in harmony with the focus of these passages on the centrality of the covenant concept, including its tangible expression in the ark of the covenant. Below, I highlight some of the common aspects, dealing first with David's psalm of thanksgiving and then the message of the 'first angel' in Rev 14.

1 Chronicles 16

Preamble

'Lord' (vs 8)
'He is the Lord our God' (vs 14).
'For great is the Lord' (vs 25).
'The Lord made the heavens' (vs 26).
'God our Saviour' (vs 35).
'God of Israel' (vs 36).

Historical prologue

'Tell of all his wonderful acts' (vs 9).
'Remember the wonders he has done, miracles and judgements he pronounced' (vs 12).
'The covenant he made with Abraham, the oath he swore to Isaac, he confirmed it to Jacob as a decree, to Israel as an everlasting covenant' (vs 16-18).
'He allowed no man to oppress them, for their sake he rebuked kings' (vs 21).

Stipulations

'Give thanks to the Lord, call on his name' (vs 8).
'Make known among the nations what he has done' (vs 8).
'Sing to him,' 'sing praise to him' (vs 9).
'Tell of all his wonderful acts' (vs 9).
'Glory in his name' (vs 10).
'Look to the Lord' (vs 11).
'Declare his glory' (vs 24).
'Ascribe to the Lord glory and strength' (vs 28).
'Ascribe to the Lord the glory due to his name' (vs 29).

'Bring an offering and come before him' (vs 29).
'Worship the Lord' (vs 29).
'Give thanks to the Lord' (vs 34).

Witnesses

'Let the heavens rejoice, let the earth be glad' (vs 31).
'Let the sea resound' (vs 32).
'Let the fields be jubilant and everything in them' (vs 32).
'The trees of the forest will sing' (vs 33).

Blessings and curses

'He remembers his covenant forever' (vs 15).
'His love endures forever' (vs 34).

Revelation 14

Preamble

'Lamb' (vs 1, 4, 5)
'God' (vs 7)
'Him, who made the heavens, the earth, the sea and the springs of water' (vs 7).

Historical prologue

Eternal gospel (vs 6): i.e., what Christ has done to save mankind (cf. the background in 13:8 and 14:1-5 concerning the Lamb's redemptive work).

Stipulations

'Fear God' (vs 7),
'Give him glory' (vs 7),
'Worship him' (vs 7).
Obedience to God's commandments (vs 12)
Faith of Jesus (vs 12)

Witnesses

Three angels (vs 6, 8, 9)
Heavens, earth, sea and the springs of water (vs 7)
The Spirit (vs 13)

Blessings and curses

'Blessed are the dead who die in the Lord from now on ... they will rest from their labour, for their deeds will follow them' (vs 13).

'If anyone worships the beast and his image and receives his mark on the fore-head or on the hand, he, too, will drink of the wine of God's fury, which has been poured full strength into the cup of his wrath, he will be tormented with burning sulphur in the presence of the holy angels and of the Lamb. And the smoke of their torment rises for ever and ever. There is no rest day or night for those who worship the beast and his image or for anyone who receives the mark of his name' (vs 9-11).

Conclusions

The evidence with regard to the similarity of key words (especially the four words phobeō, doxa, krisis, proskuneō), the use of words, and the structure between 1 Chr 16:8-36 and Rev 14:6-7 strongly suggests that 1 Chr 16:8-36 has been the basic Old Testament literary source for Rev 14:6-7. Another Old Testament passage, Ps 96, though nearly identical to 1 Chr 16:23-33, is lacking in several features wherein there is closeness between the latter passage and Rev 14:6-7. Apart from 1 Chr 16:8-36 and Ps 96, there are no other passages in the Old Testament that have a combination of the four key expressions of Rev 14:7.

The similarity between the Hebrew of 1 Chr 16:8-36 and 1QM 12:6-17 (and 1QM 19:1-8), with respect especially to the four key expressions discussed in the beginning section of this essay, suggests that this material in the Qumran litera-ture was possibly built on 1 Chr 16:8-36. But it is sufficiently different in context and structure as to rule it out as basic background to Rev 14:6-7. I have found no other places in intertestamental Jewish literature where the four key words are connected.

Both the text of 1 Chr 16:8-36 and its context point to the ark of the covenant, as is also true with regard to Rev 14:6-12 and its context (including, in the latter case, the explicit mention of the ark in Rev 11:19). The two-faceted aspect of the ark—gospel and law—is manifested in both passages. And moreover, five basic components of the ancient covenant formulary— preamble, historical prologue, stipulations, witnesses, blessings and curses—can be traced in both 1 Chr 16 and Rev 14. Thus, the attention that is drawn to the ark itself (with the mercy seat and Decalogue as integral to it), plus the occurrence of elements of the covenant formu-lary, in both 1 Chr 16:8-36 and Rev 14:6-7 (and their contexts), reveals a common underlying motif and a motivational basis for the use of the former passage as background for the latter—namely, the centrality of the ark of the covenant.

Wim Altink. Born in the Netherlands. Since 2007 president of the Netherlands Union. Studied in the Netherlands, Great Britain and the United States. Pastoral, evangelistic and administrative experience in the Netherlands for 26 years. MDiv. Andrews University, 1984. Doctoral candidate, University of Wales.

The Exodus-Motif in Psalm 23

Radiša Antić

The Bible teaches that God moulds the overall process of history. He intervenes in particular events in history (for instance, the exodus from Egypt) and he will bring his plans to a victorious fulfilment at the end of time.[1] Consequently, the biblical view of history is linear in the sense that the world has its beginning (creation) and is moving towards its *finale*, as predetermined by God.[2] If such a world-view is embraced and sincerely trusted, it could greatly contribute to the mental balance and spiritual health of human beings, because the feelings of solitude and abandonment in society and in the universe are some of the main causes of the *angst* that prevails in the world.

Psalm 23 has gained immortality by virtue of the trust and confidence expressed by its author in God who is the Lord of history and consequently of human life and who, through his providence, leads the events of this world to a future climax.[3] The sweet charm and the religious feelings expressed in Psalm 23 speak about a heart which has passed through many bitter experiences and battles, as well as the perfect peace of mind that comes from a childlike trust in God.[4] As is the case in many other instances in the Old Testament, the personal experiences of the author of Psalm 23 may be seen as collective: the local becomes universal. What makes this psalm one of the most successful texts in human history is not only its present importance for the spiritual life of a believer, but the possibility of understanding its meaning eschatologically. Namely, the author is using the exodus terminology,[5] the redemption from Egypt, apparently in order to point to the final eschatological exodus of those 'living in the land of the shadow of death' (Mat 4:16). Psalm 23 also talks about the spiritual transformation of the believer who is ready to walk on a daily basis with God, and who eagerly looks forward towards the day when the Lord of history will come and will dwell with his people under the same roof.

There have been several suggestions concerning the structure of Psalm 23.[6]

---

[1] 'History' in: Sinclair B. Ferguson and David F. Wright, eds., *New Dictionary of Theology* (Downers Grove, IL: InterVarsity Press, 1988).

[2] See Radisa Antic, *Put, Istina I Zivot* (Beograd: Preporod, 1998), 95.

[3] Arthur Weiser, *The Psalms* (Philadelphia, PA: The Westminster Press, 1962), 227; Peter C. Craigie, 'Psalms 1-50,' *Word Bible Commentary* (Waco, TX: Word Books, 1983), vol. 19, 204.

[4] See Weiser, 227.

[5] Craigie, 205.

[6] See A. L. Merrill, 'Psalm xxiii and the Jerusalem Tradition,' *Vetus Testamentum* 15 (1965), 355.

Some have suggested that the two basic pictures are God as the Shepherd and God as the Host, while others have suggested a tripartite division: the Shepherd, the Wanderer and the Host.[7] However, it seems that a structure utilising four basic images is the closest to the reality of the text: the Shepherd, the Comforter, the Host and the Father of the House.[8] This structure expresses a movement, the advancement of the intimate relationship between the believer and his God, and finally culminates at the moment when 'God himself will be with them and be their God' (Rev 21:3).

God the Shepherd

The metaphor of 'God the Shepherd' (vs 1-4) is pregnant with meaning, illustrating the character of the relationship between the psalmist and his God: God provides and protects. This metaphor is used very often in the Old Testament to describe Yahweh as 'Shepherd of Israel' (Ps 80:1; 28:9; 78:52; 79:13; 95:7; 100:3; Isa 40:11). In order to understand the concept of 'God the Shepherd' it is important to remember that some of the main characters in the Bible were shepherds: Abel, Abraham, Jacob and Isaac among the most prominent. Jesus himself said: 'I am the good shepherd; I know my sheep and my sheep know me' (John 10:14). But, for the correct comprehension of the concept of 'shepherd' in Psalm 23, it is of the utmost importance to grasp what kind of shepherd David, the author of this psalm, was. In an emotional speech he attempted to explain to king Saul what his relationship to his sheep was: 'Your servant has been keeping his father's sheep. When a lion or a bear came and carried off a sheep from the flock, I went after it, struck it and rescued the sheep from its mouth. When it turned on me, I seized it by its hair, struck it and killed it' (1 Sam 17:34, 35).

The incidents described here happened in the Judean desert far away from the public eye. There was nobody to see David's bravery and courage, nobody to applaud, nobody to praise it to somebody else. It seems that in today's world the typical, average human relationship is established on the basis of 'interest,' that is, a 'debit-credit' formula. Usually what we do, we do so that somebody else may see it, so that somebody else can applaud us and tell it to somebody else. Human relationships are often, under the influence of sin, distorted to the point where unselfish love has become a very rare commodity. Contrary to that reality of the world under sin, David loves his flock with a passionate love to the point that he is ready to risk his own life in order to save his sheep. Doukhan writes: 'Here the love is authentic or it does not exist.'[9]

---

[7]   Ibid. See also Jacques Doukhan, *Aux Portes de L'Esperance: Essai Biblique sur les Propheties de la Fin* (Dammarie-les-Lys, France: Vie et Santé, 1986), 244.
[8]   See Merrill, 355.
[9]   Doukhan, 246.

Consequently, when David says, 'The Lord is my Shepherd,' he speaks about the most caring and the most wonderful Being in the universe. God, for him, is not a Platonic 'timeless' God who, by virtue of his nature, is not able to interfere in the events of human history, or the deistic God of Voltaire who is not interested in the affairs of human beings. David's God loves his children fervently and almost fanatically. He shapes the general process of history and gets involved in particular events as well as in the lives of human beings. His love is the very foundation of the moral structure of the whole universe and without that point of departure life itself would be doomed to extinction. God's love, which is in many ways beyond human understanding—since we are petrified in the walls of Babylon—is the true source of all the virtues which give meaning and beauty to human existence. *It simply means life.*

The metaphor of the 'Shepherd' is also used to remind the people of Israel of the acts of liberation that God undertook at the time of the exodus from Egypt and his care for them during the long journey in the wilderness when God protected them as the 'Shepherd.'[10] God's acts of salvation in the past, in turn, form the foundation for the eschatological salvation in the future when God one more time, the last time, will enter into human history and liberate his children from the wilderness of suffering and death.

David continues by saying that if such a magnificent and amazing Being is our Shepherd we 'shall not be in want.' Koehler in his translation emphasizes this consequential relationship between verses 1a and 1b in the following way: 'So long as the Lord is my shepherd, I suffer no lack.'[11]

Verses 2 and 3 put the emphasis on the exodus theme again, on God's nurture and support for his people during their journey in the desert after the exodus, since in Deuteronomy 2:7 God says, 'You have not lacked anything.' Because of God's goodness, the wilderness experience is seen as an account where there were no shortages.[12] The pastures are green, the waters are still (or 'waters of rest') and the paths are without dangers.[13] It seems, in the metaphorical sense, that some special diet, the Creator's diet, is suggested here, which implies that human beings have been created with some specific sets of laws in mind. The emphasis is not primarily on the physical food we eat, but much more on those realities in life which have a strong influence on our mind or our spiritual life. God's diet and the 'restoration of our soul' are put in direct connection in the text. As God's creations we are not allowed to feed our minds with food which is not on God's menu,

---

[10] See Craigie, 206.
[11] Ibid.
[12] See Walter Brueggemann, *The Message of the Psalms* (Minneapolis, MN: Augsburg Publishing House, 1984), 155.
[13] Doukhan, 247.

such as hatred, selfishness, pride or self-sufficiency. Moreover, we are created to walk in the 'paths of righteousness' (*tsedeq*) or 'just paths'[14] or 'paths which lead to happiness.'[15] Our feet are comfortable only on the path that God has designed for human beings and that is Jesus Christ's way. Every other boulevard of human existence means not only estrangement from God but also estrangement from our essential nature which is engraved on every living cell of our bodies.

The wisdom of meaningful human existence is clearly and unmistakably expressed here in a cause and effect manner. If we are going to the *green* pastures, if we drink from the *still* waters (or 'waters of rest')[16] and if we walk in the paths of *righteousness* (or 'paths which lead to deliverance, welfare and blessedness'),[17] then and only then will he restore our soul (or 'he will bring our vitality,' 'he will calm our soul').[18]

Thus, verses 1-3 portray the first picture of God, that is, God the Shepherd, who leads his people, who walks beside his people, who walks in front, above and behind his flock; a Being who is there all the time for them; a Being who risks his life in order to save them because he loves them passionately and fervently. Since he has already demonstrated his love for his people in the event of the exodus from Egypt, his people can have confidence and trust in him that he will deliver them in the future.

God the Comforter

However, it is well known that in the reality of human life the pastures are not always green, the waters are not always still and the paths are not always peaceful. Sometimes, human beings have to go through the 'valley of the shadow of death' (*tsalmouth*) experiencing the touch of suffering, loss and death, that is, the total meaninglessness of human life (vs 4). This kind of experience has led many people throughout human history to dismiss God from their existence and to reject his involvement in the events of Planet Earth. The divinely inspired poet in Psalm 23 dares to claim, on the basis of his own experiences with God, that when humans are passing through the valley of darkness, God the Comforter is even closer to them.

Verses 1-3 are written in the third person singular: 'He makes me lie down ...'; 'he leads me ...'; 'He restores my soul'; 'He guides me.' Suddenly, in vs 4 'he' becomes 'you': '... you are with me,' 'your rod,' and 'your staff.' It seems obvious that a deep theological proclamation is found in this change of 'he' to 'you,' saying

---

[14] Ibid.
[15] See A. A. Anderson, 'The Book of Psalms,' *New Century Bible Commentary* (Grand Rapids, MI: William B. Eerdmans Publishing Co., 1972), vol. 1, 197.
[16] Ibid.
[17] Ibid.
[18] Ibid.

that while the pastures were green, the waters still and the paths peaceful, God was in front, behind and above his people.[19] But now, when a human being passes through the valley of *tsalmouth*, God the Comforter comes so close that he almost touches man, he consoles (*naham*). This proximity of God, the touch of his rod, at the moment of total despair, means everything to a mortal man.

Naham is probably the key word in Psalm 23, carrying within itself the message of hope, meaning and the future. It speaks about the special, deep relationship and friendship between God and man and emerges out of darkness and hopelessness. It may also be an allusion to God's protection during the exodus wanderings in the desert which is described in the book of Jeremiah as 'a land of drought and *darkness*, a land where no one travels and no one lives' (Jer 2:6).

In some forms of idealistic Hegelian philosophy, evil is seen as an illusion or as necessary to the perfection of the whole.[20] When one is standing and looking at a painting, according to this view, one realizes that the dark colours are necessary to the perfection of the whole. Iago is necessary in *Othello* and the imperfection of Othello's love is necessary to the defeat of evil.[21] Contrary to this aesthetic view of evil, Psalm 23 acknowledges the tragic reality in which humans find themselves but also shouts about the present remedy and future solution. The believer can already count on the presence of the almighty God when he is passing through the valley of *tsalmouth*, and he also knows that evil is an intruder into the reality of the universe. The day is coming when, as the next verse will tell us, only happiness and joy will fill the vast cosmic space.

God the Host

Verse 5 introduces one of the most delightful and enjoyable scenes in the entire Bible. God the Shepherd and God the Comforter becomes God the Host. Some neighbouring peoples around Israel[22] believed that at the end of time man will experience ultimate happiness during a shared meal with God.[23] Supported by this belief as well as by the teaching of the rest of the Scriptures on this topic, it seems sound to conclude that this verse may be seen to illustrate the eschatological 'wedding supper of the Lamb' (Rev 19:9).

After the 'green pasture experience' and after having been touched by God in the valley of death, God has yet another surprise for those who have made the decision to walk in the paths of righteousness. He organizes a big banquet, he invites all his friends and he himself serves them. The description of this banquet

---

[19] See Doukhan, 246, 247.
[20] See Alan Richardson, 'Evil, The Problem of,' in: *The Westminster Dictionary of Christian Theology* (1983), 193.
[21] Ibid.
[22] Anderson, 198.
[23] See Doukhan, 248.

is so imaginative and brilliant that one has the impression of being present and of smelling the heavenly perfume and tasting the 'cosmic' drinks. The oil represents a perfume that is the symbol of rejoicing[24] and when God serves there is abundance of everything, 'the cup overflows.'

All this is happening 'in the presence of ... enemies.' This sentence belongs to the diplomatic language of that time, as has been found in the library of Tell El Amarna. In the fourteenth century BC a petty ruler wrote to the Pharaoh saying, 'May he give gifts to his servants while our enemies look on.'[25] In the context of Psalm 23 it means that at last, at the end of time after having been led by God to the still waters and after having been touched by him in the valley of death, God and his people are sitting together at the same table, looking into each other's eyes and enjoying each other's company. All their enemies such as suffering, pain, hatred, concentration camps, gas chambers, torture and, most of all, death, are crushed and trampled. Only the memory of these enemies remains but their poisonous activities are crushed forever. They are conquered, defeated enemies. So, the presence of defeated enemies points to the happiness which is going to be so great that the human heart will be about to explode with joy.

As we have seen above, the language of exodus and wilderness permeates the whole of Psalm 23 and here in verses 5 and 6 it comes to its climax.[26] God the Shepherd liberated his people from Egyptian slavery, God the Comforter cared for them 'in the land of drought and darkness, a land where no one travels and no one lives' (Jer 2:6), and now at the end of time he is engaged in the act of eschatological exodus. This is the final, universal act of liberation of his people. In New Testament terminology it is the second coming of Jesus, the time of immeasurable and infinite bliss.

The history of humankind on Planet Earth has its beginning and it is progressing, in a negative sense, toward self-destruction. For the first time in human history the destiny of humanity and all life on this planet is in the hands of not always mentally balanced human beings. In a number of basements and rooms in different countries of the world small atomic bombs are hidden.[27] The streets of many cities of the world are covered with human blood as well as with the dead bodies of children and older people. Dead people and more dead people everywhere.

According to some analysts, the third world war has already begun, but since its form is different from previous wars in history it seems as if it will never affect us personally.[28] And this is the really tricky character of the war because we do not really see it until it comes to our front door. Climate changes are causing floods

---

[24] See Anderson, 198.
[25] El Amarna, 100: 33-35.
[26] See Craigie, 208.
[27] See Dusan Kovacevic, 'Treci Svetski Rat Je Vec Poceo,' *Blic*, September 2004, 3.
[28] Ibid.

and consequent devastation as never before and this has become one of the major concerns of the international community. The ice at the North Pole is now melting eight times faster than it did in the past. During the year 2004 around two thousand farmers in India committed suicide, since they could not produce enough food for their family because of the drought. AIDS menaces the very existence of several nations in Africa.

All these realities of the contemporary world are, according to the Bible, signs of the proximity of the eschatological exodus, when God the Host will change fundamentally, once and forever, the character and nature of human history (Mat 24). He restores our soul when we walk in the paths of righteousness, he comforts us in the valley of death and then, finally, he defeats all our enemies and organizes a big feast in our honour. But is this the end of our friendship with God?

God the Father of the house
If taken literally, verse 6 could express the trust and happiness the author found in the temple, or it could be understood as a metaphor referring to continual communion with God.[29] However, if the whole psalm is permeated with exodus themes, then it has to be understood as an eschatological reality.

After the banquet prepared by God himself in order to celebrate the successful arrival at the so long desired goal, there is another, fourth, picture, unfolding before our eyes. God the Host becomes God the Father of the house. 'Goodness' and 'love' personify here the God who will always be with his children. John in the book of Revelation states:

> Now the dwelling of God is with men, and he will live with them. They will be his people, and God himself will be with them and be their God. He will wipe every tear from their eyes. There will be no more death or mourning or crying or pain, for the old order of things has passed away (Rev 21: 3, 4).

God and man forever under the same roof. God is at last the Father of the house of the universe. Time becomes eternity.

It seems that Psalm 23 is able to encapsulate the whole experience of the Christian journey, showing that there is certain growth in the quality of our relationship with God. In order to be able to live with God throughout eternity we have first to experience the taste of the food he will be serving at the supper he will organize in our honour. In order to be present at his banquet we have to allow him to touch us when we are passing through the valley of darkness, and in order to be touched in the valley of darkness we have to walk in the paths of righteousness.

---

[29] Anderson, 199.

Radiša Antić. Born in Serbia. Since 2003 director of the E. G. White Centre, Newbold College. Pastoral, evangelistic, administrative, youth ministry and teaching experience since 1980 in the countries of former Yugoslavia and Great Britain. President for the South-East European Union, 1994-2003. Author of books and articles. PhD, Andrews University (1991).

Parallel Old Testament Laws as a Hermeneutical Key

Kai Arasola

There is little doubt or dispute over the enormous importance of law in ancient Israel.[1] Everyday life and theological concepts were shaped by the understanding the people had of the Law. There is reasonable consensus on the actual administration of justice.[2] However, the unity of scholarly opinion breaks down as soon as the origin, form, or purpose of this legal material is discussed.

Very few dispute the fact that the Old Testament was the Bible of New Testament writers and continued to be the primary written Scriptures of the Christian community for about two centuries while the canon of the New Testament was being shaped.[3] Even gentile Christians thought of the Old Testament as their proof that Jesus was the Christ[4] and that the New Testament is rooted in the Old. Subsequently, a balanced Christian hermeneutic of the Bible must include a realistic view of the Old Testament.

The Seventh-day Adventist Church is generally perceived to have a vested interest in Old Testament study. This notion is nourished by the Adventist emphasis on the Decalogue, including the Sabbath commandment, as well as by the church's interest in the prophecies of Daniel, sanctuary typology, and on its recognition of health value in the Torah's designations of clean and unclean foods.

While this perception of Adventist connection to the Old Testament may be partially correct,[5] the church's scholars have systematically favoured historical research or prophetic exegesis over, for example, theological interpretation of the Pentateuch.[6] Very few among the church's scholars have ventured to unlock the massive legal corpus in the Old Testament.

---

[1] Hans Jochen Boecker, *Law and the Administration of Justice in the Old Testament and Ancient East* (London, UK: SPCK, 1980), 27.

[2] See e.g. Roland DeVaux, *Ancient Israel, Its Life and Institutions* (London, UK: Darton, Longman & Todd, 1961), 143-163.

[3] It should also be remembered that in the beginning the majority of Christians came from a Jewish background and that a strong Jewish influence continued in particular in the eastern parts of the Roman Empire. See e.g. Rodney Stark, *The Rise of Christianity* (San Francisco, CA: HarperCollins, 1997), 49-69. Stark argues convincingly that sociological and archaeological data support close ties between the early Christian churches (typically in the Jewish ghettos) and the Jewish community.

[4] Adolf Harnack, *History of Dogma I,* (Eugene, OR: Wipf and Stock, 1997), 42f, 81.

[5] The attitude is reflected in statements such as, 'They're Seventh Day Adventists, a Christian denomination that follows the Old Testament tradition ...' 'Seventh Day Adventist invented breakfast cereal', *Winnipeg Free Press,* April 1, 2007; www.encyclopedia.com, http://www.encyclopedia.com/doc/1P3-1247827611.html. Retrieved Feb 25, 2009.

[6] A trend started by the success of Dr. Siegfried Horn.

Introductory comments on interpreting Old Testament laws

Because of the large number of laws in the Pentateuch they are sometimes divided into subsections to help interpretation. Form critical studies have proposed, though with no unanimity on the details, four basic sources: J, E, D, and P. Furthermore, several smaller law collections have also been identified, including not only the commonly known Decalogue but also the so-called Covenant Code (Ex 20:22-23,33), Deuteronomistic law (Deuteronomy), Holiness Code (Lev 17-26), the Priestly Code (Leviticus except Holiness Code), the Cultic Decalogue (Ex 34:10ff), the Shechemite Dodecalogue (Deut 27:15-26), and others.

Scholars with a conservative approach generally avoid issues related to the literary style, dating or distinctions in the setting, the *Sitz im Leben,* of various laws but whatever one thinks of the origin of the Pentateuchal laws, form critical study has done everyone a favour by giving solid background and cultural information on the laws. It has also pointed out the amazing degree to which law influenced the life and thinking of ordinary people.[7]

An example of an effort to unlock the content of Old Testament law is the more-than-century-old designation of laws as *apodictic* or *casuistic,* the former representing authoritative God-given laws including broad principles of justice while the latter deal with the actual administration of justice in the ancient courts of Israel.[8] Casuistic laws typically include a consideration of the background or motives of the case. However, such distinctions have failed to provide any generally applicable hermeneutical tool for the one who seeks to find possible present-day applications of Old Testament laws.[9]

Another method of sub-dividing Old Testament legal texts has been devised specifically for the purpose of unlocking the relevance of the laws. Assigning them to *moral, ceremonial,* and *civil* law categories makes the application of a law manageable. This method can be traced back to the days of the Westminster Confession, probably earlier.[10] In fact it can be called the traditional Protestant approach to Old Testament laws. These divisions are also found in Charles Wesley's writings and they have been typical of Methodist thinking.[11]

Many Seventh-day Adventists have adopted this hermeneutic though they sometimes add *health* laws as a fourth category. Ellen G. White followed this line

---

[7] Some historical conclusions related to form criticism are in serious conflict with traditional exegesis. No exodus, covenant at Sinai, prophets preceding both OT history and OT law. E.g. Otto Eissfeldt: *The Old Testament, An Introduction,* (Oxford, UK: Blackwell, 1974), 159-219.

[8] Patrick Dale, *Old Testament Law,* (London, UK: SCM, 1985), 5.

[9] See e.g. Hans Jochen Boecker, *Law and the Administration of Justice in the Old Testament and Ancient East,* (London, UK: SPCK, 1980), 27.

[10] Max A. Forsythe, *The Moral Law;* James B. Green, *A Harmony of the Westminster Presbyterian Standards;* A. A. Hodge, *The Confession of Faith.*

[11] Kenneth Collin, *A Hermeneutical Model for the Wesleyan Ordo Salutis.* MS; http://wesley.nnu.edu/wesleyan_theology/theojrnl/16-20/19-13.htm. Retrieved April 14, 2009.

of reasoning and makes a clear distinction between the moral law and the ceremonial law.[12] The Decalogue stands out as the supreme indicator of sin.

This approach is more helpful than form critical study for one interested in modern applications of biblical laws. Any biblical law identified as *moral* represents God's permanent will and lies at the foundation of Christian ethics, while biblical civil laws have been replaced by modern national legislation. Ceremonial laws, as advised by the New Testament, are not to be literally applied but represent symbolic values and point to Christ.[13]

However, the major problem related to this hermeneutic is that there is no undisputed, biblically based process for determining the appropriate category of each law. Many of the laws fall naturally into one category or another but there are also numerous laws on which Christian or Jewish exegetes have found no consensus.

One example is the law on clean and unclean meats. While an Adventist may claim that not eating pork (Lev. 11:7; Deut. 14:8) is a health law and good counsel even for today, most Christian exegetes would designate it as a ceremonial law with no modern relevance. On the other hand, a Jewish interpretation may disagree with both and suggest that this law has nothing to do with health or ceremonies but is a God-given test of faithfulness and therefore a moral issue. Similarly one may ask whether it is a ceremonial, health, civil, or moral law that a woman must stay twice as long in isolation after giving birth to a girl compared to delivering a boy (Lev 12:1-5).

The uncleanness and isolation itself, it could be argued, may be a matter of health. However, someone with a conviction that God initiated male supremacy at the time of creation might suggest that there is a moral lesson in this law. On the other hand, it would not be unreasonable to claim that this gender-caused difference is part of antiquated civil legislation that reflects the values of the ancient Middle East. Because uncleanness prevented a person from participating in the cult, this same law could for another exegete be a clear example of ceremonial law. The process of finding what category a law belongs to is too subjective to offer a reliable method for interpreting Old Testament laws.

The ultimate question related to the preceding discussion is to find dependable criteria for 'naturalizing' Old Testament legal or ceremonial requirements into the Christian faith, an issue thinking Christians have struggled with ever since apostolic times.[14] In the end, New Testament evidence must answer the question, but a partial answer lies also in the laws themselves. The following explores parallel

---

[12] Ellen G. White, *Patriarchs and Prophets* (Washington, DC: Review and Herald Publishing Association, 1890), 365.

[13] Ellen G. White, *Testimonies for the Church* (Mountain View, CA: Pacific Press Publishing Association, 1948), 667.

[14] Cf. Adolf Harnack, *History of Dogma I* (Eugene, OR: Wipf and Stock, 1997), 89-99.

laws found in the *Torah* and looks at changes in the laws and their implications on the character of Old Testament law.

Parallel laws

Parallel laws are a potentially significant feature of the legal material in the Pentateuch; several laws, when repeated, are radically altered and reworded. In a few instances the modifications are so extensive that the two (or more) laws cannot be observed simultaneously. In other words, on some topics the legal corpus of the Pentateuch includes new laws that must be understood to be a replacement for or an annulment of another earlier law.

Usually scholars limit themselves to comparisons between the previously mentioned law collections. For example, many of the laws in Exodus and Deuteronomy are the same and partially in the same order. Also, the so-called Book of the Covenant (Ex 20-23) and a section of the Priestly Code have similar laws.[15]

The groundwork for this study was done by collecting all legal texts from the whole of the Pentateuch into one document. This compilation was done with the broadest possible definition of the term law and includes stated principles, cult related precepts, civil laws and other texts which even remotely resemble legal genres.

In this preliminary survey comparisons between laws were done without any literary or historical analysis. The purpose, in the first instance, was only to compile a comprehensive collection of all Hebrew laws. There is no doubt that repeated laws are an extremely potent tool for source or form criticism and that they present some challenging issues related to the historical setting or date. However, this aspect of repeated laws was left outside the scope of the survey. As a matter of curiosity, one may note that whatever the original reasons for repeating laws were, they do not provide an obvious proof for a documentary interpretation of the laws. Several laws are repeated up to ten times and traditionally only four main sources are proposed for the Pentateuch.

When compiling biblical laws the first challenge is the difficulty of defining precisely what constitutes law and how laws should be divided. Rabbinic tradition suggests 613 laws in the *Torah*, 365 negative and 248 positive, or one for each day of the year and one for each bone of the body. However, the sages never produced a commonly accepted list of the 613 laws.[16] The process of analysing and subdividing the laws has always been highly subjective.

The total number of laws found in this survey was slightly higher than the Jewish one, 659. This number as such is not important and the difference stems from the aim of comparing parallel laws. In several instances a one-paragraph law

---

15 Patrick Dale, *Old Testament Law* (London, UK: SCM, 1985), 91, 96.
16 Maimonides' list is the most commonly used version of the 613 laws.

included a statement which dealt with another law topic and therefore had to be divided into two or sometimes more. Sometimes even a sentence was divided. A law prohibiting the eating of both fat and blood (Lev 3:17; 7:21-23) was counted as two laws, because the number of laws that prohibit eating blood without mentioning fat or that deal with the use of fat without mentioning blood was higher than those where the two are together.

To help categorize the laws they were divided into *civil* laws (including the Decalogue) and *cult-* or *sanctuary-related* laws. The latter included laws related to the festivals, sacrifices, or to the priests, but not, for example, laws on uncleanness if the prescribed condition for the uncleanness related to everyday life like touching a dead animal (Lev 11:31) or the menstrual period of a woman (Lev 15:18-26). With this division there were 228 cult-related laws and 431 civil laws.

As laws in each group were arranged topically, 48 temple-related laws were repeated one or more times, and 52 laws appeared only once; 100 laws in total. In the civil law group 123 laws were repeated more than once and 124 were unique, a total of 247 laws. However, it should be kept in mind that these figures are not presented as an authoritative distribution of laws and further analysis may change the numbers if a more logical way to group the laws is found.

Table: Categories of laws in the Pentateuch

Total number of laws / total law topics	659 / 347
Cult related laws total / total law topics	228 / 100
Unique /repeated laws	52 / 48
Civil life laws total / total law topics	431 / 247
Unique / repeated laws	124 / 123
Total laws with parallels	347
Parallel laws with significant changes	about 30

Most of the parallel laws come in two, sometimes three versions. A handful of laws both in the temple-related and civil section appear up to about ten times. Some of the repeated laws are identical, but most of them come with minor changes in wording, editorial changes that do not affect the actual meaning or intent of the law.

The best known, and a typical example of a repeated law with minor variants, are the two versions of the Decalogue (Ex 20:2-17 and Deut 5:6-21). The commandments are the same, the theological content as well as context are identical. It is possible to look at the differences simply as a proof against the concepts of verbal inspiration and inerrancy[17] and a reflection of the difference between oral and

---

[17] Having variants in the Decalogue, a text originally written on stone and one of the central texts of the Old Testament, is an important observation for the theory of inspiration.

written communication. But both versions of the Decalogue as well as the majority of the 171 repeated Pentateuchal parallel laws teach the same lessons and require the same application regardless of the version one reads.

Another example, familiar to Seventh-day Adventists, is the law on clean and unclean foods in Leviticus 11 and Deuteronomy 14. While the dissimilarities in the two versions of this law are greater than those of the Decalogue, they do not present any serious exegetical, theological or historical problems.

However, some of the parallel laws change so radically that it is difficult or impossible to harmonize the different versions. The survey on which these observations are based listed about 30 laws in this category. The major changes imply that the law was totally rewritten with intent to replace or annul an earlier law. The number of laws in this category is approximate for the simple reason that it is very difficult to draw a line between what is a minor and what is a major change in a law. Major changes will be illustrated by three examples.

These radically altered laws prove that some legal material in the Pentateuch was not intended to be unending. This is a significant observation. If in the same legal corpus and under the same biblical inspiration several laws are totally re-worded and earlier versions of the laws annulled (which for a conservative reader took place within the 40 years from Sinai to the borders of the Promised Land)[18] it is difficult to avoid the conclusion that from the beginning some Old Testament laws were never planned to have permanent status.

Law on Hebrew slaves

The first example of laws with major changes is the law of Israelite slaves. There are three versions of the law, two quite similar dealing with a seven-year service period (Ex 21:2-11 and Deut 15:12-18), where the second version is clearly intended to be an update of the earlier one. The third (Lev 25:8, 39-54) is primarily a law on the special privileges of the Jubilee year and can be left out of the comparison.

The main difference between the Exodus and Deuteronomy versions of the law relates to female slaves. Exodus assumes that female slaves become wives (or secondary wives) to their owner or his son. Therefore women are not released. On the other hand Deuteronomy deals with men and women equally. Women, too, are to be released after seven years of serfdom.

---

[18] If this presupposition is accepted, the large number of repeated laws and the rapid pace with which some laws keep changing is nearly overwhelming. This may have been the reason for some scholars to have shifted to moderately conservative views. They have opened the door for the possibility that some later laws may have been added to an original Sinaitic law collection. Cf. William LaSor, David Hubbard, Frederic Bush, *Old Testament Survey* (Grand Rapids MI: William B. Eerdmans Publishing Company, 1996), 6-14.

Exodus 21:2-11	Deuteronomy 15:12-18 (NIV)
If you buy a Hebrew servant, he is to serve you for six years. But in the seventh year, he shall go free, without paying anything. 3 If he comes alone, he is to go free alone; but if he has a wife when he comes, she is to go with him. 4 If his master gives him a wife and she bears him sons or daughters, the woman and her children shall belong to her master, and only the man shall go free.	If a fellow Hebrew, a man or a woman, sells himself to you and serves you six years, in the seventh year you must let him go free. 13 And when you release him, do not send him away empty-handed. 14 Supply him liberally from your flock, your threshing floor and your winepress. Give to him as the LORD your God has blessed you. 15 Remember that you were slaves in Egypt and the LORD your God redeemed you. That is why I give you this command today.
5 But if the servant declares, 'I love my master and my wife and children and do not want to go free,' 6 then his master must take him before the judges. He shall take him to the door or the doorpost and pierce his ear with an awl. Then he will be his servant for life. 7 If a man sells his daughter as a servant, she is not to go free as menservants do. 8 If she does not please the master who has selected her for himself, he must let her be redeemed. He has no right to sell her to foreigners, because he has broken faith with her. 9 If he selects her for his son, he must grant her the rights of a daughter. 10 If he marries another woman, he must not deprive the first one of her food, clothing and marital rights. 11 If he does not provide her with these three things, she is to go free, without any payment of money.	16 But if your servant says to you, "I do not want to leave you," because he loves you and your family and is well off with you, 17 then take an awl and push it through his ear lobe into the door, and he will become your servant for life. Do the same for your maidservant.
	18 Do not consider it a hardship to set your servant free, because his service to you these six years has been worth twice as much as that of a hired hand. And the LORD your God will bless you in everything you do.

The law has little direct practical application today as slavery is no longer practiced in its traditional sense. It is easy for a modern reader to deduce that the law in Deuteronomy breaks new ground towards the equality of genders and it is easy to accept Deuteronomy's version as the more developed, humane law reflecting growing respect for women and family, as well as for civilized treatment of slaves.[19]

The two versions of the law on Hebrew slaves cannot be harmonized. When the case of a female slave was to be decided one could only observe one version or the other, which means the later account has annulled the earlier one.

The Leviticus version of the law frees the slaves during the year of Jubilees, every forty-ninth year. In some cases this could mean less than seven years of service. However, this is a law primarily on Jubilees and not on slaves but as far as the issue of female slaves is concerned, this law makes no distinction between freeing male and female slaves.

The law on Passover

The next example of a changed law is the Passover. In the Pentateuch there are three major laws on the Passover (Ex 12:1-28; Lev 23:5-8; Deut 16:1-8) and an example of how the Passover was celebrated and a few minor adjustments to the law (Ex 34:25; Num 9:2-14). The comparison between the Passover laws in Exodus and Deuteronomy is of greatest interest.

The two laws are radically different in spite of the fact that the Exodus version is given the status of a 'lasting' ordinance to be celebrated 'when you enter the land.' Deuteronomy changes the very basic elements of the ordinance. Fundamental to this change is the location of the festival. Exodus Passover was a home event while the one in Deuteronomy was to be observed at a central temple site.

Exodus 12:3-51 [abbreviated]	Deuteronomy 16:1-12 (NASB)
1 Now the LORD said to Moses and Aaron in the land of Egypt, 2 'This month shall be the beginning of months for you; it is to be the first month of the year to you. 3 Speak to all the congregation of Israel, saying, 'On the tenth of this month they are each one to take a lamb for themselves, according to their fathers' households, a lamb for each household. 4 Now if the household is	1 Observe the month of Abib and celebrate the Passover to the LORD your God, for in the month of Abib the LORD your God brought you out of Egypt by night. 2 You shall sacrifice the Passover to the LORD your God from the flock and the herd, in the place where the LORD chooses to establish His name.

---

[19] Historically the actual development of women's role in Ancient Middle Eastern societies is complex and includes increasing oppression of women and removal of their rights during second and first millennium BC.

too small for a lamb, then he and his neighbor nearest to his house are to take one according to the number of persons in them; according to what each man should eat, you are to divide the lamb. 5 Your lamb shall be an unblemished male a year old; you may take it from the sheep or from the goats. 6 You shall keep it until the fourteenth day of the same month, then the whole assembly of the congregation of Israel is to kill it at twilight.

7 Moreover, they shall take some of the blood and put it on the two doorposts and on the lintel of the houses in which they eat it. 8 They shall eat the flesh that same night, roasted with fire, and they shall eat it with unleavened bread and bitter herbs.

9 Do not eat any of it raw or boiled at all with water, but rather roasted with fire, both its head and its legs along with its entrails. 10 And you shall not leave any of it over until morning, but whatever is left of it until morning, you shall burn with fire.

11 Now you shall eat it in this manner: with your loins girded, your sandals on your feet, and your staff in your hand; and you shall eat it in haste—it is the LORD'S Passover. 12 For I will go through the land of Egypt on that night, and will strike down all the firstborn in the land of Egypt, both man and beast; and against all the gods of Egypt I will execute judgments—I am the LORD.

13 The blood shall be a sign for you on the houses where you live; and when I see the blood I will pass over you, and no plague will befall you to destroy you

3 You shall not eat leavened bread with it; seven days you shall eat with it unleavened bread, the bread of affliction (for you came out of the land of Egypt in haste), so that you may remember all the days of your life the day when you came out of the land of Egypt.

4 For seven days no leaven shall be seen with you in all your territory, and none of the flesh which you sacrifice on the evening of the first day shall remain overnight until morning.

5 You are not allowed to sacrifice the Passover in any of your towns which the LORD your God is giving you; 6 but at the place where the LORD your God chooses to establish His name, you shall sacrifice the Passover in the evening at sunset, at the time you came out of Egypt.

7 You shall cook and eat it in the place which the LORD your God chooses. In the morning you are to return to your tents.

8 Six days you shall eat unleavened bread, and on the seventh day there shall be a solemn assembly to the LORD your God; you shall do no work on it.

when I strike the land of Egypt.14 Now this day will be a memorial to you, and you shall celebrate it as a feast to the LORD; throughout your generations you are to celebrate it as a permanent ordinance.'

... 20 You shall not eat anything leavened; in all your dwellings you shall eat unleavened bread.

... 24 And you shall observe this event as an ordinance for you and your children forever.

25 When you enter the land which the LORD will give you, as He has promised, you shall observe this rite."

... 43 The LORD said to Moses and Aaron, 'This is the ordinance of the Passover: no foreigner is to eat of it; 44 but every man's slave purchased with money, after you have circumcised him, then he may eat of it. 45 A sojourner or a hired servant shall not eat of it.

46 It is to be eaten in a single house; you are not to bring forth any of the flesh outside of the house, nor are you to break any bone of it.

... 51 ... evening at sunset, at the time that you came out of Egypt.'

9 You shall count seven weeks for yourself; you shall begin to count seven weeks from the time you begin to put the sickle to the standing grain.

10 Then you shall celebrate the Feast of Weeks to the LORD your God with a tribute of a freewill offering of your hand, which you shall give just as the LORD your God blesses you;

11 and you shall rejoice before the LORD your God, you and your son and your daughter and your male and female servants and the Levite who is in your town, and the stranger and the orphan and the widow who are in your midst, in the place where the LORD your God chooses to establish His name.

12 You shall remember that you were a slave in Egypt, and you shall be careful to observe these statutes.'

The key changes in the two versions of the Passover are:
- The *location* of the celebration, one at the house, the other at the temple.
- The use of hyssop to smear *blood on the doorposts* in Exodus.
- *Cooking* (*bashal*) is forbidden in Exodus and the norm in Deuteronomy.
- The Passover 'lamb.' Exodus allows *sheep* and *goats* while Deuteronomy adds *bovines* to the list.
- The list of restrictions on *aliens* is expressed less vigorously in Deuteronomy.

These changes are perfectly understandable in the light of Deuteronomy's emphasis on centralized worship. When people were away from their homes and had to choose the animal from what was available it might have been difficult to limit the selection of animals to lambs and goats. The door posts would have lost their symbolic meaning when people were away from the house. Food preparation is not limited to roasting, possibly because oxen were included.[20]

The changes and the reasons for the changes are easy to list and Old Testament application would depend on the existence of centralized worship. Today, without a temple, Jewish communities have adopted a hybrid version of the law and celebrate the *Pesach* in the house combining elements from both Exodus and Deuteronomy, adding numerous later traditions where symbolic acts replace the original law. For example, even strictly orthodox Jews usually do not commemorate the smearing of blood on the doorposts literally, as the Passover lamb is normally not slaughtered in the house.[21]

Woman's uncleanness

The third illustration of major changes in Old Testament laws is one where the actual law remains the same but the punishment radically changes and makes efforts of harmonization difficult. Most Christians and modern Jews make little issue of the law and may or may not follow it, but for orthodox Jews the observance of *niddah* or abstinence from intercourse during a woman's menstrual period and especially during the seven following days is a benchmark sign of genuine Judaism.[22] The law on a woman's uncleanness during her period is repeated three times, all in Leviticus.

Leviticus 15:19-24	Leviticus 18:19, 29	Leviticus 20:18 (NIV)
19 When a woman has her regular flow of blood, the impurity of her monthly period will last seven days, and anyone who touches her will be unclean till evening... 24 If a man lies with her and her monthly flow touches him, he will be unclean for seven days; any bed he lies on will be unclean.	19 Do not approach a woman to have sexual relations during the uncleanness of her monthly period ... 29 Everyone who does any of these detestable things—such persons must be cut off from their people.	18 If a man lies with a woman during her monthly period and has sexual relations with her, he has exposed the source of her flow, and she has also uncovered it. Both of them must be cut off from their people.

---

[20] J. D. Levenson, *The Death and Resurrection of the Beloved Son* in: Carter Jeffrey, ed. *Understanding Religious Sacrifice, A Reader* (London, UK, New York: Continuum, 2003), 438.

[21] Anon. *Judaism 101* (http://www.ou.org/about/judaism/np.htm). Retrieved April 14, 2009.

[22] Anon. *Niddah in Practice* (http://www.experiencefestival.com/a/Niddah_-_In_practice/id/1382497). Retrieved April 14, 2009. Cf. *Niddah*, Wikipedia.

While in Leviticus 15 there is no punishment for the 'crime' except that the man is unclean for seven days, in Leviticus 18 there is a death penalty for the man, the text is unclear on the woman, and in Leviticus 20 there is a death penalty for both the man and the woman.

This example deals with what, from a modern perspective, is a strange law and one that must have been totally unenforceable even in ancient settings. The purpose of the law may relate to health or it may relate to the Hebrew concept of blood. Not only is the purpose of the law unclear but the reasons for the changes in punishment are equally blurred. This law is a simple illustration of the fact that some laws in the Bible defy modern logic.

Observations from changed laws

It is actually not surprising that biblical laws are repeated and changed. What would be astonishing would be a nation with no changes in laws. Ancient societies changed their laws and modern ones do the same. The surprising fact is that so many of the laws in the Pentateuch are repeated and modified. Some laws appear to have had a very short life span which, for a conservative reader, means that divine inspiration intended them for short term use only. The reality that there are changes must not be seen as taking anything away from the Adventist tradition that the Bible has been given and preserved 'just in the way that God wanted it to be.'[23]

In the light of changing laws this means that some of the laws were of transitory nature.

Possible deductions from the changes are:

- One should look for the principles behind the laws. The principle, if it is found, may hold, even if the application has changed in shifting circumstances.
- The fact that nearly half of the law topics are repeated and that some of the repeated laws have undergone major changes can also be presented as a realistic acceptance of changing circumstances. The modified laws are a biblical pointer against Amish-type living in the past.
- On a deeper level one may also conclude that changing laws are evidence against Calvinistic biblicism which turned the Bible into a book of law on all topics and a repository of information on all manner of things, from the king's horses to death penalties or science to history.[24]

---

[23] Ellen G. White, *Selected Messages* (Washington, DC: Review and Herald, 1958), vol. I, 21.

[24] J. B. Rogers and D. McKim, *The Authority and Interpretation of the Bible, An Historical Approach* (New York: Harper and Row, 1979), 12; Kai Arasola, *End of Historicism, Millerite Hermeneutic of Old Testament Prophecies* (Uppsala: Datem, 1990), 27.

- Finally the changes show what the New Testament clearly teaches and what most Christians have intuitively understood: Not all of the Old Testament laws continue to be valid and applicable even if the Bible does not specifically annul the law.

Concluding remarks—Old Testament laws in the New Testament

The existence of repeated and changed laws proves the transitory nature of some Old Testament laws. The question remains: What is permanent? What laws are still binding or valuable for a Christian? The Old Testament does not answer the question. In the Pentateuch laws are to a large degree in a non-categorized mix and they are repeated and changed without explanatory notes.

The only law in the Old Testament that in any way stands out from the rest is the Decalogue. The narrative part of the Pentateuch describes its pronouncement by God himself and its writing on stone by the finger of God (Ex 19, 20, 34; Deut 4, 5). It was placed apart from other laws. However, that in itself does not mean that all the other laws would become invalid. A few concluding remarks reflect the views that New Testament writers have on the Decalogue and other Old Testament laws.

The first observation on New Testament usage of Old Testament laws is the permanence of the Decalogue. More than twenty texts either refer or allude to the Decalogue. Many of them go far beyond the letter of the law. For example, in the Sermon on the Mount Jesus refers to the commandment 'do not kill.' He reinforces the principle and recharges the law at a higher level that includes motives and love (Mat 5:21). The same happens with the commandment against adultery. Jesus upholds the commandment but gives it a new and deeper perspective. Even lustful thoughts are counted as sin (Mat 5:27).[25]

The longest citation of the Decalogue in the New Testament is in connection with the story of the man who comes to Jesus asking the way to eternal life. The story is found in all of the synoptic gospels with small variations (Mat 19:16-23; Mk 10:17-23; Lk 18:18-24). Jesus lists the sixth, seventh, eighth and ninth commandment (followed in the gospel of Mark with a commandment not to defraud, possibly a variant of the tenth commandment). After that he goes back to the fifth commandment. According to Matthew, Jesus completes the list with the commandment to love one's neighbour as oneself.

The story shows how firmly Jesus believed in the value of the Ten Commandments. It also confirms what the Sermon on the Mount already points to. A formal obedience to the commandments is not sufficient. True obedience to the moral law starts from the heart.

---

[25] Timo Veijola, *Dekalogi* (Helsinki, Finland: Finnish Exegetical Society, 1988), 23-30.

Paul's references to the Decalogue (e.g. Rom 7) confirm its permanent value. It is needed to point out sin and it forms a framework that guides Christian love. Jesus and New Testament writers make the Decalogue stricter, not easier.

Turning to references on other laws one notes that circumcision, all cult related requirements and festivals have come to an end and have only symbolic value (e.g. Gal 1:6-5:25). This is an important principle that was the key to the Christian mission for the gentiles. Another fundamental concept is the ambience of freedom, the Christian not being under the law but under grace. It is the divine Spirit who is the source of power for obedience (Rom 8.1-3).

Beyond these basic principles the following examples illustrate the usage:

Deut 24:1ff. Law on divorce. Man can divorce his wife if he finds something indecent in her and he writes a letter of divorce to the woman.

Mat 5:31ff. Jesus replaces or reinterprets the law by making it much more demanding. Divorce allowed only after adultery.

Ex 21:23ff; Deut 19:21. An eye for an eye, tooth for tooth etc.

Mat 5:38ff. Jesus repeals the law and gives the law a totally new basis of forgiving love and acceptance of wrong.

Lev 24:9ff. Shew bread was only for the Levites to eat.

Mat 12:3,4. Jesus excuses David's eating the bread and shows that for him the individual was more important than the literal observance of the shew bread law.

Lev 19:18; Deut. 6:5. 'Love your neighbor as yourself.' 'You shall love the Lord you God with all your heart and with all your soul and with all your might.'

Mat 22:36ff. Jesus calls these two *the* 'great and foremost commandments' on which 'the whole law and the prophets' depend.

Ex 22:28. Law on not cursing God or a ruler of your people.

Acts 23:3-5. Paul apologizes to the high priest and shows that he respected the law on not cursing a ruler.

Deut 25:4. Law against muzzling an ox while threshing.

1 Cor 9:9ff. Paul respects the law as the word of God but says that it does not apply to oxen but to pastors! The Law is used as an illustration and proof of God's care.

Deut 14:29. Part of the law of tithing tells the people to set a portion of the tithe for the poor, the orphans, the widows and the Levites.	Jas 1:27. Alludes with respect to this Old Testament law and states that pure religion is to visit the widows and the orphans.

The texts show that the New Testament represents a paradigm shift in regard to law. It not only changes law applications as was done already within the Old Testament, but whole groups of laws gain totally new meanings. Some are made stricter; others are annulled or given symbolic meanings. New Testament writers show respect for many Old Testament laws, but at the same time guide Christians away from following some of them.

Because of this it is easy to read the New Testament in a one-sided way. Ever since Paul's day the church has struggled with the question of how large a proportion of Old Testament laws is still binding. Many have followed the idea of Irenaeus who taught that the law of the Pentateuch represents God's will and a way of salvation for Old Testament times only and has little meaning for Christians.[26] Subsequently, the New Testament alone is considered binding and ethically relevant for Christians.

However, the New Testament itself does not support Irenaeus' idea of a wholesale abandoning of Old Testament laws. It is safer to follow the guidance of Augustine who dug deep into Pauline thinking and singled out the Ten Commandments as a permanent moral law.[27] However, the Decalogue is not the only law remaining. There are other laws that relate to the principles of the Ten Commandments or uphold important New Testament teachings. Interestingly, it is one of these other laws on loving God and one's neighbour (Lev 19:18; Deut 6:5) which the New Testament presents as the *most important* law of all (Mat 22:36ff). But even the Decalogue, according to the New Testament, is based on love and needs to be applied in love. After all, as Paul says, love is the fulfilment of the law (Rom 13:10).

The New Testament remains the best guide for determining the validity of Old Testament laws. But in light of the changes that take place within the legal corpus of the Old Testament, and noting that the New Testament gives only partial enforcement to laws other than the Decalogue, it is not an easy task to determine the current validity of Old Testament laws. It requires biblical knowledge and Christian maturity.

---

[26] Adolf Harnack, *History of Dogma II* (Eugene, OR: Wipf and Stock, 1997), 305.

[27] See e.g. Timo Veijola, *Dekalogi* (Helsinki: Finnish Exegetical Society, 1988), 30. William Wainwright, *Religion and Morality* (Aldershot, Burlington: Ashgate Publishing, 2005), 181f.

Kai Arasola. Born in Finland. Retired in 2009. Dean of the Faculty of Religious Studies at Asia-Pacific International University, Thailand (1995-2009). Teaching and administrative experience in Finland, Great Britain, Lebanon and Thailand. Conference president and seminary director in Finland. ThD, University of Uppsala (1989).

Dealing with 'Present Truth': 2 Peter 1:12 Revisited

Roberto Badenas

To speak about 'truth' in a postmodern world is not an easy undertaking. There is no single definition of truth on which the majority of scholars agree, and the prevailing ones continue to be widely debated. The classical philosophers paved the way for the famous definition by Thomas Aquinas of truth as 'the conformity between thing and intellect' (or 'the adequation[1] of thing and intellect').[2] This has become more or less the common dictionary definition: we call truth some form of agreement between affirmation and reality.[3]

Things started to change when Emmanuel Kant objected that the classical definition of truth is in fact a 'mere verbal definition,' a form of circular reasoning, which is not always valid.[4] The discussion went even further when Kierkegaard argued that 'truth is subjectivity. A human being cannot find truth separate from the subjective experience of one's own existing.'[5] Friedrich Nietzsche added that what we call 'truth' is only a 'mobile army of metaphors, metonyms and anthropomorphisms, an invention of fixed conventions for merely practical purposes.'[6] Then Erich Fromm defined truth as 'a functional approximation to reality.' The idea of 'absolute truth' seemed sterile to him, and therefore he considered it more realistic to speak of 'optimal truth.'[7]

Current definitions of truth

The debate about truth has led to a large spectrum of definitions—in part because there are three main levels or senses in which the word *truth* is used: as corre-

---

[1] According to *Webster's Revised Unabridged Dictionary* (C. & G. Merriam Co, 1913): 'The act of equalizing; act or result of making adequate; an equivalent.'

[2] Thomas Aquinas, *De veritate* 1:1 (cf. Lawrence Dewan, 'Is Truth Transcendental for St. Thomas Aquinas?' *Nova et Vetera*, 2,1 (2004), 1-20.

[3] See what the *Webster Dictionary Online* says on 'Truth': 'Sincerity in action, character, and utterance (1): the state of being the case; (2) the body of real things, events, and facts: ACTUALITY; (3) *often capitalized*: a) transcendent fundamental or spiritual reality; b) judgment, proposition, or idea that is true or accepted as true, the property (as of a statement) of being in accord with fact or reality, fidelity to an original or to a standard in accordance with fact' (www.merriam-webster.com).

[4] Emmanuel Kant, *Critique of Pure Reason* (Norman Kemp Smith, tr. Palgrave: Macmillan, 1929), 197.

[5] Søren Kierkegaard, *Philosophical Fragments* (tr. by V. Howard & Edna H. Hong, 1985), 75; W. Lawrie & D. Swenson, *Concluding Unscientific-Postcript* (Princeton, NJ: Princeton University Press, 1974), 181-182.

[6] See L. M. Hinman, 'Nietzsche, Metaphor and Truth' in: *Philosophy and Phenomenological Research*, 43, 2, (1982), 179-199.

[7] Eric Fromm's vision of optimal truth is described in *Man from Himself: An inquiry into the Psychology of Ethics* (New York: Holt, 1947).

spondence, as coherence, and as disclosure.[8] For many, of course, since the time of Plato and Aristotle truth is still defined as a *correspondence* between a statement and the reality (correspondence theory). According to this view, we say a statement is true when it corresponds to the reality it supposedly describes.[9] For others 'truth' means the logical *coherence* between what is said and the facts, at least within a system (coherence theory).[10] From this viewpoint a statement is true if it does not contain inner contradictions.[11] Others hold that truth is whatever is agreed upon, by some specified group, or even by all human beings (consensus theory).[12] For some, truth is *constructed* by social, historical and cultural processes, but it does not reflect any external reality (constructivist theory).[13] For others truth is identified by its effectiveness when applying concepts to actual practice (pragmatic theory).[14] The *deflationary* or *minimalist* theories of truth argue that 'to say that a statement is true is just to perform the act of agreeing with, accepting or endorsing a statement' (performative theory).[15] And for others, truth is just a *redundant* concept, a word traditionally used in conversation, mainly for emphasis, but which does not actually equate to anything in reality (redundancy theory).[16]

Our contemporaries are however, still interested in 'truth,' although they understand the word in different ways and look for truth in many directions.[17] 'In the scientific world there is a quest for truth, a desire to expand the human understanding of reality. Physicists seek truth about the processes of the created universe, physiologists seek the truth about the processes of the human body, and psychologists seek the truth about the processes of the mind. Historians seek the truth about

---

[8] For an introduction to the discussion on theories about truth, see Bradley Dowden and Norman Swartz, 'Truth,' in *The Internet Encyclopedia of Philosophy*, ed James Fieser. Http://www.utm.edu/research/iep (2005).

[9] Fernando Canale, *The Cognitive Principle of Christian Theology* (Berrien Springs, MI: Andrews University Press, 2005), 450-451. Alfred Tarski, 'The semantic conception of Truth,' in: *Philosophy and Phenomenological Research*, 4 (1944), 341-376.

[10] See Hegel, Spinoza, Leibniz, etc.

[11] James O. Young, 'The Coherence Theory of Truth,' *Stanford Encyclopaedia of Philosophy* (Sept 9, 2008), http://plato.stanford.edu/entries/truth-coherence.

[12] See specially Jürgen Habermas, *Communication and the Evolution of Society*, Thomas McCarthy, tr. (Boston, MA: Beacon Press, 1979), 1-68.

[13] The expression 'Constructivist epistemology' was first used by Jean Piaget in the famous article 'Logique et Connaissance Scientifique,' in: *Encyclopédie de la Pléiade* (1967). He refers to mathematician Adriaen Brouwer (1605-1638) and philosopher Giambattista Vico (1668-1744). Cf. *Constructivist epistemology*: www.answers.com/topicconstructivistepistemology

[14] See William James, Charles Peirce, John Dewey, etc.

[15] See P. F. Strawson, 'Truth' in: *Proceedings of the Aristotelian Society*, suppl. vol XXIV, 1950. Cf. Richard Kirkham, *Theories of Truth* (Cambridge, MA: MIT Press, 1992). Chapter 10 contains a detailed discussion of Strawson's performative theory of truth.

[16] Frank P. Ramsey, 'Facts and Propositions' (1927) reprinted in *Philosophical Papers*, David Hugh Mellor, ed., (Cambridge, UK: Cambridge University Press, 1990), 34-51.

[17] Thomas W. Currie III, *Searching for Truth: Confessing Christ in an Uncertain World* (Westminster, UK: John Knox Press, 2001).

the events and developments that shaped the human past.'[18] Nevertheless, the idea prevails in the postmodern mind that truth is a relative concept. The scientists generally agree that there is no absolute truth, but that there are objectively valid laws and principles. They deny therefore the great 'meta-narratives' of the past—including, obviously, the biblical ones—in their claim to offer an all-encompassing ultimate explanation for reality. For them truth remains mainly a quest.

Biblical definitions of truth

It is not my purpose to argue against any of the above-mentioned theories of truth, although it would be quite interesting to do so. Here I would like instead to confront them with the biblical concept of truth, and particularly with the statement of 2 Peter 1:12 which puts together the absolute concept of *truth* and the relative notion of *present* in the phrase 'present truth,' which is so well known to Adventists.

The word 'truth' (in Greek *alētheia*) is often used in the New Testament as the translation from the Hebrew *emeth*, with four main distinctive meanings:

1. *Truth* as opposite to error or falsehood (cf. Eph 4:25). We can say that this use is more or less philosophical.

2. *Truth* as moral integrity, dependability, reliability, sincerity, opposite to deception (cf. John 8:44). This use is mainly ethical.

3. *Truth* as reality, a counterpart to types, symbols, shadows (cf. Col 2:17) or mere appearance (see Phil 1:18). This use is especially hermeneutical and theological.

4. *Truth* as a synonym of the Christian faith, like in the phrase 'the truth which is present with you' (2 Pet 1:12, NASB). This fourth use, mainly ecclesial, is the one that we would like to address here.

It is interesting to notice that Jesus' own, very existential, definition of truth—'I am the way, and the truth and the life' (John 14:6)—apparently includes all the four mentioned dimensions since Jesus was at the same time: (1) true to God; (2) his reliable messenger; (3) the fulfilment of the Old Testament types; and (4) the embodiment of God's revelation. If we agree that 'truth as disclosure consists in the *uncovering* or *coming to light* of what is real,'[19] Jesus' definition of truth corresponds well to what we call 'revelation,' since in him—as well as in Scripture and nature—God reveals himself to us in many ways. And it becomes a valid paradigm for us.

'Present truth' in 2 Peter 1:12

What does *present truth* mean in the statement of 2 Peter 1:12 : 'You have been established (*estērigmenous*) in the present truth (*en tē parousē alētheia*)'? Since the sense

---

[18] Fritz Guy, *Thinking Theologically* (Berrien Springs, MI: Andrews University Press, 1999), 250.
[19] Canale, 452.

of the word *truth* is polysemous (i.e. having many meanings), in answering this question we need, first of all, to clarify the sense of the word *present* that qualifies the noun *truth*.

The adjective *parousē*, translated often by *present*, can have at least three meanings:

a. *Spatial*: A truth which is manifested, not hidden nor absent. The word *parousē* is related to *parousia*, manifestation (cf. vs 9 and Col 1:5f). In this sense *present truth* would be a truth that appears clearly to the observers. The text speaks explicitly of 'present truth manifested.'[20]

b. *Temporal*: A truth which is not past nor future, or not only past or future. A truth that is relevant for today.

c. *Existential*: A truth related to the spiritual experience of the readers (cf. 2 Tim 3:7 and 3 John 1:8): 'The truth in which the readers have been taught.'[21] In this case, *present truth* would refer to the Christian doctrine.[22]

Our contention is that the phrase 'present truth' in 2 Peter 1:12 may include more than one of these three senses and not only the last one.

In our Adventist history we have abundantly used the expression 'present truth' in this last sense, but sometimes with a restrictive scope, as if it meant just 'the Adventist message,' the disclosure of the end-time prophecies, our preaching for the preparation for the Second Coming of Christ, etc. There is no reason to object to this internal usage. It belongs to our heritage and I do not want to deny its inspiring value in our tradition. But I want to pay closer attention here to a wider meaning of the phrase *present truth*, leaving some room for the other two possible meanings, even if, in doing so, we have to accept that the two key concepts of *truth* and *present* remain in tension.

'Present truth' in the Adventist tradition

Precisely 'one of the great characteristics of the Adventist heritage is its commitment to truth, a commitment that has been typically vigorous and often courageous. This commitment was expressed in a willingness to stand against the world if evidence indicated that was the way of truth, and also in a willingness to disagree with others within the community of faith if that was required by loyalty to truth.'[23]

---

[20] The idea of truth as disclosure has been developed in the work of Heidegger and others. On the basis of the Greek word *alētheia*, truth is understood as 'discovery or revelation of something previously hidden (…). Truth, in this sense, means revealing or uncovering (…). As *disclosure*, truth exists when reality reveals itself without distortion.' See Fernando Canale, 452.

[21] Seventh-day *Adventist Bible Commentary*, vol. 6, 599.

[22] G. Harder, in TDNT 7, 656, translates *present truth* here as 'Christian doctrine or Christianity generally.'

[23] F. Guy, 250.

The idea of 'present truth'—truth whose time has come—is the most important single element in the Adventist theological heritage. While eternal truth is by definition always 'true,' a particular element of truth may have particular relevance to, and meaning for, a particular time and place. When this is so, it evokes a new recognition and understanding of its significance. Truth can thus be understood as both 'eternal' and 'dynamic.' For Adventist Christianity, the very word 'truth' ought to mean discovery and growth; 'to be authentically Adventist in the most profound sense is to be as deeply committed to the truth we have yet to learn as to the truth we already know.'[24] In this sense it appears clearly that 'any attempt to make particular past understandings, whatever their historical setting, the final criterion of the present and future interpretation of faith is not just a bad idea; it is a betrayal of the basic Adventist principle of *present truth*.'[25]

Some Christians, anxious to be faithful to the truth revealed by God, seem to overlook the challenges of the present world, and live constantly looking into the past, since they want to be sure that they do not depart from the 'present truth' of the pioneers. Others, eager to respond to the world around them, do not hesitate to trim or even to twist God's revelation in their search for relevance to face the challenges of the present. To escape the traps of these two trends, it becomes necessary to overcome the temptation of separating realities which belong together. For fidelity to the biblical text means that we cannot separate *truth* from *present*.[26]

Commitment to truth

As Christians we have a double commitment: a commitment to God's revealed truth and another commitment to the present world in which God has placed us with a mission (Mat 28:18-20). Our two commitments—*truth* and *present*—may at times be in conflict. Some of our contemporaries, sensitive to scientific and pluralistic ideas, have a hard time making the biblical notion of 'truth' compatible with their view of reality. As Christian scholars we may feel caught in the painful tension between 'present' and 'truth,' as if these two realities were almost two worlds apart. We are tempted to withdraw from either world by capitulation to the other. We often struggle to avoid both traps. We try to remain faithful to the revelation of yesterday so that we may see its implications for the realities of today. It is, however, not easy to combine loyalty to the past with sensitivity to the present. Yet, this is our Christian calling and mission: to live in the world under the Word. As disciples of Christ we are called to uplift the 'present truth' and a *truth which is present*.

---

[24] See Bradford, 24-28; Bertil Wiklander, 'The Truth As It Is in Jesus,' *Ministry* (February 1996), 5-7.

[25] Guy, 80.

[26] See Eckhart Tolle, *The Power of Now. A Guide to Spiritual Enlightenment* (Vancouver, Canada: New World Library, 2004).

If we believe that the mission and task of the Christian scholar is to search for the truth, to hold on to the truth and to teach the truth, we may agree that for us as individuals 'as well as for the community of faith, commitment to truth is the first and highest principle of theology. Because theology is a cognitive enterprise, truth is its supreme value.'[27] As members of the body of Christ we have a personal and collective commitment to truth. This collective commitment to truth

> ... is the community's decision to give to truth a higher priority than it gives to its own reputation, growth, unity, peace, or even survival, because it knows that truth is an intrinsically higher value than the past identity or future well-being of the community. This commitment ... means that the community cares supremely about truth. This kind of commitment means, furthermore, that the community cares more about truth than about its own past thinking, which constitutes its theological heritage, or its present think-ing, which constitutes its orthodoxy. This heritage must always be taken *seriously*, because it is the ground from which has grown the community's present identity; and if it were ignored or denied, the community could no longer recognize or understand itself. But the tradition must never be taken *absolutely*, because it is not an infallible norm in the quest for an ever more adequate understanding of its faith.[28]

Truth as doctrine

In the classical western view, truth was supposed to be found by reason and reflec-tion. Enlightened thinking was expected to produce virtuous actions so that the rational person would be the good person. Thus, for Plato, 'there will be no end to the troubles of states, or of humanity itself, till philosophers become kings in this world, or till those we now call kings and rulers really and truly become phi-losophers ...'[29] This idea is still alive today in what has been called *the fundamental western myth*, 'the myth of the head, of the mind, of the importance of rational and impersonal logic.'[30]

When translated into Christian terms, the classical view—rightly challenged by postmodernism—equates 'truth' with mental activity, with reason and doctrinal propositions. This intellectual view of truth is evident in the popular idea—from a fragmented mind—that religion is a personal matter, a subjective and private deci-sion depending on beliefs and doctrines. But a mainly doctrinal approach to truth

---

[27] F. Guy, 52.
[28] Ibid., 44.
[29] Plato, *The Republic*, 473C.
[30] Michael Novak, *The Spirit of Democratic Capitalism* (New York: American Enterprise Institute, 1982).

often makes even the committed believer spirituality impotent. In fact, we may become so worried about the right formulation of our beliefs and be so occupied with the defence of our dogmas, that our theological and even our evangelistic concern may divert toward what people believe about God rather than with the commitment of one's self to God in everyday life. In our western, secular view, knowledge is mainly theoretical, and it is left to everyone's discretion whether or not to derive rules of conduct from personal insights, while in the Bible the person who does not act in accordance with God is considered a fool (cf. Prov 1: 20-33). This is why it is possible for a scholar theoretically to recognize the Bible 'as the incarnation of knowledge and truth, and to see himself as its orthodox teacher ... and preach the commandments and yet steal or commit adultery or rob the temple (Rom 2:21, 22). By such inconsistencies, says Paul, the name of God is blasphemed.'[31] Our personal experience shows that our actions may depart somehow from our stated principles. Often our beliefs are less predictive of our behaviour than we may presume. Our intellectual assent to certain doctrines does not always include putting into practice all of their implications. So, for example, we can argue in public about God's sovereignty while not always allowing him to rule over our private life.

One of the problems of traditional Christianity through the ages has been its tendency to elevate *orthodoxy* (right thinking) above *orthopraxis* (right action). We do not need to go far in history to observe that the presumption of possessing the truth often led to arrogance, intolerance, or worse.

The truth as it is in Jesus

Jesus Christ, our Master and Model, gave us a perfect example of what it means to be committed to truth. In him words and deeds, both public and private, were consistent. He had one whole life, not a compartmentalized 'professional life,' a 'social life,' a 'spiritual life,' and so forth. Departing from the prevailing line of thought that was shared by most philosophers of his time—and ours—Jesus warned us that *knowing the truth* is not only an intellectual endeavour, but an existential liberating experience (John 8:32). This kind of knowledge is a commitment process which engages the entire person. Although the world in which we live often intimates that religion has only to do with religious affairs (therefore only religious professionals are called to 'full-time Christian service'), knowing the truth in a biblical sense has to do with the whole life. Compartmentalized thinking is foreign to the true disciple of Christ. He/she is called to be a disciple in whom attitude and action, belief and behaviour, cognition and commitment, go together. *He/she is someone who makes truth present.*

---

[31] G. C. Berkouwer, 'Revelation and Knowledge' in: *Studies in Dogmatics: General Revelation* (Grand Rapids, MI: Wm. B. Eerdmans Publishing Co, 1955), 137-171.

A commitment to truth requires that the theologian endeavours to remain impartial in the sense that he is 'scrupulous in assembling the evidence, honest in recognizing arguments against one's position, fair in assessing the force of these arguments, sympathetic in representing the position of those with whom one disagrees.'[32] In this sense, to uphold truth requires as much humility and courage as knowledge and intelligence.

Living truth

Our concern here is this: How can we deal with *present truth* in such a way that our personal life is transformed so that it makes us better people, and that our mission as a church is enhanced? Paul says that conversion is supposed to affect our way of thinking, and that we are to be 'transformed by the renewal of our minds' (Rom 12:1-2). This new way of thinking, according to the biblical view of the person as a whole entity, does not leave room for a dichotomy of thought and action, of *truth* and *present*.

According to the Bible, *truth is primarily relational*. Reality and truth are better known not only by rational reflection, but also through direct experience. Real knowledge of God is therefore mainly empiric, and grows out of a personal encounter with him. Personal knowledge of God is experience of God, not merely knowledge of propositions concerning God. The knowledge of God is not the result of speculative thinking, but the result of a personal experience with him and with his saving work. This is why in Scripture only the righteous person can therefore be said truly to know God (e.g. Deut 4:39; Jer 22:15-16). In this sense, therefore, to know the truth is more than to know *about* it. To know God—the Source of ultimate Truth—is to encounter and experience him, to listen to him and to obey him.

Our theological understanding of truth should be built upon the biblical view of knowledge as producing a living unity of faith and works. Faith is not a mere product of reason. It is not merely a quiet intellectual certainty on matters of doctrine. One can know *about* matters of faith, in fact one can be an excellent theologian, without *knowing* or having faith in the biblical sense. Even 'the devils believe,' James 2:19 warns us. Faith is an *attitude* of trust and commitment to a Person rather than just to a list of beliefs, truths or dogmas. This is why André Chouraqui dares to translate in his French Bible 'faith' by *adhesion* and *commitment*, and 'believing' by *joining* and *supporting*.[33] Faith takes us beyond a detached and speculative outlook into the sphere of personal involvement (John 8:31-32). True faith makes truth *present* in one's life.

---

[32] Basil Mitchell, *Faith and Criticism* (Oxford, UK: Clarendon Press, 1994), 23.
[33] André Chouraqui, *La Bible* (Paris, France: Desclée de Brouwer, 2003).

Making truth *present*

How can we deal with *truth* in such a way that our whole lives will be penetrated by it; in a way that deepens our sense of the transcendent, and at the same time gives us a clearer perception of our present reality and of our mission? How can we make truth *present*?

If it is the task of the Christian scholar to search for the truth, to know the truth and to teach the truth, one would expect, therefore, that Christian scholars, better than anybody else, would reflect in their lives the results of that commitment, of that knowledge, and of that teaching. Truth is powerful when it is argued. But it is even more powerful when it is embodied. There is power in prayer and in the gospel; there is even more power if we pray and evangelize at the same time. There is power in witness and protest; there is even more power if we testify and take action together. There is power in truth; there is even more in a truth which is *present*. For people need not only to understand the arguments of Christianity, but they must see its benefits displayed. A Christian teacher in a school, a nurse in a hospital, a secretary in an office, an assistant in a shop, or a worker in a factory, committed to make truth *present*, can have an influence out of all proportion to numbers and percentages. And who can calculate the influence for good in the whole neighbourhood of a single true Christian home, in which husband and wife are faithful and find fulfilment in each other, their children grow up in the disciplined security of love, and the family members are not just focused on themselves but also on the community? As Christians we have a mission. We are marked people both at work and at home; the world is watching us (2 Cor 3:2; Heb 12:1-2).

A church that makes *truth present*

More influential even than the example of Christian individuals and families could be that of the local church. For the church is meant by God to be his present and redeemed community, the concrete incarnation of truth and of the ideals of his kingdom. 'We must not underestimate the powerful ... impact on society of the creation of an alternative social group ... For the primary social structure through which the gospel works to change other structures is that of the Christian community.'[34]

The small group was our Lord's own chosen way of action. He began with the Twelve. The history of the church that came after them abounds in examples of the strategic influence of small groups. Throughout the centuries humanity has been led by daring minorities. Tom Sine has captured this idea very well in his book *The Mustard Seed Conspiracy*. The title alludes to the tiny seed out of which a large bush grows. Its subtitle is 'You can make a difference in tomorrow's troubled world.'[35]

---

[34] John Howard Yoder, *The Politics of Jesus* (Grand Rapids, MI: Wm. B. Eerdmans Publishing Co., 1972).

[35] See also T. Sine, *Mustard Seed versus McWorld* (Grand Rapids, MI: Baker Books, 1999).

And this is his main idea:

> Jesus let us in on an astonishing secret. God has chosen to change the world through the lowly, the unassuming and the imperceptible ... That has always been God's strategy—changing the world through *the conspiracy of the insignificant.* He chose a ragged bunch of Semite slaves to become the insurgents of his new order ... And who would have ever dreamed that God would choose to work through a baby in a stall to turn the world right side up! God chose the foolish things ... the weak things ... the lowly things ... the things that are not ... It is still God's policy to work through the embarrassingly insignificant present to change his world and create his future ...[36]

Commenting on this idea, John Stott wrote:

> *The embarrassingly insignificant present.* I feel the need to underline this topsy-turvy policy which God has adopted. At the same time, I am anxious that we should grasp that it is realistic. What minorities lack in numbers, they can make up in conviction and commitment.[37]

Motivated by their love for Christ and humankind and by their commitment to truth, the early Christians, the Reformers, and their heirs, including the Adventist Church, went everywhere preaching the Word of God and changing the world, because nothing has such a humanizing influence as the gospel. In their endeavour to make truth *present*, God's people established schools and hospitals. They took care of the blind and the deaf, the orphaned and the widowed, the sick and the dying. They fought against the slave trade, improved the conditions of workers in mills and mines, and the fate of prisoners. They protected children and women from abuse, commercial exploitation and from prostitution. They brought to all kinds of sufferers both the compassion of Jesus and modern methods of medicine, reconstructive surgery and rehabilitation. The effort to make *truth present* leads us to set ourselves against racism and political oppression. Making *truth present* pushes us to get involved in the inner city, the slums and the ghettos, and to raise our protest against the inhuman conditions of an unjust world. Making truth *present* keeps us preaching the gospel until the end.

Conclusions

We learn from Jesus that commitment to truth, full knowledge of God and of self, requires personal commitment to him. We find truth and ourselves by losing our-

---

[36] T. Sine, *The Mustard Seed Conspiracy* (London, UK: MARC, 1981), 11, 12.
[37] John Stott, *Issues Facing Christians Today* (Basingstoke, UK: Marshalls, 1984), 19-22, 75-78.

selves as we make Christ truly present in our life and around us (Mat 25:31-46), rather than by some mystical inward search. Instructions on how to deal with present truth are given over and over again in Scriptures. The wise disciple is guided by 'the Spirit of truth into all truth' (John 16:13). The power of Jesus' words is known in doing them. While Jesus was the Word of God *embodied*, we often satisfy ourselves with words rhetorically *embalmed*. More important than to formulate the gospel in correct *creed*—although this also is very important—we should endeavour to embody it in glowing *deed*.

Truth needs to become present. God has given to us, Christian scholars, intellectual and theological as well as practical responsibilities in his world. We have still some things to learn in this area to develop a Christian theological perspective of present truth within the complexities of our world. Our search for truth may be confronted with the task of deconstructing inherited theology and of rethinking, rejecting and rebuilding whatever is needed. Building mainly on a restrictive notion of *present truth* as heritage, we have often just produced a systematic theology, focused on doctrines. What would happen if our theological approach was rather built on the biblical notion of truth, made present, focused on the dynamics of divine wisdom?

By relating the concept of *present truth* mainly to eschatology and to a restrictive concept of God's 'remnant,' we have often produced an exclusive mentality, and even a self-centred church. What would happen if the stress was put on making truth present, in a theology of mission focused on justice and mercy, and not on numbers and on proselytism?

Considering that *present truth* does include something beyond biblical apocalyptic, what would happen if we explored a biblical theology of time, where the permanent essentials would permeate the urgent last time expectations and where the *kairos* (the present opportunities) would inspire the way we prepare ourselves for the coming events of *chronos*? As the nomological approach to God's law as a part of the traditional 'present truth' generates too often a casuistic, legalistic attitude to God's will, what would happen if we looked at God's law as a living way to make truth present in our everyday life, as a result of our covenant with God, through the presence of the Holy Spirit in our heart?

Following Christ's thinking and applying the biblical revelation to the pressing issues of the day, we have a great chance of remaining 'firmly established in the present truth' (2 Pet 1:12) and of making *truth* really *present*.

Roberto Badenas. Born in Spain. Since 1999 director of Education and Family Ministries Departments, Euro-Africa Division. Teaching and administrative experience in Spain and France. Dean of Theology Department, Salève Adventist University, France, 1989-1999. Author of books and articles. PhD, Andrews University (1983).

'How long, O Lord, How long?'

Richard P. Lehmann

Jesus promised to build his church (Mat 16:18).[1] To accomplish his purpose he would need time. The church was first to get organized, elders and deacons selected, evangelists, pastors and doctors sent out. The mission was to be deployed.

Today, however, after 2000 years are we not entitled to feel some level of eagerness? Is Jesus not a bit slow to fulfil his promises? This question is all the more painful considering that Seventh-day Adventists have been announcing his return for over 160 years.

A delay?

As early as the end of the first century doubts about the return of Jesus were manifested. Those who suffered pain and martyrdom had reason to wonder. Their cries reverberate throughout the centuries, 'How long, Sovereign Lord?' (Rev 6:10). Doubters raised their voices saying: 'Where is this "coming" he promised? Ever since our fathers died, everything goes on as it has since the beginning of creation' (2 Pet 3:1). Peter was responding to scoffers but his retort implies that he faced similar echoes from within the church: why else would he refute such a contention?

The scoffers made reference to creation as a matter of solid evidence. For them nothing has changed since. Peter argued that at the beginning there was *water*, a tumultuous element from which God brought forth the earth. The earth was later submerged by the same restless element. Awaiting the destiny of humanity is another unstable element, one that is impossible to restrain, *fire*. In other words, the relative stability of the present may suggest that nothing has changed since the beginning. The apparent comfort is deceptive as the unsteady world is liable to topple at any time. If it does not, it is only because of God's measure of patience. Clearly, 'The Lord is not slow in keeping his promise, as some understand slowness. He is patient with you, not wanting anyone to perish, but everyone to come to repentance' (2 Pet 3:9).

An opportunity to be seized

According to Peter the apostle, the flow of time should not be regarded as a delay but as an extension of time for conversion and return to God. This is clearly an opportunity to be seized as Peter points out, 'Since everything will be destroyed in this way, what kind of people ought you to be? You ought to live holy and godly

---

[1] All texts from the NIV, unless otherwise indicated.

lives ... So then, dear friends, since you are looking forward to this, make every effort to be found spotless, blameless and at peace with him' (2 Peter 3:11, 14).

In a similar context, Amos the prophet addressed the people of Israel who still worshipped Yahweh in his days. They did so with ostentatious generosity, bringing abundant offerings to the temple while celebrating with music of praise (Amos 5:22, 23) despite allowing oppression, injustices and maltreatment in their daily life (Amos 5:10-13). The expectation of the people, however, was for God to come and deliver them from their enemies. When the Lord took action in their favour, they thought, the world would know that they were the chosen people. Amos is the spokesman of a severe warning however: 'Woe to you who long for the day of the LORD! Why do you long for the day of the LORD? That day will be darkness, not light' (Amos 5:18).

Let us not be duped. When the day of God is at hand, when Jesus appears in the clouds of heaven, as joyful a day as it will be for those awaiting his return, it will be a dreadful day for those unprepared. As Jesus describes it in one of his superb parables, all are invited to the wedding feast offered by the sovereign, but only those attired in the proper wedding garments will be ushered in (Mat 22:8-14).

The passing of time should not be viewed as a waste of time but as a gain in the framework of the riches awaiting those who make use of this time to commune with God with renewed consecration. Here is how Paul described the implications of Christ's return to Titus: 'For the grace of God that brings salvation has appeared to all men. It teaches us to say "No" to ungodliness and worldly passions,' and 'to live self-controlled, upright and godly lives in this present age, while we wait for the blessed hope—the glorious appearing of our great God and Saviour, Jesus Christ who gave himself for us to redeem us from all wickedness and to purify for himself a people that are his very own, eager to do what is good' (Titus 2:11-14).

An opportunity to share our testimony

The author of Hebrews was faced with the same inquiry: Why has Jesus not yet returned? His response differs from that of Peter. 'For yet a little while,' he said, 'and he that shall come will come and will not tarry. Now the just shall live by faith' (Heb 10:37-38a).

For this author there is no delay, but perseverance and persistent faith is required. He follows the affirmation with a review of the heroes of faith. The entire chapter 11 honours them. We could assume that these 'heroes,' as we like to call them, were thus credited by virtue of their unfailing faith. We often assume this to be the reason they were extolled as examples in this passage. This is not the case. The author justifies their listing in these terms: 'These all died in faith, not having received what was promised' (Heb 11:13 RSV), and he substantiates his argument by saying, 'These were all commended by their faith, yet none of them received what had been promised' (Heb 11:13 RSV). Thus a believer is called upon to persevere in the faith of the promise, even when the perception of the promise is indistinct.

However, for the author of Hebrews the passing of time is not a delay, it is an opportunity for sharing and bringing others to their salvation. 'God had planned something better for us so that only together with us would they be made perfect' (Heb 11:40). Just as the faithful of ancient times failed to see the realization of their hope, which gives us the opportunity to hear and receive the word of salvation, we likewise might be deprived of that realization for the time being, so that others might benefit from salvation along with us. The passing of time is given to believers to persevere and witness. Every single day brings new challenges. These are given that we might 'endure' as did Jesus (Heb 12:1-3). As formulated in the final prayer of the book, it is also a period of time for us to do his will. 'May the God of peace, ... equip you with everything good for doing his will, and may he work in us what is pleasing to him, through Jesus Christ, to whom be glory for ever and ever. Amen' (Heb 13:20, 21).

The passing of time is therefore not a delay. According to Peter it is an opportunity for renewed conversion, while in Hebrews it is an opportunity to accomplish our mission for God, that others may receive their salvation with us.

An opportunity to serve

In a parable Jesus told following his end-time discourse, he contrasts two servants (Mat 24:45-51). One is declared faithful, the other, wicked. They are entrusted with the supervision of the staff while their master is away. After some time the wicked servant observes that his 'master is staying away a long time.' After a prolonged absence he concludes that the master might stay away permanently. He loses sight of the promised return to such a point that he becomes carefree, takes advantage of his master's wealth, and disgraces his fellow servants. As far as he is concerned the master will not return; he might as well take full advantage of the situation.

By contrast, the good servant has a different perception of time. For him, the passing of time is the *appropriate time* to care for his fellow servants. He is constantly assessing the proper time and the best way to provide for their needs. He is focused on the completion of all entrusted duties. For him, to perceive this time as a 'delay' would be a mark of distrust. The way we perceive and value time impacts our behaviour.

Paul's 'time formula'

In a formula unique to the apostle Paul he invites the Ephesians to 'redeem time' (buy back time). He gives them the reason: 'Because the days are evil' (Eph 5:16 KJV). The verb chosen is a reference to the marketplace. The use of this formula is certainly interesting. Anyone familiar with the Middle East is aware of the intense bargaining that goes on to negotiate the lowest possible price. To reach a deal a client must point out all the defects to reduce the value of the item desired. For Paul it is the opposite: days are evil, therefore we have to enrich them.

Time is not a stable value. Each person considers it differently. In fact, no one knows what time really is. It is a mystery. The apostle Peter recognizes it, 'But do not forget this one thing, dear friends: With the Lord a day is like a thousand years, and a thousand years are like a day' (2 Pet 3:8). Although a bit mindless at first glance, the formula is clear: humans simply don't know what time is!

No one can define time. A unanimous definition has never been formulated to satisfy both science and philosophy. What is time? A mystery!

Our approach to understand time is to chart it in space. We often perceive it as a straight line on which the present, past, and future are plotted. We thus convert time into a sort of spatial relationship: a pointer turning around a dial, a sand glass that runs out, a shadow sweeping across a sundial, digits continiously rolling on 12 or 24 hours.

Astrophysics measures time based on the distance light travels through space in one year. Einstein is known for having demonstrated the relativity of time and space. Bergson, the French philosopher, observed after Saint Augustine that the notion of time holds a psychological component of which the variable assessment is perceived differently depending on the nature of the event observed. Saint Augustine claimed that time is a figment of the soul; it is measured through one's expectation, observation, and recollection. Let us recognize the inconsistency found in the nature of these notions. The past escapes us with its bygones present only through our memory. The future is yet unknown, and the present goes by as we speak. Should the earth speed up, our centenarians would celebrate with 150 candles. Should the earth slow down, we would all die at twenty looking like old prunes.

For some, time is money. Depending on the circumstances, time may appear short or long. Two millennia may appear rather long. But here again, we are dealing with a relative component. Assuming that a generation is 80 years, there have been only 24 of them since the first coming of Jesus. Three generations ago we were at the dawn of the French Revolution. And only six generations separate us from Francis the First, and once again that many generations bring us to the time of Charlemagne.

Time in the Bible

Although chronological time is inherent to the Bible when dates or periods of time are mentioned, the *quality* of the time is more important than its *quantity*. The Greeks used the celestial bodies and the stars to calculate time through the careful observation of their movement. By contrast, Hebrews perceived time in terms of their eminence and influence. For them, the markers of time were the rainfalls, the brilliance of the sun, and the passing of seasons.

For this reason they perceived time as an opportunity for the appropriateness of an action. As Ecclesiastes declares, there is a time for everything, a time to plant, to build, to laugh, love, live, and even a time to cry, destroy, dance, and die (Eccl 3:1-8).

For humans time also compels a rhythm all of its own. Childhood precedes love, followed by old age. It is even capable of rejuvenating flesh when redemption is obtained (Job 33:22-25), as expressed in the praises of the Psalmist:

> Praise the LORD, O my soul;
>   all my inmost being, praise his holy name.
> Praise the LORD, O my soul,
>   and forget not all his benefits;
> who forgives all your sins
>   and heals all your diseases,
> who redeems your life from the pit
>   and crowns you with love and compassion,
> who satisfies your desires with good things
>   so that your youth is renewed like the eagle's (Ps 103:1-5).

In the Bible time is not a cyclical concept of Greek understanding, nor is it a linear value to be accounted for, it is rather an asset to be appreciated, taking advantage of the opportunities it offers, because they are all inscribed in the annals of God.

It is the influence of God in history that gives time its true meaning. His providential management topples all human endeavours. Nebuchadnezzar, who assumed that his reign was to last forever, was plunged in the darkness of his folly. Joseph, who envisioned his time to be over, was entrusted with princely status. With God time takes on a different dimension. Even death is powerless to bring it to an end. For this reason the Greek translators of the Bible and the authors of the New Testament favoured the term *kairos* rather than *chronos*. The latter implies time that goes by, whereas *kairos* focuses on the present, the opportunity to be seized to bolster the emergence of God in history.

It is not surprising that Peter, the author of Hebrews, Paul, and Jesus, all insisted on the importance of living effectively in the present moment. The present is all we have. Choices must be made continually to remain in communion with God, share his blessings, and provide appropriately the services needed around us. The choices are based on one's faith for which God imparts the standard.

To illustrate the concept Jesus shared a parable (Lk 18:1-8). The scene casts a widow annoying a civil judge to rule in her favour against an accuser. The insistence of the woman eventually brings the judge to rule on her behalf to avoid further annoyance. Jesus contrasts the attitude of the faulty human judge with God, who is likewise relentlessly solicited by humans to eradicate injustice: 'And will not God bring about justice for his chosen ones, who cry out to him day and night'? The question also comes up in the Lord's Prayer: 'Your kingdom come, your will be done on earth as it is in heaven.' This prayer of Jesus was also that of the assembled church: 'Maranatha' 1 Cor 16:22 KJV). 'Come, Lord Jesus' (Rev 22:20 RSV).

God is indeed anxious to respond: 'I tell you, he will see that they get justice, and quickly.' God's plan of salvation is right on course. Revelation adds, he 'comes'; and he is already on the way back. The battle goes on, but the victory has already been won.

The larger question is not so much knowing when the justice of God will be rendered, but: 'When the Son of Man comes, will he find faith on the earth?' (Lk 18:8). This raises a question of personal concern; is my faith alive? Is it capable of communicating hope? Am I focused on serving others, or am I absorbed with the resolution of my own questions and personal needs? Here we are at the heart of the message addressed to the Hebrews: 'You need to persevere so that when you have done the will of God, you will receive what he has promised (Heb 10:36).

Richard P. Lehmann. Born in France. Retired 2007. Pastoral, educational and administrative experiences in France, the Cameroons and Switzerland. Principal Salève University 1992-1997 and 2004-2007; president for North France Conference 1997-2001 and Franco-Belgian Union 1998-2003. Author of books and articles. PhD, University of Strasbourg (1976).

"And surely I am with you always, to the very end of the age"– An Inquiry into the Meaning of the Final Words of Jesus and Concluding Paragraphs in the Gospels of Mark and Matthew

Anders Eyvind Nielsen

Introductory Remarks

According to common social conventions associated with significant farewell scenes in everyday life, we have good grounds for believing that 'final words' (*ultima verba*) are often of much significance[1]. We may even indeed speak of the 'psychology of the farewell,' meaning that what is said before the final leave-taking acquires a particularly important meaning for generations to come. Such a rhetorical communication is well-rooted in Graeco-Roman and Jewish-Christian literary traditions.[2]

In the Hebrew version of the Old Testament we find the motif in only a handful of farewell addresses,[3] but during the Hellenistic period these different literary types of expression were shaped into a popular art form. Hence, such speeches are—compared to the Hebrew Bible—more strongly represented in the Septuagint (LXX),[4] and culminate in quality, extent and type in the time of the New Testament.[5] However, partly due to the nature of its literary and socio-linguistic context, the farewell address varies so much in both structure and content as to make it methodologically unsafe to consider it a fixed literary 'genre' (*Gattung*).[6]

---

[1] Jesus' final words are found in Mat 28:20. All biblical references are from *The New International Version Bible (NIV)*, except where I add 'my translation'. My thanks go to Klaus and Sabine Bieberstein for inspiration for this article and to Bishop of Odense, Kresten Drejergaard, for his considerable support for study time and a financial grant.

[2] E.g. William S. Kurz, *Farewell Addresses in the New Testament. Zacchaeus Studies* (Collegeville, MN: Liturgical Press, 1990); Anders E. Nielsen, *Until it is Fulfilled. Lukan Eschatology According to Luke 22 and Acts 20*. In *Wissenschaftliche Untersuchungen zum Neuen Testament* (WUNT) Reihe 2. Vol. 126, Dr. dissert. Transl. Edward Broadbridge (Tübingen: Mohr Siebeck, 2000); and George L. Parsenios, *Departure and Consolation. The Johannine Farewell Discourses in Light of Greco-Roman Literature*. In *Supplements to Novum Testamentum* (SuppNT) 117 (Leiden/Boston: Brill, 2005).

[3] Gen 27 (Isaac); Gen 49 (Jacob); Gen 50 (Joseph); Deut 33 (Moses); Josh 23-24 (Joshua); 1 Sam 12 (Samuel); 2 Sam 23 and 1 Kgs 2 (David).

[4] Besides those texts mentioned in note 3 also Tob 3 (Tobit's farewell in the form of a prayer); 2 Macc 2 (Mattatias); 2 Macc 7 (a mother and her seven sons). Also in pseudepigraphic writings, e.g. 4 Macc 18 (as a philosophic version on 2 Macc 7); Test XII (as an elaboration on Gen 49 to the extent that each of Jacob's 12 sons delivers his own farewell address); LibAntBib19 (cf. Deut 33) and TestMos (an apocalyptic version of Deut 33).

[5] Mat 28:16-20; Mk 16:14-19; Lk 22:14-38; 24:44-49 and John 13:31-17:26 (Jesus); Acts 20:18-35(36-38) and 1-2 Tim (Paul) and 2 Pet (Peter).

[6] E.g. James H. Charlesworh, ed. *The Old Testament Pseudepigrapha*, 2 vols. (London, UK: Darton, Longman & Todd, 1983). Vol.1: *Apocalyptic Literature and Testaments*, 773; Nielsen, 2000, 26-32 (cf. note 2). Klaus Bieberstein and Sabine Bieberstein, 'Angesichts des Todes

An important case-study using a farewell motif as an effective rhetorical device is Plato's treatise, *Phaedo*. This work takes the form of an elaborated dialogue where the depiction of the heroic way in which Socrates faces his unjust death sentence serves to render probable the immortality of the soul. The dialogue is between two of Socrates' pupils: Phaedo, who was an eyewitness to Socrates' death, and Echecrates, who did not arrive in time for the end. For several ancient authors *Phaedo* became something of a prototype in demonstrating how a farewell motif can be used to underscore a subject matter of particular importance. This corresponds with a general public interest in how significant figures known from literary discourses of a philosophical, historical or religious nature behaved in word and deed on their deathbeds.[7]

Indeed, the final words of a dying protagonist can very well be taken as a condensed version of what in elaborated form constitutes a farewell address. As recent research on ancient literature suggests, in both cases the point is that the terminal setting is employed either as an important summary or as a final key-interpretation of a particular, narrated *Bios*.[8] I wish to broaden the scope of this inquiry by considering the concluding paragraphs of the first two synoptic gospels, as the title of this article suggests.

In the following I shall consider the gospels of Mark and Matthew in the chronological order followed by an overriding consensus of scholars. With respect to the Lukan writings I refer to my published research on Luke-Acts.[9] I also leave aside the gospel of John, which from the particular literary and theological character of its writing requires a separate study. For the same reason I also leave aside the traditions surrounding the Lord's Supper, although this material indeed may also be viewed from a farewell perspective—especially in the case of Luke.

Finally, in my approach I take the text as 'read or heard' text. By this I mean a literary proceeding which attempts to come closer to the intended audiences of the gospels and which considers the semantic nature that the authors have chosen in order to communicate the 'good news' to these respective audiences.[10] By being listeners/readers ourselves we may at a fundamental level share some presuppositions of the intended audience. At various points in the analysis that follows I shall draw on certain elements associated with reader-response criticism and textual linguistics.

---

das Leben formulieren. Abschiedsworte Sterbender in der biblischen Literatur,' in: Martin Ebner, Jørg Frey et al., eds. *Leben trotz Tod*, JBTh Vol. 19 (2004), 46 (cf. 3-47).

[7]   Cf. the technical term, *exitus illustrium virorum*, 'concerning the departure of outstanding persons.'

[8]   Klaus and Sabine Bieberstein, 25-47.

[9]   See note 2.

[10]   Cf. Amos N. Wilder, *Early Christian Rhetoric. The Language of the Gospel* (Cambridge, MA.: Harvard University Press, 1964), *passim;* and Marinus de Jonge, 'Theology as Narration,' in: *Jesus' Inspiring and Disturbing Presence*. Transl. John E. Steely (Nashville, TN: Abingdon Press, 1974), 86-98.

The final words of Jesus in the Gospel of Mark: a cry of despair? (Mk 15:34)

To the reader familiar with the convention of antiquity that great men in the presence of approaching death may deliver brave and important words (like Socrates) as they are leaving this world, Jesus' loud cry—'My God, my God, why have you forsaken me?' (15:34)—must apparently come as something of a surprise. Just prior to this Mark has told his reader that at 'midday darkness fell over the whole land' (15:33), carrying the conventional implication that something dreadful is in progress.[11] In the end Jesus dies with a wordless cry on his lips (15:37).

Not only does the dark, demeaning picture that Mark gives of the dying Jesus seem to differ radically from the tradition also found in Jewish martyrdom literature (e.g. 2 and 4 Macc), but also the terminal setting that Mark uses appears to contradict the overall portrait of Jesus in the gospel. On behalf of God—that is, as 'the Son of God' (1:1)[12]—Jesus is literally baptised to preach and act in sight of the approaching kingdom of God (1:15). In facing death (8:31; 9:31; 10:33-34) he is thus depicted as the appointed servant of God delivering the 'many' (10:45; cf. 14:22-24), and finally conquering death itself. How do these bold elements in the narrative of Mark fit in with Jesus' final utterance, if that is to be taken as a final interpretation of the life of Jesus?

1. Three Observations

In response to this question I would like to make the following three observations: (1) Mark's translation of the quoted words in Aramaic, 'My God, my God, why have you forsaken me?' refer to Psalm 22:2. In the mouth of Jesus these words, which according to Mark are the only and the final words of Jesus on the cross, are not just a cry into the open air. On the contrary, it is a cry directed at God—and falls within a Jewish tradition of lamentation, as in the Psalms of David and the Psalms of Solomon. It is implied that God is close enough to hear and see his own Son in great distress, addressing himself to the God who holds the ultimate future in his hands.[13] Furthermore, the psalm from which Jesus quotes just the introductory phrase may evoke in an audience familiar with the poetic tradition the concluding part, for instance, 'For he has not despised or scorned the suffering of the afflicted one; he has not hidden his face from him but has listened to his cry for help' (Ps 22:24).

---

[11] Lars Hartman, *Markusevangeliet*. In: *Kommentar till Nya Testamentet* (KNT). Vols. 2a-2b (Stockholm: EFS-förlaget 2004-2005). Vol. 2b: *Markusevangeliet 8:27-16,20*, 571. The Swedish commentary is in the process of being translated into English.

[12] The reading 'Son of God' does not find support in the oldest text-critical witnesses.

[13] To be even more specific, behind the interrogative pronoun, 'Why?' (in Mk: *eis ti*), stands the Hebrew/Aramaic 'to what end?' (*lamah / lemah*), cf. LXX *hina ti;*) referring to a purpose and future goal (not like the retrospective pronoun, *maduah*''for what reason [in the past...]?' Bieberstein, 2004, 29 (cf. note 6).

(2) Klaus Bieberstein and Sabine Bieberstein[14] call attention to the two related episodes—respectively, 'the curtain of the temple was torn in two from top to bottom' (15:38) and the words of the centurion, 'Truly this man was a son of God' (15:39)—as having important implications for the interpretation of the cry of Jesus. As with the auditive/visionary revelation from an open heaven over the baptismal scene of Jesus (1:10-11), the tearing open of the temple,[15] the old symbol for the realm of God, in close relation to the death of Jesus, may just as well suggest some sort of divine response to the cry of Jesus. In both instances the verbs in the passive mood imply God as subject (cf. *passivum divinum*). So Mark's implication may be that God has successfully remained with his Son from the beginning to the end of his public ministry.

(3) The response of the centurion may go either way. In other words, according to Lars Hartman, the reader may in the first place recognize in these words of a gentile a sense of contemporary convention about great men in the act of dying transmigrating into the heroes of the Olympic world. On the other hand, the centurion may, like other figures in the passion story, be saying far more than he is aware of. The audience that recalls the words of the intervening God at Jesus' baptism, and who may at the same time identify with a man from even the same gentile background—might transpose these words to the level of a creed placed in the mouth of a non-Christian who leads an army but is unaware of the wider implications of his assent.[16]

2. The original ending of the Gospel of Mark – a proposal

If the portrait Mark gives of the last hour of Jesus is at first glance surprising when compared to the general conventions with which contemporary readers were familiar, then—following the oldest text-critical witnesses—the original but abrupt ending of the gospel (16:8) is a further puzzle for a modern audience. We read in Mark's final episode (16:1-8) of how three women early in the morning after the Sabbath arrive at the tomb to anoint the dead body of Jesus, and are stupefied. The huge stone in front of the tomb has 'been rolled back already' (16:3), and inside the tomb they see 'a youth sitting ... wearing a white robe' (16:5). Moreover this angel-like figure tells them that the crucified Jesus 'is not here' (16:6). They are asked to go back to the disciples and tell them that '[Jesus] is going on before you into Galilee; there you will see him, as he told you' (16:7). In response to this

---

[14] See note 6.

[15] According to Josephus' impressive description of the temple front curtain in Bell V:212-214 he takes this curtain 'as an image of the whole,' meaning the entire temple building, cf. Bieberstein, 2004, 32.

[16] Cf. note 25 concerning the verb in the imperfect (*hēn*) which is in use both in Mk and Mat— Jesus' cry in Aramaic on God that the Jews (due to the suffix '*i*' or '*ija'*) interpret wrongly as a calling on Elijah (15:35 par.) is, in contrast to the words of the centurion, obviously rendered as a misunderstanding (on purpose?) of the apocalyptically predisposed Jews.

bewildering command Mark adds the following astonishing comments, 'Then they went out and ran away from the tomb, beside themselves with terror. They said nothing to anybody, for they were afraid' (16:8). This comes as a major disappointment at the end of a literary work whose opening phrase proclaimed: 'Here begins the gospel of Jesus Christ the Son of God' (1:1). And yet, in the implied tension between these two phrases in Mark we may find the very key to understanding why the original ending is as it is.

Later redactional additions to this narrative (cf. 16:9 or 16:9-20)—probably under the influence of the two other synoptic gospels—suggest a growing need to make some improvement to the original ending of Mark. However, like the other gospel writers, the author of the original ending was hardly preoccupied with either stylistic or biographical matters at the expense of his literary and theological concern. For him, the meaning of Jesus' resurrection is not to be found in the empty tomb as such, but in the instruction given to the women by the young man dressed in white robes—an indication of the divine realm he represents. As a transcendental guiding figure (*interpres angelus*) known from apocalyptic traditions, the young man dressed in white in fact alters the women's point of perception—as well as the audience's—from the passing away of Jesus to the resurrection of the 'awakened' One (16:6, cf. *ēgérthē*, here as *passivum divinum*). The words of the heavenly messenger, 'he is not here' (16:6) do not testify to the *departed* Jesus but to the *risen* Jesus. From the implied divine act in transposing the figure of Jesus from the realm of death to the realm of new life it becomes clear what the resurrection of Jesus is supposed to mean to the women in the first place. For the messenger is saying, '[Jesus] is going on before you into Galilee; there you will see him, as he told you' (16:7).

The abrupt ending of Mark, with terrified women keeping quiet about their new knowledge, might lead the audience to believe that the disciples were kept in ignorance about the risen Lord. Nor might the audience recall Jesus' earlier promise that *they* would meet him in Galilee after he had been raised from the dead. On the other hand, as Hartman points out, the directing of the women to 'Galilee' may imply that in the light of Easter morning this 'place' symbolizes a profound new beginning of the gospel proclamation of the dominion of God. It is this theme (cf. 1:1; 1:14-15) that Mark is unfolding for his audience as a literary work).[17] I would therefore with Hartman (and some other scholars) suggest that Mark's introduction, 'The beginning of the gospel...' (1:1), may not just refer to the narrative of Jesus' baptism but to the entire work—right up to its endnote with the horrified women (16:8).[18] According to Mark's comment on Jesus' activity in Galilee after his

---

[17] Hartman, 587.

[18] So Hartman, vol. 2a, 24 and 29; Aage Pilgaard, *Markusevangeliet*. In *Dansk Kommentar til Det nye Testamente* (DKTN 5, Aarhus: Aarhus Universitetsforlag, 2008), 49-50.

baptism—'preaching the gospel of God' (1:14)—the substantive, 'the gospel' (tò euangélion), does not refer to Mark's gospel, but to 'the gospel of God,' as Mark explicitly states. This in turn means finally that 'the kingdom of God is upon you' (1:15)—as signified by the Christ-event in which the crucified Jesus raised from the dead is 'the Son of God' (1:1; cf. 15:39). This, I believe, constitutes *par excellence* the overall dynamic setting into which Mark is presenting his Jesus-story.

Thus the apparently helpless situation of the women in a state of shock has by divine intervention been superseded by the overwhelming 'good news' of Jesus being present in the proclamation of, and belief in, 'the gospel.' Jesus has been taken up into the sphere of eternity—into the universal capacity which Mark on his narrative level is presupposing and which on his existential level is actually living in the light of, together with his audience or community. Precisely in this overriding dimension the audience may then be prepared to take the cry of the crucified Jesus as a consequent exposition *in nuce* of the entire life of Jesus, hearing in it a cry of solidarity with those afflicted by the injustice of life. In his death cry Jesus maintains to the very end his relationship with God and his faith in God's ability to change a critical situation for the better.[19]

The final words of Jesus in the Gospel of Matthew in an intensified theological setting

Matthew's narrative version of the death of Jesus follows Mark to a great extent. Thus, Matthew tells his reader 'darkness came over the whole land' (27:45), Jesus cries out the same and only *ultimum verbum* from the cross (Mat 27:46)[20] and dies with a loud cry on his lips (27:50). However, in contrast to Mark's gospel Matthew highlights Jesus' final death cry by associating it with occurrences on a cosmic scale. Besides the fact that the 'curtain of the temple was torn in two from top to bottom,' Matthew carries on to mention a huge earthquake that split rocks apart and opened up graves so that 'many of God's saints were raised from sleep' (27:51-52). Matthew goes on to say that after the resurrection of Jesus these people were recognized by many in Jerusalem (27:53).

1. The dramatic scenario

To the rational mind these cosmic elements may either be rejected as highly superstitious or defended in a literalist way as true historical occurrences.[21] Matthew's audience, on the other hand, unaware of natural science in the modern

---

[19] Bieberstein, 35.

[20] With the minor exception that in his rendering of the Aramaic words Matthew uses the Hebrew *'eli'* / 'my God' instead of the Aramaic *'eloï,'* as Mark correctly has it.

[21] Cf. Hans Kessler, 'Jenseits von Fundamentalismus und Rationalismus: Versuch über Auferstehung Jesu und Auferstehung der Toten,' in: Hans Kessler, ed. *Auferstehung der Toten: ein Hoffnungsentwurf im Blick heutiger Wissenschaften* (Darmstadt, Germany: Wissenschaftliche Buchgesellschaft, 2004), 296-321, mentioned by Hartman, 582 (cf. note 11).

sense, would most likely be familiar with similar features in contemporary literature of a bibliographic or apocalyptic nature. By common convention deeds and deaths of great men may be underscored by supernatural features. The Roman historian Dio Cassius, for instance, in his account of Vespasian's conquest of Alexandria (cf. 60:17.5) mentions as a related incident to this important event the reappearance of people who had been raised from the dead.[22]

In his use of such cosmic elements Matthew takes up apocalyptic motifs from mainly biblical materials (esp. Ezek 37:1-14).[23] The evangelist intensifies the entire terminal setting of Jesus to a degree that clearly indicates (e.g. by using the actual verbs in the passive mood, cf. *passivum divinum*) that these 'events' are numinous in character. That is, in the very realm of approaching death the living and acting God is present with his Son—and actively so. In this highly-charged narrative it is not the natural world as such but a christological application of Scripture that is at work.[24] Furthermore, this whole scenario causes great fear in the centurion and his men, resulting in the 'confession' placed in the mouth of the centurion but also on the lips of his men that 'Truly this man was a son of God' (27:54).[25] Perhaps the audience may hear an implied conversion of the Roman tormentors, a motif also known from the Jewish-Christian martyr traditions.

In purely conventional terms Matthew's emphasis on the presence of a living and acting divinity underlines Jesus' final utterance in the most powerful way and corresponds well with his introduction—the birth and infant narratives—which among other elements inform the audience of the meaning of Jesus' name. This is achieved partly by relating this name etymologically to the Hebrew notion of salvation, specified theologically in 'he will save his people from their sins' (1:21); and partly by connecting Jesus' destiny with the Emmanuel-name, meaning 'God is with us' (Mat 1:23; cf. Isa 8:8,10).

To consummate his argument that God is present even in situations that may indicate the opposite, Matthew concludes his gospel by giving the risen Jesus the final and fundamental words to his disciples—and by inference Matthew's audience, 'And surely I am with you always, to the very end of the age' (28:20). It is

---

[22] Mogens Müller, *Kommentar til Matthæusevangeliet*. In *Dansk kommentar til Det nye Testamente* (DKTN 3, Aarhus, Denmark: Aarhus Universitetsforlag, 2000), 565, who also refers to other sources of antiquity, mentioning earthquakes in connection with the death of Julius Caesar.

[23] Ibid., 565, cf. e.g, Judg 5:4, an earthquake in relation to theophany; Zech 14:4, the split in the Mount of Olives at the appearance of the Lord, both mentioned by Müller.

[24] This phrase is almost my translation of Müller's words; ibid., 564.

[25] Müller sees in the phrase with its verb in the imperfect (*hēn*) two aspects. Firstly, the verb form indicates that with respect to the proper meaning of the designation, 'Son of God,' it was only possible *after* the death of Jesus to be taken beyond any misunderstanding. Secondly, the very 'content' of the title 'Son of God' draws its meaning from the proceeding narrative-part in Mat. Ibid., 566.

noteworthy that in this final and fundamental promise Jesus is not depicted as merely referring to God, or speaking on behalf of God, but is speaking of, and pointing to, *himself*. In other words the Emmanuel-name, 'God is with us,' now comes to mean 'Jesus is with us' as a final implicit testimony from Matthew in the form of direct speech. The 'I' who speaks, rendered here in the emphatic (cf. ėgo ... eimi), is doing so out of the ultimate power/authority conferred on him as the risen One: '... all authority in heaven and on earth has been given to me' (28:18).

These last words of Jesus (and of the gospel) comprise what is known as the 'great commission' or 'mission command,' although—to be more specific—the commission to go forth and preach the gospel is not explicitly mentioned in the text. Instead it is probably inferred in the participle, 'go forth' (*poreuthéntes*), to the universal setting of 'all the nations.' There is a previous example in Matthew, when Jesus commissions 'the twelve' to go 'to the lost sheep of the house of Israel' only (10:1-42). But the concluding commission in Matthew is clearly about the building up of the Christian life in the community. It is concerned with the 'following-up work' to help the community life to grow and be fruitful.[26] Thus, the first participle in the trinitarian baptismal form—the only one to be found in the New Testament—'make disciples' (*mathēteúsate*) is, in my view, more closely defined by the following two participles, 'baptising them' (*baptízontes*) and 'teaching them' (*didáskontes*).[27] I shall return to this motif.

2. The final paragraph as a farewell discourse

The final paragraph in Matthew may also be considered a minor farewell address, with the different minor literary features being rearranged to fit the theological and literary context. According to these minor parts or *topoi* in several farewell addresses and related literary frames there are common features. As death approaches (A), there is the summoning of relatives and friends to come to the death-bed (B), the speech itself (C), sometimes with a retrospective view which the speaker and audience share of the dying person (C/a), and/or with a prospect on the future in terms of warnings of coming danger/instructions about assignments/the speaker's instructions about the memorial service and interment (C/b), final greetings and/or blessings (D), and in the end the response of the audience in terms of sorrow/weeping (E). How does Matthew make use of these *topoi* in his chosen final section (28:16-20)?

(*ad* A) Any reference to approaching death in the context of Matthew's narrative is of course replaced by belief in Jesus' resurrection. Moreover, (*ad* B) instead of a death-bed scenario Jesus' relatives have been summoned to meet him in Galilee (28:16). (*ad* C) Some of the *topoi* are reorganized in the following two ways.

---

[26] Müller, 581.
[27] Ibid.

Firstly, Matthew anticipates (*ad* C/a) the retrospective *topos* in terms of a reference to 'Galilee' (mentioned no fewer than three times [cf. 28:7,10,16]) to indicate an 'area' in which the disciples are asked to meet the risen Jesus.[28] This directs the audience's attention to Jesus' earthly ministry, to which also the following correlative pronoun-element, 'all that' (28:20, *pánta ósa*),[29] in the farewell address points. This interpretation is supported by the mention of a particular but nameless 'mountain' (Mat 28:16) presumably as a symbolic *locus* of Jesus' preaching (Mat 5-7) and transfiguration (Mat 17:1-8). In these topographical references the audience may well see an allusion to the ministry of Jesus being in full accord with the divine realm, the will of God.

Secondly, the evangelist (*ad* E) guides the audience response to the introductory speech-frame by altering the act of weeping into an act of worship (28:17), (*ad* C/b). The future prospect is implicit in the great commission: 'Go forth therefore and make all nations my disciples ...' (28:19). And finally (*ad* D), there may be an element of blessing in Jesus' promise that he will remain with his disciples 'to the very end of the age.' In other words, the implied departed One is depicted explicitly as the present One. All the disciples receive these final words—including the doubters (28:17).

Furthermore, with regard to the episode-markers on the literary surface of the text the farewell address in question is on the one hand separated from the proceeding sections of the resurrection narrative by a spatial (locative) absolute episode marker, 'And the eleven disciples went to Galilee, to the mountain ...' (28:16, my translation). On the other hand the farewell address is, as we shall see, closely related to an overall or absolute temporal episode marker. This marker, 'After the Sabbath, when the light was about to break through upon the first day of the week ...' (28:1, my translation), organizes the rest of the narrative by indicating on which day Jesus met his disciples. Hence, the following two temporal episode-markers in the text—'And they [the women] quickly moved away from the tomb ...' (28:8, my translation) and 'While they were on their way ...' (28:11, my translation)—are both rather indistinct in character. Even with the final meeting on the mountain, the marker is a purely spatial indication referring to a quick shift in locality. The reader is not informed of any time-element, for example of how long this change of background from the tomb to the mountain took: 'And the eleven disciples went to ... the mountain' (28:16, my translation). So we may ask what are the theological implications of this formal reading of the entire text of Matthew 28?

---

[28] Galilee' is mentioned once in Mark (16:7) and once in Luke (24:7, here with an explicit reference by the two angels at the tomb to the pre-resurrected Jesus' prospect on his death and resurrection).

[29] In linguistic terms an 'anaphoric substitution on an abstract level,' referring back to the teachings of Jesus in his earthly ministry.

3. Some final suggestions about the context

I suggest that by giving prominence to the intensified setting in which the last words and cry of Jesus are uttered, in an overriding atmosphere of divine action and caring attendance, Matthew is underlining *a final time* in his resurrection-narrative. In other words, the final section (28:16-20) that he employs can be considered to be an exposition of the ultimate meaning of Jesus being raised from the dead. Which is, in the final words of the risen Jesus: 'I am with you always, to the very end of the age.' To this I offer the following four considerations.

Firstly, with respect to the overall structure of the final paragraph, the emphatic ending may be taken as an epexegetic reference to the *passivum divinum* element in the introductory phrase, '... to me is given all power in heaven and on earth' (28:18, my translation). Hence 'all power/authority' is possibly being defined as the ability of the risen Jesus to be always close to his disciples.

Secondly, with regard to the motif of a universal power in a vertical/horizontal dimension, Matthew and perhaps also his Greek speaking reader more or less familiar with the Septuagint (LXX), may well in this see a silhouette of the apocalyptic vision concerning a heavenly figure like a man approaching God, 'the Ancient of Days' (Dan 7:13) to the following effect: 'And he was given dominion, and all nations of the earth with posterity are serving all the glory [given] to him. And his power is an eternal power that shall not pass away and never be destroyed' (Dan 7:14 [LXX], my translation). In the concluding section in Matthew the following five *topoi* correlate with Daniel: (1) a passive mood of the verb 'to give,' (2) 'all power,' (3) an act of homage in terms of worship/service, and this whole setting is viewed from (4) a universal perspective, 'all nations,' and with (5) an ultimate temporal perspective.[30] Consequently, on a cosmic and universal scale both a vertical 'heaven/earth' and a horizontal dimension in terms of 'all nations/people' are involved in a new manifestation of divine power. In relation to Daniel, however, the ultimate temporal perspective of this power refers in Matthew to the risen Jesus. Thus, this comparative view of Matthew 28 and Daniel 7 seems to indicate how an apocalyptic-national vision concerning Israel has been reapplied on conditions given by a context viewed from the perspective of Jesus being raised from the dead. We may perhaps even here speak of a Christian *Midrash* on Daniel, in other words, an imaginative development of a theme suggested by Scripture.[31]

---

[30] Cf. the comparative analysis in Joachim Lange, *Das Erscheinen des Auferstandenen im Evangelium nach Matthäus. Eine traditions- und redaktionsgeschichtliche Untersuchung zu Mat 28,16-20.* Forschung zur Bibel (FzB) 11 (Würtzburg: Echter, 1973), 218-246, loc.cit. Lars Hartman, *Auf den Namen des Herrn Jesus. Die Taufe in den neutestamentlichen Schriften,* in: Stuttgarter Bibelstudien (SBS) Vol. 148 (Stuttgart, Germany: Verlag Katholisches Bibelwerk GmbH, 1992), 137.

[31] For other examples, cf. Lars Hartman, *Prophecy Interpreted. The Formation of some Jewish Apocalyptic Texts and of the Eschatological Discourse Mark 13 par.* In *Coniectanea Biblica. New*

Thirdly, Jesus' ultimate power—in which the baptism and teaching of disciples in a universal setting and the final assurance that he will always be with them—may be taken as a narrated exposition of the resurrection motif. It is in this christological perspective that the baptismal form (using the prepositional clause, 'in the name of ...' (28:19, *eis tò ónoma*), may best be understood.[32] It should also be pointed out that according to contemporary conventions the name (as *nomen proprium*) expresses the power and thus in that sense even 'the presence' of a person in whose name one acts.[33] A somewhat similar (post-resurrected) implication of the name of Jesus the reader has come across earlier in Matthew (18:20).

Finally, since Matthew (like Mark in 16:1-8) does not mention an ascension motif in his resurrection narrative of the events of Easter Day,[34] it may imply that the elevation of Jesus into the divine realm is included in the very divine act of having Jesus 'being raised from the dead' (28:7) so that he may be with his disciples 'to the very end of the age' (28:20). Thus, where *the narrated world* ends, an eschatological prospect in *the narrative world* of the risen Jesus being permanently among his disciples (and his church) can continue.

Summary

We have seen how two gospel writers, Matthew and Mark, employ farewell motifs in using final words of a dying protagonist as a convention in antiquity to summarize a retrospective view of the life lived. In Jesus' final words both authors seem to present the gospel proclamation *in nuce*. Thus, Jesus' death cry implies the presence of an acting saving God, in Matthew by means of a much more vivid and dramatic context. In close theological relation to that, Mark's somewhat abrupt narrative unfolds the meaning of Jesus as the risen One by directing the bewildered women—and informed audience—away from the empty tomb and back to the beginning of the gospel (1:1) in 'Galilee.' Matthew's extended narrative on

---

Testament Series (SB.NTSer.). Vol. 1, Dr. dissert. Transl. Neil Tomkinson (Lund, Sweden: Gleerup, 1966).

[32] Hartman, 1992, 51-52,140-141 (cf. note 30).

[33] Concerning the Semitic background, 'there is a deep meaning in the expression: to act in or with (the preposition can be translated both ways) one's name. Of course, it means, in the first place, that one mentions him in whose name one acts; but in reality it means the same as if the person in question had done it himself. The act is done as he would have done it, with his authority and on his responsibility,' Johannes Pedersen, *Israel its Life and Culture*. Vols.1-4 (London, UK: Oxford University Press / Copenhagen: Branner & Korch, 1926 and 1940, 1973 edition. Vols. 1-2 (one book), 246. Almost the same description may apply to the Hellenistic tradition, although the phrase, 'in the name of' (*eis ónoma*) as a *terminus technicus* in the business world, meaning, e.g.: 'make a credit in the name of [say] Eponychos ...' (the brackets are mine), loc. cit. Hans Bietenhardt, s.v. '*ónoma*,' in Gerhard Friedrich (ed.), *Theological Dictionary of the New Testament (TDNT)* Vol. V, transl. et ed. Geoffrey W. Bromiley (Grand Rapids, MI: Wm. B. Eerdmans Publishing Company, 1973, 245, is highly debatable as a semantic guideline for Mat 28:19, cf. Hartman, 1992, 42

[34] As Luke does, cf. Nielsen, 263-272.

the other hand develops the meaning of Jesus as the risen One by emphasizing through a related farewell address his continuing presence with his disciples. In other words, from Mark to Matthew—just to mention these two gospel writers in relation to our theme—'... we find an ongoing process of interpretation of the earthly Christ in terms of a narrative discourse which is underscored by the belief in Jesus as the risen One.'[35]

Anders Eyvind Nielsen. Born in Denmark. Since 1995 pastor in the Danish Lutheran Church. Adventist ministerial internship (1976-81). Studied at Universities of Aarhus, Denmark; Tübingen, Germany and Uppsala, Sweden. Associate Professor of New Testament Studies at the University of Aarhus (1990-95). Dr. theol. from the University of Aarhus, Denmark (1998).

---

[35] My paraphrased translation of a phrase in Mogens Müller's critical evaluation in *Bibliana's Elektroniske Nyhedsbrev* (BEN, cf. www.bibliana.net) 11 (March 18, 2009) of a newly published Danish version of Joseph Ratzinger / Pope Benedict XVI, *Jesus of Nazareth. From the Baptism in the Jordan to the Transfiguration*, transl. Adrian J. Walker (London, UK: Bloomsbury, 2007).

The Bible as 'Story': A Methodological Opportunity

Gunnar Pedersen

Our thesis is that biblical theology must concern itself with the meaning of the biblical material. That is: biblical theology proper must explore the story that its authors inhabit and through which they see the world, and by which they assign meaning to everything they speak about. In this context 'story' does not simply refer to the chronicling of a history but to the interpretation of cosmic history, that is, the world-view perspective or meta-narrative through which a person sees the world, the universe and existence.

It is our thesis that all humans inhabit a 'story' or meta-narrative, that serves as a mental lens through which they see the world and which informs their values and actions, and by which they understand and assign meaning to historic events. The biblical world of thought is no exception to this general cultural phenomenon. The biblical writers are not merely chroniclers of historical events but interpreters of a particular history; in other words, they inhabit a particular 'story' or meta-narrative by which they see and interpret the cosmic history of which they are a part. This 'story' informs their values and their actions. Through this 'story' they assign meaning to everything. Such a 'meta-story' thus appears to be the core of their theology.

The standing challenge is, therefore, to formulate a methodology for a biblical theology that will ensure that the reader will discover the 'inside' meaning of the story/stories of the Bible, that is, that he will discover its theology. Since our thesis is that biblical theology must concern itself with the 'meta-story' which the biblical authors inhabit, and through which they see the world, the critical question to be answered could be formulated as follows: *What world-view emerges from the meta-narrative of the biblical author and what are its methodological implications for biblical theology?*

While the Bible appears to be the end product of a long and complex historical process, 'the end product needs to be examined in its own right.'[1] Thus several scholars, such as Brevard Childs, James Barr, James Sanders and others, have recently called for a reassessment of the approach to biblical theology. They seek to address the present impasse in biblical theology by proposing a more narrative and canonical approach.[2] More recently N. T. Wright and others, such as Craig

---

[1] N. Frye, *The Great Code: The Bible and Literature* (Toronto, Canada: Academic Press, 1981), xvii.

[2] B. S. Childs, *Biblical Theology in Crisis* (Philadelphia, PA: Westminster Press, 1970), 99. James Barr, 'Trends and Prospects in Biblical Theology,' *JTS* 25 (1974): 265-282. James

Bartholomew and Michael Goheen, have addressed the issue by proposing that the biblical text as it stands actually constitutes a coherent story line proceeding in stages: a story that must be understood from the 'inside' of its own world-view logic in order to unlock its meaning.[3]

In line with this thinking George Stroup claimed that at the centre of Scripture is a set of narratives and that these narratives are the frame around which the whole of Scripture is constructed. Apart from these narratives the prophets would not be intelligible and without the frame of the gospel narrative it would be difficult to understand the full meaning of the parables, epistles, creeds, and hymns of the New Testament.[4] Bartholomew and Goheen further argue that 'at a philosophical and sociological level, the identity of a community or person requires the interpretation of historical experience, and narrative is the best genre for this. And, since God's action is central to Christian faith, it is not surprising that much of the Bible takes the form of narrative.'[5] Thus they claim that narrative is 'the central genre in the Bible.'[6]

For N. T. Wright 'narrative' is foundational for understanding the biblical texts. He says that 'it is a solidly established datum of history that Jews and Christians in the first century regarded the actual events in which they were taking part as possessing, in and of themselves, ultimate significance. They believed strongly that the events concerning Israel and her fate were not "bare events," but possessed an "inside" meaning, which transcended mere chronicle. And, since their interpretative grid for understanding the inside of events had to do with belief in a creator God and the fulfilment of his purposes for the whole world by means of actions concerning his covenant people, they believed — oddly from the perspective of modern western positivism — that the events in question were charged with a significance that related to all humans, and all time.'[7]

In other words the biblical authors lived and functioned within a certain set of world-view assumptions, or meta-story, apart from which their specific beliefs, institutions, experiences and actions cannot be understood nor appreciated. This observation thus reveals that the biblical material has all the characteristics of

---

Barr, *Old Testament Theology in Canonical Context* (London, UK: SCM, 1985). Wayne E. Ward, 'Towards a Biblical Theology,' *Review and Expositor*, 74 (1977): 381.

[3] Craig Bartholomew and Michael Goheen, *The Drama of Scripture* (London, UK: SPCK, 2006), ix-xii. N. T. Wright, *Scripture and the Authority of God* (London, UK: SPCK. 2005), 89-94. N. T. Wright, *The New Testament and the People of God* (London, UK: SPCK. 1992), 121-144.

[4] G. W. Stroup, *The Promise of Narrative Theology: Recovering the Gospel in the Church* (Atlanta, GA: John Knox Press, 1981), 145.

[5] Craig Bartholomew and Michael Goheen, Scripture and Hermeneutics Series. *Out of Egypt: Biblical Theology and Biblical Interpretation*, vol. 5 (Exeter, UK: Paternoster Press, 2004), 147.

[6] Craig Bartholomew and Goheen, 146.

[7] Wright, 122.

being a carrier of a particular world-view or meta-narrative expressed implicitly and explicitly in its various stories, institutions and events. So, to understand the theology of the biblical authors one needs to get to the roots of their world-view narrative.

Craig G. Bartholomew and Michael W. Goheen further recognize that the drive towards reading the Bible as an overarching story comes from a variety of disciplines such as 'systematic [theology], practical [theology], ethics and missiology — but sadly not from within biblical studies,' except for N. T. Wright, a 'rare example of a major biblical scholar in whose work story, in the grand sense, is central.' Both scholars argue that a reading of the biblical material as narrative is the 'major way of doing biblical theology.'[8]

James Barr, among others, has increasingly stressed the concept of 'story' as a referent to the world-view by which the participants in the biblical drama interpret history, in contrast to mere history as a chronicling of what happened.[9] The Exodus is not merely chronicled in the biblical story line as a historical event but is presented as an event that happens within a larger divine scheme of things for the benefit of the world, and should thus be read accordingly if one is concerned with understanding its actual theological meaning.

However, it should be remembered that the concern for the Bible as 'story' is much older than the current emerging interest. Among the Apostolic Fathers Irenaeus stands out as one who approached the Bible as narrative, that is, he read the Bible as a meta-story. The Reformed tradition, especially its Puritan wing, tended to read the Bible as a grand divine plan of salvation, that is, as a God-guided unfolding of a goal-oriented story. Thus the narrative reading of Scripture pre-dates the present concern for narrative. John Milton's two epic works *Paradise Lost* and *Paradise Regained* clearly illustrate this trend in the Reformed-Puritan tradition.

What has gradually been dawning on the postmodern contemporary consciousness is that all human beings in some way or another inhabit a comprehensive 'story,' whether they are aware of it or not. Thus it appears to be a universal phenomenon that all human life is shaped by a meta-story. The way we understand our lives and the values that we promote depend on what we think this human story is all about. The existential question then is: *Of what story am I a part?*

In Europe two major stories have been competing for the allegiance of the mind — two different ways of understanding the world, life, and existence; two stories that claim to offer the real and true understanding of the world. These are the humanist story, arising from the classical Greek and Roman cultural philosophical past, and the competing story, arising from the Hebrew biblical past. Both stories

---

8   Craig Bartholomew and Goheen, 144-145.
9   James Barr, *The Concept of Biblical Theology: An Old Testament Perspective* (Minneapolis, MN: Fortress Press, 1999), 352.

have to do with a fundamental way of understanding the cosmos, existence and what is happening in the course of human history.

Bartholomew and Goheen summarize the views of Lesslie Newbigin in these words: 'Both the biblical and the rationalist-humanist story have to do with *history*, an interpretation of what really happened.'[10] They further state that, according to Newbigin, the humanist story is rooted in a perceived evolutionary past and thus regards history 'in terms of the progressive development of human mastery over nature by science and technology that leads to a world of freedom and material prosperity.'[11] This world-view tells a story of the ascent of man, eventually coming of age as the ultimate master of the universe. 'The other story begins with the creation of the world and ends with its renewal, and leads through the narrow road marked by Israel, Jesus and the church.'[12] Thus this world-view tells a story of the coming of God to rescue his creation from all evil and to renew it, and thus the story of the one who will one day rule over all of creation. These two world stories interpret the actual history of the world and look for a goal to that history.

Both stories offer a comprehensive explanation of the origin, experience and destiny of the world and the human race. Both stories claim that they provide the true all-inclusive perspective from which to understand the origin, meaning and purpose of human life and thus the values and actions on which humans form their lives.

Actually, there is a growing awareness that even the humanist vision of reality in all its variations constitutes such a fundamental 'story' about reality; a fundamental world-view perspective in terms of which one thinks about everything, but which one does not normally think about, because such a perspective is adopted *a priori* as a self-evident truth beyond dispute, debate or even critical awareness. Nevertheless, in the postmodern era there is a growing awareness that everybody inhabits a 'story,' a world-view that claims to give answers to the fundamental questions of Who am I?, Where am I?, What is wrong?, and What is the solution?[13]—a world-view that thus gives direction to life and justifies one's actions and outlooks. While the humanist 'story' is by no means the only world-view story to compete with the biblical one, it is the most formidable western challenge to the biblical story.

Bartholomew and Goheen note that world-view stories are public and comprehensive stories as they 'offer a lens through which to view everything else, including what adherents of other world-views are "really" up to.'[14] They make a

---

[10] Craig Bartholomew and Goheen, 150.
[11] Ibid., 144-145.
[12] Ibid., 150.
[13] Brian J. Walsh and J. Richard Middleton, (Downer's Grove, IL: InterVarsity Press, 1984), 35.
[14] Craig Bartholomew and Goheen, 144-145.

striking observation, namely, that scholars who may be unaware of their western world-view lens, or who have consciously embraced the Enlightenment vision as normative, will look at biblical texts through this lens and accordingly offer a humanist account of what the biblical authors were 'really up to.'[15] Nevertheless, the biblical writers clearly inhabit a mental universe or story in which they believe that God was active in and through the historical events they recorded. The problem is that, if someone accepts the Enlightenment vision of reality, one has to reject as unreal the vision of reality that underpins the biblical story.

However, the fact remains that the biblical account contains a specific world-view story, and if anyone wants to discover what the biblical authors were 'really up to' they need to understand their meta-perspective in order to comprehend their theological thinking.

The growing awareness of the Bible as a grand story, a meta-narrative, opens up new and fresh perspectives on how to approach the Bible and how to formulate an adequate biblical theological hermeneutic. Thus a renewed interest in narrative as a primary medium of human perception of the world appears promissory for the recovery of narrative as a fundamental perspective for reading the Bible as a grand story. Alister MacIntyre, Paul Ricoeur and others have identified narrative as being essential for the human understanding of the world and for how humans order their lives in the world.[16] The problem is that positivistic science and historiography for a long time ignored such a cultural phenomenon and thus often proceeded as if Enlightenment philosophy and science themselves were exempt from such a set of metaphysical world-view beliefs controlling its methods.

Nevertheless, a new hermeneutical opportunity emerges from the observation that the Bible itself constitutes a grand meta-story or world-view paradigm; an opportunity to take the reading of Scripture beyond the present methodological stalemate. If the goal of biblical theology, in whole or in part, is defined as a search for the meaning of the biblical narrative then the researcher must seek to discover, respect and even reconstruct the basic world-view perspective within which the biblical authors operate in order to understand what they say and believe.

The issue is not whether such a world-view perspective is true to reality or whether it is acceptable to the researcher and contemporary naturalistic science. The issue concerns the researcher's ability to penetrate the theology of the persons or texts under investigation. We are not questioning the legitimacy of attempting to provide a naturalistic humanistic explanation for what is encountered in the biblical texts, or whether the researcher has the right to personally reject its theism as being for him an unacceptable view on the world. The critical point is that such

---

[15] Ibid.

[16] A. MacIntyre, *After Virtue* (Notre Dame, IN: University of Notre Dame Press, 2nd ed., 1984), 216.

an activity does not qualify as biblical theology proper, as it contains an inherent critique or polemic against the world-view story of Scripture itself.

We are not even suggesting that the researcher must *a priori* accept the biblical theistic view as a precondition for being able to retrieve the meaning of its texts. What we are saying is that the adopted method must be designed to discover, respect and even reconstruct the basic world-view perspective within which the biblical authors operate, in order to allow them to tell their own story on their own premises. Biblical theology should thus be an attempt to expose and penetrate the world-view of the biblical authors in order to discover what kind of 'story' they inhabit; a story which actually governs their thinking, logic and interpretation of the cosmos. Since their world-view story is ultimately theistic, the lens through which they see everything will be theological. Thus to discover the 'inner story' in which biblical authors think, live, move and have their being is to discover their theology.

N. T. Wright suggests that, when it comes to recovering theological meaning of the biblical texts, the pre-critical and 'modern' ways of articulating this have not met with success. He further suggests that in order to get to the theological meaning of the biblical text there are 'two levels at which we pass beyond "mere history."' In order to answer the 'why' question regarding people's beliefs 'we must move from the "outside" of the event to the "inside," and this involves re-constructing the world-views of people other than ourselves. Second, in doing so we cannot stand outside our own world-views.'[17]

So, while a contemporary reader of the Bible brings with him his own meta-narrative, the authors and writers of Scripture also had their own meta-narrative by which they interpreted the cosmos, human existence and thus historical events. Wright's crucial point appears to be that we must be clear about the dual world-views involved in reading the biblical Scriptures. Applied to the reading of the biblical 'story' this observation implies on the one hand that we need to become aware of the world-view narrative that we ourselves as readers mentally inhabit. On the other hand we need to become aware of the world-view narrative that the authors of the Bible inhabit, in order to avoid imposing our 'story' on the text and thus obscuring why the biblical authors viewed the world, life and destiny the way they did. The interpreter thus has a twofold task. Firstly, to retrieve the world-view paradigm of the text by analysing the story the text is telling, and, secondly, to analyse his or her own world-view in order to prevent it from impairing his or her ability to understand the meaning of the biblical text.

Thus, to be able to let the biblical authors tell their own story on their own premises we need to be aware of both world-view horizons in formulating and ap-

---

[17] Wright, 121.

plying a hermeneutic. We agree with N. T. Wright[18] that positivistic historiography has missed what we define as world-view awareness, and that such an awareness is critical to our proposed methodology. Actually, an awareness of world-view paradigms appears to be the key to the question of 'meaning' and in this case the theological meaning of the biblical texts. The biblical stories operate within a set of fundamental assumptions which in turn constitute the very key to their meaning, just like any other world-view narrative.

Thus, unless we detect the underlying assumed first-principles in the 'conceptional system' of the biblical authors, we will not understand the meaning of what they are saying and why they are saying what they are saying. It accordingly follows that a biblical theological hermeneutic that focuses merely on history and historical processes will be inadequate to provide a full appreciation of the themes and assumptions shaping the 'meaning' of the Bible. Biblical theology proper must seek to penetrate the 'inside' of the story/stories, and its methodology must be designed to allow the Bible to tell its own story on its own premises, not on the premises of its readers—be they past or present.

For a discipline to qualify as genuine biblical theology it must look not only at the consequent beliefs and practices of the author or the community but must uncover the very substrata of assumptions and ideas that make up the fundamental world-view of the author or community. It is not enough to ask what the author or community thought but one also needs to ask why they thought the way they did.

Thus theology, in order to qualify as biblical theology, must primarily be looking for 'meaning' which is formed by the underlying world-view assumptions, whether such assumptions are stated explicitly, or are implicit, in the texts. As a consequence, there is a need to study the inside rationale of the biblical stories in order to establish 'what made these people tick.' For example, when one studies a particular author such as Paul, the issue becomes—methodologically speaking— critical. No one can 'study Paul seriously without inquiring as to his world-view, mindset, basic and consequent beliefs, and practical aims and intentions.'[19]

The discipline of biblical theology thus calls for a different methodology than the 'historical-critical' or 'grammatical-historical' methods, which we find inherently inadequate in terms of uncovering the 'meaning' of the biblical stories, as they either philosophically reject or ignore *a priori* the world-view assertions that underpin the biblical narratives. The historical-critical approach is preoccupied with tracing historiographically how the stories may or may not have evolved naturalistically, and not with the logic of the biblical story as it stands and thus

---

[18] Wright, 122.
[19] Wright, 238.

with its theology.[20] The grammatical-historical approach limits its search to uncovering the literary assertions of the canonical texts but does not engage with the inner logic of the story and accordingly it does not wrestle with the meaning of its theology.[21] In the tradition of the grammatical-historical approach it is often left for systematic theology to sum up the findings of textual exegesis.[22] While the first approach appears to obscure the 'story' of Scripture, the other approach appears to miss the 'story' of Scripture. Whatever the merits and demerits of these two approaches may be, they both seem methodologically inadequate for penetrating into the theology of the biblical story/stories.

The real challenge for the biblical theology project is thus to formulate a methodology that will allow the biblical story/stories to tell their own 'inside' story on their own premises; a method that is not controlled by the world-view lenses of the interpreter. The issue is not whether the biblical story provides the true perspective on the world, life and existence but about what 'story' it actually assumes and affirms. While it is legitimate to critique a world-view, one needs to know the inside of such a view in order to provide a valid critique. So the challenge is to allow the Bible, in whole and in part, to tell its own story/stories on its own world-view premises and assumptions. Methodologically it can be expressed in the words of Jesus: *How do you read?* While this question raises core hermeneutical issues, it also assumes a set of epistemological axioms regarding the material that is being read and the capacity of the reader—axioms arising from the biblical theistic narrative itself.

---

[20] Craig Bartholomew and Goheen, 156. The problem with the historical-critical approach is, according to the two authors, its *a priori* philosophical positivist rejection of the entire world-view of the biblical writers and thus its search for a naturalistic explanation for the development and origin of the Bible. This approach rejects the very meaning, the underlying 'story,' of the Bible up front. This approach accordingly seems unable to explore the biblical 'story,' but ends up forcing the Bible to tell the Enlightenment, modernist, western world-view story, rather than its own story. Accordingly, they state that the biblical story is being 'held captive within the other story—the humanist narrative. And thus it will be that other story that will tend to shape our lives.' Bartholomew and Goheen, *The Drama of Scripture*, 4.

[21] Gerald Bray, *Biblical Interpretation Past and Present* (Downers Grove, IL: IVP Academic, 1996). Gerald Bray comments that the rise of the 'grammatico-historical' method was a form of historical criticism reacting to the more radical 'historical-critical' approaches by avoiding the deeper philosophical issues associated with the latter. He states that the 'mainstay of this type of criticism was textual analysis' (354). Many conservative evangelicals adopted this approach. However, he notes that 'the main weakness of the grammatico-historical approach was its philosophical and theological superficiality. By effectively ruling these issues out of consideration, proponents of the method were often unable to answer the theological assertions of the more radical critics. Minute textual exegesis did not explain how the text itself had come into being, nor did it tell anyone what it meant' (355).

[22] Fernando Canale, *Basic Elements of Christian Theology: Scripture Replacing Tradition* (Berrien Springs, MI: Andrews University Press, 2005), 26.

Thus it is our thesis that the biblical 'story' provides the structure for its own interpretation, that is, a theological hermeneutics. If the fundamental characteristic of the Bible is its 'narrative' structure, it means that the first principles, the central themes and the staged story line of Scripture must be recognized in the formulation and applications of a theological hermeneutics adequate for retrieving its theological meaning. Accordingly, an approach that methodologically respects the theistic perspective, the story line form and the staged structure of the Bible, both in its parts and as a whole, would embrace the fundamental theistic and narrative assumptions of the biblical material and could appropriately be entitled *a theistic narrative method of biblical theology.*

Gunnar Pedersen. Born in Denmark. Since 2004 Head of the Department of Theological Studies at Newbold College, Great Britain. Pastoral, educational, departmental and administrative experience in Denmark and Great Britain. President, Danish Union of Churches, 1992-1995. Lecturer in Theology Newbold College since 1995. ThD, Andrews University (1996).

'Holy Spirit, Faithful Guide'

Paul Birch Petersen

Introduction: Problems with the Spirit?

It is a commonly believed ideal that the Holy Spirit is in charge of the church in its mission. When the representatives of the church speak, we want to be able to claim, 'It seemed good to the Holy Spirit and to us' (cf. Acts 15:28).[1] Reporting projects and activities, we would like in honesty to be able to say, 'The Spirit worked wonders among us.' Very often, however, when in the estimation of some, the Spirit is at work, the results tend to create disharmony rather than unity. We seem to have problems with the Spirit!

Theologians traditionally identify the impact of the Holy Spirit in two major areas, the life of believers and the inspiration of Scripture.[2] In both of these areas the challenges we face are due to tensions between the specific and the general, the individual and the corporate. In the lives of believers the Holy Spirit is increasingly perceived as primarily affecting the individual. Policy makers and administrators watch in concern as the charismatic leaders take over, and in the name of the Spirit destroy the cautiously established unity and, perhaps, the uniformity which through corporate policies is thought to bind the church together. Elitist Christians who have received portions of spiritual gifts not allotted to everyone become authoritative representatives of God, and congregations splinter and split in the aftermath.

In contrast, the work of the Spirit through the biblical writings is often primarily seen as providing a general paradigm for all cultures.[3] Conservative concepts of inspiration tend to emphasize the general, eternal nature of the Bible rather than the culturally specific aspects. When the purpose of inspiration is thus understood to establish normative patterns applicable to all Christians at all times, all elements of the Bible take equal significance, and tensions originate with outreach projects that adapt to various cultural settings.

---

[1] Unless otherwise stated, Bible quotations in this chapter are taken from the *English Standard Version* (ESV) of 2001.

[2] The last few decades have witnessed a boom in the study of pneumatology. For an introduction, with an excellent annotated bibliography, see F. LeRon Shults and Andrea Hollingsworth, *The Holy Spirit*, Guides to Theology Series (Grand Rapids, MI: Wm. B. Eerdmans Publishing Comp., 2008).

[3] The Seventh-day Adventist debate on biblical inspiration is both extensive and intensive. *Understanding Scripture: An Adventist Approach*, Biblical Research Institute Studies, vol. 1, ed. George W. Reid (Silver Spring, MD: Biblical Research Institute, 2005) is semi-official and representative.

Thus, in our attempts to comprehend the role of the Holy Spirit in both of these areas, we are faced with similar problems. We seek to balance the specific and the general, to reach the proper relation between the individual Christian and the corporate body of believers, and to solve the tension between cultural and eternal aspects of Scripture.

I propose that the doctrine of the Trinity is the theological key to finding the balance.[4] Addressing these issues of hermeneutics and ecclesiology, and taking my clues from two key New Testament texts, I intend to outline the contours of a biblical theology of the Holy Spirit, readily acknowledging the limitations imposed by the brevity of this article.

What is at stake is not only our theoretical understanding of the Holy Spirit, but also the very unity of the church in its worship and mission. In his distinguished career Jan Paulsen has shown a keen interest in both of these topics. As a theologian, he has produced what is arguably the most significant Seventh-day Adventist work on the Holy Spirit,[5] and as an administrator he has placed the issue of corporate unity at the top of the church agenda.[6] His contributions in both of these areas contain important perspectives which help us meet the challenges and solve the problems we may have with the Spirit.

The role of the Spirit: New Testament examples
1. The Day of Pentecost. The event in Acts 2:1-4 fulfilled a promise by Jesus of a baptism in the Holy Spirit. Acts makes it clear that the Holy Spirit had already been working in Jesus (1:2). The newness of Pentecost is externally linked to the power with which the Spirit at this point breaks into history, internally to the preparation of the minds of the disciples, their ability to receive that power, and to comprehend the role of the Spirit in relation to the risen and ascended Jesus.

Pentecost compares with Mt. Sinai.[7] As God's theophany and revelation at Sinai established the covenant with Israel, so the baptism of the Spirit created the church as the people of God. What happened in Jerusalem, however, went far

---

[4]   Deemed for centuries a doctrine in exile, the Christian understanding of the Godhead as Trinity has undergone a revival in the last thirty years. A helpful historical overview is found in Roger E. Olson and Christopher A. Hall, *The Trinity*, Guides to Theology Series (Grand Rapids, MI: Wm. B. Eerdmans Publishing Co, 2002); the recent work by Allan Coppedge, *The God who is Triune: Revisioning the Christian Doctrine of God* (Downers Grove, IL: InterVarsity Press, 2007) consistently views the doctrine from the perspective of God's revelation in Christ.

[5]   Jan Paulsen, *When the Spirit Descends. Understanding the Role of the Holy Spirit* (Hagerstown, MD: Review and Herald Publishing Association, 2001), reedited and revised from a similar title published in 1976.

[6]   Along with 'Growth' and 'Quality of Life,' 'Unity' has been one of the three major focus areas for the strategic planning of the General Conference during the presidency of Jan Paulsen in the quinquennium 2005-2010.

[7]   So Walter L. Liefeld and David W. Pao, 'Luke,' in: *The Expositor's Bible Commentary*, 10, rev. ed., ed. Tremper Longman II and David E. Garland (Grand Rapids, MI: Zondervan,

beyond Sinai. It was no longer just mediating angels teaching the law;[8] God himself intervened by the Spirit to set the new covenant people on fire and write the
law in each heart. Consequently, the giving of the Spirit meant a renewal coming
from outside, yet reaching fully within.[9] Such a heart change creates unity because
it is independent of ethnic origin (cf. the international character of the audience,
Acts 2:9-11).

Moreover, this Spirit-based unity is explicitly stated as a purpose of the gift
in Peter's appeal, 'Repent and be baptised every one of you in the name of Jesus
Christ for the forgiveness of your sins, and you will receive the gift of the Holy
Spirit. For the promise is for you and for your children and for all who are far off,
everyone whom the Lord our God calls to himself' (Acts 2:38-39), a reference to
both Jews and gentiles as part of the people of God.[10]

The literary use by Luke of another Old Testament narrative enhances our understanding of how the Spirit was to create a unity of all people through Christ.
The coming of the Spirit is a language event which parallels the story of the tower
of Babel in Genesis 11:1-9.[11] There is unity in thinking and/or location;[12] heaven
comes down; many languages are suddenly spoken; people are 'bewildered';[13]
and as a result people are scattered all over the earth. The message is a reversal.
At Babel God intervened, creating new languages for the purpose of confusing;
at Pentecost the Holy Spirit gave the power of utterance in many languages in
order to unite. At Babel people were scattered all over the world in disagreement
and disharmony; at Pentecost the Holy Spirit sent his representatives into all the

---

2007), 733, and John R. W. Stott, *The Message of Acts*, The Bible Speaks Today (Leicester,
UK: InterVarsity, 1990), 61-62.

[8] Cf. Acts 7:53, Gal 3:19; Heb 2:2.

[9] Cf. Heb 8:8-10. As said by Paulsen, 'Just as Jesus is an individual external to those whom
he seeks to save, so the Holy Spirit is also external. This is important for us to remember,
so that we can avoid subjectivizing the Spirit in a way that makes him identical with our
own spiritual experience ... Although the promise is that God will put his Spirit within his
people (Ezek 36:26-27), in a very real sense he is apart from every human being in that he
comes from outside' (14-15).

[10] The expression 'those far away' (Isa 57:19) is used several times in the Old Testament
with reference to gentiles (Deut 28:49; 29:22; 1 Kgs 8:41; Isa 5:26; Jer 5:15), see Andrew T.
Lincoln, *Ephesians*, Word Biblical Commentary, vol. 42 (Dallas, TX: Word, 1990), 138-139.

[11] This reversal is emphasized by C. K. Barrett, *A Critical and Exegetical Commentary on
the Acts of the Apostles*, International Critical Commentary, 2 volumes (Edinburgh, UK:
T & T Clark, 1994-1998), 1:112; Stott 68; and Brian Edgar, *The Message of the Trinity*, The
Bible Speaks Today (Downers Grove, IL: InterVarsity Press, 2004), 216-217.

[12] The phrase *epì tò autó*, is most often translated 'together' and has a locative meaning (Acts
1:15; 2:44), but may indicate fellowship in a more technical sense, 'in church fellowship,'
so maybe 2:47, cf.. 1 Cor 11:20; 14:23. Probably the 'data is insufficient to substantiate a
technical sense,' Martin M. Culy and Mikeal C. Parsons, *The Acts of the Apostles: A Handbook
on the Greek Text* (Waco, TX: Baylor University Press, 2003), 15.

[13] Edgar (216) follows Barrett (119) in seeing the use of the Greek verb *sunexúthē* in Acts
2:6 ('confuse, confound,' from *sugxéō*) as 'deliberately' suggesting 'an allusion to Babel.'
Cf. Gen 11:7, LXX.

world in order to unite people of all languages through the good news of the death and resurrection of Jesus Christ. While people at Babel united in selfish ambitions looking to reach heaven, the effect of the giving of the Spirit was a unity of love, reaching out to lost people.

The Holy Spirit is the great communicator, and the gift of tongues in Acts 2 made the disciples uniquely able to present the message about Jesus in comprehensible languages to people who would otherwise not have been able to understand. The verb translated 'utterance' in Acts 2:4 is used in 2:14 in the sense of 'declaring clearly,' and in Acts 26:25 it is further described as 'true and rational (or sober)' in contrast to mad or meaningless talk. [14]

The gift of tongues particularly served the purpose of the corporate church established by the Spirit at this particular time in salvation history. But the gift of the Spirit in Acts 2 went beyond sheer language. It was a coming of 'fire power' which facilitated the communication of the crucified and risen Saviour, transforming the hearts and minds of those who believed, thereby opening the door for people from all nations, independent of cultural or ethnic background.

Edgar speaks to a core issue in missiology when he observes how the narrative underlines that this unity comes in diversity,

> The miracle of hearing which is described has ... the advantage of affirming the validity of each and every one of those languages and cultures that was represented ... [O]ne does not have to cease being a Mede or Elamite (or American, British, Chinese, Dutch, or Egyptian) in order to be filled with the Spirit and become a Christian. This is an important point, especially in the light of the fact that it was not long before some Christians were arguing that people ought to become Jews first before they became Christians. [15]

Another aspect of the work of the Spirit is the inspiration of Scripture, repeatedly attested by Acts (see 1:16; 4:25; 28:25). What are we able to learn from the narrative of Pentecost about the role of the Holy Spirit in this process?

It is decisive that this event was not intended to be normative. What happened on the Day of Pentecost was unique, and it does not set an absolute pattern for all revivals since then.[16] The event is unrepeatable for several reasons. First, neither Acts itself nor the New Testament in general ever makes that claim, and conversion and spiritual renewal always take place within the context of the specific theological as well as local and personal circumstances.[17] Second, historical situations are

---

[14] The only occurrences of the verb *apophthéggomai* in NT.
[15] Edgar, 217.
[16] Paulsen argues this point repeatedly and convincingly, 67-71, 85.
[17] The early church also saw the events recorded in this establishment phase as unique. Baptisms, for instance, took place in surprising situations and in quite different and at

by nature unique, and though the purpose of God's intervention by the Spirit may not alter, the specific means of reaching that purpose may. Third, the church created by the Holy Spirit on the Day of Pentecost is organised for the specific purpose of mission, and the gifts of the Spirit are functional in order to fulfil that purpose. Fourth, the event of Pentecost must be seen as part of the unique intervention by God for salvation through the life and ministry, death and resurrection, ascension and anointing of Jesus as heavenly High Priest. God was with us in Jesus. In the Holy Spirit God has come down to humans on earth. Just as the sacrificial death on Calvary was a once and for all event, so the establishment of the body of Christ on the Day of Pentecost is a corporate one-time event, necessary for the fulfilment of God's plan of salvation.[18]

Acts 2 underlines how the Holy Spirit created a unity in diversity based on the proclamation of the crucified and risen Saviour. Moreover, it highlights the fact that the Spirit in Scripture does not necessarily depict normative events.

2. The Epistle to the Ephesians. Both the Holy Spirit and the theme of unity are major components of Ephesians, uniquely combined in Paul's statement about spiritual gifts in Ephesians 4:7-14. The preceding exhortation in 4:1-6 stresses the concept of unity in several ways. Paul explicitly urges the Ephesians to 'to maintain the unity of the Spirit in the bond of peace' (4:3). Unity is underlined by the triune formula itself, and by the repetition of 'one' of which there are exactly seven (body, Spirit, hope, Lord, faith, baptism, and God, 4:4-6), the number of completeness.

Turning to the spiritual gifts, Paul begins with a reference to the individual, but closes by speaking about persons as part of the corporate body (4:7-13). The first sentence provides a significant clue to the whole section, in my view best translated as, 'But to each one of us grace was given according to the measure of the gift, namely Christ.' Reading 'of Christ' as an explicative genitive highlights two important points. What is stressed is, first, that God's grace is unlimited, next, that this gift of grace is a person, namely Christ himself.[19]

---

times inconsistent patterns (cf. Acts 8:26-40; 16:31-33; 19:1-7), making these situations impractical as norms for general policy and procedures. The church based its practice of baptism, after extensive education in catechumen classes, on general theological principles contained in the injunctions of Jesus in, for instance, Matt 28:18-20 and Mark 16:15-16, rather than reading events during this unique phase as normative for all times.

[18] Stott reflects on ways to understand the Day of Pentecost and suggests, 'first, it was the final act of the saving ministry of Jesus before the Parousia. He who was born into humanity, lived our life, died for our sins, rose from the dead and ascended into heaven, now sent his Spirit to his people to constitute them his body and work out in them what he had won for them. In this sense the Day of Pentecost is unrepeatable. Christmas Day, Good Friday, Easter Day, Ascension Day and Whit Sunday are annual celebrations, but the birth, death, resurrection, ascension and Spirit-gift they commemorate happened once and for all' (60).

[19] Most commentators, like Harold W. Hoehner, *Ephesians: An Exegetical Commentary* (Grand Rapids, MI: Baker Press, 2002), 522-523, interpret the text in Ephesians primarily in light

Paul affirms (4:8-10) the basis for the gifts to the church to be the death, resurrection, and ascension of Jesus, presupposing his previous descriptions of the unlimited richness of God's mercy or grace (Eph 1:7),[20] and of our present state as being seated with Christ, our representative, in the heavenly realm (Eph 2:4-6). Next, Paul describes (4:11-13) the gifts (plural) shared by Jesus through the Spirit. What is remarkable and has often gone unnoticed is that these gifts are persons, given to the church as 'apostles, prophets, evangelists, pastors, and teachers.'[21] Just as the main gift of God to humanity is the person of Jesus Christ, so the Holy Spirit equips individual persons to serve the corporate body.

The historical background for the emphasis on unity in Ephesians was 'the wall of hostility' between Jews and gentiles (2:14). The atoning death of Christ broke down all barriers for sinners approaching God, whether based on ethnicity, social status, or gender. Gentiles and Jews are united into 'one new man' (2:15, *anthropos*). Paul never again departs from this corporate perspective. He does not address the individual except in the context of the corporate. His 'you' is plural, not singular.[22] The 'inner man' (*anthropos* in 3:16, cf. 2:15) is not the individual, but the church. Not I, but the church is to be 'filled with all the fullness of God (3:19).

So, in Ephesians the gifts of the Spirits are persons, just as the main gift of grace from God is a person, namely Jesus Christ. They are persons, just as the Holy Spirit himself is a person, and never simply mechanic. This usage differs from other New Testament descriptions of the spiritual gifts, not because of any contradiction, but because each text contains a unique perspective. This should caution us against any mechanical or ultimate listing of spiritual gifts; any attempt to provide a normative list of human abilities and translate them into a religious category by calling them spiritual gifts fails.

The role of the Spirit in the context of the Trinity
1. The Doctrine of the Trinity.
The systematic development of the doctrine of the Trinity begins with the 'econ-

---

of what are assumed to be identical and parallel descriptions of the spiritual gifts (Rom 12:4-5 and 1 Cor 12:4-29). Hoehner, therefore, reads *cháris* as synonymous with *chárismata*, which is not used in Eph 4:1-13. This grace is then understood as a limited gift, measured out to the individual, the two genitives in the expression 'the measure of the gift of Christ' as subjective and a genitive of source, respectively.

[20] In 1:7 the riches of God's grace consist in 'forgiveness of our trespasses.' In Eph 2:4 Paul uses the term *éleos*, 'mercy,' with the synonymous *cháris*, 'grace,' in verses 5 and 7, as in 1:7 and 4:7.

[21] Hoehner acknowledges that the object of to give is 'gifted persons' (538), and that is 'a slight change from what he stated in verse 7. In verse 7 he mentions that a gift is given to each, but in verse 11 he refers to the giving of a gifted person (541).' I find it more natural in the context to be consistent in the way these two verses are read.

[22] As in Eph 3:16, 17, 19.

omy of salvation.' What we know about God comes from his self-revelation in history.[23] The early church developed the doctrine of Jesus as God on the basis of their devotion to him as God, the biblical testimony, and their understanding of the drama of salvation.[24] In Jesus God has revealed himself as a person,[25] and all doctrine of God, as well as personal, spiritual experience, need to be developed, checked, and revised in light of him who died on a cross on Calvary.[26]

In the debates of the early church, the nature of this divinity of Jesus was in the end defined from God's revelation in Scripture rather than from pagan philosophy.[27] The concept of a God without a beginning was the only concept available of Deity from the Old Testament. Identified in the New Testament with Yahweh, Jesus was believed to be the self-existent One. If he were not, we would not truly know God in person, and there would not be full atonement for our sins. The story of redemption tells about a God who in absolute love for fallen humans became a human himself to die in our place. This concept of *agapē* love stands in contrast to 'antique' or 'pagan' spirituality in which 'religion is human's way to God,' and it is the foundation for the doctrine of the Trinity.[28]

Maintaining the monotheistic belief that God is one, believing that Jesus was God, and yet realizing that the Father and the Son are two distinct personalities, led early Christians to include more than one person in that oneness of God and to understand it at least in part in relational terms.[29] The distinct divinity of the Holy Spirit became essential for genuine Christian theology because it was attested by the New Testament, because the church and the believers otherwise would have

---

[23] For the relationship between the 'economic Trinity' and the 'ontological Trinity,' see Coppedge, 127-139.

[24] Olson and Hall, 15-16.

[25] As all human terms, 'person' has a history and its limitations. God is not human except in Christ. He is not like us, he is not a person exactly the way I am a person, the Father is not a father exactly the way I am a father. We use such terms with an awareness of the mystery of God and the deficiency of all human language and thought. For a good, brief analysis of these limitations, see Coppedge, 139-148.

[26] As stated in his opening sentence and later developed by Coppedge (23), 'Christians believe that the monotheism of the Old Testament does not make God a strictly unitary being as in Judaism and Islam. Rather, the Old Testament monotheism is the monotheism of the triune God, who reveals himself more fully in the New Testament as Father, Son and Holy Spirit. Jesus is our way into this expanded understanding of God.'

[27] Two aspects of pagan philosophy played a major role in this development, the general concept that gods may have a beginning, and the *logos* philosophy which tended to see the truly divine as impassionate, immovable, and consequently as impersonal, creating a conflict with the Christian belief in God's incarnation in Christ.

[28] Johannes Sløk, 'The Unified Christian Culture,' in: Erik Lund, Mogens Pihl, and Johannes Sløk, *History of European Ideas*, 3rd ed. (Copenhagen, Denmark: Gyldendal, 1993), 132.

[29] Jesus' inclusion in the identity of God means that God must be conceived in relational terms,' say Andreas J. Köstenberger and Scott R. Swain, *Father, Son and Spirit: The Trinity and John's Gospel*, New Studies in Biblical Theology (Downer's Grove, IL: InterVarsity Press, 2008), 37. Subsequently, they speak about it as an inclusion into the oneness of God expressed in the 'Shema' of Israel (Deut 6:4).

been left without the presence of God, and because it was the only way to uphold the true divine origin of the Holy Scriptures as part of God's self revelation.

So, the doctrine of the Trinity centres around two major beliefs, the eternal divinity of Jesus Christ, and the distinct personality and divinity of the Holy Spirit.[30] Its implications are essential to the Christian faith and far-reaching in their consequences. We know God as a person through Jesus Christ, God the Son; and we know Jesus through God the Holy Spirit.[31]

The role of the Holy Spirit in the economy of salvation is to show us Jesus (see John 16:13-15). He does so through the Scriptures he has inspired, as he illuminates the minds of the believers and guides the community of the church to see Christ and thereby to meet and walk with God, fulfilling its mission to the world. In that process the Holy Spirit is not just a mechanical force; he is a person who acts 'according to his own will' (1 Cor 12:11). In the following I will reflect on the implications of this role of the Spirit in relation to Scripture, the individual believer, and the corporate church.

2. Hermeneutics: Pointing to Jesus through Scripture.

The doctrine of the Trinity illuminates our understanding of the authority and inspiration of Scripture in four related areas.

First it helps us to see the divine nature of the Bible. Only because of the Holy Spirit's place in the Deity, is the Christian community able to uphold the divine origin and authority of the Bible as an inspired revelation from God.

Next, the Spirit through Scripture helps us to see Jesus as he truly is. Without it we would paint the portrait of Jesus in our own image. Through the Bible the Holy Spirit ensures the objectivity of our subjective devotion to him. Jesus is not just a name to be repeated unceasingly in prayer for the emotional effect on the one who prays. He is a person outside of me, and the Holy Spirit through Scripture helps me to meditate upon his objective work for me and for humankind. Thus through the Bible the Spirit not only serves to uphold the Saviour we worship, but also reveals to the church the content of its proclamation. Without the work of the Spirit through Scripture, these two major aspects of church, worship and mission, would come to reflect human ideas only.

Thirdly, understanding the role of the Spirit in the economy of salvation helps us to realize the centre of Scripture. Though the Bible is a means for maintaining the doctrinal content of our salvation in Christ and thus reveals propositional

---

[30] In contrast to the present age, the distinct personhood of the Holy Spirit fairly quickly became a general consensus in the early church; see William H. Shepherd Jr., *The Narrative Function of the Holy Spirit as a Character in Acts*, SBL Dissertation Series 147 (Atlanta, GA: Scholars Press, 1994), 5-6. It took longer to settle whether he was God.

[31] Expressed by Paulsen, 'As the Son revealed the Father, so the Spirit is to reveal the Son (John 15:26),' 55.

truth, the Spirit's main purpose in inspiring the Bible is to tell about the person of God in Christ. Therefore, Jesus said that the Old Testament writings 'bear witness about' him (John 5:39), and 'beginning with Moses and all the prophets' he explained from 'all the Scriptures' 'the things concerning himself' (Lk 24:27). The New Testament writers saw all of the Old Testament in light of Christ and with him as its centre. It is impossible for Christians today to do otherwise.[32]

This truth could be understood as a 'canon within the canon.' Such a concept has been rightly criticized because it may lead to content criticism of Scripture. Yet, in the light of the doctrine of the Trinity the Spirit's purpose in inspiring the biblical writers has to be seen as presenting Christ. It follows that he is the centre of Scripture, and that the application of any biblical text to our individual or communal life today needs to weigh the significance of that text in the light of the cross of Calvary and the drama of salvation, the great controversy between good and evil. The issue is not whether it has to be done, but how it is done.

This follows in my view as a fourth consequence of viewing Scripture in light of the doctrine of the Trinity. Let me elaborate.

In reading Scripture there is a difference between what the individual specific text says, and how it is to be applied—between exegesis and hermeneutics. In inspiring the human authors of the Bible, the Holy Spirit communicated the will of God in unique situations in ways only a person is able to do. What was meant was always meant in a specific historical context and must be understood against that background. This is in the nature of interpersonal communication, and it does not detract from the authority of Scripture. On the contrary, this view upholds the concept of revelation. God is not bound by a closed continuum of events in history. He is able to communicate with humans in specific situations. Moreover, this position is built on observations of the texts themselves regarding their unique nature. 1 Corinthians, for instance, makes no claim to be spoken or written to all people at all times, neither do Kings, Song of Solomon, or Esther.

'Authority' should not be perceived as an abstract, Platonic concept, and the general authority of the canon should not be misconstrued to impose upon the individual writings of the Bible authority in areas which they themselves do not claim to address. This is not a matter of doubting the biblical testimony, but of understanding what the text actually says. Through proper exegesis we come to understand the unique subject matter of each text. We do not ask the Book of Esther for the answer to the human nature of Christ, and we do not attach authority to the book in this area for the simple reason that the book itself does not claim such authority.

---

[32] Ibid., 17.

Therefore, in applying biblical texts we need to view the significance of any particular text in light of the broader spectrum of biblical theology. Paul's injunction to slaves in Ephesians 6:5-8, for instance, should not be abused as a normative statement for all times and, consequently, provide an excuse for maintaining slavery in the twenty-first century.

The Holy Spirit is a distinct person within the Godhead, and through Scripture he has communicated with humans as a person, and has not just mechanically transferred information. When the human authors shared what had been revealed to them with the audiences of their days, they maintained their individuality and made their own choices in regard to genre and literary style. But though the Bible therefore contains a richness of variety due to both the ability of the Spirit to address specific issues and to the individuality of the writers, eternal principles are embedded in these culturally relevant messages.

Scripture contains a unified overall message, and when applying the texts or developing doctrine for the church, we use hermeneutical principles which, while respecting the uniqueness of each of the writings, nevertheless emphasize this oneness.[33] This unity in variety derives from the fact that the Bible was written under inspiration of the eternal Spirit (Heb 9:14), a distinct divine person, one of three in the God who is one.

3. Soteriology: Showing Jesus in the life of the believer.

The trinitarian implications of the role of the Holy Spirit for the life of the individual believer derive from two aspects of the doctrine, the eternal divinity of the Spirit and his distinctive personhood.

Because the Spirit is eternal God, he comes to the believing sinner in the fullness of Deity, brings the presence of God into our life, and shares gifts that belong to Christ. Yet, because he is a distinct person, the experience of the Spirit is neither to be identified absolutely with my emotional encounters, my ethical achievements and character development, nor my theological enlightenment. Coming into my life, the Holy Spirit is never my possession. He always remains another, outside of me, and he always points me to another person outside of me, namely Jesus Christ. Through the inspired Scriptures the Holy Spirit ensures that my subjective sentiments are brought into submission to the objective revelation of God. This authority of the Word of God in all aspects of my existence is ongoing and lifelong.

The Bible contains moral injunctions and theological instruction of permanent validity, but by pointing to Christ as its centre, the Spirit takes us further than just to issues of life style and ethics, or theology and doctrine. Through the Word he leads the believer into a faith relationship with Jesus as God and Saviour.

---

[33] It is, for instance, a generally accepted principle for establishing doctrine that we do not build upon one text only, but look to what the Scriptures in general say about a subject, and how this subject relates to the plan of salvation.

The same Holy Spirit, who inspired the authors to write, illuminates the minds of those who read Scriptures in order to see Jesus. He guides (John 14:26; 16:13), sanctifies (1 Cor 1:2; 6:11), comes to our aid when praying (Rom 8:26-27), and pours the love of God into the hearts of selfish sinners (Rom 5:5). He does so by growing his fruit (cf. Gal 5:22-23), and for the one who thus humbly walks in the Spirit, he transforms natural talents into gifts of service, and he may personally choose to provide new gifts, but only for the sake of the church. This way each believer remains unique, yet is continuously equipped for service to the corporate body of Christ.

4. Ecclesiology: Leading the corporate church to reflect Jesus.

The trinitarian implications of the role of the Holy Spirit for the life of the church also derive from the eternal divinity of the Spirit and his distinctive personhood, but because of the corporate nature of the church, the doctrine adds another significant perspective. First, the divine nature of the Holy Spirit means that God is still with his people even after the ascension of Jesus Christ. Deity descended in all its fullness to the church in the Holy Spirit, and he is still present to guide, illuminate, and motivate the church.

Yet, neither in the life of the individual nor in the fellowship of the church does this presence imply that sin and imperfection are no longer part of our reality. The kingdom is still a kingdom of grace, not of glory; it is not yet fully realized and will only be so at the Second Coming. Jesus, to whom the Spirit attracts our attention, is still in heaven as our High Priest. He is still within a veil, the heavenly temple is still standing, and we have not yet moved beyond the era of sin and the distance to God it creates.

Therefore, the authority of the church is not inherent, but stems from its obedience to the crucified and risen Saviour as portrayed by the Spirit in the Bible, the Word of God. The authority of the church of Christ does not rest in its organization, but in its connection with its head, Jesus Christ, and that connection through the Spirit is only present as long as the church builds its doctrinal foundation on the Word about Jesus inspired by the Holy Spirit in Scripture. Consequently, the authority of the preacher does not depend on gender, ethnic background, or age, but on the content of the message. No role in the church is to assume an authority in itself independent of and beyond that Word.

The second major aspect of the Holy Spirit in light of the doctrine of the Trinity is his distinct personhood within the one God. In the very being God is relational,[34] and being godlike means to reflect that divine unity in our church fellowship.

---

[34] The relational or communal aspect of the being of God has received renewed attention from very different faith traditions over the last decades; cf. the Orthodox scholar John D. Zizoulas, *Being as Communion: Studies in Personhood and the Church* (Crestwood, NY:

Let me elaborate on the implications by reflecting a little on some practical church matters. God calls us under the guidance of the Holy Spirit to reach out to the world with the gospel, to worship and invite to worship, and to teach what we learnt from Jesus as we baptise believers 'into the name of the Father, Son, and Holy Spirit' (Mat 28:19). If we truly are under the leadership of the Holy Spirit, we must in our mission accept his directions and expect the unexpected. When the apostolic council concluded that it 'seemed good to the Holy Spirit and to us' (Acts 15:28), the meaning was not that because we have decided, it is therefore also by way of our position the intention of the Holy Spirit. In the context, the meaning was the opposite. The apostles and early church leaders came to realize that by giving his gift of tongues to Cornelius, a gentile, before baptism, the Holy Spirit had spoken clearly about the inclusion of gentiles in the Christian fellowship (Acts 15:8-9; 10:44-48; and 11:12-17). The unexpected may not be in contrast to Scriptural principles already revealed by the Spirit, but as for the first Christians it will most likely conflict with some of our prevailing prejudices.

As a person the Holy Spirit is able to break down walls of tradition and bias and adapt to both individuals and unique situations for the sake of the message. He does not force any standard pattern for either liturgy and worship or organization. As long as the church works within the framework of the teachings of Jesus, entrusted to us by the Spirit through the Bible, the church is free to organize its outreach and worship for the purpose of its mission.

To ensure that these teachings are correctly understood, that in our worship we focus on God as he truly is, and are faithful to the Holy Spirit in our testimony about Jesus, the church develops theology as a necessary, yet secondary, discipline. Theology always needs to be in the service of the church in its mission for Christ. Therefore, true theology is not possible without the aid of the Holy Spirit. This is the real point of 2 Peter 1:19-21 in which the contrast is not between 'private' and 'corporate' interpretation of Scripture, as would fit a very hierarchic and authoritarian church. The issue is interpretation with or without the illumination of the Holy Spirit.

Yet, theology proper is a corporate enterprise. It is part of what we do when we speak together about God, and when we do, we always do so in the specific context of the church. Individual thinking motivates us to renewed reflection, yet unwillingness to assess conflicting positions, accept dialogue, and incorporate responses from fellow believers, reveals foolishness and pride, not wisdom and humility.

St. Vladimir's Press, 1985), and the Baptist theologian Stanley J. Grenz, *Rediscovering the Triune God: The Trinity in Contemporary Theology* (Minneapolis, MN: Fortress Press, 2004).

Compared with the trinitarian implications for the individual, the consequences for the corporate church include the perspective of relationship. The oneness of God is in a sense to be relived in the community of believers. This is indicated by the words of Jesus, 'that they may all be one, just as you, Father, are in me, and I in you ...' (John 17:21). The nature of this fellowship is a testimony to the world and is to be exemplified in the institution and institutions of the church as it follows the commandment given by Jesus, 'that you love one another; just as I have loved you, you are also to love one another. By this all people will know that you are my disciples, if you have love for one another' (John 13:35-36).

Conclusions

Understood from the perspective of the Trinity, the biblical doctrine of the Holy Spirit is the theological key to major issues in hermeneutics and ecclesiology. He is God, and he speaks with divine authority through Scripture. His main role in the economy of salvation is to point us to Jesus, and Christ is, consequently, the centre of the Bible.

He is a distinct person, and he does not communicate mechanically. He guides and inspires persons in specific situations, and the Bible reflects that variety. Its individual texts do not necessarily provide general, normative patterns for all times, yet they contain eternal principles which in the light of the cross of Christ are applicable beyond time and culture.

He is a distinct person within the Godhead whose being is relational. He has created a church community, united as a body with Christ as the head. He equips persons as gifts for the service of the fellowship as a whole. Being a person, he motivates the church to reach out to a lost world in ways that are at times surprising and unexpected. He willingly allows for individual methods, yet only in accordance with biblical principles, in submission to the head itself, Jesus Christ, and in the bond of mutual love which characterizes our triune God.

Paul Birch Petersen. Born in Denmark. Since 2000 Field Secretary of the South Pacific Division. Pastoral, evangelistic, youth ministry, education and administrative experience in Denmark and Australia. Author of books and articles. President, Danish Union of Churches, 1998-2000. PhD, Andrews University (1999).

The Costly Lack of Literary Imagination in Seventh-day Adventist Biblical Interpretation

Laurence A. Turner

Introduction

In this chapter I will investigate a particular aspect of current Seventh-day Adventist biblical scholarship, and its implications for the mission of the church. Let me begin with a basic observation concerning the nature of the Bible. It is not a logically developed theological or philosophical work, nor a conventional history textbook. The Bible is, by and large, a literary work, or rather, a collection of literary works. For example, one discovers ample poetry in the Psalms, prophets, Job, and so on. But even wider swathes of Scripture are narrative—in fact the dominant mode of discourse in the Old Testament is story. Genesis to 2 Kings is largely narrative, to which may be added Esther, Jonah, Ezra-Nehemiah, 1 and 2 Chronicles, plus sections of other books, such as Isaiah, Jeremiah, Ezekiel and Daniel. The Old Testament has a *story* to tell, and employs the full panoply of Hebrew narrative art in order to tell it well. Additionally, well over half of the New Testament is taken up by the narratives of the four gospels and Acts.

The broad categories of poetry and narrative prose do not exhaust the biblical genres, of course. For example, one discovers blocks of law (though set in a narrative context), and here and there presentations of abstract theological questions or affirmations, such as Ecclesiastes and Romans. However, taking the Bible as a whole such examples play second fiddle to the overtly literary narrative and poetic blocks of Scripture.

In this chapter I have limited my attention to Old Testament narrative, though what I say could be applied, in principle, to other genres. The prominence of narrative in the Bible should not surprise us, for the majority of it is the product of the Hebrew/Semitic mind. And the predominant mode of discourse in ancient Israel and first century Judaism that was used to convey matters of ultimate importance was narrative. This is precisely what Jesus did in his parables, in which he simply continued the tradition of the Old Testament in exploiting the power of stories.

This is the kind of Bible God has seen fit to give us. If we are to do justice to this kind of Bible, therefore, we need to read it in such a way that does justice to its stories. Thus, while there are many ways in which the Bible can be studied, one indispensable element must be *literary imagination*. In turn, there are a number of ways to do this. This chapter, however, will concentrate on biblical narrative criticism. This approach is broad, but in general it investigates the text as a work of art, foregrounding central elements such as plot and characterization. Other details frequently explored include intertextuality (how one narrative echoes another), wordplay, multivalence (the creative playing with more than one meaning of a word or phrase), ambiguity, irony and repetition, to name but a few. None of these is an end in itself, but such investigation aims to get at the heart of a story as a story. This brief and partial explanation of narrative criticism should be sufficient to indicate its emphases, though in practice there is great variety, and individual scholars develop interests not mentioned here.

The last twenty-five years have seen a surge of interest in the literary study of the Bible, especially its narratives. However, if you limit your reading to Adventist authors, you would never guess it. For, with very few exceptions, Adventist biblical scholars have shown no interest in engaging with the literary dimension of Scriptural stories. Yet one would have thought that highlighting the 'story' nature of Scripture should not be difficult for Adventists, given that at the centre of our proclamation is what we term 'the *story* of salvation.' The Great Controversy has a plot, with quite clearly demarcated exposition, complication and resolution. It also has characters, with finely crafted characterization provided in Scripture. And despite the conventional ways in which it has been presented, also irony, enigma, etc. In other words, all the elements of a well-constructed and imaginative plotted narrative are at the centre of Adventist proclamation, and give shape to our distinctive theology. All the more surprising, therefore, that literary engagement with Scripture is not only rarely done in Adventist theology and proclamation, but looked at with suspicion. It is high time those attitudes were challenged. Investigation of the literary aspects of the biblical text and their potential for enriching the church's mission should be incorporated into pastoral education if we are to equip our pastors to engage effectively with our contemporary culture.

Seventh-day Adventist hermeneutics: The contribution of literary interpretation

As a people of the Book, Adventists have produced a great deal of material dealing with sound hermeneutical principles. My purpose in this section is to investigate what characterises Adventist hermeneutics, as exemplified in a number of official church publications and works by representative Adventist scholars, in order to assess the church's approach to literary aspects of Scripture.

A convenient point to begin a survey of contemporary Adventist hermeneutics is the North American Bible Conference of 1974. A major contributor to the area of biblical hermeneutics at this conference, and for many years afterwards, was the distinguished scholar Gerhard F. Hasel. Hasel contributed two presentations, the first of which was on general principles of biblical interpretation,[1] a work which

---

[1] Gerhard F. Hasel, 'Principles of Biblical Interpretation,' in: *A Symposium on Biblical Hermeneutics*, ed. Gordon M. Hyde (Washington, DC: General Conference of Seventh-day Adventists, 1974), 163-193.

set out the essential framework for his work in this area for the next two decades. Apart from a brief reference to the nature of Hebrew poetry and its parallelism,[2] there is no explicit engagement with the literary dimension of biblical texts. His second contribution was a case study of responsible biblical interpretation, comprising a detailed exegesis of Isaiah 5:1-7.[3] Hasel engages with literary interpretation in only the most cursory of ways, limiting his attention to the explanation of Hebrew idiom,[4] a very brief reference to assonance in vs 1 and 7[5] and the identification of a chiasm in vs 7.[6] Despite this failure to engage in any substantial way with the literary aesthetics of the poem, Hasel can still agree that Isaiah's song 'belongs to the masterpieces of world literature.'[7] This is indeed the case, but one can point to hardly anything in Hasel's article to support the claim. The passage is treated as a text containing information, and Hasel's case study sets out the strategies which will reveal what that information is. How and why this is a 'masterpiece of world literature' is left unexplained.

Of course, scholars' interest in the literary aspect of biblical texts was still in its infancy in 1974, so Hasel's omissions might be understandable.[8] However, on this particular point, there is no perceptible change of emphasis in Adventist publications on hermeneutics over the next thirty-five years. Writing in 1980, and in an attempt to provide a high view of the authority of Scripture, Hasel emphasises even more than in his previous work the historical and linguistic competencies needed to interpret Scripture correctly. There is barely a word about the literary nature of the Bible.[9] Again, in 1985, Hasel set out principles and procedures for interpreting the Bible which in essence repeated his previously published material.[10] There is, however, a short section on the need to understand the 'literary context' of any passage, and of how an understanding of 'literary conventions' can aid interpreta-

---

[2] Ibid., 179-180.
[3] Gerhard F. Hasel, 'The Song of the Vineyard: A Case Study in Biblical Interpretation,' in: *North American Bible Conference Handbook*, ed. Gordon M. Hyde (Washington, DC: General Conference of Seventh-day Adventists, 1974), 1-18. [The articles do not have consecutive page numbers.]
[4] E.g. 'son of oil,' ibid., 5.
[5] Ibid., 5, 13.
[6] Ibid., 12.
[7] Ibid., 14, citing an undocumented source.
[8] Nevertheless, the impact of James Muilenburg's landmark presidential address to the Society of Biblical Literature, 'Form Criticism and Beyond,' *Journal of Biblical Literature* 88 (1969), 1-18, was already being felt in academic circles.
[9] Gerhard F Hasel, *Understanding the Living Word of God* (Nampa, ID: Pacific Press Publishing Association, 1980). As before, the author mentions the importance of understanding languages, words, sentences, etc., but this does not amount to a literary concern. A reader would need Hasel's competencies in order to understand a do-it-yourself manual written in a foreign language, but the resultant reading cannot be defined as a *literary* experience.
[10] Gerhard F. Hasel, *Biblical Interpretation Today* (Washington, DC: Biblical Research Institute, 1985).

tion.[11] The point, however, is not expanded. More germane to my present concern is that Hasel reveals that he is aware of literary approaches, but appears to misunderstand their scope and presuppositions.[12] Such literary approaches, Hasel states, view, 'the Bible as literature in the same way as any other literary production. The issue to be raised is whether the Bible is merely literature. Is not the Bible something other than literature? If this should be the case, and we believe it is, does this not make the biblical documents something they were not intended to be?'[13]

Certainly the Bible is 'something other than literature' in the sense that it is more than literature, but it is certainly not less than literature. The Bible is more than history, but as Hasel and others quite rightly point out, it can be subjected to, and indeed must be subjected to, historical analysis. The Bible transcends both its literary artistry and its historical context, but *both* need to be addressed by the interpreter.

More recent works on Adventist hermeneutics hardly move beyond the parameters set by Hasel's influential studies. The definitive statement on *Methods of Bible Study*[14] barely mentions literary aspects of the text. Reference is made to literary types[15] and literary structure,[16] but given the overall length of the document these are accorded minimal space, and the main issue of interpretation raised by literary questions is how to know when one should read literally and when to read figuratively. The emerging axiom is that one reads literally unless the type of literature shows that one should not. Thus, while the main purpose of the document is to oppose the use of the 'historical-critical' method, the alternative proposed is no more interested in investigating literary dimensions than the method it wishes to counter.

As Adventist hermeneutics moved into the 1990s there is evidence of a growing awareness of literary approaches to the text, but little evidence of any of them being embraced. For example, Richard Davidson[17] sets out a comprehensive list of four *General Principles* and six *Specific Guidelines* for biblical interpretation, which he believes constitute the Bible's own hermeneutical stance. He is clearly aware of 'the new literary-critical hermeneutical approaches,'[18] and the third of his six spe-

---

[11] Ibid., 107.

[12] Ibid., 116. It is certainly not true, as Hasel seems to imply, that all literary approaches to the Bible necessarily imply a desire to reject the historicity of the text.

[13] Ibid., 122.

[14] 'Methods of Bible Study,' voted at the 1986 Annual Council, and published in several publications, e.g. *Ministry* (April 1987), 22-24.

[15] '[poetic] passages employing imagery are not to be interpreted in the same manner as prose.' *Ministry* (April 1987), 23.

[16] 'The literary structure of a book often is an aid to interpreting it. The parallel nature of Daniel's prophecies is an example.' *Ministry* (April 1987), 24.

[17] Richard M. Davidson, 'Interpreting Scripture: An Hermeneutical Decalogue,' *Journal of the Adventist Theological Society* 4 (1993), 95-114.

[18] Ibid., 96.

cific guidelines is 'Literary Context and Analysis.' Indeed, Davidson asserts that, 'Scripture is not only a history book, but a literary work of art,' and additionally acknowledges 'the importance of recognizing these [literary qualities] as part of the hermeneutical undertaking.'[19] Yet at the same time he is clearly wary of such approaches, believing that they often question the historicity of the text,[20] and his treatment of the literary dimensions of Scripture is limited to a descriptive listing of basic literary genres, structure (chiasm, inclusio, etc), and an acknowledgment of 'irony, metonymy, [and] simile.'[21] All in all, this amounts to little more than an awareness of some formal literary aspects of Scripture, and an acceptance that the Bible contains great literature. What it does not do, however, is give any sense of how literary *interpretation*, beyond basic *observations* of genre, structure and metaphor, can be utilised by the Adventist exegete.[22]

Richard Davidson has contributed the most recent comprehensive treatment of biblical interpretation.[23] The guidelines he sets out are essentially the same as the six *Specific Guidelines* of his 1993 article,[24] though in parts using slightly different terms. However, while repeating much of what was said before, Davidson expands on explicitly literary concerns.

> While much of modern critical study tends to regard the narrative as fictional, the Bible student who accepts the account as factual history can benefit by examining carefully how the inspired writer has set forth the narrative to emphasize crucial points. Basic elements of narrative required to understand the 'flow' of the account include: the implied author (or invisible speaker) and the implied reader, the overall point of view or perspective, the order of events and their interrelationship ('story time'), the plot, the characters and their characterization, the setting, and the implicit commentary or rhetorical techniques used in relating the narrative.[25]

Davidson exhibits the same nervousness about the consequences of a literary approach for the perceived historicity of the biblical text, as is noticeable in some other Adventist works. This is an understandable reaction, but in my opinion largely misplaced. Davidson objects that those who interpret the final form of the text

---

19 Ibid., 103.
20 Ibid.
21 Ibid., 104-105.
22 The same characteristics are found in the otherwise very helpful Lee J. Gugliotto, *Handbook for Bible Study: A Guide to Understanding, Teaching, and Preaching the Word of God* (Hagerstown, MD: Review and Herald Publishing Association, 2000).
23 Richard M. Davidson, 'Biblical Interpretation,' in: *Handbook of Seventh-day Adventist Theology* (Hagerstown, MD: Review and Herald Publishing Association, 2000), 58-104.
24 Ibid., 95-114.
25 Ibid., 75.

from a literary perspective, usually treat the biblical text as being 'divorced from history and [the texts are] regarded as works of fiction or myth, with their own "autonomous imaginative universe" and "imitation of realty."'[26] One can demonstrate the limits of such an objection by simply reversing Davidson's concerns, by stating, 'analyses of the biblical text that foreground historical questions are usually divorced from the literary genius of the text they are analysing, and are more concerned to affirm that such and such an account is historically viable than to experience the literary power of Scripture to appeal to the heart of the reader.' Literary interpretations do not need to be seen as a threat to the overall historicity of Scripture. Responsible interpretation needs an awareness of both literary and historical strategies.

I have written three books on Genesis, largely from a literary perspective, and not for one moment would I subscribe to the view that, for example, the narratives concerning the patriarchs are 'works of fiction or myth,' with their own 'autonomous imaginative universe' and 'imitation of reality,' totally divorced from the real world. To analyse the literary art of a passage says nothing whatsoever, positive or negative, about the historicity of the events being narrated. I acknowledge Davidson's point that some literary interpreters have a low opinion of the Bible's historical worth, but this has more to do with the presuppositions of the interpreters than with literary analysis as such. One has only to consider historians and archaeologists who also believe the Bible to be 'myth' and 'fiction' to demonstrate that an historical approach does not necessarily guarantee a high view of Scripture either.

If Davidson is correct, as he undoubtedly is, that the interpreter can benefit greatly from applying the methods of narrative criticism, then why is the utilisation of such methods virtually ignored in Adventist scholarship? On the other hand, just about every Adventist exegete seems to be, *ex officio*, an expert on the historical and theological aspects of the text.

To conclude, this brief survey of Adventist works on biblical hermeneutics has shown a decided emphasis on the historical and theological dimensions of the text, yet a reluctance to engage in any meaningful way with its literary aspects.

Literary aspects of recent Seventh-day Adventist biblical scholarship
In the previous section I investigated Adventist statements concerning hermeneutics. However, what about the actual practice of biblical interpretation within the guild of Adventist exegetes in recent years? What place has been found for literary approaches in general and what literary aspects of texts in particular have been investigated?

---

[26] Ibid., 93.

Even a cursory glance at works published by Adventist scholars will show that there has been a great deal of interest in 'literary structure.' In practice, this term usually refers to chiasms or palistrophes, that is, inverse parallelism in which the second half of a literary piece is the mirror image of the first half, with the major point being highlighted in the centre, as in A:B:C:D:C':B':A'. This is not the place to critique individual suggestions; I simply wish to note the remarkable amount of interest shown in this area.[27] Strangely, however, the great interest in (largely chiastic) literary structures has not stimulated much interest in broader literary areas. In fact such preoccupations with chiasms might suggest *why* many Adventist interpreters fail to engage with the literary subtleties of texts. To a western, logical, rational mind, a chiasm appears to be an objective assessment of a literary creation that can be expressed scientifically as a diagram, with almost mathematical precision. The text's inner logic can be mapped, its balancing constituent parts plotted and 'the whole point' of the passage discovered at the fulcrum point in the diagram. Now of course chiasms are to be found in the Bible, though perhaps not as often as some scholars would have us believe. However, in my opinion, the production of diagrammatic chiasms which indicate the symmetrical literary *form* of passages, without any further engagement with the literary nature of their *content*, highlights the rationalistic preoccupations of the interpreter, rather than the literary creativity of the biblical author.

Evidence of an Adventist interest in literary matters, other than in 'literary structure,' is meagre indeed. However, a few studies show some stirrings in this area. Oestreich studies the force of metaphor and simile in the book of Hosea.[28] Without ignoring the historical and social context of the book, he addresses the function of Hosea's images by asking literary questions. In the same volume, Caesar investigates characterization in Job.[29] More than that, he also questions con-

---

[27] Literally scores of examples could be given; the following are representative. Most suggest chiastic structures, a few posit parallel structural forms of different types: Richard M. Davidson, 'The Literary Structure of the Song of Songs Redivivus,' *Journal of the Adventist Theological Society* 14, no. Fall (2003), 44-65; Jacques B. Doukhan, *Daniel: The Vision of the End* (Berrien Springs, MI: Andrews University Press, 1987); Jacques B. Doukhan, 'The Center of the Aqedah: A Study of the Literary Structure of Genesis 22:1-19,' *Andrews University Seminary Studies* 31 (1993), 17-28; Jon Paulien, *John: Jesus Gives Life to a New Generation* (Boise, ID: Pacific Press Publishing Association, 1995), 39, 68; Angel M. Rodriguez, 'Leviticus 16: Its Literary Structure,' *Andrews University Seminary Studies* 34 (1996), 269-286; William H. Shea, 'The Literary Structure of Leviticus 1-6,' in: *Creation, Life, and Hope: Essays in Honor of Jacques B. Doukhan*, ed. Jiri Moskala (Berrien Springs, MI: Old Testament Department, Seventh-day Adventist Theological Seminary, Andrews University, 2000), 83-100.

[28] Bernhard Oestreich, 'Absurd Similes for Israel in the Book of Hosea,' in *Creation, Life, and Hope: Essays in Honor of Jacques B. Doukhan*, ed. Jiri Moskala (Berrien Springs, MI: Old Testament Department, Seventh-day Adventist Theological Seminary, Andrews University, 2000), 101-126.

[29] Lael C. Caesar, 'Bildad, Superior Rhetorician,' in *Creation, Life, and Hope: Essays in Honor of Jacques B. Doukhan*, ed. Jiri Moskala (Berrien Springs, MI: Old Testament Department,

ventional approaches to Job, 'It appears entirely possible that readings of this text primarily as theology or ideological history may miss significant dimensions of the conflict which constitutes the story.'[30] Consequently, his study, 'suggests how the Book of Job might be approached primarily as a work of dramatic conflict. It seeks to heighten appreciation for the nuanced characterizations which make possible that conflict.'

Generally speaking, however, the few Adventist studies which hint at an interest in the literary nature of biblical passages promise more than they deliver,[31] while the great majority are virtually silent.

Seventh-day Adventist interpretations of specific books

Having looked at the role of literary interpretation in Adventist discussions of biblical hermeneutics, and the place of such interpretation in the work of Adventist exegetes in general, the purpose of this section is to investigate the way in which Adventist scholarship has dealt with two specific books: Jonah and Daniel. The reasons for this choice are, first, that Jonah is universally recognised as being a supreme example of Hebrew narrative art, and we are fortunate to have four Adventist commentaries on the book. Secondly, in recent years Daniel has inspired more Adventist scholarship than any other book and provides ample material for analysis.

1. Seventh-day Adventist interpretations of Jonah

The first comprehensive Adventist treatment of Jonah is in the *Seventh-day Adventist Bible Commentary*.[32] The recurring characteristics of the commentary are an emphasis on historical and archaeological information,[33] the explanation of details in the text,[34] doctrinal/theological comments,[35] and devotional applications.[36] It does not attempt any literary engagement. Of course, the commentary was published in the mid-1950s, and written for particular purposes by those who in general did not have advanced education in biblical studies, so its avoidance of the area is perhaps understandable. Nevertheless, its emphases set the tone for later contributions. Written two decades later, Hasel's commentary[37] similarly

---

[30] Seventh-day Adventist Theological Seminary, Andrews University, 2000), 127-138. Ibid., 127.

[31] For example, Ron du Preez, 'Epics & Ethics: Vital Biblical Principles for Interpreting Scripture Stories,' *Journal of the Adventist Theological Society* 10 (1999), 107-140.

[32] F. D. Nichol, ed., 'Jonah,' in *The Seventh-day Adventist Bible Commentary*, vol. 4 (Washington, DC: Review and Herald Publishing Association, 1955), 995-1007.

[33] For example, a long additional note on the history and archaeology of Nineveh (1000-1001).

[34] For example, the plant that covered Jonah (4:6), was probably a castor oil plant (1007).

[35] For example, Jonah's comments in 2:6 should not be taken to imply that he did not believe in the future resurrection of the dead (1003-1004).

[36] For example, we have the privilege of being able to pray to God in any situation, just as Jonah did in the fish (1003).

emphasises historical and archaeological information,[38] explanation of details in the text,[39] doctrinal/theological comments,[40] and devotional applications.[41] In addition, he demonstrates the burgeoning Adventist interest in 'literary structure.'[42] However, Hasel exhibits little interest in exploring the literary dimensions of the narrative.[43] Two decades on from Hasel, Dybdahl[44] marks no major departure. He likewise emphasises historical and archaeological information,[45] explanation of details in the text,[46] doctrinal/theological comments[47] and devotional applications.[48] However, there are occasional comments that have a 'literary' flavour. These are mostly concerned with basic characterization.[49]

Most recently Jo Ann Davidson's commentary[50] does demonstrate the potential of a literary approach to Jonah. She pays more than lip service to the book's narrative art, devoting a chapter to some techniques used by Hebrew narrators. While the mandatory affirmations of historicity[51] and plotting of chiasms[52] are given their due place, she explores hitherto uncharted territory in Adventist engagement with

---

[37] Gerhard F Hasel, *Jonah: Messenger of the Eleventh Hour* (Mountain View, CA: Pacific Press Publishing Association, 1976).

[38] A particular concern for Hasel, to a greater degree than the *Seventh-day Adventist Bible Commentary*, is to establish the historical veracity of the text. Hence the repeated assertions that Jonah is an historical account and not merely an allegory or parable (25, 31, 47).

[39] For example, the plural for 'seas' (Jon 2: 3) conveys the sense of the boundless ocean (36).

[40] For example, in 3:10 God's repentance is not the same as human repentance (65).

[41] For example, just like Jonah, the Christian is too often concerned with 'self' (76).

[42] For example, Jon 1:4-16 is arranged chiastically and centres on Jonah's proclamation in 1:9 (16).

[43] An isolated example of a cursory interest is his observation about the repetition of the verb 'to arise' in 1:1ff (19). Subtle use of repetition is a key element in Hebrew narrative art, but Hasel does not expand on its significance.

[44] Jon L. Dybdahl, *Hosea-Micah: A Call to Radical Reform*, The Abundant Life Bible Amplifier (Boise, ID: Pacific Press Publishing Association, 1996). The section on Jonah covers pp. 155-185.

[45] For example, information on the palaces of Sennacherib in Nineveh (165). Dybdahl is also concerned about the book's historicity, but less dogmatically than either the *Seventh-day Adventist Bible Commentary* or Hasel (e.g. 159).

[46] For example, the translation of 1:2—is it Nineveh's 'wickedness' or 'calamity' that has come up before God (164)?

[47] For example, Dybdahl reads the book from a decidedly missiological perspective, and believes that mission is the major theme of the book (158, 160, 168, 173); the nature of conditional prophecy (178).

[48] Dybdahl includes a few of these in the text of his commentary, but an aim of the series is to encourage lay readers to apply the text themselves, hence there are major blocks of questions throughout ('Applying the Word'), aimed at showing the relevance of the text to Christian life.

[49] For example, a list of contrasts between Jonah and the pagan sailors amounts to an elementary characterization (166).

[50] Jo Ann Davidson, *Jonah: The Inside Story: Wrestling with the God of Second Chances* (Hagerstown, MD: Review and Herald Publishing Association, 2003).

[51] Pp. 9-20. For a brief literary reflection which accepts the book's essential historicity but is surprisingly relaxed over the issue, see Ed Christian, 'The Shocking Message of Jonah,' *Spectrum* 31 (Autumn 2003), 26-29.

[52] Pp. 26-31. Panel writing is also explained (32-33).

the book, such as the significance of dialogue, irony, inner life and intertextuality, though with a decided emphasis on the significance of repetition (such as, the use of 'great' thirty-eight times [p. 45], and 'evil' ten times [p. 51]). Exploration of these areas results in an enlightening perspective on the character of the prophet, and an underlining of the ironies of God's involvement in human life, to mention but two gains. We are forced to confront the radical theology of the book, which uses its literary art as a vehicle for its message. Yet Davidson's commentary is simply a taster, a modest dipping of the toe into biblical narrative criticism, which demonstrates that Adventist interpreters have nothing to fear and much to gain from moving in this direction.[53]

How else might a literary engagement with Jonah enhance our understanding of the book? Two examples will suffice. First, one of the outstanding features of Jonah is the large number of questions it contains (see 1:6, 8, 10-11 [7x]; 2:4; 3:9; 4:2, 4, 9, 11). Asking questions is a common technique used by Hebrew storytellers in order to draw the reader/hearer into the story and to identify with the characters. The fact that Jonah questions more than he preaches should in itself indicate that this is not a book that simply contains historical facts and propositional theology, but a literary work seeking a reaction from its readers. This is particularly important to bear in mind when one observes that the book's climax is a question, not an assertion (4:11). The reader is left to ponder what the answer might be, and its implications. Secondly, the subtlety of Hebrew wordplay is also present throughout the book. For example, Jonah's sermon is that 'Forty days more, and Nineveh shall be overthrown!' (Jon 3:4). Clear enough, one might think. Except it isn't! For the crucial word translated 'overthrown,' *hapak* , can mean 'to overturn' (as with Sodom and Gomorrah, Gen 19:21, 25, 29), but also 'to turn around' or 'to convert' (as in Jer 31:13, cf Deut 23:5). So after forty days was Nineveh to be overturned or to be turned around; destroyed or converted? And was Jonah's prophecy fulfilled or not? And which connotation of the verb were *you* working with, dear reader? Such examples of literary sophistication could be multiplied, as they often have been in works that take the literary dimension of the Bible seriously.[54] But one finds little of that in Adventist works.

---

[53] Note should be made here of the overtly literary studies by Ernst Wendland, 'Recursion and Variation in the "Prophecy" of Jonah: On the Rhetorical Impact of Stylistic Technique in Hebrew Narrative Discourse, with Special Reference to Irony and Enigma: Part I,' *Andrews University Seminary Studies* 35 (1997): 67-98; Part II, 35 (1997), 189-209; Part III, 36 (1998), 81-110. Wendland, however, is a Lutheran scholar and does, therefore, not reflect a trend within Adventism.

[54] For representative examples of recent scholarship, see Phyllis Trible, *Rhetorical Criticism: Context, Method, and the Book of Jonah* (Minneapolis, MN: Fortress Press, 1994); James Limburg, *Jonah: A Commentary*, Old Testament Library (Louisville KY: Westminster/ John Knox, 1993); David M. Gunn and Danna Nolan Fewell, *Narrative in the Hebrew Bible* (Oxford, UK: Oxford University Press, 1993).

To summarise: If you wish to read an informed and detailed defence of the book's historicity, or marvel at complex chiasms, then read Adventist authors. If you wish to have a stimulating discussion of how the book's literary art conveys its radical message, then generally speaking, you will need to go elsewhere.

2. Seventh-day Adventist interpretations of Daniel

When moving to the book of Daniel, as another test case, the result is much the same, but the amount of evidence far greater. Lack of space prohibits a detailed discussion, but a survey of Adventist works over the last fifty years shows only slight variations on the preoccupations of the *Seventh-day Adventist Bible Commentary*:[55] historical and archaeological issues,[56] explanation of exegetical details,[57] and meticulous historical engagement with the prophecies.[58] Subsequent works tend to be variations on these same themes.[59]

What then, do we rarely find in Adventist treatments of Daniel? Three examples will suffice. First, until very recently,[60] there was a clear aversion to reading the book as a holistic literary work. The vast majority of Adventist scholarship has lingered over the prophetic chapters 7-12, for obvious reasons. Typically, chapters

---

[55] F. D. Nichol, ed., 'Daniel,' in *The Seventh-day Adventist Bible Commentary*, vol. 4 (Washington, DC: Review and Herald Publishing Associations, 1955), 743-881.

[56] For example, historical parallels to the conversion of Nebuchadnezzar (788).

[57] For example, the meaning of 'the thing has gone from me,' in 2:5 (767).

[58] See, for example, the disproportionate amount of space devoted to the sequence of nations in the prophecies of ch. 2 (772-776) and ch. 7 (819-838).

[59] For example, William H. Shea, *Daniel 1-7: Prophecy as History*, The Abundant Life Bible Amplifier (Boise, ID: Pacific Press Publishing Association, 1996); Zdravko Stefanovic, *Daniel: Wisdom for the Wise: Commentary on the Book of Daniel* (Nampa, ID: Pacific Press Publishing Association, 2007). One of the few exceptions is Jacques Doukhan, 'The Seventy Weeks of Daniel 9: An Exegetical Study,' (reprinted from *AUSS* 17 (1979), 1-22), in: Arnold V. Wallenkampf and W. Richard Lesher, eds., *The Sanctuary and the Atonement: Biblical, Historical, and Theological Studies* (Washington, DC: Review and Herald Publishing Association, 1981), 251-276. While not an entirely literary study, it does have a literary edge to it. It is also possibly the most creative contribution to the volume. See also William H. Shea, 'Poetic Relations of the Time Periods in Daniel 9:25,' 277-282, in the same volume. Shea attempts a poetic analysis of the seventy weeks. However, the study is limited to formal structures only (such as metre and the composition of cola). Neither, of course, addresses the narrative chapters Daniel 1-6. There are also three partial exceptions to this general rule in doctoral dissertations written at the Seventh-day Adventist Theological Seminary, not surprisingly all supervised by Jacques Doukhan: Paul Birch Petersen, 'The Theology and the Function of the Prayers in the Book of Daniel' (PhD dissertation, Seventh-day Adventist Theological Seminary, 1998); Winfried Vogel, 'The Cultic Motif in Space and Time in the Book of Daniel' (ThD dissertation, Seventh-day Adventist Theological Seminary, 1999). Both show an awareness of literary matters but do not develop them to any extent. Martin Pröbstle, 'Truth and Terror: A Text-Oriented Analysis of Daniel 8:9-14' (PhD dissertation, Seventh-day Adventist Theological Seminary, 2006), includes sections dealing with some literary matters. It is encouraging to encounter Adventist research which not only affirms that 'texts are works of art' (435), but which to some degree engages with the passage's style, structure and intertextuality. Needless to say, none of these is narrative-critical in its outlook.

[60] See Petersen, 'Theology and Function.'

7-12 were studied in order to defend traditional Adventist prophetic interpretation, and the narratives of chapters 1-6 exegeted to defend their historicity. This
observation is, of course, not absolute, but the undeniable tendency has been to
ignore what gives the *whole* book of Daniel literary coherence. To give but one
obvious example, How does the theme of the persecution of the faithful in the
narratives of chapters 1-6 inform the prophecies of future persecution in chapters
7-12; what contribution does this theme make to the plots of the individual narrative episodes? One has to hunt high and low to find Adventist scholars who
investigated this at all.

Secondly, Daniel repeatedly uses dramatic irony to good effect. For example,
chapter 1 sets out graphically the contrast between the presumed perspectives of
Nebuchadnezzar and those of the narrator regarding the question of who is in
control at the siege of Jerusalem.[61] And that very contrast enhances the presentation of the theological theme that runs throughout the whole book and undergirds
the prophecies—that God is in control.

Thirdly, an understanding of the dynamics of repetition in Hebrew narrative
art informs a reading of chapter 3. There are a number of notoriously repetitive
passages here, where Nebuchadnezzar, the narrator and characters underline the
details of what is commanded and the consequences of disobeying them (Dan 3:2-
3, 5, 7, 10, 15, 27) and which to the western ear are redundant. But to the Hebrew
ear they serve the literary purpose of underlining that precisely what Nebuchadnezzar commands is precisely what should happen.[62] But, of course it doesn't, and
the repetition ceases at the point of radical disobedience by the three friends, to
underline that it is their God's commands, and not those of Nebuchadnezzar, that
will come to pass.

In summary, Adventist interpretation of Daniel has dwelt either on proving the
historicity of the book, an area in which we speak to other conservative evangelicals, or in defending traditional Adventist interpretations of the prophecies, where
we speak almost entirely to ourselves. Becoming alert to the literary aspects of the
text would at the very least enrich our contributions to these two audiences, and
might even suggest innovative directions for research which result in widening
the audience interested in listening to us.

Conclusion

Allow me to give a personal testimony. After I chose to specialise in Biblical Studies, I was struck by something. Why was the academic study of the Bible less exciting than my untutored personal engagement had been, regardless of whether I

---

[61] Danna Nolan Fewell, *Circle of Sovereignty: A Story of Stories in Daniel 1-6* (Sheffield, UK:
Almond Press, 1988), 34-35.
[62] Ibid., 66.

was studying in an Adventist environment or in another setting? I finally realised what the reason was. The issues addressed by scholarship, whether of the historical-critical (formally rejected in Adventist circles) or historical-grammatical (the approved alternative) school, were not the issues that drew me to Scripture. I was captivated by the Bible's narratives, the parables of Jesus, prophetic oracles and apocalyptic visions. I was drawn to them, I now realise, because they are superb literature. But neither the historical-critical nor historical-grammatical approach treated them as such. The former method saw them as an archaeological mound to be excavated to reconstruct the historical context in which they were written, edited and evolved. And the latter approach required that narratives be 'de-storified' in order to arrive at the true goal of Bible study—propositional theology. It was only when I encountered a literary approach to Scripture that my joy returned. But with the joy came a sadness that its potential was largely shunned. So, for example, when reflecting on a passage as moving as Genesis 22, the 'sacrifice of Isaac,' Adventist authors have in general lost the plot—literally and metaphorically. One would not be surprised to read Adventist scholars discussing this passage devotionally (e.g. Abraham as an example of great faith); historically (e.g. what was the practice of child sacrifice in the ancient Near East?); archaeologically (e.g. how were Middle-Bronze Age altars constructed?); typologically (e.g. the ram in the thicket as a type of Christ); geographically (where on the map is Mount Moriah?); apologetically (e.g. no evidence in the text to support the documentary hypothesis), theologically (the meaning of sacrifice), or even structurally (another chiasm!), etc. But one would be very surprised to read a discussion of the passage from a literary point of view (e.g. the emotive use of repetition; its place in the overall plot; the narrative's contribution to the characterization of Abraham or God; the irony of obedience; the reader's response, etc.).

In one respect, the fact that Adventist biblical interpretation has shown such little interest in the Bible's literary imagination should not come as a surprise. Conservative evangelicals in general share the same aversion. For example, Longman warns that, 'Scholars, particularly those of us whose doctrine of Scripture is conservative, must resist the temptation to ignore the literary aspect of divine revelation by reducing the Scripture to history and theology.'[63] Vanhoozer too observes that evangelicals also tend to treat the Bible as 'a code book of theological ordinances.'[64] In my estimation, these observations by evangelical scholars also ring true to Adventist exegetical tradition. However, the fact that we are not alone should not be taken as licence to continue in the future as we have in the past. Guy,

---

[63] Tremper Longman, *Literary Approaches to Biblical Interpretation*, Foundations of Contemporary Interpretation, vol. 3 (Grand Rapids, MI: Academic Books, 1987), 152.

[64] Kevin J. Vanhoozer, 'Exploring the World, Following the Word: The Credibility of Evangelical Theology in an Incredulous Age,' *Trinity Journal* 16, no. 1 (Spring 1995), 14.

in his stimulating work *Thinking Theologically*, and commenting on Thompson's influential work on biblical inspiration which advocates a 'case book' rather than 'code book' approach to Scripture,[65] observes, 'While "case book" is an important improvement over "code book", it may not give sufficient emphasis to the essentially narrative function of Scripture, which is more like a "story book" than anything else.'[66] I am in full agreement with Guy. And once the point is conceded, injecting Adventist biblical interpretation with literary imagination becomes a necessity. If we fail to see the imagination in Scripture, we are less likely to use imagination in applying Scripture to the church's theology, mission and worship.[67]

Some object that literary readings can be based on presuppositions that run counter to Adventist concepts of Scripture.[68] That is true. But the same is true of the presuppositions of many historians and theologians working in biblical studies.[69] If it is possible for Adventists to utilise *appropriate* historical and theological presuppositions in the study of Scripture, as is universally agreed, then it must be possible to use *appropriate* literary presuppositions. This chapter is not the place to engage in analysis and assessment of the history of literary theory. My aim is much more modest than that: I wish to encourage Adventist biblical scholars to embrace the literary dimension of Scripture. Once that happens, we can begin to discuss what an appropriate Adventist literary hermeneutic might be. That is a discussion that can occupy us on the journey down the road. But at the moment the journey has barely begun.

Implications for the mission of the church

What benefits would we experience if we were to embrace the literary? First, it would encourage our creativity in a number of areas. For example, it would encourage originality in our preaching. Adventist preaching, when it does deal with the Bible, is predominantly thematic/doctrinal. This is not bad in itself, but in my opinion the balance is skewed. Expository preaching that taps into the literary imagination of a passage and fuels the creativity of the preacher to apply that

---

[65] Alden Thompson, *Inspiration: Hard Questions, Honest Answers* (Hagerstown, MD: Review and Herald Publishing Association, 1991).

[66] Fritz Guy, *Thinking Theologically: Adventist Christianity and the Interpretation of Faith* (Berrien Springs, MI: Andrews University Press, 1999), 91 n. 83.

[67] Cf. Fritz Guy, who suggests that a modern contextualised Adventist theology should be, among other things, '*imaginative*, recognizing not only the legitimacy but also the desirability of exploring new understandings and applications of Scripture, and regarding multiple interpretations as potentially complementary rather than contradictory' (Ibid., 235).

[68] Richard M. Davidson, 'Interpreting Scripture,' 104-105.

[69] For radically pessimistic assessments of the Bible's historical worth, see e.g., Philip R. Davies, *In Search of Ancient Israel* (Sheffield, UK: Sheffield Academic Press, 1995); Niels Peter Lemche, *The Israelites in History and Tradition* (Louisville, KY: Westminster John Knox Press, 1998).

to real life situations, would pay real dividends. It would also encourage more dialogical preaching, for biblical narrative invites a response from its audience without always providing the answer. Preachers would do well not to tame the open-endedness of biblical revelation.

Secondly, seeing the breadth of creative literary imagination in the Bible would encourage us to relate to our society in a variety of ways—that is in more than preaching. We have not been good at applying the creative arts to the tasks of evangelism and pastoral care. Opening our eyes to literature in the Bible, with its appeal to the aesthetic, might show us that God relates to us through our senses, and not just through our intellect. As Ryken reminds us, 'God trusted *literature* as a medium for conveying truth.'[70]

Thirdly, it has been well documented that our contemporary world—call it postmodern or whatever—responds to narratives rather than to 'truth expressed as propositions.' Is it possible to express Adventism through narrative? Adventist proclamation is overwhelmingly 'modern,' but our society increasingly less so. So, it is hardly surprising that large sections of western society do not even stop to listen to us. The way we present the Bible (propositional, synthetic theology), is not the way the Bible generally presents itself (through narratives, poems, and so on). Yet the Bible's own mode of discourse is, increasingly, the way our contemporary society operates. There are clear implications for mission.

Fourthly, embracing the literary dimension of the Bible would enable us to affirm its spiritual value. For there is a connection between the appreciation of the aesthetic in Scripture and the nurture of the reader's spirituality. God gave us a Bible characterised by stories, poems, visions etc. An appreciation of the literary subtlety and beauty of Scripture can feed the soul in ways that more logically developed abstractions or historical reconstructions by-pass.

My argument here is no new-fangled concept given birth in a godless age, as Martin Luther demonstrates:

> I am persuaded that without knowledge of literature pure theology cannot at all endure ... Certainly it is my desire that there shall be as many poets and rhetoricians as possible, because I see that by these studies, as by no other means, people are wonderfully fitted for the grasping of sacred truth and for handling it skilfully and happily ... Therefore I beg of you that at my request (if that has any weight) you will urge your young people to be diligent in the study of poetry and rhetoric.[71]

---

[70] Leland Ryken, 'The Bible as literature. Pt 1, "Words of Delight" in: The Bible as Literature,' *Bibliotheca Sacra* 147, no. 585 (January 1990), 11.

[71] Preserved Smith and Charles M. Jacobs, eds., *Luther's Correspondence*, vol. 2 (Philadelphia: United Lutheran Publication House, 1918), 176, cited in David J. A. Clines, 'Story and Poem: The Old Testament as Literature and as Scripture,' *Interpretation* 34, 115.

In like manner, literary and rhetorical skills should be at the forefront of Adventist biblical interpretation and application. The Adventist mission to the world should present Scripture as imaginative literature for the simple fact that that is what much of it is.

Laurence Turner. Born in Great Britain. Since 1994 Principal Lecturer and Director of Research Degrees, Newbold College, UK. Pastoral experience in England, teaching experience at Avondale, Australia and Newbold, England. Author of books and articles, generally on Old Testament theology. Frequent speaker at pastoral conventions on five continents. PhD, University of Sheffield (1989).

The Mission of God and the Faithfulness of His People: An Exegetical Reading of Revelation 14:6-13

Bertil Wiklander

Seventh-day Adventist identity as a prophetic church at the end of time finds its source and inspiration in the book of Revelation.[1] Thus, the development of the church's theology of mission in the formative period of 1850-1874 was governed by an intense study of Revelation 14:6-12.[2] And yet, an attitude of seeking a deeper understanding is part of the legacy handed down to contemporary Adventism by its pioneers, as is evident by the following comment by Ellen White:

> The book of Revelation opens with an injunction to us to understand the instruction that it contains. 'Blessed is he who reads and those who hear the words of this prophecy,' God declares, 'and keep those things which are written in it; for the time is near.' When we as a people understand what this book means to us, there will be seen among us a great revival. We do not understand fully the lessons that it teaches, notwithstanding the injunction given us to search and study it.[3]

In particular, Ellen White called attention to Revelation 14 as 'a chapter of the deepest interest' that 'will soon be understood in all its bearings.'[4] Responding to this interpretive mandate, the present article seeks to understand Revelation 14:6-13 in the context of chapter 14 and the book of Revelation as a whole.[5]

My exegetical[6] reading is based on Revelation's claim to being a self-contained literary unit (1:1-8; 22:7-21) and its implication that, in essence, John's communica-

---

[1] See, for example, A. M. Rodriguez (ed.), *Toward a Theology of the Remnant: An Adventist Ecclesiological Perspective* (Biblical Research Institute, Studies in Adventist Ecclesiology [1]). (Hagerstown, MD: Review and Herald Publishing Association, 2009).

[2] P. G. Damsteegt, *Foundations of the Seventh-day Adventist Message and Mission* (Grand Rapids, MI: William B. Eerdmans Publishing Company, 1977), 165-270; B. Schantz, *The Development of Seventh-day Adventist Missionary Thought: Contemporary Appraisal*, Diss., Fuller Theological Seminary, June 1983 (Ann Arbor, MI: UMI, 1984), 511-512, 636.

[3] E. G. White, *Testimonies to Ministers and Gospel Workers* (Boise, ID: Pacific Press Publishing Association, 1962), 113.

[4] In: *The Advent Review & Sabbath Herald*, October 13, 1904.

[5] While generally using the *New Revised Standard Version* (NRSV) in quoting the text, my reading was devoted to the earliest retrievable Greek version, which has prompted me to use my own translation as needed.

[6] I am using the tools of exegetical scholarship to recover what the earliest retrievable Greek text meant in John's time. Cf. G. Pfandl's definition that 'Exegesis is concerned with the original meaning of a text' and 'focuses on what the author wanted to say and what the text meant to the original reader.' (*The Prophetic Gift:* Sabbath School Bible Study Guide, 2009:1, *Adult Teacher's Guide*. Grantham: Stanborough Press, 2008, 126).

tive intentions are retrievable in his book. Applying a text-oriented perspective, I focus on the text[7] rather than history, recognizing that 'it is the biblical text that sets the framework for the Bible's interpretation of history.'[8] Approaching Revelation in view of Ellen White's perceptive remark that it portrays 'the deep things of God,'[9] I read it as a product of the mission of God,[10] by which he responds to the spiritual needs of the Christian church addressed in the book (1:9-3:22) and accomplishes his purpose for the created world as depicted in 21:1-22:6.

Since its early years, the Seventh-day Adventist Church has favoured a 'historicist' prophetic-symbolic mode of reading Revelation, focusing on the church-historical past and eschatological present and future.[11] Adventist scholars acknowledge, however, that the first receivers may have applied the text to a different reality than ours,[12] and that historicism incorporates the view that parts of Revelation's prophecies 'had relevance and partial application for the audiences that first received them.'[13] Ellen White, too, recognized that John's book had a message for his times and that deep spiritual lessons may be learnt from it in all times.[14] This universal *spiritual* meaning is the focus of the present article, and I proceed with the conviction that its results are compatible with historicist-prophetic readings. Although the present study has many limitations, a text-focused exegetical reading is in some sense a fundamental approach to the text[15] that may provide com-

---

[7] In terms of literary interpretation, I follow the text-oriented approach to Revelation in R. Stefanovic, *Revelation of Jesus Christ: Commentary on the Book of Revelation* (Berrien Springs, MI: Andrews University Press, 2002), xiv, 24-25. In terms of text-linguistics, I understand 'text' (from Latin *textus*, 'woven fabric, tissue') as a delimited, structured linguistic sign used for communication about the world by a sender to a receiver: see B. Wiklander, *Prophecy as Literature: A Text-Linguistic and Rhetorical Approach to Isaiah 2-4*, Coniectanea Biblica, O.T. Series 22 (Stockholm, Sweden: CWK Gleerup & Liber Tryck, 1984), 39-48, 154-157.

[8] J. Paulien, *What the Bible Says about the End-Time* (Hagerstown, MD: Review and Herald Publishing Association, 1994), 111.

[9] E. G. White, *Acts of the Apostles* (Nampa, ID: Pacific Press Publishing Association, 1911), 584.

[10] Cf. C. H. J. Wright, *The Mission of God: Unlocking the Bible's Grand Narrative* (Downers Grove, IL: InterVarsity Press, 2006).

[11] See, for example, *Handbook of Seventh-day Adventist Theology* (Commentary Reference Series 12), ed. R. Dederen (Hagerstown, MD: Review and Herald Publishing Association, 2000).

[12] W. G. Johnsson, 'The Saints' End-Time Victory over the Forces of Evil,' in: *Symposium on Revelation: Exegetical and General Studies*, Book 2, ed. F. B. Holbrook (Silver Spring, MD: Biblical Research Institute of the General Conference of Seventh-day Adventists, 1992), 22.

[13] D. Fortin, 'Ellen White's Interpretation and Use of the Seven Letters of Revelation,' *JATS*, 18:2 (2007), 202.

[14] Fortin notes that 'Ellen White's understanding of historicism allowed for the prophetic nature of the book and its spiritual relevance to contemporary first-century Christians and to all Christians throughout history' (ibid., 204).

[15] Cf. the view that 'what the biblical text meant in principle in its original setting is precisely what the text means for us today. Any application of a text to our situation must be tied to the original meaning.' (E. Müller, 'Guidelines for the Interpretation of Scripture,' in:

mon ground for dialogue with scholarly communities, theologians, and Christian denominations concerning the biblical basis for Seventh-day Adventist identity, message and mission.

A Christian 'Revelatory Prophecy': The Book of Revelation

The scroll sent by John as a circular letter to seven named Christian churches in the Roman province of Asia Minor (1:4, 11; 22:16),[16] in the second half of the first century AD,[17] was not only written for consolation, encouragement, and warning.[18] It also calls Christians to a task of witnessing to God and his righteousness for which the consolations and warnings are meant to prepare them.[19] It is named 'prophecy' (1:3; 22:7, 10) but introduced as a 'revelation of Jesus Christ' (1:1), being written on Christ's command: 'Write in a book what you see' (1:11, 19). It is defined as 'the word of God and the witness of Jesus Christ,' mediated to John through God's messengers and the 'spirit of prophecy' (1:2; 19:10; cf. 1:9; 12:17; 20:4). The individual messages to the historical churches serve as *seven* different introductions to the book (2:1-3:22), revealing different settings and kinds of spiritual needs in which John's book is meaningful. In engaging the content of his book with these diverse settings, he makes them representative of *all* the churches ('seven' being the number of completeness), which gives the intended readers a universal range.[20]

Besides introduction and conclusion (1:1-8; 22:7-21), the book contains sections of predominantly *parenetical* (1:9-3:22) and *prophetical* (4:1-22:6) revelations. The historical literary *genre* of Revelation is uncertain,[21] but 'revelatory prophecy' covers its general *text-type* among the broad literary category of revelatory writings[22]

G. W. Reid (ed.), *Understanding Scripture: An Adventist Approach* (Hagerstown, MD: Review and Herald Publishing Association, 2001), 112-113.

[16] For the epistolary character of Revelation, see D. E. Aune, *Revelation 1-5*, Word Biblical Commentary, vol. 52 A (Nashville, TN: Thomas Nelson, 1997), lxxii-lxxv; R. Bauckham, *The Theology of the Book of Revelation*. (Cambridge, UK: University Press), 1993, 12-17.

[17] For the traditional date in the time of Emperor Domitian (81-96 AD), see Stefanovic, *Revelation*, 3-5. For an earlier date, around 68-70 AD, see M. Barker, *The Revelation of Jesus Christ* (Edinburgh, UK: T & T Clark, 2000), xi.

[18] Rev 1:4, 11, 19; 2:1, 8, 12, 18; 3:1, 7, 14; 22:16.

[19] Bauckham, *Revelation*, 16.

[20] Ibid., 12-17.

[21] Two German scholars, K. I. Nitzsch (1820) and F. Lücke (1832), coined the term 'Apokalyptik' (J. M. Schmidt, *Die jüdische Apokalyptik: Die Geschichte ihrer Erforschung von den Anfängen bis zu den Textfunden von Qumran* (Neukirchen, Germany: Neukirchener Verlag, 1969), 98), but, as a designation for a literary genre, it is yet unclear what 'apocalyptic' actually stands for (cf. Aune, *Revelation 1-5*, lxx-xc; J. Paulien, 'The End of Historicism? Reflections on the Adventist Approach to Biblical Apocalyptic—Part Two,' *JATS* 17:1, 2006, 180-182; S. K. Tonstad, *Saving God's Reputation: The Theological Function of Pistis Iēsou in the Cosmic Narratives of Revelation* (Library of New Testament Studies 337, ed. M. Goodacre; London, UK and New York: T & T Clark, 2006), 17-38.

[22] Note the distinctions between Mode of Writing, Type of Text, Genre, Subgenre, and Single Texts in D. Hellholm, 'The Problem of Apocalyptic Genre and the Apocalypse of John,' *SBL Seminar Papers 1982*, ed. K. H. Richards (Scholars Press: Chico, CA, 1982), 169.

and accounts for the blend of prophecy and revelation of divine wisdom-secrets that characterizes the book.

The language of Revelation is a peculiar Greek with strong Semitic influence,[23] flavoured by symbols and sub-texts from the Hebrew Bible.[24] Although such 'inter-textual' allusions are difficult to determine with certainty,[25] it is clear that they have significantly influenced the wording, imagery, and content of the book. Recognizing that 'Revelation is really (from 1:10 to 22:6) a single vision' and that 'its imagery is common to the whole,'[26] its symbols and themes find their primary meaning from within the book as a whole.

Revelation unfolds the mission of God, 'the Alpha and Omega, the Lord God, who is and who was and who is to come, the Almighty' (1:8).[27] His will to be known as God drives his mission, a concept shared with the Bible as a whole: 'The world must know its Creator. The nations must know their Ruler, Judge and Saviour.'[28] The intended act of reading is closely connected with the *imminent* coming of Christ: John is asked not even to 'seal up the words of the prophecy of this book, because the time is near.'[29] Thus, Revelation is deeply rooted in the biblical view of God as the God who comes,[30] which is part of the 'fulfilment of *the mystery of God* as he announced to his servants the prophets' (10:7).[31] Revelation's prophetic concept of history places world events under God's dominion, and waiting in patient endurance for his salvation and judgement is therefore the faithful attitude of his worshippers.[32] As they wait and hope, God provides secret wisdom through the revelatory book where his spirit-filled prophet has 'witnessed' the revealed divine reality. Revelation is therefore itself part of the mission of God which is accomplished when the book is read, heard and taken to heart (1:3; 22:7).[33]

---

[23] Stefanovic, *Revelation*, 2-3. Cf. S. Thompson, *The Apocalypse and Semitic Syntax*, SNTS, Monograph Series 52 (Cambridge, UK: Cambridge University Press, 1985).

[24] Stefanovic, *Revelation*, 18-20. Allegedly, one-seventh of the substance of Revelation is drawn from words in the Hebrew Bible (P. Lestringant, *Essai sur l'unité de la révélation biblique* (Paris: Editions 'Je Sers,' 1942), 148). For the particular indebtedness to the book of Daniel, see G. K. Beale, *The Use of Daniel in Jewish Apocalyptic Literature and in the Revelation of St John* (Lanham, New York, and London, UK: University of America Press), 1984.

[25] J. Paulien, *Decoding Revelation's Trumpets: Literary Allusions and the Interpretation of Revelation 8:7-12* . AUSDD Series 11 (Berrien Springs, MI: Andrews University Press, 1988); idem, 'Criteria and the Assessment of Allusions to the Old Testament in the Book of Revelation,' in: *Studies in the Book of Revelation*, ed. S. Moyise, JSNTS 189 (Edinburgh, UK: T & T Clark, 2001), 113-129.

[26] Bauckham, *Revelation*, 10.

[27] Each of these titles is rooted in the Hebrew Bible and occurs seven times in Revelation (ibid., 25-30).

[28] Cf. Wright, *Mission*, 126-130.

[29] Rev 1:7; 3:11; 22:7, 10, 12, 20.

[30] Bauckham, *Revelation*, 28-30.

[31] For the central role of this passage in the structure of Revelation as a whole, see Stefanovic, *Revelation*, 40-45, 167-179, 317-332.

[32] Rev 1:9; 2:2, 19; 3:10; 13:10; 14:12. Cf. Ps 25:3, 5, 21; 27:14: 31:24; 37:7, 9, 34; 38:15; 39:7; 130:5; Lam 3:22-26.

In the prophetic section of Revelation (4:1-22:6), God asserts his divinity and reveals his mind and character in the context of the cosmic conflict with Satan, 'the deceiver of the whole world' (12:9), and his agents, 'the destroyers of the earth' (11:18). In this controversy, God is victorious through 'the Lamb that was slaughtered' (5:6-12), revealing his holiness (4:8), eternity (10:6), and worthiness of being worshipped as God (5:13; 14:7). He is the Creator who acts in faithfulness towards his creation (21:1-5),[34] the Universal Ruler of the world (11:15), the Righteous Judge of the nations (15:4), and the Saviour of his faithful people (14:1-5; 19:1-8) with whom he seeks communion (21:3, 24-26; 22:1-5).

The context of Revelation 14

The prophecy in 12:1-14:20 depicts the cosmic war from the incarnation (12:1-5) to the second coming of Christ (14:14-20) and his gathering of the redeemed before the throne of God (14:1-5). Its framework in Revelation points to chapter 14, as may be illustrated by the following comments on two springboard passages:[35]

Firstly, the emphatic proclamation that there will be no more delay, but the mystery of God will be fulfilled when the seventh angel blows his trumpet (10:5-7) leads to 11:15, where loud voices from heaven declare that the kingdom of the world has become the eternal kingdom of God and of his Christ. This climax of the five events in 11:18 summarises chapter 14:

(a) The nations raged: see 12:1-13:18; 14:8.

(b) God's wrath has come: see 14:8, 10, 19.

(c) The time has come for judging the dead: see 14:7, 13.

(d) The time has come for rewarding God's servants, the prophets and saints, and all who fear his name: see 14:1-5, 12-13, 14-16.

(e) The time has come for destroying those who destroy the earth: see 14:8-11, 17-20.

Thus, the springboard passage in 11:18 introduces and condenses the entire cosmic conflict passage in 12:1-22:6, but its five themes converge in chapter 14 which has a pivotal place in the composition: *after* Satan's war against Christ and the saints (12:1-13:18) and *leading up to* Christ's second coming and the harvest time (14:14-20).[36]

---

[33] Wright notes that 'the writings that now comprise our Bible are themselves the product of and witness to the ultimate mission of God' and 'we could as meaningfully talk of the missional basis of the Bible as of the biblical basis of mission' (*Mission*, 22, 29).

[34] Bauckham, *Revelation*, 51-53.

[35] For a definition of this literary device, see Stefanovic, *Revelation*, 26.

[36] For the concentration of links in Rev 14 with the book as a whole, see Aune, *Revelation 6-16*, Word Biblical Commentary, vol. 52 B (Nashville, TN: Thomas Nelson, 1998), 795-796.

Secondly, another springboard passage in 12:17 concludes 12:1-16 and introduces 13:1-18, thus delimiting 12:1-13:18 as one unit describing the cosmic conflict and trials of the saints. This unit is interrupted and sharply contrasted by the scene of the redeemed before the throne of God (14:1-5) which is continued and expanded by the nations' worship of God (15:2-4). Again, Revelation 14 functions as the turning-point in Satan's war against 'the rest of her children, those who keep the commandments of God and hold the witness of Jesus' (12:17; 13:7). It introduces the *salvation* of God's people (14:1-5) as an outcome of three events: (a) God's *judgement hour*, proclaimed as part of the *eternal gospel of God* for the conversion of the nations (14:6-11), (b) a *parenesis* directed to the saints (14:9-13), and (c) the *harvest hour* at the coming of Christ (14:14-20).

God's salvation of his faithful people: Revelation 14

Revelation 14 describes how God establishes his eternal reign in the world with particular emphasis on how he saves his people and judges his enemies. The theme of God's eternal reign continues from 10:6-7 and 11:15-18, i.e. from the *introduction* to the great controversy section (12:1-13:18), where God's heavenly temple is opened and the ark of his covenant is seen (11:19). Therefore, God acts in chapter 14 *from his throne*, as the eternal Creator and Ruler of the world. By the sequence of actions in 14:6-20, he reaches out to the nations and *calls* them to worship him (cf. 13:4, 8, 15), *judging* his enemies (cf. 12:1-13:18), *supporting* those who faithfully keep his commandments and have the witness of Jesus (12:17) and *vindicating* those who were conquered and killed by the beast (13:7-10).

The opening vision glorifies God's victory in Christ (14:1-5),[37] raising four questions which are answered in 14:6-20: (a) *Question:* What about those of whom the saints are redeemed (14:3-4)? *Answer:* God will call all peoples to conversion and judge his enemies (14:6-11). (b) *Question:* What about the *faithful* who suffer oppression (13:7-10)? *Answer:* God encourages them to have patient endurance (14:12). (c) *Question:* What about justice and salvation for the *dead* who have died in the Lord (13:10; cf. 6:9-11; 20:4)? *Answer:* God has declared them blessed, granting them rest and eternal reward (14:13). (d) *Question:* How and when will God distinguish between the faithful and the unfaithful? *Answer:* At the coming of Christ, he will harvest the faithful and execute judgement on the unfaithful (14:14-20).

In 14:6-20, a numerical feature calls attention to 14:14 within *seven* acts of God symbolizing completeness: *three* angels call for conversion and issue warnings (14:6-11), *three* angels execute God's reward and punishment (14:15-20), and between them is 'one like the son of man' (14:14). He can be no other than Jesus Christ who is introduced by the same phrase in John's first vision (1:13).[38] The

---

[37] See Rev 5:9-13; 7:10, 15-17; 11:15-18; 14:1-5; 15:2-4; 19:1-8; 21:6-22:6.

[38] Cf. Stefanovic, *Revelation*, 456, 459-460; Aune, *Revelation 6-16*, 839-842.

allusion to Daniel 7:13-14 calls attention to judgement, eternal kingship, and all peoples, nations, and languages serving the one like the son of man, which makes good sense in Revelation 14, since it enforces the call for conversion to the nations (14:6-7), the judgement and punishment of the unfaithful (14:8, 17-20), and Christ's gathering of the faithful worshippers (14:14-16; 15:2-4).

Drawing on the double image in Joel 3:13, the two harvests in 14:14-20 are Christ's gathering of the 'first fruit' of the faithful (the grain harvest) and the punishment of the wicked (the grape harvest).[39] This is a condition for 14:4 where the faithful are offered to God and the Lamb as 'first fruits' of the harvest of all nations, whose reaping is depicted in 14:14-16. 'The great wine press of the wrath of God' (14:19) echoes 'the wine of the wrath of her fornication'[40] that Babylon made all nations drink (14:8) and 'the wine of God's wrath' which God makes all beast worshippers drink (14:10). Babylon's wine is her unfaithful and seducing life which leads to beast worship; God's wine is his judgement on the nations which restores his kingdom.[41] Extending this imagery, water and wine are alluded to as symbols of life and death in 14:6-20. Thus, the first angel adds 'the springs of water' to the list of God's created works (14:7), which is unique in this kind of phrase.[42] This expression alludes to the life-giving images of God and Christ giving water to the thirsty from the springs of the water of life (7:17; 21:6; 22:1-2, 17) and may hint at passages like Proverbs 14:27: 'The fear of the Lord is a fountain of life, so that one may avoid the snares of death.' In contrast, the beast-worshipping nations drink 'the wine' (blood, death) of Babylon's idolatrous seduction and God's judgement (14:8-11, 17-20). This imagery argues for trust in God's power and glory as Creator, alluding to Psalm 104 where his creation of the springs of water is a *special sign* of his creative power (104:6-10), providing *life-giving water* for every being and plant on earth (104:11-18, 27-30) and giving grounds for the appeal: 'May the glory of the Lord endure forever' (104:31; cf. Rev 14:6-7).

The scene of the victorious community before the throne of God (14:1-5) lacks time reference, but time is important in the events leading up it. The announced judgement *hour* and the world-wide proclamation of the gospel of God (14:7) culminate in the second coming and the harvest *hour* (14:15). Thus, in Revelation 14, the time of judgement until the coming of Christ (14:14-20) is a special time for the *mission* of God to all nations (14:6-11) and the enduring *faithfulness* of his people (14:9-13).

---

[39] Bauckham, *Revelation*, 94-98; Stefanovic, *Revelation*, 460.
[40] This expression blends two metaphors into one: 'The acceptance of Babylon's seductive wine of fornication results in the drinking of God's wine of wrath; that is, it brings as a consequence the judgement of God' (Stefanovic, *Revelation*, 447).
[41] Ibid., 95.
[42] See Ex 20:11; Neh 9:6; Ps 146:5-7; Rev 4:11; 10:7.

The three angels' messages in Revelation 14:6-13

The *vision* of the three angels (14:6-11) is rounded off with an *exhortation* to the saints and an *audition* of divine blessing being declared on the righteous dead (14:12-13). Thus, the unity of 14:6-13 is not found in its narrative theme but in its argumentative and persuasive function. The material is organized as follows:

Two divine revelations and their significance for God's people:
A. Vision of three angels: (14:6-11)
  1. The gospel of God for every nation, tribe, language and people (14:6)
  2. *The first angel*: (14:7)
    a. All peoples called to fear and give glory to God
    b. The time of God's judgement of the earth has come
    c. All peoples called to worship God as Creator of the world
  3. *The second angel*: (14:8)
    a. Babylon has led all nations away from God
    b. Babylon will be punished and fall
    c. Babylonian allegiance places nations under the divine wrath
  4. *The third angel*: (14:9-11)
    a. The peoples' satanic beast worship denounced:
      (i) Against beast worship
      (ii) Against worship of the beast's image
      (iii) Against acceptance of the mark of the beast's name
    b. Beast worshippers are subject to God's wrath
    c. Beast worshippers will be destroyed forever
B. Exhortation to the saints: (14:12)
  1. Have patient endurance in keeping God's commandments
  2. Have patient endurance in keeping the faith of Jesus
C. Audition of voice from heaven: (14:13)
  1. The dead who die in the Lord are blessed from now on
  2. The Spirit says: They will rest from their hard labours
  3. The Spirit says: Their works go with them

The receivers of the three angels' messages are every nation, tribe, language and people on earth. Christ redeems the saints from among this body (5:9-10; 7:9; 14:4). Yet, 'all nations' will ultimately worship God (15:4), who will dwell with men as their God, and they will be his people (21:3, 24-26; 22:1-5). Thus, Revelation implies a *conversion* of the nations in response to the *message* of God's three angels (14:6-11) and his *righteous judgements* (14:8-11; 15:4; 19:2). The distinction between the converted nations (15:4b) and the special people of God (14:1-5; 15:2-4a) may be rooted in temple imagery, since Israel (the twelve tribes) worshipped in the inner court while the gentiles worshipped in the outer court, as stated in 11:1-2. This imagery belongs to the repeated identification of God's people as 'priests' (1:6; 5:10; 20:6) and the symbolic distinction between the 144,000 (7:4-8) and the great multitude (7:9-17), which in reality disappears as they worship God.[43]

The nations are under the authority of the satanic trinity (12:17-13:18) symbolized by Babylon (14:8). Among them, many worship Satan and the sea-beast (13:1-10), into which the land-beast has coerced and deceived them (13:11-18), but some might change allegiance towards the true God. Among the saints, scattered among the nations, many are faithful to God, but some are tempted to apostatise. Since God's mission is to be the God of all men (21:4), he seeks to save human beings for communion with him, before defeating his enemies and bringing final justice. Thus, while the second angel *accuses* Babylon of seducing the nations (14:8), he doesn't say that *all* nations will be punished, but *forewarns* that their satanic allegiance makes them subject to the wrath of God. Likewise, the third angel doesn't say that *all* peoples of the earth will be destroyed (14:9-11), but identifies the *fundamental crime* of beast worship in the Babylonian system and its impending punishment. In view of the first angel's call to conversion and true worship, therefore, the three angels' messages express God's *final opportunity* for those among the peoples of the earth whose names are written in the book of life (13:8; 17:8; 20:12, 15; 21:27) to 'come out of Babylon' and join God's worshipping community in eternity.

The individual messages of the three angels may be understood as follows.

The first angel's message (14:6-7)

Then I saw another angel flying in mid-heaven, with an eternal gospel to proclaim to those who live on the earth—to every nation and tribe and language and people. He said in a loud voice, 'Fear God and give him glory, for the hour of his judgement has come; and worship him who made heaven and earth, the sea and the springs of water.'

The language is associated with celebration of royal power. The unique expression *euangelion aiōnion euangelisai* (literally: 'proclaim as gospel an eternal gospel') calls attention to the gospel's extraordinary importance. In political usage in John's time, *euangelion* takes on the sense of 'message of victory' or 'message confirming the king's supremacy and reign.'[44] The qualification of *euangelion* as 'eternal'

---

[43] See Stefanovic, *Revelation*, 266; R. Lehmann, 'Remnant in the Book of Revelation,' in: Rodriguez, *Theology of the Remnant*, 91-94. For the strong influence of sanctuary symbolism in Revelation, see Barker, *Revelation*, 12-56; Paulien, *The Deep Things of God* (Hagerstown, MD: Review and Herald Publishing Association, 2004), 124-132.

[44] J. Schniewind, *Euangelion: Ursprung und erste Gestalt des Begriffs Evangelium*. Darmstadt, Germany: Wissenschaftliche Buchgesellschaft, 1970, 27-34; G. Friedrich, s.v. *euangelion* in: *TDNT* 2, 722, 724-725.

is found only here in the Bible. It defines the gospel as 'rooted and grounded in the changeless character and purpose of God,'[45] which is a recurring concept in Revelation,[46] supporting the call to *fear, glorify* and *worship* him as Ruler and Creator of the world in contrast to the impending fall of 'the great Babylon' (14:8; note the ironical allusion to Daniel 4:30!). The message alludes to Isaiah 52:7 in view of the confluence of terms like 'herald,' 'bring good news,' and 'reign of God.' The verbal set 'fear, glorify and worship' is formulaic and rooted in the declarations of praise of God's eternal power in the royal enthronement psalms[47] celebrating God's reign over the nations and their gods.[48]

The first angel calls for conversion, because men's worship of Satan and the beast (13:4, 8, 15) is really due to God, the Creator. The two appeals in the gospel of God are made on the basis of his eternal enthronement as Ruler and Judge of the nations:[49] (a) 'Fear God and give him glory' is the attitude awarded a Lord and Ruler, but its motivation sees him as the Judge who (i) achieves *victory* over his enemies (14:8) and (ii) maintains *justice* in the world (14:9-11). (b) 'Worship him' is grounded in God's ownership of the world and his life-giving and creative power. Thus, the *eternal* gospel of God anticipates the *fulfilment* of God's mission as depicted in 21:1-5 and a *revelation* of God as 'the beginning and the end' (21:6).

The gospel alludes to the Sabbath commandment in Exodus 20:8-11.[50] God's role as Creator functions in Revelation as the *reason* for worshipping him, because (a) 'he *lives* forever and ever' (10:5-7) and (b) 'all things exist and have been created by his *will*' (4:11). Thus, the allusion to Sabbath as the lawful expression of *worshipping* the Creator underlines his sovereign *power of life* and righteous *will expressed in his law*. We will see later that these concepts are important in the structure of the passage, being intertwined with two Sabbath sub-texts on God's legal authority (14:6-11) and provision of life (14:9-13).

The second angel's message (14:8)

Then another angel, a second, followed, saying, 'Fallen, fallen is Babylon the great! She has made all nations drink of the wine of the wrath of her fornication.'

---

[45] G. B. Caird, *The Revelation of St John the Divine*. Black's New Testament Commentaries (London, UK: A & C Black, 1987), 182.

[46] Rev 1:4, 8; 4:8; 22:13; cf. 5:13; 7:12; 10:5-7; 11:15-18; 15:2-4; 19:6; 21:1-22:5.

[47] Ps 93-99; note particularly Ps 96 and 1 Chr 16:8-36.

[48] W. Altink, '1 Chronicles 16:8-36 as Literary Source for Revelation 14:6-7,' *AUSS*, vol. 22, 1984, 187-196; idem, 'Theological Motives for the Use of 1 Chronicles 16:8-36 as Background for Revelation 14:6-7,' *AUSS*, vol. 24, 1986, 211-221).

[49] Cf. Rev 4:1-11; 5:13-14; 10:6; 11:15; 15:4.

[50] M. Frey, 'The Theological Concept of the Sabbath in the Book of Revelation,' in: *For You have Strengthened Me*, Festschrift G. Pfandl, ed. M. Pröbstle (St. Peter am Hart, Austria: Seminar Schloss Bogenhofen, 2007), 236-237.

The nations' worship of Satan and the beast, rather than the true God (13:4, 8, 15), makes them subject to the wrath of God (14:8b, 10, 19).[51] This divine energy flows from his righteousness and holiness and are central qualities of God in Revelation.[52] They require the condemnation of the unrighteousness on earth and the destruction of the powers of evil that contest God's rule, so that their rule may give place to the coming of God's kingdom on earth.[53] God's sovereign wrath *counters* the wrath of Satan and the nations (11:18; 12:17; 14:8-11, 17-20), and at the coming of Christ it *ends* the persecution and killing of God's faithful people and the blasphemies against God (11:18; 12:12, 17), i.e. God will *vindicate* his righteousness (15:3-4; 16:6; 19:2) and *save* the faithful who burst into joyful praise (14:1-5, 14-16; 18:20; 19:1-7).

The verb 'fallen' in the Greek text is an aorist known as 'the prophetic perfect in which a future event is described with the past tense as if it has already occurred.'[54] The future fall of Babylon is its punishment for destroying God's kingdom (see 16:1-20:15). The repetition of 'fallen' alludes to Isaiah 21:9, implying God's victory over Babylon's gods and the salvation of his people.

'Babylon' is a prophetic metaphor for a power of confusion, destruction and oppression that exalts itself above God and takes the place of God, as when Isaiah equates Babylon with Lucifer (Isa 14:12-14).[55] This is enforced by the allusion of 'the great Babylon' to Daniel 4:30 and the humiliation of the king's godless self-pride. In Revelation, Babylon represents 'the end-time world-wide religious confederacy made up of the satanic trinity (16:19) arrayed against God and his people,'[56] fulfilling the characteristics of the satanic trinity: (a) the great dragon, i.e. the ancient serpent, the Devil and Satan, the deceiver of the whole world, and his angels (12:9), (b) the sea-beast (13:1-10, 11-18), and (c) the land-beast, also called 'the false prophet' (13:11-18; 16:13-14).[57] Thus, 'Babylon' is used as a *metonym*: being typically associated with the characteristics of the satanic trinity, it refers to the whole concept of God's enemy who oppresses his people. As 'the great prostitute,' Babylon sits on 'many waters,' i.e. peoples, multitudes, nations and languages (17:1, 15), ruling over the kings of the earth who have yielded their power and authority to the beast (17:7-18:24). The kings of the earth have 'committed

---

[51] See also Rev 6:16-17; 11:18; 15:1, 7; 16:1, 19; 18:3; 19:15.
[52] Rev 4:8; 6:10; 14:10; 15:4; 16:5.
[53] Bauckham, *Revelation*, 40-43.
[54] Stefanovic, *Revelation*, 446.
[55] Ibid., 446-447. For its use by Christians and Jews as a symbol of Rome, see 1 Pet 5:13; the Sibylline Oracles 5.137-162; 2 Baruch 11:1; 67:7; and Tertullian, *Against Marcion* 3:13.
[56] Stefanovic, *Revelation*, 446-447. Cf. L. M. Garilva, 'The Development of Ellen G. White's concept of Babylon in *The Great Controversy*,' *JATS* 18:2, 2007, 223-242; Garilva finds that 'Stefanovic's view is the same as Ellen White's final view and echoes the explanation of the *Seventh-day Adventist Encyclopaedia*' (ibid., 239).
[57] See Stefanovic, *Revelation*, 487-488.

fornication' with her and the inhabitants of the earth have become 'drunk with the wine of her fornication' (17:2). This imagery fits the second angel's message in 14:8 where 'fornication' is a metaphor for apostasy from the true God.[58] Babylon's guilt includes violent oppression of God's people: sitting on a beast resembling the sea-beast, she is 'drunk with the blood of the saints and the blood of the witnesses to Jesus' (17:6).[59] Revelation's comforting message is, however, that God will give Babylon 'the wine-cup of the fury of his wrath' and Babylon and its loyal nations will be destroyed (16:13-21; cf. 14:8), which is a gospel of salvation from evil for the faithful (18:20; 19:1-6).

In view of these features, 'Babylon' has at least two levels of meaning: at the explicit *image* level, it is a city in command of a system of religious-political power with treaties binding the nations to it. At the implied *object* level, it is the satanic trinity, the great enemy of God that uses deceit and coercion to take his place and lead the earth astray. The fulfilment of 'the mystery of God' therefore requires its complete destruction.

The third angel's message (14:9-11)

Then another angel, a third, followed them, crying with a loud voice, 'If anyone worships the beast and its image, and receives a mark on his fore-head or on his hand, he will also drink the wine of God's wrath, poured unmixed into the cup of his anger, and he will be tormented with fire and sulphur in the presence of the holy angels and in the presence of the Lamb. And the smoke of their torment goes up forever and ever. There is no rest day or night for those who worship the beast and its image and if anyone receives the mark of its name.'

God's reign is founded on his sovereign *law* which is implied by *synecdoche* or *pars pro toto*: a part of God's law, i.e. the prohibition against worship of the satanic beast implies the full extent of God's law made explicit in 'the commandments of God' (14:12). Traces of the first four of the Ten Commandments are found in the third angel's message:[60] (a) the *law* of 'having no other gods before me' condemns the *crime* of worshipping the beast; (b) the *law* of 'no worship of images' condemns the *crime* of worshipping the image of the beast; (c) the *law* of 'no misuse of God's name' condemns the *crime* of accepting the mark of the name of the beast; (d) the *law* of 'Sabbath rest,' implying worship of the Creator, condemns the *crime* of beast

---

[58] See, for example, Isa 57:3-12; Ezek 16:15, 26-29. In contexts with this imagery, a city whose inhabitants worship false gods is described as a 'prostitute' (Isa 50:1; 54:4-7; Jer 3:6-10; Ezek 16; 23).

[59] Cf. Rev 6:19; 13:7, 10, 15; 16:6; 18:20, 24; 19:2; 20:4.

[60] Note Paulien's point that the first table of the law and the Sabbath function as 'the issue in the final crisis according to Revelation 12-14' (*End-Time*, 121-129).

worship, resulting in the *punishment* of 'no rest day or night' (14:11). These features are linked with the Sabbath allusions in 14:7 and 14:9-13, to which we will return later.

The expressions 'the beast, his image, and the mark of his name' (14:9-11) are introduced in 13:14-18. The beast is the sea-beast who is worshipped by the peoples of the world. Holding power and authority from Satan, it turns people into worshippers of Satan, the enemy of God (13:1, 3-4, 7), and oppresses the saints by captivity and killing them by the sword (13:10; cf. 6:11; 20:4). Via allusions to the beast-vision in Daniel 7 (verses 8 and 25), it is accused of blaspheming God, making war on the saints and conquering them, and being given authority over every tribe and people and language and nation (13:6-7).

The land-beast causes all people to be marked with the name of the sea-beast, which is a 'human' number, namely, 666 (13:16-18). John appeals here to special wisdom and understanding rather than giving an explanation (13:18), which suggests that this symbol was known among the intended receivers. While we are unable to identify it with certainty from the literary context in Revelation, external evidence suggests that it is connected with Babylon and that this would have been known in Asia Minor in the first century. The assumption that 666 corresponds to a value represented by letters in the Hebrew, Greek, or Latin alphabet, generates a multitude of meanings and no warrant for such a conjecture is found in Revelation. Instead, attention has been drawn to the Babylonian mathematical system which was based on the sexagesimal system, in which the numbers 6 and 60 were the basic counting units.[61] 60 was the number of the supreme gods in the Babylonian pantheon, and a popular amulet worn by Babylonian priests contained a configuration of numbers in a square, the sum of which is 666, both horizontally and vertically. If this was what John had in mind, 666 is the triple number of Babylon, the satanic trinity. What would it mean in Revelation 13-14?

It has been suggested that John's comment that 666 is a 'human' number may be related to the creation of human beings on the sixth day of creation.[62] Since the fullness of creation is achieved on the seventh day, the perfect divine number, with its focus on blessed rest from human works making men complete by worshipping their Creator, the number six may be associated with imperfection, human works, idolatry, and failure to give God glory. This reading is meaningful in 14:6-13, in view of the references to worship of the Creator (14:7), his law (14:9-12), and the blessing of Sabbath rest (14:13). It would also provide a connection between *three* times six, the satanic *trinity*, and their opposites: the *three* angels of God who proclaim the coming of his eternal reign when he judges his enemies and saves his people.

---

[61] Stefanovic, *Revelation*, 417-418 (with references).
[62] Ibid., 418 (with references).

The name of the beast *identifies* who belongs to and worships the satanic trinity (13:16-18). In contrast to this, the name of God and the Lamb on the foreheads of the redeemed indicates that they worship and belong to him (14:1; cf. 7:1-4). The mark of the beast is therefore a sign of unfaithfulness and disloyalty to God, of accepting a false god rather than the true God.

The third angel's message contains a chiastic pattern marked by key words, themes, and shifts in singular/plural forms of persons.[63] The parallels in 14:9b and 14:11b, indicating the *crime* of beast worship, frame the *punishment*: 'the smoke of their torment goes up forever and ever, and those who worship the beast and his image have no rest day or night' (14:11a; cf. 19:3; 20:10). This central phrase is based on Isaiah 34:8-10, where the fire from the destruction of Israel's enemy 'will not be quenched night and day' and 'its smoke will rise forever,' being associated with 'chaos and desolation.' Since fire consumes and does not preserve (20:9), the phrase does not refer to endless burning but burning making the consumption complete.[64] By its chiasm and legal style, the third angel's message warns against the *future* punishment of disloyalty to God, its *eternal* duration, and the death *without rest* under the *curse* of God in contrast to the *blessing* awarded the faithful in 14:13.

Three concepts unify the three angels' messages:

(a) *Worship:* Against any worship of Satan and his representatives, the three angels proclaim God, the Creator, as worthy of glory and *worship* (14:7), the fall of the satanic trinity and its satanic *worship* (14:8), and a stark warning to anyone who *worships* the beast (14:9-11).

(b) *Judgement:* The Greek term for 'judgement' (*krisis*) in 14:7 may refer to the entire judicial proceeding of preparing and conducting a lawsuit, pronouncing the verdict and the sentence, and effectuating the punishment as well as bringing retribution to the offended party.[65] This concept unifies the three angels' messages and links them with 'the judgement of the dead' (11:18; cf. 14:13) and the execution of God's judgement, including the two harvests at the coming of Christ (14:14-20) and the strategic destruction of evil (15:1-20:15).

(c) *Salvation:* This concept appears in 14:1-5 (logical climax of chapter 14), 14:7-8 (fall of the oppressor resulting in salvation of the oppressed), 14:9-13 (parenesis based on contrasting acts of good and evil and their retribution), and 14:14-16 (gathering of the saints at the second coming).

The three angels' messages may also be unified by allusions to Isaiah 33. Comforting God's people in their oppression (33:5-6), Isaiah points to God who is *enthroned in Zion* and how *fearing him* leads to justice, righteousness, and salvation

---

[63] Aune, *Revelation 6-16*, 797-798.
[64] Stefanovic, *Revelation*, 450-451.
[65] Büchsel, s.v. *krisis* in: *TDNT* 3, 922-923.

(cf. Rev 14:1, 7). The communal confession in Isaiah 33:22 assigns three roles to God: 'for the Lord is our *judge*, the Lord is our *lawgiver*, the Lord is our *king; he will save us.*' A connection between these roles of God as *Saviour of his people* and the three angels' messages would explain (a) the three distinct roles of God as king, judge, and lawgiver in 14:6-11, and (b) the peculiar feature that the third angel's message is worded as a *legal stipulation* rather than an act of judgement, i.e. God speaks here as lawgiver and in terms of the 'casuistic law' used across the ancient Near East and characterized by the pattern 'if a man (or anyone) commits x, he will be punished by y.' Granted this allusion, (c) the three angels proclaim, as a gospel, God's answer to his people's prayers for salvation while waiting for him in patient endurance (5:8; 6:10; 8:3, 4), and (d) the beast worshippers' punishment (14:9-11) would be alluding to the destroyer's punishment by 'devouring fire and everlasting flames' (Isa 33:10-14).

Enduring faithfulness until the end: The parenesis in Revelation 14:9-13

The parenesis in 14:9-13 addresses the saints, in the text, before the coming of Christ and his gathering of the faithful (14:14-16). It applies the vision of the three angels (14:6-11) and the audition of a voice from heaven (14:13) as arguments for the patient endurance of the saints in faithfulness to God and his will, encouraging them to keep the faith of Jesus *until death* (14:12), imitating the faithfulness of the righteous dead which leads to blessing and eternal life (14:13), while rejecting the infidelity of the beast worshippers and avoiding their curse and eternal death (14:9-11). This understanding will be substantiated in the following.

Three features suggest that 14:12 is an inspired comment by John:[66] (a) it brings a new theme and a new addressee, coordinating the contrast between the central element of the third angel's message (14:11a) and the words of a voice from heaven (14:13); (b) the chiasm identified earlier in 14:9-11 sets the third angel's message apart from 14:12, especially since the central point of 'no rest day or night' for the beast worshippers is the point of contrast with the blessed rest of the righteous dead in 14:13; (c) the deictic particle *hōde* in 14:12, 'under these circumstances' or 'in this situation,'[67] interrupts the narrative and introduces, as in similar instances in Revelation (13:10, 18; 17:9), a hortatory commentary on the preceding text in view of the anticipated impact of the events narrated in that textual unit upon faithful Christians.[68]

---

[66] Cf. Tonstad, *Reputation*, 159-164.

[67] W. Bauer, *Griechisch-Deutsches Wörterbuch zu den Schriften des Neuen Testaments und der übrigen urchristlichen Literatur* (Berlin, Germany: Verlag Alfred Töpelmann, 5th ed., 1963), s. v. *hōde*.

[68] Aune, *Revelation 6-16*, 798; see also J. Lambrecht, 'Rev 13:9-10 and exhortation in the Apocalypse,' in: *New Testament Textual Criticism and Exegesis*, Festschrift J. Delobel, ed. A. Denaux, *BETL* 161 (Leuven, Belgium: Leuven University Press, 2002), 345.

Literally, 14:12 says: 'This is the patient endurance of the saints who keep the commandments of God and the faith of Jesus.' The saints are the intended receivers of the book of Revelation (1:3; 22:9). For the enigmatic phrase *pistis Iēsou*, four translations may be considered: faith of Jesus, faith in Jesus, faithfulness of Jesus, and faithfulness to Jesus.[69] A subjective genitive fits the immediate context better.[70] As a term rooted in the Hebrew Bible and Jewish tradition, *pistis* means 'belief (in God's words), obedience, trust (hope), and faithfulness.'[71] A combination of 'faith as trust (or: hope)' and 'faithfulness (or: obedience) as loyalty' is supported by the close parallel in 13:10: facing coercion and violent death, 'the faith (of the saints)' is both trust in God and faithfulness to God. 'The faith of Jesus' (14:12) is to be 'kept' by the saints—similarly to their 'keeping' or 'preserving'[72] the commandments of God—in a situation of widespread idolatry and distrust in the true God, which suggests that what is at stake here is, above all, *loyalty to God*. In keeping with these casual observations and seeing a connection between 'faith of Jesus' and 'witness of Jesus' in Revelation,[73] I understand the literal rendering 'faith of Jesus' in terms of *trust* in God being demonstrated as *faithfulness* and *obedience* to God.[74] It has recently been suggested, however, that 'faithfulness of Jesus' is a better translation, primarily since it reflects most adequately the theme of the cosmic conflict in Revelation and keeps the character of the divine government in view, but also because of several lesser elements in the text.[75] While this suggestion is uncommon in translations and commentaries, it would be meaningful in 14:9-13 where its function as a reference to Jesus' faithfulness to God until death is the point of the exhortation (14:12), being *witnessed to* by the faithfulness of those who die in the Lord (14:13) but *denied* by the unfaithfulness of the beast worshippers (14:9-11).

The exhortation to the saints in 14:12 emphasises *endurance* in loyalty to God. The basic meaning of Greek *hypomonē* is 'steadfast endurance until the end under persecutions or temptations.'[76] In Revelation, the dangers of giving up faith come from divisive teachings[77] and the blasphemy, religious coercion and death threats by God's enemies.[78] The specific thrust of 14:12, however, is faithfulness that endures even *until violent death* by the sword,[79] based on the central value in

---

[69] Tonstad, *Reputation*, 165-194.
[70] Ibid., 179-185.
[71] R. Bultmann, s.v. *pistis* in: *TDNT* 6, 205-208.
[72] Tonstad argues for a sense that brings to view a legacy or a trust that is safeguarded and preserved as well as 'kept' in the sense of 'put into practice' (*Reputation*, 184).
[73] Ibid., 179-185.
[74] For a discussion of the fine line between 'faith' as the confidence in God demonstrated by Jesus and 'faithfulness of Jesus to God,' see Tonstad, *Reputation*, 185-189.
[75] Tonstad, *Reputation*, 168-185, 193-194; cf. Bauckham, *Revelation*, 121.
[76] F. Hauck, s.v. *menō/hypomonē* in: *TDNT* 4, 585-588.
[77] Rev 2:2-3, 9, 14-16, 20-22; 3:9.
[78] Rev 2:10; 3:10-12; 6:10-11; 12:11, 17; 13:10; 15:2; 17:6, 14; 18:4, 20, 24; 19:2; 20:4-6.
[79] Cf. Phil 2:6-11; 1 Pet 2:19-23.

Jesus' teachings that loyalty to God is more worth than life.[80] This understanding is sustained by (a) the righteous dead (14:13) being asked to rest a little longer until their number is complete of those 'who are soon to be killed as they themselves have been killed' (6:11); (b) the killing of the saints being linked with a call for 'the endurance and faith of the saints' (13:9-10); (c) the references to the righteous dead being 'beheaded for (their) witness of Jesus' (20:4); and (d) Babylon being 'drunk with the blood of the saints and the blood of the witnesses to Jesus' (17:6).[81] Keeping faithfulness *until death* affirms Jesus' exhortation to the church: 'Be faithful *until death*, and I will give you the crown of life' (2:10; cf. 3:10-11). It characterizes the faithful who overcome the enemy of God 'by the blood of the Lamb and by the word of their witness, for they did not cling to life even in the face of death' (12:11).

These observations provide an important key to understanding Revelation 14: the saints' faithfulness until death is their witness (martyria) to Jesus (6:9; 12:11, 17; 17:6; 19:10; 20:4) that 'follows' the witness (martyria) that Jesus gave until his death on the cross as Lamb of God (1:2, 5; 5:6, 9, 12; 7:14; 12:11; 13:8; 19:13). The 'witness of Jesus' is his faithful revelation of God, or 'the word of God' (1:2, 9; 12:17; 19:10; 19:11-13; 20:4), through 'the spirit of prophecy.' By obedience until death Jesus has displayed God's faithfulness to his creation, i.e. God's love for the world and his people, revealing the way in which God rules the world as opposed to how the satanic trinity rules the world. In God's mission to achieve the new world-order (21:1-5), Christ as the Lamb that was slaughtered is therefore the key. When the slaughtered Lamb is revealed 'at the centre' of God's throne in heaven (5:6; 7:17), the meaning is that Christ's sacrificial death belongs to the way God is and acts towards the world.[82] Being clothed in 'a robe dipped in blood,' Christ's name is 'The Word of God' (19:13). Thus, the worthiness of the Lamb as world ruler, similar to the worthiness of God as enthroned God (5:12-13), is based on the fact that he was 'slaughtered' which empowers him to 'ransom for God saints from every tribe and language and people and nation,' making them to be 'a kingdom and priests serving our God who will reign on earth' (5:9-10; cf. 1:5-6). Jesus is therefore 'the faithful witness, the firstborn of the dead, and the ruler of the kings of the earth' (1:5). As the saints follow him, they witness to his faithfulness to God until death and will receive their share in his victory over death and rule the world with him.[83]

In this context, the referential meaning of pistis Iēsou in 14:12 leans towards 'faithfulness of Jesus.' The 'commandments of God' may then be the implied object towards which Jesus was faithful. The patient endurance of the saints consists

---

[80] Cf. Mk 8:35; Mat 10:39; Lk 9:24.
[81] Note also Rev 6:10; 16:6; 18:24; 19:2.
[82] Cf. Bauckham, *Revelation*, 64.
[83] Rev 1:5-6, 17; 2:1, 8, 12, 18; 3:1, 7, 14; 5:1-14; 7:9-17; 11:15; 12:10-11; 14:1-5; 19:11-16.

in keeping the commandments of God and the (same) faithfulness to God and his will that Jesus witnessed to, namely, the victorious faithfulness until death by which he has become 'the holder of the keys to death' and 'the ruler of the kings on earth.' Thus, since the victory of Christ came from his faithfulness to God and his will, John encourages the saints to seek Christ's victorious faithfulness—until death, if necessary. This reading links the exhortation in 14:12 with (a) the third angel's message (14:9-11)—with its sub-text of the four commandments relating to true worship of God—and (b) the faithful 'works' of those who have 'died in the Lord' (14:13), to which we will return later. This reading also explains the feature in 14:4 where, in retrospect, the redeemed are described with a mixed metaphor for faithfulness as 'not having defiled themselves with women, for they are virgins'[84] but 'following the Lamb wherever he goes.' Their faithfulness imitates the faithfulness of Jesus Christ who is 'the faithful witness' (1:5): 'I am the first and the last, and the living one. I was dead, and see, I am alive forever and ever; and I have the keys of Death and of Hades' (1:17-18). In light of this, the blessing of the faithful who die in the Lord (14:13) acknowledges their claim to Christ's victory over death and opens their path to the reward of eternal life. Thus, following Jesus' faithfulness to God until death is the path to blessedness in death and eternal life. This reading is further supported by the details emerging in 14:13, to which we now turn.

John hears a voice from heaven declaring: 'Blessed are the dead who die in the Lord from now on' (14:13a). In the seven blessings in Revelation,[85] *makarios* ('blessed') is associated with divine reward for faithfulness.[86] Instances in the Hebrew Bible speak of the 'death of his faithful ones' as being precious to God (Ps 116:15; cf. 72:13-14). The apocryphal book of Ecclesiasticus (ca. 180 BC) links the reward of the righteous with fearing God, blessedness in death, and hope of life:

> With him who fears the Lord it will go well at the end; on the day of his death he will be blessed ... The spirit of those who fear the Lord will live, for their hope is in him who saves them ... Blessed is the soul of the man who fears the Lord! ... He lifts up the soul and gives light to the eyes; he grants healing, life, and blessing (1:13; 34:13-17).

Similar concepts are contained in Revelation's second blessing in 14:13: God's blessing rewards faithfulness until death and carries a promise of life beyond death through Christ's victory. This element is reinforced by a sub-text analogous

---

[84] The saved are symbolized by *men* who were not unfaithful with adulterous women (other gods) and *virgins* who were kept innocent and pure for their husband (God).

[85] Rev 1:3; 14:13; 16:15; 19:9; 20:6; 22:7; 22:14.

[86] See Deut 28:1-14; Isa 30:15-18; Jer 17:7-8; 1 Chr 17:26-27.

to Jesus' life, death, and resurrection: (a) 'the dead who *die* in the Lord' imitate Jesus' faithfulness until *death* on the cross; (b) the '*rest* from their labours' imitates Jesus' Sabbath *rest*; and (c) 'their righteous works' granting eternal *life* imitates Jesus' *resurrection*. This pattern of an *imitatio Christi* illustrates the characterization of the redeemed as 'those who follow the Lamb wherever he goes' (14:4).

It has been casually noted that Revelation (6:11; 14:11, 13) may reflect what is called a Sabbath rest of the righteous dead in rabbinical literature.[87] The following striking links between the Sabbath Law in Exodus 20:8-11 (alluded to in 14:7) and Revelation 14:12-13 show that the Sabbath blessing is consistently applied to those who are faithful until death:

Exodus 20:8-11	Revelation 14:12-13
Remember the Sabbath	Their works *go with* them [*remembrance*]
Keep the Sabbath holy	They *keep* God's commandments
God *rested* from work on Sabbath	They *rest* from their hard labours
God *blessed* the Sabbath	They are *blessed*
God made the Sabbath *holy*	They are *holy*

The phrase 'their works go with them' implies 'remembrance' in two ways: (a) the faithful have *remembered* and *obeyed* God's will by 'works *(erga)* that are complete in the sight of God' (3:1-3); and (b) their works *(erga)* are *remembered* in the book of judgement and the book of life.[88] The underlying point of the Sabbath symbolism in 14:9-13 is that faithfulness to the Creator brings life-giving blessing from the Creator in death, in sharp contrast to the beast worshippers who face God's wrath and will die forever.

The quoted words of the Spirit confirm and explain the blessing: 'Yes, for they will rest from their labours' (14:13b). *Kopos* ('labour') carries the sense of 'hard work to the point of weariness and exhaustion,'[89] from which death *in the Lord* gives rest. Thus, 14:13b functions as a Sabbath metaphor for redemption from the injustices and death caused by God's enemies.

The unusual phrase 'their works go with them' (14:13c) is documented in Jewish tradition. For example, *M. 'Abot* 6:9 states: 'Moreover at the time of a man's departure, neither silver or gold nor precious stones nor pearls go with him, but only [his knowledge of] the Law and good works.'[90] The so-called Apocalypse of Ezra,[91] contemporary with the book of Revelation, contains the idea that 'the works of the

---

[87] Frey, 'Sabbath,' 235. Cf. Heb 4:9-11.
[88] Rev 3:5; 13:8; 17:8; 20:12-13, 15; 21:27.
[89] Stefanovic, *Revelation*, 454.
[90] Translation by H. Danby, *The Mishnah* (London, UK: Oxford University Press, 1933).
[91] Known in English versions as 2 Ezra and appearing in the Appendix to the Vulgate as 4 Ezra.

righteous dead' are being laid up with God and will awake at the end of time for the reward of the righteous, being associated with past *faithfulness*, current *rest*, and future *reward*.[92] The same concept is used in Revelation 14:13, as noted earlier in connection with the analogy of the righteous dead with Jesus' life, death, and resurrection. However, the phrase 'their works go with them' may also be connected with the symbol of the white robes of the saints in Revelation, where Greek *erga* ('works') is a technical term for the righteous life of the faithful: 'I know your *works*, your labour and patient endurance ... your *works* and your love and your faith and your service and your patient endurance' (2:2, 19). Revelation speaks of the white robes as the righteous lives of the saints, i.e. their works, love, faith, service, and patient endurance (3:4-5, 18; 6:9-11; 7:9-17; 16:15; 19:6-8; 22:14). These are the *priestly* 'garments of glory' rooted in the concept of the saints as a 'kingdom of priests' (1:6; 5:10; 20:6)[93] and alluding to Isaiah 61:10[94] where they are connected with joy of salvation in God. These robes are outward signs of faithfulness, of having 'come out of the great ordeal (of persecution and suffering),' being tokens of eternal salvation, and their purity comes from 'being washed in the blood of the Lamb.' They are always with the saints and 'go with' them, to avoid 'nakedness and exposure to shame' (3:18). They identify the saints as God's faithful people through the stages of earth's final history and function as a parallel metaphor to being written in the book of life. The robes ('works') follow the faithful in their time of rest (6:11; 14:13), provide evidence in the judgement of the dead (20:4, 12), and dress the righteous for the wedding of the Lamb (19:6-8). They are with the righteous when they surround God's throne (7:9-17), when they enter the new city of Jerusalem and eat of the tree of life (21:27; 22:14). They function as a 'witness' to the righteousness of the elect in God's judgement proceedings, while the book of life records their reward of eternal life (20:12). Thus, the saints' patient endurance in keeping the commandments of God and the faith of Jesus (14:12) are 'righteous works' that will be rewarded (14:13c) at the Lord's coming: 'See, I am coming soon! My *reward* is with me, and I will give to everyone according to his *work* (*ergon*)' (22:12; cf. 14:14-20).

The saying in 14:13 *comforts* the saints by assurance of ultimate redemption in Christ, but the parenesis in 14:9-13 also issues a *warning*, because the faithfulness of the saints is not to be taken for granted, since Satan's war against God's people is not over yet. John gives the saints two scenarios, saying: Remain faithful until the end, even until death, for if you give up your faithfulness to God and worship the satanic beast, your end will be like that of the idolaters, i.e. eternal death under

---

[92] 2 Ezra 7:35; 7:77; 8:33.
[93] For the garments of glory belonging to angels and priests, see Barker, *Revelation*, 39, 107-108, 165-168.
[94] Ibid., 317.

God's curse. But if you die faithful in the Lord, you are already blessed in death, resting from your hard labours, waiting to inherit your promised reward of eternal life. This reading is supported by a pattern of contrasts:

	Beast Worshippers:	Creator Worshippers:
Life:	Breaking God's law	Keeping God's law
	Satanic beast worship	Faithfulness to God
Death:	Drink the wine of God's wrath	Blessed from now on
	No rest day or night	Rest from labours
Eternity:	Smoke goes up forever	Their works go with them

This contrast pattern is based on the concepts of reward versus punishment and faithfulness versus unfaithfulness, being intertwined with Sabbath symbolism. The Sabbath 'rest' of the righteous dead is contrasted with the lack of 'rest day or night' of the beast worshippers under the curse of the wrath of God.[95] This brings us back to the earlier observation that 666, the mark of the beast, is a 'human number' since humans were created on the sixth day of creation, while the fullness of life is achieved on the seventh day when God rested from his works.[96] Thus, the Sabbath symbolism in 14:9-13 enhances the dual concept of the *blessing* of the faithful who worship the Creator and the *curse* of the satanic beast worshippers who bear the mark of the beast. In 14:6-13 as a whole, therefore, at least two Sabbath sub-texts are found: one envisages God as Creator and his law requiring faithfulness (14:6-11)—the other envisages the Sabbath rest of the faithful dead with its promise of life and salvation (14:9-13). The link between these symbolic patterns is the third angel's message and the exhortation in 14:9-12.

The temporal expression 'from now on' (14:13a) adds further dimensions. In view of 6:11, I understand it to say that all who *have* died and *will* die in the Lord are 'from now on' blessed by God. In this way, 'from now on' resumes the springboard passage in 11:18: 'the *time* has come for *judging* the dead and for *rewarding* your servants the prophets and your saints and those who reverence your name, both small and great.' 'From now on' coincides with the *hour* of God's judgement (14:7) when the dead are judged and the reward of the faithful is confirmed. This part of the judgement is not mentioned by the three angels, but the blessing of the righteous dead is added by a voice from heaven (14:13) in anticipation of the grain harvest (14:14-16) and the blessing in 20:6: 'Blessed and holy are those who share in the first resurrection.' Thus, the divine declaration in 14:13, being affirmed by the Spirit, implies that God, as Judge, gives his approval of those who are faith-

---

[95] Frey, 'Sabbath,' 235.
[96] Stefanovic, *Revelation*, 418.

ful until death. They are declared blameless (cf. 14:5), being sealed (cf. 14:1) and prepared for the harvest gathering at the second coming of Christ (14:14-16). Thus 14:13 anticipates the first resurrection in 20:4-6 and the judgement of the dead in 20:11-15, assuring the saints of life and eternal communion with God.

In light of this reading of 14:9-13, the following explanatory pattern emerges in 14:6-13 as a whole: (a) The time of God's judgement has come (14:6-7); Babylon will fall (14:8) and all beast worshippers will be punished by eternal death under God's curse according to his law (14:9-11); (b) *therefore*, the saints must remain faithful until the end in keeping God's commandments and the faith (or faithfulness) of Jesus (14:12); (c) *for* in the judgement proceedings that have begun, the righteous dead are *blessed* from now on, i.e. righteous and saved forever (14:13a); their *reward* is their rest under God's blessing from their tribulations (14:13b); the *evidence* of their innocence, i.e. their faithfulness and righteous works follow them and are remembered (14:13c), and Christ will gather them as his own at the harvest time (14:14-16), placing them with him before the throne of God where they praise him (14:1-5) and where they will be joined by the converted nations (15:2-4).

Concluding reflection

Revelation 14:6-13 expresses God's care for his faithful people who are scattered among the nations at the end of time, equipping them for the task of giving faithful witness until death about God's righteousness and power, as they 'follow the Lamb wherever he goes.' The reading reported here illustrates the relevance of Ellen White's remark: 'One thing will certainly be understood from the study of Revelation—that the connection between God and His people is close and decided.'[97]

This is true also of Revelation 14:6-13. Thus, only in a 'close and decided' connection with God will the church's mission prosper, for it flows from the mission of God at the end of time when the crucial question is if he will find *faithfulness* on earth (Lk 18:8). By the faithful witness of God's people to him, his true mind and will, the faithfulness of God to his creation may be proclaimed and manifested in the conversion of the nations to their Creator, until God's mission of saving the world is completed and 'the home of God is among mortals' (21:3).

Bertil Wiklander. Born in Sweden. Since 1995 president of the Trans-European Division of Seventh-day Adventists. Experience in educational, ministerial, and communication areas. President of the Swedish Union (1993–1995). Associate Secretary in the Bible Translation Commission appointed by the Swedish Government (1975-1980). Author of articles. ThD, Uppsala University, Sweden (1983).

---

[97] Ellen G. White, *Testimonies to Ministers and Gospel Workers*, 114.

Exploring the Frontiers of Faith

PART III
Church Leadership and Ethics

Leadership under the Headship of Jesus Christ

Bjørn Ottesen

Leadership is a ministry in the church. It is described in the Bible as a spiritual gift and is primarily given by Christ to the church community. Leadership therefore exists, operates and is executed as an integral part—and in the context—of the whole organism of the body of Christ. Emphasis is not on the leader as an individual, but on the leader as a part of the community. Christ is the head of the church and he leads his people as a community. The church should recognize Christ's leadership through the community as a whole. Leaders serve to recognize, see, make visible and put focus where Christ is already leading. Christian leadership helps people take part in the activities—and mission—of God in the world. This chapter reflects primarily on the Christian leader's role in light of the New Testament teachings on the headship of Christ and the working of the Holy Spirit in the Christian community.

Christ is the true leader of the church

Jesus Christ made some very clear statements particularly during the latter part of his ministry on earth, that he would be present by his Spirit among his followers 'till the end of time' (Mat 28:18-20).[1] He confirmed that he would 'build [his] church' (Mat 16:18); that he would not leave his followers as 'orphans' (John 14:18); and that the Spirit would guide Christ's followers into truth and witness.[2] That Jesus still was in the leadership position after his ascension became a strong part of the early church's self-understanding. Christ's working and guiding through the Spirit was seen as an integral part of early church life.[3]

Even in his absence, Jesus was the true leader of the church. This concept is clearly underlined by the images that are used of the church in the New Testament: The church is like a body, but Jesus Christ is the head.[4] The church is like a temple or a building where Christ is the cornerstone.[5] In this perspective, leadership in the early church—and in the church today—was always a ministry or service with Christ being the true leader of the church. Leaders were 'members of

---

[1] All Bible quotes in this chapter are taken from the *New International Version*.

[2] See also: Mat 18:20; John 14:26-27; Acts 1:8.

[3] There are numerous specific and implied references to Christ's leadership through the Spirit in the book of Acts, and also in the epistles. Christ, through the Spirit, guided the Christian community in what they were saying, what they should do, what would happen to them—and guided their decisions: Acts 2:4; Acts 4:8-10; Acts 8:29; Acts 10:19-20; Acts 11:28; Acts 15:28; Acts 16:6-8; Acts 20:22-23.

[4] Eph 1:22-23; Col 2:19; 1 Cor 12:27.

[5] 1 Cor 3:16-17; Eph 2:19-22; 1 Pet 2:4-8.

the body' or 'stones in the building' who did not carry authority in themselves, but only as they reflected the will of Christ.

> Authority is not a goal but rather a by-product. It is a delegated authority that comes from God. It is the major power base of a leader who has learned God's lessons during maturity processing. Leaders have various power bases that give credence to their ability. Spiritual authority comes out of experience with God. A leader does not seek spiritual authority; a leader seeks to know God ... Spiritual authority results from a leader's experience with God.[6]

This interrelationship between the leadership of Christ and human leaders can be seen in connection with some events in Acts. One of the most significant changes in the history of the Christian church took place when the early church moved from being a Jewish community in Jerusalem and Judea to becoming an international movement that included peoples of all nationalities and cultures. The New Testament has numerous references to the tension in the early church about issues that related to this.[7]

It does not seem likely that the early church would have taken the necessary steps to become an international movement without the direct intervention of God. The story in Acts—particularly in chapters eight to fifteen—clearly shows that it was by the intervention of the Holy Spirit that the church was moved forward in its theology and mission.[8] The tragic circumstances of the persecution that was ignited after the stoning of Stephen (Acts 7:54-60) led the church members in Jerusalem and Judea to flee into Samaria. Through the guidance of the Holy Spirit they started to spread the gospel about Jesus Christ to the Samaritans (Acts 8). The apostles who had remained in Jerusalem (vs 1) were surprised to hear what happened in Samaria through the many Christians—Philip in particular—who had fled from Judea (vs 14-17). The new advancement of the young movement did not come through a strategic plan, but through the Spirit turning circumstances into mission opportunities.

---

[6]   J. Robert Clinton, *The Making of a Leader* (Colorado Springs, CO: Navpress, 1988), 167. Robert Clinton also defines a Christian leader as a person 1) with a God-given capacity, and 2) with a God-given responsibility to influence 3) a specific group of God's people 4) towards God's purposes for that group (202).

[7]   Examples of issues which surface: Acts 15: To what extent should gentile Christians be expected to keep the Torah? Acts 10 and 11: Should gentiles be viewed as equals to Jews? Luke 4:24-30: Does God really care about the people of other nations? 1 Cor. 9:19-23: Is there room for different lifestyles and practices in the church?

[8]   In the first chapters of his book *An Emergent Theology for Emerging churches* (Downers Grove, IL: InterVarsity Press, 2006) Ray Anderson describes the complexity of this challenge under the descriptive heading 'From Jerusalem to Antioch': How the church—under the leadership of the Holy Spirit—changed from being a Jewish sect to becoming an international community in multiple cultures.

The story of Peter and Cornelius in Acts 10 and 11 is also a momentous example of God's leading. As the events progressed, both the theology and the mission practice of the early church was changed. Through visions Cornelius and Peter (10:3, 11) were connected. Peter's theology about God's relationship to different people and the mission of the church was radically changed through his vision and God's guidance. He came to see that God is interested in all peoples and does not see any human being as 'impure or unclean.'[9] The events that followed led the entire church to change its approach to the gentiles (Acts 11:18). This significant change in theology and mission did not come from a strategic committee or from one strong leader or even a leadership team. It was Christ through the Holy Spirit who facilitated these changes.[10] When commenting on the radical changes that happened in the early church, Ray Anderson states that 'the church does not emerge out of its past.' He emphasises that in times of radical change and paradigm shifts, Christ through the Spirit leads the church into changes it could not have perceived, or organized, by itself. Only the Spirit who knows the future can lead the church into the future.[11] The role of church leadership in this case was to recognize what God was doing and then follow and implement that change.[12]

If Christ is the true head of the church, leadership in the church will be about understanding Christ and what he is doing. It will be about recognizing where

---

[9] Peter emphasizes this point several times. As he enters Cornelius' house and after visiting for some time: Acts 10:28, 34-35; before the elders in Jerusalem: Acts 11: 12-18.

[10] Alan Hirsch reflects on how the Spirit leads the church into the future. The church tends to settle for the middle class values of comfort and convenience, safety and security (43). Therefore, the church also emphasizes the leadership gifts (of Eph 4:11) of the pastor and the teacher rather than those of the apostle, prophet and evangelist, who work more on the cutting edge of church life (169 ff). He states that 'equilibrium is death' and gives the following challenging statement: 'What is it about disequilibrium that seems to stimulate life and energy? And what is it about stability that seems to stifle it? ... Is it because life itself is unpredictable and chaotic and that, when we establish organizations that seek to control and minimize the dangers of life, these organizations in the end stifle it? The history of missions is quite clear about this: Christianity is at its very best when it is at the more chaotic fringes. It is when the church settles down, and moves away from the edge of chaos, that things go awry' (258). Alan Hirsch, *The Forgotten Ways* (Grand Rapids, MI: Baker Publishing Group, 2006).

[11] Anderson, *An Emergent Theology for Emerging Churches*, 84.

[12] Ellen G. White comments on this significant event in *Acts of the Apostles*, 141-142: 'When the brethren in Judea heard that Peter had gone to the house of a gentile and preached to those assembled, they were surprised and offended. *They feared that such a course, which looked to them presumptuous, would have the effect of counteracting his own teaching* [italics mine]. When they next saw Peter they met him with severe censure, saying, "Thou wentest in to men uncircumcised, and didst eat with them." ... Peter laid the whole matter before them ... On hearing this account, the brethren were silenced. *Convinced that Peter's course was in direct fulfilment of the plan of God, and that their prejudices and exclusiveness were utterly contrary to the spirit of the gospel, they glorified God, saying, "Then hath God also to the gentiles granted repentance unto life." Thus, without controversy, prejudice was broken down, the exclusiveness established by the custom of ages was abandoned, and the way was opened for the gospel to be proclaimed to the gentiles* [italics mine].'

Christ is working in people's lives and in communities, and then leading others to join that which Christ is doing. 'So our first responsibility is to position ourselves to welcome and cooperate with the work of the Holy Spirit.'[13]

Leaders are parts of the body of Christ

Let us now further reflect on leadership as a spiritual gift to be used within the Christian community. All of the spiritual gifts are given *to the church* through individuals (1 Cor 12:7). In today's individualistic society, there tends to be an emphasis on what gifts the Holy Spirit has given to an individual.[14] In the New Testament, however, there is an emphasis on the community over the individual.[15] This can been seen in the fact that, for example, the gifts of speaking in tongues and that of prophecy are subject to the judgement of the church as a body (1 Cor 14:26-33, particularly vs 29; 1 John 4:1-3).

Ephesians 4 discusses spiritual gifts related to leadership. Over the last twenty or more years there has been an increased emphasis on this chapter as a model for leadership ministry in the church:

> It was he who gave some to be apostles, some to be prophets, some to be evangelists, and some to be pastors and teachers, to prepare God's people for works of service, so that the body of Christ may be built up until we all reach unity in the faith and in the knowledge of the Son of God and become mature, attaining to the whole measure of the fullness of Christ (Eph 4:11-13).

It can be noted that the five gifts of apostle, prophet, evangelist, pastor and teacher (APEPT) are all leadership gifts which have a part in 'preparing God's people for works of service.' This text presents a combination of several gifts that are meant to guide all the members of the local church. This indicates that local church lead-

---

[13] Robert Lewis and Wayne Cordeiro, *Culture Shift* (San Francisco, CA: Jossey-Bass, 2005), 69. See chapter 6 for a discussion on 'Divine Partnership.'

[14] There are, for example, numerous tests to get an indication of what gifts one has. These can be helpful, but it is important to connect these exercises to the biblical teaching that the gifts are given to the church through the individual members. It is the community that *owns* and has the use of all the gifts of its members collectively (1 Cor 12:7-13).

[15] That the New Testament emphasizes community over the individual can be seen in emphases like: 1. The spiritual gifts are given for the common good—rather than to give status to any individual (1 Cor 12:7). 2. It is the plurality of Christians who are the body of Christ—not each individual separately (1 Cor 3:16; 12:12). 3. This fact is also illustrated by the picture of living stones in one building (1 Pet 2:4-5; Eph 2:20-22). 4. The Spirit is at work first of all in the community of the church—and, secondly, in each member (Lk 17:21: 'you' in plural; John 14:17-18: 'you' in plural). 5. The church has a mission in the world—not each individual. Leaders and ministries grow and are defined in the context of the community and not because of one person's wish or decision. It is the church as a community that carries the responsibility of being stewards of the truth—not individuals (1 Tim. 3:15).

ership consists of more than one person, because it is rare that all gifts are present in one person. The idea of team leadership will be commented on below. Furthermore, it indicates that in the New Testament church there was more focus on the *function* of leadership than on the *office* of leadership. It is Christ who equips people to serve the community. Christ sees to it that certain functions are available—rather than putting any particular person in an office of leadership and authority.

> These verses [Eph 4:7,1] seem to underscore the fact that the church's ministry is *fundamentally* charismatic by nature. This is important to recognize because it allows us to move away from the notion of APEPT ministry as *office* to that of *function*. Jesus' gracing of his church cannot be institutionalised into office.[16]

Furthermore, this text also indicates that the ministries of leadership belong to the whole church. Just as other gifts are given to the body, so are the gifts of leadership. It is not the leader who is important, but Christ and his church.

> What we have called the ministry matrix [APEPT] suggests that the fivefold ministry belongs to, and describes in some way, the whole church. If we take the phrase *'to each one of us'* [Eph 4:7] together with the repeated distribution formula *'He ... gave some to be'* quite naturally, this implies that all Christians are included in some part in the fivefold APEPT structure ... Paul was not primarily describing, as is so often quoted, the official leadership of the church in this text, but rather the church itself, which we agree with. Paul did not labor under any misconceptions of ordained ministry that is so much a part of Christendom's assumptions of 'the ministry.' There are no clergy and no laity in the New Testament—all are ministers ... And so here Paul described everyone in the church in some way.[17]

As demonstrated above, leadership is neither an office nor a position of authority, but is an integrated part of the body of Christ where leadership is performed as a ministry.

Ellen G. White comments in several places on the need for teams of leaders.[18]

---

[16] Michael Frost and Alan Hirsch, *The Shaping of Things to Come, Innovation and Mission for the 21st Century Church* (Peabody, MA: Hendrickson Publishers, 2003), 168.

[17] Ibid., 171.

[18] "'The head of every man is Christ.' God, who put all things under the Saviour's feet, 'gave Him to be the head over all things to the church, which is his body, the fullness of Him that filleth all in all' (1 Cor 11:3; Eph 1:22, 23). The church is built upon Christ as its foundation; it is to obey Christ as its head. It is not to depend upon man, or be controlled by man. Many claim that a position of trust in the church gives them authority to dictate what other men shall believe and what they shall do. This claim God does not sanction.

She warns against individuals trusting their own judgements and acting independently of the body of the church:

> Those who are inclined to regard their individual judgment as supreme are in grave peril. It is Satan's studied effort to separate such ones from those who are as channels of light, through whom God has communicated his will, and through whom He has wrought in building up and extending his work in the earth. To neglect or despise those whom God has appointed to bear the responsibilities of leadership in connection with the advancement and spread of the truth, is to reject the means that He has ordained for the help, encouragement, and strength of his people. For any worker in the Lord's cause to pass these by, and to think that his light must come through no other channel than directly from God, is to place himself in a position where he is liable to be deceived by the enemy, and overthrown. *The Lord in his wisdom has arranged that by means of the close relationship that should be maintained by all believers in Christian fellowship, Christian shall be united to Christian, and church to church. Thus the human instrumentality will be enabled to co-operate with the divine* [italics mine]. Every agency will be subordinate to the Holy Spirit, and all the believers will be united in an organized and well-directed effort to give to the world the glad tidings of the grace of God.[19]

In the Bible there are examples of strong leaders with particular callings who—as far as we know—acted independently on their own calling from God. Moses, Elijah and Paul are some of the characters who seem to have had a strong calling from God and a strong identity in themselves, which gave them the strength to lead God's people in a certain direction. In their cases, it was not democracy or team work that set the agenda, but their own specific divine mandate and calling.

This does not, however, seem to be the pattern for leadership in the New Testament church. In addition to the concept of apostle, prophet, evangelist, pastor and teacher mentioned above, the terminology for leadership and elders in the church is consistently used in the plural.[20] Church leadership is a team effort. No single

---

The Savior declares, 'All ye are brethren.' All are exposed to temptation, and are liable to error. Upon no finite being can we depend for guidance. The Rock of faith is the living presence of Christ in the church. Upon this the weakest may depend, and those who think themselves the strongest will prove to be the weakest, unless they make Christ their efficiency. 'Cursed be the man that trusteth in man, and maketh flesh his arm.' The Lord 'is the Rock, his work is perfect.' 'Blessed are all they that put their trust in Him'(Jer 17:5; Deut 32:4; Ps 2:12).' (Ellen G. White, *The Desire of Ages*, 414).

[19] Ellen G. White, 'Separated unto the Gospel,' *Review and Herald*, May 11, 1911.

[20] Local leadership is described as teams: Fil 1:1; Acts 20,17, 28. The following terms are used about leaders in the New Testament: *Presbyteros, episkopos* and more rarely: *poimen*. Presbuteros and episkopos occur 174 times in the New Testament; they are used as synonyms and—significantly—always in the plural. See Michael Harper, *Let My People*

person carries the wisdom of God. God lives by his Spirit in the community (1 Cor 3:16-17).

Leadership within the dynamics of the church body

The leadership of the Holy Spirit in the particularly difficult circumstances de-scribed in Acts 8-15, was a dynamic process involving members of all 'ranks.' It is Christ's privilege as the head of the church to lead in the ways he chooses. New initiatives and new understandings will come forward through the body of the church. It is one of the significant tasks of leadership to look for what God is doing. Secondly, the leader will have to get in line with what God is doing. Thirdly, the leader wants to use his/her influence to help others join what God is doing.[21]

> Why is it that the church today will not trust its members? Why does the church so often decline to recognize and to accept the activity of the Spirit among unregulated groups of Christians? Why is all initiative in the church expected and presumed to derive from the clergy? It is because we have substituted for the biblical doctrine of the Holy Spirit as ruler in the church, a doctrine of our own, unknown to Scripture, the authority of professionalism.'[22]

The New Testament emphasis on leadership as a function in the community stands in contrast to some recent focus on leadership. Through the 1990s and into this millennium there has been an emphasis on strong, visionary leadership in Christian leadership literature. In some circles—particularly in Pentecostal circles in Australia and Scandinavia—there has been an emphasis on a particular brand of

---

Grow, Ministry and Leadership in the church (London, UK: Hodder and Stoughton, 1979), 174-176.

[21] As in Acts 8, 11 and 15 the more formal leadership of the church—'the apostles in Jerusalem'—had a task in discerning whether the new movements or understandings were in harmony with God. Even this was done in the context of the community. When there was consensus as to what God was doing, the leaders encouraged the whole church to move in that direction.

[22] Michael Harper, *Let My People Grow, Ministry and Leadership in the church*, 33. Michael Harper was a key figure in the debate about the church and its ministry in evangelical-Anglican England in the 1970s. *Let my People Grow* challenges the established church and calls it back to a more organic and biblical view of ministry. There is an emphasis on the whole church community as doing ministry, and service is more important than office. Leadership becomes an issue of helping all Christians to join the mission of God in their own capacity. 'The New Testament is very much more interested in ministry than in "ministers" as such, for all God's people are called to be ministers, whereas not all are called to be leaders' (42) .'But one really hopeful sign today is the switch of emphasis from office to function.' Thus Hans Küng writes, 'Ecclesial office is not a New Testament notion, but a problematical concept which emerged from later reflections.' He goes on to show that the New Testament emphasis was on service rather than status (42-43) 'The New Testament is far more concerned with function than office' (43).

'apostolic leadership.'[23] In these contexts the term 'apostolic leadership' has been used to give significant authority to the person who has received the gift of leadership. The argument has been that just as those with the gift of teaching should teach, and those with the gift of helping should help, those with the gift of leadership should lead. Some have taken this argument to the point where one sees the leader as appointed by God to make decisions and find the right direction for the church. (Often this happens in a congregational community with one strong leader.) The leader, who is often also the pastor, appoints elders and makes most decisions. Some churches with this type of leadership have grown significantly, but have also met serious leadership challenges after a few years. The opinion expressed here is that such a leadership style fails to incorporate the New Testament teachings on the 1) headship of Christ, 2) the church as a body, 3) the spiritual gifts and 4) ministry.

Ellen G. White, one of the Seventh-day Adventist pioneers, addressed this issue in a slightly different situation:

> The church of Christ is in constant peril. Satan is seeking to destroy the people of God, and one man's mind, one man's judgment, is not sufficient to be trusted. Christ would have his followers brought together in church capacity, observing order, having rules and discipline, and all subject one to another, esteeming others better than themselves. Union and confidence are essential to the prosperity of the church. If each member of the church feels at liberty to move independently of the others, taking his own peculiar course, how can the church be in any safety in the hour of danger and peril? The prosperity and very existence of a church depend upon the prompt, united action and mutual confidence of its members.[24]

In other circles there has been an intense focus on vision, strategies, mission statements and the leader's central role in providing these.[25] There are certainly many true observations in the literature which comes from different churches or organizations. It is not the aim of this chapter to diminish the need for clear strategies or visions. The aim of this study is to move back to the biblical idea of leadership as a ministry within a community. The Christian leader does not need to feel alone in finding the strategy and vision for the future. Christ has promised to build his church (Mat 16:18). The way forward will be revealed in the community. Leaders

---

[23] Roine Swensson, *Jakten på Församlingens Förnyelse* [A Search for the Renewal of the church] (Värnamo, Sweden: Semnos Förlag, 2004), 109.

[24] Ellen White, *Testimonies to the Church*, vol. 3, 445.

[25] Some of this material has come from trend-setting Christian communities like Willow Creek and Saddleback churches or prominent Christian speakers on leadership like John Maxwell.

often have a significant part in that process, but can rest in the assurance of the Spirit's work in the fellowship of the church. The need for the leader with a capital L can be provided for by a leadership which is integrated in an organic way in the community.

There is a trend among emerging churches that tries to bring leadership back to corporate ownership. Eddie Gibbs and Ryan G. Bolger have done extensive research on church models which are emerging in different denominations. In contemporary culture there is a movement from hierarchy to networks. This is also reflected in leadership styles. Gibbs and Bolger can report a new shift towards a much more organic view of leadership; leadership as a process within a community. Space does not allow for a detailed discussion of their findings here, but the following headings from their section on leadership can illustrate that shift:

From stifling control to creative freedom;

from the vision of the leader to the vision of all;

from powerful group leaders to leaderless groups;

from leadership based on willingness to leadership based on gifting;

from leadership based on position to leadership based on passion;

from authority based on position to influence based on track record;

from closed leadership to open leadership;

from leaders setting the agenda to congregational agenda setting;

from exclusive decision making to inclusive consensus building.[26]

Possibly these emerging churches have something to teach the established churches.

Conclusions

Together, the doctrines of 1) the headship of Christ, and 2) spiritual gifts and ministry, call for a Christian leadership pattern where leadership is seen as an integrated part of the Christian community. The New Testament does not call for the strong leader who can come up with all necessary answers, visions, strategies or spiritual guidance; it calls for individuals with spiritual gifts of leadership who see themselves as serving God and his community. It calls for individuals who share information, authority and processes with teams of leaders and the church community as a whole. It calls for leaders who see leadership as a ministry, and are willing to recognize God's leading even among people—and in contexts—where they, themselves, have not been a part of the events or processes. Both Christ and the community stand above the leader. The leader serves by keeping everyone's focus on God's activities and mission.

---

[26] Eddie Gibbs and Ryan K. Bolger, *Emerging churches* (Grand Rapids, MI: Baker Academic, 2005), 194-205.

Bjørn Ottesen. Born in Norway. Since 2007 president for the Danish Union of Churches. Pastoral and teaching experience in Norway, Sweden and Denmark. President Swedish Union of Churches 2001-2007. Master of Divinity (MDiv.) Andrews University, 1986. Enrolled in DMin. programme at Fuller Theological Seminary.

Goodbye Good-buy!
Towards an Adventist Approach to Responsible Consumerism

Michael Pearson

The question which I wish to tackle in this chapter is in a way a mundane one which confronts us on a daily basis, which may not appear to be a very spiritual one, and which may seem remote from any lofty considerations of mission. It concerns a subject which requires the ability to sustain many tensions both theoretical and practical. It is an attempt to bring to the church a consideration of a complex and difficult but everyday issue in a spirit which does justice to claims which seem to be, and indeed are, competing in some way.

It will, I hope, be seen by the reader as an issue which is central to our discipleship as Adventist Christians. It concerns the way in which we should use our spending power in a world which offers an increasingly wide range of consumer choices, and which at the same time displays massive discrepancies in wealth. This chapter will address the topic of ethical shopping or responsible consumerism, phrases which I shall use interchangeably. This question is inextricably linked to questions about ecology and social justice, with which our traditional Adventist wariness of socio-political involvement has made us slow to engage.

Some tensions in the conversation

It is difficult to sustain a conversation among Adventists on the question of the just disposal of one's wealth because there are such huge variations in the economic levels of members. Many Adventists and their neighbours live in parts of the world where resources are few, where people do not have much disposable income, where shopping is not a leisure activity, where the main concern is survival. At the same time, many church members elsewhere do rather well economically. This is due at least in part to the strong traditional Adventist commitment to education at all levels. Adventists are educated, become professionalized, urbanized, and, as part of a common though not inevitable process, they become secularized.[1]

There are disparities in wealth within any particular society where Adventists live. Similarly there are major differences between the consumer choices of Adventists in many different parts of the world. Such differences may do injury to the body of the church through the comparisons which members are apt to make, and the aspirations which members are encouraged to develop. The issue inevitably touches at some point on questions of social and racial inequality.

---

[1] Malcolm Bull and Keith Lockhart, *Seeking a Sanctuary* (New York: Harper and Row, 1989), 235.

Some Adventists come from countries which are developing economically after decades of centralizing control of one sort or another. They are only just beginning to feel and enjoy their spending power. They have limited money and understandably wish to get the best possible deal for it. Why take notice of privileged westerners who have long enjoyed a comfortable life, and who now, driven by a newly-sensitized conscience, want to spoil their pleasure of using a little newly-acquired wealth? Maybe the issue of ethical shopping is only for a privileged western élite to agonize over.

There is a generational question too. There is evidence to suggest that toxic industrial emissions from the eighteenth century are still doing damage to our environment.[2] I am part of a generation which in its ignorance and its eagerness to consume caused a significant part of the current problems of ecological despoliation and economic injustice. Why should you listen to such? Would you not be justified in saying that it is unreasonable and unfair for an older person who has already a sizeable carbon footprint to his name, to seek to persuade members of a younger generation to forego the benefits which he may have enjoyed for so long?

One unpalatable outcome of the world economic crisis which began in 2008 may be that the rising generation may be the first which cannot expect to enjoy a higher standard of living than their parents. If intergenerational ecological and economic injustice is a form of stealing, my own generation can only plead guilty. Our only recourse is to seek to be generous to generations who are not in a position to be generous to us.[3]

There is also a theological question. Some would regard the relative wealth which they enjoy as a gift of God, a divine response to their faithfulness. It comes from an Old Testament understanding of the material rewards of righteousness, and may in many ways be reassuring in the good times. Such people may be unwilling to listen to calls for an informal act of redistributive economic justice in the shape of ethical shopping. Such a conversation is bound to be a difficult one in the church for it touches a sensitive spot. Money after all is largely a symbol of deeper values and commitments over which there is bound to be profound disagreement.

Two big questions
Beyond these questions are two more basic philosophical questions which can be found to underlie not only this but a huge range of other ethical issues. The first

---

[2] See Noah J. Toly, 'Climate Change: Global Problem, Global Solutions,' in: Lindy Scott, ed., *Christians, the Care of Creation and Global Climate Change* (Eugene, OR: Pickwick Publications, 2008), 49-50.

[3] See Donald Hay, 'Sustainable Economics,' in: R. J. Berry, *When Enough is Enough* (Nottingham, UK: InterVarsity Press, 2007), 107-111.

concerns what Kant called the matter of moral proximity, plainly stated: 'Is it any of my business?' Can I properly be held to account for what goes on in this world remotely from me? How much of what I do is your or anybody else's business? In this case, what right do you have to cast a critical eye into my shopping bag?

In Christian terms the question translates as: 'Who is my neighbour?' and when Jesus responds to this question he offers a story which is discomforting because it goes beyond the received wisdom and seems to demand an overwhelming availability to the world (Lk 10:25-37). In the 'global village' our neighbours are alarmingly numerous.

One could work oneself into a dark despair over all the terrible injustices, disasters and atrocities which we witness in the world, usually from a distance. One could develop a debilitating sense of guilt which would profit nothing. When can I know that I have done enough? How far should my conscience about the world's ills extend? This question leads us to the moral doctrine of 'acts and omissions.' It is instructive to note that the General Confession of the Church of England asks for forgiveness *first* because 'We have left undone those things which we ought to have done'; before it adds 'And we have done those things which we ought not to have done; And there is no health in us.'[4] It is an important consideration and only serves to intensify the issue.

And so in desperation we often seek refuge in the second question: 'Will anything that I can do, any change in the way I spend my money, affect anything in the wider world at all? Will it make any difference to climate change or social injustice? I am so small and insignificant.' And so a kind of moral inertia develops. Edmund Burke offers some guidance on this particular question: 'No one made a greater mistake than he who did nothing because he could do so little.'[5]

What exactly is ethical shopping?

Ethical shopping seeks to address the above in a small way via the modification of our own habits in the market place in the hope that over time, and with a growing consensus, change will come. Ethical shopping, or responsible consumerism, entails the following—though the list is by no means comprehensive:

1. We may simply buy *less*, and so use up fewer natural resources. Frankly we do not need everything we buy. We should buy what we need, not what we want. We will seek to 'live simply so that others may simply live.'[6] We will take Jesus a little more seriously when he says that we should 'take no thought for your life, what ye shall eat; neither for the body, what ye shall put on' (Lk 12:22 KJV).

---

[4] The *Book of Common Prayer* (Glasgow, UK: Collins, n.d.), 42.

[5] Edmund Burke, cited in John Houghton, 'The Challenge of Sustainability,' in: R. J. Berry, ed., *When Enough is Enough* (Nottingham, UK: Apollos, 2007), 67.

[6] Ronald Sider, *Rich Christians in an Age of Hunger* (London, UK: Hodder and Stoughton, 1978), 11.

2. We may try to buy *local and seasonal* so that the things we buy do not have to travel long distances across the world. In this way we cut down on carbon emissions and so help to protect our environment. We will buy from small shops and companies when we can, rather than from multinational corporations.

3. We may buy *fairly-traded* produce, things which have not involved the exploitation of the planet's raw materials, or used destructive manufacturing processes.

4. We may buy *fairly-traded* products which have not involved the exploitation of workers, which have not involved slave labour, child labour, or sweatshops. It encourages a market where people have a fair wage and do not have to work in bad or dangerous conditions.

5. We may actively *boycott* certain brands, the products of certain companies which mistreat people, threaten the environment or which perhaps give financial support to political organizations we deem to be unjust.

6. We may *boycott* products from certain parts of the world where there is extreme political and social injustice.[7]

Ethical shopping means that we will use our influence, small but real, to try to do what the Lord requires of us, to '*do justly*, and to *love mercy*, and to walk humbly with thy God' (Mic 6.8 KJV, italics mine). Our power is small but not non-existent. Producers and retailers in the current economic climate have to be very sensitive to the wishes of customers, and Christians do wield some influence with their purchasing power.

Of course it is a great deal more complicated than it sounds. And it will immediately be apparent that some of our own preferred consumer practices will come under threat.

The environmental challenge

I need at this point perhaps to make explicit the connection between climate change and our shopping habits.

1. If we continue to consume without any thought for the consequences, if we continue to 'shop until we drop,' if we continue to regard shopping as a major leisure activity, then we shall quickly use up the raw materials of our planet. It will lead directly to the despoliation of our planet, in the lifetime of our children or their children.

2. If we, as westerners, continue to consume at the present rate we shall inevitably raise the expectations of those who cannot currently consume as we do. People in the so-called developing world will see our lifestyle, and of course will seek to obtain some of its benefits for themselves. The pace at which the environment will

---

[7] See Clark, Duncan, *The Rough Guide to Ethical Shopping* (London, UK: Rough Guides Ltd, 2004), 27-35.

be damaged will thus quicken greatly as expectations rise and the world's population expands.

3. If we continue to shop in the way we currently do, the simple fact is that we shall continue to exploit others in so-called developing parts of the world. They will not have the means of earning a decent living. They will feel that they have no alternative but to violate their environment in order just to survive. They will continue to do their best to subsist without any thought for the environment. You do not give much thought to carbon emissions when you do not know where your next meal is coming from. And so the cycle of environmental degradation will continue.

4. If we continue to shop as we do, and maintain our current standard of living as our right, we may anticipate that sooner or later there will be conflict over resources, wars of redistribution. In such conflict the environment is usually the first casualty.

5. If we buy something we then become responsible for it and for disposing of it. Major problems concerning climate change arise because of the problems of waste disposal in societies given to conspicuous consumption.

6. Everything is connected today in our world. With improved and swift communications, universal advertising, and mass migration, our shopping habits affect people on the other side of the world, sometimes very quickly. For example, climate change generates natural disasters which eventually raise the cost and availability to us of services like insurance.

I hope the above is sufficient to establish in your minds the strong connection between your shopping habits, social justice and the protection of the environment.[8]

Arguments against responsible consumerism
Thus far I have made certain assumptions. To seek some balance in my argument I should mention, at least briefly, some plausible counter-arguments.

1. Some would say that we are individuals responsible for the effect of our own behaviour on those around us, but we cannot reasonably be held responsible for the lives of people who are very remote from us. It is too much to expect. In the end it is a kind of moral nonsense. If you are responsible for everything, you are responsible for nothing.

2. Others would argue that no action is ever ethically pure so why bother? If you boycott one sort of product, the one that you do buy is just as bad but in a different way. If you do change your consumer behaviour there will be unexpected

---

[8] For a discussion of the arguments both ways, see Duncan Clark, *The Rough Guide to Ethical Shopping* (London, UK: Rough Guides Ltd, 2004), 3-10.

negative effects. As Thielicke argued, there are times when whatever we do, we incur guilt.[9]

3. Some object that responsible consumerism is really a distraction from problems which are political in nature, and which require concerted political action and ultimately regulation via legislation. We cannot consume our way out of trouble. There is the danger indeed that pressure groups allow governments off the hook. Climate change and issues of social justice are the business of governments which uniquely have the power to create serious change. Modification of our shopping habits is nothing but a distraction.

4. According to others, it is the poor we hurt most by our well-intentioned efforts. Flawed as they may be, our habits of consumption provide the means of subsistence to those in poorer parts of the world. They can survive because we use their cheap labour. More regulation would wreck their fragile economies.

5. Some would argue that the call for ethical shopping is political correctness gone mad. Many feel that government regulation is already intrusive in their private lives and that well-intentioned pressure groups only serve to compound the problem. Such intrusion threatens free choice. It seeks to deal with one inequity by creating another.

6. Others worry that the concern for our environment and for the working conditions of those in remote parts of the world are part of a larger political agenda with which they take serious issue. To them any sort of green agenda becomes a kind of Trojan horse concealing other socio-political motivations. They might cite liberation theology as just such a false trail. Or at best they might say that for Christians to develop a green conscience is simply to bow to intellectual fashion at the expense of more important matters.

The scope of the essay does not allow for a fuller treatment of such objections but they deserve at least to be registered, and recognized as having some merit. Our task in the market place and at the check-out is, through our choices, to sustain the tensions outlined above. My task here is to examine Adventist teaching to discover resources for facing this overwhelming ethical challenge, and to do so in a way which will encourage Adventists to make some effort towards dealing with it.

Tension: Advent and *oikos*

There is a broad consensus in many circles beyond the Adventist Church that this earth is living on borrowed time because of the damage to our ecosystem caused by humanly-generated climate change of various kinds. The Adventist Church has not really taken seriously the idea that the timing of the Second Advent may be influenced by events in the natural world like climate change, believing perhaps

---

[9] See for example Helmut Thielicke, *The Ethics of Sex* (Grand Rapids, MI: Baker Book House, 1975); *Theological Ethics*, vol. 2.

that it would somehow erode the sovereignty of God. More than that, some would suggest that any effort to reverse the trend of environmental deterioration in some way is an act of unfaithfulness. Any agency, however devastating, which hastens the Second Advent is to be welcomed. And if the church were to take the notion of serious environmental threat at all seriously how should its members and agencies relate to the need for social change? Is a call to socio-political engagement in order?

Tension: Advent and Sabbath

The whole area of environmental ethics is a difficult one for Adventists because it brings into tension our two defining doctrines, the very two which give us our name. The seventh day, the Sabbath, encourages us to be good stewards of the creation which has come from the hand of God. It encourages us to rest and know that God is God. It teaches us not to exploit God's creation mercilessly for our own purposes. We must work in harmony with it, preserve it, and respect it.

In the Old Testament, the principle of the sabbatical year, designed precisely to rest the land and protect it from over-exploitation every seven years, confirms Sabbath teaching. So too does the Jubilee year every fifty years (after seven times seven years) when people had to return the land and other property to its original owner, confirming the importance of equal distribution of wealth and resources. The pervading Sabbath principle calls for the protection of the land, and those who work it, against exploitation (Lev 25).

But the doctrine of the Second Advent may be thought by some adherents of the faith to have a very different outworking. If Jesus is indeed to return to the earth soon, then the imperative to be good stewards of the earth may weaken as other priorities intervene. There is no point in putting great energy into protecting our world if everything will soon be destroyed, later to be renewed, all by the hand of God and God alone. On the contrary, all our energies should go into proclaiming a soon-coming Saviour with no energies being diverted into other matters. Protecting that which is to be consumed makes no sense, indeed may seem to be an erosion of faith.

There have been a number of occasions in Adventist history when contemporary concerns and enthusiasms were thought to threaten to side-track the church. Joseph Bates argued in this way about the abolition of slavery movement in the USA. He believed that he had come 'face to face with a tremendous enveloping cause. When Christ comes, liquor will be forgotten and the slave will be free. The lesser causes are swallowed in the greater.'[10] The questions of environment and social justice might well be judged by some to be just such a 'lesser cause.'

---

[10] A.W. Spalding, *Origin and History of Seventh-day Adventists*, vol. 1 (Washington, DC: Review and Herald Publishing Association, 1962), 315.

Any solution must come in the form of a tension which has to be sustained. Jesus told us to 'occupy till I come.'[11] Some of the gospels seem to emphasize the importance of daily Christian virtue over the eschatological excitement which takes centre stage elsewhere in the New Testament. It has been a long time, over 160 years, since the early Adventists first announced that the Advent was imminent, but this tension actually goes back right to the very beginnings of the Christian church. It demands that we give thought to how we relate to time. Persistent short-termism under pressure from the belief in an imminent advent can only lead to a degree of moral confusion.

Therefore much depends on how we choose to understand the kingdom of God, the kingdom of heaven. Jesus said that the kingdom of God 'has already come upon you' (Lk 11:20-21 NEB). If one simply understands the kingdom of God to refer to what comes after the second advent, then the whole environmental issue will mean little. If we believe, on the other hand, that the kingdom of God is among us now, that it is being built even while we are here on earth, then it will matter very much to us. Not that we can create heaven on earth but that we can be agents of God's kingdom now, and the changes in men's and women's hearts will be reflected in the outer world, in the environment. The kingdom of God now will carry over into the kingdom of God yet to come. But this has always been a deep divide in the Christian church, and the Adventist Church is no exception.

Sabbath

The Sabbath has something to teach us when it comes to environmental ethics if we will allow it do so. God gave us the Sabbath to protect us from many things like over-work, over-trading, being too materialistic, and generally treating ourselves as the centre of the world. The Sabbath is partly about protection against excess, about rhythm of life, moderation, reflection, perspective.

A person who respects time—like the Sabbath—may well find it easier to respect space, the world, the creation. So Sabbath keeping prepares us to use our environment wisely, the Sabbath urges us to respond to our environment lovingly, to make us less inclined to consume thoughtlessly.

It is important to realise that it is not so much that we keep the Sabbath but that the Sabbath keeps us.[12] Adventists have however attached other significances to Sabbath observance. It has sometimes become a time of passivity, a day of disengagement from the wider society and its concerns. It has become to some primarily a test of loyalty to God, to the Truth. Adventists have even become proprietorial

---

[11] Lk 19:13 KJV. For a fuller discussion of this tension see Michael Pearson, *Millennial Dreams and Moral Dilemmas* (Cambridge, UK: Cambridge University Press, 1990), 17-31.

[12] See Jonathan Sacks, *Faith in the Future* (London, UK: Darton, Longman and Todd, 1995), 132-37.

about it on occasion. The Sabbath then becomes commodified. This is in fact the deepest of contradictions. Abraham Heschel insists that the special feature of the Sabbath as God's holy gift is that time cannot be possessed by anybody; it can only be entered into, it is air to be breathed.[13] Attitudes towards Sabbath keeping among Adventists do expose a tension as we relate to our environment and to matters of social justice.

Stewardship and tithing

Adventists have long believed that we have been made stewards of our possessions, and are to use our wealth not only for ourselves but also for others' benefit. The biblical principle of tithing, returning ten percent of income, enjoined on all members, is a matter of trust, and has made us aware that our wealth belongs to God. It teaches us to distinguish between our needs and our wants. It shows us what we have a right to expect from life. Most would agree that it has proved a good method of financing the church and enriching the church spiritually. The regular practice of giving offerings for the support of the church and its many activities further underlines the point.

Probably two in three of all Adventists pay tithe, a tenth of their income, to God via the church. The money is funnelled through the central church organization at a local level and serves principally to pay the salaries of those in pastoral ministry. However, like all good practices it runs the risk of being routinized. Members may come to think of their considerable financial contribution in terms, crudely speaking, of taxation. It should enable the church to deal with the problems of the world and the church. The rest, ninety percent of their salary, is theirs and often it is barely enough. Good stewardship involves getting the best deal for our money from our remaining ninety percent. Many believe that they are better off with ninety percent plus God's blessing for faithfulness than with a hundred percent, even that God points the faithful in the direction of good deals. If the ninety percent is needed to survive in a sometimes harsh world they may feel that they cannot spend much on other causes, for example by paying higher prices for ethically-traded goods.

Judgement

Protestantism with its doctrine of the priesthood of all believers and the doctrine of individual judgement places great emphasis on personal relationship with God and the personal responsibility of the individual. Adventists certainly are encouraged to have 'a personal relationship with Jesus Christ' from the very outset of our spiritual journey. Furthermore, the unique Adventist teaching of the investigative

---

[13] Abraham Heschel, *The Sabbath: its meaning for modern man* (New York: Farrar, Straus, and Giroux, 1951).

judgement emphasizes the importance of individual moral behaviour for it is that which will shape our eternal destiny. Adventists are, in this sense, rugged individualists.

Yet the whole environmental debate involves our taking responsibility for large social issues only soluble by corporate action. Responsibility rests with groups of people not individuals. The notion that we may sin simply by virtue of our membership of certain groups is unfamiliar, and traditionally Seventh-day Adventists have been less than comfortable with it. The idea that we may sin by being consumers, by occupying a certain position in an international trade pattern, is a view that sits uneasily with us. For example, we buy the cheapest bananas in a supermarket to suit our pocket rather than fairly-traded ones to ensure that a peasant farmer somewhere in Central America gets a fair price for his crop. We find it difficult to accept that any moral responsibility attaches to that simple market choice.

The notion of corporate responsibility is an inescapable one in the modern world but not one that we take seriously enough. ADRA's logo is 'changing the world, one life at a time,'[14] which perhaps unintentionally captures the tension.

Evolution and creation

Adventists hold as a central belief that God is the Creator of the world; it is a motif which runs through all the teachings of the church. In its usual expression it involves the belief that God created our world in six literal days about six thousand years ago. We also assert, though it often takes the form of a parenthesis, that God is the Sustainer of our planet. In other words, God is by intentional action involved in maintaining the world day by day. If God did not do so our earth would be like a balloon which is losing its air. On this view then we, as stewards, have the obligation to support God in sustaining our world. If we are serious about this then environmental concerns—global warming, deforestation, biodiversity, etc.—become leading moral concerns of Adventists.

The fact however is that this is not a moral duty which we have eagerly embraced. It may be that we conclude, for no obvious reason, that any expression of environmental concern inevitably draws on an evolutionary view of the world. It may be that it is taken to involve the concept of slow change over a long period of time towards some sort of humanly-devised salvation. Adventists tend to think in terms of historical events not processes. Process is not really a part of the active vocabulary of Adventists. Events are taken to be decisive. And, of course, the idea that we inhabitants of earth can by an enormous act of will engineer better times in the future is counter-intuitive for Adventists. In some strange way we come to think that the ecological ideal of sustainability strikes against the identity of the

---

[14] See: www.adra.uk.org.

Sustainer. It is perhaps an understandable error of logic, but an error nonetheless given our role as God's appointed stewards.

We are not evolutionists, we do not believe in the survival of the fittest as an adequate explanatory social mechanism. Thus we cannot believe in simply allowing the global market to decide moral matters for us. We believe in intervention, in a God who intervenes. We have no option but to be interventionists ourselves as we seek to 'do justly,' and that applies as much to our shopping as to anything else.

It may of course be that there is some residual fear here of a form of pantheism, which has painful resonances for Adventism. But that is another story.[15]

Body, mind and spirit
Adventists have a clear view of the value of the body. We are not classical Greeks who thought that the mind was superior and the body an inconvenience. We believe that Jesus came in the flesh, lived bodily among us, died at the hands of his executioners, and that he was resurrected, body as well. So bodies do matter; the material world is important. The environment must therefore also be important. 'Body, mind and spirit' is the enduring touchstone of Adventist teaching and practice. Our material surroundings do influence our spiritual selves and vice-versa.

Thus the commitment to health reform in Adventism has a long and interesting history. Vegetarianism is widely practiced among Adventists because we believe it wise to eat certain types of food and not others for our own personal benefit, because our bodies are the temples of the Holy Spirit, and God needs freedom to dwell within us (1 Cor 6:19-21). Now the environmental movement is teaching us another reason not to eat animals, because meat production uses up much more of the earth's resources—land, water, seed—than do vegetables, fruits, pulses, rice and so on. And so traditional Adventist teaching about wholeness now has a new edge: a healthy spirit in a healthy mind, a healthy mind in a healthy body, a healthy body in a healthy environment. The logic is inescapable.

Self-worth
Fundamental to all Adventist teaching is the knowledge that we are loved by God. We know that we have worth, are not without value because God loves us. Our worship and study practices endlessly confirm that. Even when we make mistakes, are selfish, violent, lustful, envious, God still loves us. It is the profoundest sort of reassurance which is easy to grasp at the conceptual level but more difficult to lay hold of at an affective level. This is perhaps attested to by the fact that some Adventists while believing that God loves them struggle with the idea that God

---

[15] See for example Richard W. Schwarz, *John Harvey Kellogg MD* (Nashville, TN: Southern Publishing Association, 1970).

likes them or might be pleased with them. This may have a number of everyday practical outworkings, one of which is relevant here.

If this central Christian belief is truly rooted in the heart of the believer then we do not need to place reliance on externals, possessions, or fashionable brands to convince ourselves and others that we are worth something. To wear it, or drive it, is one thing, but to rely for our identity on it is quite another. The advertising media and retailers offer identities which are 'off the peg.' Our identity comes from elsewhere. The Christian Church affirmed long before *L'Oréal* that we 'are worth it.' Pope Benedict XVI rightly observed that 'the external deserts in the world are growing, because the internal deserts have become so vast.'[16]

Prophetic voice

The Adventist Church has always claimed to be characterized by the 'spirit of prophecy.' This in fact reduces to the claim that in the nineteenth century Ellen White was in receipt of visions and divine guidance from which the church has greatly benefited. This has proved an unfortunate reduction, and this observation is by no means designed to dispute her ministry in any way whatsoever; quite the contrary. If the church has exercised a prophetic role it must continue to speak with a prophetic voice. We have the job of echoing the messages of the prophets. Even the most cursory look at the Old Testament prophets, at Amos and Isaiah for example, will reveal that there is a clear condemnation—that the poor suffer at the hand of the rich, that the rich surround themselves with luxuries at the expense of the poor.

There is room for Seventh-day Adventists to be radical without compromising our identity. James White made it clear that if the church is to claim to have the 'spirit of prophecy' it must not only have individuals who see the world in radical terms but also those who are prepared to hear that voice and obey it.[17] It is very easy for Adventism to adjust to the social status quo and lose its radical edge. The prophetic voice on the environment and issues of social justice has little trace of an Adventist accent.

Some uncomfortable examples

At some stage this essay must become an uncomfortable read to the typical western consumer. If that is not yet the case then now is perhaps the moment as we stop to ask some questions:

---

[16] Brian Heap and Flavio Comim, 'Consumption and Happiness: Christian Values and an Approach towards Sustainability,' in: R. J. Berry, *When Enough is Enough* (Nottingham, UK: Apollos, 2007), 87.

[17] Pearson, Michael, *Millennial Dreams and Moral Dilemmas* (Cambridge, UK: Cambridge University Press, 1990), 46. See also 68, 191.

- Did you know that the average person in the West will use six toiletries before leaving the house each day, containing about 100 synthetic chemicals, many of which can survive the journey from the sewage works finally to the sea, where they may well contaminate the environment?
- Did you know that 20,000 litres of water are needed to produce one tee-shirt?
- Did you know that in the EU we discarded 100 million mobile phones in 2004? They contain highly damaging chemicals in their manufacture, and when they are thrown on to landfill sites, leach dangerous chemicals.
- Did you know that air travel is the world's fastest growing source of greenhouse emissions?
- Did you know that a tourist uses at least five times as much water and electricity as a local resident?
- Did you know that much of the world's chocolate production depends on child labour?
- Did you know that if you buy a cup of coffee from a chain shop which costs say 2 Euro, as little as 5 cents may go to the peasant producer in South America?
- Did you know that when a car has driven 10,000 kilometres it has produced its own weight in carbon emissions?
- Did you know that 20% of male workers on banana plantations in Ecuador become infertile because of the fertilizers with which they come into contact?
- Did you know that there are a lot of other similarly disturbing statistics about the contents of your shopping basket which you do not know?[18]

Conclusion

Now this essay is in grave danger of having precisely the opposite effect to the one intended. It may well be that I am depressing the reader. It may be that all this is overwhelming you to the extent that you slump back and become inert.

The problem *is* overwhelming. It requires many different types of action by many people. We can make progress by choosing for ourselves a few priorities. You cannot do everything. You cannot do nothing. It is vital to realise that this is

---

[18] For these and similarly disturbing statistics taken from reputable sources, see, for example, Leo Hickman, *A Good Life: a Guide to Ethical Living* (London, UK: Eden Project Books, 2005), and Duncan Clark, *The Rough Guide to Ethical Shopping* (London, UK: Rough Guides Ltd, 2004). See also Elizabeth Breuilly, Martin Palmer, eds., *Christianity and Ecology* (London, UK: Cassell Publishers, 1992); Dieter Hessel, Larry Rasmussen, eds., *Earth Habitat* (Minneapolis, MN: Augsburg Fortress, 2001); Ian Bradley, *God is Green* (London, UK: Darton, Longman and Todd, 1990).

not just another among many difficult social issues. It is foundational, and requires our immediate attention.

But there is a final tension. As Christians we are called to joy as well as to duty. I am not writing in order to make readers miserably analytical or introspective. Yet I do not want us to be merely secularized consumers. I believe that Adventists have some limited power and influence in our own communities. We need some change in the consumer culture of our western church on this matter. We need our church leaders to set an example by giving serious consideration to ways of reducing their air and car travel.

It is an unpalatable truth that secular people do more to protect the work of our Creator and Sustainer than do church members. This essay is simply a call to live our faith when we go shopping. It is a call to see shopping as an opportunity to bear witness to our values. Ellen White once said that there is 'more religion in a loaf of good bread than many of you think;'[19] the same could be said of the other contents of our shopping basket.

Michael D. Pearson. Born in Great Britain. Since 1997 vice-principal Newbold College, England. Since 1972 extensive teaching and lecturing experience on contemporary ethical issues for generations of Newbold students and other groups in Europe and America. Author of books and articles. DPhil, University of Oxford (1986).

---

[19] White, Ellen G., *Testimonies for the Church*, vol. 2 (Mountain View, CA: Pacific Press Publishing Association, 1948), 373.

The Boundaries of Christian Hospitality in a Postmodern Setting

Steven Thompson

Australian fire fighter David Tree stopped his truck and offered a bottle of water to a singed and dazed koala walking the ash-strewn roadside during the February 2009 bush fires in Victoria, Australia.[1] Thanks to a colleague's mobile phone photo, this simple act of cross-species interaction has been broadcast worldwide. Neither fire fighter nor koala seemed aware that their brief hospitality encounter refuted a much-publicized assertion by the world's best-known postmodernist philosopher that 'pure hospitality,' free from ulterior motives, the demands of conventionality, or other contaminants, does not exist in this world.[2]

The ethics and philosophy of hospitality have received considerable attention during the past twenty years by postmodern philosophers, led by Jacques Derrida (1930-2004). The purpose of this essay is to compare Derrida's influential construct of 'pure hospitality' with the model of hospitality inherent in monotheistic, revealed religion, particularly in its Judeo-Christian form. The essay will argue, first, that 'pure hospitality' actually exists in this world. Second, it will argue that this 'pure hospitality' is a core ethical component of revealed religion, and third, that it exists only within boundaries, conditions and limits. This concept will be designated 'boundaried hospitality.' The essay concludes by suggesting a few implications of boundaried hospitality for selected Christian modes of engagement with society.

Hospitality in European philosophical thought

Does hospitality cease to be hospitality if it is limited by any boundaries? This question, traditionally at home among ethicists and political philosophers, was brought into widespread prominence by Jacques Derrida in the 1990s. But it has occupied western thinkers at least since Plato (427-347 BC), whose life experience in Athens impacted his view of hospitality to strangers. Early in his life Athens attracted visitors and intending immigrants due to its cultural and economic success, but after a devastating thirty year war with Sparta, as Athens resigned herself to defeat, a different sort of intending immigrant arrived: desperate refugees seeking security. Plato, writing his *Laws* near the end of his life, called for strict limitations to the hospitality offered to refugees, and for restrictions on the numbers

---

[1] Sam the Koala, who turned out, after further scrutiny, to be Samantha, now has her own website at http://koalasam.com.

[2] Derrida expressed disbelief in the existence of 'pure hospitality,' among other places, in Anne Dufourmantelle, *Of Hospitality: Anne Dufourmantelle Invites Jacques Derrida to Respond*, transl. Rachel Bowlby (Stanford, CA: Stanford University Press, 2000), 77.

allowed to settle.[3] His work has influenced subsequent thinking and policy about hospitality, refugees, and intending immigrants.

A more tolerant and open attitude towards strangers developed among Stoics around the beginning of the Christian era, at a time when the old, largely independent Greek city-states had given way to the socially unifying consequences of Alexander the Great's conquests, followed by Rome's political expansion. Focus among some thinkers turned away from local, ethnic and tribal, and more in the direction of national and international.[4] As a corollary to this process, the concept of the autonomous individual emerged, fostered by social developments in the expanding cities of the empire, giving rise to early expressions of the concept of the brotherhood of all humans. Stoics captured this development in their slogan *caritas humani generis* 'love for humankind.'[5] In this changed climate the concept of 'stranger' underwent change. While Plato had championed the concept of boundaried hospitality, Stoics can probably be credited with laying the foundation for the postmodern notion of extending hospitality to all humans without limits, in order to avoid violence, or at least neglect. Plato's boundaried hospitality was adopted by German Enlightenment philosopher Immanuel Kant (1724-1804), while Derrida carried the Stoic position to its logical conclusion in his concept of 'pure' hospitality.[6]

Immanuel Kant's landmark 1795 essay *Zum ewigen Frieden* ('Perpetual Peace') provided the modern political concept that there is a natural human right to hospitality, a hospitality that was clearly boundaried.[7] In his essay's 'Third Definitive Article for a Perpetual Peace' Kant spelled out hospitality boundaries for both host and stranger. He designated hospitality only within these conditions to be a right, and he located the stranger seeking hospitality somewhere between the extremes of 'enemy, to be treated with hostility' and 'fellow inhabitant for a certain length of time.'[8] Kant employed the terms 'temporary sojourn' and 'right to associate' to further describe his view that hospitality is boundaried. He declared that the guest

---

[3] Plato, *Laws* 12:952D-953E. For an easily accessed translation, see Plato, *The Laws*, transl. Trevor J. Saunders, Penguin Classics (Harmondsworth, Middlesex: Penguin Books, 1970), 503-505.

[4] John E. Stambaugh and David L. Balch, *The New Testament in its Social Environment* (Philadelphia, PA: Westminster Press, 1986), 55.

[5] The phrase is from Cicero's ethical treatise *De Finis Bonorum et Malorum* ('About the Ends of Goods and Evils') 5.23.65 and is expounded with comment by Ladislaus J. Bolchazy, *Hospitality in Antiquity: Livy's Concept of its Humanizing Force* (Chicago, IL: Ares Publishers, 1995), 55-64.

[6] Hans Boersma, *Violence, Hospitality, and the Cross* (Grand Rapids, MI: Baker Academic, 2004), 28-38. See also Thomas E. Reynolds, 'Welcoming Without Reserve?: A Case in Christian Hospitality,' *Theology Today* 63 (2006): 98-99.

[7] Immanuel Kant, *Perpetual Peace: With an Introduction by Nicholas Murray Butler*, transl. Nicholas Murray Butler (New York: Columbia University Press, 1939).

[8] Ibid., 23.

had no 'right to be a permanent visitor,' thus clearly differentiating hospitality, which to his thinking was temporary and dependent on mutual obligation, from permanent residency or citizenship, which rested on a quite different conceptual foundation from that of hospitality.

The two centuries separating Kant from Derrida were laden with the rise and decline of European colonialism and industrialisation, accompanied by social up-heavals and wars. By the 1920s radically pessimistic views of human nature began to quench both Enlightenment humanistic optimism and classic Christian hope. It was in this atmosphere that Derrida worked. His main reason for insisting that pure hospitality must be free from limits was to acknowledge the potential for violence in every human encounter. For Derrida, denial of hospitality amounted to, or could quickly lead to, violence.[9] The only violence-free hospitality, for him, was the pure hospitality which exists only when a host gives everything, includ-ing himself, to a guest. Paradoxically, Derrida's 'pure' hospitality, while avoiding violence to the guest, would ultimately obliterate the host by an unboundaried drain of his resources. In one frank declaration of the ultimate consequence of his pure hospitality, Derrida declared that, if it actually existed, pure hospitality would lead to death: 'It is to death that hospitality destines itself ...'[10] Elsewhere he identified the stranger (whom he labelled 'the other'), whose arrival is anticipated by the host, with death.[11]

Biblical hospitality in cultural context

Whether one reads in Genesis chapter 18 of the biblical patriarch Abraham's hos-pitality to approaching strangers, or of the hospitality experiences of strangers in Homer's *Iliad* and *Odyssey*, the components of hospitality, and the sequence in which they are offered, are strikingly similar. The definition of hospitality em-ployed in this essay, informed by biblical and Graeco-Roman sources, specifically excludes entertainment of family, friends and acquaintances, and entertainment to facilitate business or politics. The typical components of ancient hospitality in biblical and Graeco-Roman sources, including the respective roles of the stranger and host, will be sketched below.

---

[9] For Derrida's own words see his strangely-titled essay 'Hostipitality.' He produced this peculiar neologism by joining 'hostility' to 'hospitality.' Jacques Derrida, 'Hostipitality,' in *Acts of Religion*, Gil Anidjar, ed. (New York: Routledge, 2002), 361. See also his 'Step of Hospitality/No Hospitality,' in: Dufourmantelle, *Of Hospitality*, 77. For discussion see Gary Gutting, *French Philosophy in the Twentieth Century* (Cambridge, UK: Cambridge University Press, 2001), 309-310. Hent deVries, *Philosophy and the Turn to Religion* (Baltimore, MD: John Hopkins University Press, 1999), 22. Boersma, *Hospitality and the Cross*, 31. Amos Yong, *Hospitality and the Other: Pentecost, Christian Practices, and the Neighbor* (Maryknoll, NY: Orbis Books, 2008).

[10] Derrida, 'Hostipitality,' 360.

[11] Derrida, 'Faith and Knowledge: The Two Sources of Religion,' as cited by deVries, *Turn to Religion*, 311-312.

Stranger/guest

In the ancient world the 'stranger' (Hebrew *gēr*; Greek *xenos*; Latin *peregrinus*) was exposed to risks which are hardly imaginable to today's typical western travellers and sojourners. Stranger vulnerability was therefore the point of departure for ancient hospitality, as was the belief that strangers came under divine protection.[12] Stranger protection was the responsibility of the chief God himself—Yahweh in the case of the Hebrews, Zeus in the case of the Greeks.

Conversely, fear of the stranger was also a feature of ancient hospitality which is now being explored by Christian writers.[13] Strangers evoked mixed, sometimes powerful, emotions which tended towards polarisation. They evoked fear because of their unknown identity, origin and mission. Fear must be overcome before hospitality could be accepted or offered, as in the case of fire fighter David Tree and Sam the koala. To help overcome this fear, several ancient cultures worked with the belief that strangers could be gods, or god's representatives, in disguise.

Host

The role of ancient host typically fell to the chief family of a settlement or town, whose gate would have been the point of initial contact for a stranger seeking hospitality. The prestige and social standing of the host family would be influenced by the quality, dignity and safety of hospitality offered to strangers.[14]

The first and most fundamental obligation of the host was to prevent harm to the stranger. For Greeks a major role of Zeus, chief god of the Greek pantheon, was reflected by one of his titles, *Zeus xenios* ('Zeus protector of hospitality').[15] Zeus had responsibility for strangers, and woe betide the person who exploited one of his charges! Greek authors from Homer (circa eighth century BC) to Plato and beyond agreed that 'all strangers ... come under the protection of Zeus.'[16] A concise theology of hospitality is articulated later in the same work when Homer's main character, Odysseus, reminded a potential host, from whom he requested hospitality: 'You know the laws of hospitality: I beseech you good sir to remember your duty to the gods. For we throw ourselves on your mercy; and Zeus ... is the traveller's god: he guards their steps and he invites them with their rights.'[17] Plato,

---

[12] Briefly sketched by Otto Hiltbrunner, *Gastfreundschaft in der Antike und im frühen Christentum* (Darmstadt, Germany: Wissenschaftliche Buchgesellschaft, 2005), 46.

[13] See the discussion in John Koenig, *New Testament Hospitality: Partnership with Strangers as Promise and Mission* (Philadelphia, PA: Fortress Press, 1985), 3-5.

[14] For reflection on the concept of a Christian host, see Christine D. Pohl, 'Hospitality From the Edge: The Significance of Marginality in the Practice of Welcome,' *Annual for the Society of Christian Ethics* (1995): 127-136.

[15] 'In this role the father of gods and men ... overseeing the behaviour and needs of the *xenos* ('stranger') 'according to John Taylor, *Classics and the Bible: Hospitality and Recognition* (London, UK: Duckworth, 2007), 2.

[16] Homer, *The Odyssey* 6.207-208. For a convenient translation see Homer, *The Odyssey*, transl. E. V. Rieu, Penguin Classics (Harmondsworth, Middlesex: Penguin Books, 1946), 146.

[17] Ibid., 9.269-273.

centuries later, at the high watermark of classical Greek culture, echoed this perspective when he declared that Zeus was the god of strangers, and that, assisted by intermediary spiritual powers known as *daimones*, Zeus would punish most severely those who violated the sacredness of agreements with strangers, including hospitality.[18]

Hebrews were likewise under divine obligation to protect the stranger. This was a repeated theme in Pentateuchal legislation. 'A stranger you must not exploit, because you were strangers in the land of Egypt' (Ex 22:20).[19] Nearly identical commands are found in Ex 23:9 and Lev 19:33. Old Testament strangers sometimes experienced innovative protection under this provision of Torah. The Syrian army which invaded Israel, and was marched in a state of divinely-inflicted blindness to Israel's king by the prophet Elijah (flourished 875 BC), was protected from harm when he re-badged them as 'guests,' thus requiring the king to protect them and extend hospitality (2 Kgs 6:21-24).

Divine punishment for breach of hospitality could be severe, and in some cases was visited on entire cities. The Greek destruction of Troy was sparked when Paris seduced Helen, the wife of his host. The salutary Old Testament instance was Sodom, whose male population made a brazen attempt to molest the strangers offered hospitality by Abraham's nephew Lot (Gen 19). While the destruction of Sodom was the consequence of additional transgressions, breach of hospitality was central. Later Jewish re-telling highlighted this reason for divine destruction of the city.[20] Recent interpreters concur: 'The transgressions of Sodom's inhabitants mainly consist in sexual debauchery, human hubris, and violation of (the law of) hospitality.'[21]

The act of hospitality

Ancient hospitality accounts nearly always include an offer by the host of water, a bath and fresh apparel, followed by food and drink, then rest. Medical help was offered if needed. Hospitality typically concluded with an offer of food for the next stage of the journey, and an escort or guide if warranted by circumstances. These constitute standard acts of hospitality which any self-respecting ancient householder extended to every traveller on request, without question or cost. Woven

---

[18] Plato, *Laws* 5.729e translation from Plato, *Laws*, 193-194.

[19] This assumes the validity of the definition of Hebrew *gēr* to include 'stranger.' For a counter view see T. R. Hobbs, 'Hospitality in the First Testament and the Teological Fallacy,' *Journal for the Study of the Old Testament* 95 (2001): 20-21.

[20] Josephus, *Jewish Antiquities* 1.200. The anti-hospitality of the inhabitants of Sodom received its strongest statement in the Targum Pseudo-Jonathan to Gen 18:20 which included the legend of the girl *Pĕlētîth* who was punished for taking bread to a poor man, according to Martin J. Mulder, 'Sodom and Gomorrah,' in *The Anchor Bible Dictionary*, vol. 6, ed. David Noel Freedman (New York: Doubleday, 1992), 102.

[21] Ibid., 100.

into the act were occasions for the stranger to disclose his identity, origin and mission. The host would reciprocate with personal information, or by providing local information to the stranger. Multitudes of narrated hospitality acts in ancient literature support this sketch.[22] Within this framework were nested attitudes and practices governing the stranger-host relationship. The host did not 'pry' into the stranger's business, and the stranger did not appropriate for himself anything in the household which the host did not explicitly offer. Quality of food served, quantity of food consumed, and appropriate length of stay were among the boundaries governed by the shared concept of hospitality.

In summary, ancient hospitality was a short-term, custom-governed, non-commercial, non-reciprocal symbiosis or 'triangle' of host, stranger, and the divinely-sanctioned, stranger-protecting theology of hospitality.[23] 'Social dyad' is another designation for stranger and host within hospitality's mutually-applicable set of boundaries.[24] Ancient hospitality reduced, but did not obliterate, the distinction between host and guest.[25]

The basis for hospitality

The belief in divine command as the basis for hospitality emerges clearly in a range of ancient sources.[26] One modern specialist employs the expression *ius hospitii, ius dei*, 'the right to hospitality which is established by God' to indicate this widespread belief in divine-command hospitality.[27] Divine protection of strangers as a sacred duty of a host is well attested among Roman authors. They also wrote admiringly of its practice among people groups they encountered. They viewed the ancient northern European *Germani*, for example, as actively modelling divine-command hospitality, including protection of strangers. Julius Caesar (100-44 BC) observed that among the *Germani* 'divine command (Latin *fas*) prohibits violation

---

[22] Andrew E. Arterbury, 'The Ancient Custom of Hospitality, the Ancient Novels, and Acts 10:1-11:18,' *Perspectives in Religious Studies* 29 (2002). See also Amy G. Oden, *And You Welcomed Me: A Sourcebook on Hospitality in Early Christianity* (Nashville, TN: Abingdon Press, 2001), 145.

[23] This definition of hospitality, as well as the term 'triangle' is drawn from Taylor, *Hospitality*, 12.

[24] The argument in favour of the necessity of a social dyad for genuine hospitality to exist has been stated by Anthony J. Gittins, 'Beyond Hospitality?,' *Currents in Theology and Mission* 21 (1994): 164-82. He argues that an isolated individual, without social context, is not a stranger, but an anomaly. The implications of this understanding of biblical hospitality for Christians is explored by Reynolds, 'Welcoming Without Reserve,' 196-200.

[25] For a judicious integration of cultural evidence with theological construct on Christian hospitality's limitations, see Yong, *Hospitality and the Other*, 122-124. Reynolds, 'Welcoming Without Reserve,' 197-198. See also Igor Lorencin, 'Hospitality Versus Patronage: An Investigation of Social Dynamics in the Third Epistle of John,' *Andrews University Seminary Studies* 46 (2008): 172-173.

[26] See for example the survey of Homeric hospitality in Taylor, *Hospitality*, 1-35.

[27] The Latin expression is used by Bolchazy, *Hospitality in Antiquity*, 14, and frequently elsewhere in his monograph.

of strangers; whoever comes to them for any reason they guard from injury, and relate to as sacred.'[28] Roman historian Tacitus (55-117 AD), in his description of the *Germani* theology of hospitality, stated their view that strangers were under the protection of the gods, and that it was *nefas* ('violation of divine command') to turn away a stranger requesting hospitality.[29] These Greek and Roman accounts provide context for the following survey of biblical hospitality references.

Biblical hospitality as divine command

The purpose of this section, after exploring selected accounts of hospitality in Scripture, is to argue that hospitality is a revealed, divinely-commanded dimension of biblical faith and life.[30] Hospitality references appear throughout the Hebrew Bible.[31] So important is divine-command hospitality that it appears in the heart of the Decalogue's fourth commandment, extending Sabbath rest to the stranger (Ex 20:10; 23:12; Deut 5:14).[32] Divine-command hospitality is implied even by the imagery of the best known Hebrew Psalm: 'You set a table for me in view of my enemies; you anoint with oil my head; my cup overflows' (Ps 23:5). Here Yahweh leads by example, modelling the sort of hospitality he commanded in Torah.[33]

In the New Testament, Matthew's intricately structured and repetitive account of Jesus' parable of the final judgement (Mat 25:34-46) employs hospitality to the stranger as the basis for the final judgement. The clearly-identifiable components of hospitality—welcoming the stranger at the door, offering food, drink, and clothing—testify to the centrality of divine-command hospitality in the teaching of Jesus. When the Sadducee lawyer questioned Jesus about which command of the law was greatest (Lk 10:25-27), Jesus' reply, whether he intended it or not, echoed a Greek legal formulation preserved in ancient inscriptions: 'Hospitality [is] the greatest of the laws.'[34] As further evidence for divine-command hospitality, Jesus quoted the Pentateuchal summary of the Decalogue, 'love your neighbour as yourself,' then went on to redefine 'neighbour' to include 'stranger' (Lk 10:25-37).

---

[28] Julius Caesar, *Gallic War* 6.23.

[29] Tacitus, *Germania* 21.

[30] For the biblical material see, in addition to standard Bible dictionary articles, Andrew J. Arterbury and William H. Bellinger, 'Returning to the Hospitality of the Lord: A Reconsideration of Psalm 23, 5-6,' *Biblica* 86 (2005): 388-391. For an excellent summary of both Graeco-Roman as well as biblical hospitality as divinely-commanded see Hiltbrunner, *Gastfreundschaft*, 22-33.

[31] For limited discussion and references, see Hobbs, 'Hospitality in the First Testament,' 3-4.

[32] This assumes the validity of the definition of Hebrew *gēr* to include 'stranger.' For a counter view, see Ibid., 20-21.

[33] The hospitality features of this passage have been exegeted by Andrew J. Arterbury and William H. Bellinger, 'Returning to the Hospitality of the Lord: A Reconsideration of Psalm 23, 5-6,' *Biblica* 86 (2005): 387-395.

[34] *Inscriptiones Graecae* 1193, 1331, cited by Bolchazy, *Hospitality in Antiquity*, 20.

While the rest of the New Testament lacks explicit divine commands to be hospitable to the stranger, its presence operates in the background of dozens of passages in the gospels, Acts, Pauline and other epistles, and Revelation. It emerges into the foreground at times: 'Do not forget to be hospitable to strangers; by being so, some, without knowing it, have had angels as their guests' (Heb 13:2).[35] Based on the widely distributed biblical evidence from Old and New Testaments, a conclusion is offered here that there is biblical support for a Christian theology of hospitality as divine command.[36]

Boundaried nature of divine-command hospitality

Divine-command hospitality in Scripture is, like its ancient Greek equivalent, always boundaried. Christian hospitality therefore, like certain other divine benefits, is not entirely open or unconditional. Its practice is hedged with necessary features which guard the honour of God and prevent abuse of either stranger or host. Because much recent Christian literature on hospitality overlooks evidence that biblical hospitality is boundaried, this essay will now sketch its key elements.[37]

1. Boundaried hospitality in the New Testament

Studies of New Testament hospitality typically fail to do justice to explicit references to boundaried hospitality.[38] Probably the most explicit New Testament demand for boundaried hospitality is that of the Elder, who instructed his congregation to deny hospitality to anyone not holding the correct understanding of the nature of Christ. 'If someone comes to you not maintaining this teaching, do not let him into the house, and do not speak a greeting to him' (2 John 10). Unfortunately this provoked a response in kind from the opposing party: '[Diotrephes] himself will not welcome the brothers, and those wishing to do so he prevents, and puts them out of the church' (3 John 10). While interpreters have examined in detail

---

[35] Translation by Donald Wayne Riddle, 'Early Christian Hospitality: A Factor in the Gospel Transmission,' *Journal of Biblical Literature* 57 (1938): 141.

[36] Hospitality as a Christian obligation is supported by Letty Mandeville Russell, 'Postcolonial Challenges and the Practice of Hospitality,' in: *A Just and True Love: Feminism at the Frontiers of Theological Ethics. Essays in Honor of Margaret A. Farley*, Maura A. Ryan and Brian F. Linnane, eds. (Notre Dame, IN: University of Notre Dame Press, 2007), 123. While several theologians cited in this essay agree that Christian hospitality is not optional, some deny that it is based on a divine command. See for example Yong, *Hospitality and the Other*, 127.

[37] Pioneer exploration of Christian hospitality's boundaries by Caroline Westerhoff has as its thesis that 'Boundaries and hospitality go together: they are in a necessary but irresolvable tension with each other.' Caroline Westerhoff, *Good Fences: The Boundaries of Hospitality* (Cambridge, MA: Cowley Publications, 1999; reprint, Morehouse Publishing, Harrisburg, PA, 2004), xii.

[38] Development of the concept of hospitality's boundaries is absent for example from Koenig, *Hospitality*. Abraham J. Malherbe, *Social Aspects of Early Christianity*, second, enlarged ed. (Philadelphia, PA: Fortress Press, 1983). Taylor, *Hospitality*, 113-146. Arterbury, 'Hospitality in Acts 10.' Lorencin, 'Hospitality Versus Patronage,' 165-174.

most features of this exchange, little has been noted on these two explicit references to denial of hospitality.[39]

Paul wrote to Roman Christians 'now you must offer hospitality (*proslambanō*, designating the host's role in hospitality) to the weak-in-faith one, but not for the purpose of heated debates over arguable views' (Rom 14:1). His imperative 'offer hospitality!' is boundaried by the limitation 'not for debates'! New Testament hospitality occasions were not to be hijacked by doctrinal and ethical debating. Paul repeats his initial directive in 15:7. In 14:1 to 15:7 he sketched two conflict-separated groups of Christians which have preoccupied interpreters ever since—the weak and the strong. By contrast, less exegetical effort has been expended on the opening and closing commands of this section. Some read the second imperative (15:7) as part of a preliminary conclusion to the epistle, rather than as a continuation of 14:1.[40] Whether this is correct or not, the second command to show hospitality is often overlooked. Food and drink, key elements of hospitality, are prominent in 14: 2f, 14f, 17, 20-23. Paul, by the exclamation 'The kingdom of God is not food and drink' (14:7) deliberately highlighted the role of meals and hospitality.[41]

A clear violation of boundaried hospitality is behind 2 Tim 3:6. 'For among [the persons impacted by last-day moral decay] are those who make it a habit to gain entry by devious means (*endunō*, 'to creep, sneak, insinuate oneself') into homes and take over for their own ends little women loaded down with sins, led about by a range of longings, always receiving instruction but never able to arrive at a knowledge of the truth.' This blunt and colourful glimpse of an unsavoury aspect of early Christian life depicted persons who targeted and exploited others by gaining access to their homes and instructing them. Such a practice could potentially violate several aspects of hospitality. The author's advice for his readers is equally blunt: 'Keep firmly turned away from such types!' (vs 5, where the present imperative of *apotrepō* plus accusative implies 'remain turned away from'). Jude 4 employs the verb *pareisdunō*: 'certain persons, ungodly ones, infiltrated ...' The precise transgression of hospitality is hinted at later in the epistle. During the *agapē* fellowship meals these 'ungodly persons were devoid of reverence' (*aphobōs*), and they 'shepherded themselves,' probably in the sense that they lived at the expense of their followers (Jude 12). The passage's translation is complicated by the richly allusive wording, but its reference to abuse of hospitality is clear.[42]

---

[39] The hospitality issue behind this passage has recently been addressed by Lorencin, 'Hospitality Versus Patronage.'

[40] This is the position taken by James D. G. Dunn, *Romans 9-16*, vol. 38a, *Word Biblical Commentary* (Dallas, TX: Word Books, 1988), 844.

[41] See Koenig, *Hospitality*, 56.

[42] For an account of the history of interpretation of this passage, along with the options for translating its metaphors and allusive expressions, see Richard J. Bauckham, *Jude, 2 Peter*, vol. 50, *Word Biblical Commentary* (Waco, TX: Word Books, 1983), 84-87.

Boundaried hospitality is implicit several places in the New Testament where it is not explicit. According to John 10:1 the stranger is under obligation to approach the main door of the sheepfold when requesting hospitality, to avoid being mis-identified as a thief. In Rev 3:20 the risen Jesus announced: 'I stand at the door and knock ...' Only if a host voluntarily opened would Jesus enter for hospitality. As a respectful stranger, he did not force entry, but waited at the door for the host's initiative.

2. Boundaried hospitality in the early church

Several recently-published histories of the early spread of Christianity omit reference to hospitality's role. This is the case for works on conversion and evan-gelism.[43] It is also true for general histories of early Christian mission.[44] This omis-sion is as unfortunate as it is surprising. One hundred and thirty years ago church historian Adolf Harnack (1851-1930) demonstrated the importance of early Chris-tian hospitality in a two-part journal article, which appeared later in expanded form in his *Meisterwerk* on the mission and expansion of early Christianity.[45] Brief but informative surveys of early Christian hospitality have recently begun to ap-pear.[46]

The presence of boundaried hospitality among early Christians is illustrated from two post-New Testament sources. The first is the earliest surviving church manual, the *Didachē*, ('Teaching of the Twelve Apostles'), composed about 100 AD. The section on visiting strangers demonstrated that early Christians practiced boundaried hospitality. The document's author suggested simple indicators to help congregations distinguish true from false itinerant teachers and lay believ-ers. Concerning itinerant teachers (designated 'apostles and prophets') the *Didachē* instructed: 'Let every apostle, when he cometh to you, be received as the Lord; but he shall not abide more than a single day, or if there be need, a second likewise; but if he abide three days, he is a false prophet. And when he departeth let the apostle receive nothing save bread, until he findeth shelter; but if he ask money, he

---

[43] There is no serious discussion of hospitality in Michael Green, *Evangelism in the Early Church*, rev. ed. (Eastbourne, UK: Kingsway Communications, 2003). He refers to hospitality extended to Paul during house arrest in Rome on page 332, and quotes Richard Baxter (*The Reformed Pastor*) on the success of hospitality evangelism. Hospitality's role in early church expansion is not discussed in Rodney Stark, *The Rise of Christianity* (Princeton, NJ: Princeton University Press, 1996).

[44] Hospitality is not seriously discussed in Robin Lane Fox, *Pagans and Christians* (New York: Harper & Row, 1986). The word does not occur in the index to Eckhard J. Schnabel, ed., *Early Christian Mission*, 2 vols. (Downers Grove, IL: InterVarsity, 2004). I could find no treatment of the role of hospitality in W. V. Harris, ed., *The Spread of Christianity in the First Four Centuries* (Leiden, Netherlands: Brill, 2005).

[45] Adolf Harnack, *The Mission and Expansion of Christianity in the First Three Centuries*, transl. James Moffatt, vol. 1 (London, UK: Williams & Norgate, 1908; reprint, New York: Harper and Brothers, 1962), 177-180.For details of his seminal 1879/80 journal articles on early Christian hospitality, see 177, n. 1.

[46] See Hiltbrunner, *Gastfreundschaft*, 165-81. Pohl, 'Hospitality from the Edge,' 121-136.

is a false prophet' (11.4-6). Another test was given in the chapter: 'And no prophet when he ordereth a table in the Spirit shall eat of it; otherwise he is a false prophet' (11.9). By adhering to well-known and widely-acknowledged boundaries of hospitality, early church leaders endeavoured to shield hospitable congregations from exploitation.

A similar test was to be applied to lay Christian travellers seeking hospitality from a congregation. 'But let everyone that cometh in the name of the Lord be received ... If the comer is a traveller, assist him, so far as ye are able; but he shall not stay with you more than two or three days, if it be necessary. But if he wishes to settle with you, being a craftsman, let him work for and eat his bread. But if he has no craft, according to your wisdom provide how he shall live as a Christian among you, but not in idleness. If he will not do this, he is trafficking upon Christ. Beware of (*prosechō*) 'be on guard against such men' (12.1-5).[47] This passage, again, employs standard components of hospitality to determine frankly the genuineness of strangers seeking hospitality in the name of Jesus. Through these guidelines in the *Didachē*, church leaders offered a simple, culturally-relevant test of stranger authenticity—did they respect, or violate, boundaried hospitality?

The second case is from a remarkable account of a peripatetic philosopher and holy man, Peregrinus, who took his own life in an extravagant self-immolation at the end of the Olympic Games in 165 AD. The account of his life by the pagan author Lucian of Samosata (born c. 120 AD) is useful for its account of the conversion of Peregrinus to Christianity. Lucian acknowledged the important place accorded to hospitality by early Christian congregations when he mocked: 'So if any charlatan and trickster, able to profit by occasions, comes among [Christians], he quickly acquires sudden wealth by imposing upon simple folk.'[48] In this caricature of early Christian hospitality Lucian contrasted the craftiness of Peregrinus with the naïveté of the Christians. But even they practiced boundaried hospitality, as Lucian acknowledged when he narrated that 'after [Peregrinus] had transgressed in some way against [the Christians]—he was seen, I think, eating some of the food that is forbidden them—they no longer accepted him (16).'[49] Here again is a case of the violation of a clear boundary, which incidentally seemed to be food-related, resulting in the withdrawal of Christian hospitality.

---

[47] Translation by J. B. Lightfoot, *The Apostolic Fathers: Revised Texts with Short Introductions and English Translations*, second edition (London, UK: Macmillan and Co, 1893; reprint, 1926), 233-234.

[48] Lucian, *The Passing of Peregrinus* 13 (A. M. Harmon transl., Loeb Classical Library, vol. 5, 15).

[49] The historicity of Peregrinus is vouched for by contemporary scholarship, as for instance Leofranc Holford-Strevens, *Aulus Gellius* (London, UK: Duckworth, 1988), 104-05. C. P. Jones agrees: 'The essentials [of the life of Peregrinus] are above suspicion' according to C. P. Jones, *Culture and Society in Lucian* (Cambridge, MA: Harvard University Press, 1986), 121.

The main argument of this section of the essay has been that for the Christian, hospitality is divinely commanded, but that even divine-command hospitality has boundaries. This is in contrast to Derrida's assertion that in order to be pure, hospitality cannot have boundaries. Derrida's notion that hospitality leads to death, however, does overlap somewhat the Christian doctrine of the atoning death of Jesus. According to John's gospel, the ultimate measure of love is one's willingness to lay down one's life for a friend (John 15:13).[50] Under the influence of Derrida's pure hospitality the doctrine of the Atonement is now being viewed as an act of divine hospitality that leads to death—the death and resurrection of Jesus Christ—which then enables others to experience the joy of life-nurturing, divine hospitality.[51]

Boundaried hospitality and Christian engagement

The thesis that Christian divine-command hospitality even in its purest form remains boundaried will now be employed in order to scrutinise aspects of selected Christian modes of engagement with society. Such a step seems required because even boundaried divine command Christian hospitality can be 'vulnerable to distortion and misuse.'[52]

1. 'Virtual church' in the light of boundaried Christian hospitality

The arrival of 'virtual church' has cast a cloak of anonymity over congregational member and visitor alike, removing the member-visitor distinction usually visible in traditional, face-to-face congregational worship gatherings. 'Virtual church,' whether created by the sheer enormity of contemporary super churches, or by the electronic media, inhibits or prevents some forms of hospitality. When worshippers anonymously assemble in enormous audiences instead of in congregations, or when they sit outside the church building in the family car viewing proceedings on a giant outdoor screen, or when they lounge at home viewing televised worship, they are denied the personal encounters so central to the Pauline model of the body of Christ. This removes opportunities to give and receive human hospitality. It also cancels the uniting impact of Christianity's central celebration of God's hospitality in communion, or Eucharist.

2. Public evangelism in the light of boundaried Christian hospitality

Public evangelism encounters hospitality, including its boundaries, especially at the point of the evangelist's physical or media-enabled virtual arrival on the doorsteps of potential hosts. I once pastored a congregation whose members, when I raised the possibility of a public evangelistic effort, bristled with resistance

---

[50] For additional statements of this motif of John's gospel, see 10:15, 17; 13:39; 1 John 3:16.
[51] See especially Boersma, *Hospitality and the Cross*.
[52] Christine D. Pohl, *Making Room: Recovering Hospitality as a Christian Tradition* (Grand Rapids, MI: William B. Eerdmans Publ. Comp., 1999), 127.

and resentment because, years earlier, a forceful visiting evangelist insisted on removing the church's exterior signboard, along with any other indication of the confessional affiliation of their building. From the perspective of hospitality, their resistance was justified. For a guest to interfere with his host's identity, especially to the extent of concealing identifying features of the dwelling, would overstep one of hospitality's boundaries.

Electronic media enables the public evangelist, as stranger, to seek simultaneous entry into multiple homes. Entry is important—in the words of Alfred C. Fuller, founder of America's legendary Fuller Brush Company, 'getting in is the trick.'[53] He continued: 'Assume a welcome. Never say "May I come in?" but rather, "I'll step in a minute."'[54] At this point it is important to recall the New Testament image of Jesus as stranger on the doorstep (Rev 3:20). Like Jesus, the evangelist has a message of life-and-death importance for the householder. But the evangelist coming in the name of Jesus should not violate the boundaries of hospitality in gaining entry to homes, and should make appropriate disclosure about his identity and mission. A doorstep approach that conceals more than it reveals breaches hospitality.[55] The hospitality components in Jesus' instruction to the earliest travelling evangelists (Mat 10; Mk 3; Lk 6) is worth reviewing in this connection.

Another serious challenge to hospitality arises for the tele-evangelist. The process of televising or filming imposes a series of reality-limiting filters between evangelist and viewer. These range from simple make-up, studio lighting, backdrop and camera viewing angles, to more profound cognitive and emotional filters and props. These can be used to conceal as effectively as to reveal. As a result, the viewer who invites in the tele-evangelist sees only what the evangelist chooses to reveal. By comparison, ancient hosts, through routine hospitality acts of bathing and re-clothing, feeding and table talk, gained considerable insight into their guest's identity. Concealment was more difficult with face-to-face ancient hospitality than with today's tele-evangelist, who can assume an on-camera *persona* which may differ significantly from off-camera, unfiltered reality. The potential for deception due to inadequate or misleading personal disclosure calls for the highest integrity from the tele-evangelist.

Finally one must ask, in light of the pronouncement noted earlier in the *Didachē* that strangers who asked for money breached hospitality: Should the tele-evange-

---

[53] Eddie Stride, *C.E.N.* March 10, 1966 citing the Fuller Brush Co. training manual, quoted by George W. Target, *Evangelism Inc.* (London, UK: Allen Lane The Penguin Press, 1968), 236.

[54] Ibid., 237.

[55] Marketing experts recognize the damage done to commerce by concealed identity. For a discussion of honest versus dishonest representation for marketers, see http://womma. org/

list solicit money while 'in' a home as stranger/guest? However one answers, the need to ask this question illustrates the significant gap between face to face hospitality as a form of gospel witness on the one hand, and the evangelist's virtual presence in homes facilitated by mass media on the other.

3. Multiculturalisation in the light of boundaried Christian hospitality

Diverse regions of today's world experience what is designated by the newly-coined term 'multiculturalisation'—the rapid mingling of cultures previously separated by custom, law or distance. 'The world is truly becoming a global village in terms of mobility and economic and social life.' These words are from a booklet summarising half a century of official Roman Catholic social teaching on hospitality to refugees. It makes repeated calls for recognition of their rights, and for their basic human needs to be met by state and church.[56] Its author quotes a challenging papal statement on the role of congregations which is highly relevant to this essay: 'The parish, which etymologically means a house where the guest feels at ease, welcomes all and discriminates against none, for no one there is an outsider.'[57]

Local church hospitality efforts seem so feeble in the face of mass migration, whether caused by disaster, or due to a wish for social and economic improvement. Those with experience delivering hospitality to immigrants and refugees confess to being overwhelmed, and their work compromised, if they and those to whom they provide hospitality do not observe adequate boundaries. A sensitive, Scripture-based account of this complex and sometimes painful process by Christine Pohl named one of the consequences of offering even boundaried Christian hospitality: 'By welcoming strangers, however, the community's identity is always being challenged and revised, if only slightly. While this is often enriching, it can occasionally stretch a place beyond recognition.'[58] She referred to the stress arising from such stretching, before outlining some key boundaries established in Scripture for ancient Israel when absorbing strangers. 'Incorporation into membership in Israelite society was possible when strangers identified fully with the social meanings of the Israelite community.'[59] For ancient Israel, circumcision completed and summed up the total social and spiritual integration package expected of the stranger who intended to stay. With the passage of time, in the experience of the early church, parts of the package ceased to accomplish its original spiritual and social purpose, and the Holy Spirit guided the apostles in reframing it in light of their experience of Jesus Christ.

---

[56] Sandie Cornish, *The Call to Hospitality, Catholic Social Justice Series No. 44* (North Sydney, NSW: Australian Bishops Conference, 2002), 17.
[57] John Paul II, 'World Migration Day Message 1999,' as cited by Ibid., 23.
[58] Pohl, *Making Room*, 136.
[59] Ibid., 137.

The pages of the New Testament record the struggle to find what Pohl terms a suitable set of 'minimal boundaries that would allow good relations among converts' in a changing social climate.[60] She acknowledged the vital role of group identity for Christians, and their emotionally-charged responses when that identity is threatened: 'When strangers are welcomed in, especially if they come in significant numbers or if they are quite different from the welcoming community, there will be strains on identity. The community will be transformed by the people it welcomes ... There is less impact if strangers stay only briefly, but if strangers stay long-term ... then a fairly complex set of questions about beliefs and behaviours emerge.'[61] The practice of Christian hospitality today is clearly challenged by rapid multiculturalisation. Integrating long-stay immigrants into congregations is a process which extends beyond the doctrine and practice of Christian hospitality. It needs to be informed by, and allowed to draw on, the resources of the separate biblical motif of 'the sojourner.'

Other Christian activities that could be profitably examined from the perspective provided by the motif of hospitality include church growth, ecumenical relationships, mission, and long-term foreign aid. In fact, just about every dimension of Christian life could benefit from scrutiny from the perspective of boundaried hospitality.

Conclusion

This essay has argued support for the following interconnected propositions: first, that hospitality is a foundational biblical motif for the divine-human relationship; second, that 'divine-command' hospitality should be part of Christianity's mode of being; third, that even God's 'pure hospitality' is boundaried. The essay has also examined some of the possible impacts of divine-command, boundaried hospitality on 'virtual church,' on public evangelism, and on multiculturalisation.

Christians who accept the necessity of 'divine-command' hospitality as a dimension of Christian living will be sensitive to the Spirit's guidance in discerning which of Christian hospitality's boundaries are relevant at particular times and places. 'We are travellers, pilgrims and strangers, on earth,' declared Ellen White. 'Let the churches arise as one, and work earnestly as those who are walking in the full light of truth for these last days. Let your influence impress souls with the sacredness of God's requirements.'[62] Boundaried hospitality is one of God's expectations. It seems unwise to ignore, violate, or over-extend its bounds in the very activity of bringing the hospitality of Christ to people who have not experienced it.

---

[60] Ibid.
[61] Ibid., 141.
[62] Ellen G. White, *Testimonies for the Church* vol. 6 (Mountain View, CA: Pacific Press Publishing Association, 1900), 452.

Steven Wayne Thompson. Born in USA. Retired 2009. Pastoral experience in Great Britain, 1972-1978. Lecturer (1978-1984) and principal (1984-1990) at Newbold College. Dean of theology faculty and lecturer at Avondale College (1991-2008). Currently supervising postgraduate research students. Numerous scholarly publications. PhD, University of St Andrews, Great Britain (1976).

Exploring the Frontiers of Faith

PART IV
Education

The Role of Education in the Seventh-day Adventist Church

Niels-Erik Andreasen

Most leaders as well as church members will agree that education has always played a crucial role in the study of Scripture, the formation of theology, and Christian mission, and it stands to reasons that it therefore should occupy a correspondingly important place within the church organization. In this essay I will explore that importance in further detail.

Education in the gospel commission

A good place to begin is the gospel commission (Mat 28:18-20). It is generally understood, correctly, as a call to Christian witness, evangelism and what we now call church growth. Generations of Adventist children learned to memorize this passage, and its instruction to 'go' has inspired missionaries since the beginnings of Christianity, indeed it very likely inspired Paulsen and his family to travel as missionaries from Norway in the far north to Africa in the south. Its three instructions from the risen Lord to his newly fledged apostles are to make disciples of all nations, baptise them in the name of the Father, Son and Holy Spirit, and teach them whatever Jesus had taught his disciples. Not surprisingly, these instructions to the apostles follow the pattern set by Jesus himself in his own life and ministry. He became an early disciple of his relative John the Baptist, was baptised by him, whereupon he set about teaching his own disciples for the next three and a half years. To become a disciple (along with the newly coined verbal form 'discipling') means to become (or make someone) a follower in the way a student—or better, an apprentice—follows the master to learn from him or her. Baptism with water is a symbol communicating cleansing of past failures, along with complete devotion to a new life as a Christian apprentice. That is to be followed by an extended period of teaching and learning—'everything I have taught you.' The gospels report that the Baptist objected to Jesus' request for baptism, but was put at ease with the explanation that this act would be carried out in fulfilment of a divine plan and become an example for others to follow (Mat 3:14-15). The language of this entire incident is steeped in education practices as follows: The student beginning as an apprentice seeks out a teacher, then follows a commitment to stay the course, and the extended instruction can begin in earnest. That, explained the departing Christ to his apostles, is how the Christian witness in the world must be conceived and carried out.

It should not come as a surprise, for when we read this last instruction by the risen Christ back into the gospels, the life of a teacher at work is on display from beginning to end. Jesus' followers called him master and teacher (John 3:2). His teaching was interesting, sometimes provocative and generally convincing. People flocked to hear him and many became his disciples (John 4:39-41). Some established teachers of the day objected, as teachers habitually do to a newcomer on the scene, but he kept on teaching with barely a distraction (cf. John 8:2-11). Others observed that he taught differently from other teachers (Mat 7:28-29, Mk 1:21-22, Lk 4:31-32), and in one sense that is true, but in another sense those other teachers, the rabbis and scribes, notably of the Pharisaic party, taught in a similar way— namely by wrapping human interest stories around scriptural truths and explaining the kingdom of heaven in everyday language. Joachim Jeremias, the prolific twentieth century student of ancient Jerusalem, Judea and Galilee in the time of Jesus, identified many common settings of his teaching along with its unique features.[1] In at least one sense Jesus' teaching was unique, namely its call for a radical submission to God's will. There was more urgency in Jesus' teaching than in the teaching of his contemporaries; some will say there was an eschatological urgency, an invitation to enter the kingdom of heaven now, not by withdrawing from society as was the practice among, for example, the Qumran community. Rather, Jesus' teaching about the kingdom called for resolute decision-making directed to everyday life choices (Lk 18:18-30). In short, the teaching materials and instructional methods used by Jesus may not have differed much from those of his contemporaries, but he had a new and convincing way of helping his students grasp the essentials. A good example of that difference is on display in the conversation between two teachers (rabbis), Jesus and Nicodemus (John 3). We do not really know what Nicodemus wanted to discuss with Jesus, but it likely had to do with what comes up toward the end of their conversation, namely the teachings of Torah (the Old Testament) and their relationship to Jesus' teachings, a subject that is still troubling rabbis in our time.[2] Jesus characteristically cut to the chase of this subject by informing Nicodemus that only a person filled by the Spirit of God can learn spiritual lessons, and such indwelling by the Spirit requires a new birth, like a baptism. The response by Nicodemus ('how can a person be born again when he is old?') discloses the difference between the two teachers—not their different understanding of a common practice, such as baptism, but a different understanding of what it really means to be baptised and how that changes a person's thinking totally, including the thinking about Torah, and extending to all the religious instructions found in Scripture. That illustration better than most explains the key trademark of Jesus' teaching: He quickly lays open the key thought to be learned,

---

[1] Joachim Jeremias, *Jerusalem in the Time of Christ: An investigation into economic and social conditions during the New Testament period* (Philadelphia, PA: Fortress Press, 1975).

[2] Jacob Neusner, *A Rabbi Talks With Jesus* (Montreal, Canada: McGill-Queen's University Press, 2000).

and then explains how to arrive at it in a deeply personal and unmistakable way. The following chapter (John 4) illustrates the way Jesus put his urgent teaching into practice during his interaction with a Samaritan woman he met at Jacob's well. His request for water, the discussion of the woman's personal life and the invitation to worship God in spirit and truth is a fascinating example of an educational process leading to discipleship, new understanding and Christian witness.

But as for the materials and methods in which Jesus wrapped his teachings, they are hardly unusual or startling. Indeed, they are so ordinary and so much a part of daily life, so as to be almost amusing. A woman who lost her money and found it again, a son who ran away from home and then came back, a tree that gave no fruit, farmers, shepherds, fishermen and builders doing their daily work, travelling tradesmen, employers setting wages for their labourers, unpopular soldiers and hated tax collectors on the job—hardly anything escaped his attention, and everything was made an object lesson for the benefit of his apprentices. I have often thought that had Jesus lived in our day, he would feel very comfortable with a high school or a general education college curriculum of science, history, communication, social studies, economics, history and geography. He would engage each subject, often noticing the amusing part of the lessons, to discover something crucial for understanding life and eternity. He would be an effective teacher in our time as he was in his own, gently cajoling his listeners to see the obvious point to be taken home and not be left in the dark by self-imposed blindness (Mat 7:3-5). The role of a teacher was his destiny during his short life on earth, and he fulfilled it perfectly.

Jesus repeatedly explained this destiny by referring to what had been written about him and about his mission in the Scriptures. Contemporary theologians have debated who Jesus really was on the grounds that what we read about him in the gospels was written by those who viewed him through eyes of faith and who bore witness to him from the vantage point of a later time. But Jesus himself found the meaning and direction of his life through a study of the Scriptures that spoke of 'the one who is to come.' One of those passages in Isaiah 11:2-9 sets out in a fascinating display of educational terminology what the coming 'messianic' son of David will be like. 'The Spirit of the Lord will rest upon him—the Spirit of wisdom and understanding, the Spirit of counsel and power, the Spirit of knowledge and of the fear of the Lord—and he will delight in the fear of the Lord.' It goes on to say that as a ruler he will not judge by what is seen and heard (externals, in other words), but he will decide based upon what is right and just, that is to say, he will decide after he has determined the underlying facts following a thorough examination of the evidence (vs 3-4). And when it comes time to mete out discipline, he will do so, not with a sword, that is to say by using physical power, but by the words of his mouth, reflecting the power of his intellect (vs 4-5). Such a ruler, who exercises his authority through fair-minded and thoughtful understanding, not surprisingly will bring peace to the world (vs 6-8), a peace that exceeds anything imagined before, until 'the earth will be full of the knowledge of the Lord, as the waters cover the sea' (vs 9). The education concepts on display here may not remind us of a contemporary school curriculum, but it comes close to the classical education of the 'prince' preparing to take up his duties as a ruler (1 Kgs 3:6-14).

In light of this remarkable prophetic depiction of the coming Messiah, it is not surprising that the last images of the risen Christ in the Scriptures portray someone who is able to open a book and read it (Rev 5:1-5). In one sense this text belongs right with the beginning of the 'revelation of Jesus Christ,' as the Apocalypse is called. To be sure, its first chapter opens with a description of Christ standing among the candlesticks, the seven churches whose troubles are getting progressively worse. But that merely leaves the reader to wonder with some trepidation what the outcome will be—will the church succeed or fail in such a dangerous world? The answer is written in a book that only Christ can open and read, and with that begins the reader's education about the future and final fate of the church. The answer is found in a closed book. Not surprisingly given its complex content, it was a difficult book for anyone to crack open, so to speak. Only Christ (the lamb) could do that. Once opened, however, it was handed over to the revelator for him to digest (just as we today speak about digesting difficult materials which we have to master), and with the further instruction to explain its content through words of prophecy (Rev 10:11). In short, the last book of the Scriptures is an invitation to learn what the fate of the church will be; it is all written in a difficult book that only Christ can open. But once opened, the revelator can read it, understand it and pass its instructions on to his readers through a series of visions and symbols. Thus, once again, Christ, with the assistance of his apostle John, becomes a teacher. Given the educational nature of the Apocalypse, as seems to be the case, we readily understand why no student of this book may add to or subtract from what it says (Rev 22:18-19). The final assignment by Christ to his students is to read what is in the book—not add to it.

It would be most unfortunate and mistaken to speak of Jesus the teacher to the neglect of Jesus Christ the great Redeemer and Justifier of sinners by grace through faith. Jesus the teacher must never displace Christ our Redeemer in Christian thinking. Accordingly, the Scriptures which lay out the mission of Christ, portray his role as suffering servant, the lamb to be slain for many, and his victory over sin and death repeatedly and with great clarity (Gen 3:15; Isa 53; John 3:16). And yet, in preparation for this redemptive role, during his life on earth, a life that was directed by the words of sacred Scripture, and continuing after his resurrection, through the indwelling of his Spirit, the Paraclete who leads us into all truth, Jesus is our teacher (John 16:13).

Education and wisdom

It is important in any discussion of education in the Scripture to reference the wisdom books which provide strong evidence that education also occupies an important place in the Old Testament. The wisdom books found there (Job, Proverbs, Ecclesiastes) are intended for the instruction of the young and the not so young but still ignorant (Prov 1:2-6; 9:1-6). Their purpose is to help everyone who lacks wisdom to understand the laws God has placed within the created world, including human life, to live wisely and prudently in accordance with these laws, but always in humility before God the Creator and Redeemer. Indeed, biblical wisdom is closely related to creation and it can only begin properly with belief in God the Creator (Prov 3:19; Eccl 12:1). Additionally, the many stories in Scripture of faithful young men and women also belong to this wisdom genre. The stories of Jacob, Joseph, Ruth, Solomon, Daniel and Esther, etc., are educational stories intended to give examples of wise living. They anticipate the life of Jesus, first in the story of the 12-year young boy who was found conversing with the learned teachers in the temple (Lk 2:41-52) and later in his many stories, parables and other wise sayings. The very last two of his parables tell about wise and foolish women and men, some of whom took advantage of what they had learned, namely to be diligent and act prudently (Mat 25:1-30). This is no accidental arrangement of the material by the gospel writer, but part of a teaching plan befitting Jesus himself. These stories represent his concluding lesson, as it were, to his disciples, and they draw upon the educational concepts of the Scriptures he knew so well, stories of young men and women who had become wise and acted accordingly or foolish and lost all. Ruth and Esther were models of wise women who, like the young wise virgins in the story of Jesus, had prepared themselves to wait for the opportunity to meet their bridegrooms. Jacob, Joseph, Solomon and Daniel were models of the two men in the story of Jesus who put their considerable talents to good and productive use by multiplying their assets.

These models of wisdom in the Scripture, encapsulated in the life and teachings of Jesus himself, form the platform for his ministry of education, not just religious education, but ordinary education that is provided today at home and in schools. As Jesus in his person was God incarnate in human form, so his earthly ministry was incarnate in the role of a teacher. There can be no real Jesus without it—there can be no real Christianity apart from it.

Education in early Christian theology

If indeed educational ideas are so deeply embedded in the words of Scripture and therefore occupy so integral a part of the life of Jesus which was directed in every way by the word of God in Scripture, educational concepts will also be found near the heart of Christian theology, if we will only look for them.

Christian theology began in earnest with the apostle Paul. Of course the other apostles contributed to it too, but Paul was its master. Before Paul, the first recorded theological treatise by the apostle Peter (Acts 2) on the day of Pentecost sets out the fundamentals of what later became the 'Apostles' Creed,' originally intended as a teaching tool. In it are brief affirmations about God by the testimony of the prophet (Joel) and the patriarch (David) and then follows the affirmation of God's son Jesus, whom he raised to be both Lord and Christ. Finally the Holy Spirit is introduced and with it the church into whose fellowship three thousand were added that day. In whatever way and place that 'sermon' was constructed, delivered and recorded, it represents a rudimentary theological statement about God, Christ and the Holy Spirit. It is followed a little later by the surprising experience of Peter, reported in Acts 10, which poses a question about who is invited by the Spirit into the new Christian fellowship. The answer, intended to educate, is that everyone who believes, regardless of gender, ethnic background (Jew and gentile), and profession may belong to the community of believers. That early Christian concept too became part of Christian theology.

However, it was the apostle Paul who laid the foundation of Christian theology and he, more than the other apostles, who built Christian thinking around educational concepts, thereby setting a pattern for Christian theologians of all time. Indeed, it may be said that it was education that helped keep Christian theology orthodox, in the sense of being faithful to Scripture. And there is historical evidence to suggest that when Christian theology was in danger of coming adrift from its Scriptural moorings, only education could bring it back home.

The apostle Paul generally did not take the time to disclose his principles of Christian teaching or theology as we may say today—for he was too busy evangelizing to do so, except on a few occasions when he was pressed by questions, opposition, or confusion about his thinking. At such times he would explain how a Christian thinks about theology. Such an illustration is found in 1 Cor 2:1-16. In this familiar passage Paul responds to some divisive ideas that had surfaced in the church of Corinth. Parties had arisen, leading to divided loyalties, personality cults, followed by questions about the fundamental idea of Christianity, Jesus, the incarnation, God himself, and the Christian relationship to local (Greek) wisdom or philosophy, as we may say in our time. On a personal level the apostle represents himself as somewhat of an outsider to these conflicts by reminding his readers that he did not baptise any of them, except two individuals and one family (1 Cor 1:14-16). Starting from that neutral vantage point, he developed his principles of Christian education, or theology, in chapter 2 by outlining the following familiar points.

First he reminded his readers that when he arrived in Corinth as a messenger of Christianity, he only presented the simple teaching of Christ and him crucified (vs

2). He offered no superior wisdom (theology), only a simple proclamation about Jesus. He did so to make room for the Spirit of God, rather than his own cleverness, to work on the hearts of his listeners. This part of his argument is familiar and has been referenced, sometimes thoughtlessly, by some 'anti-intellectual' Christians speaking against 'theology,' here called wisdom. That was not the apostle's intention, as becomes obvious next.

Thus the apostle's opening irenic statement is interrupted by his next forceful outburst: However, we do speak a message of wisdom to those who are mature. About this wisdom he had three things to say, all of them connected with educational concepts. First, this wisdom for mature Christians differs from the wisdom of the 'rulers of this age.' We might identify them as the 'tyrants and terrorists' of the time who always seek to control the thinking and values of their subjects for their own gain. That kind of wisdom comes to nothing, Paul asserted in a plea for a different kind of thought pattern. Second, he explained that the wisdom he teaches is comprehensive, namely consisting of those secret things of God that have been hidden in the world and destined by God for our glory (edification), since before time began (vs 7). As in the case of Jesus, so here the apostle identified the subject of his teaching to the mature as all the secrets God has left in the world, including, we might presume, the physical world (science), the social world (history and social studies), the artistic world (of writers, poets, artists, musicians, etc., some of whom he quoted earlier during his visit to Athens, Acts 17:22-34)—all of these mysteries are open to study by mature Christians in their quest for the fuller and deeper meaning of Christian faith. Third, the Spirit of God guides the search for such knowledge. The Spirit represents God at work among us, guiding, searching, revealing and disclosing. This is how he explained it: If two people want to understand each other they must have a common spirit, a sort of a meeting of their two minds in the search for a shared understanding. Similarly, if human beings want to understand the wisdom of God they must have a measure of God's Spirit within them, again enabling a sort of meetings of two minds, God's and ours. That is the foundation of Christian education, or Christian theology, intended to disclose the secrets God has placed in the world since the beginning of time. But can that be done, even with the presence of the Spirit? How can humans have a meeting of their minds with God's, as it were? That is an educational question, a question of epistemology (the study of how we come to understand things).

Paul addressed that question in the conclusion of this long discussion with a quotation from the Scriptures, namely part of a series of rhetorical questions asked by the prophet Isaiah. 'For who has known the mind of the Lord, that he may instruct him' (Isa 40:13)? The correct response to these questions implied by the prophet is that no one can access God's mind in this way. Isaiah is here refuting the existence of idols so common in his time by contrasting them with the true

God. A human being may have a thing or two to say about an idol, after all the idols are made by human artists and they have, as the prophet explains, neither eyes nor minds (Isa 44:18). But the true God is entirely different. No human being can instruct him, nor claim to know his mind—humans can only approach God in worship. That is the prophet's reply which the apostle now stood on its head, by essentially contradicting it with his own concluding punch line: 'But we have the mind of Christ' (vs 16). In short, believers in whom the Spirit dwells can access the mind of God. They can 'instruct' him, as it were—tell him things, discuss things with him in give and take, match wits with him, as good students will do with their teacher. That is how theology is made; that is how Christian education works. It emerges when followers of Christ, who have been given access to the mind of Christ through his Spirit, like good students are invited to 'match wits with God' to uncover the secrets he has hidden in the world.

'Making theology,' then, is an educational activity, faith seeking understanding, and it is residing deep in the Scriptures and in the life of Jesus. It is different from coming to faith, that is, becoming a disciple of Jesus. Any person can hear and accept the simple message about Jesus and him crucified—the way of salvation is indeed open to all. But God has more in store for his human family, intended since the foundation of the world for its glorification, and it can be taught and learned. What then could be more natural than for Christians to establish schools where faith can grow through learning until all God's eternal mysteries are laid open? Jesus set the example in the beginning of his ministry by calling together a small group of apprentices, students whom he could teach. He selected his teaching materials from every part of the human experience, especially the so-called secular subjects, as we call them today, since for a believer all knowledge is God's knowledge. From that point on, with only occasional interruptions, Christians have been studying without any indication of exhausting the secrets God has placed in his world.

Education in the life of the Church

In his small book entitled *Building the Christian Academy*,[3] Arthur Holmes traced in broad strokes the remarkable development of Christian education (the 'academy,' as he termed it) from the time of the early church to the present. Once again, it is instructive to notice that the outer form of this education has remained very similar to that of secular or common education, but its inner spirit differs in important ways. Thus the classical curriculum familiar from early Christian times was retained by Christian educators, but the teaching and learning experiences found new and important pathways that became the heart and soul of Christian education.

---

[3] Arthur Holmes, *Building the Christian Academy* (Grand Rapids, MI: Wm. B. Eerdmans Publishing Co., 2001).

Holmes organized his review of this heart and soul of Christian education around four educational rubrics.

1. 'The usefulness of liberal arts as preparation for service to both church and society';
2. 'The unity of truth';
3. 'Contemplative (or doxological) learning';
4. 'The care of the soul and spiritual formation.'[4]

The first of these, the liberal arts inherited from classical education, included grammar, rhetoric and logic, arithmetic, geometry, astronomy and music. In this case 'liberal' does not refer to a political and philosophical orientation toward social issues, but rather to that which liberates the human mind from the darkness of ignorance.

The idea of the unity of all truth is derived from the Christian teaching of creation with its affirmation that God is one, and that the whole world therefore belongs to him and to his Christ. Consequently knowledge about the world has cohesiveness despite what appears puzzling and contradictory in both the physical environment and in human life. Furthermore, no subject in all creation falls outside the scope of a Christian's education. Contemplative learning moves the student to consider what lies beyond the objective and observable part of the world, namely its Creator, his Spirit and his immeasurable gift of life. The student's natural response to this rubric is celebration, thanksgiving and praise. The last important rubric of early Christian education, the care of the soul, seeks to nurture the inner being, for example by shaping human values, discovering social responsibilities, guiding spiritual formation and faith development.

The partnership between the classical curriculum and the heart and soul of Christian education, endorsed by the life of Christ and the wisdom of Scripture, was to remain with Christian education until very recent times. At each moment in this long history, a crucial responsibility of Christian educators and institutions was to make certain that the heart and soul of this education would remain intact and flourish within this partnership.

St. Augustine (354-430 AD) was a teacher before he became a Christian, and he continued teaching after his conversion, until he was appointed bishop of Hippo (North Africa). His influence upon Christian theology and education was to last centuries and may have contributed to the early establishment of formal Christian educational institutions. Cathedral schools in urban centres and monastic schools in more rural locations became the first formal educational institutions for the young, leading them to a deeper understanding of Christian faith and a life of piety, while preparing them for the priesthood or other types of Christian voca-

---

[4] Holmes, 2.

tion. Eventually universities, chartered by the church, were established in cities as Bologna, Italy (1088), Paris (1150), Oxford (1167), Salamanca, Spain (1218) and Prague (1348), and throughout Western Europe wherever Christianity took hold. At the time they were founded on the scholastic principles of learning, which were eventually discarded under the influence of the Renaissance and later the discovery of the modern sciences. Nevertheless these universities kept education central in the life of the Christian church of the west. Apparently the eastern church paid less attention to education, focusing more on meditation and spiritual reflection, very possibly to the detriment of its influence and mission beyond the borders of the Middle East, Southeastern and Central Europe and Russia. It developed into a number of national and regional churches which to this day do not promote Christian education much, except in community Sunday schools for children and theological schools for the clergy.

The Protestant Reformation, under the influence of the Renaissance, revitalized the central role of education in shaping the Christian mind. Both Jean Calvin and Martin Luther were educators at heart and they drove the principles of Reformation forward from the believers' heartfelt longing for God's grace through individual and personal understanding of his word, made accessible to all as a result of the reformers' commitment to translating the Scripture into the vernacular. Through the study of Scripture the believers learned that the balance between divine grace of forgiveness and a thoughtful commitment to a life of obedience is demonstrated in the life of Christ and the word of God. Indeed, this pathway to reformation made the reformers life-long educators. Calvin's *Institutes of the Christian Religion*[5] is a theological treatise as well as an educational text book. Luther's earliest theological insight came while he lectured on the book of Psalms to his students. And his small catechism became a textbook for young adults preparing them for church membership. Without these educational concepts, along with a commitment to reading and understanding the Scripture, the Reformation would not have succeeded. In fact it may be said that the reformers recovered the traditional educational roots of early Christianity, with the result that the entire church became a kind of Christian school in which the Scripture was the basic text book, and every believer became a student. In turn the commitment to that kind of learning in time led to the 'scientific' study of the Scriptures, their languages, background and interpretation, in universities throughout Western Europe. Meanwhile, worship was also reformed and given a simple format of hymns and prayers surrounding the centrality of preaching. A by-product of these educational developments was the greatest democratization of Christianity since the time of the first church. The teaching of individual righteousness by faith and the priesthood of all believers,

---

[5] Jean Calvin, John McNeill, ed. *Institutes of the Christian Religion* (Philadelphia, PA: Westminster Press, 1960).

regardless of their social and economic standing, are reminders that educational and democratic principles generally go hand in hand.

The importance of education to Christian faith was soon transported to the new world by both Protestant and Catholic immigrants, leading to the establishment of Christian colleges and universities in North America and Catholic institutions in both North and South America and beyond. The early Adventist colleges continue this pattern to the present. It has often been noted with concern that some of the early Christian colleges in the new world became secular, e.g. Harvard, Princeton, Yale. But others, such as Calvin, Hope, Notre Dame, Wheaton, Oberlin, along with the Adventist colleges and universities and many others, remain vibrant Christian institutions. Additionally, many newer institutions, mainly non-denominational and evangelical, have embraced this traditional Christian educational mission because they understand that Christian faith cannot flourish without it. Twentieth century Christian missionary educators, including Adventists, extended this pattern by establishing a network of Christian schools and colleges in Asia, Central and South America, Africa and India on the heels of their mission assignment. As a result, the number of Adventist colleges and universities alone is approaching 110 worldwide.

It has been observed correctly that these original mission schools and colleges in the developing world prepared many first generation indigenous leaders after the independence of their nations from the colonial powers. For example Nelson Mandela commented in his biography, *Long Walk to Freedom,* upon the importance of these mission schools and colleges for the twentieth century rebirth of the Republic of South Africa, and made special reference to the steady, non-political educational service by Adventist missionary teachers.[6] Perhaps education provided the most understated impact by Christian missionaries on the lives of the new Christians in the former European colonies. Paulsen himself participated in the process of extending Adventist education to the newly established Adventist missions in West Africa, first to Adventist Missionary College at Bekwai-Ashanti, now Valley View University in Oyibi, Ghana and later to the Adventist College of West Africa, now Babcock University, in Nigeria. Such educational services by Christian educators have helped transform what began as mere Bible schools for the Adventist church into recognized schools of theology and ministry, and more recently into church-related government-chartered comprehensive universities, enrolling thousands of students in a growing number of faculties. They testify to the enduring strength of the original church commitment to general liberalizing education, a common curriculum infused with a unique Christian heart and soul, first witnessed in the earliest Christian schools.

---

[6] Nelson Mandela, *Long Walk to Freedom* (Boston and New York: Little Brown & Co., 1995), 168-169.

Some Christian educators have been tempted at times to abandon this unique educational enterprise in favour of institutions offering 'special' or 'limited' religious education, such as Christian Bible colleges, while others have lost their way in a blind pursuit of a completely secular curriculum of study without a Christian heart and soul, now so common in the majority of western universities. Nevertheless, the original concept, traced back to the first Christian centuries, of the Christian academy remains intact and vibrant throughout the world, even while challenged by critics, especially since the nineteenth century. What is the responsibility of Christian educators when confronted by the many detractors in our time who affirm the rigours of a liberating education on the one hand, but have lost its heart and soul on the other?

The central role of Christian education in the Adventist Church today
The remarkable title of George Marsden's book, *The Outrageous Idea of Christian Scholarship*,[7] dramatically captures the key challenge faced by Christian educators in our time, namely the widespread claim that a liberal education and rigorous scholarship simply cannot build upon a common curriculum using 'scientific' principles of inquiry, while at the same time staying committed to a Christian heart and soul. Such an idea is considered outrageous by many secular educators, maintains Marsden. For example, there is the challenge arising from a commitment to pluralism by most educators of our time. The idea of committing to a single set of values that a distinctive Christian heart and soul would bring to education, rather than accepting a variety of perspectives and alternatives, would be outrageous to most contemporary educators. Another challenge is the widespread presumption by secular educators that faith and learning, like church and state, must be kept separate, in order to free education of extraneous influences on the independence of scholarship. And the assumption that scholarship will become misguided by a commitment to the existence of God, rather than just to the existence of the self, on the part of the teacher or investigator, also represents a challenge to Christian education from most secular educators and researchers—part of what makes it outrageous to many minds.

While acknowledging the seriousness of these challenges, Marsden gently sets them aside by offering thoughtful alternatives that persuade and enlighten. Seventh-day Adventist educators must do the same. We have at times been less than forthright about just how widespread, ingrained and influential these challenges to Christian education are. We have even chosen now and again to dismiss them out of hand as 'wrong' or 'sinful.' While there is something to be said for such a dismissive attitude at times, a forthright and informed evaluation of these wide-

---

[7] George Marsden, *The Outrageous Idea of Christian Scholarship* (New York, NY: Oxford University Press, 1997).

spread and pervasive challenges to Christian education in our time and a thoughtful affirmation of its true heart and soul would be especially helpful to Seventh-day Adventist education at this time, because of its rapid expansion around the world where it is confronted with broad based exposure to the common secular principles of education.

Further, to be effective and convincing, such thoughtful and honest discussion of these challenges, along with an affirmation of the heart and soul of Christian education, must be legitimized in our church, and Paulsen's presidency has offered such legitimacy. The mandate from his administration is that the educational arm of the church is central to its mission, and that it is important to review all relevant issues confronting it prayerfully, forthrightly and thoughtfully, not in a dismissive way, but in the bright light of intellectual clarity, along with a strong commitment to the historic heart and soul of Christian education.

Such an approach to Adventist education in the twenty-first century might begin with certain tried and agreed upon fundamental educational principles for Christians, for example:

1. Our belief in God the Creator of heaven and earth leads to the understanding that the whole world is God's and all its truth is his.

2. God's truth is liberating by setting us free of the self-imposed ignorance and prejudice so many have chosen for themselves.

3. Education with a heart and soul always leads to humility on the part of the honest educator because of what yet remains unknown, and it also replaces the centrality accorded by many secular educators to the human self with a divine reality.

Education with a heart and soul makes us responsible for what we know, especially toward those who still live in ignorance or arrogance. A thoughtful consideration of Christian education in light of such principles would help change the idea of Christian education from being considered outrageous to becoming acknowledged as both natural and valuable. Further, it promises to be of help to Adventist educators who in many places are hard pressed by the educational principles and practices of our time.

As an expression of its commitment to Christian education while legitimizing a serious discussion of its outer form and inner heart and soul, the General Conference of Seventh-day Adventists during the presidency of Paulsen formulated and regularly read a new mission statement for the Adventist world church that includes a section on education—the teaching ministry of the church, as follows: 'Teaching—Acknowledging that development of mind and character is essential to God's redemptive plan, we promote the growth of a mature understanding of and relationship to God, His word, and the created universe.' This educational statement belonging to the core mission of the Church is a standing invitation for its educators and educational institutions thoughtfully to affirm the 'ordinary' framework—the regular curriculum of Christian education, while continually seeking for its heart and soul with each new generation of students. That search begins with Jesus and the Scriptures and is guided by centuries of Christian educational practice. To do so is as important for Adventist education in the twenty-first century as it was for Christian education in its first century.

Niels-Erik Andreasen. Born in Denmark. Since 1994 president of Andrews University. From 1970 onwards served Adventist higher education in Pacific Union College and Avondale College (Australia). Lecturer and dean of the Loma Linda University School of Religion. President of Walla Walla College. In 1994 elected fifth president of Andrews University. Author of books and articles. PhD, Vanderbilt University, USA (1971).

Thinking Ahead: Liberal Arts Education and the Future of Adventist Mission

Michael M. Kulakov Jr.

How do the goals of a liberal arts education relate to the mission of the Seventh-day Adventist church?[1] How significant is it that Ellen White, at a crucial turning point in the early history of the Adventist movement, 'steered the denomination away from the Bible college model of higher education and toward what we could call a 'Christian liberal arts approach'?[2] As we look into the future and reflect on the 136-year history of Adventist education, and note the recurring 'rounds of tension' between Adventist mission and academic vision, and observe the shifts to the right and to the left[3], one wonders what may keep our bifocal perspective in balance.

I have seen in the lives of some of my Adventist teachers and other worthy Christian leaders in the Soviet era a strong commitment to both genuine spiritual vitality and intellectual freedom. Their robust faith has been severely tested in forced labour camps and challenged by authoritarian regimes.[4] They have been equally passionate about boldly sharing their newly found freedom in Christ, about 'Christ's solidarity with the oppressed,' about intellectual integrity, and our indebtedness to and the need to study and understand the wider religious, cultural and intellectual context. At the very core of their mature and balanced vision was their living encounter with the triune, living God of Abraham, Isaac and Jacob, who reigns supreme over the entire created order, including the life of the mind and all aspects of the natural world.

I believe that this is where we need to look for a resolution of the tension between Adventist mission and academic vision. God's sovereignty over both the supernatural and the natural world provides the Adventist missionary, teacher and scholar with a single unifying platform, a vantage point from which to see the goals of Adventist mission and the goals of academic pursuit as intrinsically interdependent and inseparable. Once you realize that the living, triune God himself is

---

[1] This chapter was first presented as a paper at the ASRS/SBL Annual Convention meeting in Boston, MA on Friday, November 21, 2008.

[2] See George R. Knight, 'The Missiological Roots of Adventist Higher Education and the Ongoing Tension between Adventist Mission and Academic Vision,' *Journal of Adventist Education* (April/May 2008), 22.

[3] Ibid., 21.

[4] See Mikhail P. Kulakov Sr., with Maylan Schurch, *Though the Heavens Fall* (Hagerstown, MD: Review and Herald Publishing Association, 2008). See also Glen H. Stassen, 'Critical Thinking and Prophetic Witness, Historically-Theologically Based,' *Religious Studies News* 23:2 (March 2008), passim. Hereafter *RSN*.

the real reason behind the historic emphasis of Adventist education on the whole person, you are refreshingly surprised by the amazing theological height, christological depth and pneumatological breadth of this truly liberating vision. And the decision of our founders to settle on the liberal arts approach also begins to make sense. If one looks closely not at the content but the goals of the classical liberal arts education, and its core value, one perceives that its original emphasis was on developing 'skills of freedom': critical thinking[5], leadership and citizenship.[6] That is why in essence, if viewed within the value system of the Adventist faith, 'the goals of liberal education—to develop independent thinkers who hold values of fairness and compassion—are the goals of Adventist educational philosophy.'[7]

Adventist mission and academic vision through the prism of the Trinity

At this time of fundamental cultural shifts, the 'clash of civilizations,' the exclusive truth claims of competing religions and the epistemological challenge of postmodernism, which is frightening to some and liberatingto others, there is ground for us to stand on which is normative, scriptural and not authoritarian.[8] There is unity and diversity, freedom and completeness in the way by which the triune God—the incarnate Christ, the Holy Spirit and the Father—choose to redeem and reclaim the material universe. If our sanctified imagination can appreciate the breath-taking images of climbing to the top of Kilimanjaro, on a three dimensional I-MAX (image maximum) cinema screen of a museum (although some of us get quite dizzy in the course of the experience), we can be infinitely more blessed with the many more megapixels of greater theological and intellectual resolution and the depth of perspective through a living encounter with our triune God.

Christological depth

In the Lordship of Christ over the world, which he died to redeem, there is a challenge for us to reclaim a truly Christ-centred biblical cosmology, free from Manichaean and Gnostic extremes. 'I came so they can have real and eternal life, more and better life than they ever dreamed of.'[9] He is the author of the Scriptures, but he is also the author of the book of nature and of the life of the mind. He is the Lord of the natural sciences and the Lord of the arts. And as Christian teachers and missionaries in this world that is getting more and more complex, we have a solemn

---

[5] Cf. E. G. White who wrote that 'true education' enables students 'to be thinkers, and not mere reflectors of other men's thought.' Cited from *Education* (Mountain View, CA: Pacific Press Publishing Association, 1903), 16, 77.

[6] See W. R. Connor, 'Liberal Arts Education in the twenty-first century,' AALE Occasional Papers in Liberal Education #2, 4-5.

[7] Terrie Dopp Aamodt, 'Face Values: Liberal Education's Imperative,' *Journal of Adventist Education* (April/May 1996), 12.

[8] See Stassen, *RSN*, p. v.

[9] John 10:10 (*The Message*).

duty to study and understand all the other modes of his revelation. 'Love the Lord your God ... with all your mind and with all your strength.'[10] The Psalmist reminds us that the heavens and the skies 'day after day ... pour forth speech; night after night they display knowledge ... Their voice goes out into all the earth, their words to the ends of the world.'[11] I will never forget how, right after the collapse of the Soviet Union, some of the prominent writers in Moscow and scientists in Novosibirsk Academgorodok, who discovered order and meaningful design through their own study of theoretical physics, were eagerly seeking communication with Christians in the country, from whom they were previously isolated, and also with their Christian counterparts in the West. Sadly, we were not ready for a dialogue and collaboration. In the Lordship of Christ over all dimensions of life there are no 'narrow loyalties,' no sectarian arrogance or isolationism and no coercion. There is a holistic richness in the mission of the incarnate Jesus and in his radical ethic of the Sermon on the Mount (Mat 5) which challenges us to be real agents of reconciliation in our communities.

Pneumatological breadth

There is breadth and inclusiveness in the promise and the gift of the Holy Spirit 'for you and your children and for *all who are far off.*'[12] It is so surprising and refreshing to see that the Spirit also transforms and turns many outside of the church into his agents. 'The wind blows wherever it pleases' (John 3:8). Both our Adventist mission and our academic vision need the transforming, enabling (1 Cor 12:14) and liberating energies of the Spirit. 'Where the Spirit of the Lord is, there is freedom.' (2 Cor 3:17; Isa 42:1ff; 61:1ff). Christ's Spirit leads to open-mindedness through continuous repentance. It builds a new community and establishes a new form of citizenship (Gal 3:28). Glen Stassen reminds us that the breadth of the Spirit, which knows no boundaries, also calls us, just as it called the leaders of the early church, to repent 'for a narrow and nationalistic faith.' 'God is independent from, and calls us to repentance for our captivity to the assumptions of our society and the powers and authorities of our nation.'[13]

Theological height

We will never be able fully to grasp the theological height and holistic completeness of the sovereignty of God and 'the Lordship of Christ' over the entire created order, the whole person and all dimensions of reality (Col 1:15-16). Vladimir Lossky reminds us of the need to prostrate our intellect 'before the living God,

---

[10] Mark 12:30.
[11] Psalm 19:2, 4.
[12] Acts 2:39. See also Stassen, *RSN*, p. v.
[13] Ibid.

radically ungraspable, unobjectifiable and unknowable.' Lossky contrasts the philosophical abstractions of the 'God in general' of Descartes, of Leibniz, and of the 'dechristianised Deists' with the living persons of the Trinity.[14] For Lossky, the doctrine of the Trinity forms the heart of negative theology. It is a 'cross for human ways of thought.'[15] It is a primordial revelation and, at the same time, the source of all revelation and all reality. The fullness of being, the end and the meaning of existence, can be found in the Trinity alone. 'Between the Trinity and hell there lies no other choice.'[16] After the Minneapolis meetings, Ellen White, without equivocation and ambiguity, uplifted the 'three living persons of the heavenly trio,' emphasizing that 'the Holy Spirit ... is as much a person as God [the Father] is a person,' and stating that 'Christ is the pre-existent, self-existent Son of God.'[17] This has a direct bearing on one's missiological and academic perspectives as well as on the relationship between the two. True worship of the God of the Trinity protects a person from a fragmented, one-sided view of reality, and enables us to grow by grace to the full stature of womanhood and manhood in Christ. The recognition of the mystery of the Trinity and the presence of Christ's liberating spirit in the heart bring humility, reverence, open-mindedness and a genuine thirst to ever expand one's knowledge of God, his Word and the world which Christ died to redeem.

I have agonised over the question as to what kind of educational paradigm reflects most fully the potency, completeness and universality of 'incarnational trinitarianism' and the gospel's call to the whole person. The Adventist holistic educational approach has no other more secure foundation than biblically based 'incarnational trinitarianism' and the value system of liberal education.

Dangers to liberal arts education and its timeless values

In his very insightful study of the relationship between Adventist philosophy of education and liberal education, Terrie Dopp Aamodt correctly observes that 'Seventh-day Adventist higher education exists within the values of liberal education.'[18] He reminds us that our 'commitment to the tradition of liberal education dates back to 1910, when Ellen White advised the denomination to upgrade its school

---

[14] Vladimir Lossky, *In the Image and Likeness of God*, ed. John Erickson and Thomas E. Bird (Crestwood, NY: St. Vladimir's Seminary Press, 2001), 88-89.

[15] Vladimir Lossky, *Mystical Theology of the Eastern Church* (Cambridge, UK: James Clarke, 1991), 66.

[16] Ibid., 66. See also Mikhail Kulakov, 'Vladimir Nikolaievich Lossky', in: John Witte Jr. and Frank S. Alexander, eds., *The Teachings of Modern Christianity on law, politics and human nature* (New York: Columbia University Press, 2006), 617.

[17] See the several references in Ellen G. White, *Evangelism* (Washington, DC: Review and Herald Publishing Association, 1946), 615, 616; see also Ellen G. White Comments, *The SDA Bible Commentary* (Washington, DC.: Review and Herald Publishing Association, 1980), vol. 6, 1075, cited by George Knight, in 'Adventists and Change,' *Ministry* (October 1993), 11.

[18] Aamodt, 12.

of medicine to produce fully certified physicians. Her directive ensured that the feeder colleges would also seek accreditation and develop strong liberal education programs.'[19]

In her definitive statements concerning the goals of Adventist education, emphasizing the redemptive purpose and a biblically-based holistic approach, she underscored the original goals of the classical liberal arts education: critical thinking, caring leadership and citizenship. 'She set forth Moses, Daniel, and Paul, who had both higher education and religious understanding, as examples to be emulated. One reason that 'Paul was such a power' was that 'he had knowledge that could match' that of the 'greatest scholars,' combined with the 'knowledge of Christ.'[20]

As we look into the future and assess our present circumstances in the changing globalized world, we quickly realize that what is most valuable is usually most vulnerable and threatened. The forces of the market are at times brutal and unsparing. Increasing specialization and fragmentation of education is another major threat to liberal education.[21] There is a sharp drop in humanities enrolments. W. R. Connor, president of the *National Humanities Center*, observes that 'between 1966 and 1993 the percentage of humanities majors in the Liberal Arts I institutions declined from about 40 percent to about 30 percent. In Liberal Arts II institutions, it went from about 25 percent to 10 percent.'[22] He also notes a decline in funding for research in humanities. There is also a growing gap in faculty salaries between humanists and their colleagues teaching natural sciences. Connor also observes that national performance in the humanities has declined.[23]

Is it essential to preserve liberal education at all costs? The two terms used in classical antiquity *Artes Liberales* and *Artes Illiberales* distinguished between two principal types of educational curricula. The term *Artes Liberales* designated education proper to a freeman (Latin: *libera*, free), as distinct from the *Artes Illiberales*, which constituted training that was considered suitable for those who were not free and which is now broadly defined as vocational education. In the medieval western university the seven liberal arts consisted of the *Trivium*: grammar, rhetoric and logic and the *Quadrivium*: geometry, arithmetic, music and astronomy. In the colleges and universities of the modern era the liberal arts curriculum typically comprises the study of theology, languages and literature, as well as history, philosophy, science and mathematics.

'A liberal education,' Connor explains, 'means what a free person ought to know as opposed to what a well educated and trusted slave might know. Such

---

[19] Ibid.
[20] George Knight, citing E.G. White in 'The Missiological Roots,' *JAE*, 24.
[21] Aamodt, 12.
[22] Connor, 1.
[23] Ibid., 2-3.

a slave might well know a trade, manage a business, run a bank, or cut a deal.'[24] What kind of education does one need for running a country, leading a church, directing an evangelistic advance and becoming a light among those in the academia and the media who shape the public opinion?

I am challenged by Mark Noll's searching question about our preparedness and the depth of our commitment to educate Christian servant leaders of tomorrow to think 'within a specifically Christian framework across the whole spectrum of modern learning, including economics and political science, literary criticism and imaginative writing, historical inquiry and philosophical studies, linguistics and the history of science, social theory and the arts.'[25]

Do we have a clear vision of the distinctive role that Adventist higher education should play in the mission of the church to the marginalised and to those who shape public opinion, the mainstreams and the élites? Why should cultivation of the life of the mind matter to Seventh-day Adventists? Because to be Christ's true disciples we must know both Christ and the world which he created and died to redeem. God in Christ reconciled the world to himself and gave us the ministry of reconciliation.

Why is preserving liberal education with Seventh-day Adventist Christian values crucial for the mission of our church?

1. It lays the necessary foundations for understanding and reaching the secular mind. Great western universities function 'as the mind of the western culture.'[26] It provides the framework and trains the mind to understand and critically evaluate popular culture, technical and scientific values.[27]

2. It gives a platform and the intellectual tools for analysing the highly complex issues of the urban and globalized world and for adequately meeting the high expectations of urban Christians and urban pastors.[28]

3. It creates the environment firstly, for a 'profound study of the issues themselves' and, secondly, 'a study informed by profoundly Christian convictions.'[29]

4. It provides a comprehensive framework and a unified vision for addressing the 'plight of the sinner'and 'the plight of the victim,' and for distinguishing between the two (Karl Barth).

5. Because understanding 'the great controversy' in the twenty-first century world involves knowledge and understanding of the most complex issues of glo-

---

[24] Ibid., 5.
[25] Mark A. Noll, *The Scandal of the Evangelical Mind* (Grand Rapids, MI: William B. Eerdmans Pub. Co., 1994), 7.
[26] Ibid., 51.
[27] Ibid., 34.
[28] Monte Sahlin, *Mission in Metropolis: The Adventist Movement in an Urban World* (Lincoln, NE: Center for Creative Ministry, 2007), 63.
[29] Noll, 34.

bal economy, foreign and domestic policy, the arts as a form of social criticism, bioethics (the ethical implications of genetic engineering, cloning, stem cell research and artificial intelligence, etc.).

A vision for the future
1. Uniting critical thinking and religious imagination
I believe that our universities must cultivate intellectual excellence, creativity and religious imagination; I believe that critical thinking and religious imagination must not be compartmentalised, but must be drawn into a conversation, thus, I believe we need to cultivate what Karen-Marie Yust creatively describes as 'critical imagination.'

2. The inseparability of the life of the Spirit from the life of the mind
I believe that deep commitment to Christian faith is not only compatible with an equally deep commitment to a free search for the whole truth, but should be inseparable from such free search and intense scholarship. Karl Barth admonished us in his introduction to *Evangelical Theology*: 'Prayer without study would be empty. Study without prayer would be blind.'

3. Adventist Universities and First Order Public Discourse
I believe that every Adventist university should be a facilitator of a thoughtful and informed dialogue with the surrounding culture. I dream of the time when the atmosphere at our Adventist universities will be even more appealing, and so irresistibly attractive (through spiritual and intellectual depth, vibrancy and freedom) that the finest young minds in North America and elsewhere will choose to study at *our* universities and, as our graduates, will then make a significant contribution to first order public discourse.

4. Adventists and the great institutions of higher learning
Our growing vibrant, global Adventist community deserves (and certainly desperately needs) to have centres of research right on the campuses of the established, great western institutions of higher learning.[30] I believe that one day right on the campuses of great European universities and other great centres of learning among the Methodist, Anglican, Lutheran, Presbyterian and Catholic research centres and institutes will be fine Adventist research centres where young people from all backgrounds will study and collaborate together.

5. A new vision for sponsoring research universities
I believe that the rapidly growing, vibrant, global Adventist community deserves to have, and will ultimately grow in its midst, a new kind of philanthropist who will see his greatest mission in establishing and sponsoring outstanding research universities, and in supporting intellectual life, because 'for a Christian,

---

[30] Ibid., 51.

the most important consideration is not pragmatic results, or even the weight of history, but the truth.'[31]

6. Pastors, church leaders and the Adventist university

I believe that we, as Adventist teachers, pastors and church leaders at all levels, will see ever more clearly the great truth of the Incarnation—'that the Son of God became flesh and dwelt among us';[32] that God values the material realm, everything that he has created in this world, 'the dignity *in this world* of all human beings and the potential value *in this world* of all that they do.'[33] Our university will be at the heart of the church and the church will be at the heart of the university.

Mikhail M. Kulakov Jr. Born in Russia. Since 2005 lecturer at Columbia Union College, USA. Educated in the USA and Great Britain. First principal of Zaoksky Adventist University, Soviet Union, 1988-1993. Author of various books and articles. Co-director of the Bible Translation Institute, Moscow. D.Phil, Oxford University (2002).

---

[31] Ibid., 50.
[32] Ibid., 252.
[33] Ibid.

Challenges to Adventist Education in the Middle East

Svein Myklebust

The Middle East is often defined as the area around the eastern part of the Mediterranean Sea, the Arabian Peninsula, and the area east as far as Iran.[1] Seventh-day Adventists arrived in this region in the 1870s, and over time missions were established and the Middle East found its place in the organization of the Seventh-day Adventist Church.[2] The Middle East Union Mission (MEUM) was organized in 1943 and currently consists of 14 countries. It does not now include the traditional Middle Eastern countries of Iran and Turkey, but it does include Sudan.[3] The church is currently operating schools in four of these 14 countries: Egypt, Jordan, Lebanon, and Sudan. In the organizational structure of the MEUM, Egypt is a separate 'field' (EF), Jordan and Lebanon are parts of East Mediterranean Field (EMF), and Sudan is divided into Sudan Field (SF) in the north and South Sudan Field (SSF) in the south. This study will therefore focus on these four countries, but with emphasis on Egypt, Jordan, and Lebanon. There are two Adventist schools in Egypt, Nile Union Academy (NUA) and Zeitoun School (ZS). NUA was founded in 1946 as a boarding academy on the American model. It has no elementary section. Zeitoun School is a large elementary school operating on the Egyptian school system. In EMF, Jordan has two schools, Amman Adventist Secondary School (AASS) founded in 1942 and the Irbid Adventist School (IAS), an elementary school located in the north of the country. The church at one time operated six schools in Lebanon, but the number has now been reduced to two, both located in the Beirut area. Mouseitbeh Secondary School (MASS) was established in 1929 and Bouchrieh Adventist Secondary School (BASS) in 1939. Both these secondary schools have kindergarten and elementary sections, and both operate on the government system, as do the schools in Jordan.[4]

Middle East University (MEU) located in Beirut is the only tertiary institution operated by the church in this region. MEU currently offers undergraduate degrees in four areas as well as an MA in Education and an MBA degree. MEU was

---

[1] Caplex *Leksikon* (Oslo: J.W. Cappelen's Forlag, 2000), 712.
[2] Richard W. Schwarz and Floyd Greenleaf. *Light Bearers: A History of the Seventh-day Adventist Church* (Nampa, ID: Pacific Press Publishing Assiciation, 2000), 143. See also: Manoug H. Nazerian, *The Seventh-day Adventist Church in Lebanon: 1897-1997* (Beirut, Lebanon: The EMF of Seventh-day Adventists, 1999).
[3] Seventh-day *Adventist Yearbook 2009*. Silver Spring, MD (General Conference of Seventh-day Adventists, 2009).
[4] Ibid.

established as a college in west Beirut in 1939 and was relocated to its present site in 1946. It has always operated on the American model, and was quickly recognized by the government of Lebanon as a degree-offering institution. In 2001 the government issued a decree awarding the college university status.[5]

The Adventist school in Khartoum has traditionally been independent from the church. It is currently self-supporting and administered by a school board consisting of the church pastor, lay persons, and school administrators. The school has for some time been located in a property rented by the church, and has at times received financial backing from Sudan Field. However, it is not listed as a subsidiary of Sudan Field in the organizational directory of the Middle East Union. Eyira Adventist Vocational Academy (EAVA) in SSF was established in the 1996 with support from the Adventist Development and Relief Agency (ADRA). It received an ADRA operating subsidy for an initial period, but problems arose after this help came to an end. In Sudan there are also several schools that are operated by local communities with considerable Adventist involvement.[6]

The importance of these schools

Looking back over the 80 years that have passed since the first of these schools was founded, it is difficult to give an exact account of their impact on the church or indeed on the wider community. As in other countries with Adventist schools, they became the key training ground for pastors and other church workers, but because of the limited access church members had to good and free public education, the schools probably have had a greater impact than similar schools in the Western world. It is worth noting that the education students received often became a ticket to a new life abroad. Many became faithful workers in church organizations and institutions in the Western world, or eventually joined the ranks of professionals and business people in an adopted country, especially the United States of America.

In a region where most members came from a humble background, belonging to a worldwide church community that was not only a spiritual home, but also had very tangible assets, provided prestige as well as opportunities. Ownership of land and institutions has traditionally been a measure of a church's standing in society. The sale of Adventist church properties over the past decade and the idea of closing schools have therefore been very painful to many church members.[7]

---

[5] Middle *East University Academic Catalogue 2007-2008*, 27-28. See also: www.meu.edu.lb.
[6] Information from the two 'fields' in Sudan suggests that the *self-help* schools may have an enrolment of 8,000 to 10,000 students.
[7] In the course of the last decade, the so-called 'Division Compound' was sold as building plots. The Bishmezzine School in Lebanon was closed for financial reasons, and questions were raised about the future of a number of schools in the Middle East Union.

When Adventism came to the Middle East, Sabbath keepers often had difficulty finding work because their presence would be required on Saturdays. Church institutions therefore provided welcome work opportunities that undoubtedly brought many people into the church who would otherwise have found it much more difficult to join. The job opportunities also made it easier for young people to stay in the church after reaching working age. However, in the long run, the fact that the church became a major employer may not have enhanced the spiritual climate in the church. For some, a job in one of the schools became their only tie to the church.

In the schools, students and local teachers as well as other church members came in close contact with many foreigners. The missionaries tended to be hard working idealistic Christians held in high esteem. However, they were also exponents of their home cultures, and thus, perhaps unwittingly, hindered the indigenization of Adventism and helped to create an Adventist subculture where North American and European cultural idiosyncrasies at times became as important a part of people's faith as biblical absolutes. Consequently, a life abroad often became the aim of graduates, and the church in the Middle East over time lost some of its most capable members and their children to other regions of the world.

The schools soon became agents in establishing contacts with people in their local community. Many young people from different faith groups have been educated in Adventist schools, and both they and their parents have become aware of the Adventist Church and what it stands for. The large number of Muslim students in our schools demonstrates the fact that many Muslims are quite happy to expose their children to Christian education, because they believe they will get a good education and will be taught desirable values.[8] The presence of Middle East University in Lebanon has opened the eyes of political leaders to the existence of the Adventist Church. Doors have been opened to the very top in government and there have been frequent contacts with government ministers and education officials on and off campus. Contacts with educational leaders from different faith groups have brought better understanding and appreciation to both parties.[9] Except for the years of civil war in Lebanon (1975-1991), MEU has been a major arena for contacts between Adventists from the different countries in the region. It has also helped to expose Adventists from the world church to Adventism in the Middle East as well as to the Arabic language and life and culture in the Arab world.

---

[8]   In 2008-2009 the Zeitoun School had 26.5% and MASS had 96.5% Muslim students.
[9]   Examples of contacts would be the meetings that took place with the President and the Prime Minister of Lebanon in connection with the process to expand the recognition of Middle East College, and a meeting that MEU officials attended with the Syrian Minister of Education.

Challenges

The greatest challenge to the church in Egypt and the East Mediterranean Field is the shrinking membership. In 1980 Egypt Field had 1,100 members in 14 churches. Ten years later the membership peaked at 1,348 members, but in 2000 the membership had fallen to 921, and in 2005 it stood at 790. In 1980 East Mediterranean Field reported 1,242 members in 14 churches. At that time EMF included Cyprus as well as Turkey in addition to Jordan, Lebanon, and Syria. However, the total membership in Cyprus and Turkey at the time was so small that it has no great statistical significance for this study. For the next 15 years the reported membership kept increasing to reach 1,411 in 1995, even though the number of churches had fallen to eight. Then, in 2000 the reported number had fallen to 668, and continued to fall to 552 in 2005. The number of churches in Jordan and Lebanon was now seven.[10] There are no Adventist churches in Syria where the church has been banned since about 1970. In both EF and EMF the sudden drop in reported membership was caused by a purging of the records in order to make them reflect more closely the real membership. Even so, the recorded figures probably still grossly overstate the number of people actually present for Sabbath services on any given Saturday morning.

The decreasing membership in EF and EMF is not only the greatest challenge to the church, it is the key underlying cause for most of the challenges that their school systems are facing. It has implications for the recruiting of staff and students, and makes it difficult to keep the schools on a sound financial footing.

The conditions in the two fields in Sudan were very different. In 1980 the Sudan Mission reported nine members. In 1985 there were three churches with a total membership of 327. Five years later there were 1,932 members in 21 churches, and in 1995 there were 4,930 members.[11] By 2000 Sudan had been split into two fields. Sudan Field in the north reported 21 churches with 4,910 members, and South Sudan Field had 11 churches with 2,968 members. In 2005 the membership in SF had increased to 5,547 and that in SSF had reached 6,010.[12] Even so, the church in Sudan had serious problems caused by the brutal civil war which led to huge numbers of people being displaced internally in addition to the many who eventually moved as refugees to neighbouring countries. The operation of a growing church became particularly difficult because of all the educated members who could have filled positions of leadership, but chose to go and live in America as refugees.

---

[10] See Statistical Chart 1.
[11] Ibid.
[12] Ibid.

Statistical Chart 1: *Church membership (Mem.) and number of congregations (Ch.).*[13]

	1980		1985		1990		1995		2000		2005	
	Mem.	Ch.	Mem.	Ch.	Mem.	Ch.	Mem.	Ch.	Mem.	Ch.	Mem.	Ch.
EMF	1,242	14	1,360	15	1,354	8	1,411	8	668	8	552	7
EF	1,100	14	1,159	14	1,348	14	1,242	22	921	25	790	19
SF	9	-	327	3	1,932	21	4,930	28	4,910	21	5,547	14
SSF									2.968	11	6,010	16

Staffing

In 1980 Amman Adventist Secondary School had nine Adventist teachers out of a total of 22. This ratio was generally maintained until the mid-nineties, but by 2000 there was only one Adventist teacher left. The figures for BASS show that for the entire period about half of the teachers came from an Adventist background. In 1980 the figure was 14 out of 26 and in 2005 10 out of 19. In MASS there was more of a predominance of non-Adventist teachers, the ratio stayed approximately two to one for the whole period. The figures for NUA are much more encouraging from an Adventist point of view, because except for 1980 only one or two teachers were not members of the church.[14]

In the annual statistical reports issued by the Department of Education in the General Conference of Seventh-day Adventists, the elementary schools in each church union are not listed separately but are lumped together. In 1980 more than half of the teachers in the elementary schools in the Middle East were Adventists, but by the mid-nineties this had dropped to about one third. The percentage later increased as did the total number of teachers, presumably because of the inclusion of figures from independent schools in Sudan.[15]

The numbers for Middle East University demonstrate the difficulty in finding Adventist teachers for the tertiary level. In 1980, 21 of 22 teachers were Adventists, but in 2005 only 10 of 32 came from an Adventist background.[16] Later on we will see that a dwindling pool to choose from may not be the only cause for the staffing problems. Out of a population of about 150 active church members in Lebanon, it is statistically unlikely that one would find enough qualified persons to man two schools with about a thousand students, and even far less likely that one would find a sufficient number of professors to staff a university, even if it is a small one.

---

[13] Seventh-day *Adventist Yearbook 1980/1985/1995/2000/2005* (Silver Spring, MD: General Conference of Seventh-day Adventists).
[14] See Statistical Chart 2.
[15] Ibid.
[16] Ibid.

Statistical Chart 2: *Total number of teachers and Adventist teachers (Adv.) in the schools in the Middle East Union.*[17]

	1980		1985		1990		1995		2000		2005	
	Total	Adv.	Total	Adv.	Total	Adv.	Total	Adv.	Total	Adv.	Total	Adv.
Elementary	34	19	62	35	141	76	6	26	261	147	260	120
AASS	22	9	14	11	22	10	19	6	10	1	11	1
BASS	26	14	24	14	9	1	31	9	17	5	19	10
MASS	30	12	31	13	12	1	68	18	9	11	50	24
NUA	8	4	9	7	10	9	11	10	7	7	8	7
MEU	22	21	10	8	17	16	21	17	22	13	32	10

Inconsistencies in the chart suggest that for some years the teachers in the primary sections of the schools have been reported with the secondary teachers. However the general trend is still clear.

Quality of teachers

The limited financial base, the small pool of Adventist members, and the fact that many educated church members have left for overseas, have had a serious impact on the quality of teaching in the schools. In the Amman school the non-Adventist teachers are paid so little that only newly qualified teachers tend to be hired. When they have gained some experience these teachers often move on to better paid positions in other schools. In Lebanon, some Adventists were hired as teachers without proper qualifications because of a lack of better qualified Adventists, and also to make work available to church members who needed a job. These facts have also made it very difficult to fire staff when their services were no longer needed or wanted. Because the church has paid contract teachers reasonably well, and because there is a large pool to choose from, the contract teachers in the schools in Lebanon have generally been of good quality.[18]

As we saw above, Nile Union Academy has normally had a full staff of Adventist teachers, at least partly because the Middle East Union has made budgets available for overseas teachers, a privilege that the other secondary schools have generally not enjoyed. The reason for this generosity is presumably a long tradition combined with the fact that NUA for a long time was the only boarding school in the union with a secondary school program.

---

[17] General *Conference of Seventh-day Adventist, Department of Education World Report* (1980/1985/1990/1995/2000/2005).

[18] See Statistical Chart 3 for details about the professional training of elementary teachers.

The limited pool to choose from has also made it very difficult to find qualified local people to manage the schools. In EMF the current principals demonstrate dedication and skills, but one is beyond retirement age without a replacement in sight, and if the others for some reason should want a change, it would be very difficult to find suitable replacements. In Egypt the church relies on outside expertise to operate NUA, and for a while the same was true for Zeitoun School.

At Middle East University the two-thirds of the teachers that come from outside the church have always been hired on a temporary basis. The fact that there is a large pool of teachers that lecture in more than one university has made it possible to fill vacancies at the University with capable lecturers. Filling positions of leadership with practising members of the church has become even more difficult than in the past. In its 70 years of existence Middle East University has had presidents from overseas except for most of the years between 1978 and 1993.[19] Resources have been available for study scholarships for suitable people to fill positions in the University as well as in the schools, but there have been very few candidates with the interest and potential to take advantage of these offers.

Statistical Chart 3: *Number of elementary school teachers with adequate professional (Pro.) training.*[20]

	1980		1985		1990		1995		2000		2005	
	Total	Pro.	Total	Pro.	Total	Pro.	Total	Pro.	Total	Pro.	Total	Pro.
Elementary Teachers	34	9	62	50	141	53	76	48	261	89	260	64

Students

In the five-year period 2003 to 2007, a total of 36 people were baptised into the Seventh-day Adventist Church in the East Mediterranean Field, an average of seven per year.[21] It is obvious that with such a small and ageing constituency the four schools will have very few Adventist students. As noted before, the statistical office of the Department of Education at the General Conference offers only a total figure for the enrolment in the elementary schools in the Middle East Union. In 1980, when there were no students in Sudan, only 38 of 690 elementary students came from an Adventist background. Fifteen years later the figure was 60 out of 1632 students. However, because of Sudan the figure for 2000 was 3089 students from an Adventist background out of a total enrolment of 7060.[22]

---

[19] Middle *East University Academic Catalogue 2007-2008*, 19.
[20] General *Conference of Seventh-day Adventists, Department of Education World Report* (1980/19 85/1990/1995/2000/2005).
[21] General *Conference of Seventh-day Adventists: Annual Charts and Statistics* (D60317), See http//:www.adventiststatistics.org.
[22] See Statistical Chart 4.

In 1980 AASS reported 36 students from an Adventist background out of a total of 172. In 1995 the figure was 21 of 154, and in 2005 it was four out of 58. In 1980 Lebanon reported 74 out of 428 for BASS and 11 out of 520 for MASS. In 2005 BASS had four Adventist students out of 113 and MASS had one out of 221. NUA had no non-Adventist students in 1980 and 1985. By 1995 half of the students came from outside the church, and in 2005 only 29 of a total student body of 79 came from an Adventist background.[23]

The figures for Middle East University also illustrate the fall in available Adventist students in its traditional constituency. In 1980 27 out of 75 came from the Adventist community. In 1995 the figure was 32 of 157, and in 2005 the number was 15 of 175.[24] In 2007 there were no Adventist students from Jordan, one from Egypt, and one from Sudan. The main reason for the diminishing number of Sudanese students on campus was that all church-sponsored students over the last decade or so, with the possible exception of one, eventually ended up as refugees in the Western world rather than as church workers in their own country. In part to avoid a similar situation in the future, MEU started two off-campus programs with almost 70 students to help educate pastors for the two fields in Sudan. Therefore, the total number of Adventist students enrolled in MEU programs had increased from 1980 to 2005. In 2008 another intensive programme for the training of pastors was launched. This group meets on campus and is expected eventually to have 15-20 students.

A survey of the churches in EF and EMF conducted by the Middle East Union in the late 1990s demonstrated that there were very few potential students in these countries for all levels in the school system. The situation in Sudan is very different, and if financial constraints can be overcome by tapping into the flow of aid that is becoming available—especially if a more permanent peace can be achieved—there are huge potentials for the further expansion of the educational programme of the church.

The sudden variations in numbers in the following chart for the secondary schools are presumably caused by the inclusion of elementary figures with the figures for the secondary school sections. The huge increase in the elementary school figures are presumably caused by the inclusion of students from the independent schools in Sudan. The reported figures for MEU do not include the off-campus programmes.

---

[23] Ibid.
[24] Ibid.

Statistical Chart 4: *Total number of students and Adventist students (Adv.) in the schools in the Middle East Union.*[25]

	1980		1985		1990		1995		2000		2005	
	Total	Adv.	Total	Adv.	Total	Adv.	Total	Adv.	Total	Adv.	Total	Adv.
Elementary	690	38	1,908	120	3,099	225	1,632	60	6,843	3,154	7,060	3,089
AASS	172	34	128	34	135	29	154	21	61	7	58	4
BASS	428	74	396	34	71	6	461	7	93	6	113	4
MASS	520	11	701	6	58	0	1,086	10	194	5	221	1
NUA	48	48	34	34	75	51	44	22	39	24	79	29
MEU	75	27	58	10	71	?	157	32	167	24	175	15

Financial issues

A fourth area of challenges that is closely related to the current size of the Adventist population, but also has other causes, is the shaky financial standing of virtually all the schools. In the past, the Middle East was at the receiving end of the generosity of the church in America, perhaps even to a greater extent than other overseas fields. A special relationship appears to have existed even when the Middle East Union was not under the direct administration of the General Conference. During the years that the offices of a church division were located in Beirut, about 30 expatriate families were living in Beirut, caring for the various church administrative entities as well as a publishing house, college, and schools. This huge establishment opened a large number of work opportunities for local Adventists. The dependence on money from outside, the fact that the church became a key employer, the large number of overseas personnel, and the departure of so many educated nationals with potential for leadership roles, helped to maintain a colonial mentality in the group that remained. This mindset has been very difficult to change, even after it became clear that the world church no longer has the means to be as generous as it used to be.

The new financial situation has had an impact on the church in the entire region, but more than anywhere else in Lebanon, where payments into the Middle East Union's empty sustentation (retirement) fund has brought the EMF to the brink of financial ruin. The schools were assigned their share of the sustentation burden, but found it difficult to pay, and at the same time finance their other needs. In the nineties the church in Lebanon and its schools relied on a fund of

---

[25] General *Conference of Seventh-day Adventists, Department of Education World Report.* (1980/1985/1990/1995/2000/2005).

more than a million dollars that had been accumulated by the schools during the Civil War, and was earning a sizeable amount of interest every year to finance all their needs. However, in the course of about ten years EMF spent its 'nest egg' and accumulated a huge debt to the Middle East Union because of the required sustentation payments. A financial plan to save the two schools in Lebanon has been put in place, relying on their income from tuition, tight budgeting, and shedding of personnel not crucial to the operation. The school in Amman has survived on funds generated from tuition and gifts from abroad as well as some support from the church. This school, as well as Zeitoun School in Egypt and the school in Khartoum, appear able to manage without financial support from the church in the 2008-2009 academic year.[26] However, while living on a survival diet may be possible for a limited period of time, funds must eventually be made available for maintenance and the purchase of new equipment.

EAVA started its existence with aid from ADRA for its operation, but once the initial period of support ran out, there were financial difficulties. It appears that an agreement between SSF and the Middle East Union will secure the operation for the period 2009-2012.[27] Overseas aid has tended to be available for the building of facilities, but not to the same degree for long-term operation.

Middle East University now manages without any substantial financial support from the church, except for the allocation of a few expatriate budgets. Survival on student tuition alone has made it difficult for the institution to pay competitive salaries to its permanent employees. One senior faculty member recently left for another local university before the contracted years of service required for his sponsorship came to an end, and there are Adventists working in other local universities who might have been attracted to MEU if the remuneration had been competitive. MEU has sold some land and received some large donations that have made it possible to renovate most of its academic facilities. From funds provided from the sale of the old division compound, the Middle East Union has helped to upgrade a number of residential buildings and renew roads and other infrastructure in order to make housing available for their employees. The University still holds a piece of land of more than 10 hectares that could be developed or sold to provide a steady income to secure the operation for years to come. MEU continues to be an asset to the Middle East Union by helping to educate its ministry and other personnel on and off campus at a very low cost. The renovated office building that houses the Middle East Union and the residences of most of their employees are located on University land.

---

[26] Information supplied by the Education Department of the Middle East Union.
[27] Information supplied by the South Sudan Field.

A glorious past

In light of the glorious past it has been very hard for many church members to face current realities and accept that at times downscaling of facilities becomes a must for survival. The closing of the Bishmezzine School in Lebanon and the discussions about the future of the Zeitoun School illustrate this point. The downscaling has been particularly painful in Lebanon where the church at one time operated six schools. Over the last decade issues relating to the operation of the schools have taken much of the field committee's time. Finances and personnel matters were the key concerns, but the fact that so many Adventists have come to rely on the church for their livelihood became a serious obstacle to dealing with the issues in an effective way. A new and painful day occurred when it became evident that Adventists could no longer be guaranteed life-long job security.

The burden of a glorious past has also been very obvious at Middle East University. The College was at one time staffed by professors from overseas and had an international student body living in dormitories on campus. A new reality made it necessary to redefine the mission of the institution. Educating workers for the church and providing the membership with a university to send their children to for academic pursuits in an environment that exemplifies an Adventist lifestyle is still a key reason for its existence, but the institution could not survive without day students to fill the classes.[28] The presence of a majority of students with a non-Adventist background caused a certain amount of tension about the continuation of traditional practices and regulations. Some of those who attended or worked at MEU in the past and now reside overseas have found it particularly difficult to handle the perceived lack of spirituality and what they see as improper conduct.

Other challenges

Elementary and secondary schools are subject to the education laws of the land in which they operate. In Egypt the closely defined curriculum and frequent visits by government inspectors make it difficult for Zeitoun School to follow what would normally be seen as an Adventist curriculum. When NUA attempted to achieve status as a fully-fledged Egyptian secondary school, the leadership eventually decided to discontinue these overtures and instead search for ways to introduce an external secondary diploma. The problem is less obvious in Lebanon, but even there regular Bible classes are basically non-existent because of curricular and performance-related pressures, and the fact that most students come from another faith background. The government of Lebanon allows more freedom in the development of university curricula, which makes it possible for MEU to require religion related courses in all its undergraduate degree programs.[29]

---

[28] Middle *East University Academic Catalogue 2007-2008*, 101-183.
[29] Ibid., 175-181.

Concluding remarks

The challenges facing Adventist schools in the Middle East have been formidable, but there is reason for some optimism. The financial issues are perhaps the least worrying. Improved procedures, controls, and more accountability have helped to ease some of the tensions. If, in addition, an overall strategy for the creation of endowments through the sale of properties and donations from the 'diaspora' could be put in place, and the sustentation payments reduced, continued operation could become considerably easier.

Staffing the schools with a larger number of qualified Adventists is a greater challenge because of the limited number of available teachers, but the shortage can be reduced if every potential candidate for a job is groomed from an early age. A more competitive wage scheme for university teachers would help at MEU. In Sudan where the church has a much larger membership, but where access to education has been limited, building a strong force of teachers and administrators becomes primarily a question of funds and facilities. A plan for teacher education, similar to the existing Middle East University programme for pastoral training, has been sketched out, but so far financing has not become available.

Providing a fully defensible philosophical base for the continued operation of some of the schools has not yet been accomplished. The existence of strong emotions and a desire to avoid confrontations have at times allowed questions to be settled by default. The elementary school in EF and the schools in EMF would have to close immediately if their primary purpose was to serve the children of the church family. Their reason for existence therefore has to relate to their mission in the wider community. In view of all the church funds that are tied up in the schools and all the administrative time that continues to go into them, the owners will at some stage have to define more precisely their expectations of an Adventist owned and operated business and then agree on ways to take the schools forward in light of their findings.

Svein Myklebust. Born in Norway. Retired 2008. First president Middle East University, Beirut. Served as lecturer, dean and president in the education system of the Seventh-day Adventist Church for more than forty years in colleges/universities in Norway, Nigeria, Kenya, England, and Lebanon. PhD, University of Wisconsin (1980).

Exploring the Frontiers of Faith

PART V
Mission and Christian Witness

Evangelism and Inter-faith Relations in a World Parish

Bert B. Beach

It is popular in Christian churches today to lift up the Great Commandment—love—but there is a growing tendency, not least in leading ecumenical circles, to overlook or neglect the Great Commission: 'Go ye into all the world, and preach the gospel to every creature' (Mk 16:15). The very last recorded words of Jesus call his followers to be witnesses 'to the uttermost parts of the earth' (Acts 1:8). Many of these 'uttermost parts' are dominated by such historical world religions or religious philosophies as Islam, Buddhism, Hinduism, and to a lesser extent, by Judaism. We have here the potential for at least friction and, more likely, confrontation, especially where and when 'revealed' religions meet each other.

The world is the Seventh-day Adventist parish

The early Seventh-day Adventist pioneers soon developed a world vision of what they called *the work*. In a short time they moved from the stifling 'closed door' concept to the broader view of the *field* as the United States, the melting pot of nations, tribes and peoples, and, finally, to the exciting vision of a world missionary church going to the ends of the earth. Indeed, the Christian church is called to be a world movement. This was confirmed for all time at the Jerusalem Council (Acts 15), when it was made clear that the Christian church was not to be a Jewish subset, but a world church with a universal gospel, and not a local or ethnic gospel largely confined within historical geographic boundaries. It is, nevertheless, interesting to note that most Christian churches are not organized as *world* churches, but as *national* or even *local* churches. Even in the Seventh-day Adventist church occasionally a tension can be felt between the 'local mission' and the 'global vision.'

John Wesley was right, 'The world is my parish.' However, this concept was not appreciated by the ecclesiastical establishment of his day. Today, there are still various religious forces and legal arrangements that promote establishment, canonical territory, comity arrangements, registration or legal authorisation, nationalism, and cultural traditions. From a biblical perspective, 'the field is the world,' 'the harvest is the end of the world' (Mat 13:38, 39), and there is urgency to go from everywhere to everywhere. This is an integral part of the Adventist ethos.

Understanding and facing differences in religion

While the mandate is clear, the question remains: how can Christians in general and Seventh-day Adventists in particular, fulfil the God-given global missionary assignment? When facing other world religions and their adherents, there are no doubt some general principles that apply across the board, and there are some specific attitudes and approaches in dealing with religious difference that are more applicable to individual religions, like Judaism. One thing is clear—ignoring the teachings of other religions, a holier-than-thou attitude, looking down on other world religions as simply heathen and their followers as ignorant, benighted souls, is counter-productive and leads nowhere, except into a wall of hostility and separation.

For Adventists, the writings of Ellen G. White are of practical evangelistic significance and help. While she is very clear regarding the necessity to fulfil with deliberate urgency the task of world evangelization, she offers very little specific guidance in regards to meeting the non-Christian religions of her time. She makes practically no direct reference to Islam, Hinduism, Buddhism, Taoism, Sikhism, Shintoism, or Confucianism. She makes one reference about 'Mohammedanism,' (a term which today would be considered offensive to Muslims) and its non-belief in the divinity of Christ, and urges Christians to be zealous in teaching the pre-existence of the only Saviour of the world.[1] She does, however, enunciate an overriding principle, which provides a basis for *overcoming difference*: 'Christ recognized no distinction of nationality or rank or creed ... Christ came to break down every wall of partition: He came to show that his gift of mercy and love is as unconfined as the air, the light, or the showers of rain that refresh the earth.'[2]

In the Vatican II *Declaration on the Relationship of the Church to Non-Christian Religions*, two constructive principles are presented: 1. The Roman Catholic Church wishes not to reject that which is 'true and holy' in other religions, and 2. Catholics are encouraged to have prudent and loving 'dialogue and collaboration with the followers of other religions' and in Christian witness 'acknowledge, preserve, and promote the spiritual and moral goods found among these men,' including 'the values in their society and culture.'[3] Of course, there are some difficult problems in ascertaining what is 'true and holy' and what are 'spiritual and moral goods,' but nevertheless, *dialogue* is a much more promising road on which to travel and reach some understanding, than *diatribe*.

Dealing with Judaism—Some suggestions

The one non-Christian religion Ellen G. White actually deals with is Judaism. She says that many Jews are 'to be won.' She was probably referring to latent anti-Semitism when she said that Adventists 'should not despise the Jews,'[4] and that

---

[1]   The *Home Missionary*, September. 1892, 194.
[2]   Ellen G. White, *Testimonies for the Church*, vol. 9, (Mountain View, CA: Pacific Press Publishing Association, 1968), 190.
[3]   Walter M. Abbott, ed., *The Documents of Vatican II* (New York, NY: Herder and Herder Association Press,1967), 662, 663.
[4]   Manuscript 87, 1907.

'there is to be no erecting of barrier ... Our work is to be given freely to the Jews as to the gentiles.'[5]

She also presents two principles in dealing with the Jews that, it seems to me, could very well have some general application to contacts with other world religious belief systems:

1. The approach should not be to destroy the 'Jewish economy,' but to develop it with the truth.[6] In other words, we are to work on the plan of *progression* rather than *discontinuance*. Of course, this is obviously clearer with regard to Judaism than other religions, but nevertheless, can we not postulate that the evangelistic task, in general, is not to 'destroy,' but to 'develop' and build?[7]

2. Jews can be an effective force or 'power' to labour for Jews.[8] The principle is to use those best acquainted by personal experience with the religion concerned. This can be a most effective bridging contact. However, there is one demur. Converts, because of the possible trauma associated with change and conversion, can at times be a little inflexible or extreme, and this can mitigate against their effectiveness in building bridges of understanding.

In her book *The Acts of the Apostles*,[9] Mrs. White, in regards to meeting with the Jews, underlines the importance of linking the Old Testament and the New Testament. Seventh-day Adventists should be in a better position to do this than most other Christians. The Sabbath, unclean foods, the Day of Atonement, the cleansing of the heavenly sanctuary, and Christ's high priestly ministry are all links in the chain connecting the Old and the New Testament. However, one needs to be aware that many rabbis may resent this approach as having, from their perspective, a dangerous pseudo-Jewish nature.

Islam

In approaching Muslims, it is sensible to emphasize the *oneness* and unity of God, as clearly affirmed, for example, by Moses and Isaiah. To simply and artlessly present in early contacts the Godhead as three separate persons of the same essence will usually be counter-productive. It is good to remember that much about the nature of God has not been revealed to us. Muslims respond affirmatively to oneness, immutability, and all-mercifulness of God. Again, as with Jews, Adventist

---

[5] *Manuscript Releases*, vol. 14, 138.
[6] Manuscript 87, 1907.
[7] See Ellen G. White, *Evangelism* (Washington, DC: Review and Herald Publishing Association, 1946), 554.
[8] Talk by Ellen G. White at the General Conference Session of the Seventh-day Adventist Church, Manuscript 87, 1907.
[9] Nampa, ID: Pacific Press Publishing Association, 2005, 381. Mrs. White asks Adventists to show Christ 'portrayed in the pages of the Old Testament ... unlocked by the key of the New' (Manuscript 87, 1907).

dietary practices are a positive factor, especially since Muslims have a strong ab-horrence of swine. A real plus is the Adventist position regarding abstinence from drinking alcoholic beverages. That is why the anti-alcohol approach, e.g., through the *International Commission for the Prevention of Alcoholism and Drug Dependency* (ICPA), has opened doors.

The very term *Islam* involves in its meaning 'surrender' to God. Here we have another basis for dialogue—the concept of total surrender.

The notion of the Messiah, the Anointed One, the Al-Masiah, is another topic for discussion and explanation regarding what this means and implies. The Second Coming of Jesus is an important Christian belief and is also found in the Hadith, the early Muslim tradition. These are theological links, which can be explored in order to understand agreements and differences.

Buddhism

The key Buddhist concept of emptiness (shunyata), which is such an antidote to stepping on the western treadmill of goods-getting and selfishness, reminds us that Jesus called for self-denial and said that, 'Whosoever will save his life shall lose it' (Mk 8:34, 35). There should be room for fruitful dialogue.

Buddhism places great emphasis on the inner experience of enlightenment. Does this not have some relationship to what Christians call conversion? Of course, there is a difference, but there is here also a commonality. There also seems to be in Mahayana Buddhism a more open attitude and some concept of salvation, or rather enlightenment, by faith and grace, on which a relationship can be built and developed.

Taoism and Confucianism

Taoism emphasises order, nature, and simplicity, avoiding self-seeking. It is, in essence, a system of ethics affirming order. There should be useful openings here for Adventists and their emphases on obedience to God's law which orders the universe and calls for respect of parents, regard of God's creation, simple lifestyle, and self-denial in Christ.

In addition to Taoism, Confucianism is a significant system of ethics influenc-ing hundreds of millions of Chinese, though it appears to be rapidly collapsing under growing western cultural influence, especially among the youth. The tradi-tional emphasis has been on duty and proper relationships between people (e.g. husband-wife, parent-child, employer-employee). The Golden Rule (Don't do unto others what you don't want them to do to you) is underlined, giving opportunity to present the Golden Rule in its more positive Christian wording. Respect and responsibility certainly are also Christian values.

Absence of contacts

One can argue about the liabilities of the ecumenical movement, but it must be acknowledged that it has opened the doors to greater understanding of 'the other.' False stereotypes and caricatures have been removed. Perhaps one of the weak points in interfaith relations is the absence of contacts between Adventist church leaders and leaders of non-Christian religions. Contacts with such religious personalities and the *intelligentsia* of other world religions have been minimal. Withdrawing into one's own religious cocoon and the absence of leadership contacts with representatives of other religious bodies can be seen as a mark of sectarianism. This is a negative view of Adventism which needs to be proactively refuted by stepping out of isolation. The recent appointment of an assistant for interfaith relations to the president of the General Conference is a clear step in the right direction.

General principles of interfaith relations

There are some key principles of interfaith relations which should guide Seventh-day Adventists when they interact with other religions and their members.

1. High ethical standards. In meeting with believers of other faiths only the highest ethical standards are acceptable. We need to be truthful, transparent, and just *vis-à-vis* other religions. Never should Adventists knowingly make false statements regarding the teachings or official practices of other religious bodies.

2. Knowledge of culture. It is important to know the culture and history of other people and how these relate to their religion. Religion, culture and history are often closely intertwined. It is hard for people of another religious persuasion and cultures to take you seriously, if they find you both illiterate and naïve regarding what has for centuries made their civilisation tick.

3. Standing for morality. Immorality is rampant around the world, not least in western societies. Religious fundamentalists/extremists, especially in Islam, see the West, led by the United States, as promoting gross and satanic immorality. In approaching those belonging to other religions, Adventists must be seen as standing tall for morality in Babylonian societies. Morality includes both honesty and obedience, and also respect for human dignity and life. Adventists should let those they are trying to reach see that they 'are conscientious,'[10] consistent, and cooperative, and not manipulative and full of self-serving ulterior motives.

4. No material inducements. While Adventists will wish to lead others to Jesus Christ and biblical beliefs, any solicitation and subsequent conversion should never be influenced by the allurement of material inducements, gifts, or any siren song, which would make 'conversion' a sham.

---

[10] Ellen G. White, *Gospel Workers* (Washington, DC: Review and Herald Publishing Association, 1915), 120.

5. Pro-family stance. In many third world countries and religions, the family plays a dominant and all-pervasive role. Adventists need to be seen as pro-family, when anti-family forces are chipping away at the flanges of the family or even undermining the whole concept of marriage and the traditional family unit. Adventists must not be seen as endeavouring to break family ties and causing isolation, but rather as supporting, as far as possible, family linkage and respecting family needs and support.

6. Adaptability and context. In approaching adherents of other religions, it is helpful to 'adapt' Christianity in general and Adventism in particular. Adaptability is a valuable quality for interfaith contacts. In 1 Corinthians 9:19-22, Paul shows his adaptability to win from all classes of people as many as possible to Christ: though a free man, he makes himself a servant, for the Jews he conformed to their customs, as long as he did not have to violate principle. It was the same for the gentiles, that is members of other religions: he tried to make himself like them, though always conscious of his duty to God. He sums up his strategy, 'I have become everything in turn to men of every sort, so that in one way or another I may save some' (vs 22, NEB). This strategy is not practising deception, but it is helping to achieve proper contextualisation of the gospel and self. The gospel must remain the same, but its context can change. There is no point in shocking others by nonconformity to their customs in regard to dress, food preparation, terminology, and even some external and culture-related aspects of religious services. In witness or in evangelistic outreach, personal or organised, it is helpful to conform to certain customs and even perhaps prejudices, if basic principles and conscience are not in danger of being violated or compromised.

7. Establishing credibility. When approaching non-Christians (or other Christians for that matter), it is wise to first refer to 'points of doctrine on which you can agree.'[11] It is counter-productive to introduce too early possibly 'objectionable features of the Seventh-day Adventist faith.'[12] The issue is not one of 'hiding' the truth, but how to best 'reach' other faiths. It is destructive to produce the whole message immediately and burst in on another religion like the proverbial bull in a china (or China!) shop. People of whatever religion may (and probably) have been warned and given all kinds of innuendos or falsehoods about the religion that is trying to reach them.

It is a pedagogically sound approach to proceed slowly and in stages. First, you need to establish credibility and sincerity and 'dwell on the necessity of practical godliness' and sincerely 'give them evidence that you are a Christian, desiring

---

[11] Ibid., 120.
[12] Ellen G. White, *Evangelism* (Washington, DC: Review and Herald Publishing Association, 1946), 246.

peace, and that you love their souls.'[13] This can take some time, for you first need to gain the confidence of your interlocutors.

8. Flexible multiple idea approach. In dealing with other ways of thinking, one should not use only a single fixed approach, but be ready to vary and alter the manner of coming closer to the followers of another religion. The approach should be aligned to the actual circumstances to be dealt with.[14]

The issue of proselytism

So far we have not mentioned directly the issue of proselytism. It is a problem in interchurch and inter-faith relations. There are some religious groups that strongly reject proselytism. However, there is a problem of definition. There are many different meanings given to proselytism: dictionary definition (converting people from one belief to another), evangelism, corrupt witness, inappropriate methods, wrong target, self-seeking motives, etc.

It is wiser and more correct, it seems to me, to use the term *false proselytism*, than simply *proselytism*, without further definition or clarification. There is the real danger of weakening or eliminating evangelism—the lifeblood of a living, active church—when condemning proselytism, without an unambiguous definition emphasizing the pejorative aspects and meaning. The common denominators of 'false proselytism' are the use of *force*, in one of its many forms, and spreading *falsehood*.

Proper dissemination of religion

Since evangelization is a clear mandate of New Testament Christianity, what are proper methods of dissemination of faith and belief? The following seven points are based on the fourteen principles that emerged from the work of the International Religious Liberty Association's *Conference of Experts*, which met twice in Spain in 1999 and 2000.[15]

1. Witness to one's own faith experience is a most valid approach, against which it is hard for anyone to argue effectively.

2. Honesty and fairness are necessary ingredients of any evangelistic endeavour. Honesty means telling the truth, being transparent and not devious, not disseminating false information. Fairness means, for example, comparing the ideal of one's church with the ideal of the other church, not with the reality of the other church. In other words, fairness requires that you compare reality with reality, and ideal with ideal. This sounds obvious, but how many of us fall short in this connection when we make comparisons? Honesty and fairness also mean using cur-

---

[13] *Gospel Workers*, 120.
[14] *Gospel Workers*, 118, 119.
[15] See the journal *Fides et Libertas*, 2001, 85-87.

rent theological texts and statements of another religion or denomination, when presenting where they stand, not using outdated texts or unrepresentative views that lack current validity and thus have little credibility today.

3. As already stated, material inducements (a form of bribery) are not proper for evangelism. This reminds us of the 'rice Christians' in years gone by. But, unfortunately, the practice of offering gifts and other material or financial attractions can still persist in more subtle forms.

4. Cajolery and undue pressure are forms of false proselytism, and unworthy of the freedom and winsomeness of the gospel invitation.

5. Proper dissemination of the faith is not 'evangelistic imperialism.' The latter has as its goal simply enlarging one's church by gaining members from another religious group. The goal of authentic evangelization is not to diminish another group, but to spread the gospel of salvation, 'present truth,' so that conversion takes place and souls are brought to Christ and the church family of their free choice.

6. Proper proselytism/evangelism must always be based on a conversion experience coming from a conscientious conviction. Then the truth will truly provide freedom.

7. In looking at other churches, we need to recognise that 'all agencies that lift up Christ are part of the divine plan for the evangelization of the world.' [16]

The Petrine principles in witness

The issues we have discussed are really a matter of ethos and not legal code. Laws regarding proselytism and limiting evangelism are both ineffective and potentially destructive of religious liberty, and Christians should protest and oppose such restrictions. The issue is one of human—even Christian—relationships. It is not a matter of law, but of ethics and appropriate attitudes. Two basic human rights are involved: 1. the religious liberty right to practice, communicate, and teach one's religion; 2. the right to privacy and to be left alone and not be evangelised. These rights should not clash, if respect prevails for the dignity and conviction of others, and dissemination of one's faith takes place in a responsible and courteous way.

In 1 Peter 3:15, the apostle Peter provides three key principles to be kept in mind when witnessing about your faith. These Petrine principles are simple, but salutary. In essence, Peter says: Present your faith with *humility*, *respect* for the other persons, and *honesty* which provides a good conscience.

The danger of syncretism

When looking at the relationship between Christianity and other world religions, one needs to be aware of the issue of syncretism—that is, the attempted union or

---

[16] See *General Conference Working Policy* (Seventh-day Adventist Church), policy O 100.

reconciliation of diverse or opposite doctrines or beliefs. There are many people in the world today (as there have often been in history) who believe that all religions are legitimate paths to truth and salvation. They would say that the various Christian formulations of truth are relative and, therefore, quite inadequate. Christianity may be 'better,' but only to a degree, and therefore it behoves individuals and churches to find ways to synthesize, enlarge, and harmonize Christian doctrines and lifestyle with the belief systems of other religions. This is a standard postmodern value thinking. Frederick the Great's dictum nicely summarizes this view: 'Everyone is saved in his own way.' This was the world-view of the Greco-Roman civilisation in New Testament times. In contrast, the apostle Peter made the Christian view unmistakably clear: 'For in all the world no other name has been given to men but this, and it is by this name that we must be saved' (Acts 4:12, Phillips translation)! Indeed, the Christian global message is, in final analysis, that in no one else 'but Jesus Christ can salvation be found.' However, in today's catholic climate and emphasis on relativism, the syncretistic approach to religion and interfaith relations is definitely more problematic than a head-on collision with atheism, because the former appears to offer an attractive global dimension of faith, tolerance, freedom and benign human relations.

Can non-Christians be saved?
A question that is often raised, especially in evangelical circles, is whether any non-Christian can be saved. We often hear it said that one who has not heard and responded to the name of Christ cannot be saved. Furthermore, we are told that the millions that die every year and 'go to Christ-less graves' will suffer the pangs of hell-fire throughout the ceaseless ages of ages!

Seventh-day Adventists strongly disagree with this theological view. The motivation—and it is powerful—for missionary evangelism is not that without hearing and accepting the specific Christian biblical message Muslims and Hindus cannot be saved, but it is because Christ commands his disciples to be his witnesses proclaiming the good news of salvation, leading people here and now to a better and fuller life, calling people to greater light and discipleship, challenging them to respond positively to the stirrings of their conscience.

Christ: The light that lights every man or woman
In reaching out to people, of whatever religion, the following three truths should be kept in mind:

1. Not all Seventh-day Adventists will be saved.

2. Not all or only Christians belonging to a church will be saved.

3. The important Pauline principle, 'For God has no favourites ... when gentiles who do not possess the law carry out its precepts by the light of nature, then,

although they have no law, they are their own law, for they display the effect of the law inscribed in their heart. Their conscience is called as witness ...' (Rom 2:13-15, NEB). What Paul is saying is that gentiles (e.g. Buddhists or Hindus) may have no knowledge of Christ, of biblical principles as such, but through their conscience and experience, they demonstrate the operation in their thoughts and actions of the spirit and law of God, the presence of which is endorsed by their own struggles of conscience, and which condemns or excuses them. God will judge 'the secrets of the human hearts,' and any salvation will come from and by Jesus Christ, who died for every human being. Cherishing the light received and making the most of opportunities provided is 'all that is required.'[17] In John's gospel, Christ is presented as 'the true light' that comes into the world and illumines the existence of every human being for both salvation and judgement, even though men and women may not know, comprehend, or acknowledge him (see John 1:5, 9).

There is truth present in every religion, for the true light is at work even in gross darkness. However, from a Seventh-day Adventist perspective, salvation comes only in Christ, and the salvific value of religion, if at all, is in proportion to the extent it points its followers in the direction of divine truth and light, that is in the final analysis Christ.

From everywhere to everyone

For Christians there is an enormous but glorious evangelistic task to accomplish. The population of the earth increases in several regions rapidly. Ellen G. White wrote about classes of people who would need to be the object of special work during the eschatological time of the end. Maybe some of these special classes are the adepts of religions to which she herself made little direct reference during her lifetime. Since those days there has been *one key change,* summarized in the word *globalisation,* with all its problems and evangelistic potential. In this exciting context, the church now *can* and *must* go from 'everywhere to everywhere and everyone.' To buoy up God's 'evangelistic witnesses' in the global mission, there are two divine promises: the everlasting gospel will be preached *in all the world,* and *then the end will come,* as the whole world is lightened with God's glory.

Bert B. Beach. Born Switzerland. Retired. Director of the department of Public Affairs and Religious Liberty of the General Conference of Seventh-day Adventists (1980-1995). Educational assignments, departmental work and administrative experience in Italy, the United States and Great Britain. Executive secretary Trans European Division. Active in committees and societies that deal with religious liberty and interchurch relationships. Author of books and articles. Doctor of the University of Paris, 1968.

---

[17] *Gospel Workers,* 332.

From Mission Comity to Interdenominational Relations: The Development of the Adventist Statement on Relationships with Other Christian Churches

Stefan Höschele

In the year 2010, the Christian world, and especially those engaged in mission, will commemorate one of the major Christian meetings of the twentieth century, the 1910 World Missionary Conference in Edinburgh.[1] This conference was undoubtedly one of the most important gatherings of the modern missionary movement: for the first time, a multi-denominational group of more than 1,000 persons representing global Protestantism met for common strategizing, theological work, and missiological reflection.

At the same time, Edinburgh 1910 has been called the birth hour of modern ecumenism, for it is here that the impetus of the nineteenth century missionary movement began to translate into the beginnings of the Ecumenical Movement of the twentieth century. In a group representing scores of missionary organizations and quite a number of distinct church traditions, one prominent issue was naturally that of missionary cooperation. Some missions, particularly the young faith missions, were nondenominational altogether, but most organizations conducting work among non-Christians were tied to some denominational body with its confessions, church polity, and hierarchy. However, given the sheer vastness of unreached peoples in non-Christian (or at least non-Protestant) environments, Protestant workers of different societies often cooperated more easily in Africa and Asia than they would have done in Europe or North America.

Yet there were also very different cases. Between Protestants and Roman Catholics, frequently a veritable rush for mission territories occurred in the hope of securing areas in which the other would not dare to intrude. However, even when spheres of influence were recognized by governments, mutual infringements did happen—as was the case in East Africa until the early 1920s. Even before Edinburgh, thoughtful Protestant mission leaders therefore devised the *comity principle*, a missionary type of ecumenism, which implied that Protestant missionary organizations confined their activities to particular territories in order to leave the plans of other Protestant missions undisturbed.[2] After Edinburgh, comity agreements became the rule in much of the Protestant missionary world.

---

[1] This text was first presented as part of a public lecture on September 8, 2008 at Newbold College.

[2] The most comprehensive treatment of comity is R. Pierce Beaver, *Ecumenical Beginnings in Protestant World Mission: A History of Comity* (New York: Thomas Nelson, 1962).

For Seventh-day Adventists, comity was evidently a difficult issue. On the one hand, they appreciated the modern missionary movement and wanted to be part of it; after all, six Seventh-day Adventists attended the Edinburgh conference.[3] At the same time, Adventists felt that they had the final warning message to bring to the world—and the world, to them, implied both the 'heathen' and Christians of other denominations. How could they, under these circumstances, agree to cooperate with other Christians in dividing territories and enter comity agreements? But even if they did not do so, how were they going to relate to the modern missionary movement and the churches that had sparked it?

This chapter seeks to contribute to an answer to this question by exploring the history of the most important comity statement that Adventists produced in that period (for the text, see the appendix). Beyond its initial goal, this statement ultimately became crucial for Adventist thinking on ecumenism in general; it has been quoted time after time in later Adventist interchurch encounters. However, its origin and effects have not yet been investigated in any study.

The context

The Seventh-day Adventist Church entered the twentieth century as a missionary movement that had expanded to all continents and was about to enter the second third of the world's nations.[4] American Adventist missionaries served in much of Asia and South America; many Europeans were drawn to Africa and the Middle East. In most of these areas, other Christian bodies operated near Adventist mission establishments, and in some regions this fact led to significant friction, often not because the missionaries actively tried to make converts from members of other Protestant societies but because indigenous Adventist members were persuaded about the validity of their faith for their people and thus disrespected the spheres of influences that the Whites either agreed or assumed.[5] In some areas, this led to serious conflicts; in others, Adventists were actively involved in attempts to create agreements or statements to clarify and settle such conflicts.

---

[3] For more details and a critical discussion of the Adventist participation at Edinburgh, see Keith A. Francis, 'Ecumenism or Distinctiveness? Seventh-Day Adventist Attitudes to the World Missionary Conference of 1910,' in *Unity and Diversity in the Church*, ed. R. N. Swanson (Oxford, UK: Blackwell, 1996), 477–487.

[4] For interpretations of Adventist mission and missiology, see Børge Schantz, 'The Development of Seventh-Day Adventist Missionary Thought: Contemporary Appraisal,' PhD. diss., Fuller Theological Seminary, 1983, and Stefan Höschele, *From the End of the World to the Ends of the Earth: The Development of Seventh-day Adventist Missiology* (Nürnberg, Germany: Verlag für Theologie und Religionswissenschaft, 2004).

[5] Interestingly, Adrian Hastings argues that Africans seldom liked comity agreements; he reasons that rivalry between different Christian groups 'had at least the merit that it provided Africans with a certain freedom of religious choice and even standards of evaluation to judge each particular missionary package.' See Adrian Hastings, *The Church in Africa, 1450–1950* (Oxford, UK: Clarendon, 1994), 421.

The most noteworthy discussions in this regard developed in Asia. Different from Africa, where many mission societies entered late and where there were vast unentered territories even in the early twentieth century, a much greater variety of missionaries had swarmed into the various Asian regions in the century before. This translated into an increased need of coordination between the scores of Protestant societies.[6] Two cases in point were China and India. The National Missionary Council of India produced a comprehensive *Statement on Comity among Missions in India in 1916*.[7] In China, a Special Committee on Comity was appointed by the China Continuation Committee (the Chinese equivalent to national missionary councils in other countries) in 1917. This Special Committee recommended the Indian statement in a revised form, and by 1922, 115 missions had accepted the statement.[8] Adventists, however, were conspicuously absent from this group.

The second decade of the twentieth century was not only a period of war in Europe and elsewhere; for Adventists, it also signified continuing expansion of missionary activities and attempts at managing this ever-diversifying missionary enterprise. It is therefore not surprising that precisely in this decade the division structure of the Seventh-day Adventist Church was created, which effectively transferred much of the executive power and operations management to regions outside the United States. Precisely this transfer of authority also played a role in the Adventist response to the issue of comity. In 1917, the Asiatic Division of Seventh-day Adventists dealt with the issue, both in response to the discussions in India and China and because the matter was a pressing one for Adventists altogether.

The making of a statement

The way in which the most important Adventist comity statement developed is remarkable; this is why this study presents a detailed account of this development. The first reference may be found in a letter of the then Asiatic Division Vice-President, Judson S. James, in September 1917,[9] the very year that the Special Committee on Comity in China had adopted its statement. The thrust of this letter is that Adventists felt the need to relate meaningfully to other missions and missionaries. However, in the absence of a confession of faith, a church manual, and a working policy, there was no binding basis on which an Adventist position could be built except elements of a theological tradition and concepts gleaned from Ellen White and the nineteenth century founders of the denomination.

---

[6] Beaver, *Ecumenical Beginnings*, 81–110 (India) and 111–133 (China).
[7] Ibid., 97, 102–109.
[8] Ibid., 124.
[9] J. S. James—'Dear Brethren,' September 18, 1917, General Conference Archives of Seventh-day Adventists, Silver Spring (hereafter GCA) 21/1919/Comity.

James not only stressed the importance of the 'very large and important' comity question; he emphasized in particular that such a text could not constitute a *definitive* statement. While he encouraged church leaders to send their input because 'the Asiatic Division should make some sort of a declaration of principles held by our people regarding the Comity of Missions,' such a declaration, according to James, had to embody exactly this—not fixed rules, but principles. The Adventist non-creedal stance inherited from the nineteenth century Restorationist Movement certainly contributed to this hesitancy in crafting a binding text.[10]

At the same time, James's cautious attitude was connected with a good deal of missionary wisdom, which implied an understanding of the contextuality of all matters related to cross-cultural ministry. He argued that comity 'doubtless cannot be dealt with alike in all the fields. Certain rules and regulations can be followed in India that would not be practicable in China, and vice versa.' Therefore, the statement was to express what Adventists thought regarding missionary cooperation 'in this part of the world'—i.e. in Asia.[11] The same view was expressed by William Spicer, the denomination's missionary statesman, when the statement was finally voted in 1919. He commented on the action, 'I believe it is well to have these comity statements made by the local sections rather than by the Home Board. Then each field may deal with the matter as they are pressed to say something, and other fields are not affected by it.'[12] Apparently the principle of freedom in missionary practice and strategy as well as the non-creedal tradition were so important in those years that Spicer and other Adventist leaders of the period preferred to leave even a matter of such ecclesiological importance somewhat open.

This, however, did not hinder church leaders in different regions from formulating texts of their own. In India, the response to James's letter came most quickly; only two months after his request for input, the India Union Mission had created their own statement.[13] Apparently they were not satisfied with the first draft of a declaration prepared by the Asiatic Division and revised by Arthur G. Daniells,[14] then General Conference president. Daniells's text was worded in a very general way and surprisingly lacked any recognizable Adventist content; the Indian Union wording differed completely and contained a clear emphasis on the distinctiveness of the Adventist message and mission.

---

[10] On the connection between the Restorationist Movement and Seventh-day Adventism, see Stefan Höschele, 'Constructions of Catholicity and Denominational Particularity: Key Stations in the Seventh-Day Adventist Doctrinal Journey,' in *Christian Traditions between Catholicity and Particularity*, ed. Leo Koffeman and Martin Prudky (Frankfurt a.M., Germany: Lembeck, 2009), forthcoming.

[11] J. S. James—'Dear Brethren,' September 18, 1917, GCA.

[12] W. A. Spicer—[J. L.] Shaw, March 21, 1919, GCA 21/1919/Spicer, W. A.

[13] 'Statement on Comity,' November 17, 1917, GCA 21/1919/Comity; W. W. Fletcher—J. L. Shaw, October 4, 1918, GCA 21/1918/Fletcher, W. W.

[14] 'Revised Form, Comity Declaration,' n.d., GCA 21/1919/Comity.

The discussion continued but was somewhat delayed by the General Conference session in 1918 and the creation of new administrative structures in Asia in 1918–1919: the Eastern Asia Division (which included China and the surrounding countries; later it was called Far Eastern Division) and what was soon to become the Southern Asia and the Australasian Divisions (1920/1922). With all the changes in leadership and organization, the comity matter was deferred for more than a year, even though it remained an extremely urgent issue, especially in China, where Adventists were vigorously opposed by some other Protestant missions.[15] In early 1919, however, the Eastern Asia Division took it up again and voted a statement apparently drafted by Division Secretary Clarence C. Crisler;[16] its structure resembled the 1917 version, but the text included a few thoughts more in line with the statement from India. Thus, it constituted—like so many theological consensus texts—a well-crafted compromise.

In examining the 1919 statement, one can discover very quickly that this is an outstanding Adventist theological text. In fact, it might even be considered one of the most important denominational texts in the first half of the twentieth century. Pre-dating the *Fundamental Beliefs* of 1931 and the first *Church Manual* of 1932, and produced only a few years after Ellen White's death, this is probably the first post-pioneer text of public significance. While an interpretation of the text as such must be done elsewhere,[17] it is important to note that the text did not create entirely new thinking but continued along the 'friendly relations' line vis-à-vis other Christians that was already present in a General Conference resolution of 1870.[18]

---

[15] C. C. Crisler—J. G. White, November 17, 1918, GCA 21/1919/Comity. In this letter, Clarence Crisler lamented the fact that, in some parts of the interior [of China] ... there are a considerable number of missionaries of limited education and of rather narrow views who seem to have an altogether wrong conception of our methods of work.' In fact, the China Continuation Committee wanted to take serious actions against Adventists in China, but apparently this could be averted.

[16] I. H. Evans—A. G. Daniells, W. T. Knox, and J. L. Shaw, December 2, 1918, GCA 21/1918/Evans, I. H. mentions that Crisler had sent a statement draft. Crisler had been Ellen White's secretary until her death. His keen interest in administrative matters is visible in his posthumously published book *Organization: Its Character, Purpose, Place and Development in the Seventh-Day Adventists Church* (Washington, DC: Review and Herald Publishing Association, 1938).

[17] An in-depth theological analysis of the statement's theological content, like a comparison with the declaration from India and the earlier (Daniells') draft, would be desirable, but space constraints have made it impossible to include the theological part of an earlier stage of the paper in this printed version. May it suffice to mention that the 1919 statement contains an enormously missional ecclesiology, a balanced soteriology, and—somewhat hidden in this seemingly technical text—an anthropology that strongly emphasizes freedom of choice. Related to these theological concepts is an implicit doctrine of God that emphasizes both his saving activities and his demands of humans. Altogether, the statement is typically Adventist in its theological thrust.

[18] This resolution says, 'RESOLVED, that for the sake of our blessed Redeemer we desire to cultivate fraternal feelings, and maintain friendly relations, with all who name the name of Christ; and in particular with those who in common with us hold to the unpopular

The beginning of a career

It is important to note that the comity issue and this 1919 statement were large-ly a matter of regional interest at that particular time. Mainly because of certain frictions between missionaries in China, the then Eastern Asia Division felt com-pelled to publish such a text. In early 1918, the division leadership still hoped that the General Conference would make a pronouncement on the issue in its session because they thought this was beyond their own responsibility.[19] When this did not happen, I. H. Evans, the division president, expressed strong regret and al-most begged for a General Conference Committee action even in late 1918,[20] but, it seems, to no avail. Apparently, many General Conference leaders still wanted to keep out of the discussion as far as possible. Thus, there was no other way but to design a text in Eastern Asia, with the advantage that it was exactly what Adven-tists in the area wanted it to be like,[21] and the disadvantage of a somewhat lesser degree of authority, at least according to the kind of thinking that Evans's letter reveals.

Yet this presumed weakness did not take long to be remedied. The *Review & Herald* published the text in the year after it was voted, and even German Adven-tist leaders found it so interesting that they included it in their missionary maga-zine.[22] The decisive action, however, happened in 1926, when officers of the Gen-eral Conference decided to include it in their new *Working Policy* booklet,[23] where it appeared in an almost identical form. This was done without any traces of a discussion regarding the validity of a regional policy to the worldwide denomina-tion—in spite of the fact that the initial idea behind the booklet had been to collect

---

doctrine of the second advent of our Saviour near.' Business Proceedings, Eighth Annual Session of the General Conference of Seventh-day Adventists, March 15, 1870, GC Committee Minutes, GCA.

[19] C. C. Crisler—E. C. Lobenstine, March 22, 1918, GCA 21/1919/Comity. However, the war conditions hindered many missionary representatives from attending, and the session ultimately did not address comity.

[20] 'How I feel that the General Conference Committee, having had this question referred to them, should make any declaration that is to be made, and take the responsibility from local men ... In my opinion great care should be exercised in wording any declaration that is sent out. ... I trust that the General Conference Committee will make any declaration that is to be made, and have it uniform throughout the world.' I. H. Evans—A. G. Daniells, W. T. Knox, and J. L. Shaw, December 2, 1918, GCA 21/1918/Evans, I. H.

[21] John Luis Shaw, then an associate secretary at the General Conference, actually praised the statement by asserting that it 'has the advantage of having been carefully worked out on the ground with leaders of our work in China and other eastern fields. In some respects these men were better prepared to work out a Comity statement than the General Committee on this side.' J. L. Shaw—E. C. Lobenstine, August 13, 1919, GCA 21/1919/Comity.

[22] Review & Herald 97, August 19, 1920, 5–6 (1061–1062); Der Advent-Bote in der Heidenwelt, October 1920, 30–31.

[23] General Conference Working Policy (Washington DC: General Conference of Seventh-day Adventists, 1926). Cf. also Constitution, By-Laws, and Working Policy of the Far Eastern Division of Seventh-Day Adventists (Singapore, 1919).

'policies of the General Conference.'[24] Apparently the statement was deemed very appropriate and so helpful that its adoption as a global guideline did not meet any opposition.

Thus began the career of the most important text in the field of Adventist interdenominational relations. In the *Working Policy*, the statement was placed at the end of the mission section, indicating that it was meant for 'overseas' work, i.e., for missionary service in traditionally non-Christian countries. However, once the text was thus 'canonized,' it served as a reminder to all Adventists that the missiological and theological issues behind the statement existed everywhere, even in regions with a Christian background such as North America and Europe. The questions of how to view other denominations and their activities, and how to relate to them appropriately, simply could not be avoided by the growing Adventist Movement.

Later changes in the statement

The fact that the statement was included in the *General Conference Working Policy* did not mean that the text thenceforth remained exactly the way it had been conceived in the beginning. Like the 'Adventist Fundamental Beliefs', texts created in particular periods were being dealt with in a flexible way even if major parts remained unchanged. Although not every single amendment needs to be discussed (changes took place in 1977, 1988, and 1997);[25] an overall comparison of the 1919/1926 version and the current text is enlightening (cf. the synopsis in the appendix at the end of this essay).

Probably the most important modification is the title. The text had been conceived as a statement for a particular mission context; through its adoption into the *Working Policy*, it became a declaration of global validity, but its career had not yet reached the climax. This happened when the title was changed from 'Our Relationship to Other Societies' first to 'Relationship to Other Religious Organizations' (1977) and then to 'Relationships with Other Christian Churches and Religious Organizations' (1988). Now the statement had acquired a global and ecumenically comprehensive meaning. Of course there were good reasons for this modification: After the end of the traditional western missionary era in the 1960s and the forma-

---

[24] The General Conference Committee voted in its meeting of September 27, 1922, that 'a committee of five be appointed to prepare a statement embodying the current policies of the General Conference ... and that this be presented to a later Council.' See GC Committee Minutes, GCA. Of course even in those years the Divisions were regarded as *part of* the General Conference, but the relationship of Division and General Conference policies had not been defined.

[25] The major changes took place in 1988; the 1977 and 1997 modifications were more or less cosmetic. See the GC Committee Minutes of October 16, 1977; October 6, 1988; and October 2, 1997, GCA. These amendments were all made at Annual Council meetings, which regularly modify the *General Conference Working Policy* content.

tion of independent church organizations in much of Africa and Asia in the same era, the relationship to other mission societies was simply no longer a relevant issue. What was important now was how to relate to other *churches*.

Curiously, the increasing weight in the new heading is counteracted to some extent by the 1997 reformulation 'When interdivision work brings us in contact with other Christian societies and religious bodies.' Before, this sentence had been worded 'Wherever the prosecution of the gospel work brings us into touch with other societies and their work.' Thus, it may seem that there was a tendency to reduce the authority of the statement and assign its function merely to those who serve in continents or regions other than their own. This, of course, corresponded to how 'mission work' had been understood by many in the missionary movement of the nineteenth and early twentieth centuries. Moreover, the fact that the text still appears in the *Working Policy* section on interdivision employees testifies to its origin in missionary operations. In a way, the statement seems rather oddly placed in that section with its current heading, but probably there was simply no one who suggested an alternative location.

What is more important, however, is the fact that several other adaptations took place in 1988, which illustrates how a text from another era could still serve important purposes even two or three generations later and in a markedly different situation. One element that appears is 'religious bodies': Non-Christians come into focus as an analogy to non-Adventists; thus, the principles of 'Christian courtesy, frankness and fairness' apply to relations with people of all backgrounds. While this somewhat broadens the perspective, another change went in the opposite direction. The original had confessed, 'We recognize every agency that lifts up Christ before men as a part of the divine plan for the evangelization of the world.' In 1988, a seemingly minor change to 'those agencies' was probably an attempt to relativize an assertion that to some appeared too generous and sweeping.

The most significant change, however, is the addition of two entirely new sentences which sharpen a particular view of Adventist identity. The 1988 revision added '*Biblical truths in the setting of* the special message of preparation,' emphasizing that Adventists had specific teachings that distinguished them from others. Eight years after the 1980 reformulation of the denomination's *Fundamental Beliefs*, this revision made up for the lack of explicit Adventist doctrinal content and emphasis in the original. In a similar spirit of emphasizing denominational particularity, the formulation 'our policy is to make the great masses of the people our special aim in evangelistic work' was abandoned and replaced with a formulation that deleted this last bit of comity heritage from the text: 'The Seventh-day Adventist Church also acknowledges the rights of other religious persuasions to operate without geographic restrictions.'

Thus the text's career had continued more than half a century after its birth. Some modification of details occurred; at the same time, there was a great degree of stability: many of the central items—good relations with other Christians, conviction as a basic principle, no explicit comity, and a concept of commission to share the Adventist view of the gospel with people of all backgrounds, whether non-Christians or Christians—persisted. The most important aspect of the text's career also illustrates this mix of continuity and discontinuity: the comity statement had become a statement on interchurch relations.

The impact on Adventist interchurch relations

What effects did the 1919 statement and its later versions have? What was its *Wirkungsgeschichte*? After being included in an official publication of the denomination's leading administrative unit and in the absence of rival texts,[26] the statement probably *had to* make at least *some* impact on Adventist ecclesiological and ecumenical reasoning. Moreover, once it was a statement of the worldwide church, it constituted not merely a precedent but a comprehensive set of guidelines on relating to other Christian denominations everywhere. While a full account of the use of the statement would demand a study of its own, a few observations can be made here:

1. The statement and references to it appeared in a variety of Adventist publications very soon, indicating that it was well-accepted throughout the denomination.[27] Naturally, it was also included at full length in *Questions on Doctrine*, a book documenting denominational positions in the context of an informal dialogue with Evangelical leaders in North America, under the heading 'Adventist Relationship to World Missions Program'—meaning the missionary ventures of *other* Protestants. This book and the dialogue illustrated that the Seventh-day Adventist Church stood at some distance from other Evangelicals because of its particular beliefs but still desired mutual recognition as Christians and Protestants. Although the statement had not yet been updated to refer to interchurch relations in general, it provided a basis for this crucial stage in the Adventist history of interdenominational relations.

---

[26] Interestingly, the 1931 'Fundamental Beliefs' contained no general section on the church, only a section on the gifts of the Holy Spirit and its relation to the 'remnant church' (No. 19). Therefore one can argue that conclusions on the question of the relationship between the Seventh-day Adventist Church and other Christian denominations could not easily be derived from the 1931 Fundamental Beliefs.

[27] See, e.g., *Quarterly Review of the European Division of the General Conference of Seventh-Day Adventists* [hereafter QR], 3rd quarter, 1926, 2 (the European Division adopted the statement in 1926); Ernst Kotz, 'Our Work in India,' *Review and Herald*, April 2, 1931; C. C. Crisler, 'Forty Years Ago in Kansu,' *The China Division Reporter*, April–May 1933, 9; Oliver Montgomery, *Principles of Church Organization and Administration* (Washington, DC: Takoma Park, 1942), 129–131.

2. Very early some church leaders realized that the importance of the statement was not limited to missionary operations in non-Christian regions. The European Division magazine commented on the adoption of the text in 1926, 'The Statement of our Relationship to other Societies found in this issue ... applies primarily to the situation in the mission fields, yet the principles outlined are, generally speaking, of equal importance also for the homeland.'[28] The 1919 statement clearly had the potential for developing a dynamic of its own from the very beginning. Its mix of emphasizing good relations with other Christians on the one side and the urgency of sharing the Adventist message with them on the other represented the logic inherent in Seventh-day Adventist missionary operations from the beginning.

3. In most of the major documents relating to Adventist interchurch relations from the 1960s onward the 1919 statement or its revised version is referred to. Whether in dialogues such as the WCC-SDA conversations 1965–1971 and the Lutheran-Adventist dialogue 1994–1998[29] or in regional and international positions papers:[30] as a policy, the statement was commonly a major point of reference when interchurch relations were discussed. Its twofold approach of recognizing other denominations' activities and emphasizing the particular Adventist mission clearly suited the needs of interdenominational conversations.

4. As the earliest document included in the book *Statements, Guidelines and Other Documents*[31] — and indeed the only one coming from the period before 1980 — the importance of the 1919 statement was clearly recognized. Its inclusion in the book may be interpreted as meaning that the decisive and defining role of the statement was now undisputed.

---

[28] QR, 3rd quarter, 1926, 18.

[29] So *Much in Common: Documents of Interest in the Conversations Between the World Council of Churches and the Seventh-Day Adventist Church* (Geneva: World Council of Churches, 1973), 73–74; *Lutherans and Adventists in Conversation: Report and Papers Presented 1994-1998* (Silver Spring. MD: General Conference of Seventh-Day Adventists; Geneva: The Lutheran World Federation, 2000), 22; here the reference to the text is found in the final report.

[30] E.g. B. B. Beach, 'Seventh-day Adventists and the Ecumenical Movement,' Study document, released in connection with the General Conference Session, 1985; published in W. R. Beach und B. B. Beach, *Pattern for Progress, The Role and Function of Church Organization* (Washington, DC: Review and Herald Publishing Association, 1985), 100–109; 'Siebenten-Tags-Adventisten und die Bemühungen um die Einheit der Christen [1991],' *Erklärungen, Richtlinien und andere Dokumente*, CD-ROM version (Lueneburg, Germany: Advent-Verlag, 2002), 62 (a declaration voted by the Euro-Africa Division Executive Committee); *Unser Verhältnis zu anderen Kirchen, Freikirchen und Gemeinschaften*, Adventgemeinde heute 1 (Hannover, Germany: Gemeinschaft der Siebenten-Tags-Adventisten in Deutschland, 1993), 13 (a booklet issued by the denomination in Germany).

[31] Ray Dabrowski (ed.), *Statements, Guidelines and Other Documents: A Compilation* (Silver Spring, MD: Communication Department, General Conference of Seventh-day Adventists, 2005; first ed. 1996). For an analysis of these Adventist statements, see Stefan Höschele, 'An Emerging Genre: Adventist Denominational Statements and their Theological Implications,' *Spes Christiana* 17 (2006): 29–50.

Insights

The history of the 1919 statement conveys several insights, which are offered in lieu of a conclusion. One is of a general (ecclesiastical-)historical nature (1); others enlighten the way Seventh-day Adventism (2) and interchurch relations work (3), while a last observation is devoted to the question of how mission and theology are linked (4).

1. A general ecclesiastical-historical insight. It is fascinating to see *how a movement*—especially one that rejected creeds and written rules of church order—*developed a tradition* with statements that ultimately became very powerful. The 1919 statement started out as a regional product but was included in an authoritative manual of the General Conference and thus attained an official and global character just nine years after the initial discussions in China and Asia; moreover, once it had reached this status, it remained the focal point of reference whenever related issues were being dealt with.

This swift career also shows how a worldwide religious movement constantly renegotiates local varieties and concerns and its coherence on the global level. Rather than representing a top-down approach, the statement was developed in what was then the periphery in spite of some missionaries' pleas that the General Conference be involved in the wording. Not only did the statement find acceptance into the body of foundational denominational texts, it also influenced larger theological questions and administrative issues: Adventist ecclesiology, missiology, and ecumenics, i.e., the way in which Adventist future generations perceived appropriate relations with other Christian churches.

2. Seventh-day Adventism. While the overall theological importance and impact of a single text should not be overestimated, the 1919 statement still illustrates that even a short theological text often bears resemblance to the larger corpus of documents and context of thinking that it belongs to. Compared with other drafts of comity statements in the period, the 1919 statement was most representative of the mainstream Adventist position; therefore, the career of this most balanced statement—as far as the Adventist context is concerned—is not surprising.

When evaluating the statement more specifically with regard to Adventism and its attitude to other Christian churches, it reveals what seems to be an overall tendency of ambivalence in the way Adventists view and relate to them.[32] The very positive affirmation 'We recognize every agency [or those agencies] that lifts up Christ as part of the divine plan for the evangelization of the world' together with

---

[32] The one exception to this attitude is Roman Catholicism, which is viewed much more critically due to prophetic interpretations stemming from the nineteenth century; cf. 'Roman Catholicism,' in Dabrowski, *Statements*, 90–91, and Reinder Bruinsma, *Seventh-Day Adventist Attitudes Toward Roman Catholicism, 1844–1965* (Berrien Springs, MI: Andrews University Press, 1994).

the 'high esteem' with regard to individual Christians is coupled with a refusal to recognize their activities as sufficient.

3. Ecumenism. On a more positive note, this seeming ambivalence may actually turn out to be a dialectic in which every Christian denomination finds itself. While Christians *must* recognize the fact that adherents of other denominations *are* Christians—even if the criteria for being 'Christian' are disputed—almost all (except underground Christians) will adhere to a particular congregation, which also belongs to some larger network of congregations. These networks are mostly still denominations or confessional bodies of some sort, and even if they are not, they are quasi-denominations or will turn into denominational bodies after some time. Thus, almost all Christians belong to some kind of a denomination, and these denominations have to relate to one another in some way. If a denomination has a reason for existence at all, it will uphold what it deems to be its own mission while, at the same time, recognizing the good in other Christian churches.[33] These two principles may produce some tension at times but do not contradict each other. In fact, the Adventist way of embodying this dialectic may be a unique contribution to interchurch relations, and its study to ecumenics.

The Adventist model of ecumenicity that shines through the 1919 statement is a model that may actually appeal to large numbers of Christians who have no formal link to the Ecumenical Movement so far. Many of these are members of free churches, notably in the Evangelical and Pentecostal Movements. By emphasizing the necessity to build good relations between denominations even in the absence of territorial thinking and membership in organizations, Adventists provide an alternative to the common ecumenical paradigm, which strongly relies on mutual recognition based on a peculiar sacramental theology, territorial divisions, and formal membership in ecumenical bodies. Such alternative paradigms are much needed in the Ecumenical Movement, which has lamented its own stagnation for about two decades. Probably an Edinburgh conference representative of today's global Protestantism and an ensuing new birth of an ecumenism for the twenty-first century would look different from 1910 and would move in a direction that is more in line with the Adventist approach.

4. Mission and Theology. Apart from these specific observations, an overall insight concerns the way in which mission and theology, the church's action and reflection, are intertwined. Neither of the two is primary, and both are dynamic. This dynamism does not mean, of course, that there is no continuity—there definitely is much of it in the history of the statement and of Adventist interdenominational encounters, as in Christian thinking and Adventist beliefs in general. However,

---

[33] A good example of this approach is George Vandeman, *What I Like about … the Lutherans, the Baptists, the Methodists, the Charismatics, the Catholics, Our Jewish Friends, the Adventists* (Boise, ID: Pacific Press Publishing Association, 1986).

the 1919 statement and its theological thrust, which resulted from a missionary situation, is a fine example of the hermeneutical circle—or, rather, the hermeneutical spiral[34]—that connects the beliefs of a religious community to its context in addition to its holy texts. This connection implies that influences work two ways; while theology impels believers to engage in mission, it is also true that theology is created in mission. Since the development of theology in mission can be seen already in the early Christian church and even in biblical times, would it be an overstatement to say that only a theology that is connected with the mission of the church is appropriate and faithful to God?

Stefan Höschele. Born in Germany. Since 2003 lecturer at Friedensau Adventist University, Germany. Pastoral service in Germany and Algeria. Missionary service (education) Tanzania Adventist College, Arusha. Author of scholarly publications including Christian Remnant—African Folk Church: Seventh-day Adventism in Tanzania, 1903–1980. PhD University of Malawi (2005).

[34] Grant R. Osborne, *The Hermeneutical Spiral: A Comprehensive Introduction to Biblical Interpretation*, 2nd edition, (Downers Grove, IL: InterVarsity Press, 2006 [first ed. 1991]), suggests replacing the older metaphor of the 'hermeneutical circle' with a 'spiral' to indicate the dynamic nature of interpretation and understanding, which leads beyond closed circle-like systems. Evidently, this is helpful for theological hermeneutics as much as for biblical hermeneutics, and even more so for a theological hermeneutic that is informed by God's mission.

Appendix
Synopsis: *Our Relationship to Other Societies* (1919) and *Relationships with Other Christian Churches and Religious Organizations* (2005)

Sources: *Advent Review and Sabbath Herald* 97, no. 34 (1920), 5–6 (1061–1062); *General Conference Working Policy*, 2005 (Section O 100)

Our Relationship to Other Societies	Relationships with Other Christian Churches and Religious Organizations
In the desire to avoid occasion for misunderstanding or friction in the matter of relationship to the work of other societies, we, the General Conference Committee of Seventh-day Adventists for the Far Eastern Division, submit the following statement for the guidance of workers in the division:	To avoid creating misunderstanding or friction in our relationships with other Christian churches and religious organizations, the following guidelines have been set forth:
1. We recognize every agency that lifts up Christ before men as a part of the divine plan for the evangelization of the world, and we hold in high esteem the Christian men and women in other communions who are engaged in winning souls to Christ.	1) We recognize those agencies that lift up Christ before men as a part of the divine plan for evangelization of the world, and we hold in high esteem Christian men and women in other communions who are engaged in winning souls to Christ.
2. Wherever the prosecution of the gospel work brings us into touch with other societies and their work, the spirit of Christian courtesy, frankness, and fairness should at all times guide in dealing with mission problems ; and in this matter we adopt the following principles and plan of operation:	2) When interdivision work brings us in contact with other Christian societies and religious bodies, the spirit of Christian courtesy, frankness, and fairness shall prevail at all times.
a. That we recognize that the essence of true religion is that religion is based upon conscience and conviction. It is therefore to be constantly our purpose that no selfish interest nor temporal advantages shall draw any person	3) We recognize that true religion is based on conscience and conviction. It is therefore to be our constant purpose that no selfish interest or temporal advantage shall draw any person to our communion and that no tie shall hold any member save the belief and conviction that in this way the true connection with Christ is found. If a change of con-

to our communion, and that no tie shall hold any member, save the belief and conviction that in this way he finds true connection with Christ. When change of conviction leads any member of our society to feel no longer in accord with us in faith and practice, we recognize not only his right but his duty to change his religious affiliation to accord with his belief.

b. That before admitting to church membership any one who is a member of another church, every care be exercised to ascertain that the candidate is moved to change his religious affiliation only by force of religious conviction and out of regard to his personal relationship to his God; and that wherever possible, consultation be had with those in charge of the church or mission with which the applicant is connected.

c. That persons under censure of another mission for clearly established fault in Christian morals or character, shall not be considered eligible for membership in our mission until they have given evidence of repentance and reformation.

d. That an agent employed or recently employed by another church or mission or other organization shall not be employed by our church or mission without preliminary consultation with the church or mission with which the agent is or was formerly connected.

e. We advise that when setting salaries, the local mission auditing committees give consideration to the salaries paid by other missions operating in the same field.

viction leads a member of our church to feel no longer in harmony with Seventh-day Adventist faith and practice, we recognize not only the right but also the responsibility of that member to change, without opprobrium, religious affiliation in accord with belief.

We expect other religious bodies to respond in the same spirit of religious liberty.

4) Before admitting to church membership members of other religious organizations, care shall be exercised to ascertain that the candidates are moved to change their religious affiliation by religious conviction and out of regard to their personal relationship with God.

5) A person under censure of another religious organization for clearly established fault in Christian morals or character shall not be considered eligible for membership in the Seventh-day Adventist Church until there is evidence of repentance and reformation.

3. As to the matter of territorial divisions and the restriction of operations to designated areas, our attitude must be shaped by these considerations:

a. As in generations past, in the providence of God and the historical development of his work for men, denominational bodies and religious movements have arisen to give special emphasis to different phases of gospel truth, so we find in the origin and rise of the Seventh-day Adventist people, the burden laid upon us to emphasize the gospel of Christ's second coming as an event 'even at the door,' calling for the proclamation of the special message of preparation of the way of the Lord as revealed in Holy Scripture.

b. As this advent proclamation is described in Scripture prophecy, particularly as the revelation of Christ sets it forth in the terms of Revelation 14:6-14, it is commissioned that this special message of the 'everlasting gospel' which is to precede the coming of the Saviour shall be preached 'to every nation, and kindred, and tongue, and people.' While this commission makes it impossible for us to restrict our witness to this phase of the gospel to any limited area, and impels us to call it to the attention of all peoples everywhere, our policy is to make the great masses of the people our special aim in evangelistic work.

6) The Seventh-day Adventist Church is unable to confine its mission to restricted geographical areas because of its understanding of the gospel commission's mandate.

In the providence of God and the historical development of His work for men, denominational bodies and religious movements have arisen from time to time to give special emphasis to different phases of gospel truth. In the origin and rise of the Seventh-day Adventist people, the burden was laid upon us to emphasize the gospel of Christ's second coming as an imminent event, calling for the proclamation of Biblical truths in the setting of the special message of preparation as described in Bible prophecy, particularly in Revelation 14:6-14. This message commissions the preaching of the "everlasting gospel to every nation, and kindred, and tongue, and people" bringing it to the attention of all peoples everywhere.

Any restriction which limits witness to specified geographical areas therefore becomes an abridgment of the gospel commission.

The Seventh-day Adventist Church also acknowledges the rights of other religious persuasions to operate without geographic restrictions.

The Limitation of God and the Free Will and Holy Ignorance of Man: Towards an Understanding of the Plight of the Un-warned

Børge Schantz

Christians in all generations have struggled with some important issues relating to the final judgement. The promise of eternal life for the true believers who have responded positively to the call of God is plainly set forth in the Scriptures and well-understood (Ps 37:39; 1 Thess 4: 16,17.)[1] There is also evidence that those who do not accept Christ will be lost (Deut 30:15; Lk 9:25). But what about the billions who were born into the world and died without having a fair chance to hear the divine call to repentance and accept or reject the offer to be one of God's children?

This chapter will attempt to deal with the subject of the fate of the un-warned and hopefully move towards a better appreciation and understanding of the various complicated issues. These have to do with creation, the fall, man's free will, the limitations of God, successes and failures in world missions, and even the possibility that God has in some cases left us in a kind of 'holy ignorance' for our own benefit.

Creation, man's free will and God's limitations

God is the Creator, Sovereign Ruler and Owner of the universe and everything is subjugated to him. Creation is governed by natural laws instituted by the Creator with no scope for deviations. The creation of Adam and Eve, however, is an exception. Men and women were endowed with free will. This means that the Creator will not assert his power over the desires and choices of human individuals. It also implies that men and women will be held morally accountable for their actions.

> But while everything in nature is governed by natural law, man alone, as an intelligent being, is capable of understanding its requirements, is amenable to moral law. To man alone, the crowning work of his creation, God has given a conscience to realize the sacred claims of the divine law, and a heart capable of loving it as holy, just, and good; and of man prompt and perfect obedience is required. Yet God does not compel him to obey; he is left a free moral agent.[2]

---

[1] All Scripture references in this essay are from the *New International Version*.
[2] Ellen G. White, *Selected Messages* (Washington, DC: Review and Herald Publishing Association, 1958), vol. 1, 76

God wanted subjects who would voluntarily respond to his rule, love and care. Obedience to God and to the divine principles would be by their own choice, based on their love for their Creator (Gen 2:15, 17). This free will is thus the condition for human happiness.

God's gift of a free will to man had the effect that—humanly speaking—the omnipotent and omnipresent Creator and Ruler of the universe really accepted some limitations on himself. By divine choice God accepted self-imposed restraints and confinements as far as his relations with men and women were concerned. This theology of a 'limited' God is a comprehensive debate in itself that space will not allow us to explore fully. Richard Rice has dealt with it in detail in *The Openness of God*.[3]

We will for our purpose, just in human language, assume that God for the sake of mankind limited himself. The greatest example of this divine limitation is that Christ, part of the Trinity, as *the Word became flesh and made his dwelling among us* (John 1:14). God has chosen to limit his use of power and foreknowledge in order to give man the freedom to choose. Where the will of man begins the divine will of God ends. God's selfrestraint is a condition for man's liberty. In his omnipotence God could have destroyed Satan and ended his rebellion the moment it took place. However, the long-suffering God waits. God's limitation is also man's opportunity for salvation. This divine limitation means that God will never use force to effect changes in human beings. He will appeal to men and women to choose the right path. For the sake of their own happiness he wants them to use their free will to worship him as their Creator.[4]

The fall and conditions for a return to paradise

God took a risk by limiting himself. The immediate negative result of this limitation was the Fall. It had fatal consequences not only for mankind, but for the entire creation. The entrance of sin into the world, in principle, changed the divine goal. After Adam and Eve left paradise, God still wanted the new earth to be inhabited with people with a free will, desiring to be with their Creator. The change was in the manner that citizenship in paradise was to be obtained. The original plan was that the descendants of Adam and Eve would be physically born in the garden. After the fall the good Lord offered a readmission to paradise—but now to people born again through repentance and forgiveness of sins.

In other words: It was an exercise of man's use of his free will that brought separation between God and man. And it will also need an exercise of free will to

---

[3] Richard Rice, *The Openness of God* (Washington, DC: Review and Herald Publishing Association, 1980), 39-44.

[4] Børge Schantz, 'The Limitations of God,' *Adventist-Muslim Review*, vol. 2 (Autumn 1994), 1-4.

regain the status men and women lost in the original Garden of Eden. The concept that man was endowed at creation with a capacity to make choices, whether to obey or to disobey, whether to love or to reject God, is underlined in many places in the Scriptures (Deut 28:1, 2; 13-15; Isa 1:19, 20; Matt 7:24-27; Rom 6:12; Rev 22:17).

How many people were born into the world?

Exact figures as to how many people have ever lived on earth are impossible to calculate. Various attempts have been made by demographers. Applying different approaches, they suggest numbers that vary from 50 to 300 billion. The evolutionist demographers are responsible for the high numbers, while creationists—who accept a worldwide flood some 4500 years ago—put the number at between 50 and 100 billion. Both groups of demographers seem, however, at least to agree that at the time of Christ and the apostles, the world had no more than about 300 million inhabitants.[5] To be on the conservative side we will for the purpose of this chapter accept that since creation at least 100 billion persons have been born into the world. Interestingly, in 2008 a Dutch scientist calculated that 107.5 billion people have thus far lived on earth.[6]

The history of divine calls to accept the true religion

God's people, whether in Israel or in the infant Christian church, were his chosen instruments for witnessing. The outreach programmes reported in both the Old and New Testaments reveal the opportunities that were offered to the gentile nations around Israel to accept eternal life. Thought-provokingly, however, the call never really reached beyond what is termed the ancient world. The divine invitation was limited to only a few nations. It did not reach the more remote corners of the earth but only a few geographical areas in the ancient and Mediterranean world.

Throughout Old Testament times there was a constant witness to call people to use their free will to honour and serve God. From Seth (Gen 4:29) to the time of Malachi (Mal 4:5) beautiful and inspiring incidents are recorded of victory and progress. The temple in Jerusalem was the centre for the worship of Israel. It became a symbol of Judaism and the centre for outreach to the surrounding nations. However, too often the children of Israel chose to use God's blessings for their own benefit.

The zenith of the Old Testament witness to the living God came with the conquests of Alexander the Great, who ruled from Greece to India and from Turkey

---

5   Carl Haub, *How many Christians Have Ever Lived on Earth?* consulted on line at http://www. prb.org/Articles/2002/HowManyPeopleHaveEverLivedonEarth.aspx3.
6   See http://www.telegraaf.nl/binnenland/2648022/_Ruim_honderd_miljard_mensen_ooit_ op_aarde_html.

to Egypt. In this era the children of Israel experienced the tragic Diaspora (722 BC and later 598-582 BC). God, however, turned this tragic dispersion into a missionary blessing. As a result of the Diaspora Jews were found in Greece, in Arabia, and even as far as Mumbai in India. Here they were known as 'Shanwar Teli'—the caste of oil pressers who did not work on Saturdays.[7] Yet, multitudes of people, even in the ancient world then, had no knowledge of Jerusalem and the Hebrew faith. To these must be added the millions living in areas today called the Americas, Africa, the Far East and Europe. The call to accept or reject the Hebrew God was never heard.

In New Testament times, a few years after the resurrection of Christ, the first missionaries moved out of Palestine. Again, according to the records, they only reached neighbouring nations and people groups on the shores on the Mediterranean Sea. The apostle Paul became the missionary *par excellence*. He claimed that he carried the gospel to the limits of the Roman Empire—the then known world. He renders an extremely positive account of the progress of the gospel (Rom 1:8; 16:25-27; Col 1:6 and 23; 1 Tim 3:16). He preached in Arabia, from Jerusalem to Illyricum and in Asia Minor. In Europe Paul visited Greece, Crete, Italy, and perhaps even Gaul and Spain. In Athens he expressed the belief that God 'commands all people everywhere to repent' (Acts 17:30). Thus, the apostle Paul could be interpreted to report that in his time Christ, in one way or another, was made known to the 45 million inhabitants in the Roman Empire. Still, there were millions in other countries and continents in his age who never had a fair chance to hear the gospel. This means that, if we accept that there were 300 million inhabitants in the world at the time of the first Christians, about 250 million people did not hear the witness of Paul and his fellow missionaries. They went to their graves un-warned.

Facts and figures of modern missions

The story of missionary activities and their results in the 2000 years since the first Christians went out is a fascinating one. It is an account of endeavours in preaching, teaching and healing. But the biblical goal of 'bringing salvation to the ends of the earth' is still far from reached. Twenty centuries of Christian missions were not always reports of gospel victories and continual progress. There were periods with delays, with retarded and diverted activities, and standstills. Not until around the nineteenth century were serious attempts made to reach the most remote corners of the world.

Specialists dealing with so-called *missiometrics* claim that in the 2000 years of Christian missions the average percentage of people in the world belonging to the various Christian traditions never exceeded one third. Today, in 2010, the world

---

[7] Børge Schantz, *Development of Seventh-day Adventist Missionary Thought: A Contemporary Appraisal* (PhD diss., Fuller Theological Seminary, 1983), 294.

population stands at about 6.8 billion. Interestingly, this means that of all people who ever lived, when we accept the number 100 billion, 7% are alive today. Of these 6.8 billion about 2.2 billion (33%) are Christians.

With the combined efforts of as many as 4600 Christian mission agencies operated by the one-third Christians in the world, roughly another one-third of the inhabitants in the non-Christian world are exposed to the gospel call. Still remaining is a third of the world's population—more than 2 billion men and women living today—who will not have a meaningful opportunity to accept Christ. They are completely ignorant of the message of salvation and can be classified as un-reached, *un-warned* and therefore un-evangelized.[8]

Based on the assumption that 100 billion people since creation have been born into the world, a conservative conclusion is that between 30 and 50 billion people never had the privilege of hearing a call to accept or reject the offer of the kingdom of God. They went to their graves without ever having a fair chance to be invited.

Various theological positions

Most Christian traditions have accepted the missionary challenge. They are involved in attempts to reach and invite the un-warned and 'hidden' peoples. Still, world-evangelization, involving the combined efforts and missionary activities by all Christian traditions, is—as we have seen—far from reaching its goal. There are millions of hidden, unreached and therefore un-warned people living today.

Thus we are left with a burning question: How will God deal with these un-saved in the last judgement? There is a clear command to God's church: 'Go and make disciples of all nations.' However, there is no explicit biblical 'thus saith the Lord' to answer the question of the unreached. This lack of direct biblical guidance has resulted in various, often contradictory, responses by various Christian traditions. Theories are based on their interpretations of the Bible, their doctrines and even traditions. The results be can roughly classified in four main theologies: exclusivism, inclusivism, pluralism and universalism.[9]

Exclusivism

The exclusivist denominations regard not only non-Christian religions as products of fallen men who willfully rebelled against God. They also believe that confessing

---

[8] David D. Barrett, et al., 'Christian World Communions: Global Table 4,' *International Bulletin of Missionary Research* (January 2009), 32.

[9] A very useful summary of these four positions is provided by Robin A. Brace. See http://homepage.ntlworld.com/robin.brace/1theoterms.htm. Some other good resources include: Gabriel Fackre, et. al., *What About Those Who Have Never Heard?* (Downers Grove, IL: InterVarsity Press, 1995); Paul F. Knitter, *No Other Name? A Critical Survey of Christian Attitudes toward the World Religions* (Maryknoll. NY: Orbis Books, 1985); John Sanders, *No Other Name: An Investigation into the Destiny of the Unevangelized* (Grand Rapids, MI: William B. Eerdmans Publishing Company, 1992).

Christians in other traditions with their 'false doctrines' have placed themselves outside the divine conditions for salvation. There is salvation only through belief in their own specific doctrines. People outside their narrow circle are beyond the saving grace of Jesus Christ.[10]

The Roman Catholic Church claims that outside the church there is no salvation (*Extra ecclesiam nulla salus*). Scripturally, this ancient Christian doctrine is based on the metaphor of the vine and the branches in John 15; it was developed by Augustine (354-430). This means that membership in the Catholic Church is a condition for salvation. 'Membership' constitutes formal acceptance of the creeds and regular participation in the life of the church.[11]

A few Protestant Reformed churches that support the doctrine of predestination (which includes a denial of human free will) could also be classified as exclusivists as they believe that some are foreordained to salvation, others to damnation.[12]

The main texts quoted by the exclusivists are John 14:6 ('I am the way, the truth and the life; no one comes to the Father but through Me') and Acts 4:12 ('Nor is there salvation in any other, for there is no other name under heaven given among men by which we must be saved'). Other texts that are often used to support this position are Psalm 90:5; Isaiah 44:6; 45:21-22; John 6:68; 14:6; and 1 Corinthians 10:19-22. Special emphasis is given to the severe warnings and condemnations of idol worship revealed in the Old and New Testaments.

Inclusivism

Protestant and evangelical churches have responded to the questions on salvation outside Christianity with multiple solutions. A general term that covers their understanding is inclusivism—defined for our purpose as 'the recognition that one's belief system is the only true and valid one. However, beliefs of other Christians (even some world religions) contain some truth. It follows that, although the work of Christ is the only means of salvation, still explicit knowledge of Christ is not necessary in order for one to be saved.'[13] Inclusivism has several forms: *traditional* inclusivism, *relativistic* inclusivism, *private* inclusivism and *corporate* inclusivism. The general positions do not necessarily imply that salvation is available apart from Christ. It is, however, generally maintained that God is able and willing to apply the merits of Christ's work to whomever he sees fit.

The moderate evangelical inclusivists maintain a conservative understanding and attitude. The Catholic maxim *Extra ecclesiam nulla salus* is paraphrased

---

[10] Consulted online at http://www.Theopedia.com/Exclusivism.
[11] Sandro Magister, http://www.Chiesa.espresso republica.it/articolo/19632?eng=y.
[12] E. A. Livingstone, *Concise Dictionary of the Christian Church*. (Oxford, UK: Oxford University Press, 1977), 412.
[13] Consulted online at http://www.Theopedia.com/Inclusivism.

in terms of *Ubi salus ibi ecclesia* (Wherever there is salvation, there is the church). In this concept the church is a community that covers the world and is not made up of baptised professed Christians only. There also are 'anonymous Christians' who find salvation in their respective religions in, for instance, Africa, Asia and the Americas. There are even people who mysteriously, through the work of the Holy Spirit, are living, without realizing it, according to biblical principles and are humbly sensing a dependence on an unnamed divine power. The moderate inclusivists believe that those who do not know Christ, and have never been exposed to the gospel, are also under the influence and care of the Holy Spirit. They may feel a need for deliverance and may accept that there is a divine power. This will prepare them for salvation. Favourite Bible texts are Acts 14:17 ('Yet he has not left himself without testimony: he has shown kindness by giving you rain from heaven and crops in their seasons; he provides you with plenty of food and fills your hearts with joy') and Romans 2:12-16; Psalm 87:4-6; and Acts 17:26-28.

In addition, it is argued, there were individuals in the Bible from the nations around Israel who were accepted as children of God, although they were 'outsiders.' Among them were Melchizedek (Gen 14:18-20); Job (Job 1:1); the widow at Zarephath (1 Kgs 17:9-24); Namaan, the Syrian (2 Kgs 5:1-18); Ruth, the Moabite (Ruth 4:9-10) and Cornelius (Acts 10:1-48).

Universalism and pluralism

The liberal inclusivists are open to rather broad interpretations. They can be classified according to two main approaches: universalism and pluralism. Generally, their ideas fall outside what most evangelical Christians accept as the divine purposes for mankind, salvation in Jesus Christ and the main thrust of the Scriptures. Under the influence of Asian religions these theories have become popular in recent decades.

Universalists apply Christian terminology, and their theories are for that reason classified by some as a kind of Christianity. They claim biblical support for their views, maintaining that all persons and creatures are related to the divine, and will be reconciled to God. This means that all people will ultimately be saved. After all, 'God so loved *the world*.' However, some suggest that there may be those who will need a second probation, even a period in a kind of purgatory, in order to be admitted to paradise. Universalism is inclusivism on the far left.

Pluralists believe all religions are equally valid and lead to God and salvation. No religion is inherently better than, or superior to, any other religion. Christianity, Judaism, Islam, Hinduism, Buddhism and the various traditional religions have equal status. This idea of pluralism has to some extent evolved from the major Asian religions (Indian guru movements, Buddhist and Lamaistic groups). Pluralists recognize that differences in rituals and beliefs, symbols and metaphors are results of cultures. On the most important issues there are similarities in that all religions emphasize a love for divinities, a concern for fellow human beings, as well as rules for relationships.[14]

Exclusivists and the conservative inclusivists share the same limited eschatological, territorial and geographical concepts with both the Old and New Testament. Their 'theologies of salvation' only deal with, and explain, the eternal fate of people who have had a chance to hear the biblical divine invitation. The billions throughout history—who happen to reside outside the geographical outreach circle of the evangelists and therefore never had invitations to accept or reject the divine call—fall outside their scope. On the other hand, the universalists and pluralists, in their theories and theologies, take into account all who at any time or any place were born into the world.

Puzzling questions

The various positions raise relevant and important but different questions for all Christian churches that are involved in missions. The non-predestinarian exclusivists believe there is salvation in the gospel only as defined in their own doctrines. For that reason obedience to the Great Commission ('Go and make disciples of all nations'), is vital for the life of the church and its right to existence. Their 'truth' must be proclaimed. Where they succeed they will, however, have to answer serious questions from new Christians in areas of the world where Christianity only recently gained a foothold. *We* have been warned. But what about *our ancestors*? Will they have a chance of salvation, since they never heard the divine call?

The inclusivists in the moderate forms will meet other questions. How much biblical knowledge and understanding of God's plan of salvation is needed in order to be a candidate for heaven? Perhaps on an even more practical level: Why be involved in missions, when there are other ways to heaven and to salvation? These are valid questions—especially when in some cases non-Christian religions are not only regarded as target for evangelism, but when it is maintained that Christ is already present in them. With such orientations, why use effort, manpower and finances for world evangelization?

Traditions that belong to predestinarian branches of Christianity have no real urge to be involved in world-wide missions. They will witness—not to convince, but to search and find those who are already destined to be saved. They believe in the divine decree that certain people are predestined to eternal salvation, while others are eternally condemned, as expressed in the *gemina predestinatio* (double predestination). They leave it to God whom he wishes to save. Their 'theology of evangelism' conveniently takes care of the fate of the un-warned.[15]

---

[14] Brad Johnson in: http://www.leaderu.com/theology/salvific.html.
[15] Ibid.

Adventist positions

As there is a lack of implicit biblical guidance, Christians are divided in their understanding of what happens to the billions who died without a fair chance to hear the gospel call to accept or reject salvation. Disagreements are not defined solely by denominational borders. Christians in the same traditions often have conflicting views regarding the positions expressed by either exclusivism or inclusivism. This is also true for Seventh-day Adventists.

In a well-organized and detailed set of 28 Fundamental Beliefs we find doctrines that deal with gospel proclamation, salvation in Jesus Christ, the investigative and final judgement, and the resurrections of both good and evil people. However, the fate of the billions of un-warned is untouched. The Fundamental Beliefs seem to indicate that the eschatological concerns of Seventh-day Adventists are limited to people who have had a chance to hear the call from God. This really means a rather limited group in the Christian world and, to some extent, mission areas. The Fundamental Beliefs do not really reveal a concern for the fate of the lost myriads in the non-Christian world. The billions of uninvited and un-warned people are not touched on in a meaningful way in Adventist eschatology.

One result of this negligence is that Adventist church members today are turning to other sources for answers, probably influenced by both exclusivist and inclusivist theologies, or are drawing their own conclusions. The Adventist 'pioneers' on the other hand stood for the extreme version of exclusivism. They maintained that there was no salvation possible outside the 'Three Angels' Messages.' In their early history, Adventists, with their keen interest in some Old Testament laws, were experiencing, in need of, and perhaps even proud of their exclusivism. Paul in the epistles seems to indicate that in his time the badge of distinction between Jews and gentiles was based on Old Testament laws (Sabbath and dietary rules), or at least the way in which they were interpreted as a means of salvation. This isolated the Jews from others.[16] Adventist pioneers, wearing the same badge of law abidance, which isolated them from other Christians, were slow in stressing the vital point that, although we are judged by our works, we are saved by grace.

Any new revival movement with a strong remnant theology, arising in a Christian community, needs to have narrow concepts of its own calling in order to be effective fishers of men and good shepherds of the flock. A strong belief and proclamation of even minor distinctive doctrines is needed in order to survive as a separate movement amidst the multitude of Christian traditions. For a church with a strong remnant theology and an 'eternal gospel to proclaim to those who live on earth' (Rev 14:6) the exclusivist concepts are constant reminders not only to be involved in mission. It also stimulates zeal to keep its doctrines pure.

---

[16] David Bosch, *Transforming Mission* (Maryknoll, NY: Orbis Books, 1992), 156.

However, Adventists are also aware of and realize and accept that world-wide mission endeavours by the many missionary societies—including their own—are far from reaching 'every nation, tribe, language and people.' This makes part of the inclusivist option attractive. The biblical picture of God as not only the righteous Judge, but also a loving Father, provides the assurance that the Lord of missions will take care of the unreached, 'hidden' and un-warned people. In accepting this position there is comfort, perhaps even an excuse for lack of missionary involvement. Consequently, it has also become generally accepted, if not officially stated by most Seventh-day Adventists, that people in other churches who die without a full knowledge of the Advent message may also be recipients of God's grace.

The position of Ellen G. White

The writings of Ellen G. White are an important guide for Adventists, not only on practical issues but also regarding theological and eschatological issues and challenges. Studies of her views on the fate of the un-warned seem to show leanings towards inclusivism, although there are hints of exclusivism.

It is interesting that in the 1880-1910 period—the time when Ellen G. White was most active in her authorship—Protestants began to manifest a growing interest in approaches to non-Christian religions and to the question of salvation apart from Christ. Inclusivism was beginning to have a decisive influence.[17]

The following quotation has a direct bearing on the fate of the un-warned and 'ignorant':

> Those whom Christ commends in the judgement may have known little of theology, but they have cherished his principles. Through the influence of the divine Spirit they have been a blessing to those about them. Even among the heathen are those who have cherished the spirit of kindness; before the words of life had fallen upon their ears, they have befriended the missionaries, even ministering to them at the peril of their own lives. Among the heathen are those who worship God ignorantly, those to whom the light is never brought by human instrumentality, yet they will not perish. Though ignorant of the written law of God, they have heard his voice speaking to them in nature, and have done the things that the law required. Their works are evidence that the Holy Spirit has touched their hearts, and they are recognized as the children of God.[18]

---

[17] Børge Schantz, *Development of Seventh-day Adventist Missionary Thought*, 723.

[18] Ellen G. White, *The Desire of Ages* (Mountain View, CA: Pacific Press Publishing Association, 1940), 638.

Regarding the people who throughout the ages never had heard the call from God through the Old and New Testament, or through missionaries, Ellen White wrote:

> Among earth's inhabitants, scattered in every land, there are those who have not bowed the knee to Baal. Like the stars of heaven, which appear only at night, these faithful ones will shine forth when darkness covers the earth and gross darkness the people. In heathen Africa, in the Catholic lands of Europe and of South America, in China, in India, in the islands of the sea, and in all the dark corners of the earth, God has in reserve a firmament of chosen ones that will yet shine forth amidst the darkness, revealing clearly to an apostate world the transforming power of obedience to his law.
>
> ... In the depths of heathenism, men who have had no knowledge of the written law of God, who have never even heard the name of Christ, have been kind to his servants, protecting them at the risk of their own lives. Their acts show the working of a divine power. The Holy Spirit has implanted the grace of Christ in the heart of the savage, quickening his sympathies contrary to his nature, contrary to his education.[19]

These positive inclusivist statements must be balanced with some exclusivist sayings, which confirm that in the writings of Ellen G. White too there is a both/and to keep things in balance and even produce some healthy and creative tensions. In a commentary on Acts 4:12 we read:

> As Cain thought to secure the divine favour by an offering that lacked the blood of a sacrifice, so do these expect to exalt humanity to the divine standard, independent of the atonement. The history of Cain shows what must be the results. It shows what man will become apart from Christ. Humanity has no power to regenerate itself. It does not tend upward, toward the divine, but downward, toward the satanic. Christ is our only hope. 'There is none other name under heaven given among men, whereby we must be saved.' 'Neither is there salvation in any other' (Acts 4:12).[20]

On the issue of ignorance she has this interesting, but problematic, comment:

---

[19] Ellen G. White, *Christ's Object Lessons* (Washington, DC: Review and Herald Publishing Association, 1941), 386.
[20] Ellen G. White, *Patriarchs and Prophets* (Washington, DC: Review and Herald Publishing Association, 1958), 72.

I saw that the slave master will have to answer for the soul of his slave whom he has kept in ignorance; and the sins of the slave will be visited upon the master. God cannot take to heaven the slave who has been kept in ignorance and degradation, knowing nothing of God or the Bible, fearing nothing but his master's lash, and holding a lower position than the brutes. But He does the best thing for him that a compassionate God can do. He permits him to be as if he had not been, while the master must endure the seven last plagues and then come up in the second resurrection and suffer the second, most awful death. Then the justice of God will be satisfied."[21]

Healthy and creative tensions

The wavering between two positions is not necessarily a negative experience. Both theories have values, even when 'proof texts' are applied as a defence for positions. They seem to be able to co-exist and even result in healthy and creative tensions. The moderately inclusivist understanding embraces hope in the final judgement for the billions of un-warned people, while the positive exclusivist concepts are constant reminders to stay within the framework of biblical absolutes. This is specially needed when 'number game' missionaries venture into questionable areas where universalism or pluralism theories and theologies are accepted. This could be the case when it is accepted in some approaches to Muslims that the Koran is an inspired book and Mohammed a true prophet.

The Roman Catholic Church with its *Extra ecclesiam nulla salus* is firmly and unquestionably in the exclusivist corner. However, in a 1964 sermon, Joseph Ratzinger (now Pope Benedict XVI), discussed whether there is salvation outside the church and gave the following verdict:

Everything we believe about God, and everything we know about man, prevents us from accepting that beyond the limits of the Church there is no more salvation, that up to the time of Christ all men were subject to the fate of eternal damnation. We are no longer ready and able to think that our neighbour, who is a decent and respectable man and in many ways better than we are, should be eternally damned simply because he is not a Catholic. We are no longer ready, no longer willing, to think that eternal corruption should be inflicted on people in Asia, in Africa, or wherever it may be, merely on account of their not having 'Catholic' marked in their passport.[22]

---

[21] Ellen G. White, *Early Writings* (Washington D.C., Review and Herald Publishing Association, 1945), 276.

[22] Cardinal Joseph Ratzinger, in http://www.beliefnet.com/Faiths/Christianity/Catholic/2007/01/Are-Non-Christians-Saved.aspx.

In the twenty-first century even Roman Catholics are open to aspects of the inclusivist concepts.

Christian 'holy ignorance'

In general, Christians have ambivalent—even self-contradictory—solutions to questions related to the fate of the billions of un-warned and unreached people. They are, in a sense, somewhat wavering between two opinions. In the Bible there is, as mentioned, no 'thus saith the Lord' on these vital questions. There is, however, a prophecy that 'this gospel of the kingdom will be preached in the whole world as a testimony to all nations, and then the end will come' (Mat 24:14) and a command to 'go and make disciples of all nations' (Mat 28:19).

The Almighty knows the end from the beginning. He also knows human nature with its many limitations and narrow understandings. It seems that inspiration, in certain matters, allows the Bible student to live in a state of 'holy or blessed ignorance.' Various reasons could be cited for this 'holy ignorance.' The Bible refers to secret things that belong only to God and revealed things that belong to men (Deut 29:29). The evangelist John writes about people's inability to understand the truth (John 13:7), and states that human weaknesses sometimes demand silence on certain issues (John 16:12). Indeed, our limitations can hinder full comprehension (1 Cor 13:12). The apostle Paul believed that Christ would return in his lifetime (1 Thess 4:15-17). There are, undoubtedly, cases where the Lord of missions accepts that his children's perceptions of the great eternal plan of salvation remain rather limited, as men and women 'only know in part.' The knowledge of the fate of the un-warned and unreached may well be one of these areas of 'holy ignorance.'[23]

Towards a biblical solution

Some cardinal elements of the exclusivist position—such as a keen missionary zeal, the safeguarding of biblical absolutes, and maintaining church jurisdiction—have already been dealt with. The inclusivist position, on the other hand, gives us inspiration to attempt a brief outline of the main biblical arguments for accommodating an 'eschatology of the un-warned,' thereby emphasizing a comforting confirmation of God's love and justice.

There are texts in Scriptures that will provide the billions of people who never had a chance to hear the divine call with a hope of salvation. The points are based on texts in the Bible that accept ignorance as excuses, consciences as guides, and attributes of Christ as redeeming factors.

---

[23] Børge Schantz, *Development of Seventh-day Adventist Missionary Thought*, 219f .

Ignorance as an alibi

The New Testament contains references to ignorance as an excuse for not follow-ing the plan of salvation and even for not obeying the commands of God. In Acts 14:16-17 Paul and Barnabas declare that God 'in bygone generations allowed all nations to walk in their own ways.' They were permitted to follow their own rea-soning, perhaps even their own system of religion. They had not received written divine laws, and no messengers were sent to them.[24]

Paul writes in Romans 3: 25, 'God had passed over the sins that were previously committed.' The apostle is not just talking of individual sins before conversion or the sins of Israelites before Christ was crucified. The words can also be interpreted to include the sins of the world before the atoning sacrifice of Christ. This does not mean that God let these sins go unpunished. With the death of Christ, however, God also dealt with past sins. The concept of previous sins that were 'passed over' could graciously cover the transgressions of all people ever born into this world. There can be no true gospel unless there is righteousness for the ungodly.

In Athens these sentiments of Paul are applied to an audience that, although well-educated, still could be termed ignorant, at least in spiritual matters. 'In the past God overlooked such ignorance, but now he commands all people every-where to repent' (Acts 17:30). Paul is no doubt referring to the worship 'at the altar of the unknown god' (vs 23). The meaning of the phrase 'God overlooked' is not that God regarded idolatry as innocent, or the crimes and vices to which idolatry led as of no importance. However, their ignorance was a mitigating circumstance, and he often allowed the nations to live in a state of disadvantage without imme-diately coming forth in direct judgement against them.[25]

The role of conscience

All people have a conscience—understood as the ability that distinguishes wheth-er one's actions are right or wrong. It is also the attitude which informs one's moral judgment before performing any action. The Holy Spirit will not implant rules of ethics in the human mind. However, the conscience will work on what people, including those who have lived in ignorance, have personally accepted as right and wrong according to their religion and culture. The apostle Paul in Romans 2:14-16 writes:

> Indeed when gentiles, who do not have the law, do by nature things required
> by the law, they are a law for themselves, even though they do not have

---

[24]   Werner De Boor, *Die Apostelgeschichte* (Wuppertal, Germany: R Brockhaus Verlag, 1979), 259-260.

[25]   Barnes' Notes, *Commentary on Acts of the Apostles* (Electronic Database. Copyright (c) 1997 by Biblesoft).

the law, since they show that the requirements of the law are written on their hearts, their consciences also bearing witness, and their thoughts now accusing, now even defending them. This will take place on the day when God will judge men's secrets through Jesus Christ, as my gospel declares.

Romans 2:9-16 can be interpreted to mean that the Holy Spirit will work on everyone's conscience or concepts of what is right and wrong. These notions can be based on reason, traditions, observations and even religious laws on murder, theft, adultery, honouring parents, etc. This text applies to those unfortunate billions who have never had a verbal or scriptural revelation of divine rules for life and of God's plan of salvation.[26]

This position does not imply that salvation is available apart from Christ. It reveals that God is able and willing to apply the merits of Christ's work to whomever he wishes and sees fit. Outside the framework of Christian communities people have the hope of eternal life as a result of an 'obedience-unto-life' principle. They may have experienced the divine presence in nature: 'For since the creation of the world his invisible attributes are clearly seen, being understood by the things that are made, even his eternal power and Godhead, so that they are without excuse' (Rom 1:20-21).

The Christian who transgresses the law can receive forgiveness when he/she makes a confession. Obedience to the law of conscience, insofar as it coincides with God's law and a fundamental knowledge of the absolute difference between good and evil, will in the case of the gentile be looked upon positively on the day of judgement. Man has no control over the voice of the conscience. Conscience is an uncompromising witness.[27]

The attributes of Jesus Christ

Scripture ascribes important attributes to Jesus Christ, a member of the Trinity, that vividly describe his intimate, loving and decisive role in the redemptive process. Jesus Christ is credited in the Bible with the following divine roles: God (Mat 28:16-18); Creator (John 1:3); Sustainer (Col 1:17); Lawgiver (Jas 4:12); Saviour (Acts 4:12); Advocate (1 Tim 2:5); and Judge (2 Tim 2:4).

'For God so loved the world that he gave his one and only Son, that whoever believes in him shall not perish but have eternal life. For God did not send his Son

---

[26] Werner De Boor, *Der Brief an die Römer* (Wuppertal, Germany: R Brockhaus Verlag, 1975), 72f. A. M. Hunter, *The Epistle to the Romans* (London, UK: SCM Press, 1955), 36-37, Werner De Boor, op. cit., 36-37.

[27] D. A. Carson et al., *New Bible Commentary. 21ˢᵗ Century Edition* (Leicester, UK: InterVarsity Press, 1994), 1122. Barnes' Notes, *Commentary on Romans* (Electronic Database. Copyright (c) 1997 by Biblesoft).

into the world to condemn the world, but to save the world through him' (John 3:16-17). In God's plan of salvation it is the Lawgiver who takes the penalty for the lawbreaker, whom he created. The Saviour is the Judge but also the Advocate for the sinner. And these divine characteristics are applied in a loving service and divine desire for the redemption of mankind, which includes the un-warned, un-reached and unevangelized wherever and whenever they lived. They also are the receivers of God's love and justice.

This outstanding love was illustrated in an sublimely exalted manner at the crucifixion when Christ on the cross interceded for the Roman soldiers with the words: 'Father, forgive them, for they do not know what they are doing' (Lk 23: 34).

The soldiers were gentiles from the 'nations.' In his prayer he found the only possible excuse for their cruel acts, namely, their ignorance. The Advocate and Judge manifested his saving qualities for his creation. He showed the compassion of his heart. He implored God to pardon them and cites the only possible excuse — ignorance — that could be found for their ruthless acts. The plea for pardon was uttered for people who in their cruelty even went beyond the stipulations of the harsh Roman criminal laws.

This Jesus Christ is the Saviour of all mankind. He loves the un-warned. The same plea expressed in divine love for the Roman soldiers will also be made for those people who never had a chance to hear about his salvation.

Our God who is righteous is also love. Through Jesus Christ God accepts the sinner, not as a criminal, but as a son he loves.[28] Therefore we can with confidence leave the billions of people who never heard about Jesus Christ in the love and care of the Creator, Lawgiver and Judge. For he is also our Advocate and our Saviour.

Børge Schantz. Born in Denmark. Retired. Founding director of the Seventh-day Adventist Global Centre for Islamic Studies, 1987-1996. Pastoral, evangelistic, teaching and admin-istrative experience in Denmark, Faroe Islands, Sierra Leone, Nigeria, Lebanon, Cyprus, USA and Great Britain. Author of books and articles. PhD, Fuller Theological Seminary, USA, California (1983).

---

[28] William Barclay, *The Letter to the Romans* (Edinburgh, UK: The Saint Andrew Press, 1972), 56.

The Nimble Foot

Sigve K. Tonstad

The city of Trondheim is small by international standards. With a population of 168,000, no high rise buildings, and a lush wreath of green on the hills to the south, a visit down-town poses little risk to the small-town feel. Within Norway, however-er, Trondheim is large enough to make it the third largest city. It is located almost exactly in the centre where the country narrows, on the southern edge of the wide Trondheimsfjord. The river Nid courses through the city in sweeping and exaggerated loops before emptying into the ocean. According to *Wikipedia*, the word *Trond* means 'a good place' and *heim* means 'home,' the name supporting the claim to which most of the inhabitants would subscribe. It is 'a good place to live,' better yet, 'a good home.'

Trondheim's history makes up for of what it lacks in numerical clout. Under the name Nidaros, Trondheim was until 1217 the seat of the king and the capital of Norway. Saint Olav (d. 1030), revered as a martyr and one of Norway's first Christian kings, is buried there. His burial site is hallowed by the Nidaros Cathedral, one of the largest and finest Gothic cathedrals in Northern Europe, rising with imposing grandeur in the rustic and inconspicuous down-town area. The city became the northernmost archbishopric of the Roman Catholic Church in 1151, a distinction it retained until Norway turned Protestant in 1537. That year, Olav Engelbrektsson, the last archbishop, fled for refuge to the austere Munkholmen, the small island located in the middle of the fjord, easily visible from the city.

Someone concerned with matters of church and Christianity will find many things of interest in Trondheim. I therefore hasten to hope that the reader will not feel misled if I propose to pay Trondheim a visit for a different and more worldly reason. Trondheim's main claim to fame within Norway and all over Europe to-day is neither the Cathedral nor its outstanding Polytechnic University. That reason is found at Lerkendal, the city's soccer stadium, and in the city's soccer team, Rosenborg. And a huge claim it is.

In the 1990s and well into the new millennium, Rosenborg won the Norwegian soccer league thirteen years in a row. Fielding largely home-grown players, the team went on to 'eat cherries with the big ones,' as the saying goes in Norway. Defeating the odds, Rosenborg outshone other Scandinavian teams by a wide margin, competing neck and neck with rich and glamorous European teams in the European League of Champions, year after year performing in a manner quite unprecedented in the history of European soccer. In one image that is now enshrined in the halls of soccer lore, the team from Trondheim in 1996 beat AC Milan, one of Europe's wealthiest clubs, on the latter's home turf, eliminating it from the play-offs. The club's owner, the current Italian Premier Silvio Berlusconi, sat in the stands. Immaculately dressed as always, the tycoon saw his team come up short against Rosenborg, the latter team led by a dishevelled coach dressed in his trademark and expectation-lowering parka.

In 1996 the man in the parka and his team were only at the beginning of out-performing a number of the most jaded powerhouses of European soccer. I wish to explore this phenomenon and the lessons it may hold. Before we do, however, I must explain the title of my essay.

Just past the middle of the spectacular run, Nils Arne Eggen, the man in the parka, wrote a book in which he explains the success of his team. In Norwegian, the title of the book is *Godfoten*, with the subtitle, *Samhandling—veien til suksess*.[1] *Godfoten* means 'the good foot,' but the literal translation fails to convey the full meaning of the term. Translating it 'the *best* foot' is more to the point, or even as 'my favourite foot,' the latter rendition preserving the endearing flavour. Better still, I believe, is the translation I have chosen, *The Nimble Foot*. The subtitle is slightly more straightforward. The author does indeed call for *Interaction*—hailing interaction as *the Road to Success*, but this, too, falls short of what the subtitle means in Norwegian. *Samhandling* is not just *inter*action. It is better explained as *coordinated* action or as *orchestrated* action. It is my self-designated assignment to put some lessons of *The Nimble Foot*, a piece of contemporary Norway, before the reader of this *Festschrift*.

The Principles of *The Nimble Foot*

Nils Arne Eggen, the author of *The Nimble Foot*, is a volatile figure, intense and en-thusiastic in ways that belie the image of Norwegians as a dour, soft-spoken, and unflappable breed. Americans who are familiar with Garrison Keillor's portrait of Norwegians in his *Lake Wobegon* series should be warned. Eggen does not fit Keil-lor's stereotype by a wide margin. To say that he is colourful and temperamental understates the facts. Eggen is high-voltage and explosive, extremely quick-witted, an extrovert who at times seems to have no filter, a man who says what he thinks and who hardly thinks anything that he does not say. It is possible, of course, that the public persona is a calculated projection, an image cultivated because it serves Eggen's overriding goal. That goal, to be sure, has been to win soccer games with Rosenborg.

And yet there is an earthy wholesomeness to Eggen's winning ways, as if to make it clear that soccer success must not be bought at the price of sacrificing per-sonal integrity. Eggen takes care to preserve his connection to his rural roots in

---

[1] Nils Arne Eggen, *Godfoten: Samhandling—veien til suksess* (Oslo, Norway: Aschehoug, 1999).

nearby Orkdal, where he still has his home. He reveres his upbringing, beginning with recollections from World War II and the immediate postwar years. His outlook is egalitarian, almost militantly so; he embodies an ideology that is vehemently anti-snobbery, he frowns on the self-conceit of the divas of the European soccer élite and their tendency to hoard privileges that are actually the fruit of many people's labours. If he is committed to excellence that is second to none, it is because he finds his role models in the rural community in which he grew up; in his father and mother and other people in his village who modelled the integrity, perseverance, and selflessness that are the ingredients in his own recipe for success.

By education Eggen holds an advanced degree in Norwegian literature and pedagogy, having practiced both in the classroom. He can recite Norwegian poetry with ease, and he often quotes Ibsen verbatim when he wants to make a point. Again, however, his humour and self-deprecating demeanour may be intentionally misleading without being insincere. All his talents, perhaps his weaknesses, too, have been harnessed for the goal of making Rosenborg a winning team.

Among the ideas Nils Arne Eggen singles out as basic to Rosenborg's success in the field of soccer are three that may be relevant for a church that is groping for ways by which to make its efforts a success. These principles, stated mostly in soccer terminology, are (1) the principle of playing to win; (2) the principle of strategic preparedness; and (3) the principle of orchestrated action.

1. Playing to win

It might seem like a moot point to say that Eggen's team is playing to win. Does not every team enter the field with the goal of winning? On the surface, the answer is yes, of course. But below the surface there is another story. Rosenborg may take the field against any team within Norway with the expectation of winning, and it has thirteen consecutive league trophies to prove the point. The team cannot, however, travel to the soccer capitals of Europe with the same expectation. When Norwegian teams in the past have ventured out to face the brand-names of European soccer, the implicit goal has been to play so as not to lose.

There is a difference. An explicit winning strategy has been out of the question when the team by all accounts is up against a superior opponent. Dearth of talent and lack of resources make a defensive strategy the most prudent course of action. According to the accepted wisdom, Rosenborg, like all Norwegian teams, ought to concentrate on playing defence when it goes abroad. It must do everything in its power to disrupt the other team's formations. The plan of action must be *destructive* rather than *constructive*. Playing compact defence, hoping by hook or by crook to keep the other team from scoring goals, the plan is to ride out the storm. If by some stroke of luck there is an opening on the other side, the weaker team might be able to launch an occasional counter punch. The key ingredient, nevertheless, its mentality if not the articulated strategy, is survival.

Nils Arne Eggen and Rosenborg decided to go against the grain of established wisdom. He instructed his team to pursue a strategy of offensive play even against reputedly superior continental teams. A strategy of not losing was not enough; *his* team would play to win, and it would play to win no matter how imposing the opponent. Again, eschewing the notion that a team from Norway must practice the soccer of destruction, Eggen insisted that his team, like the best of teams, would play constructive soccer. They would win on the merit of an offensive strategy, or they would not win at all.

The experts were doubtful, pointing to the fact that Rosenborg did not have the human talent and the resources to match the big teams in Europe. This was true, and it remains true. At the beginning of the Eggen era, Rosenborg recorded lopsided losses that seemed to prove the pundits right. But Eggen refused to be deterred. What his team lacked by way of individual skills, a deficit he was quick to acknowledge, it would make up for by taking the strategy of *the nimble foot* a step further.

2. Strategic preparedness

It may seem odd that a person of strong social democratic beliefs like Nils Arne Eggen should emphasize individual discipline and skill to the extent that he does, but these are nevertheless key ingredients in his approach to Rosenborg. There is no substitute for sustained, individual effort. Eggen and his associates would seek out the best talent in the immediate region and beyond, and they would bring the talent to Rosenborg much like other organizations that are determined to improve their performance. The coach would be second to none in encouraging the player to improve his skills, and his organization would, more than other teams in Norway, lead the way in providing the framework within which individual improvement could be maximized.

In this respect Eggen's philosophy resembles the thinking of another exceptional leader in Norway. Knut Schrøder, a specialist in Ear-Nose-and-Throat-surgery and for many years the chief executive officer of the University Hospital of Tromsø in the far north, states his view of organizational improvement this way: Many organizations, he says, live by the ideology of *strategic planning*. They try to envision the future, and the leaders do their best to produce successful prescriptions for the future they envision. Schrøder's ideology, by contrast, as the leader of a medical institution, must for obvious reasons be different. Medicine is a field in constant change, developing faster than any one individual can imagine or anticipate. In order to keep up in this field a strategy of strategic planning is doomed to fail. One can hardly make successful plans for a future that is not known.

The alternative, says Schrøder, is *strategic readiness*. Where the strategic planner places his confidence in his or her *plan*, the one who lives by the law of strategic readiness places his or her confidence in *people*. Human preparedness is the watchword; quality is not found in the plan but in the people. Preparedness on the level of the individual is the key. The prepared person will know what to do in the changing situation in ways that the strategic plan cannot envision or anticipate. The strategic plan will time and again find itself hopelessly outdated and outmanoeuvred by changing circumstances.

Moreover, where the strategic plan puts confidence in the wisdom of the few, strategic preparedness lives by the wisdom of the many. It is a participatory form of leadership, entirely dependent on the input from the members of the team. Indeed, it is precisely from the acknowledgement of *not* knowing that strategic preparedness gets its strongest argument. From the awareness of *not* knowing those who live by the logic of strategic readiness seek out people who know or commission them to go forth to discover what needs to be known.

3. Orchestrated action

On the individual level, Trondheim's Rosenborg cannot compete with the powerhouses of European soccer. Matching player for player, hardly anyone on the Rosenborg team will have the level of skill needed to play for the top teams in Europe. Where there is an exception, and there have been some, the player has already been enticed by a wealthier club abroad.

But soccer is a team sport. Rosenborg has excelled as a *team*, making up for individual shortcomings by paying attention to internal team dynamics more than better endowed teams have found it necessary to do. No sentence encapsulates the philosophy of *The Nimble Foot* better than the following: '*When you enter the field you must play to the full measure of your own potential. But it is even more important to enter the field with the purpose of making your fellow players play well.*'[2]

Making *your fellow players play well*? What does this mean? How does one do it? At Rosenborg, this means that each player must be profoundly aware of the strengths as well as the weaknesses of his team mates. Playing to make the other player do well means that the ball is served to the next person in a way that corresponds to his strengths. His weaknesses and lack of skills must be avoided. Rosenborg's success is to a large degree the result of orchestration of the players' strengths and the simultaneous avoidance of their weaknesses. Again, only when the players know each other well, and only when they perform to enhance the strengths of their team mates, will they be successful against teams that can afford better endowed and better paid individual players.

Eggen features Jahn Ivar 'Mini' Jacobsen as an example. This diminutive and entertaining man from the north of Norway would by international standards be a mediocre player. But when his team mates serve him the ball in the areas of his strengths, right in front of him, and rarely high balls in the air, he is fast as lightning,

---

[2] Eggen, 226.

excelling on the level with the very best. If played to in areas of his weakness, Mini (his nickname because of his small stature), will be inhibited, and repeated failure to perform will make him uptight. At Rosenborg, however, he has flourished and has even acquired skills that were notably absent at the beginning. Eggen says that when Mini came to Rosenborg in 1988, he referred to himself as the *Baron of the Air* in order to pre-empt concerns about his lack of skills with respect to heading the ball. As he gained confidence, he became an able header, too, qualified for a pilot's license, says Eggen, 'at least for small aircraft at lower altitudes.'[3]

This part is *Godfoten* in a nutshell because the concept of *The nimble foot* requires interest in the other players on the team, awareness of the other players' strengths and weaknesses, and commitment to play in a way that helps team mates excel.

In search of *the Nimble Foot* in the Seventh-day Adventist Church

This introduction to Norwegian soccer must now give way to an inquiry into the state of the church to which Jan and Kari Paulsen have devoted a lifetime of service. How can we translate (1) the principle of playing to win; (2) the principle of strategic preparedness; and (3) the principle of orchestrated action into resources for the the church? What cues might we want to take from the worldly game of soccer to help us in a vastly more important spiritual enterprise? In my view there is a lot to learn.

1. Playing to win.

In the soccer parlance of Nils Arne Eggen, playing to win marks a shift from a negative to a positive mission. While the accepted wisdom in Norwegian soccer has clung to a defensive posture, attempting to snatch victory from the jaws of certain defeat by tearing the opponent's play apart, Eggen proposed to win by playing a positive game. Playing not to lose, as we have seen, was not enough. Forcing the other team to lose also fails to state the vision. Rosenborg would take an offensive stance; *it would believe in itself,* and it would go forth with a constructive and not a destructive plan of action.

I see a similar vision articulated by Ellen G. White for the Seventh-day Adventist Church long ago. Her subject is the church's relationship with other bodies of believers, in this instance the Roman Catholic Church.

> This message must be given, but while it must be given, we should be careful not to thrust and crowd and condemn those who have not the light that we have. We should not go out of our way to make hard thrusts at the Catholics. Among the Catholics there are many who walk in all the light that shines upon them, and God will work in their behalf.[4]

---

[3] Eggen, 219.

What is this but a shift in emphasis from negative to positive, from a destructive to a constructive conception? The notion of making 'hard thrusts' is one that could well be applied to a soccer team that tries to discomfit the other team. Here it relates to how a church engages another body of believers. And the message could not be clearer: *Don't do it that way*; don't play a game of destruction! Indeed, there is an implicit criticism of the way the church has played its game and a call to change the terms of engagement.

> We may have less to say in some lines, in regard to the Roman power and the papacy, but we should call attention to what the prophets and apostles have written under the inspiration of the Spirit of God.[5]

Having 'less to say in some lines' is an interesting formulation, a subtle, muted rebuke, and yet it signals a change of direction and emphasis quite like the foregoing statement. Playing to win is not the same as playing not to lose; playing offence is not the same as relying on a defensive strategy; playing a constructive game is not the same as concentrating on disrupting the other side's play. A team's merit is not proven by the demerits of the other team; in soccer a team that puts most of its efforts into disrupting the opposing side quickly earns the contempt of the people in the stands. Playing not to lose may result in a winning score, but it may nevertheless lead to loss of standing.

'Brethren,' Ellen G. White writes in a touching personal appeal, 'I feel hurt when I see that so many decided thrusts are made against the Catholics.'[6] This suggests not only a rebuke to a strategy that is unfair and counter-productive but also an author who is capable of putting herself in the shoes of those who are at the receiving end of the attack. A negative approach will fail; 'there is such a thing as shutting the door in their faces as they are about to enter.'[7]

In Norway, the decision on the part of Rosenberg to play a constructive game was a decision not to take the road of least resistance. It meant raising one's own game to a new level, developing qualities that had not been part of the team's tradition. It also posed a challenge to traditionalists, the people who were used to a certain style of play and who could not envision victory by any other means. This is a hard sell in the context of the *aficionados* of soccer, and it is even harder in religion or in politics.

---

4   Ellen G. White, *Testimonies*, vol. 9; *Counsels to Writers and Editors* (Nashville, TN: Southern Publishing Association, 1946), 63.
5   White, *Letter* 57 (1896); *Counsels to Writers and Editors*, 65.
6   White, *Letter* 20 (1896); *Counsels to Writers and Editors*, 64.
7   White, *Letter* 20 (1896); *Counsels to Writers and Editors*, 65.

Has the call to Seventh-day Adventists to become more positive and constructive toward another body of believers been heeded? Should there be a similar call
with respect to other religions? More than one century ago, revered interpreters
of the prophecies of Revelation claimed to find a reference to Islam in Revelation's
fifth trumpet. The rhetoric of these interpreters is likely to raise some eyebrows.

> Like the noxious and even deadly vapors which the winds, particularly
> from the southwest, diffuse in Arabia, Mahometanism spread from hence
> its pestilential influence—arose as suddenly and spread as widely as smoke
> arising out of the pit, the smoke of a great furnace. Such is a suitable symbol
> of the religion of Mahomet, of itself, as compared to the pure light of the
> gospel of Jesus. It was not, like the latter, a light from heaven, but a smoke
> out of the bottomless pit.[8]

Long before the time of television and air travel, when the Muslim world seemed
far away and quite irrelevant, there was neither the incentive of public relations
nor the impulse of generosity. 'Noxious and even deadly vapors;' 'pestilential influence,' 'smoke out of the bottomless pit;' so much for a religion that in the estimation of these interpreters could be dismissed as a message straight from hell.

A century later, the aura of risk-free remoteness persists in yet another critical view, this one, too, claiming support in the prophecies of Revelation. Islam is
again depicted as a religion bereft of redeeming features.

> The blast of the fifth trumpet was fulfilled in the rise and progress of the
> Arabs. Arabia has been called 'the pit of the abyss,' because of its deserts
> and empty areas. It was here that Mohammedanism arose and spread like
> 'a smoke.' This false and fanatical faith threatened at one time to obscure the
> light of the gospel.[9]

No harm might ensue by calling Islam 'this false and fanatical faith' in earlier
years before its rise of western consciousness. At that time there was no need to
fear Muslim retaliation against western high-handedness whether in the arena of
politics or with respect to interpretation of the Bible. It is a venture of considerably

---

[8] Alexander Keith, *The Signs of the Times*, 3rd ed. (Edinburgh, UK: William Whyte and Co.,
     1833), 299; see also Uriah Smith, *Thoughts, Critical and Practical, on the Book of Daniel and the
     Revelation* (Battle Creek, MI: Review and Herald Publishing Association, 1882), 617; idem,
     The Prophecies of Daniel and the Revelation (Nashville, TN: Southern Publishing Association,
     1944), 497.
[9] Roy Allan Anderson, *Unfolding the Revelation* (Mountain View, CA: Pacific Press Publishing
     Association, 1974 [orig. 1953]), 89-90.

higher risk to see the statement repeated much later,[10] at a time when the distance between the Muslim world and the West is rapidly shrinking. The condescending view and negative colourization of Islam bear the marks of distance and detachment, let alone an attempt to win a hearing among adherents to the Muslim faith. Both of the statements featured above belong to the category of destructive engagement.

The late Robert Darnell, probably the foremost Adventist student of Islam to date, devoted his career to a new approach to Muslims. He and his wife Mary spent many years as missionaries in the Middle East, learning first hand that the traditional paradigm of confrontation and destructive play was failing. By acquainting himself with the spiritual aspirations of Islam, Darnell concluded that the traditional view was fruitless and theologically untenable. He urged the churches instead to have a dialogue with Muslims on the foundation of mutual respect and understanding, a transformation of outlook not unlike Ellen G. White's call for a new attitude toward Roman Catholics. By contextualizing his witness, Muslims would come to a better understanding of God from within their own context. In this process Darnell did not see himself representing a fixed point around which other entities were moving. Rather, his point was moving, too, particularly in the sense that he did not see his witness located within an impregnable Fortress Christianity. The witness advocated by Darnell and his small circle of associates in the Middle East was a constructive vision. He, the Seventh-day Adventist, would abandon the defensive posture and the security of his fortress, embracing instead the engagement and the witness of the itinerant believer. He would be a pilgrim living in tents, joined in dialogue with other believers actual and potential across the lines that divide, whether the divide be ethnic, political, or religious.[11]

Perhaps Ellen G. White's call to Adventists to avoid 'hard thrusts' at members of the Catholic faith and her prediction that Adventists might have 'less to say' about the Roman Catholic church should be extended to other groups, as well. 'Brothers and sisters,' I hear her say, 'I feel hurt when I see that so many decided thrusts are made against the Muslims.'[12]

Selective realignments, whether with respect to Roman Catholics or Muslims, will in the long run only be piecemeal improvements. In order to move from a defensive to an offensive mode of operation, and in order to work along the lines of *The nimble foot*, a more profound re-thinking may be necessary. As Seventh-day Adventists, we have for some time thought of ourselves as *the remnant church*.[13]

---

[10] I am inclined to believe that the view expressed in the 1974 edition reveals a failure of redaction rather than a matter of conviction.

[11] See Sigve Tonstad, 'A Blessing in the Midst of the Earth: Traveling the Prophetic Highway in Isaiah,' *Spectrum* 34 (2006), 46-53.

[12] White, *Letter* 20 (1896); *Counsels to Writers and Editors*, 64.

[13] Ellen G. White, *The Remnant Church* (Mountain View, CA: Pacific Press Publishing

Has this notion become a liability? Is the concept of *the remnant* the ideological bottom line of a posture that is defensive in its default position? I do not mean to suggest that the notion of the remnant is alien to the Bible or to intimate that we should not aspire to be part of what the Bible describes as the remnant.[14] It is rather that a 'remnant' mindset and self-understanding seem prone to settle for the *status quo*; the one who belongs to the remnant has arrived irrespective of what happens in the church or in the world; *remnant* as a state of existence lacks the incentive and the means to critique and correct itself. It is desirable to be part of the remnant as to the final outcome of things, but it is hazardous to a person's spiritual vocation.

Aside from the fact that the remnant idea has lost resonance in a pluralistic age, sounding exclusivist and self-congratulatory, it has a static connotation. 'The remnant' is the residue that is left when the struggle is over; it conveys a sense of mission accomplished that could be as ill-fated as other premature declarations to this effect in recent memory, the motif suggesting a group that is leaving rather than a group that is engaged. I would like to suggest a complementary, perhaps an alternative, vision: We should aspire to be a *catholic* church as much or more than we seek to be 'the remnant.' To adopt the catholic aspiration might be a transformation like the one that took place in Rosenborg—a move from a defensive to an offensive mode of operation. A catholic aspiration conveys a commitment to embrace the world, to feel its hurt, and to minister to the world's needs in its messy and complex entirety. Where no failure, apparent or real, need upset the sleep of the person who sees herself as a member of the remnant, no success, apparent or real, will be sufficient to make the person who embraces the catholic aspiration believe that the work is done.

Let me clarify this suggestion with two circumscriptions. No, I am *not* suggesting that we should be a *Roman* Catholic Church, with the imperial and hegemonic connotation that still adheres to the Roman connection. No, I am *not* implying that we should put away all thought of being part of the biblical remnant. But I am proposing that the remnant *motif*, as a vocational vision, is a depleted resource. It is not sufficiently descriptive of the task at hand because the struggle is *not* over, the mission is *not* accomplished, we have *not yet* shared God's 'eternally valid message' with 'those who live on the earth—to every nation and tribe and language and people' (Rev 14:6).

Association, 1950); Charles Teel, ed., *Remnant and Republic: Adventist Themes for Personal and Social Ethics* (Loma Linda, CA: Loma Linda University, Center for Christian Bioethics, 1995). It is well to be reminded that Ellen G. White, though invested in the subject, does not authorize a book to be published in her name. One can easily envision compilations of her writings that might conceive the church in different terms.

14 Cf. Gerhard Hasel, *The Remnant: The History and Theology of the Remnant Idea from Genesis to Isaiah* (Berrien Springs, MI: Andrews University Press, 1974).

Let me attempt two suggestions as to what a catholic vision might entail in practical terms. The suggestions are not original; they are embedded in our legacy and partially actualized at the institution where I am teaching. First, at Loma Linda University, many students attend who are not defined by us or who do not define themselves as members of 'the remnant.' They may belong to other bodies of believers or to no body at all. We welcome them, and we do our best to equip them for a mission of healing in the world. They are *our* students, and we strive to make them feel that our school is *their* university. And they do deliver beyond our fondest expectations, some going where faculty or students in the 'remnant' category might fear to tread. Let Aimee Murray, a recent graduate of Loma Linda University's School of Public Health, serve as an example. I had the privilege of having her in my class on *Biblical Ethics* shortly before her graduation. Aimee is now ministering to drought-stricken children in Ethiopia, far from the amenities of western civilization. Who will deny that Aimee is part of fulfilling *our* mission, or, better yet, who will deny that the mission she is fulfilling is truly a world-embracing and catholic mission inspired by God? I wish to be part of the remnant, of course, but Aimee's sense of calling makes me want even more to be part of her commitment to serve a world in need. I see no meaningful definition of 'the remnant' that does not include Aimee.

Second, Loma Linda University trains health professionals. This is not a sideshow in a catholic conception of the task before the church, whether we envision that task in biblical terms or in terms of our own historic legacy. All we need to do to become truly catholic in our vision is to revive our commitment to what Ellen G. White fondly called *the medical missionary work*. No amount of preaching, and certainly no amount of talking on television, can substitute for personal ministry in the field of human need. Let the following statements, reproduced here with just a few comments, set the tone.

> Our Lord Jesus Christ came to this world as the unwearied servant of man's necessity. He 'took our infirmities, and bare our sicknesses,' that He might minister to every need of humanity. Matthew 8:17. The burden of disease and wretchedness and sin He came to remove. It was His mission to bring to men complete restoration: He came to bring them health and peace and perfection of character.[15]

What is this, if not a catholic vision of the church, a mission without boundaries as to who should benefit and without exclusionary clauses as to needs that are to

---

[15] Ellen G. White, *The Ministry of Healing* (Mountain View, CA: Pacific Press Publishing Association, 1937 [orig. 1905]). It is worth noting that this programmatic book for Seventh-day Adventism was published just as the College of Medical Evangelists, now Loma Linda University, was getting ready to open its doors.

be addressed? Just as important, however, what is this but a mission that cannot be accomplished by means other than *personal* ministry, a mission that cannot be outsourced either to the pulpit or to television?

The author of this statement proposed a shift of priorities and emphasis in her lifetime that is worth revisiting.

> I have been shown that in our labor for the enlightenment of the people in the large cities, the work has not been as well organized or the methods or labor as efficient as in other churches that have not the great light we regard as so essential. Why is this? Because so many of our laborers have been those who love to preach (and many who were not thoroughly qualified to preach were set at work), and a large share of the labor has been put forth in preaching.[16]

The author who thus seems aware of what other groups are doing, commending them for pursuing methods of labour that are better than the ones she finds in her own ranks, might even approve of the present attempt to draw lessons from the game of soccer. More important, however, is the commitment to reach people in the large urban areas of the world and *not* to do it through the avenue of preaching only. Indeed, Ellen G. White more than hints that in her day, at least, there was a disproportionate allotment of people, time, and resources to preaching at the expense of more effective means of ministry.

The counsel coming from this source is virtually inexhaustible. Her vocational vision is catholic, inclusive, and firmly grounded in people's felt needs. It is an outward-looking, constructive vision, the vision of someone playing to win. 'To take people where they are, whatever their position, whatever their condition, and help them in every way possible—this is gospel ministry.'[17] A commitment to win cannot be stated more eloquently or wholeheartedly than this.

2. Strategic preparedness.

By now my allotted portion of this *Festschrift* is nearly exhausted. There is only room to recall briefly the other elements that belong to the *nimble foot* strategy. In the context of the church, strategic *preparedness* rather than strategic *planning* means a process that is participatory, that prioritizes the development of individual skills, and that envisions execution by the many rather than by the few. Leaders will acknowledge that no one can prepare for a future that he or she does not know. Readiness to minister in such a context must be entrusted to people who are individually prepared and who will bring to the task skills that exceed the vision of any

---

[16] Ellen G. White, *Letter* 34 (1892); *Medical Ministry* (Mountain View, CA: Pacific Press Publishing Association, 1932), 301.
[17] Ellen G. White, *Manuscript* 62 (1900); *Medical Ministry,* 238.

one leader. On the level of the local church, one change that is easily imagined is a move from passive listening to active learning and participatory ministry.

3. Orchestrated action.

Perhaps the most important issue, certainly the most urgent in my view, is Nils Arne Eggen's emphasis on working to make the players of his team execute in a way that makes fellow players successful. In order to accomplish this, every member of the team must be aware of the skills and limitations of everyone else on the team, from the leaders to the players on the field. Eggen believes that he cannot urge this point too strongly. The team cannot succeed in winning against another team if a player is distracted by other things and certainly not if he is focused on finding fault with his team mates. The entire notion of playing as a team frays if members devote their energy to speaking against a team member, if they behave in ways that weaken trust, or if a player dissents from the principle that it is his task to play in a way that makes his fellow player succeed.

In 1974, when I was a senior in college at Andrews University, Winton Beaven gave an address on the occasion of the University's centennial celebration. I can no longer remember many of his points, but I have not forgotten that he spoke favourably of A. Graham Maxwell, a dedicated Bible scholar. Beaven, who at that time was an administrator at the Kettering College of Medical Arts, recounted the life of Charles Kettering, the wealthy industrialist who donated millions of dollars to the Adventist Church. Toward the end of his life, as Kettering's health was declining, some leaders in the church sought for a way to show gratitude toward their benefactor. Specifically, they wished to find someone who could speak meaningfully to Kettering about matters of faith. Their choice was Graham Maxwell. A meeting requiring a transcontinental flight on the part of Maxwell was arranged. After the meeting, Kettering gave the following commendation, 'What that man said made more sense than anything I had ever heard.'

At the time I heard this story I was too uninformed to have an opinion on the theological questions that were debated. But the thought that someone in our ranks had said something about faith that made sense to a person on the outside impressed me and made me happy. Charles Kettering did not give his commendation about me, but he gave it regarding someone on my team. His commendation would not be true of me or of many others in the church as to his need, but at least there was one person who could speak in a way that made sense to someone who was willing to listen.

The seed that was thus sown was reinforced when I read a book that same year by Edward A. Sutherland, the first president of Emmanuel Missionary College, now Andrews University.[18] Among other accomplishments, Sutherland was

---

[18] Edward A. Sutherland, *Studies in Christian Education* (Madison, TN: Nashville Agricultural and Normal Institute, 1915; repr. Payson, AZ: Leaves-of-Autumn Books, 1984).

instrumental in moving Battle Creek College to rural Berrien Springs, Michigan. I read his book outside any class assignment, and sent a copy to my future wife in California and thirty copies to friends in Norway. For the view that is of interest here Sutherland was indebted to an essay written by Thomas B. Macaulay.[19] The subject is how, after the Reformation, diversity and dissent are handled in the Roman Catholic Church compared to the Protestant context.

Sutherland says that the Roman Catholic Church became wiser than the Protestant churches in dealing with people who on certain points had distinctive convictions or emphases. Where the Protestant mindset has a low threshold for internal division and schism, the Papacy seeks to harness differences for its catholic mission. It has been able to bring together 'all the strength of establishment, and all the strength of dissent,'[20] seeing them as complementary rather than conflicting interests. In Macaulay's words:

> Place Ignatius Loyola at Oxford. He is certain to become the head of a formidable secession. Place John Wesley at Rome. He is certain to be the first General of a new society devoted to the interests and honour of the Church.[21]

These seeds have grown into the conviction that the threshold for criticizing a fellow church member should be raised to a higher level than it was when I was in college or than it is now. Our team cannot succeed if we mistake our task, kicking a member of the team instead of passing the ball to him or her. If part of my assignment is to be aware of the strengths and weaknesses of my fellow players, the other part is to play in such as way as to enhance the witness and ministry of my fellow players. The principle of *the nimble foot* has less to do with my individual skills and limitations and more to do with how we perform together as a team. If we play together nimbly, emphasizing a constructive and offensive strategy, we might earn a hearing among believers in Christian communities, in the Muslim community, and among people who have heard a lot of religion but, like Charles Kettering, have not heard it in a form that made sense to them.

As I write this, Nils Arne Eggen is no longer the coach of Rosenborg, and Jan Paulsen will not forever hold his position of leadership in the Seventh-day Adventist Church. He and Kari have in their ministry emphasized the positive and

---

[19] Macaulay's essay was written on the occasion of the English translation of Leopold von Ranke, *The Ecclesiastical and Political History of the Popes of Rome, during the Sixteenth and Seventeenth Centuries*, 3 vols (transl. Sarah Austin; London, 1840); cf. Thomas B. Macaulay, 'Leopold von Ranke's History of the Popes,' in *Critical and Historical Essays*, vol. 2 (1843). My source for these books is the Project Gutenberg, 2000. Macaulay's essay is also included in *Critical and Historical Essays*, Hugh Trevor-Roper, ed. (New York: McGraw-Hill, 1965), 273-314. The page reference here is to the latter volume.

[20] Macaulay, 303.

[21] Ibid.; cf. Sutherland, *Studies in Christian Education*, 19-20.

constructive, they have been keenly interested in the individuals they have met on their way; and they have tirelessly sought the success that is possible only when all the members of the team unite for the common goal. In short, they have practised the vision of *the nimble foot*. May their work continue, even after Jan leaves office at the General Conference, and may their influence endure. They are not likely to settle in Trondheim, almost at the half-way mark between the rural communities where Jan and Kari spent their childhoods. Instead, they have set their sights on the place beyond that, more than Trondheim, is 'a good place to live' and 'a good home.'

Sigve K. Tonstad. Born in Norway. Since 2005 assistant professor of medicine and religion at Loma Linda University. Pastoral and medical experience in Norway and the USA. Author of books and articles. Extended travels as lecturer in biblical, theological and medical subjects. MD, Loma Linda University. PhD, University of St. Andrews, Great Britain (2005).

Congratulatory List

The following persons and organizations have accepted the invitation to insert their name on the Congratulatory List *(tabula gratulatoria)*. They thereby want to express in a special way their best wishes to Dr. Jan and Mrs. Kari Paulsen.

They are listed alphabetically under the denominational entity where they currently are, or have been, employed or where they reside at present. Friends and supporters are listed under a special heading.

By securing in advance a copy of the *Festschrift* they have further underscored their tangible support for this united effort to honour Dr. Paulsen and to express appreciation for his services to the Seventh-day Adventist world church.

General Conference of Seventh-day Adventists

Eliane and Bert B. Beach, Silver Spring, Maryland, USA
Elizabeth and Matthew Bediako, Takoma Park, MD, USA
Paul S. Brantley, Silver Spring, Maryland, USA
Rae Lee and Lowell Cooper, Silver Spring, Maryland, USA
Sharon M. Cress, Silver Spring, Maryland, USA
Grazyna and Rajmund Dabrowski, Silver Spring, Maryland, USA
Loida and Karnik Cortez Doukmetzian, Silver Spring, Maryland, USA
Carolyn and Larry Evans, Silver Spring, Maryland, USA
Ernestine and Mark Finley, Silver Spring, Maryland, USA
Kim and Clifford Goldstein, Silver Spring, Maryland. USA
John Graz, Silver Spring, Maryland, USA
Janet and Allan Handysides, Silver Spring, Maryland, U.S.A.
Eugene and Alice Hsu, Silver Spring, Maryland, USA
Noelene and William G. Johnsson, Silver Spring, Maryland, USA
Verna and Gerry Karst, Burtonsville, Maryland, USA
Joyce and Mary Lee Keeler, Silver Spring, Maryland, USA
Jean and Mark Kellner, Columbia, Maryland, USA
Anthony and Debora Kent, Silver Spring, Maryland, USA
Debby and Bill Knott, Silver Spring, Maryland, USA
Linda Mei Lin Koh, Silver Spring, Maryland, USA
Bettina and Gary Krause, Silver Spring, Maryland, USA

Kathleen and Jonathan Kuntaraf, Silver Spring, Maryland, USA
Ros and Peter Landless, Silver Spring, Maryland, USA
Sherry and Bob Lemon, Silver Spring, Maryland, USA
Armando and Rosa Miranda, Silver Spring, Maryland, USA
Ellen and Hiskia Missah, Silver Spring, Maryland, USA
Judith and Pardon Mwansa, Silver Springs, Maryland, USA
Ivy and G. T. Ng, Silver Spring, Maryland, USA
Mindi and Jim Nix, Silver Spring, Maryland, USA
Ellen and Bob Nixon, Clarksville, Maryland, USA
Norma Jean and Orville Parchment, Silver Spring, Maryland, USA
Erika and Maxine Puni, Columbia, Maryland, USA.
Laura Dean and Mike Ryan, Silver Spring, Maryland, USA
Weslynne and Donald Sahly, Silver Spring, Maryland, USA
Ella Smith and Nord A. Simmons, Silver Spring, Maryland, USA
Leisa and James Standish, Silver Spring, Marylamd, USA
Frank Teeuwen, Silver Spring, Maryland, USA
Clinton Wahlen, Silver Spring, Maryland, USA
Sharon K. and Jeffrey K. Wilson, Silver Spring, Maryland, USA
Elinor and Neal Wilson, Silver Spring, Maryland, USA
Nancy and Ted Wilson, Silver Spring, Maryland, USA

East-Central Africa Division
(Burundi, Democratic Republic of Congo, Eritrea, Ethiopia, Kenya,
Rwanda, Uganda, Tanzania)

Jane and Killion Agalo, Kendu Bay, Kenya
Christine and Philippe Agbovor, Nairobi, Kenya
Erick Agembe, Kendu Bay, Kenya
Joyce and Dan Agwena, Ranen, Sare-Awendo, Kenya
Mehret and Melak Alemayehu, Addis Ababa, Ethiopia
Maganga and Muhiya Alingunde, Lubumbashi, DR Congo
Rose and Lameck Anyona, Nyamira, Kenya
Caroline and Meshack Onjego Asimba, Nairobi, Kenya
Pauline and Richard Ayako, Nairobi, Kenya
Joan and Zablon Ayiera, Nyamira, Kenya
Ilunga and Kasongo Banza, Lubumbashi, DR Congo
Abigael and Thomas Barongo, Kisii, Kenya
Bakurikiza Rose and Dusabe Benjamin, Goma, DR Congo

Darlene and Steven Bina, Nairobi, Kenya
Mayanga Sangwa and Luhunga S. Bin-Saidi, Lubumbashi, DR Congo
Temesgen Bulti, Addis Ababa, Ethiopia
Joy and Bob Butler, Nairobi, Kenya
Anna and Hesron Byilingiro, Kigali, Rwanda
Agnes and Reuben Charo, Mombasa, Kenya
Stella and William Chienjo, Nairobi, Kenya
Candide and Dieudonne Cishaka, Bujumbura, Burundi
Elizabeth and Joel Dalaguan, Kendu Bay, Kenya
Grace and Vincent Dionzon, Kinshasa, DR Congo
Eva and Alvin Eliamani, Nairobi, Kenya
Lydia and Solomon Wolde Endreas, Asmera, Eritrea
Jeannette and Ambroise Fumakwa, Kinshasa, DR Congo
Gelanye and Philip Gai, Nairobi, Kenya
Joy and Bernard Gashaija, Nairobi, Kenya
Aster and Bekele Gebre, Addis Ababa, Ethiopia
Addis Alem and Robel Gezahegn, Addis Ababa, Ethiopia
Mary and John Macharia Gichuiri, Nairobi, Kenya
Eugenie and Jerome Habimana, Nairobi, Kenya
Aster and Alemu Haile, Addis Ababa, Ethiopia
Danny Harelimana, Bujumbura, Burundi
Bisinge and Nigatu Hordofa, Akaki, Ethiopia
Tamari and Jeremiah T. Izungo, Arusha, Tanzania
Atimang'o Josephine and Udongo Jauca, Goma, DR Congo
Kyaga and Kwabene Marie Jeanne, Goma, DR Congo
Rose and Edison Kaahwa, Kasisi, Uganda
Margaret and Samuel Kajoba, Kampala, Uganda
Mary and Joshua Kajula, Arusha, Tanzania
Miriam and John Kakembo, Kampala, Uganda
Mbuyi and Bruno Kalala, Kinshasa, DR Congo
Esther and John Kalema, Kampala,Uganda
Eva and Noah Kasereka, Nairobi, Kenya
Rachel J. and Msembele Kaspal, Arusha, Tanzania
Sheba and Francis Katengu, Arusha, Tanzania
Teddy and Fred Kazooba, Kampala, Uganda
Christine and Joseph Keino, Nairobi, Kenya
S. S. Keraka, Jr., Nairobi, Kenya
Clara and Rei Towet Kesis, Nairobi, Kenya
Rosette and Hudson Kibuuka, Nairobi, Kenya

Diana and Nehemiah Kinyanjui, Nairobi, Kenya
Miyinga and Emmanuel Kudikowesa, Kinshasa, DR Congo
Lusamba Julienne and Baledi T. Lambert, Lukanga, DR Congo
Terry and Samuel Lumwe, Nairobi, Kenya
Justine Lwanga, Bugema, Uganda
Margaret and Jonathan Maangi, Kisii, Kenya
Mary and Geoffrey Mabuba, Arusha, Tanzania
Rebecca C. and James Machage, Arusha, Tanzania
Roselyne and Ken Maena, Nairobi, Kenya
Alice and Samuel Makori, Nairobi, Kenya
Annie and Musasia Makulambizia, Goma, DR Congo
Emily and Alex Malayi, Eldoret, Kenya
Kujane and Luendu Malu-Malu, Kinshasa, DR Congo
Esther and Bernard S. K. Mambwa, Arusha, Tanzania
Adoniah Manyama, Goma, DR Congo
Dorcas and Alfred Marundu, Nairobi, Kenya
Rebecca and Zachary Marwa, Mombasa, Kenya
Irene and Jones Masimba, Nairobi, Kenya
Nonceba and Zacchaeus Mathema, Nairobi, Kenya
Mwamini and Martin H. Mayenze, Lubumbashi, DR Congo
Mohony Basua and Baniyungu Jean Mbavw, Kinshasa, DR Congo
Nakku and Geoffrey Mbwana, Nairobi, Kenya
Kavira and Kahindo Syalembereka Mbwete, Goma, DR Congo
Risper and Nehemiah Michira, Nairobi, Kenya
Adede and Millicent, Nairobi, Kenya
Shelly and Christopher Misoi, Eldoret, Kenya
Kakule Mithimbo, University of Lukanga, DR Congo
Dorcas and Dan M'masi, Nairobi, Kenya
Mary and Maxwell Mochache, Nairobi, Kenya
Batoto and Bulanda Mpyana, Lubumbashi, DR Congo
Betty and Paul Musyoka Muasya, Nairobi, Kenya
Jerusha and Jonathan Muga, Nairobi, Kenya
Marie-Claire and Muzaila Mujinga, Lubumbashi, DR Congo
Kavira and Kasereka Kimuhotire Mulenghera, Goma, DR Congo
Rhoda and Duncan Mumbo, Kendu Bay, Kenya
Germaine and Elam Musoni, Nairobi, Kenya
Angeline and Joel Musovosi, Nairobi, Kenya
Mwocmini and Kazase Mutumishi, Goma, DR Congo
Mary and Ezekiel Mutwanga, Mbarara, Uganda

Lydia and Samuel Mwebaza, Kampala,Uganda
Daudi M. Ndekeja, Arusha, Tanzania
Leah and Peter Ndeto, Nairobi, Kenya
Mary and Kigundu Ndwiga, Nairobi, Kenya
Salome and Jacob Ngussa, Arusha, Tanzania
Miriam and Festus Njagi, Nairobi, Kenya
Leoncie and Evariste Nsabimana, Bujumbura, Burundi
Ntakirutinana and Jethron Nsabiyaremye, Bujumbura, Burundi
Odile and Martin Nsengiyumua, Bujumbura, Burundi
Spos and Lambert Ntiguma, Bujumbura, Burundi
Linda and Isaac Nyabola, Nairobi, Kenya
Bilhah and Obed Nyamache, Kisii, Kenya
Shem Ngoko, Nyamira, Kenya
Jeanine and Elie Nyandwi, Bujumbura, Burundi
Lumine and Etzer Obas, Lubumbashi, DR Congo
Judith and Tom Obuya, Kisumu, Kenya
Jane and Joseph Ochanda, Nairobi, Kenya
Queentant and Erich Ochieng, Kisumu, Kenya
Yetunde and Tayo Odeyema, Nairobi, Kenya
Carolyne and John Odiango, Ranen, Sare-Awendo, Kenya
Daniel Oduor, Kendu Bay, Kenya
Rebecca and Fredrick N. Ofwono, Mbale, Uganda
Benter and Tom Eli Ogal, Kendu Bay, Kenya
Ruth and Nathan Oirere, Nairobi, Kenya
Rehema and Joel Okindo, Nairobi, Kenya
Helen and Steve Okoto, Kisii, Kenya
Jane and Samuel Omollo, Ranen, Sare-Awendo, Kenya
Pamela and Lewis Ondiek, Kisumu, Kenya
Elvinah and Elkana Ong'esa, Nairobi, Kenya
Catherine and Edward Ontita, Nairobi, Kenya
George Opande, Mombasa, Kenya
Y. I. Osindi, Nairobi, Kenya
Boaz Ouma, Eldoret, Kenya
Mabel and Brempong Owusu-Antwi, Nairobi, Kenya
Mary and Iloch Oyena, Lira, Uganda
Birgit and Philip Philipsen, Nairobi, Kenya
Ruth and Kepha Pondi, Nairobi, Kenya
Julia and Job Rotich, Eldoret, Kenya
Suzana and Lucas N. Rugemalila, Arusha, Tanzania

Elizabeth and Blasious Ruguri, Nairobi, Kenya
Beatrice and Samson Sirare, Nairobi, Kenya
Jesse Tabaranza, Lubumbashi, DR Congo
Leah and Benjamin K. Tanui, Nairobi, Kenya
Alem Tehaye and Adugnaw Tegete, Nairobi, Kenya
Bitota and Kamunga Theodore, Kinshasa, DR Congo
Mandine and Ongasa Bongele Thomas, Goma, DR Congo
Genet and Fesaha Tsegaye, Nairobi, Kenya
Mimi and Jean-Pierre M. Tshimanga, Nairobi, Kenya
Tshibale and Ntumba Tshiswabantu, Kinshasa, DR Congo
Teddy and Joseph Twesigye, Kampala, Uganda
Esseye and Tesfa Umeta, Gimbie, Ethiopia
Irene and Geoffrey Wanyoike, Nairobi, Kenya
Felekech and Abraham Woncheso, Addis Ababa, Ethiopia
Masika and Malembe Bamuswekere Yaya, Goma, DR Congo

Euro-Africa Division
(Czech Republic, France, Germany, Italy, Romania, Spain, Switzerland)

Concepción Roig and Roberto Badenas, Berne, Switzerland
Angela and Daniele Benini, Rome, Italy
Maria José and Mario Brito, Berne, Switzerland
Esther Valls and Jesús Calvo, Madrid, Spain
Doris and Markus Czettl, Berne, Switzerland
Lydia and Elí Diez-Prida, Lueneburg, Germany
Ruth and Ulrich Frikart, Prilly, Switzerland
Johannes Gerhardt, Friedensau, Germany
Didier Gilson, Dammarie-les-Lys, France
Stefan Höschele, Friedensau, Germany
Petra and Peter R. Kunze, Berne, Switzerland
Marianne Fröse-Lange and Werner E. Lange, Lueneburg, Germany
Tania and Richard Lehmann, Collonges-sous-Salève, France
Monika and Günther Machel, Ostfildern, Germany
Michael Makowski, Lueneburg, Germany
Maeve and Gabriel E. Maurer, Berne, Switzerland
Eliane and Roland Meyer, Collonges-sous-Salève, France
Anca and Cristian Modan, Bucharest, Romania
Stéphanie and Gabriel Monet, Collonges-sous-Salève, France

Dana and Karel Nowak, Prague, Czech Republic
Rolf J. Pöhler, Friedensau, Germany.
Magdalena and José Manuel Prat, Barcelona, Spain
Alicia Martínez and Juan Andrés Prieto, Madrid, Spain
Gloria Ramírez and Julián Rumayor, Madrid, Spain
Ottilie and Bernd Quoß, Berlin, Germany
Herta and Klaus van Treeck, Hannover, Germany
Christiane and Bruno R. Vertallier, Berne, Switzerland
Vera and Ralf Wegener, Collonges-sous-Salève, France

Euro-Asia Division
(Belarus, Georgia, Kazakhstan, Kyrgyzstan, Moldova, Russia,
Tajikistan, Turkmenistan, Ukraine, Uzbekistan)

Alla and Viktor Alexenko, Moscow, Russia
Larisa and Andrei Arfandi, Moscow, Russia
Sybel and Guillermo E. Biaggi, Darmstadt, Germany
Svetlana and Lev Bondarchuk, Zaokski, Russia
Svetlana andVyacheslav V. Buchnev, Minsk, Belarus
Ludmila and Valery Burak, Rostov, Russia
Saodat and Eduard Dilev, Dushambe, Tajikistan
Natalia and Yuri Drumi, Zaokski, Russia
Lubov and Vladimir N. Elisev, Khavarovsk, Russia
Lilia and Sergei P. Iovu, Almaty, Kazakhstan
Natalia and Valery Ivanov, Moscow, Russia
Natalia and Julian A. Ivaschenko, Tashkent, Uzbekistan
Zhanna and Mikhail F. Kaminskiy, Moscow, Russia
Svetlana and Vyacheslav N. Kara, Moscow, Russia
Olga and Viktor Katsal, Moscow, Russia
Natalia and Oleg S. Kim, Almaty, Kazakhstan
Anna and Oleg V. Kirilov, Tashkent, Uzbekistan
Svetlana and Vasily Kostiuk, Kiev, Ukraine
Natalia and Viktor A. Kozakov, Novosibirsk, Russia
Lilia and Vladimir A. Krupsky, Kiev, Ukraine
Raisa and Igor V. Krasilnikov, Podolsk, Russia
Maria and Jacob Kulakov, Moscow, Russia
Svetlana and Sergei Kuzmin, Tula, Russia
Vera and Sergei N. Larionov, Astana, Kazakhstan

Maria and Illya Leahu, Moscow, Russia
Aksenia and Pavel Liberanskiy, Rostov, Russia
Olga and Daniil V. Lovska, Almaty, Kazakhstan
Damaris and Gustavo J. Massaro, Moscow, Russia
Amalia and Andrei A. Miller, Astana, Kazakhstan
Maritza and Branislav Mirilov, Moscow, Russia
Lilia and Andrei Moldovanu, Kishinev, Moldova
Irina and Valery N. Nazimko, Bishkek, Kyrgyzstan
Raisa and Ivan I. Ostrovsky, Moscow, Russia
Nina andMoises I. Ostrovsky, Minsk, Belarus
Marina and Rubin R. Ott, Almaty, Kazakhstan
Zhanna and Nikolai N. Patsukevich, Minsk, Belarus
Ludmila and Daniil D. Pavelko, Astana, Kazakhstan
Olga and Oleg P. Prokofiev, Bishkek, Kyrgyzstan
Ludmila and Daniil Reband, Kiev, Ukraine
Alla and Vladimir P. Romanov, Khavarovsk, Russia
Nagila and Oleg A. Schepelev, Almaty, Kazakhstan
Lidia and Alexander F. Schwarz, Tbilisi, Georgia
Svetlana and Peter Sirotkin, Moscow, Russia
Tamara and Vladimir E. Snytko, Podolsk, Russia
Galina and Artur A. Stele, Darmstadt, Germany
Lidia and Vasily D. Stolyvar, Podolsk, Russia
Alena and Andrei T. Ten, Tashkent, Uzbekistan
Tessie and Edwin S. Tigley, Darmstadt, Germany
Irina and Grigory Titkov, Rostov, Russia
Oksana and Mikhail E. Tretyak, Khavarovsk, Russia
Nina and Ivan Vartsaba, Moscow, Russia
Oksana and Igor P. Vasilchenko, Bishkek, Kyrgyzstan
Nadezhda and Dmitry Vertylo, Kiev, Ukraine
Maria and Viktor Vitko, Moscow, Russia
Natalia and Eugene D. Zavadiuk, Almaty, Kazakhstan
Ramona and Vitalie Zgherea, Moscow, Russia

Inter-American Division
(Belize, Colombia, Costa Rica, Dominican Republic, Guatemala, Puerto Rico)

Belkis and Cesario Acevedo, Santo Domingo, Dominican Republic
Luis Miguel Acevedo, Santo Domingo, Dominican Republic

Carmen Lilia and Hector Julio Arias, Bogota, Colombia
Nelson Fernando Hurtado Barillas, Jalapa, Guatemala
Mary Luz Villalba and Edilso Barrera, Bogota, Colombia
Anett and Balvin Braham, Miami, USA
Clementina and Juan Caicedo, Bogota, Colombia
Maria and Héctor Carela, Santo Domingo, Dominican Republic
Alejandra Casila, Santo Domingo, Dominican Republic
Yanet and Abilio Cima, BelizeCity, Belize
Yanet andDavid Cornelio, San Pedro de Macorís, Dominican Republic
Ana and Heraldo Douff, Port Limon, Costa Rica
East Puerto Rico Conference, Rio Piedras, Puerto Rico
Alida and Joel Fernández, West Santo Domingo, Dominican Republic
Caridad and Ciro Garcia, San Francisco de Macorís, Dominican Republic
Rosa and Bilsan Gregorio, Jutiapa, Guatemala
Orlando Esteban Itara Hernández, Chiquimula, Guatemala
Elda Letrera and Jose Ramiro Hernández, Quetza Henauger, Guatemala
Cecilia Moreno and Pedro Iglesia, Bogota, Colombia
Belkis and Moisé Javier, Santo Domingo, Dominican Republic
Velda and Luis Jesse, Belize City, Belize
Ludmila and Israel Leito, Miami, USA
Roxana and Jaime Eduado Torres Linares, Zacapa, Guatemala
Gloria and Wilfredo Ruiz Marenco, Alajuela, Costa Rica
Brenda and Jose Guillermo Solis Mayorga, Zacapa, Guatemala
Irma and Mario Augusto Calderon Miranda, Vista Hermosa II, Guatemala
Esther and Persio Morrobel, San Francisco de Macorís, Dominican Republic
Bélgica and Oreste Natera, San Juan, Puerto Rico
Ruth and Feliberto Matínez Páez, Sonador Bonao, Dominican Republic
Gloria Suarez and Jaime Perilla, Bogota, Colombia
Miriam and Juan Perla, Miami, USA
Pedro A. Méndez Plata, Santiago, Dominican Republic
Dora Stella Lopez and Eduardo Ramirez, Bogota, Colombia
Moisés Gabriel Méndez Ramos, San Marcos, Guatemala
Ana and Juan Jose Moran Reichmann, Vista Hermosa II, Guatemala
Isabel and Santiago Reyes, Jalapa, Guatemala
Sandra and David Thomas Reyes, Zacapa, Guatemala
Alicia and Erwin Leonardo Garcia Sinal, Jalapa, Guatemala
Dennis Slusher, Belize City, Belize
South Puerto Rico Mission, Puerto Rico
Silvestre González Tabar, Santo Domingo, Dominican Republic

Jose Maria Vallejo, San Jòse, Costa Rica
Sandra and Daniel Nerio Velásquez, Chiquimula, Guatemala
Alma and Filiberto Verduzco, Miami, USA
Graciela and Angel Ajanel Vicente, Zacapa, Guatemala
Sergio Armando Villela, San Jòse, Costa Rica
Dilia and Saulo Vizcaíno, Azua, Dominican Republic
Shirnet and Leon Wellington, Miami, USA

North American Division
(Canada and United States)

All 58 Conference Presidents, North American Division
Loretta and Eric D. Anderson, Keene, Texas, USA
Carla Baker, Silver Spring, Maryland, USA
Judy and Kevin Beers, Silver Spring, Maryland, USA
Cynthia and Gordon Bietz, Collegedale, Tennessee, USA
Maxine and James Black, Silver Spring, Maryland, USA
Sandra and Larry Blackmer, Silver Spring, Maryland, USA
Jean and Shawn Boonstra, Thousand Oaks, California, USA
Debra and George Brill, Silver Spring, Maryland, USA
Desinee and G. Alexander Bryant, Silver Spring, Maryland, USA
Sarah and Ernest Castillo, Silver Spring, Maryland, USA
Gloria and Mario Ceballos, Silver Spring, Maryland, USA
Shirley and Marshall L Chase, Thousand Oaks, California, USA
Elizabeth A. and Ramon Chow, Silver Spring, Maryland, USA
Lisa and Ron Clouzet, Silver Spring, Maryland, USA
Joyce and Gary R. Councell, Silver Spring, Maryland, USA
Melanie and Manny Cruz, Silver Spring, Maryland, USA
Brenda and Dan Day, Silver Spring, Maryland, USA
Cindy and Maitland DiPinto, Silver Spring, Maryland, USA
Myung Soon and Hyunsok Doh, Los Angeles, CA, USA
Shirley G and Thomas Evans, Silver Spring, Maryland, USA
Odette and Teofilo Ferreira, Silver Spring, Maryland, USA
Anita and Robert S. Folkenberg, Huddleston, Virginia, USA
Carolyn Forrest, Silver Spring, Maryland, USA
Debra Fryson, Silver Spring, Maryland, USA
Chare and Steve L. Gallimore, Thousand Oaks, California, USA
Dave and Eileen Gemmell, Silver Spring, Maryland, USA

Evelyn and Frank M. Gonzalez, Thousand Oaks, California, USA
Audrey and Ricardo B. Graham, President, Thousand Oaks, California, USA
Pricilla and David E. Greenlaw, Orlando, Florida, USA
Sook and Paul Hopkins, Silver Spring, Maryland, USA
Patricia L Horst, Silver Spring, Maryland, USA
Osceola and Roscoe J. Howard, III, Lincoln, Nebraska, USA
Donna and Daniel R. Jackson, Oshawa, Ontario, Canada
Paula J. and Alfred Johnson, Silver Spring, Maryland, USA
Andee and Del L. Johnson, Silver Spring, Maryland, USA
Jan and Warren D. Judd, Thousand Oaks, California, USA
Ella and Carl Johnston, Keene, Texas, USA
Jewel and Alvin Kibble, Silver Spring, Maryland, USA
Lois and Donald G. King, South Lancaster, Massachusetts, USA
Lynette and Frederick M. Kinsey, Silver Spring, Maryland, USA
Hatsumi and Sakae Kubo, Chico, California, USA
Lyudmila and Mikhail Kulakov, Silver Spring, Maryland, USA
Me and Sung Kwon, Silver Spring, Maryland, USA
David and Nancy Lamoreaux, Silver Spring, Maryland, USA
Barbara and Don Livesay, Berrien Springs, Michigan, USA
Elaine and Willie Oliver, Silver Spring, Maryland, USA
Ivanette and Ken Osborn, Silver Spring, Maryland, USA
Lissy C. and Michael Park, Silver Spring, Maryland, USA
Walter L Pearson, Jr., Silver Spring, Maryland, USA
Lidija and Zdravko Zack Plantak, Silver Spring, Maryland, USA
Barbara and Dennis Plubell, Silver Spring, Maryland, USA
Kristin and Michael Priest, Silver Spring, Maryland, USA
Kathy G. and Edward Reid, Silver Spring, Maryland, USA
Cheryl and Gordon L. Retzer, Decatur, Georgia, USA
Ruthie and Jose V. Rojas, Silver Spring, Maryland, USA
Marti and Don C. and Schneider, Silver Spring, Maryland, USA
Rosa Delia and Lincoln Steed, Silver Spring, Maryland, USA
Judy and Halvard B. Thomsen, Silver Spring, Maryland, USA
Linnea and Max C. Torkelsen, II, Ridgefield, Washington, USA
Betty and Max A. Trevino, Keene, Texas, USA
Gayle and Michael Tucker, Thousand Oaks, California, USA
Lilya and John Wagner, Silver Spring, Maryland, USA
Maurine and Ray Wahlen, Silver Spring, Maryland, USA
Phyllis and William Washington, Silver Spring, Maryland, USA
Becky and Dave Weigley, Columbia, Maryland, USA

Ted and Lyn Wick, Silver Spring, Maryland, USA
Margaret and DeWitt Williams, Silver Spring, Maryland, USA

Northern Asia – Pacific Division
(Hong Kong, Japan, Korea, Mongolia),

Michelle Abel, Ulaanbaatar, Mongolia
Connie and John W. Ash III, Shatin, Hong Kong
Otguntuya Tserenpil and Bold Batsukh, Ulaanbaatar, Mongolia
Lee Suan Ang and Edmund Cao, Shatin, Hong Kong
Mae and Jason Chan, Shatin, Hong Kong
Young Hwa Lee and Young Tae Choi, Seoul, Korea
Mei-Chih Huang and Tony Chou, Shatin, Hong Kong
Verna Wu and Daniel Chuah, Shatin, Hong Kong
Connie Wong and Chiloe Fan, Shatin, Hong Kong
Jane Fung, Shatin, Hong Hong
Mei Tin Cheung and Ivan Gim, Shatin, Hong Kong
Ju Nyeo Jang and Myung Kwan Hong, Seoul, Korea
Mi Ja Chang and Sung Sun Hong, Seoul, Korea
Kyung Sook Shim and Chun Kwang Hwang, Seoul, Korea
Rhonda and Clyde Iverson, Goyang City, Korea
Michelle Abel and Chris Jensen, Ulaanbaatar, Mongolia
Charlotte Lai and Daniel Jiao, Shatin, Hong Kong
Ruby and Samuel Jiao, Shatin, Hong Kong
Jae Young Kim and Taek Cheol Jung, Seoul, Korea
Eun Shin Park and Myung Kil Kang, Daegu, Korea
Chung Hyo and Ki Kon Kim, Seoul, Korea
Miyong and Paul Kotanko, Ulaanbaatar, Mongolia
In Sook Jung and Hark Bong Lee, Gwangju, Korea
Ahn Sook Yoo and Jairyong Lee, Goyang City, Korea
Ruth Hsiao and Li Chun Liu, Shatin, Hong Kong
Xiao Hong Wang and Michael Mok, Shatin, Hong Kong
Joy Wong and Kok Hoe Ng, Hong Kong
Joyce Ng and Ming Sham, Shatin, Hong Kong
Keiko and Masaki Shoji, Yokohama, Japan
Maike Stepanek, Goyang City, Korea
Ryoko and Akeri Suzuki, Goyang City, Korea
Linda and Terry Tsui, Shatin, Hong Kong

Ki See Lee and Bo Suk Um, Seoul, Korea
Rachel Yeung and Johnny Wong, Shatin, Hong Kong
Mary and Robert Wong, Shatin, Hong Kong
Lily Swen and Sze Fai Wu, Shatin, Hong Kong
Ok Ran Lee and Si Yul Yum, Daejeon, Korea
Lin Wang and John Zhang, Shatin, Hong Kong

South American Division
(Argentina, Brazil, Bolivia, Chile, Ecuador, Peru)

Monica and Bolivar Alana, Brasilia, Brazil
Silvana and Edgar Araya Bishop, Chillan, Chile
Hildenir and Euler Bahia, Engenheiro Coelho, Sao Paulo, Brazil
Maria Cristina and Alacy Barbosa, Hortolandia, Sao Paulo, Brazil
Otto Carbo and Leonor Bustinza, Ñaña, Lima, Peru
Vania and Helio Carnassale, Sao Paulo, Brazil
Gabriela and Marcelo Cerda, Buenos Aires, Argentina
Célia and Gilberto Damaceno, Cachoeira-Bahia, Brazil
Anny and Carlos Gill, Buenos Aires, Argentina
Ana María and Roberto Gullon, Cochabamba, Bolivia
Rute and Ignacio Kalbermatter, Curitiba, Brazil
Adriene and Erton Kohler, Brasilia, Brazil
Claudia and Josue Solange Martins Lavras, Minas Gerais, Brazil
Fátima and Eber Liessi, Santiago, Chile
Dóris and Jose Carlos de Lima, Tatui, Sao Paulo, Brazil
Sara and Mauricio Lima, Rio de Janeiro, Brazil
Fabiana and Alexandre Lopes, Sao Paulo, Brazil
Denise and Marlinton Lopes, Belem do Pará, Brazil
Leni and Marlon Lopes, Jacarei – Sao Paulo, Brazil
Esther and Leonel Lozano, Quito, Ecuador
Blanca and Arbin Lust, Buenos Aires, Argentina
Eliana Gonçalves Frozza and Pedro Renato Maringa, Parana, Brazil
Mirian and Jose Paulo Martini, Engenheiro Coelho, Sao Paulo, Brazil
Evelyn and Ruy Nagel, Porto Alegre, Brazil
Warlei and Marino de Oliveira, Brasilia, Brazil
Rosecler and Geovanni Queiroz, Recife, Brazil
Clara Elvira and Orlando Ramos, Lima, Peru
Sylvana Andrea and Oscar Ramos, Libertador San Martin, Entre Ríos, Argentina

Clarita and Samuel Sandoval, Lima, Peru
Susan and Magdiel Perez Schulz, Brasilia, Brazil
Débora and Elder Roger Silva, Brasilia, Brazil
Joice and Rubens Silva, Santo Domingo, Ecuador
Ivete and Domingos Sousa, Sao Paulo, Brazil
Raquel and Tito Benavidez Vinto, Cochabamba, Bolivia

South Pacific Division
(Australia, Kiribati, Papua New Guinea, Vanuatu)

Dawn and Bryan Ball, Cooranbong, Australia
H. Ross Cole, Cooranbong, Australia
Lester D Devine, Woongarrah, Australia
John Dickenson, Leeman, Port Vila, Vanuatu
David and Jenny Gibbons, Pennant Hills, Australia
Denis Hankinson, Victoria, Australia
Graeme J Humble, Pacific Adventist University, Papua New Guinea
Coralee and Bradley Kemp, Sydney, Australia
Kiribati Coralee and Nauru Mission Staff, Kiribati
Deirdre and Allan G Lindsay, Cooranbong, Australia
Julie and Barry Oliver, Sydney, Australia
Pacific Adventist University Library, Papua New Guinea
Carmel and Ray Roennfeldt, Cooranbong, Australia
Branimir and Danijela Schubert, Pacific Adventist Univ., Papua New Guinea
Wolfgang H. M. Stefani, Adelaide, Australia
Lawrence Pita Tanabose, Wahroonga, Australia
Kristin and Steven Thompson, Cooranbong, Australia
Marlene and Ken Vogel, Melbourne, Australia
Neil Watts, Brisbane, Australia
Gary Webster, Watanobbi, Australia

Southern Africa-Indian Division
(Angola, Botswana, Madagascar, Malawi, Mozambique South Africa, Zambia, Zimbabwe)

Darlene and Jacinto Adap, Pretoria, South Africa
Monde Simate and Harrington Akombwa, Lusaka, Zambia

Glaucia and Gilberto Araujo, Pretoria, South Africa
Penny and André Brink, Somerset West, South Africa
Veronica and Baxter Chilunga, Blantyre, Malawi
Ruth and Micah Choga, Pretoria, South Africa
Caroline and Habson Chola, Pretoria, South Africa
Otilia Ualanre and Candido Fabiao, Maputo, Mozambique
Marilyn and Eugene Fransch, Pretoria, South Africa
Filomena Vilhena and Adolfo Gouveia, Huambo, Angola
Sithembile and Passmore Hachalinga, Pretoria, South Africa
Elize and Julian Hibbert, Pretoria, South Africa
Tefo and Boitirelo Kabo, Gabarone, Botswana
Ellah Kamwendo, Pretoria, South Africa
Ntombizodwa and Trevor Kunene, Bloemfontein, South Africa
Maria and Jose Lemos, Huambo, Angola
Mervis and Mabuku Litebele, Blantyre, Malawi
Nellie and Alex Llaguno, Pretoria, South Africa
Rita Josefina Diniz and Biriate Lote, Maputo, Mozambique
Almarie and Francois Louw, Bloemfontein, South Africa
Jean Mabuto, Pretoria, South Africa
Annie and Paminus Machamire, Gabarone, Botswana
Savie and Solomon Maphosa, Pretoria, South Africa
Gertrude and Saustin Mfune, Blantyre, Malawi
Boipelo and Super Moesi, Pretoria, South Africa
Valerie and Hensley Moorooven, Pretoria, South Africa
Beatriz Luisa Meque and Paulo Muchanga, Maputo, Mozambique
Rhoda and Rashford Musonda, Pretoria, South Africa
Seviria and Evans Muvuti, Bulawayo, Zimbabwe
Lilian and Bedinical Ndatoya, Lusaka, Zambia
Litha and Hendrik van der Ness, Bloemfontein, South Africa
Rhoda and Goodwell Nthani, Pretoria, South Africa
Patricia and Jongimpi Papu, Pretoria, South Africa
Arlete and Justino Paulo, Pretoria, South Africa
Laetitia and Pieter du Plessis, Pretoria, South Africa
Shunila and Bapi Rana, Gabarone, Botswana
Angeline and Robert Rasolonomenjanahary, Antananarivo, Madagascar
Denise and Paul Ratsara, Pretoria, South Africa
Ramiandramanjato and Samuel Ravonjiarivelo, Antananarivo, Madagascar
Viviane and Bernard Rivet, Antananarivo, Madagascar
Patience and Good-son Shumba, Pretoria, South Africa

Avules and George Siamuzoka, Lusaka, Zambia
Bongi-Nkosi and Burns Sibanda, Bulawayo, Zimbabwe
Effie and Richard Sithole, Bulawayo, Zimbabwe
Elaine Asta Pasquatto and Elias Teodoro, Huambo, Angola
Gillian and Terence de Villiers, Heidelberg, South Africa

Southern Asia Division
(India)

Rosenito and Gordon Christo, Hosur, Tamil Nadu, India
Ramsangpuii Colony and L C Colony, Shillong, Meghalaya, India
Esther Devadas and Justus Devadas, Pune, Maharashtra, India
Vinodhini and Ch John, Hydrabad, Andhra Pradesh, India
Ramani and T P Kurian, Hosur, Tamil Nadu, India
Premila and Hidyat Masih, Delhi, India
Eileen and Daniel Padmaraj, Bangalore, Karnataka, India
Jennifer and M J Prakasam, Bangalore, Karnatka, India
Gracifill and B R Sangma, Jowai, Meghalya, India
Valsala and S Stanley, Trichur, Kerala, India
Jean and S Sundaram, Chennai, Tamil Nadu, India
Sumithra and Ramesh Yadev, Pune, Maharashtra, India

Trans-European Division
(Albania, Bosnia-Herzegovina, Croatia, Denmark, Estonia, Faroe Islands,
Hungary, Iceland, Israel, Kosovo, Latvia, Lebanon, Lithuania, Macedonia,
Montenegro, The Netherlands, Norway, Pakistan, Poland, Scotland, Serbia,
Slovenia, Sweden, United Kingdom)

Ayodeji Adesina, Watford, United Kingdom
Albanian Mission, Tirana, Albania
Cathy and Martin Altink, Capelle aan den IJssel, The Netherlands
Els and Wim Altink, Huis ter Heide, The Netherlands
Arna and Helge Andersen, Randers, Denmark
Audrey Andersson, Lindesberg, Sweden
Hilde and Rolf Andvik, Sandefjord, Norway
Tom Angelsen, Tromsø, Norway
Margaret and Martin Anthony, Ferndown, United Kingdom

Radisa Antic, Bienfield, United Kingdom
Ida and Kai Arasola, Vastila, Finland
Einar Valgeir Arason, Sandgerði, Iceland
Ruth and Bjørnsten Arntsen, Røyse, Norway
Kalervo Aromäki, Helsinki, Finland
Petra and Gunnar Dam Asholm, Tølløse, Denmark
Rosa and Nikola Aslimovski, Pristina, Kosovo
Jørn Aspnes, Lundamo, Norway
Berit and Gunnar Aune, Oslo, Norway
Kjell Aune, Beirut, Lebanon
Anne Berit and Paul Aywaz, Stenløse, Denmark
Lynda and John Baildam, Binfield, United Kingdom
Aranka and Milan Bajic, Beirut, Lebanon
Jan Barna, Binfield, United Kingdom
Randi Beckhaug, Jevnaker, Norway
Zeljko Begic, Novi Sad, Serbia
Belgrade Theological Seminary, Belgrade, Serbia
Sheila and Martin Bell, Crieff, Scotland
Cynthia and Karl Benz, Maidenhead, United Kingdom
Karin and Karl Bergland, Stokke, Norway
Hanne and Ove Berntsen, Røyse, Norway
Heidi and Daniel Birch, Nærum, Denmark
Branko Bistrovic, Zagreb, Croatia
Terje Bjerka, Oslo, Norway
Per Bolling, Gävle, Sweden
Janez Borse, Slovenj Gradec, Slovenia
Igor Bosnic, Budapest, Hungary
Bosnia and Herzegovina Conference, Banja Luka, Bosnia-Herzegovina
Employees, British Union Conference, Watford, United Kingdom
Aafje and Reinder Bruinsma, Zeewolde, The Netherlands
Sylvi Nordvåg Bunken, Røyse, Norway
Kirsti and Stein Bøhmer, Røyse, Norway
Vibe and Knud Capion, Vejlefjordskolen, Denmark
Ida and Sigvald Christensen, Silkeborg, Denmark
Paul Clee, Watford, United Kingdom
Michael and Evelyn Collins, Arua, Uganda
Jacqueline and John Crissey, Binfield, United Kingdom
Alina and Stanislaw Dabrowski, Blonie, Poland
Sidsel and Terje Dahl, Hønefoss, Norway

Sonja and Jens V. Danielsen, Torshavn, Faroe Islands
Samuel Davis, London, United Kingdom
Nikola Desancic, Zelenika, Montenegro
Rudy Dingjan, Soest, The Netherlands
Momir Djurisic, Belgrade, Serbia
Gretha Isfold and Gustav Draget, Moss, Norway
Daniel Duda, St Albans, United Kingdom
Duna Conference, Budapest, Hungary
Britta Dunton, Garston, United Kingdom
Randi Dyresen, Sandefjord, Norway
Sigrun and Finn F. Eckhoff, Røyse, Norway
Karin and Llew Edwards, Crieff, United Kingdom
Marion Elisenberg, Larkollen, Norway
Oleg Elkine, Haifa, Israel
Richard Elofer, Jerusalem, Israel
Ronald W. Emmerson, Wokingham, United Kingdom
Leo and Clarissa Espana, Tirana, Albania
Anette and Allan Falk, Ringsted, Denmark
Inger and Lehnart Falk, Virum, Denmark
Basim Fargo, Beirut, Lebanon
Pia and Robert Fisher, Stouby, Denmark
Timo Flink, Mikkeli, Finland
Kay Flinker, Daugård, Denmark
Geir Tøndel Fossum, Skotselv, Norway
Annelies and Gerard W. Frenk, Amersfoort, The Netherlands
Jane Froma-Taylor, Koudekerk aan den Rijn, The Netherlands
Laszlo Gallusz, Belgrade, Serbia
George Keough Library Staff, Middle East University, Beirut, Lebanon
Harald Giesebrecht, Oslo, Norway
Vera Gietzmann, St Albans, United Kingdom
Tordis and Øyvind Gjengstø, Loddefjord, Norway
Søster and Øivind Gjertsen, Oslo, Norway
Sergey Gregorev, Ashdod, Israel
Mart and Willemien de Groot, Londonderry, Ireland
Laila and Eric Gudmundsson, Selfoss, Iceland
Odd Hagen, Koppom, Sweden
Sirpa Halminen, Vaasa, Finland
Sulo Halminen, Piispanristi, Finland
Annalisa Halonen, St Albans, United Kingdom

Robert Hansen, Raufoss, Norway
George and Beatrice Harris, Nottingham, United Kingdom
Signe and Walder Hartmann, Daugård, Denmark
Gry and Atle Haugen, Røyse, Norway
Nanna-Lise and David Havstein, Oslo, Norway
Atte Helminen, Vantaa, Finland
Aimo Helminen, Raisio, Finland
Bertold Hibner, Kaunas, Lithuania
Øystein Hogganvik, Lunner, Norway
Veslemøy Hogganvik, Røyse, Norway
Jonquil and Roy and Hole, Crowthorne, United Kingdom
Karen and Bernie Holford, Crieff, United Kingdom
Renée and Jurriën den Hollander, Maarssen, The Netherlands
Gerd and Willy Hugstmyr, Finnsnes, Norway
Gill and Jim Huzzey, Kings Langley, United Kingdom
Iceland Conference, Reykjavík, Iceland
Bjørg and Kristen Falch Jakobsen, Straumsjøen, Norway
Mary and Henning Jacobsen, Århus, Denmark
Ryszard Jankowski, Poznań, Poland
Myrthle Jaworska, Engelsviken, Norway
Ingerlis and Sven Hagen Jensen, Viborg, Denmark
Richard Vagn Jensen, Modum, Norway
Anna Johansen, Kokkedal, Denmark
Patrick Johnson, Wokingham, United Kingdom
Solveig Krusholm and Johann Johannsson, St Albans, United Kingdom
Janne Schantz Johnsson, Kollefjord, Faroe Islands
Jón Hjörleifur Jónsson, Reykjavík, Iceland
Tove and Gunnar Jørgensen, Røyse, Norway
Mladen Juricevic, Zagreb, Croatia
Sibrina and Klaus Kalliokoski, Säynätsalo, Finland
Ellen and Kåre Kaspersen, Rakkestad, Norway
Julian and Beatrice Kastrati, Tirana, Albania
Birthe and Ole Kendel, Kettinge, Denmark
Estelle and Duco Kerssen, Zoetermeer, The Netherlands
Eduard Keshishyan, Watford, United Kingdom
Turid Keyn, Jevnaker, Norway
Elsie and Willy Keyn, Hommersåk, Norway
Engebret Kittilsland, Røyse, Norway
Janos Kovacs-Biro, St Albans, United Kingdom

Bernard Koziróg, Podkowa Leśna, Poland
Lone and Bjørn Krøll, Vedbæk, Denmark
Srecko Kuburic, Zagreb, Croatia
Lynn and Reidar J. Kvinge, Sandnes, Norway
Reidun and Rolf H. Kvinge, Saltnes, Norway
Leonard and Jean Lane, Telford, United Kingdom
Monica and Per de Lange, Røyse, Norway
Sigrid and Toralv de Lange, Bjorbekk, Norway
John Lascu, Tel Aviv, Israel
Pawel Lazar, Warsaw, Poland
Anne Leskinen, Tampere, Finland
Robin Lewis, Southampton, United Kingdom
Berit and Per Lisle, Binfield, United Kingdom
Kari and Tor Lisle, Oslo, Norway
Paul Lockham, Watford, United Kingdom
Claude Lombart, Thetford, United Kingdom
Don and Kathleen Lowe, Wokingham, United Kingdom
Nils-Erik Lundberg, Vaggeryd, Sweden
Kaarina and Heikki Luukko, Ranas, Sweden
Macedonian Mission, Skopje, Macedonia
Sergije Maletic, Novi Sad, Serbia
Stanisa Margaric, Zagreb, Croatia
Gry Beate and Victor Marley, Røyse, Norway
Brian and Inge Martin, Bristol, United Kingdom
Ruth and Karl Martinussen, Hommersåk, Norway
Harrison Mburani, Dagenham, United Kingdom
Julio Mendez, Jerusalem, Israel
Ingold and Erich Metzing, Binfield, United Kingdom
Nebojsa Milovanovic, Zagreb, Croatia
Petter Moltzau, Tromsø, Norway
Clyde Moore, Shrewsbury, United Kingdom
Finn Myklebust, Porsgrunn, Norway
Randi and Svein Myklebust, Kolnes, Norway
Andreas Müller, Daugård, Denmark
Else and Richard Müller, Daugård, Denmark
Anne-May and Thomas Müller, Nærum, Denmark
Annette and Timon Müller, Nykøbing Sj, Denmark
Bert Nab, Dordrecht, The Netherlands
Samuel Ngui, Bracknell, United Kingdom

Tadeusz Niewolik, Kraków, Poland
Sture Nilsson, Jönköping, Sweden
Edith Nordvåg, Lillehammer, Norway
North Conference, Novi Sad, Serbia
Albertus de Nysschen, Torquay, United Kingdom
Margit Høibraaten Olsen, Sandefjord, Norway
Hella and Odd-Henrik Olsen, Moss, Norway
Sidsel and Reidar Olsen, Røyse, Norway
Maj-Britt and Bjørn Ottesen, Nærum, Denmark
Roma Paley, St Albans, United Kingdom
Helen and Mike Pearson, Binfield, United Kingdom
Lisbeth and Gunnar Pedersen, Binfield, United Kingdom
Else and John Pedersen, Hobro, Denmark
Ellen and Kaj Pedersen, Daugård, Denmark
Josip Perisic, Zagreb, Croatia
Felicia and Lamar Philips, Tirana, Albania
Elma and Pekka Pohjola, Tampere, Finland
Esti and Miroslav Pujic, St Albans, United Kingdom
Alicia and Rob de Raad, Norg, The Netherlands
Dusan Radosavljevic, Meljak, Serbia
Marek Rakowski, Warsaw, Poland
Grethe and Villi Rasmussen, Daugård, Denmark
Islwyn and Maureen Rees, Weston-super-Mare, United Kingdom
Edel Reichelt, Sandefjord, Norway
Viestrus Rekis, Riga, Latvia
Cornelia and Matthijs de Reus, Emmen, The Netherlands
Paulina and Usko Rinta-aho, Watford, United Kingdom
Roger Robertsen, Hönefoss, Norway
Krzysztof Roszkowski, Warsaw, Poland
Olavi Rouhe, Tampere, Finland
John and Clair Sanches, Zeist, The Netherlands
Helen Savage, Paignton, United Kingdom
Iris and Børge Schantz, Bjaeverskov, Denmark
Hans Jørgen Schantz, Faxe, Denmark
Sylviane Senty, Bracknell, United Kingdom
Andrzej Siciński, Warsaw, Poland
Connie and Thorgeir Sjøvold, Fredrikstad, Norway
Skogli Health- and Rehabilitationcenter AS, Lillehammer, Norway
Ian Sleeman, Binfield, United Kingdom

Slovenian Conference, Ljubljana, Slovenia
Björgvin Hjelvik Snorrason, Reykjavík, Iceland
Hanna and Harold Soriton, Binfield, United Kingdom
South Conference, Nis, Serbia
South-East European Union, Belgrade, Serbia
Nancy and Torstein Stavdal, Örebro, Sweden
Peter and Vera Stearman, Watford, United Kingdom
Birgith and Alf Steen, Sandefjord, Norway
Sonja and Ton Steens, Zeist, the Netherlands
Peggy and André Stijnman, Schiedam, The Netherlands
Lasse Stølen, Vestfossen, Norway
John Surridge, Cardiff, United Kingdom
Rachel and Ron Surridge, Grantham, United Kingdom
Olly and Gunnar Svendsen, Selbustrand, Norway
Pat Swan, St Albans, United Kingdom
Tibor Szilvasi, Beirut, Lebanon
Maksymilian Szklorz, Warsaw, Poland
Dorothy and Fretson Taylor, Emberton, United Kingdom
Joan and Michael Taylor, Weston-Super-Mare, United Kingdom
Ida and Johann Thorvaldsson, Selfoss, Iceland
Elsie and Tor Tjeransen, Rykkinn, Norway
Imre and Maria Tokics, Budapest, Hungary
Michael Toy, London, United Kingdom
Djordje Trajkovski, Belgrade, Serbia
Laurence Turner, Binfield, United Kingdom
Nina Usacheva, Tel Aviv, Israel
Ivana Vargovic, Zagreb, Croatia
Lisa Vartiainen, Piikkiö, Finland
Richard Vine, Bournemouth, United Kingdom
Vivienne and Robert Vine, Wellingborough, United Kingdom
Sophia and Aristotle Vontzalidis, Watford, United Kingdom
Zarko Vujosevic, Belgrade, Serbia
Patricia Walton, St Albans, United Kingdom
Lise and Tue Westing, Vejle, Denmark
Fanny and Wim Wiersema, Zuidoostbeemster, The Netherlands
Kirsten and Georg Wiik, Oslo, Norway
Rosanna and Bertil Wiklander, St Albans, United Kingdom
Gösta Wiklander, Göteborg, Sweden
Judith Willis, Watford, United Kingdom

Gunvor Wollan, Sandefjord, Norway
Sigrid Borghild Wollan, Lillehammer, Norway
Anne-May and Harald Wollan, St Albans, United Kingdom
Liljan and Tore Wollan, Lillehammer, Norway
Christine and Frank Wood, Wokingham, United Kingdom
Orville and Phyllis Woolford, Maracas, Trinidad
Valentina and Reza Yousefi, Hedensted, Denmark
Christa and Peter Zarka, Budapest, Hungary
Jovan Zeravica, Novi Sad, Serbia
Valdis Zilgalvis, Riga, Latvia
Živorad Janković Adventist Gymnasium, Novi Sad, Serbia

West-Central Africa Division
(Cameroon, Ghana, Liberia, Ivory Coast, Nigeria)

Harriet and E. Mensah Aborampah, Sunyani, Ghana
Grace and Philemon N. Aboungo, Tamale, Ghana
Esther and Ezekiel A. Adeleye, Akrue, Nigeria
Georgina and R. Afonaa-Mensah, Sekondi, Ghana
Monica and Fred Agyei-Baah, Sunyani, Ghana
Taiwo and Onaolapo Ajibade, Abidjan, Côte d'Ivoire
Mary and James Amoah, Kumasi, Ghana
Philomena and Nathan K. Anim, Accra, Ghana
Josephine and Adu Twumasi Ankrah, Koforidua, Ghana
Dora and Solomon Annan, Tamale, Ghana
Drucilla and Chris Annan-Nunoo, Accra, Ghana
Comfort and Sameul M. Ansah, Koforidua, Ghana
Sarah and S. B. Arloo, Koforidua, Ghana
Dorcas and Philip Baffour-Awuah, Monrovia, Liberia
Sarah and Stephen H. Bindas, Lagos, Nigeria
Joyce and Kwasi Boateng, Kumasi, Ghana
Mary and Benjamin Kwabena Brobbey, Kumasi, Ghana
Esther and Markus Musa Dangana, Lagos, Nigeria
Leticia and Emmanuel Denteh, Kumasi, Ghana
Helen and Nkeruwen John Enang, Abidjan, Côte d'Ivoire
Verna and R. Danforth Francis, Abidjan, Côte d'Ivoire
Irja and Erkki Haapasalo, Monrovia, Liberia
Chinyere and Chiemela Ikonne, Abidjan, Côte d'Ivoire

Sarah and Zakari Kassoule, Abidjan, Côte d'Ivoire
Cecilia and Anthony Kessie, Accra, Ghana
Elizabeth and Allah-Ridy Kone, Yaounde, Cameroon
Diana and Kwame Boakye Kwanin, Kumasi, Ghana
Constance and Samuel Adama Larmie, Accra, Ghana
Theresa and Ibrahm Bamayi Maigadi, Kaduna, Nigeria
Margaret and Emmanuel Manu, Abidjan, Côte d'Ivoire
Victoria and Dickson Sarfo Marfo, Kumasi, Ghana
Angele and Jean-Emmanuel Nlo Nlo, Abidjan, Côte d'Ivoire
Catherine and Gideon C. Nwaogwugwu, Umungasi, Aba, Nigeria
Diana and Thomas Techie Ocran, Sekondi, Ghana
Elizabeth and Ernest Okei Okonkwo, Lagos, Nigeria
Janet and Joseph Ola, Lagos, Nigeria
Elizabeth and Isaac Owusu-Amponsem, Accra, Ghana
Abidemi and Ezekiel A. Oyinloye, Ibadan, Nigeria
Patience and Paul Adu Sampah, Tamale, Ghana
Dorothy and Seth Asare Tawiah, Sunyani, Ghana
Blessing and Jacob Edogamhe Umoru, Benin City, Nigeria
Theresa and Ambrose Kpongunaa Waahu, Accra, Ghana
Josephine and Gilbert Wari, Abidjan, Côte d'Ivoire
West-Central Africa Division, Abidjan, Côte d'Ivoire
Martha and Osei Yeboah, Sekondi, Ghana

Adventist International Institute of Advanced Studies
(Senior Education Institution on the Philippines)

Peggy and Stephen Guptill, Silang, Cavite, Philippines
Elsye and Max Langi, Silang, Cavite, Philippines
Trevlynn and Frederick Rudolphus Oberholster, Silang, Cavite, Philippines
Puring and/ Paoring Ragui, Silang, Cavite, Philippines

Andrews University
(A General Conference senior education institution)

Demetra and Niels-Erik Andreasen, Berrien Springs, Michigan, USA
Cobie and Peter van Bemmelen, Berrien Springs, Michigan, USA
Elsie L. and Edwin F. Buck, Berrien Springs, Michigan, USA
Madeline and Robert Johnston, Berrien Springs, Michigan, USA

Margarita and Keith Mattingly, Berrien Springs, Michigan, USA
Lynn and Lester Merklin, Berrien Springs, Michigan, USA
Eva and Jiří Moskala, Berrien Springs, Michigan, USA
James J. North, Jr., Berrien Springs, Michigan, USA
Dalry and Stephen Payne, Berrien Springs, Michigan, USA
Marit and Paul Birch Petersen, Berrien Springs, Michigan, USA
Teresa and John Reeve, Berrien Springs, Michigan, USA
Phyllis and Russell L. Staples, Berrien Springs, Michigan, USA

Loma Linda University
(University and Community)

Grethe and Leif Bakland, Loma Linda University, California, USA
Lyn Behrens and Dave Basaraba, Loma Linda University, California, USA
Beverly Buckles, Loma Linda University, California, USA
Kathleen and Ronald Carter, Loma Linda University, California, USA
Joan Coggin, Loma Linda, California, USA
Del E. Webb Memorial Library, Loma Linda, California, USA
Elizabeth and Gary Dickinson, Loma Linda University, California, US
Angela and David Dyjack, Loma Linda University, California, USA
Ruthita and Duane Fike, Loma Linda University, California, USA
Vicki and Daniel Fontoura, Loma Linda University, California, USA
Berit and Geir Frivold, Loma Linda, California, USA
Sarah Roddy and Daniel Giang, Loma Linda University, California, USA
Ruthy and Charles Goodacre, Loma Linda University, California, USA
Donna and Roger Hadley, Loma Linda University, California, USA
Myrna and Shawki Hanna, Loma Linda, California USA
Bien and David P. Harris, Loma Linda University, California, USA
Judy and Richard Hart, Loma Linda University, California, USA
Marilyn and Clifford Herrmann, Loma Linda University, California, USA
Joyce Hopp, Loma Linda University, California, USA
Linda and Mark Hubbard, Loma Linda University, California, USA
Marilyn and Billy Hughes, Loma Linda University, California, USA
Victoria and Craig Jackson, Loma Linda University, California, USA
Melanie and Michael Jackson, Loma Linda University, California, USA
Darice and Kevin Lang, Loma Linda University, California, USA
Rhonda and Jesse Mock, Loma Linda University, California, USA
Erin and Steve Mohr, Loma Linda University, California, USA
Mildred and Svein Nilsen, Loma Linda, California, USA

Anita Norskov Olsen, Loma Linda, California, USA
Sandy and James Pappas, Loma Linda University, California, USA
Pamela and Jon Paulien, Loma Linda University, California, USA
Kathy Lau and Ricardo Peverini, Loma Linda University, California, USA
Prudence and Leslie Pollard, Loma Linda University, California, USA
Julieta and Humberto Rasi, Loma Linda, California, USA
Michelle and Mark Reeves, Loma Linda University, California, USA
Carol Ann and Darold Retzer, Loma Linda University Church, California, USA
Anita and Randy Roberts, Loma Linda University Church, California, USA
Doris and Don Roth, GC Loma Linda, California, USA
Carrie and Zareh Sarrafian, Loma Linda University, California, USA
Sue and Mel Sauder, Loma Linda University, California, USA
Cindy Schmidt, Loma Linda University, California, USA
Laura and Verlon Strauss, Loma Linda University, California, USA
Alyna and Bernard Taylor, Loma Linda University Church, California, USA
Birthe and Torben Thomsen, Loma Linda, California
Serena and Sigve Tonstad, Loma Linda, California, USA
Carol and Richard Weismeyer. Loma Linda University, California, USA
Ellen G. White Estate, Loma Linda University, California, USA
Linda and Rick Williams, Loma Linda University, California, USA
Betty and Gerald Winslow, Loma Linda University, California, USA
Janice and David Wren, Loma Linda University, California, USA
Cheri and Anthony Zuccarelli, Loma Linda University, California, USA

Oakwood University
(A General Conference senior education institution)

Karen and John Anderson, Huntsville, AL, USA
Susan and Delbert Baker, Huntsville, AL, USA
Marcia and Leon Burnette, Huntsville, AL, USA
Wyvonne and Roengsak Cartwright, Huntsville, AL, USA
Sabrina Cotton, Huntsville, AL, USA
Patricia and Don Daniel, Huntsville, AL, USA
James Hutchinson, Huntsville, AL, USA
Barbara and Harold Lee, Huntsville, AL, USA
Edrene and Roy Malcolm, Huntsville, AL, USA
Carolyn and Jason McCracken, Huntsville, AL, USA
Beverly and Timothy McDonald, Huntsville, AL, USA
Jan and Craig Newborn, Huntsville, AL, USA

Margaret and Philip Nixon, Huntsville, AL, USA
Patricia and Eaton Tomlin, Huntsville, AL, USA
Barbara and Mervyn Warren, Huntsville, AL, USA

Friends and Supporters

Inge and Jørgen Visti Andersen, Borup, Denmark
Ingegärd and Peter Beyerhaus, Tuebingen, Germany
Herbert Blomstedt, Luzern, Switzerland
Malcolm Bull, London, United Kingdom
Denzil and Reg Burgess, Deltona, Florida, USA
Ingeborg and Bent Christiansen, Oceanside, California, USA
Muriel and Hugo Christiansen, Ooltewah, USA
Docile Felix, Cape Town, South Africa
Ragnhild and David Gronert, Kristiansand, Norway
Patrick and Daniele Guenin, Annecy le Vieux, France
Kirsten Hills, Edgewater, Maryland, USA
John Hougaard, Odder, Denmark
Anna Margrethe and Carl Jorgen Houmann, Apopka, Florida, USA
Jytte V. Jensen, Vallensbæk, Denmark
Majlis and Ove Jordahl, Hokksund, Norge
Bitten and Johnny Kaspersen, Hillerød, Denmark
Lex Lijkendijk, Skensved, Denmark
Keith Lockhart, London, United Kingdom
Bodil and Vagner Lund, Lyngby, Denmark
Anders Eyvind Nielsen, Ringe, Denmark
Marion and Calmar Zadok Nielsen, Auburn, California, USA
Yvonne J. Oster, Nyhyttan, Sweden
Svend Overlade, Søby, Denmark
Wanda and Glenn Pedersen, Laurel, Maryland, USA
Anne Mette and Thorkild Pedersen, Rollands Plains, Australia
Georgia and Jason Schellas, Lompoc, California, USA
Christina and Ulf Schmidl, Lohra, Germany
Sissel and Matts Sjölander, Osby, Sweden
Martha and Stig Sjölander, Osby, Sweden